COMPLETE
VISUALIZING
TECHNOLOGY

Seventh Edition

Debra Geoghan

Bucks County Community College

330 Hudson Street, NY, NY 10013

Vice President, Career & IT Skills: Andrew Gilfillan
Executive Portfolio Manager: Jenifer Niles
Managing Producer: Laura Burgess
Development Editor: Cheryl Slavik
Director of Product Marketing: Maggie Moylan
Director of Field Marketing: Leigh Ann Sims
Field Marketing Manager: Molly Schmidt
Product Marketing Manager: Heather Taylor
Operations Specialist: Maura Garcia
Senior Product Model Manager: Eric Hakanson
Lead, Production and Digital Studio: Heather Darby
Course Producer: Amanda Losonsky

Digital Content Producer: Tanika Henderson
Senior Art Director: Mary Siener
Associate Director of Design: Blair Brown
Cover Design: Cenveo® Publisher Services
Cover Image Credits: pickingpok/Shutterstock, Fmgt/Shutterstock, Thitisan/Shutterstock, topseller/Shutterstock, Julien Tromeur/Shutterstock
Full-Service Project Management: Amy Kopperude
Composition: iEnergizer Aptara®, Ltd.
Printer/Binder: LSC Communications
Cover Printer: Phoenix Color
Text Font: 10/12 Helvetica Neue LT W1G Roman

Library of Congress Cataloging-in-Publication Data

Names: Geoghan, Debra, author.
Title: Visualizing technology. Complete/Debra Geoghan, Bucks County
  Community College.
Description: Seventh edition. | NY, NY : Pearson, [2019]
Identifiers: LCCN 2017051677| ISBN 9780134816449 (casebound) | ISBN
  0134816447 (paper)
Subjects: LCSH: Computer science—Popular works. | Microcomputers—Popular
  works.
Classification: LCC QA76.5 .G3765 2019 | DDC 004—dc23 LC record available at https://lccn.loc.gov/2017051677

1 18

ISBN 10:   0-13-481644-7
ISBN 13: 978-0-13-481644-9

Brief Contents

Contents

CHAPTER 3

File Management   112

CHAPTER 6

Digital Devices and Multimedia   280

CHAPTER 11

Databases 548

CHAPTER 12

Program Development 598

What's New in This Edition?

Visualizing Technology Seventh Edition

Always current; always innovative.

Visualizing Technology is a highly visual, engaging computer concepts textbook. Filled with all the important topics you need to cover, but unlike other textbooks, you won't find pages full of long paragraphs. Instead, you'll find a text written the way students are hardwired to think: it has smaller sections of text that use images creatively for easier understanding, and chapters are organized as articles with catchy headlines. The seventh edition continues to provide a hands-on approach to learning computer concepts in which students learn a little and then apply what they are learning in a project, simulation, or watch a Viz Clip video to dive deeper. Each chapter has two *How-To* projects focused on *Digital Literacy* and *Essential Job Skills*, so that students are gaining the skills needed for professional and personal success. They learn about the important topics of ethics, green computing, and careers in every chapter. And, as technology continually evolves, so does the content. In this latest edition, all content has been reviewed and updated to cover the latest technology.

The optimal way to experience *Visualizing Technology* is with MyLab IT. All of the instruction, practice, review, and assessment resources are in one place, allowing you to arrange your course from an instructional perspective that gives students a consistent, measurable learning experience from chapter to chapter. At the end of the course, students are given the opportunity to earn a *Digital Competency* badge to demonstrate that they are digitally literate and ready to move on in their academic courses and future careers.

Highlights of What's new in This Edition

- All content and images updated for currency
- New and updated quizzes
- New coverage of Artificial Intelligence, including Machine and Deep Learning
- Many new and updated Viz Clip videos
- MyLab IT *Digital Competency* Badge
- Pearson etext 2.0 provides an interactive and accessible learning experience

INSTRUCTION

Prepare visual and kinesthetic learners with a variety of instructional resources

- **Pearson etext 2.0** provides an environment in which students can interact with the learning resources directly.
- **Viz Intro Videos** provide overview of chapter objectives.
- **Viz Clip Videos** dig deeper into key topics in a YouTube-like style.
- **PowerPoint Presentation** – to use for in-class, online lecture, or student review lecture.
- **Audio PowerPoint Presentations** deliver audio versions of PPTs—lecture option for online students.
- **TechBytes Weekly** provides ready-to-use current news articles, including discussion questions and course activities.

PRACTICE

Engage students with hands-on activities and simulations that demonstrate understanding

- **How-To Projects** provide two active-learning projects per chapter—a *Digital Literacy* Project and an *Essential Job Skill* Project. Each project focuses on skills students need for personal and professional success. Topics include basic website creation, mobile application creation, video creation, and using social media for brand marketing.
- **How-To Videos** *show* students how to complete the projects.
- **IT Simulations** are detailed, interactive scenarios covering the core chapter topic. Students work through the simulations to apply what they have learned and demonstrate understanding in an active learning environment.
- **Windows 10 high-fidelity training simulations** allow students to explore Windows in a safe, guided environment that provides feedback and Learning Aids (Watch and Practice) if they need help.

REVIEW

Self-check and review resources keep learning on track

- **Viz Check Quiz Parts 1 & 2** provide a self-check of 3–4 objectives so that students can see how well they are learning the content. (Feeds grade to MIL gradebook.)
- **Viz Intro Videos** can also be used for review, as they provide an overview of what is covered in the chapter.
- **Other in-book, end-of-chapter projects and resources:** Mindmap Visual Review; Objective Recaps; Key Terms; Summary; Review Exercises—Multiple Choice, True or False, and Fill-in-the-Blank.

CHANGES BY CHAPTER

Chapter 1 What Is a Computer?

- Added coverage of Ninetendo Switch
- Increased coverage of Artificial Intelligence

Chapter 2 Application Software

- Updated all software versions
- Added more coverage of Web apps

Chapter 3 File Management

- Added Career Spotlight Document Control Specialist

Chapter 4 Hardware

- Added hyper-threading
- Added flash BIOS

Chapter 5 System Software

- Added references to current/newer releases of major operating systems, removed references to some older, obsolete systems

Chapter 6 Digital Devices and Multimedia

- Removed PictBridge

Chapter 7 The Internet

- Updated to most recent browser versions
- Updated speeds of Internet connection types

ASSESSMENT

Measure performance with ready-to-use resources

- **End-of-Chapter Quiz** is a comprehensive chapter quiz that covers all chapter objectives.
- **Application Projects** (MyLab IT Grader project) are written to Windows 10 and Office 2016 and allow students to demonstrate productivity, competency, and critical thinking.
- **Testbank exam** contains customizable prebuilt, autograded, objective-based questions covering chapter objectives.
- **Other in-book, end-of-chapter projects and resources:** Running Project; Critical Thinking; Do-It-Yourself; Ethical Dilemma; On The Web; Collaboration.

Chapter 8 Communicating and Sharing: The Social Web

- Added Waze, Uber, Lyft, Airbnb
- Expanded discussionn of payment services including PayPal, Venmo, SquareCash, and Google Wallet

Chapter 9 Networks and Communication

- Introduced WiGig 802.11ad
- Introduced IP addresses

Chapter 10 Security and Privacy

- Added clickbait and sharebaiting
- Added WannaCry ransomeware, Fruitfly and OSX.Dok malware

Chapter 11 Databases

- Added blockchain
- Added autonomous cars

Chapter 12 Program Development

- Added more coverage of software development models
- Increased coverage of AI- added machine learning and deep learning

Appendix A Microsoft® Office 2016 Applications Projects

Appendix B Using Mind Maps

Visual Walkthrough

VISUALIZING TECHNOLOGY HALLMARKS

- **Addresses visual and kinesthetic learners**—images help students to learn and retain content while hands-on projects allow students to practice and apply what they learned.
- **Easy to read**—it has the same amount of text as other concepts books but broken down into smaller chunks of text to aid in comprehension and retention.

- **Clear, easy-to-follow organization**—each chapter is broken into a series of articles that correspond to chapter objectives.
- **Highly visual**—students will want to read!

Learning Objectives clearly outlined in chapter opener and restated at the beginning of each article

Learning Outcomes are clearly defined at the beginning of each chapter.

Chapter Intro Video introduces the main concepts of the chapter

Explanation of the **Running Project** for that chapter

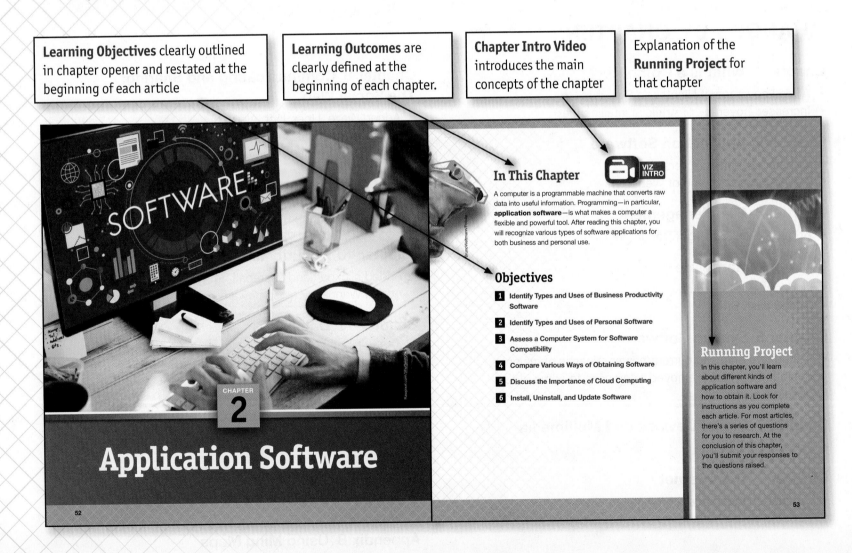

CHAPTER 2

Application Software

In This Chapter

A computer is a programmable machine that converts raw data into useful information. Programming—in particular, **application software**—is what makes a computer a flexible and powerful tool. After reading this chapter, you will recognize various types of software applications for both business and personal use.

Objectives

1. Identify Types and Uses of Business Productivity Software
2. Identify Types and Uses of Personal Software
3. Assess a Computer System for Software Compatibility
4. Compare Various Ways of Obtaining Software
5. Discuss the Importance of Cloud Computing
6. Install, Uninstall, and Update Software

Running Project

In this chapter, you'll learn about different kinds of application software and how to obtain it. Look for instructions as you complete each article. For most articles, there's a series of questions for you to research. At the conclusion of this chapter, you'll submit your responses to the questions raised.

52

53

Catchy headlines begin each article

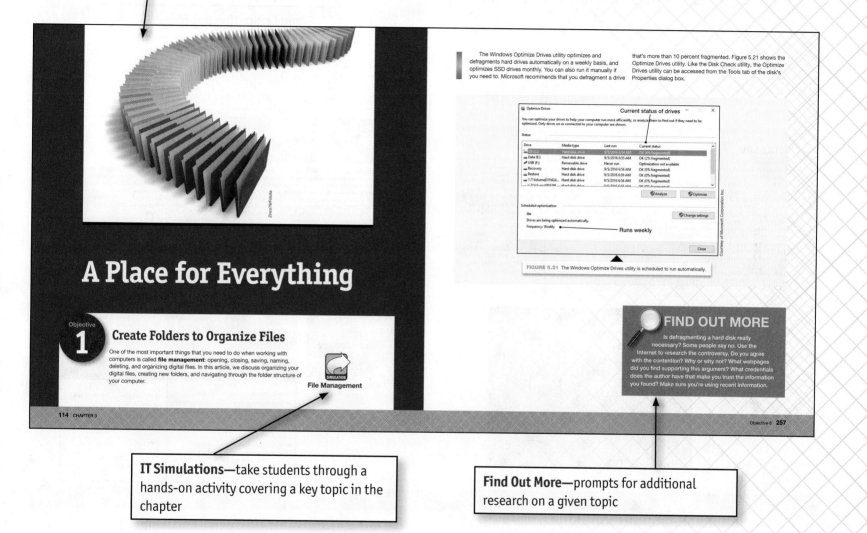

A Place for Everything

Objective
1

Create Folders to Organize Files

One of the most important things that you need to do when working with computers is called **file management**: opening, closing, saving, naming, deleting, and organizing digital files. In this article, we discuss organizing your digital files, creating new folders, and navigating through the folder structure of your computer.

SIMULATION
File Management

The Windows Optimize Drives utility optimizes and defragments hard drives automatically on a weekly basis, and optimizes SSD drives monthly. You can also run it manually if you need to. Microsoft recommends that you defragment a drive that's more than 10 percent fragmented. Figure 5.21 shows the Optimize Drives utility. Like the Disk Check utility, the Optimize Drives utility can be accessed from the Tools tab of the disk's Properties dialog box.

FIGURE 5.21 The Windows Optimize Drives utility is scheduled to run automatically.

🔍 **FIND OUT MORE**

Is defragmenting a hard disk really necessary? Some people say no. Use the Internet to research the controversy. Do you agree with the contention? Why or why not? What webpages did you find supporting this argument? What credentials does the author have that make you trust the information you found? Make sure you're using recent information.

IT Simulations—take students through a hands-on activity covering a key topic in the chapter

Find Out More—prompts for additional research on a given topic

Images are used to represent concepts that help students learn and retain ideas

Green Computing provides eco-friendly tips for using technology

Moore's Law

In 1965, Intel cofounder Gordon Moore observed that the number of transistors that could be placed on an integrated circuit had doubled roughly every two years. This observation, known as **Moore's Law**, predicted this exponential growth would continue. The law was never intended to be a true measure, but rather an illustration, of the pace of technology advancement. The increase in the capabilities of integrated circuits directly affects the processing speed and storage capacity of modern electronic devices. As a result of new technologies, such as building 3D silicon processors or using carbon nanotubes in place of silicon (Figure 1.7), this pace held true for roughly 50 years, but by 2016 most experts agreed this pace is no longer viable. The increase in the capabilities of integrated circuits directly affects the processing speed and storage capacity of modern electronic devices.

Moore stated in a 1996 article, "More than anything, once something like this gets established, it becomes more or less a self-fulfilling prophecy. The Semiconductor Industry Association puts out a technology road map, which continues this [generational improvement] every three years. Everyone in the industry recognizes that if you don't stay on essentially that curve they will fall behind. So it sort of drives itself." Thus, Moore's Law became a technology plan that guides the industry. Over the past several decades, the end of Moore's Law has been predicted. Each time, new technological advances have kept it going, but as new ideas and technologies have emerged, sticking to Moore's Law has become increasingly less practical or important. Moore himself admits that exponential growth can't continue forever.

In less than a century, computers have gone from being massive, unreliable, and costly machines to being an integral part of almost everything we do. As technology has improved, the size and costs have dropped as the speed, power, and reliability have grown. Today, the chip inside your cell phone has more processing power than the first microprocessor developed in 1971. Technology that was science fiction just a few decades ago is now commonplace.

Moore, Gordon E. 1996. "Some Personal Perspectives on Research in the Semiconductor Industry," in Rosenbloom, Richard S., and William J. Spencer (Eds.). Engines of Innovation (Boston: Harvard Business School Press), pp. 165–174.

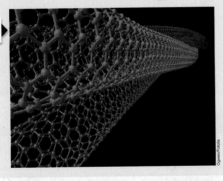

FIGURE 1.7 Carbon nanotubes may someday replace silicon in integrated circuits.

Ogwen/Fotilia

GREEN COMPUTING
Smart Homes

The efficient and eco-friendly use of computers and other electronics is called **green computing**. Smart homes and smart appliances help save energy and, as a result, are good for both the environment and your pocketbook.

Smart homes use home automation to control lighting, heating and cooling, security, entertainment, and appliances. Such a system can be programmed to turn various components on and off at set times to maximize energy efficiency. So, the heat can turn up, and the house can be warm right before you get home from work, while not wasting the energy to keep it warm all day while you're away. If you're away on vacation or have to work late, you can remotely activate a smart home by phone or over the Internet. Some utility companies offer lower rates during off-peak hours, so programming your dishwasher and other appliances to run during those times can save you money and help energy utility companies manage the power grid, potentially reducing the need for new power plants.

Can't make your home a smart home overnight? No worries! You can take some small steps without investing in an entire smart home system. Try installing a programmable thermostat, putting lights on timers or motion sensors, and running appliances during off-peak hours.

Smart appliances can monitor signals from the power company transmitted over the **smart grid**—a network for delivering electricity to consumers that includes communication technology to manage electricity distribution efficiently. When the electric grid system is stressed, smart appliances can react by reducing power consumption. Although these advances are called smart home technology, the same technologies can also be found in commercial buildings.

stockcreations/Shutterstock

Running Project

Use the Internet to look up current microprocessors. What companies produce them? Visit **computer.howstuffworks.com /microprocessor.htm** and read the article. How many transistors were found on the first home computer processor? What was the name of the processor, and when was it introduced?

5 Things You Need to Know	Key Terms	
• First-generation computers used vacuum tubes. • Second-generation computers used transistors. • Third-generation computers used integrated circuits (chips). • Fourth-generation computers use microprocessors. • Moore's Law states that the number of transistors that can be placed on an integrated circuit doubles roughly every two years—although today it is closer to every 18 months.	central processing unit (CPU) ENIAC (Electronic Numerical Integrator and Computer) green computing integrated circuit	microprocessor Moore's Law smart appliance smart grid smart home transistor vacuum tube

Subtopics have same color background as main topics—makes it easy to follow each piece

Ethics boxes provide thought-provoking questions about the use of technology

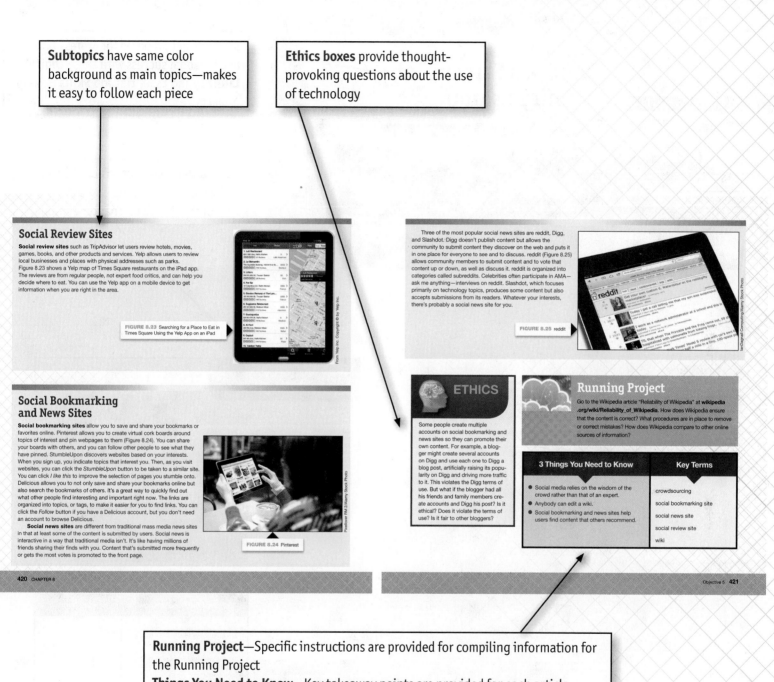

Social Review Sites

Social review sites such as TripAdvisor let users review hotels, movies, games, books, and other products and services. Yelp allows users to review local businesses and places with physical addresses such as parks. Figure 8.23 shows a Yelp map of Times Square restaurants on the iPad app. The reviews are from regular people, not expert food critics, and can help you decide where to eat. You can use the Yelp app on a mobile device to get information when you are right in the area.

FIGURE 8.23 Searching for a Place to Eat in Times Square Using the Yelp App on an iPad

From Yelp Inc. Copyright © by Yelp Inc.

Social Bookmarking and News Sites

Social bookmarking sites allow you to save and share your bookmarks or favorites online. Pinterest allows you to create virtual cork boards around topics of interest and pin webpages to them (Figure 8.24). You can share your boards with others, and you can follow other people to see what they have pinned. StumbleUpon discovers websites based on your interests. When you sign up, you indicate topics that interest you. Then, as you visit websites, you can click the *StumbleUpon* button to be taken to a similar site. You can click *I like this* to improve the selection of pages you stumble onto. Delicious allows you to not only save and share your bookmarks online but also search the bookmarks of others. It's a great way to quickly find out what other people find interesting and important right now. The links are organized into topics, or tags, to make it easier for you to find links. You can click the *Follow* button if you have a Delicious account, but you don't need an account to browse Delicious.

    Social news sites are different from traditional mass media news sites in that at least some of the content is submitted by users. Social news is interactive in a way that traditional media isn't. It's like having millions of friends sharing their finds with you. Content that's submitted more frequently or gets the most votes is promoted to the front page.

FIGURE 8.24 Pinterest

Pixelfover RM 2/Alamy Stock Photo

Three of the most popular social news sites are reddit, Digg, and Slashdot. Digg doesn't publish content but allows the community to submit content they discover on the web and puts it in one place for everyone to see and to discuss. reddit (Figure 8.25) allows community members to submit content and to vote that content up or down, as well as discuss it. reddit is organized into categories called subreddits. Celebrities often participate in AMA—ask me anything—interviews on reddit. Slashdot, which focuses primarily on technology topics, produces some content but also accepts submissions from its readers. Whatever your interests, there's probably a social news site for you.

FIGURE 8.25 reddit

ler/Digital Computing/Alamy Stock Photo

ETHICS

Some people create multiple accounts on social bookmarking and news sites so they can promote their own content. For example, a blogger might create several accounts on Digg and use each one to Digg a blog post, artificially raising its popularity on Digg and driving more traffic to it. This violates the Digg terms of use. But what if the blogger had all his friends and family members create accounts and Digg his post? Is it ethical? Does it violate the terms of use? Is it fair to other bloggers?

Running Project

Go to the Wikipedia article "Reliability of Wikipedia" at **wikipedia .org/wiki/Reliability_of_Wikipedia**. How does Wikipedia ensure that the content is correct? What procedures are in place to remove or correct mistakes? How does Wikipedia compare to other online sources of information?

3 Things You Need to Know	Key Terms
● Social media relies on the wisdom of the crowd rather than that of an expert.	crowdsourcing
● Anybody can edit a wiki.	social bookmarking site
● Social bookmarking and news sites help users find content that others recommend.	social news site
	social review site
	wiki

Running Project—Specific instructions are provided for compiling information for the Running Project
Things You Need to Know—Key takeaway points are provided for each article
Key Terms—Students are reminded of the key terms they should understand after reading each article

Capture a Screenshot of Your Desktop
Digital Literacy Skill

HOW TO VIDEO

A useful skill is creating screen shots of your desktop. For example, it's helpful for providing directions on how to do something or for keeping a record of an error message that appears on your screen. Windows includes a program called the Snipping

Tool that you can use to capture a screenshot. Macs include the Grab tool.

The Windows Snipping Tool can capture four types of snips: Free-form, Rectangular, Window, or Full-screen. The Mac Grab tool can capture three types of grabs: Selection, Window, or Screen.

You can save your screenshots, email them, paste them into

documents, and annotate and highlight them. If necessary, download the student data files from **pearsonhighered.com /viztech**. From your student data files, open the *vt_ch01_howto1_ answersheet* file and save the file as **lastname_firstname_ch01_ howto1_answersheet**.

> Students get prepared for professional and personal success with these **Digital Literacy** and **Essential Job Skills** How-To projects.

> **Career Spotlight**—Each chapter provides an interesting career option based on chapter content

Facebook Pages

Unlike a Facebook profile, which is linked to a person, a Facebook Page is used to promote an organization, a product, or a service. A Facebook Page can have more than one administrator, so you can share the responsibilities among several people or departments. The Facebook Page for this textbook can be found at **facebook.com/visualizingtechnology**. A Page is public, so it can be viewed by anyone, even those who are not logged in to Facebook.

To create a Facebook Page, you need a personal Facebook account. Facebook's Terms of Service permit you to have only one personal Facebook account, but you can create multiple Facebook Pages. So, for example, a college representative might create a page for each department, club, or office. Once you are logged in to your personal account, the option *Create Page* can be found in the menu options. You can choose from several page categories (Figure 8.29). A page for a business or an organization will have

FIGURE 8.29 Create a Page Categories

CAREER SPOTLIGHT

SOFTWARE TRAINERS Software trainers—sometimes called corporate trainers—are in demand as companies deploy more software programs. This high-paying career may involve some travel and requires good computer skills, organization, and communication skills. Software trainers usually have at least a bachelor's degree and on-the-job training. Some companies offer train-the-trainer courses that can lead to certification. You might work for a training company, in the training department of a large company, or as a consultant to many companies.

7th Son Studio/Shutterstock

Running Project
Research a game or program that you would like to run on your computer. What are the system requirements for the program? Does your computer meet the minimum requirements? In what ways does it exceed them?

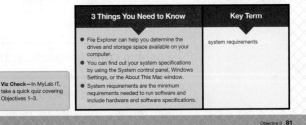

3 Things You Need to Know	Key Term
• File Explorer can help you determine the drives and storage space available on your computer. • You can find out your system specifications by using the System control panel, Windows Settings, or the About This Mac window. • System requirements are the minimum requirements needed to run software and include hardware and software specifications.	system requirements

Viz Check—In MyLab IT, take a quick quiz covering Objectives 1–3.

> **Viz Check quizzes**—Each chapter includes two short online quizzes covering 3–5 objectives

How-To Projects—Each chapter provides two step-by-step projects, complete with visual instructions, to complete interesting and useful items

How-To Videos—Each How-To Project has a corresponding video walk-through of the project

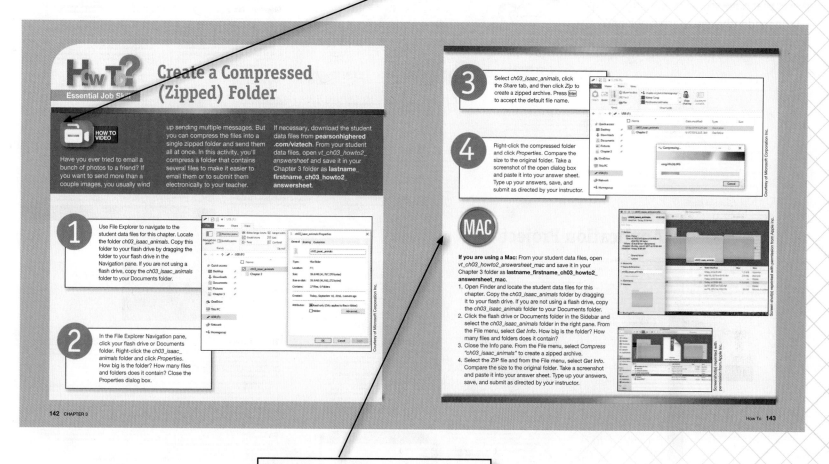

Mac coverage—Where appropriate, instructions and solutions are included so Mac users can complete the exercises

The **End-of-Chapter content** ranges from traditional review exercises to application and hands-on projects that have students working independently, collaboratively, and online

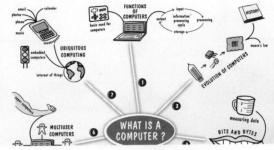

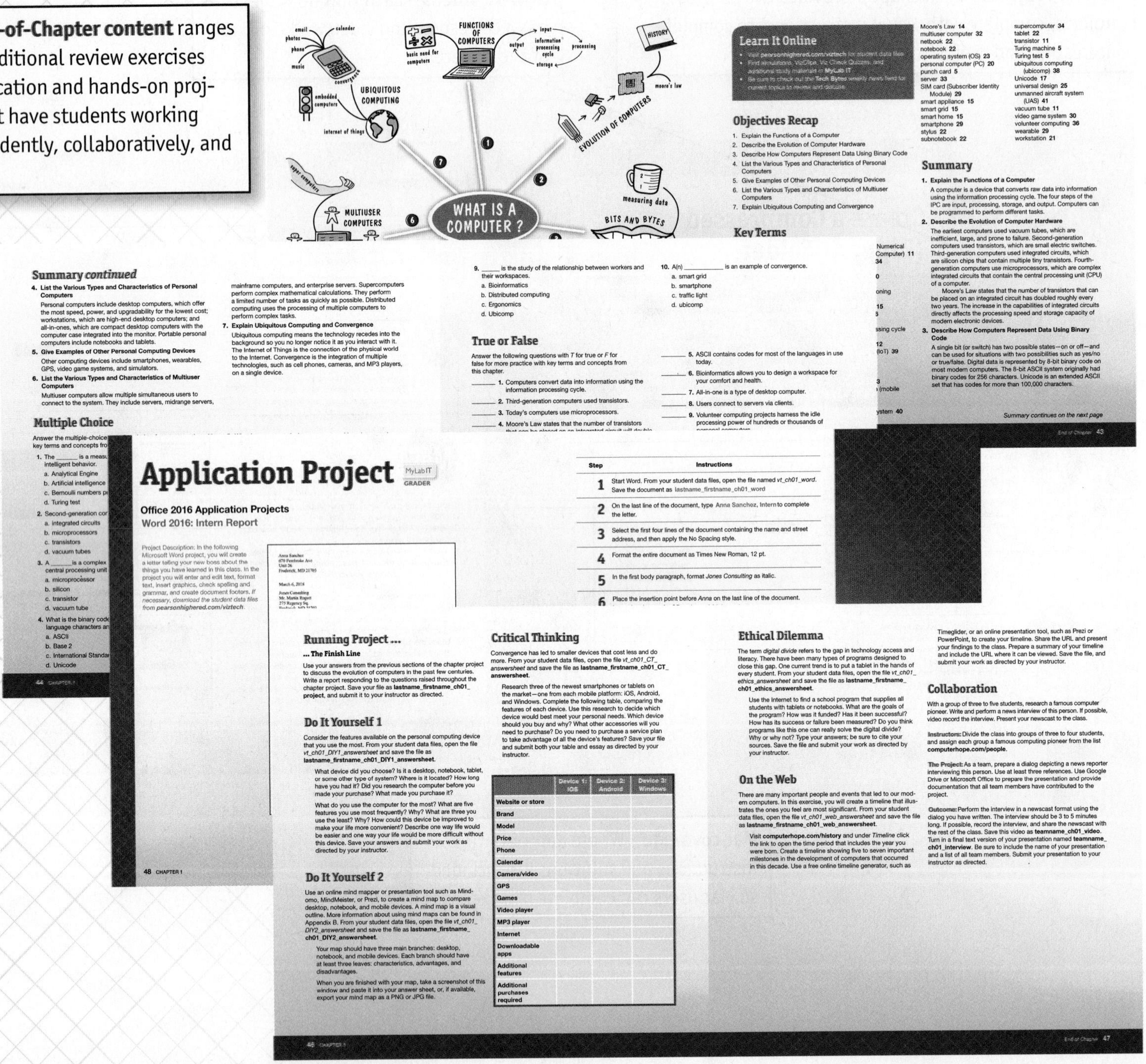

Learn It Online

- Visit pearsonhighered.com/viztech for student data files.
- Find simulations, VizClips, Viz Check Quizzes, and additional study materials at MyLab IT.
- Be sure to check out the Tech Bytes weekly news feed for current topics to review and discuss.

Objectives Recap

1. Explain the Functions of a Computer
2. Describe the Evolution of Computer Hardware
3. Describe How Computers Represent Data Using Binary Code
4. List the Various Types and Characteristics of Personal Computers
5. Give Examples of Other Personal Computing Devices
6. List the Various Types and Characteristics of Multiuser Computers
7. Explain Ubiquitous Computing and Convergence

Key Terms

Moore's Law 14	supercomputer 34
multiuser computer 32	tablet 22
netbook 22	transistor 11
notebook 22	Turing machine 5
operating system (OS) 23	Turing test 5
personal computer (PC) 20	ubiquitous computing (ubicomp) 38
punch card 5	Unicode 17
server 33	universal design 25
SIM card (Subscriber Identity Module) 29	unmanned aircraft system (UAS) 41
smart appliance 15	vacuum tube 11
smart grid 15	video game system 30
smart home 15	volunteer computing 36
smartphone 29	wearable 29
stylus 22	workstation 21
subnotebook 22	

Summary

1. Explain the Functions of a Computer

A computer is a device that converts raw data into information using the information processing cycle. The four steps of the IPC are input, processing, storage, and output. Computers can be programmed to perform different tasks.

2. Describe the Evolution of Computer Hardware

The earliest computers used vacuum tubes, which are inefficient, large, and prone to failure. Second-generation computers used transistors, which are small electric switches. Third-generation computers used integrated circuits, which are silicon chips that contain multiple tiny transistors. Fourth-generation computers use microprocessors, which are complex integrated circuits that contain the central processing unit (CPU) of a computer.

Moore's Law states that the number of transistors that can be placed on an integrated circuit has doubled roughly every two years. The increase in the capabilities of integrated circuits directly affects the processing speed and storage capacity of modern electronic devices.

3. Describe How Computers Represent Data Using Binary Code

A single bit (or switch) has two possible states—on or off—and can be used for situations with two possibilities such as yes/no or true/false. Digital data is represented by 8-bit binary code on most modern computers. The 8-bit ASCII system originally had binary codes for 256 characters. Unicode is an extended ASCII set that has codes for more than 100,000 characters.

Summary continues on the next page

Summary continued

4. List the Various Types and Characteristics of Personal Computers

Personal computers include desktop computers, which offer the most speed, power, and upgradability for the lowest cost; workstations, which are high-end desktop computers; and all-in-ones, which are compact desktop computers with the computer case integrated into the monitor. Portable personal computers include notebooks and tablets.

5. Give Examples of Other Personal Computing Devices

Other computing devices include smartphones, wearables, GPS, video game systems, and simulators.

6. List the Various Types and Characteristics of Multiuser Computers

Multiuser computers allow multiple simultaneous users to connect to the system. They include servers, midrange servers,

mainframe computers, and enterprise servers. Supercomputers perform complex mathematical calculations. They perform a limited number of tasks as quickly as possible. Distributed computing uses the processing of multiple computers to perform complex tasks.

7. Explain Ubiquitous Computing and Convergence

Ubiquitous computing means the technology recedes into the background so you no longer notice it as you interact with it. The Internet of Things is the connection of the physical world to the Internet. Convergence is the integration of multiple technologies, such as cell phones, cameras, and MP3 players, on a single device.

Multiple Choice

Answer the multiple-choice key terms and concepts from

1. The _____ is a measure of intelligent behavior.
   a. Analytical Engine
   b. Artificial intelligence
   c. Bernoulli numbers p
   d. Turing test

2. Second-generation com
   a. integrated circuits
   b. microprocessors
   c. transistors
   d. vacuum tubes

3. A _____ is a complex central processing unit
   a. microprocessor
   b. silicon
   c. transistor
   d. vacuum tube

4. What is the binary code language characters an
   a. ASCII
   b. Base 2
   c. International Standar
   d. Unicode

9. _____ is the study of the relationship between workers and their workspaces.
   a. Bioinformatics
   b. Distributed computing
   c. Ergonomics
   d. Ubicomp

10. A(n) _____ is an example of convergence.
   a. smart grid
   b. smartphone
   c. traffic light
   d. ubicomp

True or False

Answer the following questions with *T* for true or *F* for false for more practice with key terms and concepts from this chapter.

_____ 1. Computers convert data into information using the information processing cycle.

_____ 2. Third-generation computers used transistors.

_____ 3. Today's computers use microprocessors.

_____ 4. Moore's Law states that the number of transistors that can be placed on an integrated circuit will double

_____ 5. ASCII contains codes for most of the languages in use today.

_____ 6. Bioinformatics allows you to design a workspace for your comfort and health.

_____ 7. All-in-one is a type of desktop computer.

_____ 8. Users connect to servers via clients.

_____ 9. Volunteer computing projects harness the idle processing power of hundreds or thousands of

Application Project

MyLab IT GRADER

Office 2016 Application Projects
Word 2016: Intern Report

Project Description: In the following Microsoft Word project, you will create a letter telling your new boss about the things you have learned in this class. In the project you will enter and edit text, format text, insert graphics, check spelling and grammar, and create document footers. *If necessary, download the student data files from pearsonhighered.com/viztech.*

Step	Instructions
1	Start Word. From your student data files, open the file named *vt_ch01_word*. Save the document as lastname_firstname_ch01_word
2	On the last line of the document, type *Anna Sanchez, Intern* to complete the letter.
3	Select the first four lines of the document containing the name and street address, and then apply the No Spacing style.
4	Format the entire document as Times New Roman, 12 pt.
5	In the first body paragraph, format *Jones Consulting* as italic.
6	Place the insertion point before *Anna* on the last line of the document.

Running Project ...

... The Finish Line

Use your answers from the previous sections of the chapter project to discuss the evolution of computers in the past few centuries. Write a report responding to the questions raised throughout the chapter project. Save your file as lastname_firstname_ch01_**project**, and submit it to your instructor as directed.

Do It Yourself 1

Consider the features available on the personal computing device that you use the most. From your student data files, open the file *vt_ch01_DIY1_answersheet* and save the file as **lastname_firstname_ch01_DIY1_answersheet**.

What device did you choose? Is it a desktop, notebook, tablet, or some other type of system? Where is it located? How long have you had it? Did you research the computer before you made your purchase? What made you purchase it?

What do you use the computer for the most? What are five features you use most frequently? What are three you use the least? Why? How could this device be improved to make your life more convenient? Describe one way life would be easier and one way your life would be more difficult without this device. Save your answers and submit your work as directed by your instructor.

Do It Yourself 2

Use an online mind mapper or presentation tool such as Mindomo, MindMeister, or Prezi, to create a mind map to compare desktop, notebook, and mobile devices. A mind map is a visual outline. More information about using mind maps can be found in Appendix B. From your student data files, open the file *vt_ch01_DIY2_answersheet* and save the file as **lastname_firstname_ch01_DIY2_answersheet**.

Your map should have three main branches: desktop, notebook, and mobile devices. Each branch should have at least three leaves: characteristics, advantages, and disadvantages.

When you are finished with your map, take a screenshot of this window and paste it into your answer sheet, or, if available, export your mind map as a PNG or JPG file.

Critical Thinking

Convergence has led to smaller devices that cost less and do more. From your student data files, open the file *vt_ch01_CT_answersheet* and save the file as **lastname_firstname_ch01_CT_answersheet**.

Research three of the newest smartphones or tablets on the market—one from each mobile platform: iOS, Android, and Windows. Complete the following table, comparing the features of each device. Use this research to decide which device would best meet your personal needs. Which device should you buy and why? What other accessories will you need to purchase? Do you need to purchase a service plan to take advantage of all the device's features? Save your file and submit both your table and essay as directed by your instructor.

	Device 1: iOS	Device 2: Android	Device 3: Windows
Website or store			
Brand			
Model			
Price			
Phone			
Calendar			
Camera/video			
GPS			
Games			
Video player			
MP3 player			
Internet			
Downloadable apps			
Additional features			
Additional purchases required			

Ethical Dilemma

The term *digital divide* refers to the gap in technology access and literacy. There have been many types of programs designed to close this gap. One current trend is to put a tablet in the hands of every student. From your student data files, open the file *vt_ch01_ethics_answersheet* and save the file as **lastname_firstname_ch01_ethics_answersheet**.

Use the Internet to find a school program that supplies all students with tablets or notebooks. What are the goals of the program? How was it funded? Has it been successful? How has its success or failure been measured? Do you think programs like this one can really solve the digital divide? Why or why not? Type your answers; be sure to cite your sources. Save the file and submit your work as directed by your instructor.

On the Web

There are many important people and events that led to our modern computers. In this exercise, you will create a timeline that illustrates the ones you feel are most significant. From your student data files, open the file *vt_ch01_web_answersheet* and save the file as **lastname_firstname_ch01_web_answersheet**.

Visit computerhope.com/history and under *Timeline* click the link to open the time period that includes the year you were born. Create a timeline showing five to seven important milestones in the development of computers that occurred in this decade. Use a free online timeline generator, such as

Timeglider, or an online presentation tool, such as Prezi or PowerPoint, to create your timeline. Share the URL and present your findings to the class. Prepare a summary of your timeline and include the URL where it can be viewed. Save the file, and submit your work as directed by your instructor.

Collaboration

With a group of three to five students, research a famous computer pioneer. Write and perform a news interview of this person. If possible, video record the interview. Present your newscast to the class.

Instructors: Divide the class into groups of three to four students, and assign each group a famous computing pioneer from the list computerhope.com/people.

The Project: As a team, prepare a dialog depicting a news reporter interviewing this person. Use at least three references. Use Google Drive or Microsoft Office to prepare the presentation and provide documentation that all team members have contributed to the project.

Outcome: Perform the interview in a newscast format using the dialog you have written. The interview should be 3 to 5 minutes long. If possible, record the interview, and share the newscast with the rest of the class. Save this video as **teamname_ch01_video**. Turn in a final text version of your presentation named **teamname_ch01_interview**. Be sure to include the name of your presentation and a list of all team members. Submit your presentation to your instructor as directed.

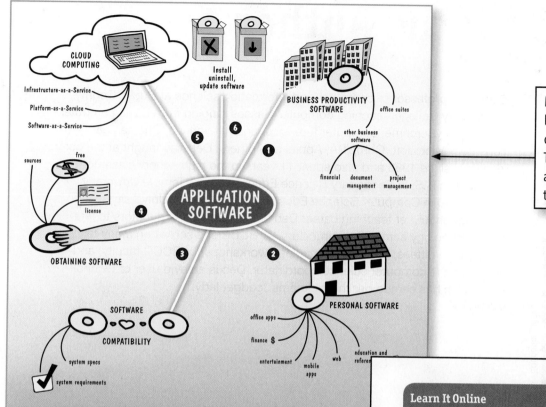

Mind maps are visual outlines of the chapter content, organized by objectives. They help students organize and remember the information they learned

- Visit **pearsonhighered.com/viztech** for student data files
- Find simulations, VizClips, and additional study materials in **MyLab IT**
- Be sure to check out the **Tech Bytes** weekly news feed for current topics to review and discuss

Objectives Recap

1. Identify Types and Uses of Business Productivity Software
2. Identify Types and Uses of Personal Software
3. Assess a Computer System for Software Compatibility
4. Compare Various Ways of Obtaining Software
5. Discuss the Importance of Cloud Computing
6. Install, Uninstall, and Update Software

Key Terms

app 84	office application suite 55
application software 53	open source 65
bug 99	patch 99
cell 57	personal information manager
cloud 86	(PIM) 60
cloud computing 86	Platform-as-a-Service (PaaS) 87
cloud service provider (CSP) 87	platform-neutral 85
database 59	project management software 62
desktop application 84	query 59
document management system	record 59
(DMS) 61	report 59
donationware 83	retail software 83
EULA (end-user license	service pack 99
agreement) 83	shareware 83
field 59	Software-as-a-Service (SaaS) 88
form 59	spreadsheet 57
freemium 83	subscription 83
freeware 83	system requirements 80
Gantt chart 62	table 59
hotfix 99	web apps 71
Infrastructure-as-a-Service	word processor 55
(IaaS) 87	

Summary

1. Identify Types and Uses of Business Productivity Software

The most common business software is an office application suite—which may include a word processor, spreadsheet, presentation program, database, and personal information manager. Other business applications include financial software, document management, and project management software.

2. Identify Types and Uses of Personal Software

Personal software includes office applications, especially word processors, spreadsheets, and presentation programs. Other personal applications include entertainment and multimedia software such as media managers, video and photo editing software, and video games. Financial and tax preparation software as well as educational and reference software are also popular. You can run web apps in a browser, on any device with Internet access.

3. Assess a Computer System for Software Compatibility

Before purchasing and installing software, you should research the system requirements needed to run the program and compare them to your system specifications using File Explorer and the System Control Panel or System Settings window. On a Mac, use the About This Mac window.

4. Compare Various Ways of Obtaining Software

You can obtain software from brick-and-mortar and online stores, publisher websites, and download websites. Download mobile apps only from trusted markets. It's important to read the EULA to understand the software license restrictions.

5. Discuss the Importance of Cloud Computing

Cloud computing moves hardware and software into the cloud, or Internet. Cloud computing allows you to access applications and data from any web-connected computer. Some benefits include lower cost, easier maintenance, security, and collaboration.

6. Install, Uninstall, and Update Software

Managing the programs on your computer includes installing, uninstalling, and updating the software. You can install programs through an app store, by using media, or by downloading from a website. Updating software fixes bugs, adds features, or improves compatibility. You should uninstall software using the program's uninstaller.

About the Author

Pearson Education, Inc.

Debra is a professor of computer and information science at Bucks County Community College, teaching computer classes ranging from basic computer literacy to cybercrime, computer forensics, and networking. She has certifications from Microsoft, CompTIA, Apple, and others. Deb has taught at the college level since 1996 and also spent 11 years in the high school classroom. She holds a B.S. in Secondary Science Education from Temple University and an M.A. in Computer Science Education from Arcadia University.

Throughout her teaching career Deb has worked with educators to integrate technology across the curriculum. At BCCC she serves on many technology committees, presents technology workshops for BCCC faculty, and serves as the computer science coordinator. Deb is an avid user of technology, which has earned her the nickname "gadget lady."

Dedication

This project would not have been possible without the help and support of many people. I cannot express how grateful I am to all of you. Thank you.

My team at Pearson—Jenifer, Cheryl, Laura, and everyone else: you have been amazing, helping to bring my vision to reality and teaching me so much along the way.

My colleagues and students at Bucks County Community College: for your suggestions and encouragement throughout this process. You inspire me every day.

And most importantly—my family. My husband and sons for your patience, help, and love—even when it meant taking a photo "right this minute," or reading a chapter when you wanted to be doing something else, or missing me while I was away. And the rest of my family and friends who agreed to let me use their photos throughout the book. I couldn't have done this without your love and support.

And finally my dad—who taught me to love technology and not be afraid to try new things. I miss you and love you, daddy.

Reviewers of All Editions

Phil Valvalides   Guilford Technical Community College

Svetlana Marzelli   Atlantic Cape Community College

Pat Lyon   Tomball College

Arta Szathmary   Bucks County Community College

June Lane   Bucks County Community College

Ralph Hunsberger   Bucks County Community College

Sue McCrory   Missouri State

Laura White   University of West Florida

Karen Allen   Communtiy College of RI

Ralph Argiento   Guilford Technical Community College

Kuan Chen   Purdue University Calumet

Carin Chuang   Purdue University North Central

Christie Jahn Hovey   Lincoln Land Community College

Dr. Seth Powless   University of Toledo

Amiya K. Samantray   Marygrove College

**Special thanks to Lisa Hawkins,
Frederick Community College**

Mimi Spain   Southern Maine Community College

Kathie O'Brien   North Idaho College

Pat Franco   Los Angeles Valley College

Claire Amorde   Florida Institute Of Technology

Michael Haugrud   Minnesota State University Moorhead

Anjay Adhikari   Miami Dade College

Lynne Lyon   Durham College

Kate Le Grand   Broward College

Carolyn Barren   Macomb Community College

Bob Benavedis   Collins College

Theresa Hayes   Broward College

Mary Fleming   Ivy Tech Community College

Penny Cypert   Tarrant County College

Bernice Eng   Brookdale Community College

Deb Fells   Mesa Community College

Karen Allen   Bunker Hill Community College

Beverly Amer   Northern Arizona University

Michael Beddoes   Salt Lake Community College

Leilani Benoit   New Mexico State University

Gina Bowers   Harrisburg Area Community College

Linda Collins   Mesa Community College

Fred D'Angelo   Pima Community College

Robert Devoe Peterson   Fresno City College

Hedy Fossenkemper   Paradise Valley Community College

Rachelle Hall   Glendale Community College

Terri Helfand   Chaffey College

Ilga Higbee   Black Hawk College

Kay Johnson   Community College of Rhode Island

Darrel Karbginsky   Chemeketa Community College

Susan Katz   University of Bridgeport

Sherry Kersey   Hillsborough Community College

Ellen Kessler   Harrisburg Area Community College

Kate Legrand   Broward Community College

Mike Lehrfeld   Brevard Community College

Jian Lin   Eastern Connecticut State University

Nicole Lytle   California State University, San Bernadino

Peggy Menna   Community College of Rhode Island

Deborah Meyer   Saint Louis Community College, Forest Park

Pam Silvers   Asheville-Buncombe Technical Community College

Will Smith   Tulsa Community College

Lynne Stuhr   Trident Technical College

Ann Taff   Tulsa Community College

Jim Taggart   Atlantic Cape Community College

Michelle Vlaich Lee   Greenville Technical College

VISUALIZING
TECHNOLOGY

CHAPTER

1

What Is a Computer?

In This Chapter

VIZ INTRO

If you've gone grocery shopping, put gas in your car, watched a weather report on TV, or used a microwave oven today, then you've interacted with a computer. Most of us use computers every day, often without even realizing it. Computers have become so commonplace that we don't even consider them computers. In this chapter, we discuss what a computer is and look at the development of computers in the past few centuries. After reading this chapter, you will recognize the different types of computing devices and their impact on everyday life.

Objectives

1 Explain the Functions of a Computer

2 Describe the Evolution of Computer Hardware

3 Describe How Computers Represent Data Using Binary Code

4 List the Various Types and Characteristics of Personal Computers

5 Give Examples of Other Computing Devices

6 List the Various Types and Characteristics of Multiuser Computers

7 Explain Ubiquitous Computing and Convergence

Running Project

In this project, you'll explore computers used in everyday life. Look for instructions as you complete each article. For most articles, there is a series of questions for you to research. At the conclusion of the chapter, you'll submit your responses to the questions raised.

BrunoWeltmann/Fotolia

Moon Light PhotoStudio/Shutterstock

What Does a Computer Do?

1

Explain the Functions of a Computer

A **computer** is a programmable machine that converts raw **data** into useful **information**. Raw data includes numbers, words, pictures, or sounds that represent facts about people, events, things, or ideas. A toaster can never be anything more than a toaster—it has one function—but a computer can be a calculator, a media center, a communications center, a classroom, and much more. The ability to change its programming distinguishes a computer from any other machine.

Necessity Is the Mother of Invention

The original computers were people, not machines, and the mathematical tables they computed tended to be full of errors. The technical and scientific advancements of the Industrial Revolution at the end of the 19th century led to a growing need for this type of calculated information and to the development of the first mechanical computers.

In the early 19th century, mathematician Charles Babbage designed a machine called an **Analytical Engine**. This mechanical computer could be programmed using **punch cards**—stiff pieces of paper that convey information by the presence or absence of holes. Punch cards were developed by Joseph Marie Jacquard as part of the Jacquard loom to manufacture textiles with complex patterns (Figure 1.1). The Analytical Engine would have been the first mechanical computer, but the technology didn't exist at the time to build it. In his 1864 book *Passages from the Life of a Philosopher*, Babbage wrote, "The whole of the development and operations of analysis are now capable of being executed by machinery. As soon as an Analytical Engine exists, it will necessarily guide the future course of science." In 2011, a group of researchers at London's Science Museum began a project to build Babbage's computer. The project will take at least 10 years and cost millions of dollars.

Mathematician Ada Lovelace, a contemporary of Babbage, wrote a program for the Analytical Engine to calculate a series of Bernoulli numbers—a sequence of rational numbers used in number theory. Because of her efforts, many consider her the first computer programmer. Lovelace never tested the program because there were no machines capable of running it; however, when run on a computer today, her program yields the correct mathematical results. In 1979, the Ada computer language was named in her honor.

In 1936, mathematician Alan Turing wrote a paper titled *On Computable Numbers*, in which he introduced the concept of machines that could perform mathematical computations—later called **Turing machines**. In 1950, he developed the **Turing test**, which tests a machine's ability to

Mark Scheuern/Alamy Stock Photo

FIGURE 1.1 Punch cards create textile patterns in a Jacquard loom.

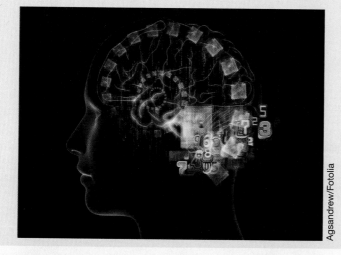

Agsandrew/Fotolia

display intelligent behavior. It took 64 years for the first computers to pass the Turing test, in 2014. Many consider Alan Turing to be the father of computer science and **artificial intelligence**—the branch of science concerned with making computers behave like humans. Alan Turing was the subject of the 2014 movie *The Imitation Game* Today, AI is being used in game playing, speech recognition, smart appliances such as air conditioners and refrigerators, medical and engineering research, weather forecasting, robots and automation, credit card fraud detection, and the list goes on. AI systems are helping humans solve problems in areas that range from entertainment to saving lives.

STORAGE: The raw data is stored temporarily until it can be processed. The processed information is stored for later retrieval.

INPUT: Data is collected from a customer order form.

OUTPUT: The processed data–now information–is output to the store employee to fulfill the order.

PROCESSING: The data is manipulated, or processed, so it can be used to evaluate the customer's order.

FIGURE 1.2 The information processing cycle converts data collected from a customer order form into information used to fulfill the order.

THE INFORMATION PROCESSING CYCLE

Computers convert data into information by using the **information processing cycle (IPC)**. The four steps of the IPC are input, processing, storage, and output. Raw data entered into the system during the input stage is processed, or manipulated, to create useful information. The information is stored for later retrieval and then returned to the user in the output stage. Figure 1.2 shows a general analogy of how this works. In this example, a customer is ordering an item online. The data collected from the customer is the input. The input is temporarily stored in the system until it can be processed. During processing, the data is used to evaluate the customer order. The output is sent to the employee to pick, pack, and ship the order.

It was nearly a century after Babbage designed his Analytical Engine before the first working mechanical computers were built. From that point, it took only about 40 years to go from those first-generation machines to the current fourth-generation systems.

Running Project

Many developments of the Industrial Revolution, such as the Jacquard loom, helped pave the way for modern computers. Use the Internet to find out how the following people also contributed: George Boole, Vannevar Bush, Nikola Tesla, and Gottfried Wilhelm Leibniz.

4 Things You Need to Know

- Computers are programmable machines.
- The four steps of the information processing cycle are input, processing, storage, and output.
- The IPC converts raw data into useful information.
- Artificial intelligence is the science of making computers behave like humans.

Key Terms

Analytical Engine

artificial intelligence

computer

data

information

information processing cycle (IPC)

punch card

Turing machine

Turing test

Digital Literacy Skill

Capture a Screenshot of Your Desktop

HOW TO VIDEO

A useful skill is creating screen shots of your desktop. For example, it's helpful for providing directions on how to do something or for keeping a record of an error message that appears on your screen. Windows includes a program called the Snipping Tool that you can use to capture a screenshot. Macs include the Grab tool.

The Windows Snipping Tool can capture four types of snips: Free-form, Rectangular, Window, or Full-screen. The Mac Grab tool can capture three types of grabs: Selection, Window, or Screen.

You can save your screenshots, email them, paste them into documents, and annotate and highlight them. If necessary, download the student data files from **pearsonhighered.com /viztech**. From your student data files, open the *vt_ch01_howto1_ answersheet* file and save the file as **lastname_firstname_ch01_ howto1_answersheet**.

1 From your student data files, right-click the file *vt_ch01_friend*, point to *Open with*, and then click *Photos*.

2 In the Windows search box on the taskbar, type **snip** and then, in the Search results, click *Snipping Tool*.

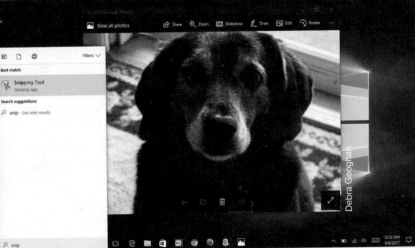

Courtesy of Microsoft Corporation Inc.

3 In the Snipping Tool window, click the drop-down arrow next to *New* and click *Free-form Snip*. Drag the mouse to draw a line around the dog's head with the Snipping Tool scissors. Click the *Copy* icon on the toolbar. Switch to your answer sheet and paste the snip under **Free-form Snip**. You can resize the image to fit your answer sheet.

Courtesy of Microsoft Corporation Inc.

Debra Geoghan

4 Return to your image. In the Snipping Tool window, click *New*. Click the drop-down arrow next to *New* and click *Rectangular Snip.* Drag the box around the dog's head and release the mouse button. Click the *Copy* icon on the toolbar. Paste the rectangular snip into your document under **Rectangular Snip**.

5 Use the same procedure to capture a Window Snip and a Full-screen Snip of the dog and paste both in your document. In a paragraph, describe the difference between the snips you took. Save the file and submit it as directed by your instructor.

If you are using a Mac:
1. From your student data files, double-click the file *vt_ch01_friend* to open it in Preview.
2. From Launchpad, click the *Other* folder, and then open Grab.
3. From the Grab *Capture* menu, click *Selection*. Drag the box around the dog's head and release the mouse button. Use the *Edit* menu to copy the capture and then paste it into your answer sheet. Use the same procedure to capture a Window and Screen grab and paste both in your document. In a paragraph, describe the difference between the grabs you took. Save the file and submit it as directed by your instructor.

Screen shot(s) reprinted with permission from Apple Inc.

Debra Geoghan

A Brief History of Computers

2 Describe the Evolution of Computer Hardware

In this article, we look at the evolution of computers in the past century—from the massive first-generation machines of the 1930s and 1940s to the modern fourth-generation devices—and how Moore's Law has predicted the exponential growth of technology.

History of Computers

Computers have come a long way since Babbage and Turing. Between the mid-19th and mid-20th centuries, the Industrial Revolution gave way to the Information Age. Since that time, the pace of technology has grown faster than it ever has before.

FIGURE 1.3 ENIAC was the first working, digital, general-purpose computer.

FIRST-GENERATION COMPUTERS

During the 1930s and 1940s, several electromechanical and electronic computers were built. These first-generation computers were massive in size and used vacuum tubes and manual switches to process data. **Vacuum tubes**, which resemble incandescent light bulbs, give off a lot of heat and are notoriously unreliable. **ENIAC (Electronic Numerical Integrator and Computer)**, built at the University of Pennsylvania from 1943 to 1946, is considered the first working, digital, general-purpose computer (Figure 1.3). ENIAC used about 18,000 vacuum tubes, weighed almost 30 tons, and occupied about 1,800 square feet. Originally created to calculate artillery firing tables, ENIAC wasn't completed until after the war ended and was reprogrammed to solve a range of other problems, such as atomic energy calculations, weather predictions, and wind-tunnel design. The programming was done by manipulating switches and took six programmers several days to complete.

The Harvard Mark I, also known as the IBM Automatic Sequence Controlled Calculator, was a general-purpose digital calculator used by the U.S. Navy toward the end of World War II. It was 51 feet long and 8 feet tall. Grace Hopper worked on the Mark I and was one of the first computer programmers. Hopper is sometimes credited with coining the term *bug* to refer to a glitch in a computer program.

Important first-generation computers include the Z1 and Z3 built in Germany; the Colossus machines in the United Kingdom; and the Atanasoff–Berry Computer (ABC), the Harvard Mark 1, ENIAC, and UNIVAC in the United States (Table 1.1).

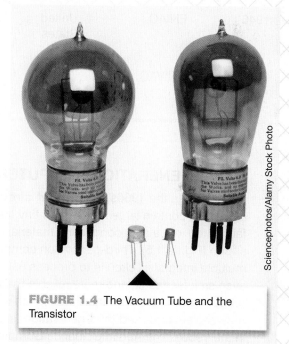

FIGURE 1.4 The Vacuum Tube and the Transistor

SECOND-GENERATION COMPUTERS

Invented in 1947, **transistors** are tiny electronic switches. The use of transistors in place of vacuum tubes enabled second-generation computers in the 1950s and 1960s to be more powerful, smaller, more reliable, and reprogrammed in far less time than first-generation computers. Figure 1.4 illustrates the difference between the size of a vacuum tube and a transistor.

TABLE 1.1 Important First-Generation Computers

Date	Computer	Origin	Creator	Description
1936–1941	Z1–Z3	Germany	Konrad Zuse	The Z1 through Z3 were mechanical, programmable computers. Working in isolation in Germany, Konrad Zuse didn't receive the support of the Nazi government, and his computers were destroyed during the war.
1942	Atanasoff–Berry Computer (ABC)	United States	Professor John Atanasoff and graduate student Clifford Berry at Iowa State College	The ABC was never fully functional, but Atanasoff won a patent dispute against John Mauchly (ENIAC), and Atanasoff was declared the inventor of the electronic digital computer.
1944	Colossus	United Kingdom	Tommy Flowers	Used by code-breakers to translate encrypted German messages, these computers were destroyed after the war and kept secret until the 1970s.
1944	Harvard Mark 1	United States	Designed by Howard Aiken and programmed by Grace Hopper at Harvard University	The Mark 1 was used by the U.S. Navy for gunnery and ballistic calculations until 1959.
1946	ENIAC	United States	J. Presper Eckert and John Mauchly at the University of Pennsylvania	ENIAC was the first working, digital, general-purpose computer.
1951	UNIVAC	United States	Eckert/Mauchly	The world's first commercially available computer, UNIVAC was famous for predicting the outcome of the 1952 presidential election.

THIRD-GENERATION COMPUTERS

Developed in the 1960s, **integrated circuits** are chips that contain large numbers of tiny transistors fabricated into a semiconducting material called silicon (Figure 1.5). Third-generation computers used multiple integrated circuits to process data and were even smaller, faster, and more reliable than their predecessors, although there was much overlap between second- and third-generation technologies in the 1960s. The Apollo Guidance Computer, used in the moon landing missions, was designed using transistors, but over time, the design was modified to use integrated circuits instead. The 2000 Nobel Prize in physics was awarded for the invention of the integrated circuit.

BRIAN_KINNEY/Fotolia

FIGURE 1.5 Integrated Circuits on a Circuit Board

FOURTH-GENERATION COMPUTERS

The integrated circuit made the development of the microprocessor possible in the 1970s. A **microprocessor** is a complex integrated circuit that contains processing circuitry that enables it to behave as the brain of the computer, control all functions performed by other components, and process all the commands it receives. The microprocessor is also referred to as the **central processing unit** or **CPU** (Figure 1.6). The first microprocessor was developed in 1971 and was as powerful as ENIAC. Today's personal computers use microprocessors and are considered fourth-generation computers. Microprocessors can be found in everything from alarm clocks to automobiles to refrigerators.

Singkham/Fotolia

FIGURE 1.6 Fourth-generation computers use microprocessors.

FIND OUT MORE

Integrated Circuits

Play the integrated circuit game nobelprize.org /educational/physics/integrated_circuit to learn more about this invention. Who invented the integrated circuit? Where might you still find a vacuum tube today? How did the invention of the transistor affect the radio? What's the significance of the handheld calculator?

Nobel Media AB

Moore's Law

In 1965, Intel cofounder Gordon Moore observed that the number of transistors that could be placed on an integrated circuit had doubled roughly every two years. This observation, known as **Moore's Law**, predicted this exponential growth would continue. The law was never intended to be a true measure, but rather an illustration, of the pace of technology advancement. The increase in the capabilities of integrated circuits directly affects the processing speed and storage capacity of modern electronic devices. As a result of new technologies, such as building 3D silicon processors or using carbon nanotubes in place of silicon (Figure 1.7), this pace held true for roughly 50 years, but by 2016 most experts agreed this pace is no longer viable. The increase in the capabilities of integrated circuits directly affects the processing speed and storage capacity of modern electronic devices.

Moore stated in a 1996 article, "More than anything, once something like this gets established, it becomes more or less a self-fulfilling prophecy. The Semiconductor Industry Association puts out a technology road map, which continues this [generational improvement] every three years. Everyone in the industry recognizes that if you don't stay on essentially that curve they will fall behind. So it sort of drives itself." Thus, Moore's Law became a technology plan that guides the industry. Over the past several decades, the end of Moore's Law has been predicted. Each time, new technological advances have kept it going, but as new ideas and technologies have emerged, sticking to Moore's Law has become increasingly less practical or important. Moore himself admits that exponential growth can't continue forever.

In less than a century, computers have gone from being massive, unreliable, and costly machines to being an integral part of almost everything we do. As technology has improved, the size and costs have dropped as the speed, power, and reliability have grown. Today, the chip inside your cell phone has more processing power than the first microprocessor developed in 1971. Technology that was science fiction just a few decades ago is now commonplace.

Moore, Gordon E. 1996. "Some Personal Perspectives on Research in the Semiconductor Industry," in Rosenbloom, Richard S., and William J. Spencer (Eds.). Engines of Innovation (Boston: Harvard Business School Press), pp. 165–174.

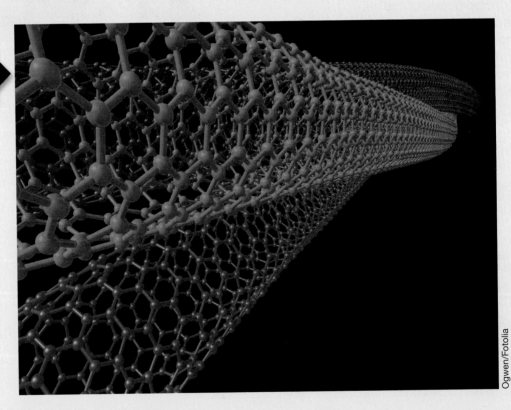

FIGURE 1.7 Carbon nanotubes may someday replace silicon in integrated circuits.

Ogwen/Fotolia

GREEN COMPUTING
Smart Homes

The efficient and eco-friendly use of computers and other electronics is called **green computing**. Smart homes and smart appliances help save energy and, as a result, are good for both the environment and your pocketbook.

Smart homes use home automation to control lighting, heating and cooling, security, entertainment, and appliances. Such a system can be programmed to turn various components on and off at set times to maximize energy efficiency. So, the heat can turn up, and the house can be warm right before you get home from work, while not wasting the energy to keep it warm all day while you're away. If you're away on vacation or have to work late, you can remotely activate a smart home by phone or over the Internet. Some utility companies offer lower rates during off-peak hours, so programming your dishwasher and other appliances to run during those times can save you money and help energy utility companies manage the power grid, potentially reducing the need for new power plants.

Can't make your home a smart home overnight? No worries! You can take some small steps without investing in an entire smart home system. Try installing a programmable thermostat, putting lights on timers or motion sensors, and running appliances during off-peak hours.

Smart appliances can monitor signals from the power company transmitted over the **smart grid**—a network for delivering electricity to consumers that includes communication technology to manage electricity distribution efficiently. When the electric grid system is stressed, smart appliances can react by reducing power consumption. Although these advances are called smart home technology, the same technologies can also be found in commercial buildings.

stockcreations/Shutterstock

Running Project

Use the Internet to look up current microprocessors. What companies produce them? Visit **computer.howstuffworks.com /microprocessor.htm** and read the article. How many transistors were found on the first home computer processor? What was the name of the processor, and when was it introduced?

5 Things You Need to Know

- First-generation computers used vacuum tubes.
- Second-generation computers used transistors.
- Third-generation computers used integrated circuits (chips).
- Fourth-generation computers use microprocessors.
- Moore's Law states that the number of transistors that can be placed on an integrated circuit doubles roughly every two years—although today it is closer to every 18 months.

Key Terms

central processing unit (CPU)	microprocessor
	Moore's Law
ENIAC (Electronic Numerical Integrator and Computer)	smart appliance
	smart grid
green computing	smart home
	transistor
integrated circuit	vacuum tube

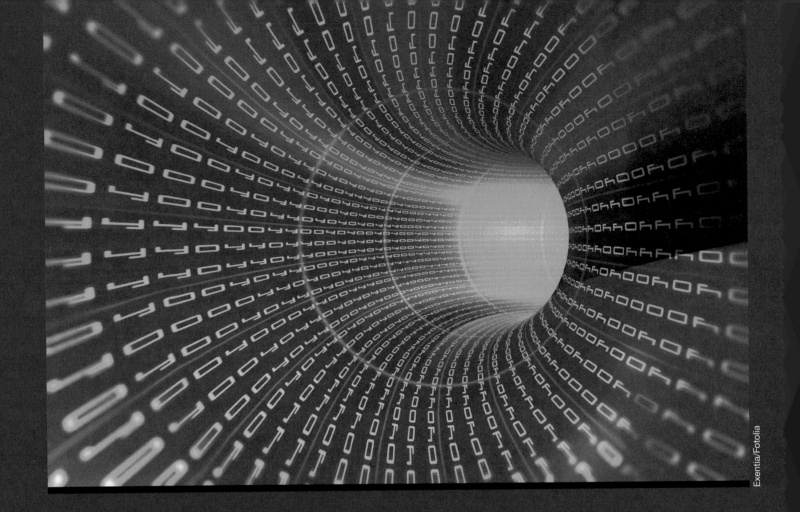

Exentia/Fotolia

Bits and Bytes

3 Describe How Computers Represent Data Using Binary Code

VIZ CLIP

Bits and Bytes

Humans have 10 digits—our fingers!—which is why the most commonly used number system is the decimal, or base 10, number system. Computers have switches, not fingers, and use the **binary number system** also referred to as **base 2**, a number system that has only two digits—0 and 1. All information entered into a computer system must be converted into binary digits.

Binary Code

Computers do not speak English or Spanish or Chinese or any other human language, so how does a computer interpret what a human inputs? On a typewriter, when you press the *A* key, you get an A on the page. Computers only understand 0s and 1s, so when you press the *A* key, it must somehow be converted to 0s and 1s. Digital data is represented using a **binary code**. A binary code represents digital data as a series of 0s and 1s that can be understood by a computer.

Binary code works like a bank of light switches. If there is only a single light switch in a room, there are two possible states: The light can either be on or it can be off. This code works in situations with only two possibilities, such as yes/no or true/false, but it fails when there are more than two choices, such as vanilla/chocolate/strawberry. Adding another switch—or bit—increases the possible combinations by a factor of two, which equals four possibilities. A third switch, or bit, gives us eight possibilities, and so on (Table 1.2). A **bit**, short for binary digit, is the smallest unit of digital data. Eight bits equal a **byte**, which gives us 256 possibilities. A byte is used to represent a single character in modern computer systems. For example, when you press the

A key, the binary code 01000001 (65 in decimal) is sent to the computer.

ASCII (American Standard Code for Information Interchange) was developed in the 1960s using a 7-bit system that represented 128 characters and included English alphabet symbols in both uppercase and lowercase, numbers 0 through 9, punctuation, and a few special characters. It was later expanded to an 8-bit extended set with 256 characters, but ASCII needed to be adapted to be used for other languages, and many extended sets were developed. The most common extended ASCII set is **Unicode**. Unicode is the standard on the Internet and includes codes for most of the world's written languages, mathematical systems, and special characters. It has codes for about 100,000 characters. The first 256 characters are the same in both ASCII and Unicode; however, the characters in the last rows in Table 1.3 include Latin, Greek, and Cyrillic symbols, which are represented only in Unicode.

TABLE 1.2 A binary code using 8 switches, or bits, has 256 different possible combinations.

Number of Bits (switches)	Possibilities	Power of Two
1	2	2^1
2	4	2^2
3	8	2^3
4	16	2^4
5	32	2^5
6	64	2^6
7	128	2^7
8	256	2^8

TABLE 1.3 ASCII and Unicode Representations

Character	ASCII (in decimal)	Unicode (in decimal)	Binary Code
#	35	35	00100011
$	36	36	00100100
0	48	48	00110000
1	49	49	00110001
A	65	65	10000001
B	66	66	1000010
a	97	97	1100001
b	98	98	1100010
œ		339	
ŕ		341	
α		945	

Measuring Data

Bits (b) are used to measure data transfer rates such as an Internet connection, and bytes (B) are used to measure file size and storage capacity. The decimal prefixes of *kilo*, *mega*, *giga*, *tera*, *peta*, and so on are added to the base unit (*bit* or *byte*) to indicate larger values. Binary prefixes *kibi*, *mebi*, and *gibi* have been adopted, although their use isn't widespread. A megabyte (MB) is equal to 1,000,000 bytes, and a mebibyte (MiB) is equal to 1,048,576 bytes, a slightly larger value. Tables 1.4 and 1.5 compare the two systems.

A megabyte (MB) is equal to 1 million bytes—the equivalent of about 500–800 pages of plain text. The size of a single picture taken with a digital camera can be 24 megabytes or more. A gigabyte is equal to 1,000 megabytes; most storage is measured in gigabytes. Larger hard drives are measured in terabytes. A terabyte equals 1,000 gigabytes. As the commonly used types of digital files have changed from plain text to images, music, and video, the file sizes have become larger, and the need for storage has grown. Fundamentally, however, all files are still just 0s and 1s.

TABLE 1.4 Decimal Storage Capacity Prefixes

Decimal Prefix	Symbol	Decimal Value	
		Exponential	Numeric
Kilo	K or k	10^3	1,000
Mega	M	10^6	1,000,000
Giga	G	10^9	1,000,000,000
Tera	T	10^{12}	1,000,000,000,000
Peta	P	10^{15}	1,000,000,000,000,000
Exa	E	10^{18}	1,000,000,000,000,000,000
Zetta	Z	10^{21}	1,000,000,000,000,000,000,000
Yotta	Y	10^{24}	1,000,000,000,000,000,000,000,000

TABLE 1.5 Binary Storage Capacity Prefixes

Binary Prefix	Symbol	Binary Exponent	Decimal Value
Kibi	Ki	2^{10}	1,024
Mebi	Mi	2^{20}	1,048,576
Gibi	Gi	2^{30}	1,073,741,824
Tebi	Ti	2^{40}	1,099,511,627,776
Pebi	Pi	2^{50}	1,125,899,906,842,624
Exbi	Ei	2^{60}	1,152,921,504,606,846,976
Zebi	Zi	2^{70}	1,180,591,620,717,411,303,424
Yobi	Yi	2^{80}	1,208,925,819,614,629,174,706,176

Alen-D/Fotolia

CAREER SPOTLIGHT

JOBS

BIOINFORMATICS   Computers have become integral to almost every modern career. Nowhere is this more evident than in the field of biology. **Bioinformatics** is the application of information technology to the field of biology. Computers are used to analyze data, predict how molecules will behave, and maintain and search massive databases of information. The rapid growth of biological information over the past few decades has created a demand for new technologies and people who know how to use them. This field requires at least a four-year degree. If you have a strong interest in science and technology, bioinformatics might be a good career choice for you.

Alexander Raths/shutterstock

Running Project

Use the Internet to research the usage of decimal and binary prefixes discussed in this chapter. Describe two instances when binary prefixes are more commonly used.

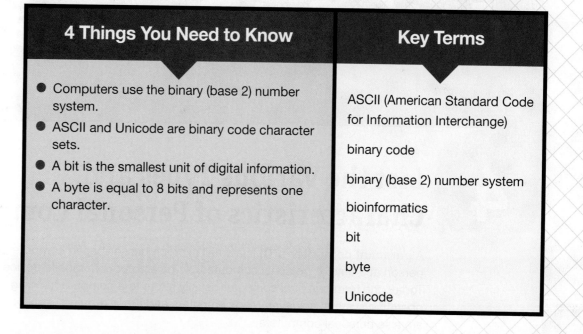

4 Things You Need to Know

- Computers use the binary (base 2) number system.
- ASCII and Unicode are binary code character sets.
- A bit is the smallest unit of digital information.
- A byte is equal to 8 bits and represents one character.

Key Terms

ASCII (American Standard Code for Information Interchange)

binary code

binary (base 2) number system

bioinformatics

bit

byte

Unicode

Javi indy/Shutterstock

Let's Get Personal

4

List the Various Types and Characteristics of Personal Computers

A **personal computer (PC)** is a small microprocessor-based computer used by one person at a time. A personal computer can be a notebook, mobile device, or desktop. Today, the term *personal computer* usually refers to a computer running a Windows operating system; however, Mac computers and those running Linux operating systems are also personal computers.

SIMULATION

What Is a Computer?

Desktop Computers

A **desktop computer** is a personal computer that fits into a workspace, such as a desk or counter. Desktops range in price from under $300 for basic personal systems to thousands of dollars for high-end machines used for video editing, gaming, and number crunching. Desktop computers offer the most speed, power, and upgradability for the lowest cost. A **workstation** is a high-end desktop computer or one that's attached to a network in a business setting.

An **all-in-one computer** is a compact desktop computer with an integrated monitor and system unit (Figure 1.8). Some all-in-ones are wall-mountable. All-in-ones save desktop real estate but may be difficult to upgrade because of their small size. They are popular in places where space is at a premium, such as emergency rooms, bank teller windows, and classrooms.

FIGURE 1.8 An all-in-one desktop computer with the components mounted behind the monitor is popular in settings in which desktop space is limited.

Andrew Brookes/Corbis/Getty Images

Ekaphon maneechot/Shutterstock

Notebook Computers

Notebook or **laptop** computers are portable personal computers. Notebook computers can rival desktops in power and storage capacity—but can cost significantly more than a comparable desktop system. In spite of the higher cost, notebooks have become more affordable, and thus more popular. In 2015, notebooks outsold desktops more than two to one. Modern notebook computers come with built-in wireless networking capabilities, webcams, and bright widescreen displays, and can handle most ordinary computing tasks with ease. High-end notebooks with large screens and powerful processors are referred to as desktop replacements, because many individuals now purchase this type of system instead of a traditional desktop computer.

A **convertible notebook** computer has a screen that can swivel to fold into what resembles a notepad or tablet. These computers include a touch screen or a special digital pen, or **stylus**, that enables you to write directly on the screen, making them useful for taking notes or drawing diagrams and for making information such as sales catalogs portable. A two-in-one notebook had a detachable screen that converts to a tablet. A **tablet** is a handheld mobile device that falls somewhere between a notebook and a smartphone. A tablet has an LCD—liquid-crystal display—screen, a long battery life, and built-in wireless connectivity. Tablets are a good choice for travel. A tablet may have a detachable keyboard, making it more notebook-like with the keyboard in place. Tablets come with a variety of pre-installed **mobile applications**, or **mobile apps**—programs that extend the functionality of mobile devices. Thousands of apps can be downloaded and installed to make the device even more versatile. With these devices, you can edit documents, take photographs, surf the web, send and receive email, and watch videos.

The smallest type of notebook computer is a **netbook**. These lightweight, inexpensive computers are designed primarily for Internet access. Low-cost notebooks, tablets, and subnotebooks have largely replaced netbooks. A **subnotebook** is a notebook computer that is thin and light and that has high-end processing and video capabilities. The screen on a subnotebook is typically larger than on a netbook, in the range of 13–15 inches. Ultrabooks that run Windows, Chromebooks, and Apple's MacBook Air are examples of subnotebooks (Figure 1.9).

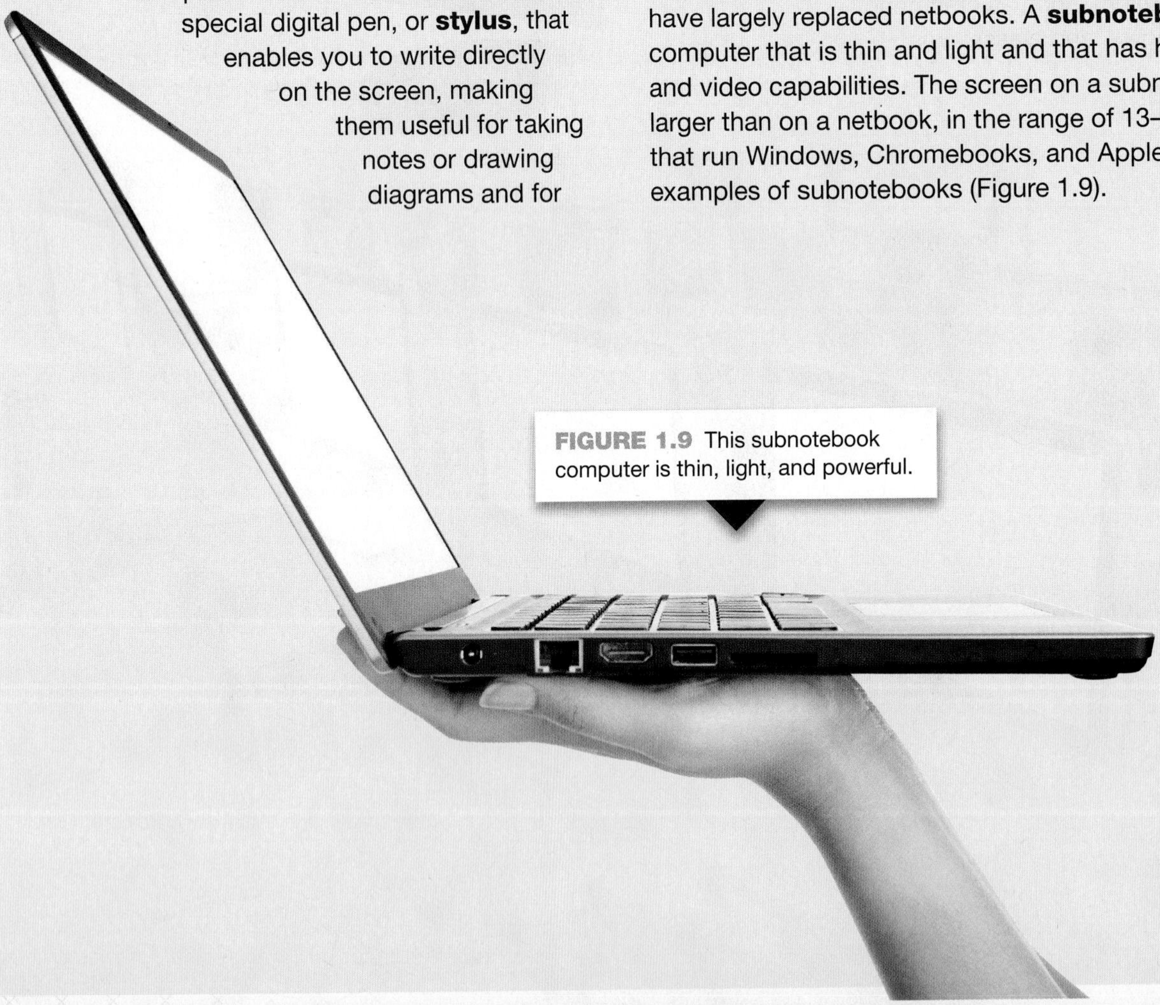

FIGURE 1.9 This subnotebook computer is thin, light, and powerful.

Creativa Images/Fotolia

MAC, PC, or Something Else?

In the personal computer market, there are two main platforms of personal computers to choose from: Macs and PCs. A computer platform includes both the hardware and software that make up the system. What's the difference between the two, and which one should you choose? Most of the configurations of computers discussed in this chapter are available in both platforms. The primary difference between them is the operating system they run. An **operating system** is software that provides the user with an interface to communicate with the hardware and software on a computer. A computer can't run without an operating system installed. Operating systems are discussed in detail in another chapter.

Mac computers are built by Apple and run the macOS operating system. Using a program called Boot Camp that's included with macOS, users can also run Microsoft Windows on a Mac. Macs have a reputation for being secure, stable, and fun. They come with a variety of useful programs already installed and are very user friendly. Macs are often used in creative businesses, such as advertising and graphic design, and are growing in popularity in the home market.

PCs can be built by any number of companies, including Sony, Asus, Lenovo, and Toshiba. PCs that run some version of the Windows or Linux operating systems constitute over 85 percent of the U.S. market share. Because PCs are produced by many manufacturers, they are available in numerous models, configurations, and price ranges. PCs that run Windows have the largest selection of software available.

Chromebooks are less common than Macs or PCs, but are growing in popularity. Chromebooks are subnotebooks that run the Chrome OS—a version of the Linux operating system released by Google. These notebooks are designed to work best when connected to the Internet and rely on web apps and online storage rather than traditional software. The Chromebox is a desktop computer running Chrome OS. Figure 1.10 highlights some of the features of Macs, PCs, and Chromebooks.

Personal computers have become so commonplace that roughly 80 percent of U.S. households have at least one personal computer. In addition, by 2014, tablet sales rivaled PC sales. The type of computer you choose depends on many factors, including personal preferences, the types of software you use, compatibility with school or work computers, and cost.

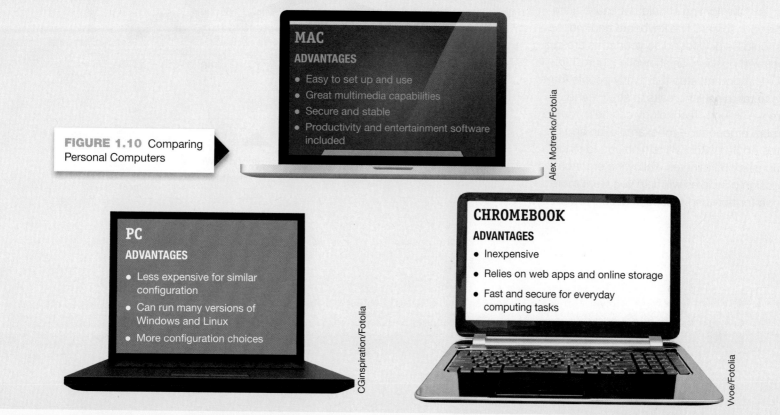

FIGURE 1.10 Comparing Personal Computers

MAC
ADVANTAGES
- Easy to set up and use
- Great multimedia capabilities
- Secure and stable
- Productivity and entertainment software included

Alex Motrenko/Fotolia

PC
ADVANTAGES
- Less expensive for similar configuration
- Can run many versions of Windows and Linux
- More configuration choices

CGinspiration/Fotolia

CHROMEBOOK
ADVANTAGES
- Inexpensive
- Relies on web apps and online storage
- Fast and secure for everyday computing tasks

Vvoe/Fotolia

Ergonomics

An improperly set up workspace can affect your health, comfort, and productivity. **Ergonomics** is the study of the relationship between workers and their workspaces. Ergonomic design creates a work environment designed to reduce illnesses and musculoskeletal disorders. The furniture you use, the lighting in the room, and the position of your equipment all affect your work environment.

Whether you are working in class at a desktop computer, sitting on the couch playing video games, or reading a book on an e-reader at the beach, your goal should be to keep your body in a neutral body position without twisting or turning to reach or see your screen. You should not need to lean forward, and your feet should be flat on the ground or on a footrest. Your monitor should be at or below eye level so you do not need to tilt your neck to see it, and the lighting should not cause glare on your screen. The keyboard and mouse should be positioned so your arms are in a relaxed position, as shown in Figure 1.11. One important step that many people forget is to take regular breaks to stretch and move around. Technology can help you be more ergonomic—for example, an app on the Apple Watch will remind you to stand up every 50 minutes. Following ergonomic design principles will help you work more comfortably and reduce strain on your body.

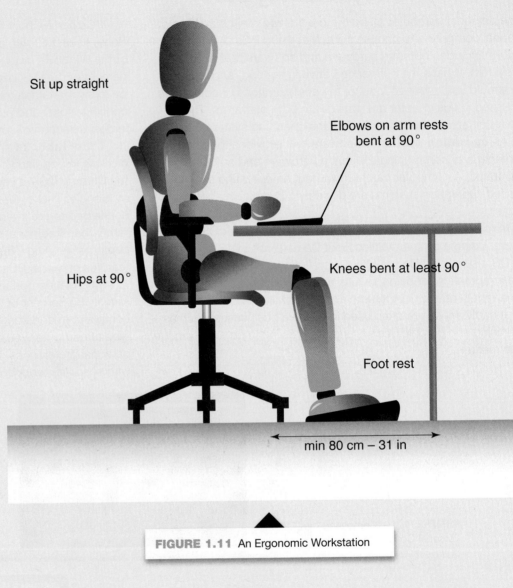

Sit up straight

Elbows on arm rests bent at 90°

Hips at 90°

Knees bent at least 90°

Foot rest

min 80 cm – 31 in

Maluson/Shutterstock

FIGURE 1.11 An Ergonomic Workstation

UNIVERSAL DESIGN

Universal design principles not only help create environments that accommodate people with disabilities, but also benefit those with no special needs. For example, wider doorways allow wheelchairs and walkers through and make it easier to carry merchandise and move furniture. In technology, applying universal design means designing spaces that are easily accessible. This term also refers to input and output devices that can be used and adjusted by everyone. Devices should be simple and intuitive to use for everyone. Universal design extends to software and website design as well.

Running Project

It's hard to imagine a job that doesn't require a working knowledge of personal computers. Look up the term *digital literacy*. Use several different websites to get an idea of what this term means, and then write up a description of digital literacy for the career that you plan to pursue.

6 Things You Need to Know

- Desktop computers give you the most bang for your buck.
- Notebook or laptop computers are portable PCs.
- Tablets fall somewhere between notebooks and smartphones and run mobile apps.
- The primary difference between a Mac and a PC is the operating system software.
- Chromebooks and Chromeboxes run the Google Chrome OS and function best when connected to the Internet.
- Ergonomics and universal design help create workspaces that are healthy and easier for users.

Key Terms

all-in-one computer

Chromebook

convertible notebook

desktop computer

ergonomics

laptop

Mac

mobile application (mobile app)

netbook

notebook

operating system

personal computer (PC)

stylus

subnotebook

tablet

universal design

workstation

 Viz Check—In MyLab IT, take a quick quiz covering Objectives 1–4.

Ergonomics

HOW TO VIDEO

The Occupational Safety and Health Administration (OSHA) website has a computer workstation checklist. In this activity, you will use the checklist to evaluate your workspace at home or school. If necessary, download the student data files from **pearsonhighered.com /viztech**. From your student data files, open the *vt_ch01_howto2_answersheet* file and save the file as **lastname_firstname_ch01_howto2_answersheet**.

1 Open your browser and go to **www.osha.gov/SLTC/etools /computerworkstations**.

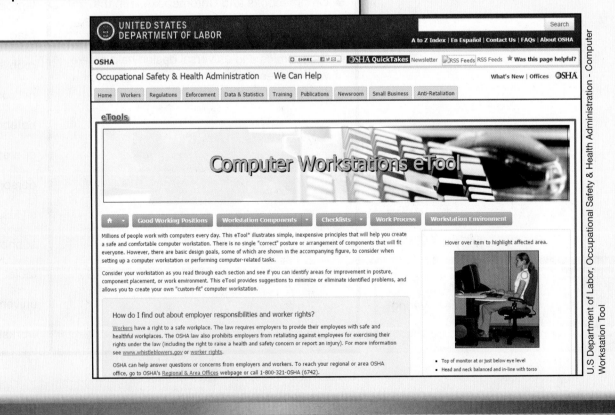

U.S Department of Labor, Occupational Safety & Health Administration - Computer Workstation Tool

2 Click *Good Working Positions* and read the information on this page. What does neutral body positioning mean, and what are the four reference postures?

U.S Department of Labor, Occupational Safety & Health Administration - Computer Workstation Tool

Computer Workstations eTool

| 🏠 ▾ | Good Working Positions | Workstation Components ▾ | Checklists ▾ | Work Process | Workstation Environment |

Good Working Positions

To understand the best way to set up a computer workstation, it is helpful to understand the concept of neutral body positioning. This is a comfortable working posture in which your joints are naturally aligned. Working with the body in a neutral position reduces stress and strain on the muscles, tendons, and skeletal system and reduces your risk of developing a musculoskeletal disorder (MSD). The following are important considerations when attempting to maintain neutral body postures while working at the computer workstation:

- *Hands, wrists,* and *forearms* are straight, in-line and roughly parallel to the floor.
- *Head* is level, or bent slightly forward, forward facing, and balanced. Generally it is in-line with the *torso*.
- *Shoulders* are relaxed and *upper arms* hang normally at the side of the body.
- *Elbows* stay in close to the body and are bent between 90 and 120 degrees.
- *Feet* are fully supported by the floor or a footrest may be used if the desk height is not adjustable.
- *Back* is fully supported with appropriate lumbar support when sitting vertical or leaning back slightly.
- *Thighs* and *hips* are supported by a well-padded seat and generally parallel to the floor.
- *Knees* are about the same height as the hips with the *feet* slightly forward.

3 Click the *Checklists* arrow and click *Evaluation*. Complete the checklist to evaluate your workspace. For each question that you answer no to, click the appropriate link to read the information on how to correct the problem. How did your workstation fare? What are some areas for improvement? How could you improve your score? When you have finished the checklist, click the link to Print Checklist. If you are using Safari or Chrome, save the checklist as a PDF file. Using Edge, Internet Explorer or Firefox, print using the Microsoft Print to PDF or Microsoft XPS Document Writer option. Save the file as **lastname_ firstname_ch01_howto2_ checklist**. Submit both the answer sheet and checklist files as directed by your instructor.

U.S Department of Labor, Occupational Safety & Health Administration - Computer Workstation Tool

Computer Workstations eTool

| 🏠 ▾ | Good Working Positions | Workstation Components ▾ | Checklists ▾ | Work Process | Workstation Environment |

Checklists » Evaluation

This checklist can help you create a safe and comfortable computer workstation. You can also use it in conjunction with the purchasing guide checklist. A "no" response indicates that a problem may exist. Refer to the appropriate section of the eTool for assistance and ideas about how to analyze and control the problem.

🖨 Print Checklist   Clear Form

☑ **WORKING POSTURES** - The workstation is designed or arranged for doing computer tasks so it allows your...
1. **Head** and **neck** to be upright, or in-line with the torso (not bent down/back). If "no" refer to Monitors, Chairs and Work Surfaces.
   ○ Yes   ○ No
2. **Head, neck, and trunk to** face forward (not twisted). If "no" refer to Monitors or Chairs.
   ○ Yes   ○ No

☑ **MONITOR** - Consider these points when evaluating the monitor. The monitor is designed or arranged for computer tasks so the...
1. **Top** of the screen is at or below eye level so you can read it without bending your head or neck down/back.
   ○ Yes   ○ No
2. **User with bifocals/trifocals** can read the screen without bending the head or neck backward.
   ○ Yes   ○ No

Beyond the Desktop

Give Examples of Other Computing Devices

Today, the term *computer* no longer refers only to desktops used for office work. Many of us carry computers with us everywhere we go. In fact, mobile devices have become the primary computing devices for many people.

Mobile Devices

Mobile devices are portable, handheld computers used for business and entertainment and come in many different shapes and sizes—from tablets and smartphones to fitness monitors that you wear on your wrist. Some of these devices serve specialized functions, such as GPS navigation, while others, such as smartphones, are more general-purpose devices. Mobile devices are the fastest growing segment of personal computers.

Scanrail/Fotolia

SMARTPHONES AND TABLETS

Mobile devices such as smartphones and tablets combine features such as Internet and email access, digital cameras, GPS and mapping tools, and access to thousands of mobile apps. Mobile devices are useful when carrying a regular notebook computer isn't practical. Mobile devices are the fastest-growing segment of personal computers.

Basic mobile phones are limited to making phone calls and perhaps texting and taking photos. **Smartphones** are small computers that combine a cellular phone with such features as Internet and email access, a digital camera, mapping tools, and the ability to edit documents. You can download additional mobile applications, or mobile apps, to extend their capabilities, which makes them true convergence devices. The cellular networks offered by major carriers offer data transfer speeds that rival home connections. This improved connection speed enables you to check email, watch TV, video chat, and play online games almost anywhere. Your cellular plan may include separate charges for voice and data. Using apps that use your data connection can quickly use up the amount of data in your plan, leading to reduced speed or extra cost. Apps can also decrease the battery life of your device. Many mobile phones use a **SIM card—Subscriber Identity Module**—which identifies the phone, and includes account information and cellular carrier. Cellular-enabled tablets use the same network as your smartphone to access the Internet. You need to purchase a data plan from your cellular carrier to use this feature.

WEARABLES AND GPS

Computers worn on the body are known as **wearables**. These hands-free computers are used for fitness tracking and health monitoring, communications, military operations, and entertainment. The Apple Watch is a general-purpose wearable computer (Figure 1.12).

Originally built by the military, the **Global Positioning System**, or **GPS**, consists of at least 24 satellites operating at all times (Figure 1.13), plus several spares. These satellites transmit signals that are picked up by a GPS receiver on the ground to determine

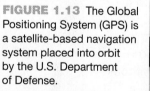

FIGURE 1.12 The Apple Watch is a wearable computer.

Jacek Lasa/Alamy Stock Photo

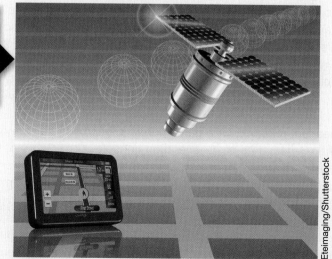

FIGURE 1.13 The Global Positioning System (GPS) is a satellite-based navigation system placed into orbit by the U.S. Department of Defense.

Eteimaging/Shutterstock

the receiver's current location, time, and velocity through triangulation of the signals. Since the mid-1990s, GPS devices have been available for civilian use. There are scientific applications for GPS technology, such as surveying, map making, self-navigating robots, and clock synchronization. GPS is used in automobiles, airplanes, and boats for navigation and tracking. Many mobile apps use GPS for navigation, location services, and just plain fun. For example, some apps use your location to determine what information to display, such as discounts, local weather, or nearby restaurant recommendations.

Geocaching is an electronic scavenger hunt played around the world. Players, called geocachers, hide geocaches—typically a small waterproof container—and post GPS coordinates on the Internet. You can then find the geocaches using your GPS device or app on your mobile device to help you navigate. The geocaches have logbooks to sign and often small prizes. Geocachers that find a prize leave something else in return, so you never know what you will find. Check out **geocaching.com** to find out how to play.

Umnola/Fotolia

Video Game Systems and Simulations

A **video game system** is a computer designed primarily to play games. The first arcade video games were released in the early 1970s, and video game systems for the home soon followed. Magnavox released its Odyssey game console in 1972. It was programmed to play 12 different games. Atari released a home version of Pong for the 1975 holiday season. Sold exclusively through Sears, Pong was the hottest gift of the year. For many people, video game systems were the first computers they had in their homes.

Current video game systems have high-end processing and graphics capabilities and the abilities to play movies and music, enable online game play, and browse the Internet. Game consoles such as Microsoft Xbox One and Sony PlayStation 4 have built-in hard drives, can play DVDs and Blu-ray discs, and display high-definition video, and the newest version of Xbox One supports 4K Ultra HD video. Kinect for Xbox has motion and voice sensors that enable you to play certain games without holding a **game controller**—a device used to interact with a video game. In 2016, PlayStation VR was the first virtual-reality headset released for a game console. Microsoft has announced the release of its next generation console, Xbox Scorpio, for late 2017 and Sony is expected to release PS5 in 2018 or 2019. Each update brings improved hardware and a better gaming experience.

Handheld video games enable you to take your games wherever you go. The popularity of smartphones and tablets has reduced this market dramatically. The Nintendo Switch is a hybrid system that allows you to connect the handheld system to a dock that turns it into a console system.

Video game systems aren't just for entertainment. In healthcare, medical students use video game simulations to learn to be better doctors, simulations help stroke patient rehab to improve fine motor reflexes, and surgeons use simulations to practice intricate techniques. In other applications, pilots train on flight simulators, business students solve complex problems, and biology students perform virtual dissections. Simulations enable you to immerse yourself in a situation that may not be safe or accessible otherwise.

TZIDO SUN/Shutterstock

FIND OUT MORE...

GPS and Beyond

GPS is a U.S. based system. Did you know that Russia has a system called GLONASS and the European system is called Galileo? Together these three systems provide global coverage, and yet there are still places on earth where GPS is inaccessible. DARPA (The Defense Advanced Research Projects Agency) is working on a new positioning system that won't use satellites at all. Use the Internet to find out how this new system will work and when it is expected to be functional.

Running Project

Use the Internet to find out how medical students are using video game simulations. What are some of the medical schools using such systems? How are these systems used? How do professors and students feel about them? What other fields use simulators to train students?

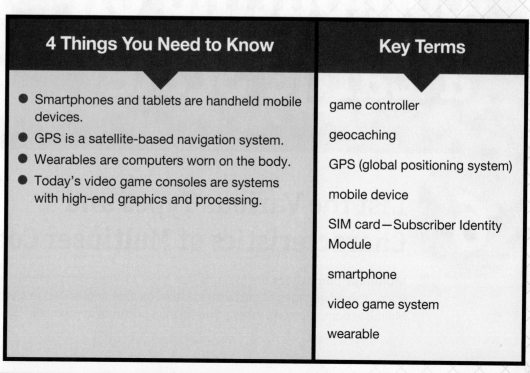

4 Things You Need to Know	Key Terms
● Smartphones and tablets are handheld mobile devices. ● GPS is a satellite-based navigation system. ● Wearables are computers worn on the body. ● Today's video game consoles are systems with high-end graphics and processing.	game controller geocaching GPS (global positioning system) mobile device SIM card—Subscriber Identity Module smartphone video game system wearable

Scanrail1/Shutterstock

Computing on a Large Scale

6

List the Various Types and Characteristics of Multiuser Computers

Multiuser computers are systems that allow multiple simultaneous users to connect to them. The advantages of multiuser systems include centralized resources and security. Multiuser computers are more powerful than personal computers.

Servers

Server computers provide services, such as Internet access, email, or file and print services, to client systems such as your home or office computer. A **client** is a device that connects to or requests services from a server. Servers range in size and cost from very small servers costing a few hundred dollars to massive enterprise servers costing hundreds of thousands of dollars (Figure 1.14).

Small and midrange servers that users connect to via personal computers can perform complex calculations, store customer information and transactions, or host an email system for an organization. They can support hundreds of simultaneous users and are scalable, allowing for growth as a company's needs change.

FIGURE 1.14 In multiuser systems, multiple simultaneous users connect to a server computer.

Horoscope/Shutterstock

Mainframes are large computers that can perform millions of transactions in a day. Mainframe computers have largely been replaced by **enterprise servers**, and the terms are sometimes used synonymously (Figure 1.15). These systems allow thousands of users to utilize the system concurrently. These are most commonly found in businesses that have massive amounts of data or transactions to process, such as banks and insurance companies.

Scanrail/Fotolia

FIGURE 1.15 Enterprise servers can allow thousands of simultaneous users and perform millions of transactions every day.

Supercomputers

Supercomputers are very expensive computer systems designed to perform a limited number of tasks as quickly as possible. They perform complex mathematical calculations, such as those used in weather forecasting and medical research. A supercomputer can consist of a single computer with multiple processors or can be a group of computers that work together. The world's top supercomputers are found at major universities and research institutes around the world. Figure 1.16 provides a sampling from the listing of the top 500 supercomputers, which is located at **top500.org**.

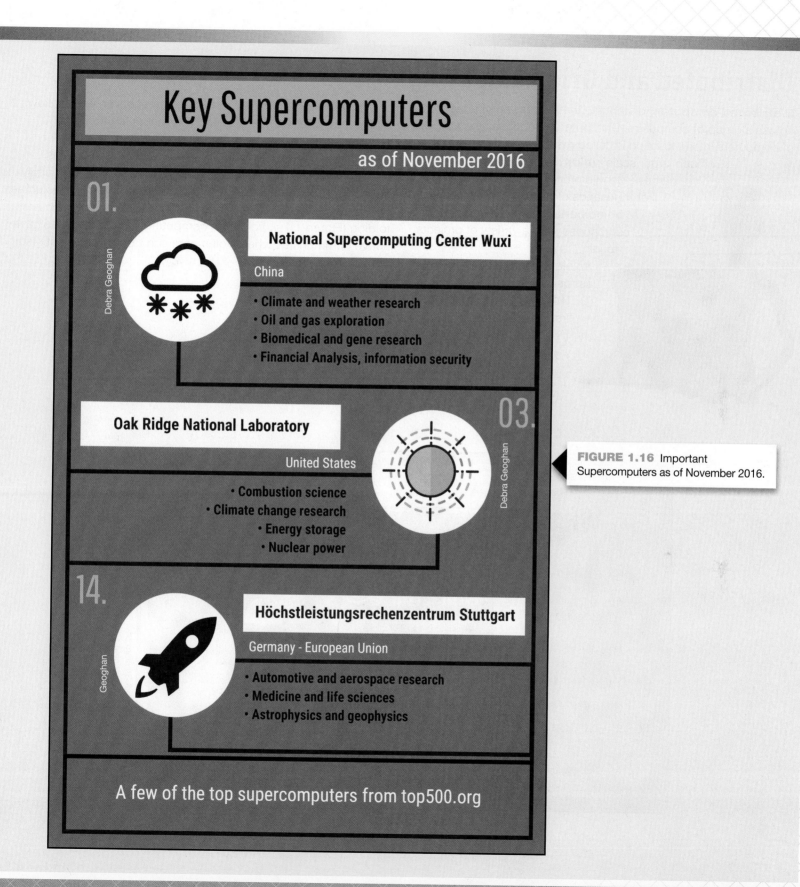

FIGURE 1.16 Important Supercomputers as of November 2016.

Distributed and Grid Computing

Distributed computing distributes the processing of a task across a group of computers. Distributed computing using a group of computers in one location is called **grid computing**. On a much larger scale, **volunteer computing** projects harness the idle processing power of hundreds or thousands of personal computers.

At **boinc.berkeley.edu**, a volunteer can choose from a variety of projects to join.

A volunteer interested in astronomy might join SETI@home. One of the first volunteer computing projects, SETI@home has had more than 6 million participants since 1999. A volunteer downloads and installs a program that runs as a screensaver, which allows SETI (Search for Extraterrestrial Intelligence) to utilize the processing abilities of your computer when it is idle without having to pay for processing time. The SETI screensaver is actually a complex piece of software that downloads and analyzes radio telescope data for SETI. Folding@home is another volunteer computing project that works to fight diseases by studying protein folding (Figure 1.17). Volunteer computing project websites have active communities where volunteers can talk to the scientists and to each other.

Deniseus/Shutterstock

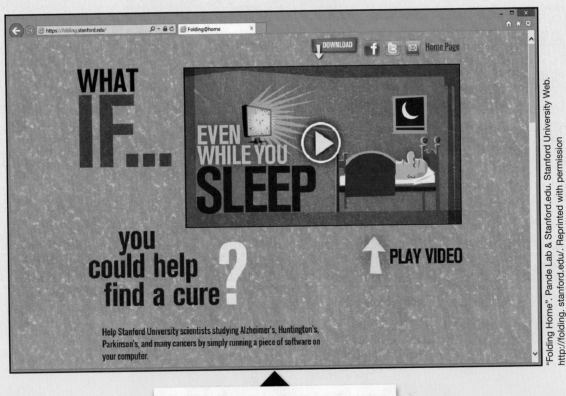

FIGURE 1.17 The Folding@home website

"Folding Home". Pande Lab & Stanford.edu. Stanford University Web. http://folding. stanford.edu/. Reprinted with permission

Multiuser systems enable users to leverage the power of computers that far exceed what a PC can do. Centralized information management, security, and distributed processing across multiple systems have given the scientific and business communities the power to solve many of society's most pressing problems in an extremely short amount of time.

ETHICS

The Internet of Things

IoT may make modern life more convenient and comfortable, but at the cost of some of your privacy. Retailers can track you in their stores by the location of your cell phone, noticing what aisles you visit and avoid, which helps plan the store layout and targeted advertising presented to you. Personal health trackers record your vital statistics, and promise not to share your personal information. The built-in camera on your Smart TV that enables you to use Skype or play interactive content can be used to record your actions and audio, even when you are not using it. And all Internet connected devices—yes, even your refrigerator—are potential hacker targets. In fact, the hack that made major websites such as Amazon and Netflix inaccessible in October 2016 was perpetrated by using hacked IoT devices in millions of homes. Is the potential loss of privacy worth the convenience of the technology?

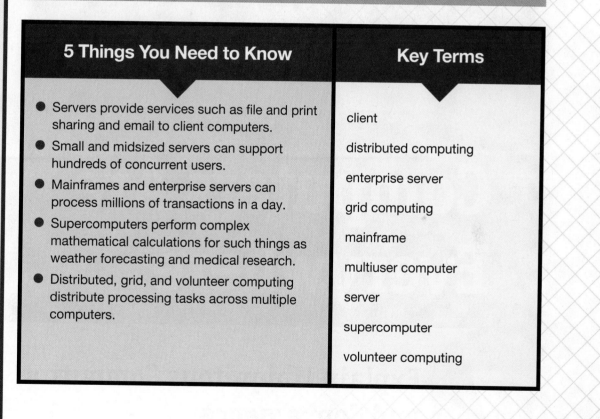

Running Project

Use the Internet to learn about current volunteer computing projects. Select one that you are interested in, and write two or three paragraphs highlighting the project and some of its achievements.

5 Things You Need to Know

- Servers provide services such as file and print sharing and email to client computers.
- Small and midsized servers can support hundreds of concurrent users.
- Mainframes and enterprise servers can process millions of transactions in a day.
- Supercomputers perform complex mathematical calculations for such things as weather forecasting and medical research.
- Distributed, grid, and volunteer computing distribute processing tasks across multiple computers.

Key Terms

client

distributed computing

enterprise server

grid computing

mainframe

multiuser computer

server

supercomputer

volunteer computing

Everythingpossible/Fotolia

Computers Are Everywhere

Objective

7 Explain Ubiquitous Computing and Convergence

VIZ CLIP

Ubiquitous Computing

Computers have become so commonplace that sometimes the technology isn't recognized as being a computer. The word ubiquitous, according to Merriam-Webster, means existing or being present everywhere. **Ubiquitous computing (ubicomp)**, also referred to as invisible computing, means technology recedes into the background. The technology actually becomes part of the environment. Digital signage has replaced traditional billboards, you can pay for gas with the wave of a credit card, and you can upload pictures to the cloud from your mobile phone. **Smart homes**—in which the lights, climate, security, and entertainment are automated—are examples of ubiquitous computing.

Embedded Computers

An **embedded computer** is a specialized computer that is part of another device, such as a gasoline pump, home appliance, traffic light, or the self-checkout line at the supermarket. Computer chips can monitor your vital signs and calories burned when exercising, regulate the flow of gas in your car, and regulate the temperature of water in your dishwasher. Embedded computers make modern lives easier. These specialized computers have become so common that it would be hard to imagine living without them (Figure 1.18).

The **Internet of Things (IoT)** is the connection of the physical world to the Internet. Objects are tagged and can be located, monitored, and controlled using small, embedded electronics. Some examples of IoT devices you may already use include fitness and health trackers, smart thermostats, and monitors for babies or the elderly. These devices have existed for some time, but adding the IoT features means they can be monitored and controlled remotely via a web browser or mobile app.

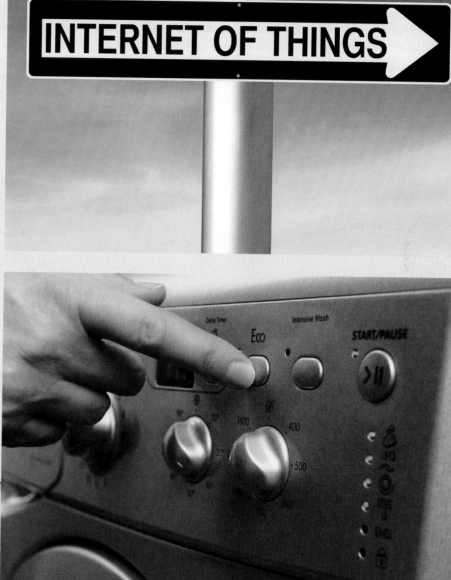

Rnl/Fotolia

Highwaystarz/Fotolia

> **FIGURE 1.18** Embedded computers can be found in many objects encountered every day, such as this washing machine.

Convergence

The **convergence**, or integration, of technology on multifunction devices such as smartphones has accustomed us to carrying technology with us. You no longer need to carry around several different devices because convergence devices now incorporate cell phones, personal information management tools, email, web browsing, document editing, MP3 players, cameras, GPS, games, and more (Figure 1.19). In some parts of the world, there are more mobile phones than people, and this has resulted in the rapid development of technologies such as

mobile payment systems—using a mobile device rather than cash or credit cards to pay for items. In many cases, mobile phones have replaced personal computers.

As we rely more and more on technology, we expect it to work. We take for granted that the traffic light timing will protect us, the GPS will guide us to our destination, and the ATM will dispense our funds only to us. Ubiquitous computing is already an integral part of our lives. It will be interesting to see where technology takes us in the not-too-distant future.

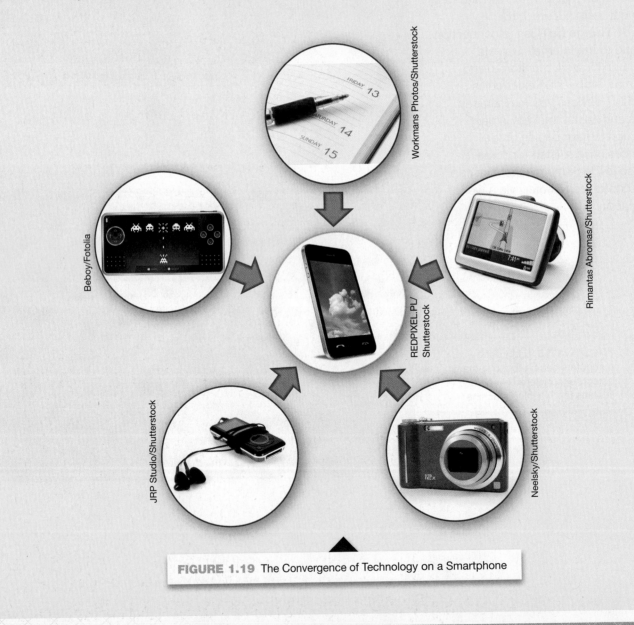

FIGURE 1.19 The Convergence of Technology on a Smartphone

UNMANNED AIRCRAFT SYSTEMS

Just a few years ago, aircraft piloted by remote control or onboard computers or **unmanned aircraft systems (UAS)**, also known as drones, were used only by the military. Today, commercial applications are being developed. Drones are useful in agriculture, land management, energy, and construction industries; for example, to inspect the underside of bridges and other locations where it is difficult or unsafe for people to go. Amazon is developing a drone delivery service. Drones carrying cameras are helpful in search and rescue missions, and could replace traffic and news helicopters (Figure 1.20). As technology improves, many more drone applications will surely be developed.

There are, however, privacy and safety concerns about the proliferation of UAS in our skies. The Federal Aviation Administration (FAA) has implemented some rules for non-military UAS users at www.faa.gov/uas. "The FAA reviews and approves UAS operations over densely-populated areas on a case-by-case basis." The FAA estimates that as many as 7,500 small commercial UAS may be in use by 2018.

FIGURE 1.20 A UAS records video of icebergs and glaciers.

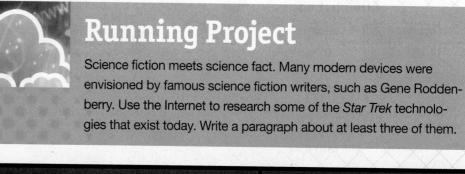

Running Project

Science fiction meets science fact. Many modern devices were envisioned by famous science fiction writers, such as Gene Rodden-berry. Use the Internet to research some of the *Star Trek* technologies that exist today. Write a paragraph about at least three of them.

Viz Check—In MyLab IT, take a quick quiz covering Objectives 5–7.

4 Things You Need to Know

- Ubiquitous computing is technology that's invisible to us.
- Embedded computers are found in everything from traffic lights to dishwashers.
- The Internet of Things connects the physical world to the Internet.
- The convergence of technology allows us to carry a single multifunction device that can do the job of many separate devices.

Key Terms

convergence

embedded computer

Internet of Things (IoT)

mobile payment system

smart home

ubiquitous computing (ubicomp)

unmanned aircraft system

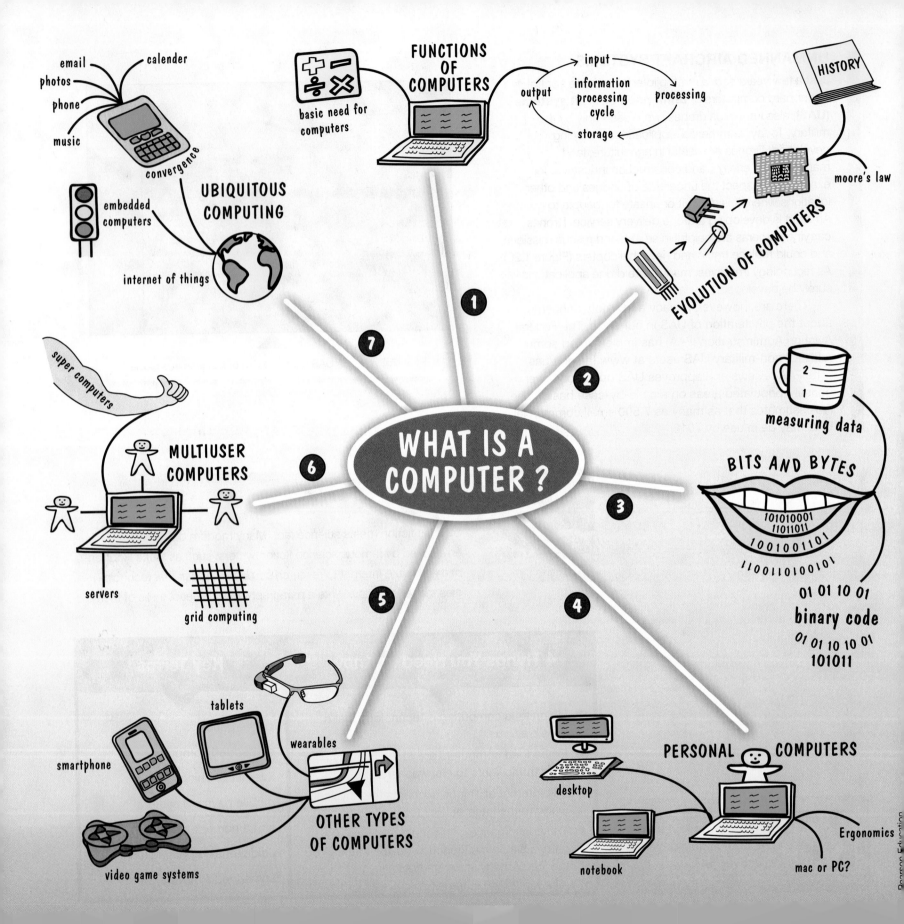

Learn It Online

- Visit **pearsonhighered.com/viztech** for student data files
- Find simulations, VizClips, Viz Check Quizzes, and additional study materials in **MyLab IT**
- Be sure to check out the **Tech Bytes** weekly news feed for current topics to review and discuss

Objectives Recap

1. Explain the Functions of a Computer
2. Describe the Evolution of Computer Hardware
3. Describe How Computers Represent Data Using Binary Code
4. List the Various Types and Characteristics of Personal Computers
5. Give Examples of Other Personal Computing Devices
6. List the Various Types and Characteristics of Multiuser Computers
7. Explain Ubiquitous Computing and Convergence

Key Terms

Summary

1. Explain the Functions of a Computer

A computer is a device that converts raw data into information using the information processing cycle. The four steps of the IPC are input, processing, storage, and output. Computers can be programmed to perform different tasks.

2. Describe the Evolution of Computer Hardware

The earliest computers used vacuum tubes, which are inefficient, large, and prone to failure. Second-generation computers used transistors, which are small electric switches. Third-generation computers used integrated circuits, which are silicon chips that contain multiple tiny transistors. Fourth-generation computers use microprocessors, which are complex integrated circuits that contain the central processing unit (CPU) of a computer.

Moore's Law states that the number of transistors that can be placed on an integrated circuit has doubled roughly every two years. The increase in the capabilities of integrated circuits directly affects the processing speed and storage capacity of modern electronic devices.

3. Describe How Computers Represent Data Using Binary Code

A single bit (or switch) has two possible states—on or off—and can be used for situations with two possibilities such as yes/no or true/false. Digital data is represented by 8-bit binary code on most modern computers. The 8-bit ASCII system originally had binary codes for 256 characters. Unicode is an extended ASCII set that has codes for more than 100,000 characters.

Summary continues on the next page

Summary *continued*

4. **List the Various Types and Characteristics of Personal Computers**

   Personal computers include desktop computers, which offer the most speed, power, and upgradability for the lowest cost; workstations, which are high-end desktop computers; and all-in-ones, which are compact desktop computers with the computer case integrated into the monitor. Portable personal computers include notebooks and tablets.

5. **Give Examples of Other Personal Computing Devices**

   Other computing devices include smartphones, wearables, GPS, video game systems, and simulators.

6. **List the Various Types and Characteristics of Multiuser Computers**

   Multiuser computers allow multiple simultaneous users to connect to the system. They include servers, midrange servers, mainframe computers, and enterprise servers. Supercomputers perform complex mathematical calculations. They perform a limited number of tasks as quickly as possible. Distributed computing uses the processing of multiple computers to perform complex tasks.

7. **Explain Ubiquitous Computing and Convergence**

   Ubiquitous computing means the technology recedes into the background so you no longer notice it as you interact with it. The Internet of Things is the connection of the physical world to the Internet. Convergence is the integration of multiple technologies, such as cell phones, cameras, and MP3 players, on a single device.

Multiple Choice

Answer the multiple-choice questions below for more practice with key terms and concepts from this chapter.

1. The _____ is a measure of a computer's ability to display intelligent behavior.

   a. Analytical Engine

   b. Artificial intelligence

   c. Bernoulli numbers program

   d. Turing test

2. Second-generation computers used _____ to process data.

   a. integrated circuits

   b. microprocessors

   c. transistors

   d. vacuum tubes

3. A _____ is a complex integrated circuit that contains the central processing unit (CPU) of a computer.

   a. microprocessor

   b. silicon

   c. transistor

   d. vacuum tube

4. What is the binary code that can represent most currently used language characters and is the standard used on the Internet?

   a. ASCII

   b. Base 2

   c. International Standards

   d. Unicode

5. What is a compact desktop computer with an integrated monitor and system unit called?

   a. All-in-one

   b. Mainframe

   c. Supercomputer

   d. Workstation

6. What type of portable computer has a screen that can swivel to fold?

   a. Convertible notebook

   b. Netbook

   c. Subnotebook

   d. Tablet

7. _____ consists of 24 satellites that transmit signals to determine the receiver's current location, time, and velocity through triangulation of the signals.

   a. UAS

   b. GPS

   c. A wearable system

   d. A flight simulator

8. _____ perform complex mathematical calculations, such as those used in weather forecasting and medical research.

   a. Enterprise servers

   b. Mainframes

   c. GPS

   d. Supercomputers

9. _____ is the study of the relationship between workers and their workspaces.
   a. Bioinformatics
   b. Distributed computing
   c. Ergonomics
   d. Ubicomp

10. A(n) _____ is an example of convergence.
    a. smart grid
    b. smartphone
    c. traffic light
    d. ubicomp

True or False

Answer the following questions with *T* for true or *F* for false for more practice with key terms and concepts from this chapter.

_____ 1. Computers convert data into information using the information processing cycle.

_____ 2. Third-generation computers used transistors.

_____ 3. Today's computers use microprocessors.

_____ 4. Moore's Law states that the number of transistors that can be placed on an integrated circuit will double roughly every 18 years.

_____ 5. ASCII contains codes for most of the languages in use today.

_____ 6. Bioinformatics allows you to design a workspace for your comfort and health.

_____ 7. All-in-one is a type of desktop computer.

_____ 8. Users connect to servers via clients.

_____ 9. Volunteer computing projects harness the idle processing power of hundreds or thousands of personal computers.

_____ 10. The idea that computers are all around us is called convergence.

Fill in the Blank

Fill in the blanks with key terms from this chapter.

1. A computer is a programmable machine that converts raw _____ into useful _____.

2. _____ is considered the first working, digital, general purpose computer.

3. _____ is the branch of science concerned with making computers behave like humans.

4. Developed in the 1960s, _____ are chips that contain large numbers of tiny transistors fabricated into a semiconducting material called silicon.

5. _____ design creates a work environment designed to reduce illnesses and musculoskeletal disorders.

6. _____ is a system that represents digital data as a series of 0s and 1s that can be understood by a computer.

7. A _____ consists of 8 bits and is used to represent a single character in modern computer systems.

8. _____ are computers that provide services, such as Internet access, email, or file and print services, to client systems.

9. _____ shares the processing of a task across a group of computers.

10. _____ is the integration of technology on multifunction devices such as smartphones.

Running Project ...

... The Finish Line

Use your answers from the previous sections of the chapter project to discuss the evolution of computers in the past few centuries. Write a report responding to the questions raised throughout the chapter project. Save your file as **lastname_firstname_ch01_ project**, and submit it to your instructor as directed.

Do It Yourself 1

Consider the features available on the personal computing device that you use the most. From your student data files, open the file *vt_ch01_DIY1_answersheet* and save the file as **lastname_firstname_ch01_DIY1_answersheet**.

What device did you choose? Is it a desktop, notebook, tablet, or some other type of system? Where is it located? How long have you had it? Did you research the computer before you made your purchase? What made you purchase it?

What do you use the computer for the most? What are five features you use most frequently? Why? What are three you use the least? Why? How could this device be improved to make your life more convenient? Describe one way life would be easier and one way your life would be more difficult without this device. Save your answers and submit your work as directed by your instructor.

Do It Yourself 2

Use an online mind mapper or presentation tool such as Mindomo, MindMeister, or Prezi, to create a mind map to compare desktop, notebook, and mobile devices. A mind map is a visual outline. More information about using mind maps can be found in Appendix B. From your student data files, open the file *vt_ch01_ DIY2_answersheet* and save the file as **lastname_firstname_ ch01_DIY2_answersheet**.

Your map should have three main branches: desktop, notebook, and mobile devices. Each branch should have at least three leaves: characteristics, advantages, and disadvantages.

When you are finished with your map, take a screenshot of this window and paste it into your answer sheet, or, if available, export your mind map as a PNG or JPG file.

Critical Thinking

Convergence has led to smaller devices that cost less and do more. From your student data files, open the file *vt_ch01_CT_ answersheet* and save the file as **lastname_firstname_ch01_CT_ answersheet**.

Research three of the newest smartphones or tablets on the market—one from each mobile platform: iOS, Android, and Windows. Complete the following table, comparing the features of each device. Use this research to decide which device would best meet your personal needs. Which device should you buy and why? What other accessories will you need to purchase? Do you need to purchase a service plan to take advantage of all the device's features? Save your file and submit both your table and essay as directed by your instructor.

	Device 1: iOS	Device 2: Android	Device 3: Windows
Website or store			
Brand			
Model			
Price			
Phone			
Calendar			
Camera/video			
GPS			
Games			
Video player			
MP3 player			
Internet			
Downloadable apps			
Additional features			
Additional purchases required			

Ethical Dilemma

The term *digital divide* refers to the gap in technology access and literacy. There have been many types of programs designed to close this gap. One current trend is to put a tablet in the hands of every student. From your student data files, open the file *vt_ch01_ethics_answersheet* and save the file as **lastname_firstname_ch01_ethics_answersheet**.

Use the Internet to find a school program that supplies all students with tablets or notebooks. What are the goals of the program? How was it funded? Has it been successful? How has its success or failure been measured? Do you think programs like this one can really solve the digital divide? Why or why not? Type your answers; be sure to cite your sources. Save the file and submit your work as directed by your instructor.

On the Web

There are many important people and events that led to our modern computers. In this exercise, you will create a timeline that illustrates the ones you feel are most significant. From your student data files, open the file *vt_ch01_web_answersheet* and save the file as **lastname_firstname_ch01_web_answersheet**.

Visit **computerhope.com/history** and under *Timeline* click the link to open the time period that includes the year you were born. Create a timeline showing five to seven important milestones in the development of computers that occurred in this decade. Use a free online timeline generator, such as Timeglider, or an online presentation tool, such as Prezi or PowerPoint, to create your timeline. Share the URL and present your findings to the class. Prepare a summary of your timeline and include the URL where it can be viewed. Save the file, and submit your work as directed by your instructor.

Collaboration

With a group of three to five students, research a famous computer pioneer. Write and perform a news interview of this person. If possible, video record the interview. Present your newscast to the class.

Instructors: Divide the class into groups of three to four students, and assign each group a famous computing pioneer from the list **computerhope.com/people**.

The Project: As a team, prepare a dialog depicting a news reporter interviewing this person. Use at least three references. Use Google Drive or Microsoft Office to prepare the presentation and provide documentation that all team members have contributed to the project.

Outcome: Perform the interview in a newscast format using the dialog you have written. The interview should be 3 to 5 minutes long. If possible, record the interview, and share the newscast with the rest of the class. Save this video as **teamname_ch01_video**. Turn in a final text version of your presentation named **teamname_ch01_interview**. Be sure to include the name of your presentation and a list of all team members. Submit your presentation to your instructor as directed.

Application Project

MyLab IT
GRADER

Office 2016 Application Projects
Word 2016: Intern Report

Project Description: In the following Microsoft Word project, you will create a letter telling your new boss about the things you have learned in this class. In the project you will enter and edit text, format text, insert graphics, check spelling and grammar, and create document footers. *If necessary, download the student data files from **pearsonhighered.com/viztech**.*

Anna Sanchez
670 Pembroke Ave
Unit 26
Frederick, MD 21703

March 6, 2018

Jones Consulting
Mr. Martin Rogert
275 Regency Sq.
Frederick, MD 21703

Dear Mr. Rogert:

Subject: Eager intern

Thank you so much for giving me the opportunity to work with you as an intern this semester. I have learned a lot about computers in my class at school and I'm eager to share my knowledge with you at *Jones Consulting*. For example, I have learned about the different types of personal computers and other devices.

Thank you so much for this amazing opportunity. I am eager to get started and believe that I can really help you effectively leverage technology in the office.

Sincerely,

Anna Sanchez, Intern

vt_ch01_word_solution.docx

Microsoft Word 2016, Windows 10, Microsoft Corporation

Step	Instructions
1	Start Word. From your student data files, open the file named *vt_ch01_word*. Save the document as **lastname_firstname_ch01_word**
2	On the last line of the document, type **Anna Sanchez, Intern** to complete the letter.
3	Select the first four lines of the document containing the name and street address, and then apply the No Spacing style.
4	Format the entire document as Times New Roman, 12 pt.
5	In the first body paragraph, format *Jones Consulting* as italic.
6	Place the insertion point before *Anna* on the last line of the document. Insert the picture of a QR code *vt_ch01_image1*.
7	Change the text wrapping style of the picture to Top and Bottom.
8	Use the shortcut menu to correct the misspelling of the word *semsester* to *semester*.
9	Using the Spelling and Grammar dialog box, accept the suggested correction for the repeated word.
10	Use the Spelling and Grammar dialog box to correct the misspelling of the word *beleive* to *believe*. Ignore all other spelling and grammar suggestions.
11	Insert the file name in the footer of the document using the FileName field.
12	Save the document and then close Word. Submit the document as directed.

Application Project

Office 2016 Application Projects
PowerPoint 2016: Business Technology Plan

Project Description: Your new boss has asked you to help her create a PowerPoint presentation discussing technology needs at Clearview Medical Supplies. In this project, you will edit and format text and bullets, insert and format pictures, check spelling, add new slides and change slide layout, apply transitions, and add speaker notes. *If necessary, download the student data files from* **pearsonhighered.com /viztech**.

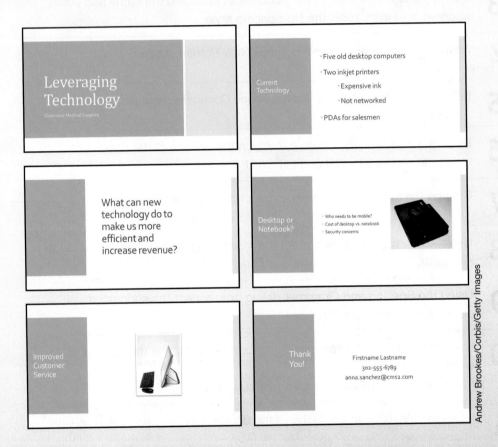

Andrew Brookes/Corbis/Getty Images

Step	Instructions
1	Start PowerPoint. From your student data files, open the file *vt_ch01_ppt*. Save the presentation as **lastname_firstname_ch01_ppt**
2	On Slide 1, change the subtitle text (*Clearview Medical Supply*) to **Clearview Medical Supplies**
3	On Slide 1, use the shortcut menu to correct the spelling of *Technology*. Change the font of the title text, *Leveraging Technology,* to Cambria and change the size to 72.
4	On Slide 2, change the font size of the title text to 32. Change the line spacing of the bullets on Slide 2 to 1.5 and the font size to 32.
5	After Slide 3, insert a new Title and Content slide and add **Improved Customer Service** as the title text.
6	On the new Slide 4, in the content placeholder, insert the picture *vt_ch01_image2*.
7	On Slide 4, apply the Simple Frame, White picture style to the picture.
8	Find and replace the word *sales* with **revenue**
9	Use the Spelling tool to check the spelling in the document. Correct the spelling errors on Slide 2, but ignore all instances of the spelling of *Clearview*.
10	Change the layout of Slide 5 to Two Content. In the right placeholder, insert the picture *vt_ch01_image3*.
11	Switch to Slide Sorter view and delete Slide 6. Move Slide 5 into the Slide 4 position. Switch back to Normal view.
12	On Slide 6, replace *Anna Sanchez* with your name.
13	In the Notes Pane on Slide 2, add the following speaker note (include the period): **Clearview needs to be a forward-thinking company.**
14	Apply the Fade transition with a duration of 01.00 to all of the slides in the presentation.
15	Insert the page number and the footer **Firstname Lastname** using your name, on the notes and handouts pages for all slides in the presentation. View the presentation in Slide Show view from beginning to end, and then return to Normal view.
16	Save the presentation and then close PowerPoint. Submit the presentation as directed.

Application Software

In This Chapter

VIZ INTRO

A computer is a programmable machine that converts raw data into useful information. Programming—in particular, **application software**—is what makes a computer a flexible and powerful tool. After reading this chapter, you will recognize various types of software applications for both business and personal use.

BrunoWeltmann/Fotolia

Objectives

1 Identify Types and Uses of Business Productivity Software

2 Identify Types and Uses of Personal Software

3 Assess a Computer System for Software Compatibility

4 Compare Various Ways of Obtaining Software

5 Discuss the Importance of Cloud Computing

6 Install, Uninstall, and Update Software

Running Project

In this chapter, you'll learn about different kinds of application software and how to obtain it. Look for instructions as you complete each article. For most articles, there's a series of questions for you to research. At the conclusion of this chapter, you'll submit your responses to the questions raised.

Making Business Work

ctive

Identify Types and Uses of Business Productivity Software

Companies of all sizes rely on computers for many aspects of running a business—from billing to inventory to payroll to sales. Most businesses depend on a variety of software applications to complete tasks.

Office Suites

The most commonly used application software in business is an **office application suite**, such as Microsoft Office, Apple Productivity Apps —Pages, Numbers, and Keynote— (Figure 2.1), Google Docs, or Apache OpenOffice. These suites include applications that are designed to work together to manage and create different types of documents and include features that enable multiple users to collaborate. A suite has the advantage of having a common interface and features. For example, in Office applications, settings to configure how the application behaves or displays are found by clicking the File tab and clicking Options. In a business environment, Microsoft Office is the standard, but most programs have the ability to save a file in multiple formats, making them compatible with other products or backward compatible with older software versions. For example, you can save a file created in Google Docs as a Microsoft Word file.

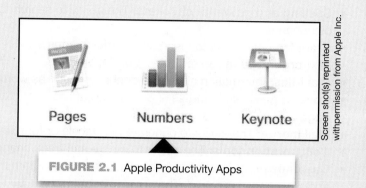

FIGURE 2.1 Apple Productivity Apps

WORD PROCESSING

A **word processor** is an application that's used to create, edit, and format text documents; the documents can also contain images. A full-featured word processor, such as Microsoft Word or Pages for Mac, can create everything from simple memos to large, complex documents.

Figure 2.2 shows a Word document created using some of the most commonly used features of a word processor. The page number is inserted in the header, and the pages are numbered automatically as the content changes. The *Title* style is used to format the title of the essay. Styles enable you to apply a predefined set of formatting steps to text. The image and heading are centered on the page, but the title and text are left-aligned. The spellchecker displays a red wavy line under the word *Appy*, indicating that the word wasn't found in the spellchecker dictionary. It's possible to add words not found in the spellchecker dictionary and create a custom dictionary so that these additional words—such as your last name or industry-specific terms and brand names—aren't flagged for incorrect spelling.

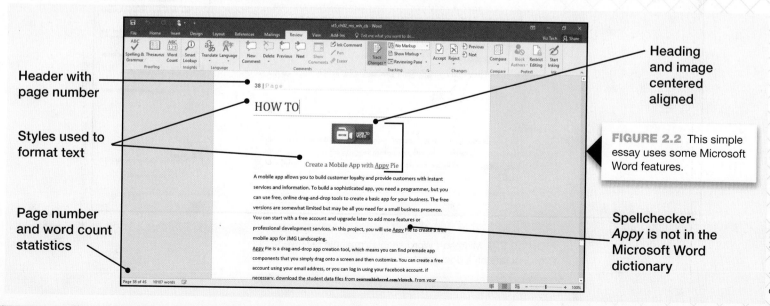

Header with page number

Styles used to format text

Page number and word count statistics

Heading and image centered aligned

FIGURE 2.2 This simple essay uses some Microsoft Word features.

Spellchecker-*Appy* is not in the Microsoft Word dictionary

Some standard features of word processors include:

- **What you see is what you get:** The layout on the computer screen shows the document layout as it would appear if printed.
- **Formatting styles:** Text style, font, color, size, and alignment.
- **Spelling and grammar checkers:** The ability to search for and replace errors in spelling and grammar, and to create custom dictionaries.
- **Graphics:** The ability to insert and format images.
- **Text organization tools:** Tables, bullets, and lists.
- **Statistics:** Information about the document such as word count.
- **Content guides:** Footnotes, indexes, and tables of contents.
- **Page layout:** Headers and footers, page numbers, and margins.
- **Mail merge:** The ability to generate mail labels or form letters for lists of people.
- **Collaboration tools:** The ability to merge and track changes made by multiple people.
- **Customization:** The ability to configure how a program performs or displays, such as how menus display or how often and where a file is saved. These default settings can be changed using the Settings, Preferences, or Options menus in most applications.

Businesses utilize more advanced features—such as track changes, mail merge, and document protection—to create many kinds of business documents. Figure 2.3 shows comments and edits from multiple reviewers working on the same document. This is one way that users can collaborate on a project.

Comments from collaborators indicated by different colors

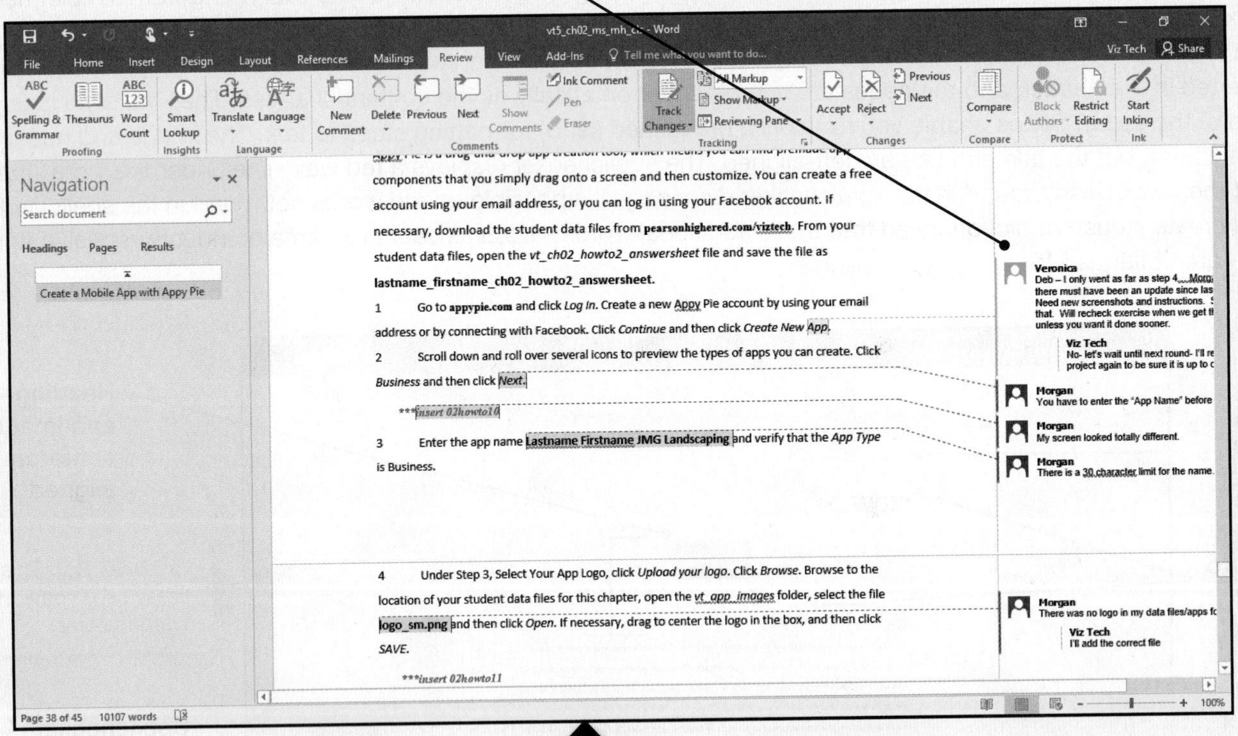

FIGURE 2.3 Microsoft Word enables multiple reviewers to collaborate on a document.

Courtesy of Microsoft Corporation Inc.

SPREADSHEET SOFTWARE

A **spreadsheet** application, such as Numbers for Mac, Google Sheets, or Microsoft Excel, creates electronic worksheets composed of rows and columns. Spreadsheets are used for applications such as budgeting, grade books, and inventory. Spreadsheets are critical to researchers in both the natural and social sciences as a statistical analysis tool. They are useful tools for managing business expenses, payroll, and billing, although there are also tools that are specifically made for such tasks. Spreadsheets are also very good at organizing data, by sorting, filtering, and rearranging, making them useful for things that don't involve calculations at all—such as address lists and schedules.

In a spreadsheet, the intersection of a row and a column is called a **cell**. Cells can contain numbers, text, or formulas. Three-dimensional spreadsheets can have multiple worksheets that are linked together, making them very flexible and powerful. Spreadsheet applications have the ability to create charts or graphs to display data visually. Although there are other spreadsheet programs available, in a business environment, Microsoft Excel is used almost exclusively. Figure 2.4 shows a spreadsheet created for a U.S. history course that lists all the U.S. presidents and their political parties. The number of presidents in each party was calculated, and a pie chart showing that information was generated.

One advantage to using a spreadsheet program is that it can be customized. For example, a teacher might use a spreadsheet to create custom formulas and calculations rather than having to adjust grading methods to fit into a commercial grade book program's format. Another advantage is cost savings. Because most office computers already have a spreadsheet program installed as part of an office suite, there's no need to purchase additional software. Programs that are part of an office suite have a similar interface, so users will have some familiarity with the program interface and need less training to use the individual programs.

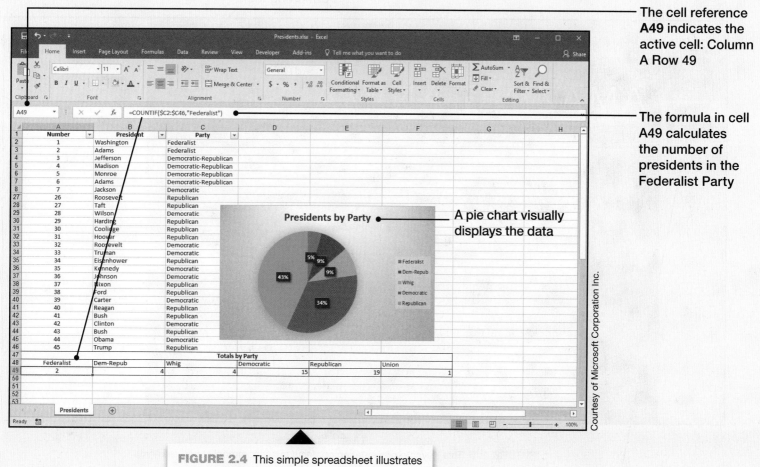

The cell reference **A49** indicates the active cell: Column A Row 49

The formula in cell A49 calculates the number of presidents in the Federalist Party

A pie chart visually displays the data

Courtesy of Microsoft Corporation Inc.

FIGURE 2.4 This simple spreadsheet illustrates text, numbers, a formula, and a pie chart.

PRESENTATION SOFTWARE

A presentation application, such as Microsoft PowerPoint, Keynote on a Mac, or the online tools Prezi or Sway, is used to create electronic presentations. If you want to present facts, figures, and ideas and engage your audience at the same time, you need visual aids. With presentation software, it's easy to create them. Each slide can contain text, graphics, video, audio, or any combination of these, making your visual aids dynamic and enhancing your presentation. A good speaker creates a presentation that audiences will be interested in and will remember.

Figure 2.5 shows a Keynote presentation about animals. The presentation here is shown in Navigator view, which enables the author to see the slide order and easily make changes by dragging the slides into position. This presentation contains two slides—containing images and text—and uses a built-in design template with predefined colors, fonts, and layouts. Good design principles for presentations include using easy-to-see color schemes and large font sizes, limiting the amount of text on each slide, limiting the use of slide transitions and animations, and using images to enhance your words.

Formatting tools

Slide thumbnails

FIGURE 2.5 This Keynote presentation contains many commonly used elements.

DATABASE SOFTWARE

A database program such as Microsoft Access is used to create and manage a **database**—a collection of information that is organized in a useful way. Your telephone book or email contact list is a simple database. A library catalog, patient records in a doctor's office, and Internet search engines are all examples of commonly used databases. You can use a desktop database application to create small databases for contact management, inventory management, and employee records.

A **record** in a database contains information about a single entry, such as a customer or product. A database is a collection of related records organized into one or more **tables**. Other objects can be generated to organize the data, including forms, reports, and queries.

Using a contact list as an example, each contact has a record. Every record consists of fields of information. A **field** is a single piece of information in a record in a database. In this case, each record would contain fields for name, address, email, phone, etc. Although a simple database like this could also be created in a spreadsheet, using a database program gives you more flexibility. **Forms** can be created for easy data entry. **Reports** can be generated to display selected information. Figure 2.6 shows a contact list database that consists of five records in a table and a phone list report created from the table. Most flexible of all, **queries** can be created to pull out records that meet specific criteria.

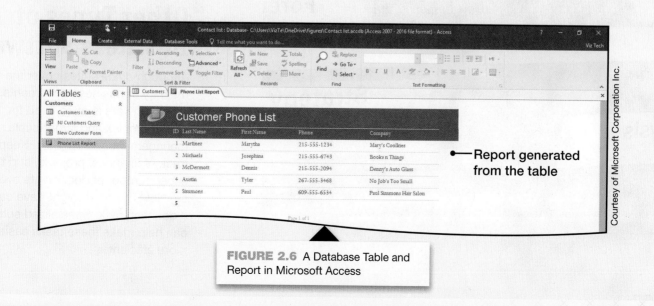

FIGURE 2.6 A Database Table and Report in Microsoft Access

PERSONAL INFORMATION MANAGER

A **personal information manager (PIM)** may be a stand-alone program or part of an office suite. In business, the most widely used of these programs is Microsoft Outlook (Figure 2.7). A PIM manages your email, calendar, contacts, and tasks—all in one place. It includes the ability to share calendars and schedule meetings. Many smartphones incorporate PIM features and can be used in conjunction with desktop systems. Additionally, there is a Microsoft Outlook app for the Android, iOS, and Windows mobile platforms. You can sync your contacts, appointments, and tasks between multiple systems, taking the information with you wherever you go. You can configure your mobile device with notifications to alert you to appointments and new messages. Notifications can be on-screen alerts, vibrations, sounds, or a combination of these.

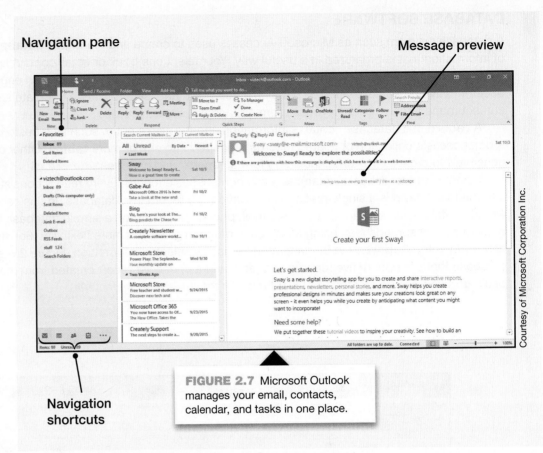

Navigation pane

Message preview

Navigation shortcuts

Courtesy of Microsoft Corporation Inc.

FIGURE 2.7 Microsoft Outlook manages your email, contacts, calendar, and tasks in one place.

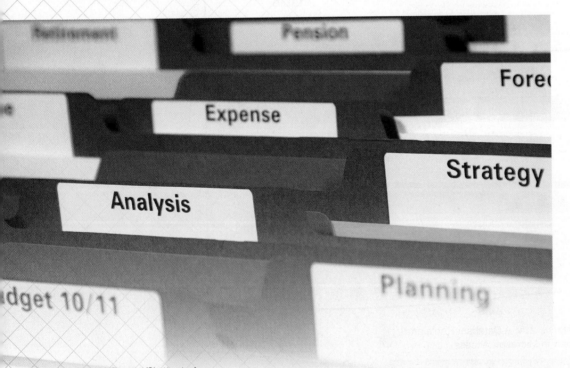

Chad McDermott/Shutterstock

Other Types of Business Software

Although office suites cover the majority of business documents, other software is often used for more complex and larger-scale management and projects. Keeping track of finances, projects, and the sheer number of documents even the smallest business might have can be a daunting task. Specialized software can help make these tasks easier and more efficient.

FINANCIAL

Every business must track expenses and taxes. An Excel spreadsheet system is sufficient for many situations, but some businesses prefer to use basic accounting software such as Intuit QuickBooks (Figure 2.8), Sage 50 (formerly known as Peachtree), or FreshBooks, which is completely cloud-based. Accounting software enables you to track your business finances and generate reports and graphs so that you can make business decisions. You can use accounting software for expense tracking, invoicing, payroll, and inventory management. By organizing all financial information in one place, it is easy to see the big picture and to handle year-end tasks such as income tax returns.

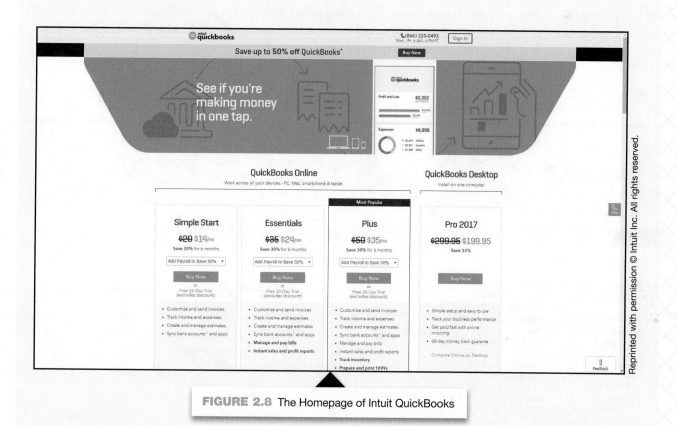

FIGURE 2.8 The Homepage of Intuit QuickBooks

DOCUMENT AND PROJECT MANAGEMENT

For both practical and legal reasons, even the smallest business needs document management—the ability to save, share, search, and audit electronic documents throughout their life cycle. Keeping track of all the documents in a business, ensuring that the right people have access to them, and ensuring that the correct version is available are all part of a **document management system (DMS)** such as Microsoft SharePoint, Alfresco, Dropbox, Citrix ShareFile, and Google Drive for Work. Storage is what defines a DMS. Instead of keeping files on local drives, files are stored on a server or on the web, making them more accessible and secure.

Project management software helps you complete projects, keep within budget, stay on schedule, and collaborate with others. The most popular project management program is Microsoft Project and the leading web-based application is Basecamp. Both of these tools excel at helping projects run smoothly. Figure 2.9 shows a workshop planning project in Microsoft Project. The left column contains the tasks and dates for the project, and the right side shows the schedule and progress of the project in a graphic known as a **Gantt chart**.

Project management software features include:

- A timeline that tracks due dates, milestones, and deadlines
- Team-planning capability that, by simply dragging and dropping, creates a team with the right individuals and resources
- A portfolio manager that monitors the allocation of scarce resources and current project costs

Thousands of software applications are used in businesses, including some that are created in-house or made for a specific type of business, but the programs discussed in this article are universal. Modern businesses depend on both people and technology to remain competitive.

FIGURE 2.9 Planning a Workshop Using Microsoft Project

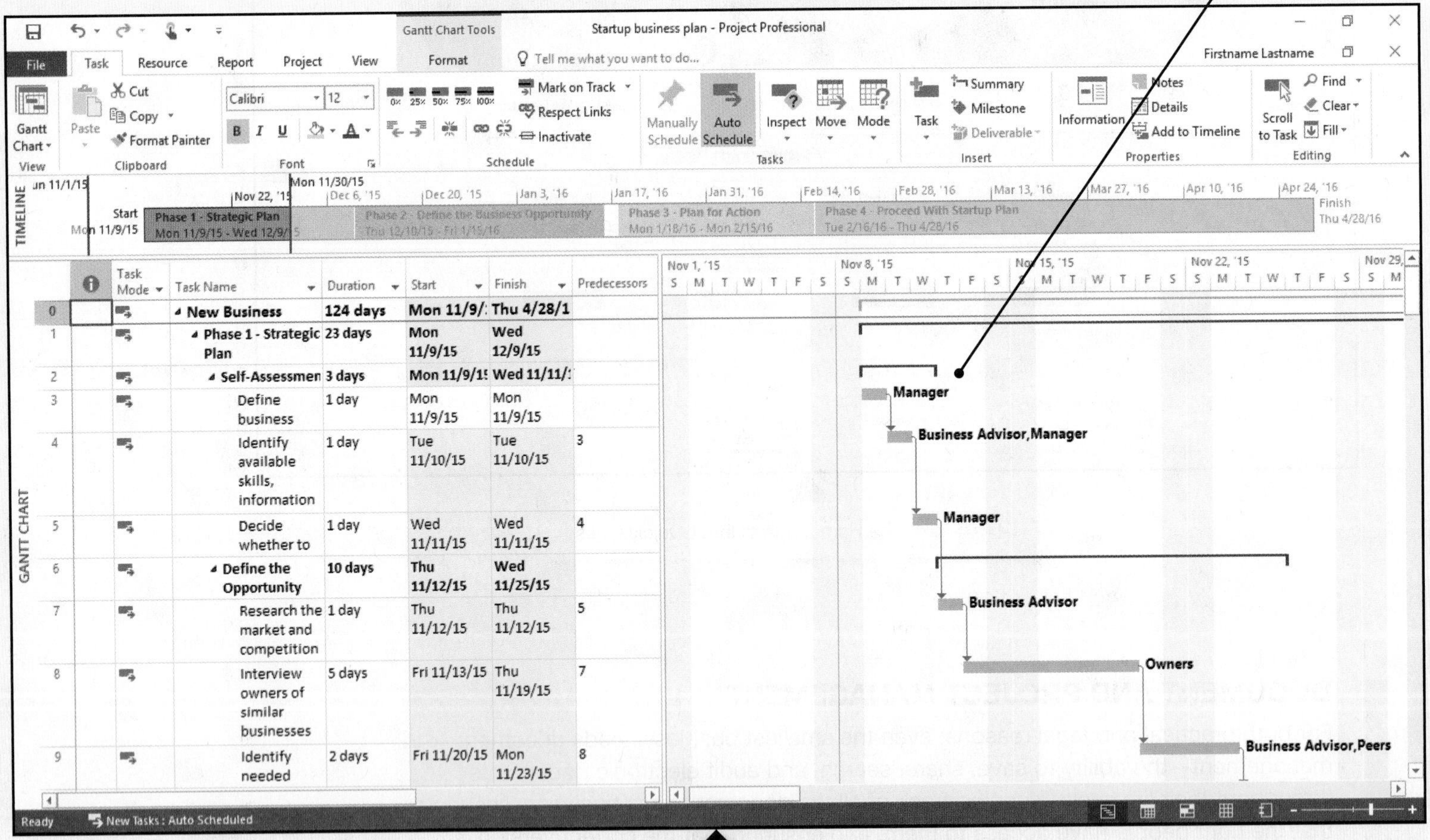

Courtesy of Microsoft Corporation Inc.

Running Project

Microsoft Office is a full suite of programs, but not every user needs the whole package. Use the Internet to research the current versions of Microsoft Office that are available. If you use a Mac, be sure to include the Mac version. Write a two- to three-paragraph essay comparing the versions. Explain which applications are in each, the cost, the number of licenses available, and any other details you deem important.

5 Things You Need to Know

- Office application suites may include word processing, spreadsheet, presentation, and database software.
- Personal information manager software manages email, contacts, calendars, and tasks.
- Businesses use financial software to track business finances and generate reports and graphs that can be used to make business decisions.
- Document management systems enable businesses to save, share, search, and audit electronic documents.
- Project management software helps businesses keep projects on schedule.

Key Terms

application software

cell

database

document management system (DMS)

field

form

Gantt chart

office application suite

personal information manager (PIM)

project management software

query

record

report

spreadsheet

table

word processor

Making It Personal

2 Identify Types and Uses of Personal Software

Software is what makes a computer useful. The variety of software available today is vast, but it takes only a couple of programs to make a computer indispensable—and even fun to use. In this article, we look at some of the software you might want to install on your own system.

SIMULAT

Applica
Softwa

Office Applications

A full office application suite, which includes word processing, spreadsheet, database, presentation, and personal information management applications, is usually more than the average home user needs or wants. A basic word processor and perhaps a spreadsheet and presentation program are often included in home or student versions of an office suite. Microsoft Office comes in several different versions, including a monthly subscription plan called Office 365, allowing you to purchase just the applications you actually need. For the Mac, Pages, Numbers, and Keynote are built-in apps.

Apache OpenOffice (Figure 2.10) is a free, open source alternative office suite available in Windows, Mac, and Linux versions. **Open source** means that the source code is published and made available to the public, enabling anyone to copy, modify, and redistribute it without paying a fee. Some open source websites, such as Apache OpenOffice, ask for donations to support the development of the product. Apache OpenOffice contains word processor, spreadsheet, presentation, drawing, database, and formula writer applications.

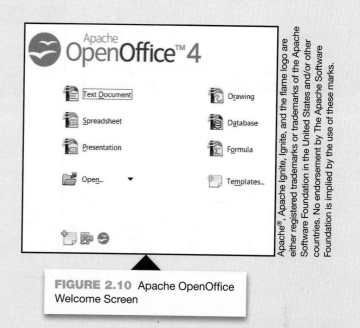

FIGURE 2.10 Apache OpenOffice Welcome Screen

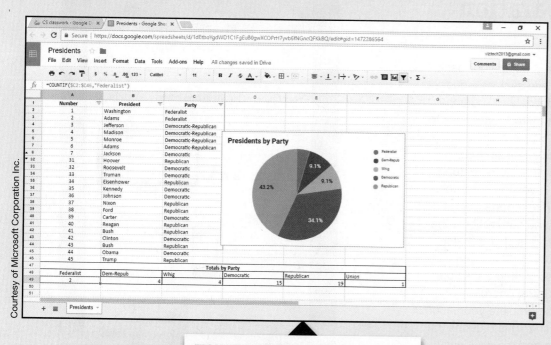

Courtesy of Microsoft Corporation Inc.

FIGURE 2.11 Google Drive Spreadsheet

Online alternative office suites are another solution. The most popular are Microsoft Office Online and Google Drive, which includes Google Docs, Google Sheets, Google Slides, and other apps. These free websites offer easy-to-use interfaces, with word processing, spreadsheet, presentation, and communication applications. You access them through a browser and don't need to install anything on your computer. The beauty of these websites is that you can access and edit your files from anywhere, including many mobile devices, and easily collaborate and share with others. Figure 2.11 shows a spreadsheet in Google Drive.

There are many free or low-cost alternatives if you are willing to spend some time finding them and learning how to use them. All of these alternatives have the ability to save files in common file formats, enabling you to move your work between programs and across platforms.

Microsoft Office Online includes Word, Excel, PowerPoint, and OneNote. The free web apps are not full-featured versions. Figure 2.12 shows a PowerPoint presentation being edited using the Office Online version. The option to Edit in PowerPoint will download and open the file in the full version of PowerPoint, if it is installed on the system.

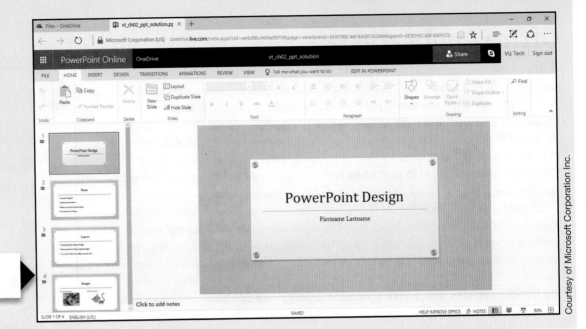

FIGURE 2.12 Microsoft Office Online PowerPoint

Courtesy of Microsoft Corporation Inc.

Finance and Tax Preparation Software

Personal finance software can help you keep track of your bank accounts, monitor your investments, create and stick to a budget, and file your income taxes. As with office applications, personal finance software ranges from expensive commercial packages to free and online options.

Two of the most popular commercial packages are Intuit Quicken and YNAB—You Need a Budget. Both include features such as online banking, online bill payment, investment portfolio tracking, and budgeting. You can also generate reports, calculate loan interest, and write checks. At tax time, you can easily gather the information you need from these applications. If you prefer to use an online application, **Mint.com** (Figure 2.13) is a popular choice. After you enter all your accounts, use Mint to track your spending. Mint also has mobile apps for iOS and Android.

Tax preparation software enables you to complete your income tax returns yourself on your computer or online. This reduces the chance of making errors in your calculations and makes it easy to save—and later retrieve—your returns. You can file your return electronically or print and mail it. Previous years' returns can be imported into a new return and generate year-to-year comparisons. Tax preparation programs walk you through the process step by step and provide you with suggestions and help throughout.

FIGURE 2.13 Track your budget and spending on Mint.com.

IanDagnall Computing / Alamy Stock Photo

The three main tax preparation programs are Intuit TurboTax, H&R Block, and TaxAct. For simple tax returns, there are free online options. For more complex returns, you can install the full programs on your computer or use online versions. In general, the more complicated your return is, the more expensive the software you will require. If you start a free return and later discover that you need to upgrade to a full version, you can do so without losing any of the information you have already entered (Figure 2.14).

No matter how simple or complex your financial situation, there's a financial software solution that you can use.

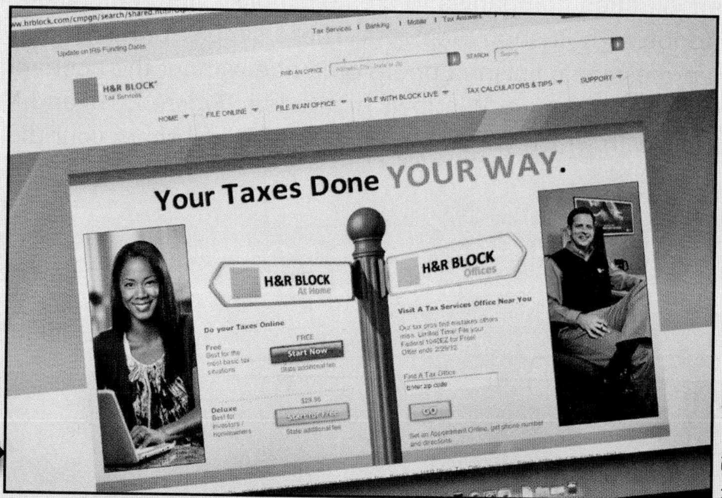

FIGURE 2.14 H&R Block Tax Prep

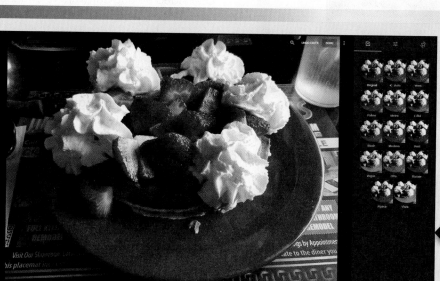

NetPhotos/Alamy Stock Photo

Debra Geoghan

Entertainment and Multimedia Software

Entertainment and multimedia software make computers fun to use for education and entertainment. You can edit and organize your photos (Figure 2.15), movies, and music; play games; or learn a new skill.

FIGURE 2.15 Editing a Photo in Google Photos

VIDEO AND PHOTO EDITING

Video and photo editing software enables you to create masterpieces from your personal photos and videos. You can spend hundreds of dollars for professional programs, but you can also find free or low-cost alternatives that have almost all the features you need.

Use image editors—sophisticated versions of graphic programs—to edit and create images. You can add a variety of special effects to photographic images, as well as remove blemishes, crop portions of them, and adjust the coloring, and then save them in a variety of file formats. Powerful image editing software, such as Adobe Photoshop, is used primarily by professionals, but the popularity of digital photography encouraged companies to create simpler photo editing software such as Adobe's Photoshop Elements. These simpler programs enable you to create a professional finished photo or image without the cost and learning curve of complex software. Windows computers (Figure 2.16) and Macs include Photos apps with which you can edit, organize, and share your digital photos. Many

Editing categories

Editing tools

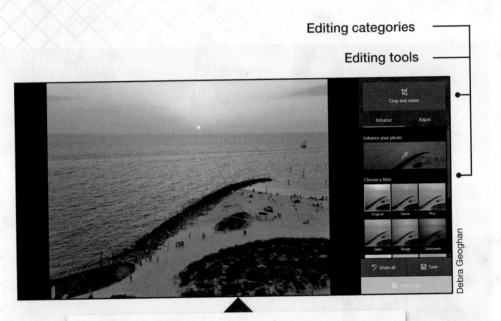

Debra Geoghan

FIGURE 2.16 Editing an image with the Windows Photos app.

online photo services such as Google Photos, Shutterfly, and Flickr include basic editing tools like cropping, resizing, red-eye removal, and special effects like making the picture look black-and-white and adding special borders. You can also order photo prints and create personalized gifts like calendars, books, and coffee mugs.

Use video editing software to enhance your personal videos. You can spend hundreds of dollars for professional programs, but for most people, free or low-cost alternatives have all the features necessary.

Video editors are programs that enable you to modify digitized videos. Video editing software ranges from free online services such as YouTube, to free programs such as Apple iMovie, to very expensive professional-quality programs such as Adobe Premiere and Sony Vegas. Because video editing requires significant system resources, there are few online options available. Figure 2.17 shows a movie being created using iMovie.

MEDIA MANAGEMENT

Use media management software to organize and play multimedia files such as music, videos, and podcasts. You can transfer or rip your music CDs to your computer; organize your songs into playlists for activities like exercising, driving, or dancing; and find new music that you might like using the online store

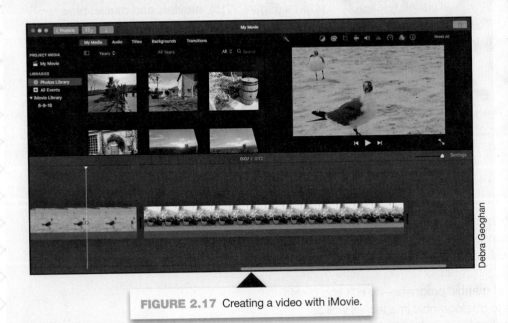

Debra Geoghan

FIGURE 2.17 Creating a video with iMovie.

feature. You can watch a movie trailer, a professor's lecture, or a music video. The content available to you grows daily.

Use Apple iTunes (Figure 2.18) to organize music, videos, and other media files. If you have an iOS device—iPod, iPhone, or iPad—then you will use iTunes to transfer music from your computer to your device. In iTunes, you can shop for new music, find podcasts to subscribe to, rip your music CDs to your computer, and watch movie trailers. Podcasts are prerecorded radio- and TV-like shows you can download and listen to or watch any time. There are thousands of podcasts to which you can subscribe. Your instructors might have podcasts of their class lectures. By using Apple's Internet-based storage system iCloud, items purchased using iTunes will automatically sync to all of your registered devices and computers. Google Play and Amazon Prime are online services that enable you to purchase, store, and play your media in the cloud. This gives you access from any Internet-connected device.

GAMES

When you think of someone who plays video games, do you picture a young man on an online quest? What about the grandmother playing puzzle games, or the dad playing online baseball, or the preschooler learning colors and shapes? Games and simulations are more than just first-person shooters in which you play the game from the perspective of the game character and much of the action involves some sort of weapon. Minecraft (Figure 2.19) is a popular game available across many devices and platforms, which is described as a virtual land and involves creating, exploring, digging, and building. Video games are played by all sorts of people. The average age of a video game player is 32 to 35 years old, 20 percent are over 50, and about 40 percent are female. Video game sales, which include mobile apps, games for video game systems, and computer games, reached over $15 billion in the United States in 2016.

Games are one type of software for which you really need to pay attention to the system requirements for installation. They take a lot of processing, memory, and video power to run well and display complex graphics, and trying to play a game on an inadequate system is a frustrating experience.

FIGURE 2.18 iTunes

Public Broadcasting Service

FIGURE 2.19 Playing Minecraft on a tablet.

Anatolii Babii/Alamy Stock Photo

Educational and Reference Software

Educational and reference software is a broad category that includes software to study, plan, design, and create just about anything you are interested in. More than any other category we have discussed, educational and reference software options are mobile and cloud-based applications. Let's look at a few of the most popular offerings.

TRIP PLANNING, FAMILY, AND HEALTH

When I was a little kid and the family planned a vacation, we had to go to the store to buy maps, tour books, and yellow highlighters. We would spend hours mapping out our route, planning our stops based on the outdated information in the tour books, and hoping the food would be decent and the hotel rooms would be clean. Today, I still spend hours researching and planning our trips, but I use mobile apps or online mapping software, such as the Windows Maps app (Figure 2.20) or Google Maps, and I read online reviews from other travelers. Thanks to the software available, I can easily reroute a trip if something unexpected happens, such as traffic detours or if I decide to take in an interesting attraction or go exploring off my original route.

Use genealogy programs to create family trees or slideshows of your family photos, view timelines and maps, and search through millions of historical records on the Internet. Family Tree Maker and the Windows Ancestry app integrate with the **Ancestry.com** website.

Health and fitness trackers enable you to monitor your exercise, keep track of your food intake and sleep patterns, and help you train to run your first 5K (Figure 2.21). There are apps for guided meditation and those that remind you to get up and move around. Other apps can help you keep track of your medical conditions, symptoms, and medication.

FIGURE 2.20 Windows Maps App

FIGURE 2.21 A fitness tracker linked to a smartphone app.

HOME AND LANDSCAPE DESIGN

Want to build a deck? Plant a garden? Remodel your kitchen? Rearrange your furniture? Paint the dining room? Home and landscape design software has you covered. Free or retail, online or installed on your system, there are programs to help you design and plan all your home improvement projects (Figure 2.22). Several online apps allow you to compare paint colors. Just upload a picture and experiment with the color choices until you find your favorites. You should use whatever program has the color codes for the brand of paint you plan to buy.

FIGURE 2.22 Design your house with software.

Web Apps

You may sometimes find yourself without your own computer—at work, school, travel, or a friend's house. **Web apps** are programs that you run in a web browser. They need no installation, so you can run them on just about any device with Internet access. Many common software applications can be found in online versions, including office applications, photo editing, financial programs, and of course games. For example, with a free Google account you have access to office apps, maps, blogging software, photo editing and organization, and a calendar (Figure 2.23).

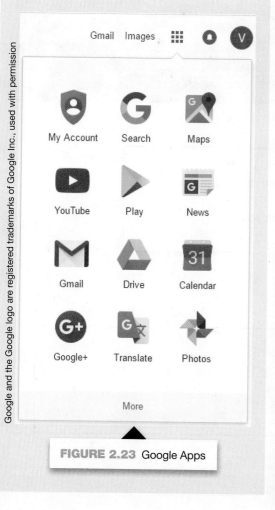

FIGURE 2.23 Google Apps

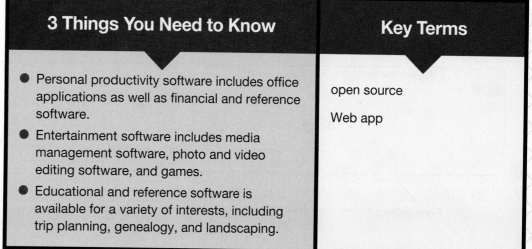

Running Project

One place to learn about free software alternatives is MakeUseOf. This website is a daily blog that includes a directory of hundreds of useful websites and apps. Go to makeuseof.com, at the top of the screen click the Menu, and select a category that interests you. Select two articles to read, and write a one- to two-paragraph summary of one of the articles. Did you decide to try the application described? If so, why? Did you find it useful? Would you recommend it to a friend?

3 Things You Need to Know

- Personal productivity software includes office applications as well as financial and reference software.
- Entertainment software includes media management software, photo and video editing software, and games.
- Educational and reference software is available for a variety of interests, including trip planning, genealogy, and landscaping.

Key Terms

open source

Web app

HOW TO VIDEO

Create a Document Using WordPad or TextEdit

Digital Literacy Skill

Microsoft Windows includes a word processing application called WordPad. macOS includes TextEdit. These are basic programs that can be used to create simple documents, such as homework assignments, even if you don't have a full word processor, such as Microsoft Word, installed.

The figure below identifies the parts of the WordPad window:
- The File menu contains commands to open, save, print, and email your documents.
- The Quick Access toolbar has buttons for save, undo, and redo by default, but you can customize it by clicking the arrow on the right.
- The ribbon has two tabs: Home and View. The Home tab contains the commands for formatting the document and inserting objects; the View tab contains commands to change the way the document displays on your screen.

1 To start WordPad, from the Windows Start menu or Search bar, begin to type **wordpad**. In the Search results, click *WordPad*. In the blank document area of the WordPad screen, type **Chapter 2 How to Use WordPad** and press [Enter]. On the next line, type your name and press [Enter] twice.

File menu   Quick Access Toolbar   Ribbon

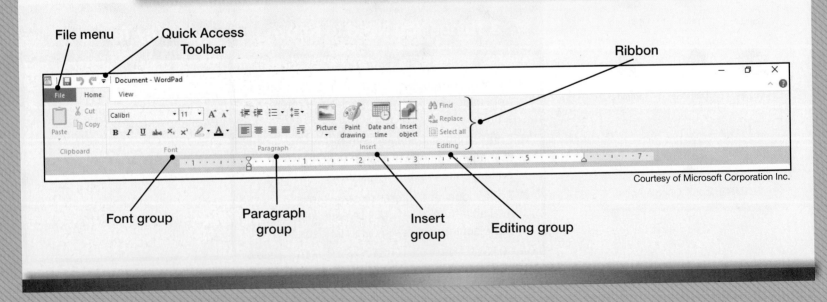

Courtesy of Microsoft Corporation Inc.

Font group   Paragraph group   Insert group   Editing group

 **2**

Type the following paragraph:
WordPad is a basic word processor that is included with Windows. I can use it to type homework assignments and other documents that are compatible with most word processing programs.

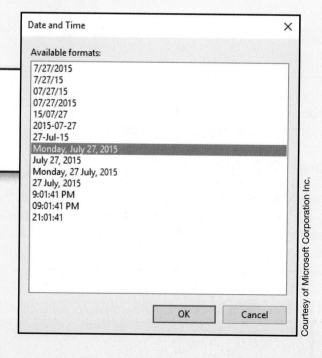

Courtesy of Microsoft Corporation Inc.

3

Press Enter. On the Home tab, in the Paragraph group, click the *Start a list* button and type the following three bullet points (press Enter after each):

- **Free**
- **Easy to use**
- **Compatible**

4

Press Enter again to exit the bulleted list. In the Insert group, click the *Date and time* button; select a date format that includes the day of the week. Click *OK*.

5 Drag your mouse to select the paragraph of text, the bulleted list, and the date. In the Font group, click the *Font family* arrow and change the font from Calibri to Times New Roman. Click the *Font size* arrow and change the font size to 12.

6 Select the first two lines and, in the Paragraph group, click the *Center* button. In the Font group, change the font size to 14 and click the *B* button to make the text bold.

7 Click *File*, point to *Save as*, and choose the appropriate format. The default format is *Rich Text document*, which is compatible with all word processors. If you're required to submit your work in the Microsoft Word format, select *Office Open XML document* from the list instead. Navigate to the folder where you are saving your Chapter 2 work and save the file as **lastname_firstname_ch02_howto1**. Submit this file as directed by your instructor.

If you are using a Mac:

In macOS, TextEdit has a menu bar with six menu choices:

- The TextEdit menu includes options to customize the program.
- The File menu includes items such as Open, Close, Save, and Print.
- The Edit menu is where you find options to edit the text in your document, such as Cut, Copy, Insert, and the Spelling and Grammar checker.
- The Format menu has tools to format text, tables, lists, etc.
- The View menu enables you to zoom in and out.
- The Window menu enables you to modify how a document displays on your screen.

The TextEdit toolbar contains shortcuts for common formatting commands.

Menu bar

Toolbar

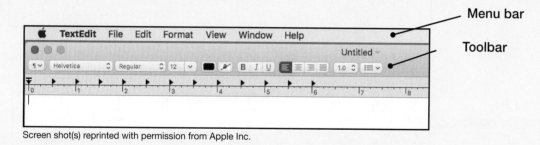

Screen shot(s) reprinted with permission from Apple Inc.

1. Open *TextEdit* from the Launchpad. In the TextEdit dialog box, click *New Document*. Click the *Format* menu and then click *Wrap to Page*. In the blank document area of the TextEdit document, type **Chapter 2 How to Use TextEdit** and press Enter. On the next line, type your name and press Enter twice.
2. Type the following paragraph:
   TextEdit is a basic word processor that is included with macOS. I can use it to type homework assignments and other documents that are compatible with most word processing programs.

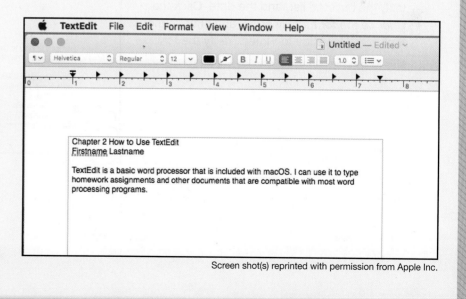

Screen shot(s) reprinted with permission from Apple Inc.

3. Press Enter. Click the *List bullets and numbering* button. Below *None*, click the second (round) bullet choice, and type the following three bullet points (press Enter after each):
   - **Free**
   - **Easy to use**
   - **Compatible**

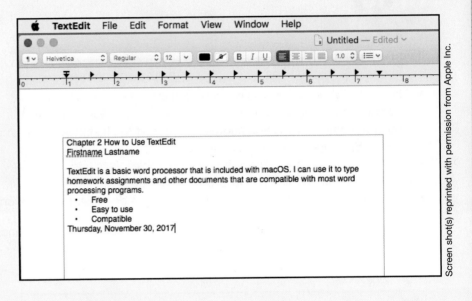

4. Press Enter again to exit the bulleted list. Type the current date, using the format *Thursday, July 1, 2016*, and press Enter.
5. Drag your mouse to select the paragraph of text, the bulleted list, and the date. Click the *Choose the font family* arrow and change the font from Helvetica to Times. Verify the font size is set to 12.

6. Select the first two lines and click the *Center text* button. Set the font size to 14 and click the *B* button to make the text bold.

7. Click *File*, click *Save*, and choose the appropriate format. The default format is *Rich Text Document*, which is compatible with all word processors. If you're required to submit your work in the Microsoft Word format, select *Word 2007 (.docx) Document*. Click the *Where* arrow, navigate to the folder where you are saving your Chapter 2 work, and save the file as **lastname_firstname_ch02_howto1**. Submit this file as directed by your instructor.

Tsiumpa/Fotolia

Will It Run?

Assess a Computer System for Software Compatibility

System sp

Your best friend just told you about an awesome new game she bought. Should you run right out and buy it, too? At $60, the game is an investment that warrants at least a little bit of research on your part, as do most other software purchases. So what do you need to know?

Your System Specs

Before you rush out—or go online—to buy software, you need to do a little bit of work. You need to document your system specs so you can compare them to the system requirements of the software. That is the only way you'll know whether your system can run the program.

Most store-bought software requires a DVD drive to do the installation. Although a few programs will run from a DVD or flash drive, most programs are installed on your computer's hard drive. Many newer, lighter notebook computers no longer include a DVD drive. To install software on a system without a DVD drive, you can purchase an external drive, but the easiest thing to do is to install software that you download directly from the web. The amount of drive space required for the installed software is listed in the system requirements. You can verify that you have enough free space by opening File Explorer. The Windows computer in Figure 2.24 has a CD drive. It has 78.4 GB of free space on the hard drive (C:) labeled OS, and 133 GB free on the second drive (E:) labeled Data. There is also a removable disk with 235 MB free.

Another way to find this information is to use the Settings window. From the Start menu, open *Settings*, click *System*, and then click *Storage* (Figure 2.25). You can view your system drives on the Storage tab. Here you can also change the default save location for apps, documents, music, pictures, and videos if you have multiple drives available on your system.

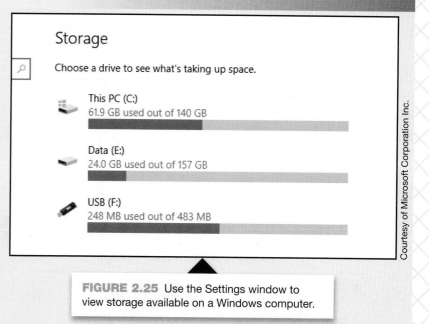

FIGURE 2.25 Use the Settings window to view storage available on a Windows computer.

On a Windows computer, obtain the other information you need by using the System control panel. To do this, open *File Explorer*, click *This PC*, and then on the Computer tab, click *Properties*. Most of the information you need is found on this page: operating system version, processor type and speed, and amount of memory installed. You can also find this information on the About tab of the System Settings window as shown in Figure 2.26.

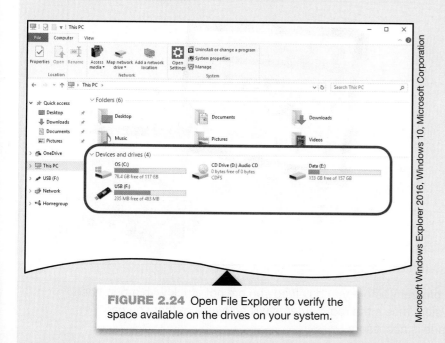

FIGURE 2.24 Open File Explorer to verify the space available on the drives on your system.

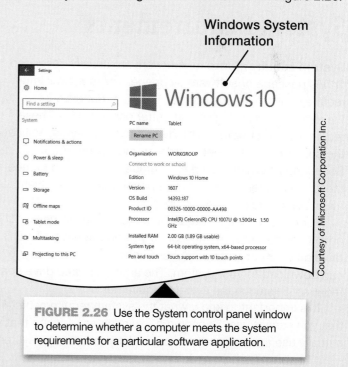

FIGURE 2.26 Use the System control panel window to determine whether a computer meets the system requirements for a particular software application.

To locate system information on a Mac, click the *Apple* menu, and then click *About This Mac.* The Overview tab (Figure 2.27) lists the OS version, processor, memory, and graphics on the system. The Storage tab (Figure 2.28) shows the disk drive information.

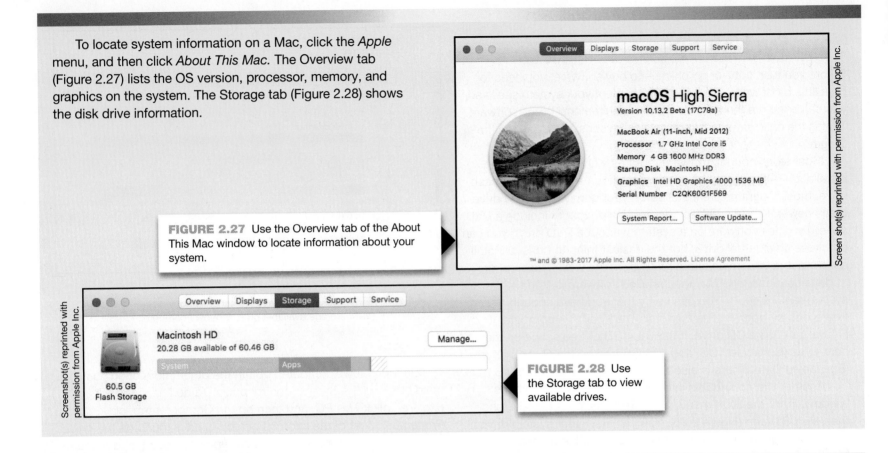

FIGURE 2.27 Use the Overview tab of the About This Mac window to locate information about your system.

FIGURE 2.28 Use the Storage tab to view available drives.

System Requirements

System requirements for software are usually described on the package or software webpage. These are minimum requirements to get the program running, but exceeding the requirements will give you better performance. These requirements list both the hardware and software specifications the computer must meet in order to run the program. Sometimes, you may need to upgrade your system to meet these requirements. As software becomes more sophisticated, the system requirements go up.

For most software you buy in a store, you will need a DVD drive to perform the installation. If you do not have a DVD drive on your computer, purchase software online that you can download to your system. The amount of free drive space required is listed in the system requirements.

It is important to know what the system requirements are for a program before you buy it so you are not stuck with a purchase that you cannot use. Spending a few minutes verifying that your system meets the requirements will help ensure that you can actually use the software you buy or let you know if a system upgrade is necessary.

7th Son Studio/Shutterstock

SOFTWARE TRAINERS Software trainers—sometimes called corporate trainers—are in demand as companies deploy more software programs. This high-paying career may involve some travel and requires good computer skills, organization, and communication skills. Software trainers usually have at least a bachelor's degree and on-the-job training. Some companies offer train-the-trainer courses that can lead to certification. You might work for a training company, in the training department of a large company, or as a consultant to many companies.

Running Project

Research a game or program that you would like to run on your computer. What are the system requirements for the program? Does your computer meet the minimum requirements? In what ways does it exceed them?

Viz Check—In MyLab IT, take a quick quiz covering Objectives 1–3.

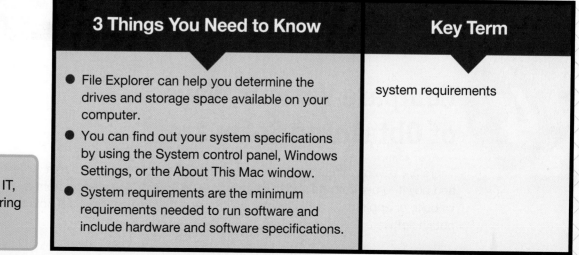

3 Things You Need to Know

- File Explorer can help you determine the drives and storage space available on your computer.
- You can find out your system specifications by using the System control panel, Windows Settings, or the About This Mac window.
- System requirements are the minimum requirements needed to run software and include hardware and software specifications.

Key Term

system requirements

Natalia Merzlyakova/Fotolia

Where to Get It

4

Compare Various Ways of Obtaining Software

There are several different ways to obtain software. You can go out to a store and buy it, order it online and have it shipped to you, or download it from a website or app store. In this article, we look at software licensing and how to obtain software.

VIZ CLIP

Connect to an External Monitor or Projector to Display Presentations

Licensing

When you purchase and install software on your computer, you may not actually own the program. Instead, you license it. The software is owned by the company that created it. Carefully read the **EULA (end-user license agreement)**—the agreement between the user and the software publisher—on all software to know your rights before you install it, including the number of computers you can legally install it on, the length of time you have access to it, and any privacy notices (Figure 2.29). You should look for important hidden information in the fine print. For example, by clicking *I Agree* on some EULAs, you allow the installation of additional "features" such as toolbars and spyware on your computer.

The two most common software licenses are:

- **Proprietary software license:** Grants a license to use one or more copies of software, but ownership of those copies remains with the software publisher. This is the type of license found on most commercial software and is the most restrictive in terms of your rights to distribute and install the software.
- **Open source software license:** Grants ownership of the copy to the end user. The source code for that software must be made freely available. The end user has the right to modify and redistribute the software under the same license.

In both cases, there may or may not be a fee for the use of the software. The cost of software is a big factor in choosing which programs to install.

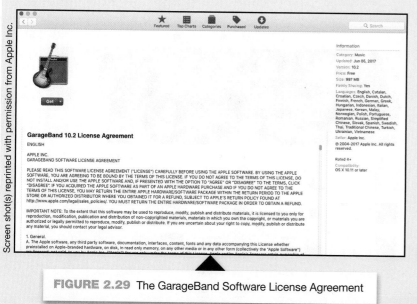

Screen shot(s) reprinted with permission from Apple Inc.

FIGURE 2.29 The GarageBand Software License Agreement

Free or Fee

Not all proprietary software has a fee, and not all open source software is free. The cost of software is determined by the publisher. There are several basic models for software distribution:

- **Retail software:** The user pays a fee to use the software. Microsoft Office, Adobe Photoshop, and TurboTax are all examples of retail software.
- **Subscription** : Some retail software, such as Microsoft Office and Adobe Creative Cloud, can be purchased through a subscription service. A monthly or yearly fee provides access to the software for a limited time. The advantage to subscriptions is that updates and newer versions of the software are included as long as the subscription is valid.
- **Freeware:** Can be used at no cost for an unlimited period of time. Some popular freeware programs include Apple iTunes and 7-Zip.
- **Shareware:** Software may be offered in trial form or for a limited period that allows you to try it out before purchasing a license. It's sometimes referred to as trialware. This marketing model of selling software has become so popular that you can purchase most retail software this way. You can download a 30- or 60-day free trial of products from Microsoft, Adobe, and many other publishers. New computers often come preloaded with lots of trialware—sometimes referred to as *bloatware* because it uses system resources and is often unnecessary or of limited value to the user.
- **Donationware:** A form of freeware in which the developers accept donations, either for themselves or for a nonprofit organization. VLC Media Player and FileZilla are two popular examples of donationware.
- **Freemium:** A common way to monetize—earn money from—a mobile app is via in-app purchases. The app itself is free to download and install, but additional features, game levels, or other content can be purchased for small, one-time payments or via subscriptions.

Sources of Software

Software is available in a variety of places. You can purchase software in specialized computer and electronics stores, office supply stores, and discount and mass merchandise stores. The price and variety of programs available in these places will vary widely. If you're looking for a popular piece of software, such as game or tax preparation software, then you'll likely find it for a good price, but if you're looking for something less popular, you may have a hard time finding it on the shelf.

A much larger selection of software is available through online retailers, such as **Amazon.com**. These sites sell the same software in a box and ship it to you. Some software may also be available for immediate download. Online retailers often have a larger selection of software than retail stores, and prices are comparable. When you purchase software directly from the software publisher's website, you can immediately download it. The cost can be competitive with retailers, but it pays to shop around.

Websites such as **cnet.com**, **tucows.com**, and **zdnet.com** have huge libraries of freeware and shareware to download. For open source software, go to **sourceforge.net**. An advantage to using sites like these is that they include editor and user reviews to help you choose the program that is right for you. Also, these websites test the programs for malicious intent, but it still makes sense to be careful. Read the reviews and look out for any suspicious terms in the licenses and installers.

A **desktop application** is a computer program that is installed on your PC and requires a computer operating system such as Microsoft Windows or macOS. When you install a desktop application, many files may be placed on your system, and changes might be made to the operating system settings. Desktop applications can be complex and designed to do many different things. An **app** is a self-contained program usually designed for a single purpose. Apps are much smaller than desktop applications and generally don't require any complicated installation. Apps use far fewer system resources than desktop applications and thus can run on lower-end systems and mobile devices. Microsoft Windows 10 and macOS support both desktop apps and apps that run on all device families—including computers, phones, and tablets. Most popular apps are available for multiple platforms. For example, Evernote is a popular note-taking app that is available for Windows desktops, Macs, iOS devices, Android devices, and Windows phone devices. When you install the corresponding version of the app on each of your devices and platforms, you can access your content from all of them.

The Windows Store is included with Windows, and the App Store is part of macOS (Figure 2.30) and iOS. These stores give you access to thousands of programs, both free and paid, directly from your device. You can also update previous purchases through the store interface. Software apps for mobile devices should be downloaded from trusted sources. It is safest if you use the recommended app store or marketplace for your device. The apps must pass through rigorous testing to be placed in the market, thus reducing the risk of malicious or harmful code running on your device.

Helen Sessions/Alamy Stock Photo

Screen shot(s) reprinted with permission from Apple Inc.

FIGURE 2.30 Mac App Store

Web apps run in browsers, and therefore are **platform-neutral**—they will run on any device with a supported browser and Internet access. Web apps typically don't require any installation, and using web apps ensures that you are always using the most current version of the program. The disadvantage to relying on web apps is the requirement to have Internet access.

When choosing the type of app to use, consider the length of the project, the location of any collaborators, the system resources available, and the technical expertise available.

When you download software from a website, it's good practice to back up the downloaded file and license in case you ever need to reinstall the program. Wherever you finally decide to purchase software, be sure that you understand the license terms before you click the *I Accept* button.

FIND OUT MORE...

Visit the Open Source Initiative (OSI), at **opensource.org**. What is OSI, and what does it do? How does it define *open source*?

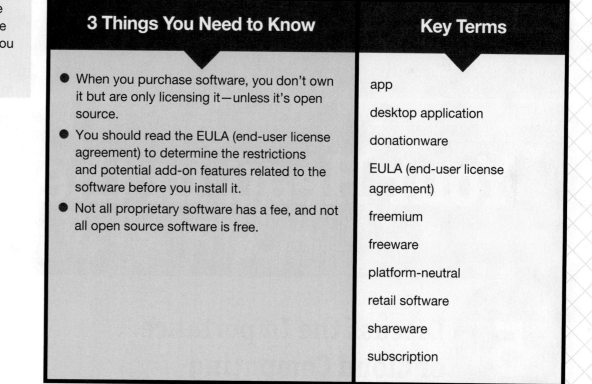

Running Project

Use the Internet to find out what the terms *volume license* and *single-seat license* mean. What are they? How are they alike? How are they different?

3 Things You Need to Know	Key Terms
• When you purchase software, you don't own it but are only licensing it—unless it's open source.	app
	desktop application
• You should read the EULA (end-user license agreement) to determine the restrictions and potential add-on features related to the software before you install it.	donationware
	EULA (end-user license agreement)
• Not all proprietary software has a fee, and not all open source software is free.	freemium
	freeware
	platform-neutral
	retail software
	shareware
	subscription

Dragonstock/Fotolia

Your Head in the Cloud

Objective

5 Discuss the Importance of Cloud Computing

The **cloud** refers to the Internet. **Cloud computing** takes processing and storage off your desktop and business hardware and puts it in the cloud. As the need for storage, security, and collaboration has grown, cloud computing has become an important part of business and personal systems.

Cloud Computing

Three types of services can be delivered through the cloud: Infrastructure-as-a-Service, Platform-as-a-Service, and Software-as-a-Service (Figure 2.31). Together, these three services can provide a business with an integrated system for delivering applications and content using the cloud. The companies that deliver these cloud services, such as Amazon, Google, and Salesforce, are known as **cloud service providers (CSPs)**. Cloud solutions save money in software, hardware, and personnel costs; increase standardization; and increase efficiency and access to technology. Although there is some concern about the security of using cloud services for storing sensitive information, large CSPs offer very secure environments.

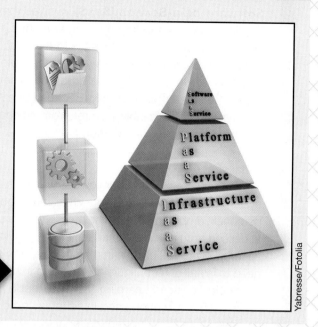

FIGURE 2.31 Cloud Computing Services

INFRASTRUCTURE-AS-A-SERVICE (IaaS)

Technology infrastructure costs for servers and network hardware can be as much as 80 percent of a typical IT budget. With **Infrastructure-as-a-Service (IaaS)**, a company uses servers in the cloud instead of purchasing and maintaining them. This reduces costs for hardware, software, and support personnel. Companies that don't have the expertise in-house can have sophisticated servers to house large databases, centralized document management, and security, using and paying for just what they need, so they can increase their usage during surges in demand, such as holiday or tax season, and decrease it during lulls. A commonly used IaaS service is off-site backup services.

PLATFORM-AS-A-SERVICE (PaaS)

Platform-as-a-Service (PaaS) provides a programming environment to develop, test, and deploy custom web applications. This gives businesses the ability to build, deploy, and manage SaaS applications. PaaS also makes collaboration easier and requires less programming knowledge than traditional programming tools. Three popular PaaS programs are App Engine from Google, Force.com from SalesForce, and Microsoft Azure.

SOFTWARE-AS-A-SERVICE (SaaS)

Software-as-a-Service (SaaS) involves the delivery of applications over the Internet—or web apps. Of the cloud services, SaaS is the most visible to the user. Any time you open your browser to access your email, upload photos, or share a file, you are using SaaS. SaaS has several advantages over installing software locally. Because SaaS is delivered on demand, it's available anytime from any computer that has Internet access. In addition to the convenience, SaaS also eliminates the need to apply updates to local software installations.

Mathias Rosenthal/Fotolia

You use SaaS whenever you use web mail. A web mail system does not download your email messages to your personal computer. Instead, the messages are stored and accessed from a hosted email server that provides backup and security, gives you access from anywhere, and eliminates the need to install and configure an email program on your computer.

A cloud-based Learning Management System, or LMS, is an SaaS application used in schools and corporate training environments to deliver educational materials, track student interactions, and assess student performance. Students are able to access the LMS from any Internet-connected device using a web browser. Some LMS systems also provide enhanced mobile access through mobile apps. You may use an LMS at your college; for example, Blackboard or Canvas or Moodle.

Microsoft Office Online and Google Drive are examples of personal SaaS. These services include productivity tools and online file storage, and they enable you to collaborate and share files with others. For businesses, there are more powerful, fee-based tools including G Suite by Google Cloud and Microsoft Office 365. Table 2.1 compares the costs of using Microsoft Office 2016, Google Apps, and Microsoft Office 365 for a small business with 10 users.

TABLE 2.1 Small Business Costs

Cost Comparison for a Small Business	Microsoft Office Home and Business 2016	G Suite by Google Cloud	Microsoft Office 365 Business Premium	Microsoft Office 365 Business Essentials
Initial cost	$229.99 per license	—	—	—
Price per user per year	—	$120	$150	$60
Annual cost for 10 users	$2,299 for the first year (or $766 per year for three years*) plus support costs	$1,200	$1500	$600
Cost for three years	$2,299	$3,600	$4,500	$1,800
	Desktop applications	Web apps only—no desktop applications	Includes web apps and desktop applications and Office on Demand streaming of full-featured versions of Office on Windows computers	Web apps only—works with your existing versions of desktop applications

*There is a new Microsoft Office release about every three years.

Applying an update to an application on each computer can be a costly, time-consuming process. However, with a SaaS solution, updates happen on the remote system and do not affect local users. Users instantly have access to new features as soon as they log into their account on a SaaS site. No local configuration is needed.

For businesses, using the cloud to deliver apps offers several benefits: a simple and quick way of accessing applications from anywhere, a relatively small cost per user, and the elimination of the need to maintain and support the applications on site. SaaS may not be a term most people use very often, but the services it provides are used every day by individuals and businesses alike. As cloud computing continues to mature, you'll find more and more of your computing up in the cloud.

Together, IaaS, SaaS, and PaaS can provide a business with an integrated system for delivering applications and content using the cloud. Well-known providers of cloud services include Microsoft, Amazon, Google, and Salesforce.com. Cloud solutions save money in software, hardware, and personnel costs; increase standardization; and increase efficiency and access to technology. The CSPs can build huge datacenters in remote locations near inexpensive and green power supplies such as hydroelectric plants. Building such datacenters is impractical for most businesses.

Running Project

Does your school use cloud computing—also known as above-campus computing? If so, which services (e.g., email, apps) do you access from the cloud? Give two examples of your personal use of cloud computing.

3 Things You Need to Know

- The cloud is the Internet.
- Cloud computing uses hardware and software resources that are in the cloud instead of local.
- Cloud computing consists of three types of services: Infrastructure-as-a-Service (IaaS), Platform-as-a-Service (PaaS), and Software-as-a-Service (SaaS).

Key Terms

cloud

cloud computing

cloud service provider (CSP)

Infrastructure-as-a-Service (IaaS)

Platform-as-a-Service (PaaS)

platform-neutral

Software-as-a-Service (SaaS)

How To?

Create a Mobile App with Appy Pie

HOW TO VIDEO

A mobile app allows you to build customer loyalty and provide customers with instant services and information. To build a sophisticated app, you need a programmer, but you can use free, online drag-and-drop tools to create a basic app for your business. The free versions are somewhat limited but may be all you need for a small business presence. You can start with a free account and upgrade later to add more features or professional development services. In this project, you will use Appy Pie to create a free mobile app for JMG Landscaping.

Appy Pie is a drag-and-drop app creation tool, which means you can find premade app components that you simply drag onto a screen and then customize. You can create a free account using your email address, or you can log in using your Facebook account. If necessary, download the student data files from **pearsonhighered.com/viztech**. From your student data files, open the *vt_ch02_howto2_answersheet* file and save the file as **lastname_firstname_ch02_howto2_answersheet**.

1 Go to **appypie.com** and click *Join*. Create a new Appy Pie account by using your email address. Click *Sign Up* and then verify your account. On the Dashboard, click *Create New App*.

2 Enter the app name **Lastname Firstname App**. Click *Business* and then click *Next*. On the Selection tab, in the Facebook page name box, type **Visualizing Technology**, scroll down to select the Facebook page for this text, click *Next*. Scroll down and select Theme Green, click *Next*.

Courtesy of AppyPie.com

3 On the Design tab, under App Pages, click the *About Us* icon to edit this page. In the *Description* box, select the existing text, press Delete, and then type **We are JMG Landscaping, family-owned and operated since 1985.** (include the period). Replace the word *Title* with **Founder** and enter your name in the text box to the right. In the box below, enter a brief description of your background. Click the small icon below the picture and select the icon of a building. Replace the text in the Website URL box with the URL of your school, and then in the *Founded* box, type **1985**. Under Mission, enter the text: **To Provide the Best Customer Service for our clients**. At the bottom of the page, click *Add Page*.

4 Under App Pages, click *Twitter*. Delete this page by clicking the trashcan icon. In the Confirm Delete dialog box, click *Delete*. Under App Pages, click *Website* and enter the following information in the appropriate fields:
Page Name: **JMG Landscaping**
Change the first website icon to an envelope, change the word Website to Email, and enter **info@jmglandscaping.net** in the textbox on the right.
Replace the second line web address with **http://jmglandscaping.net**
At the bottom of the page, click *Add Page*.

5 Delete the Photo and Video app pages. Click *Facebook*. Confirm the *Facebook page URL* box contains **https://facebook.com/visualizingtechnology** and then click *Preview* to verify that the link works. If the preview does not work, verify that the URL protocol is *https.* Take a screenshot of this page and paste it into your answer sheet. Click *Add Page.*

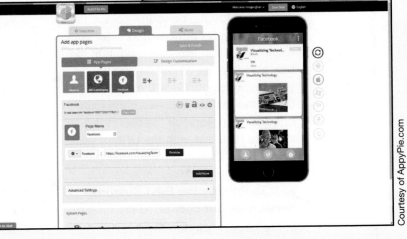

Courtesy of AppyPie.com

6 If necessary, click *App Pages* to display the app page categories. Under Commerce, click *Coupon*. Under Select Coupon leave 10% Discount selected, and in the *Heading* box type **Pre-Season Clean-up**. In the *Brief Description* box type **Get your yard ready for spring!** Click to expand the Savings section and change the Discount to **20**. Expand the Validation section. Check the Show Scanner Code Type box and select QR Code. In the *Date Of Issue* box, if necessary, click the date picker and select today's date. Change the *Valid Till* date to the end of the following month. Take a screenshot of this page and paste it into your answer sheet. Click *Add Page.*

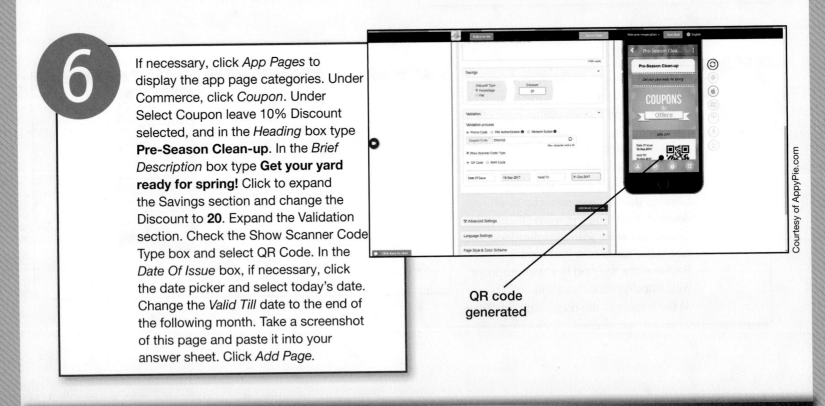

QR code generated

Courtesy of AppyPie.com

7 Click the *Design Customization* tab. Under Brand Identity, click *App Icon*. Click the *Upload App Icon* tab. Click the existing icon, browse to the location of your student data files for this chapter, select the file *logo_sm.png*, and then click *Open*. If necessary, drag to center the logo in the box, click *Save,* and then click *OK*.

8 Click *Splash Screen* and then click the *Upload Splash Screen* tab. Under For Portrait, click the existing image, browse to the location of your student data files for this chapter, select the file *splash.jpg*, and then click *Open*. If necessary, drag the sizing handle of the image selection box to make the image fill the box. Be sure *Use the same image for both Portrait and Landscapes modes* is selected, and then click *OK*.

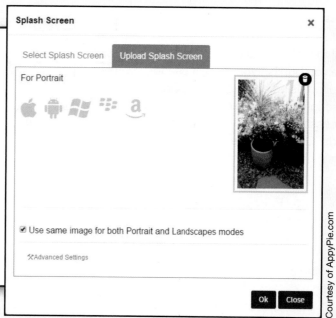

9 Under App Background, browse the images and select a suitable background image. Scroll down, and under Select navigation layout, select *List*. Under App Overlay, select the green (first) theme.

Courtesy of AppyPie.com

10 Carefully check all of your work, and then scroll to the top and click *Save & Finish*. Once you publish your app, it cannot be edited using a free account. On the Subscription page, select the *Free plan*. If necessary, close any prompts to invite friends. Click *Continue to My Apps*.

Courtesy of AppyPie.com

11 Click the *App as a website* link for your app. Click *Preview App* in the emulator window to test your app. Take a screenshot of the *App as a website* page and paste it into your answer sheet. Copy the URL of the page from the browser address bar (not the app package), paste it into your answer sheet, and submit it as directed by your instructor.

Courtesy of AppyPie.com

You have created an app that can be downloaded and used on a mobile device. Return to your dashboard and wait 5–10 minutes before proceeding. (Note: It may take up to 2 hours before your app is available.) You will receive an email when your app is ready. Click the *Test Your App* button and read about the options to download your app. The URL and QR code provided can be embedded in your website or other media to share your app with customers. Appy Pie uses HTML5 to build apps, which is a platform-neutral language that works on all modern personal computing systems. That means you can create one app that can be used on the web and on iOS, Android, and Windows devices. To create apps for some platforms requires a paid Appy Pie account.

Managing Software on Your System

Install, Uninstall, and Update Software

Some specialized devices have their instructions coded into the firmware, but most programs must be installed on a computer. Managing the programs on your computer includes installing, uninstalling, and updating the software. It is important to keep software current and to uninstall unneeded programs to keep your system running efficiently, free up disk space, and prevent flawed software from enabling malware or hacker attacks.

Installing Software

The process of installing software copies files to the computer and may alter system settings and create new folders. The installation process might require you to enter administrator credentials to proceed. There are three ways to install software on a personal computer: download from an app store, load from a local device using media such as a CD or DVD or USB flash drive, or download from a website.

When you purchase an app from the Windows Store, click the *Get* button (Figure 2.32), *depending on the type of app you want,* and the installation will proceed automatically. If it is a paid app, you will have to complete the purchase before you install the program. On a Mac, from the App Store, for a free app, click *Get* and then click *Install App*; for a paid app, click the price and then click *Buy App*. You must enter your Apple ID and password to complete the purchase and installation.

To install from a disc, insert the disc in the drive and follow the instructions on the screen. If the installation does not begin automatically, open File Explorer, click the disc in the Navigation pane, and then double-click the setup or installation file. On a Mac, double-click the disc image that appears on the desktop. Installing from a disc will likely require you to enter a product key to validate the software. Many notebook computers no longer include an optical drive for installing software in this manner.

To install a program from a website, click the link to download the file. You may be given the option to run or save the file. The advantage of saving the file is that you can use it to reinstall the program if the need arises. If the file is zipped, you might need to unzip or extract it before you can install the program. Locate and double-click the installer file, which is usually named Setup.

FIGURE 2.32 Install an app through the Windows Store.

GREEN COMPUTING

Online And Downloaded Programs vs. Store-Bought Software

When you walk into a store and pick up software in a box or order from an online retailer and have the package shipped to you, there are several environmental impacts. First, there's product packaging and the packaging material used to ship the product. Although cardboard and paper are recyclable, the EPA estimates that only about 70 percent of it is actually recycled. The rest of it—and other materials, such as plastic shrink-wrap and packing peanuts—ends up in landfills. Then there's the media inside the package. What happens to the CD or DVD when the software is no longer needed? It ends up in the trash— and into the landfill it goes. Finally, the transportation costs of shipping the product to you or to the store—air pollution, fuel consumption, and emission of greenhouse gases—all add up.

All these environmental impacts are eliminated using online applications or purchasing software online and downloading it to your computer. No packaging, no transportation costs, no obsolete media, and the convenience of having the software delivered to you on the spot make these alternatives better choices for the environment.

Pablo Eder/Shutterstock

Updating and Uninstalling Software

Software publishers regularly release updates to their programs, often to address security holes, or **bugs**—flaws in the programming. An update might add new features, compatibility with new devices or file formats, or more levels to a game. A **patch**, or **hotfix**, addresses individual problems as they are discovered. A **service pack** is a larger, planned update that addresses multiple problems or adds multiple features—previous patches and hotfixes are included in the service pack.

Updating software requires an Internet connection. Apps purchased through an app store can be updated through the store (Figure 2.33), but most other programs require files to be downloaded from the Internet. You can configure software to check for updates automatically, or you can manually search for updates yourself. In a business environment, computers are generally not set to update software automatically because updates are centrally managed by the IT department where they can be tested before being installed on business systems.

When you no longer need a program on your computer, you should uninstall it by using the proper uninstaller to ensure that all files and settings are completely removed. Troubleshooting computer problems sometimes involves uninstalling and reinstalling software or updates. To view or uninstall the programs on a Windows computer, open File Explorer, in the Navigation pane click *This PC*, and then, on the Computer tab of the ribbon, click *Uninstall or change a program* to open the Programs and Features window (Figure 2.34). Locate the program that you want to uninstall, click the program name, and then click either the *Uninstall* or *Uninstall/Change* button that appears above the program list. The options available will vary depending on the program. Some programs will have a *Repair* option that you can use to fix the software installation. To uninstall a program from the Start menu, right-click an app and then click *Uninstall*, which will open the Programs and Features window. You can also uninstall programs from the System Settings window. Click the *Apps & features* tab, click the app you want to uninstall, and then click the *Uninstall* button (Figure 2.35). To uninstall a program on a Mac, if no uninstaller is provided, simply drag the program from the Applications folder to the trash.

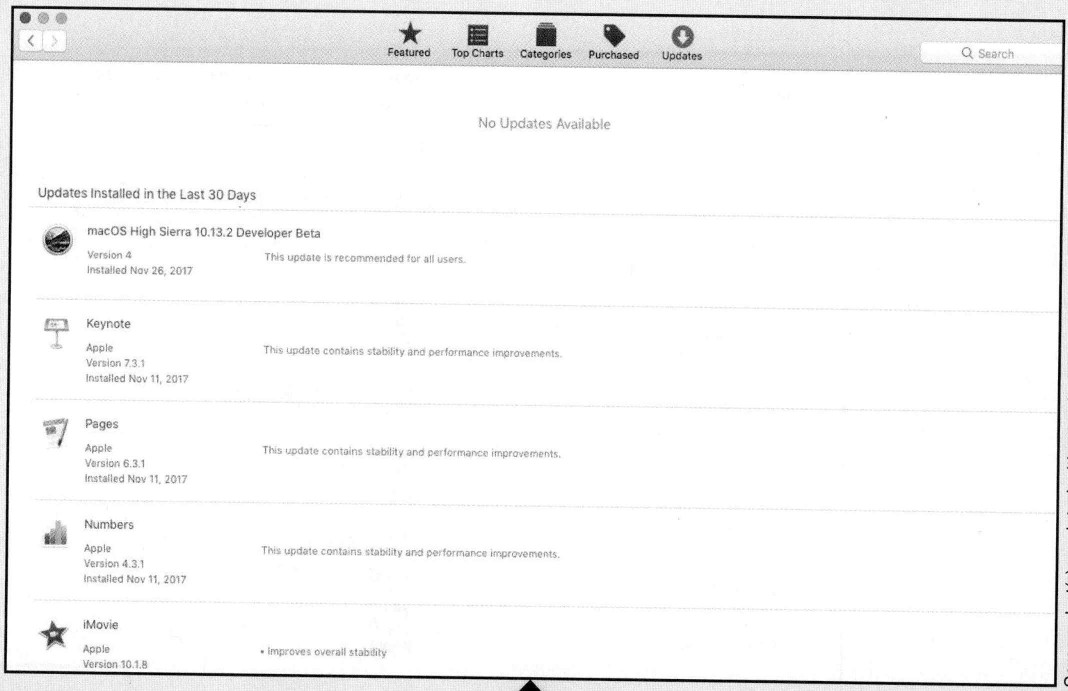

Screen shot(s) reprinted with permission from Apple Inc.

FIGURE 2.33 Update Apps through the App Store

Uninstall or change a program

To uninstall a program, select it from the list and then click Uninstall, Change, or Repair.

Organize ▾   Uninstall   Change   Repair

Name	Publisher	Installed On	Size	Version
☑ ASUS Smart Gesture	ASUS	8/2/2016	131 MB	4.0.12
Camtasia Studio 8	TechSmith Corporation	3/16/2016	617 MB	8.6.0.2054
Conexant HD Audio	Conexant	8/3/2016		8.66.4.60
Google Chrome	Google, Inc.	10/3/2015	78.6 MB	66.101.32869
Intel® Graphics Driver	Intel Corporation	8/3/2016	3.44 MB	10.18.10.4276
Microsoft Office 365 - en-us	Microsoft Corporation	9/9/2016	507 MB	16.0.7167.2040
Microsoft Project Professional 2016 - en-us	Microsoft Corporation	9/9/2016	507 MB	16.0.7167.2040
Microsoft Visio Professional 2016 - en-us	Microsoft Corporation	9/9/2016	507 MB	16.0.7167.2040
Microsoft Visual C++ 2008 Redistributable - x64 9....	Microsoft Corporation	11/8/2015	1.04 MB	9.0.30729.6161
Microsoft Visual C++ 2008 Redistributable - x86 9....	Microsoft Corporation	11/8/2015	6.17 MB	9.0.30729.6161
Mozilla Firefox 41.0.2 (x86 en-US)	Mozilla	8/3/2016	85.7 MB	41.0.2
Mozilla Maintenance Service	Mozilla	8/3/2016	250 KB	41.0.2
OpenOffice 4.1.2	Apache Software Foundation	11/8/2015	319 MB	4.12.9782
Screen Recorder Launcher		8/12/2016		2.0
Skype™ 7.17	Skype Technologies S.A.	1/15/2016	158 MB	7.17.105
Snagit 9.1.3	TechSmith Corporation	10/3/2015	115 MB	9.1.3.19
Windows 10 Upgrade Assistant	Microsoft Corporation	8/3/2016	5.00 MB	1.4.9200.17346
Windows Driver Package - ASUS (ATP) Mouse (11...	ASUS	8/3/2016		11/11/2015 1.0.0.262

FIGURE 2.34 Use the Programs and Features control panel window to uninstall software.

← Settings

⚙ Home

Find a setting 🔍

System

🖵 Display

☰ Apps & features

☰ Default apps

🗔 Notifications & actions

⏻ Power & sleep

🗔 Battery

🗔 Storage

🗺 Offline maps

🗔 Tablet mode

🗔 Multitasking

🗗 Projecting to this PC

Apps & features

Manage optional features

Search, sort, and filter by drive. If you would like to uninstall or move an app, select it from the list.

Search this list 🔍

☰ Sort by name ⌄

🗔 Show content from all drives ⌄

3D Builder		25.7 KB
Microsoft Corporation		8/5/2016
Alarms & Clock		16.8 KB
Microsoft Corporation		9/4/2016
App connector		16.0 KB
Microsoft Corporation		8/5/2016
App Installer		16.0 KB
Microsoft Corporation		8/13/2016
ASUS Smart Gesture		131 MB
ASUS		8/2/2016

Modify   Uninstall

Calculator   16.0 KB

FIGURE 2.35 Use the System Settings window to uninstall software.

ETHICS

Sharing Software

Jacob and Thomas share a dorm room, and each has his own notebook computer. The college provides students in the Computer Science department with several programs for their classwork. One of the programs that Jacob receives as a part of his major is an expensive drawing program. Thomas has always wanted to learn the drawing program, but because it is so expensive he has not had a chance to try it out, so he asks Jacob to lend him a copy to install on his own computer. Jacob is unwilling to do so, because he knows the software license only allows him to install one copy of the program on his own computer, specifically for his classwork. What should Jacob do? Is there a legal way for the guys to share the program?

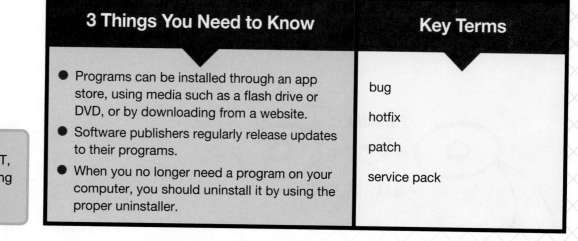

Running Project

On your computer, open the Programs and Features control panel window (on a Mac, open the Applications folder). How many programs are installed on your system? What are they? How many do you use on a regular basis? Which ones do you think should be uninstalled and why?

Viz Check—In MyLab IT, take a quick quiz covering Objectives 4–6.

3 Things You Need to Know

- Programs can be installed through an app store, using media such as a flash drive or DVD, or by downloading from a website.
- Software publishers regularly release updates to their programs.
- When you no longer need a program on your computer, you should uninstall it by using the proper uninstaller.

Key Terms

bug

hotfix

patch

service pack

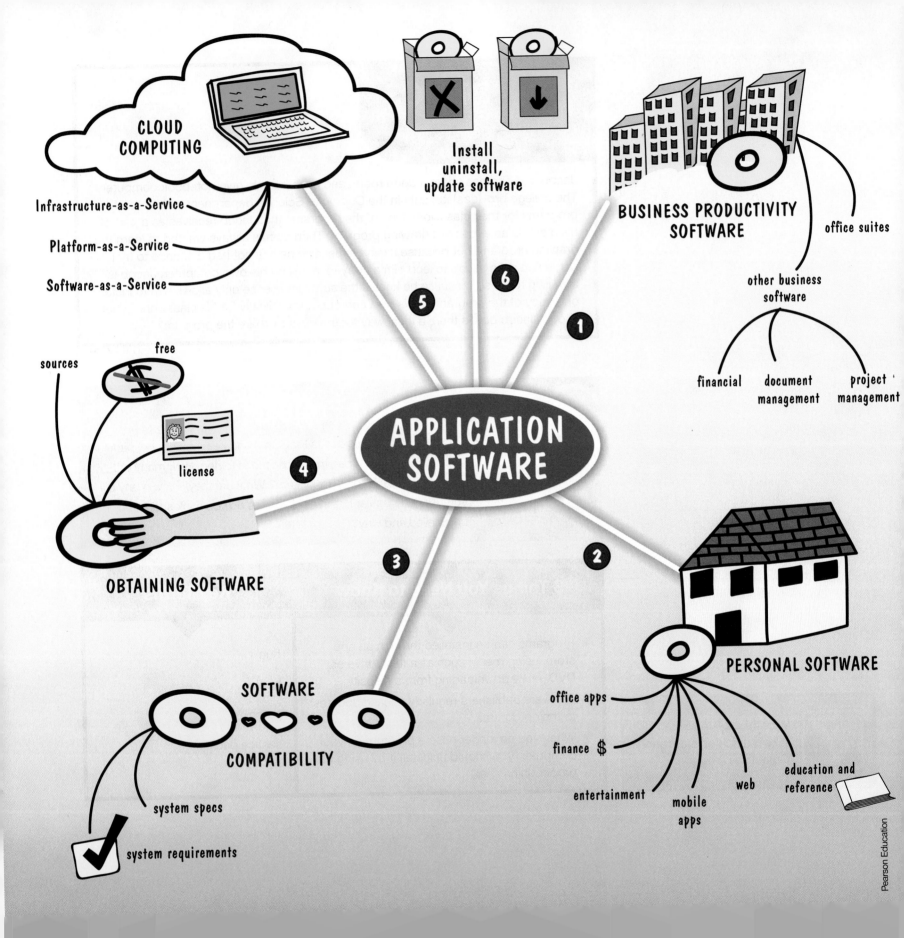

CLOUD COMPUTING

Infrastructure-as-a-Service

Platform-as-a-Service

Software-as-a-Service

Install uninstall, update software

BUSINESS PRODUCTIVITY SOFTWARE

office suites

other business software

financial

document management

project management

sources

free

license

OBTAINING SOFTWARE

APPLICATION SOFTWARE

PERSONAL SOFTWARE

office apps

finance $

entertainment

mobile apps

web

education and reference

SOFTWARE

COMPATIBILITY

system specs

system requirements

Pearson Education

Learn It Online

- Visit **pearsonhighered.com/viztech** for student data files
- Find simulations, VizClips, and additional study materials in **MyLab IT**
- Be sure to check out the **Tech Bytes** weekly news feed for current topics to review and discuss

Objectives Recap

1. Identify Types and Uses of Business Productivity Software
2. Identify Types and Uses of Personal Software
3. Assess a Computer System for Software Compatibility
4. Compare Various Ways of Obtaining Software
5. Discuss the Importance of Cloud Computing
6. Install, Uninstall, and Update Software

Key Terms

app **84**
application software **53**
bug **99**
cell **57**
cloud **86**
cloud computing **86**
cloud service provider (CSP) **87**
database **59**
desktop application **84**
document management system (DMS) **61**
donationware **83**
EULA (end-user license agreement) **83**
field **59**
form **59**
freemium **83**
freeware **83**
Gantt chart **62**
hotfix **99**
Infrastructure-as-a-Service (IaaS) **87**

office application suite **55**
open source **65**
patch **99**
personal information manager (PIM) **60**
Platform-as-a-Service (PaaS) **87**
platform-neutral **85**
project management software **62**
query **59**
record **59**
report **59**
retail software **83**
service pack **99**
shareware **83**
Software-as-a-Service (SaaS) **88**
spreadsheet **57**
subscription **83**
system requirements **80**
table **59**
web apps **71**
word processor **55**

Summary

1. Identify Types and Uses of Business Productivity Software

The most common business software is an office application suite—which may include a word processor, spreadsheet, presentation program, database, and personal information manager. Other business applications include financial software, document management, and project management software.

2. Identify Types and Uses of Personal Software

Personal software includes office applications, especially word processors, spreadsheets, and presentation programs. Other personal applications include entertainment and multimedia software such as media managers, video and photo editing software, and video games. Financial and tax preparation software as well as educational and reference software are also popular. You can run web apps in a browser, on any device with Internet access.

3. Assess a Computer System for Software Compatibility

Before purchasing and installing software, you should research the system requirements needed to run the program and compare them to your system specifications using File Explorer and the System Control Panel or System Settings window. On a Mac, use the About This Mac window.

4. Compare Various Ways of Obtaining Software

You can obtain software from brick-and-mortar and online stores, publisher websites, and download websites. Download mobile apps only from trusted markets. It's important to read the EULA to understand the software license restrictions.

5. Discuss the Importance of Cloud Computing

Cloud computing moves hardware and software into the cloud, or Internet. Cloud computing allows you to access applications and data from any web-connected computer. Some benefits include lower cost, easier maintenance, security, and collaboration.

6. Install, Uninstall, and Update Software

Managing the programs on your computer includes installing, uninstalling, and updating the software. You can install programs through an app store, by using media, or by downloading from a website. Updating software fixes bugs, adds features, or improves compatibility. You should uninstall software using the program's uninstaller.

Multiple Choice

Answer the multiple-choice questions below for more practice with key terms and concepts from this chapter.

1. Which application would be the best choice for creating a resume?
   a. Database
   b. Personal information manager
   c. Spreadsheet
   d. Word processor

2. Software that has the source code published and made available to the public—enabling anyone to copy, modify, and redistribute it without paying a fee—is called _____ software.
   a. freeware
   b. open source
   c. trial version
   d. platform-neutral

3. Which database object pulls out records that meet specific criteria?
   a. Field
   b. Form
   c. Query
   d. Report

4. _____ is an online alternative to office application suites.
   a. Google Drive
   b. OpenOffice
   c. TextEdit
   d. WordPad

5. _____ software helps you manage email, calendars, and tasks.
   a. Document management
   b. Personal information management
   c. Project management
   d. Word processing

6. Programs that can run in a browser are known as _____.
   a. open source software
   b. web apps
   c. IaaS
   d. suites

7. The system requirements for software do not include the _____.
   a. amount of free drive space
   b. amount of RAM
   c. operating system version
   d. computer manufacturer

8. _____ can be used for a limited period that allows the user to try it out before purchasing a license.
   a. Donationware
   b. Freeware
   c. Retail software
   d. Shareware

9. Which cloud computing service is an online programming environment used to develop, deploy, and manage custom web applications?
   a. IaaS
   b. PaaS
   c. SaaS

10. A(n) _____ is a large, planned software update that addresses multiple problems or adds multiple features.
    a. bug
    b. hotfix
    c. patch
    d. service pack

True or False

Answer the following questions with *T* for true or *F* for false for more practice with key terms and concepts from this chapter.

_____ 1. In a business environment, Microsoft Access is the most popular spreadsheet application.

_____ 2. A cell is the intersection of a row and a column in a spreadsheet.

_____ 3. Apache OpenOffice can not open and work with documents created in Microsoft Office.

_____ 4. Documents created with a word processor can also contain images.

_____ 5. A project management system enables a company to save, share, search, and audit electronic documents throughout their life cycle.

_____ 6. A Gantt chart shows the schedule and progress of a project.

_____ 7. If your computer doesn't meet the minimum system requirements for a piece of software, it will probably still run on your system.

_____ 8. Trialware is a form of freeware where the developers accept donations, either for themselves or for a nonprofit organization.

_____ 9. Web apps are also known as PaaS.

_____ 10. It is generally safe to download mobile apps from unknown sources.

Fill in the Blank

Fill in the blanks with key terms from this chapter.

1. A(n) _____ is an application that creates electronic worksheets composed of rows and columns.

2. A(n) _____ is a row of data in a database table that describes a particular entry in the database.

3. A(n) _____ is a database object that displays selected information.

4. A(n) _____ is used to save, share, search, and audit electronic documents throughout their life cycle.

5. _____ software has its source code published and made available to the public, enabling anyone to copy, modify, and redistribute it.

6. _____ are the minimum hardware and software specifications required to run a software application.

7. _____ is software offered in trial form or for a limited period that allows the user to try it out before purchasing a license.

8. The license agreement between the software user and the software publisher is the _____.

9. Part of cloud computing, _____ is the use of Internet-based servers.

10. A(n) _____ is a flaw in software programming.

Running Project ...

... The Finish Line

Assume that you just got a new computer with no software on it. Use your answers to the previous sections of the project to help you select five pieces of software that you consider indispensable to have. Which programs did you pick and why? If you could only afford to buy one program, which would it be? Which would you likely use a web-based tool for?

Write a report describing your selections and responding to the questions raised throughout the chapter. Save your file as **lastname_firstname_ch02_project** and submit it to your instructor as directed.

Do It Yourself 1

System requirements for new software often include a computer system with lots of available processing power, storage space, and memory. In this activity, examine your own computer to help you make smart software purchases. Windows and macOS provide many details about your computer through built-in utilities. For this exercise, use the File Explorer window. For a Mac, use the About This Mac window to complete the table. From your student data files, open the file *vt_ch02_DIY1_answersheet* and save the file as **lastname_firstname_ch02_DIY1_answersheet**.

Open File Explorer. If necessary, click *This PC*. In the right pane is a listing of all the drives available on your computer. If you are using a Mac, open the *About This Mac* window from the Apple menu and click the *Storage* tab. Complete the table below to record details about your system—include the name, capacity, and free space for each drive. Save the file and submit the assignment as directed by your instructor.

Hard Disk Drives	Other Devices	Network Locations

Do It Yourself 2

Windows and macOS come with several applications. In this activity, you'll examine these accessories. From your student data files, open the file *vt_ch02_DIY2_answersheet* and save the file as **lastname_firstname_ch02_DIY2_answersheet**.

1. From the Windows 10 Start menu, click *All apps*. (From the Windows 8 Start Screen, in the bottom left corner, click the down arrow to display all apps. If necessary, click the arrow next to Apps to display by name.) Scroll to display Windows Accessories. For a Mac, click the *Launchpad* and review the programs on the first screen, then click *Other*. What programs are listed? Which of these programs have you used in the past? Are there any that you are unfamiliar with?

2. Use Windows Help to learn about Calculator, Math Input Panel, Paint, and Sticky Notes. If you are using a Mac, on the Finder menu bar, click *Help*, and search for Apps included with your Mac. Look up Calculator, Grapher, Preview, and Stickies. Write a one- to two-paragraph summary of each application. Save the file and submit it as directed by your instructor.

Critical Thinking

You're starting a small photography business. You need an inexpensive but powerful photo editing program to touch up your Images. Compare two photo editing programs in the $75–$200 range. From your student data files, open the file *vt_ch02_CT_answersheet* and save the file as **lastname_firstname_ch02_CT_answersheet**.

1. Evaluate two photo editing programs from online retailers and compare them with respect to your requirements. Complete the table below, comparing the features of each program, to organize your research.

	Program 1	Program 2
Name of program		
Cost		
Local install or online?		
Important features		
Online ratings (website)		
Support		

2. Which program should you buy and why? Is there anything else (hardware, software, office supplies) that you'll need to purchase to use the program? Save your file and submit both your table and essay as directed by your instructor.

Ethical Dilemma

You have decided to buy an expensive video editing program and look online for a good deal. You find a listing from a seller that has good ratings, so you buy the software. When the software arrives, you're disappointed to find that it is a pirated copy and includes a program to generate a license key to unlock the program—a key-gen program. From your student data files, open the file *vt_ch02_ethics_answersheet* and save the file as **lastname_firstname_ch02_ethics_answersheet**.

You bought the software in good faith and really need it to complete your homework assignment. What do you do? Would you install the software? Why or why not? Is it acceptable to install the software for the assignment and uninstall it when you're finished? Save the file and submit it as directed by your instructor.

On the Web

The SourceForge website is a great place to find open source software. From your student data files, open the file *vt_ch02_web_answersheet* and save the file as **lastname_firstname_ch02_web_answersheet**.

1. Go to **sourceforge.net**. What are the projects of the month and editor's choices? Click the title of each project to view the webpage of the project. Complete the following table for two projects of your choice.

Project	Brief Description	Rating	Last Updated

2. Select an application category from the menu on the left. Choose one application that looks interesting and that you do not already use. Read the description and reviews. What are the strengths and weaknesses of the program? Save the file and submit it as directed by your instructor.

Collaboration

Instructors: Divide the class into five groups, and assign each group one software license topic for this project. The topics include freeware, shareware, donationware, open source software, and EULAs.

The Project: As a team, prepare a multimedia presentation for your license type. The presentation should be designed to educate consumers about the license type. Use at least three references, only one of which may be this text. Use Google Docs or Microsoft Office to plan the presentation, and provide documentation that all team members have contributed to the project.

Outcome: Prepare a multimedia presentation on your assigned topic, using Prezi or another tool approved by your instructor, and present it to your class. The presentation may be no longer than 3 minutes. Turn in your file showing your collaboration named **teamname_ch02_collab**. Include the URL to your presentation. Submit your presentation to your instructor as directed.

Application Project

MyLab IT
GRADER

Office 2016 Application Projects
PowerPoint 2016: Introduction to PowerPoint Design

Project Description: Your boss has asked you to edit a PowerPoint presentation discussing good PowerPoint design. In this project, you will edit and format text and bullets, insert and format pictures, check spelling, add new slides and change slide layout, apply transitions, and add speaker notes. If necessary, download the student data files from *pearsonhighered.com/viztech*.

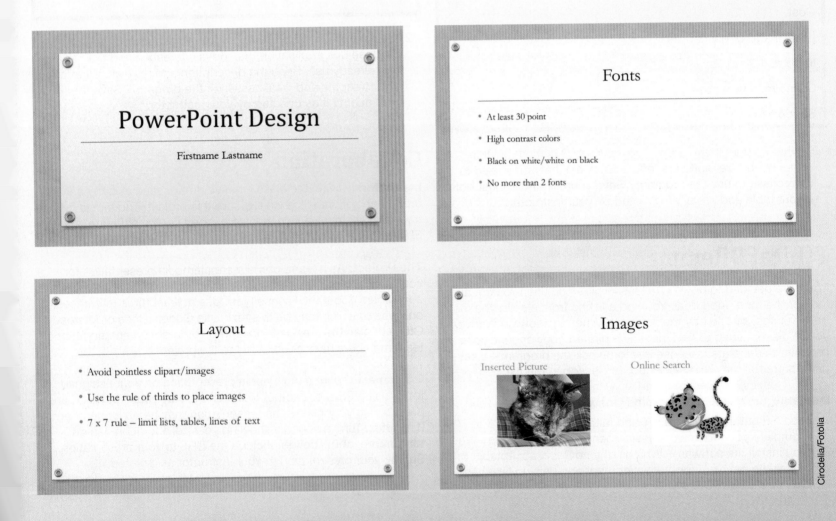

PowerPoint Design

Firstname Lastname

Fonts
- At least 30 point
- High contrast colors
- Black on white/white on black
- No more than 2 fonts

Layout
- Avoid pointless clipart/images
- Use the rule of thirds to place images
- 7 x 7 rule – limit lists, tables, lines of text

Images
Inserted Picture   Online Search

Cirodelia/Fotolia

Step	Instructions
1	Start PowerPoint. From your student data files, open the file *vt_ch02_ppt.* Save the presentation as **lastname_firstname_ch02_ppt**
2	On Slide 1, using your own name, type the subtitle text **Firstname Lastname** Change the font of the title text, *PowerPoint Design,* to Cambria and change the size to 48.
3	On Slide 2, change the line spacing of the bullets to 1.5 and the font size to 28.
4	On Slide 3, use the shortcut menu to correct the spelling of *Layout.* Change the line spacing of the bullets to 1.5 and the font size to 28.
5	Insert a new Comparison slide after Slide 3 and add the title text **Images**
6	On the new Slide 4, in the bottom left content placeholder, insert the picture *vt_ch02_image2.* In the content place holder, type **Inserted Picture**
7	On the new Slide 4, in the bottom right content placeholder, search for and insert an online image of a cat. In the content place holder, type **Online Search**
8	Format both images to a height of **2.5**″. Align the middle of the images.
9	Switch to Slide Sorter view and delete Slide 5. Switch back to Normal view.
10	In the Notes pane on Slide 2, add the following speaker note: **Keep your fonts simple and easy to read.**
11	In the Notes pane on Slide 3, add the following speaker note: **Your layout should focus the viewer's attention.**
12	In the Notes pane on Slide 4, add the following speaker note: **Images should enhance what you have to say.**
13	Apply the Wipe transition with a duration of **01.50** to all of the slides in the presentation.
14	Insert the page number and then type your name as the footer on the notes and handouts pages for all slides in the presentation. View the presentation in Slide Show view from beginning to end, and then return to Normal view.
15	Save the presentation and close PowerPoint. Submit the presentation as directed.

Application Project

Office 2016 Application Projects

Excel 2016: Comparing Office Application Suite Costs

Project Description: In this Microsoft Excel project, you will format cells and a worksheet. You will create a formula and insert a header and footer. *If necessary, download the student data files from* **pearsonhighered.com/viztech**.

Comparisons

Cost Comparison for a Small Business

	G Suite by Google Cloud	MS Office 365 Small Business Premium
Initial Cost - per license	-	-
Price Per User Per Month	10.00	12.50
Annual Cost for 10 Users	$ 1,200.00	$ 1,500.00
Apps included	Docs, Sheets, Slides, Mail, Calendar, Chat, Drive, Sites, Groups	Word, Excel, PowerPoint, Outlook, OneNote, Publisher, Access, Lync
Live Support/Updates	24/7 phone and email support	Telephone and online answers
Online Support	Self-service online support	How-to resources, connections with other Office 365 customers
Reliability	99.9% uptime guarantee	Guaranteed 99.9% uptime

Step	Instructions
1	Start Excel. From your student data files, open the Excel file named *vt_ch02_excel*. Save the workbook as **lastname_firstname_ch02_excel**
2	Apply the Berlin theme to the workbook.
3	Merge and center the text in cell A1 over columns A:C. Change the cell style to Heading 1.
4	Set the width of columns A:C to 30. Wrap text in cells B7:C10.
5	Apply the Comma cell style to the range B3:C4. Apply the Currency and Total cell styles to the range B5:C5.
6	Select the range A2:C2 and set the text to wrap in the cells. Center and middle align the text in the selected range. Change the cell style to Heading 3.
7	In cell B5, create a formula to calculate the annual cost of G Suite for 10 users. Copy the formula to cell C5.
8	Change the orientation of the Sheet 1 worksheet to Landscape.
9	Center the worksheet horizontally on the page.
10	Rename the Sheet1 tab as **Comparisons**
11	Insert a header with the sheet name in the center cell. Insert a footer with the file name in the left cell.
12	Save the workbook and close Excel. Submit the workbook as directed.

Massimo_g/Fotolia

File Management

In This Chapter

VIZ INTRO

The concepts of file management are not unique to computing. We use file cabinets, folders, boxes, drawers, and piles to manage our paper files—anything from bills to photographs to homework assignments to coupons. In this chapter, we look at managing electronic files. After you complete this chapter, you will be able to organize and manage your files to make working more efficient.

BrunoWeltmann/Fotolia

Objectives

1 Create Folders to Organize Files

2 Explain the Importance of File Extensions

3 Explain the Importance of Backing Up Files

4 Demonstrate How to Compress Files

5 Use Advanced Search Options to Locate Files

6 Change the Default Program Associated with a File Type

Running Project

In this chapter, you'll learn about the importance of file management. Look for instructions as you complete each article. For most articles, there's a series of questions for you to research or a set of tasks to perform. At the conclusion of this chapter, you'll submit your responses to the questions raised and the results of the tasks you've performed.

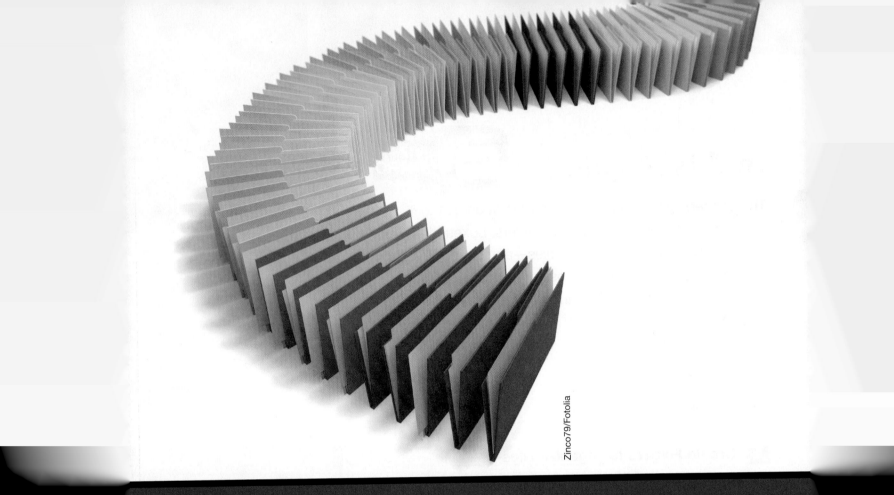

Zinco79/Fotolia

A Place for Everything

Create Folders to Organize Files

One of the most important things that you need to do when working with computers is called **file management**: opening, closing, saving, naming, deleting, and organizing digital files. In this article, we discuss organizing your digital files, creating new folders, and navigating through the folder structure of your computer.

SIMULATION

File Management

Navigating Your Computer

Before you can create files, you need a place to put them. You can start with the existing folder structure of your computer that is created by the operating system and customize it to fit your needs. **Folders** are containers that organize files on your computer. Windows comes with some folders already created, organized in a **hierarchy** of folders within folders—known as subfolders or children—which enable you to further organize your files. The sequence of folders to a file or folder is known as its **path**. Some versions of Windows use **libraries** to organize similar files located in different locations. There are four libraries: Documents, Music, Pictures, and Videos.

FILE EXPLORER

On a computer running Microsoft Windows, the window you use to navigate the file system is called **File Explorer**. You can use File Explorer to navigate through your system and to handle most file management tasks. Open File Explorer by clicking the *File Explorer* icon on the taskbar on the desktop or from the Windows Start menu. Figure 3.1 identifies some of the parts of the File Explorer window:

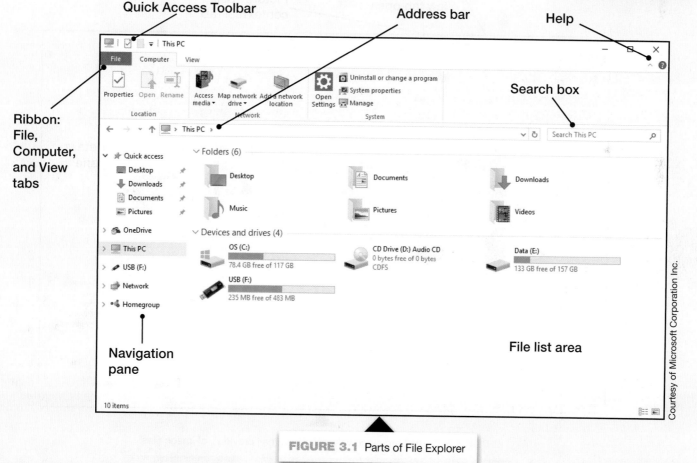

FIGURE 3.1 Parts of File Explorer

- **Quick Access Toolbar:** Contains icons for frequently used commands. The icons displayed can be customized to the way you work.
- **Ribbon:** Contains common tasks on the items in the file list area. The tabs change depending on the objects displayed.
  - **Home tab:** Contains commands to copy, paste, move, delete, rename, select, open, and edit.
  - **File tab:** Contains commands to open and close the windows and provides access to system Help.
  - **Computer tab:** Contains commands to navigate your computer and access system settings and the Control Panel.
  - **View tab:** Contains commands that enable you to change the way objects in the file list are displayed. For picture files, choosing *Large Icons*, as shown in Figure 3.2, displays a small preview, or thumbnail, of the image. Displaying the Details pane shows you more information about a selected file.
- **Address bar:** Contains the path to the current location in the File Explorer window and is used to navigate through folders and libraries. You can move down in the folder hierarchy by clicking the arrow after your location. You can move back up in the folder hierarchy by clicking the arrows or links in the Address bar.
- **Search box:** Use to search for files located in the current File Explorer window.
- **Help:** Found under the File tab or by clicking the ? icon in the upper right corner.
- **Navigation pane:** Use to navigate the folders and drives available on a computer. The Navigation pane is divided into several sections: Quick Access, OneDrive, This PC, and Network. Clicking on any of these sections changes the contents in the right pane. Clicking the small triangle before an item in the Navigation pane expands it to display the locations it contains. You can customize what displays in this pane using the View tab.
- **File list area:** Displays the contents of the current location selected in the File Explorer window.

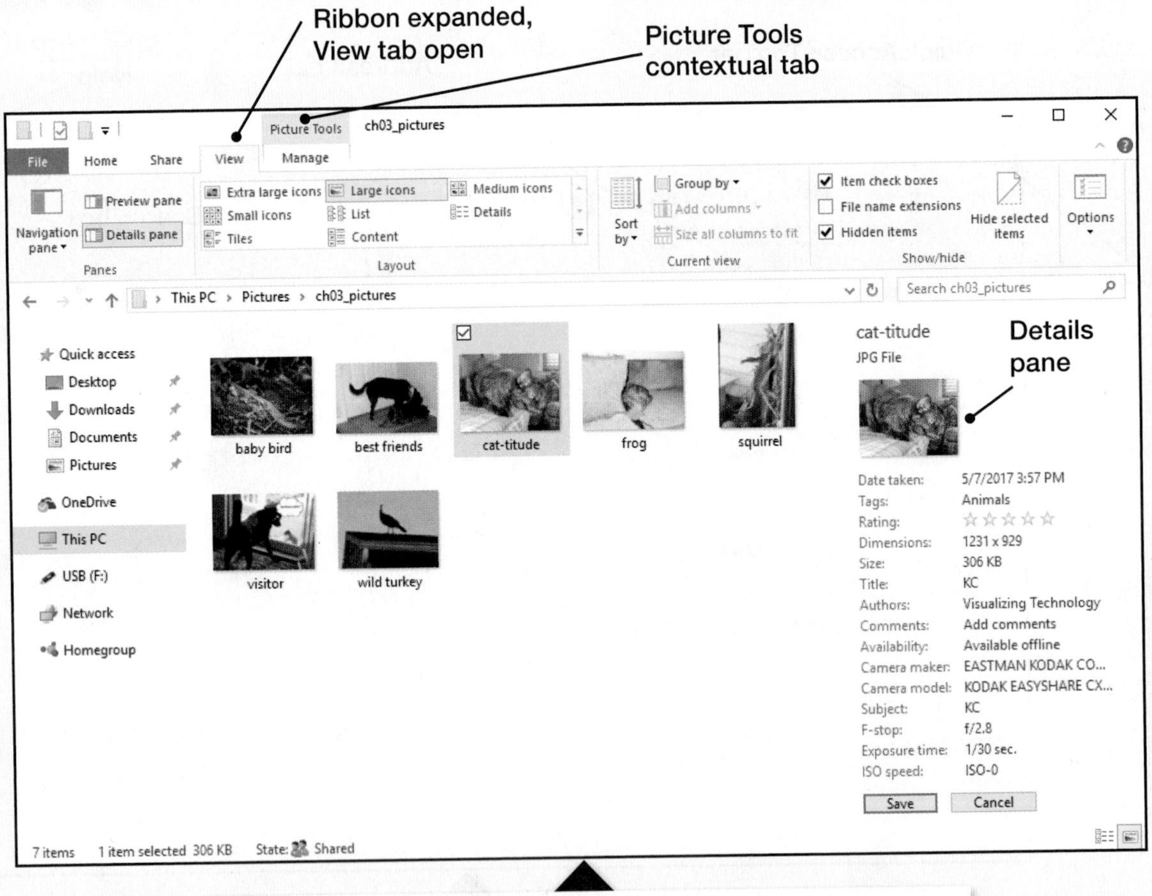

FIGURE 3.2 The Large Icon view displays small previews of image files.

THE WINDOWS USER FOLDER

When a user account is added to a Windows computer, Windows automatically creates a personal user folder for that account, along with subfolders inside it (Figure 3.3). To see your user folder in File Explorer, click *This PC*, click the up arrow (↑), and then double-click the folder with your user name.

What folders are located under your user name? The Documents folder is the place to store files such as word processing files, spreadsheets, presentations, and text files. There are also folders set up for pictures, music, and videos. These specialized folders are the best places to save your pictures, music, and videos so they're easy to find. Without this folder structure, all of your files would be lumped together, making it much harder to keep track of what you have; it would be like dumping all your snapshots into a shoebox. Your user folder items are normally accessible only by you. If another person logs on to the computer using a different account, that person won't see your files.

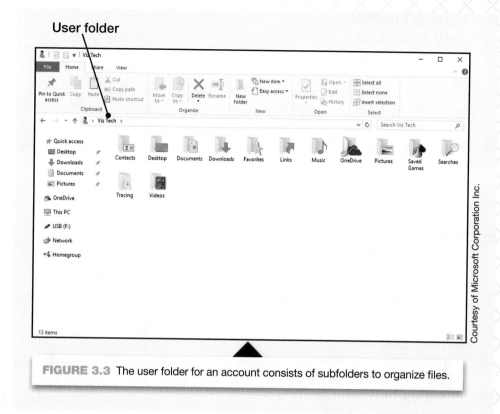

User folder

FIGURE 3.3 The user folder for an account consists of subfolders to organize files.

QUICK ACCESS

File Explorer includes Quick access items on the Navigation pane to help you work more easily. By default, this section includes shortcuts to Downloads, Desktop, Documents, and Pictures, and as you work, recent and frequently used locations are added to the list. In Figure 3.4 the Chapter 3 folder has been added to the Quick access list. You can modify this behavior by using *Change folder and search options* in the File menu, and you can customize Quick access by adding other locations. In File Explorer, simply right-click the location and click *Pin to Quick access*.

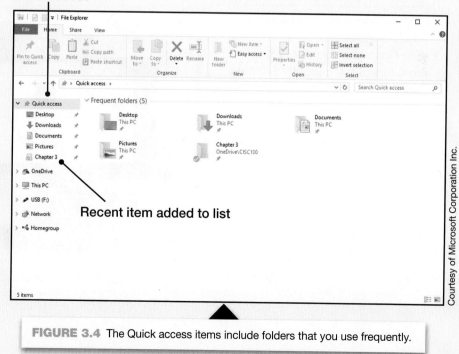

Quick access

Recent item added to list

FIGURE 3.4 The Quick access items include folders that you use frequently.

macOS FINDER AND FOLDERS

On a Mac computer, **Finder** is used to find and organize files, folders, and apps. To open Finder, from the Finder menu bar, click *File* and click *New Finder Window* or click the *Finder* icon on the dock. The Finder window opens to All My Files. Click the user name in the left pane to display the user folder and subfolders. The user folder includes subfolders to store documents, downloads, movies, music, and pictures. The Public folder can be used to share files with other users of the same computer. Figure 3.5 identifies some of the parts of the Finder window:

- The Toolbar contains buttons to change the way Finder behaves.
- The View options on the toolbar change the way Finder displays information.
- The Search box is used to search for files on your Mac.
- The Sidebar contains icons for things you frequently use, such as disks, folders, shared resources, and other devices.
- The Contents area displays the contents of the currently selected location.

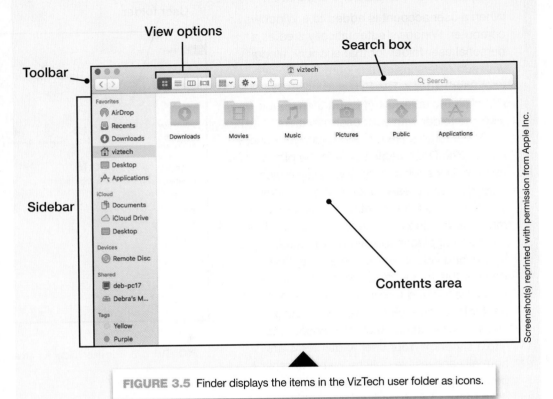

View options

Search box

Toolbar

Sidebar

Contents area

Screenshot(s) reprinted with permission from Apple Inc.

FIGURE 3.5 Finder displays the items in the VizTech user folder as icons.

Rawpixel.com/Shutterstock

MOBILE DEVICES AND FILE STORAGE

Mobile devices are meant to be mobile—fast and light—and don't have a lot of room to store files. Some mobile devices can use an SD card to extend storage. For larger storage, they rely on using the Internet—or **cloud**—to organize and store your files, making your mobile files accessible on all of your devices, not just the one in your hand. Cloud storage is discussed later in this chapter.

Creating and Using Folders

You're not limited to using the folder structure that's automatically created by Windows or macOS. You can create your own organizational scheme to fit your needs. This is especially useful when you use flash drives, external hard drives, and other locations that aren't part of the user folder hierarchy. Suppose you print 25–30 photos a month (or 300–360 photos a year). How would you keep track of them? If you put them in a big box, in a few years you'd have thousands of photos in the box. It would be nearly impossible to keep track of them or find anything unless you organized them into photo albums. The same is true with the files on your computer. Creating folders to organize your files makes storing and finding them much easier. You can create a new folder when you save a file. This enables you to organize your files as they're created instead of after the fact. The Save As dialog box that opens when you save a file looks very much like File Explorer and includes the *New folder* button (Figure 3.6). Figure 3.7 demonstrates how to create a new folder on a flash drive.

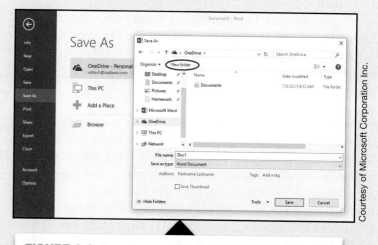

FIGURE 3.6 Create a new folder when saving a file in Word.

Courtesy of Microsoft Corporation Inc.

FIGURE 3.7 Steps to Create a New Folder on a Flash Drive (Windows)

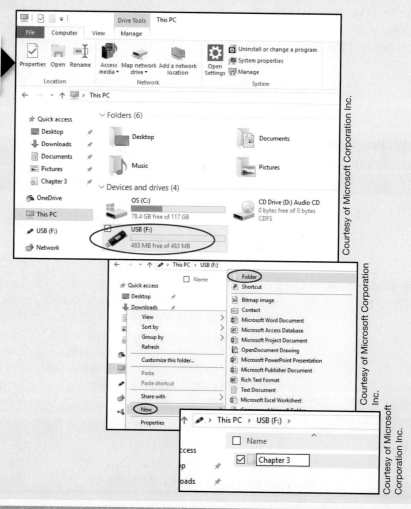

Courtesy of Microsoft Corporation Inc.

1. Insert the flash drive into the computer. Close any windows that open automatically. Open File Explorer and, if necessary, click *This PC*. You should see the flash drive listed under Devices and drives. The drive letter will vary depending on the other drives on the system.
2. Double-click the icon for the flash drive to open it. Right-click a blank area of the window, point to *New*, and click *Folder* (Another way—on the ribbon, click *New folder*)
3. Type **Chapter 3** to name the folder and press Enter. You have created a new folder on your flash drive to store your files.

To create a new folder on a Mac, use the File menu in Finder (Figure 3.8) or press Shift + Command ⌘ + N.

Organizing your files into folders is easy once the folders have been created. You can use File Explorer or Finder to copy and move files to different locations on your computer. When you copy a file, you make a duplicate that can be put in another location, leaving the original file intact; moving a file changes the location of the file. Both of these tasks can be accomplished in several ways, as explained in Table 3.1 and Table 3.2. To select multiple files to copy or move, hold down the Ctrl key in Windows as you click on each file. If the files are adjacent, in Windows you can click the first file, hold down the Shift key, and click the last file. To select all the files in a window, press Ctrl + A. On a Mac, use the Command ⌘ or Shift key to select multiple files, or use Command ⌘ + A to select all.

Learning to work with folders will make organizing your files much easier and more efficient. File Explorer and Finder enable you to navigate and view your files in several different ways so you can use the methods you find the most useful.

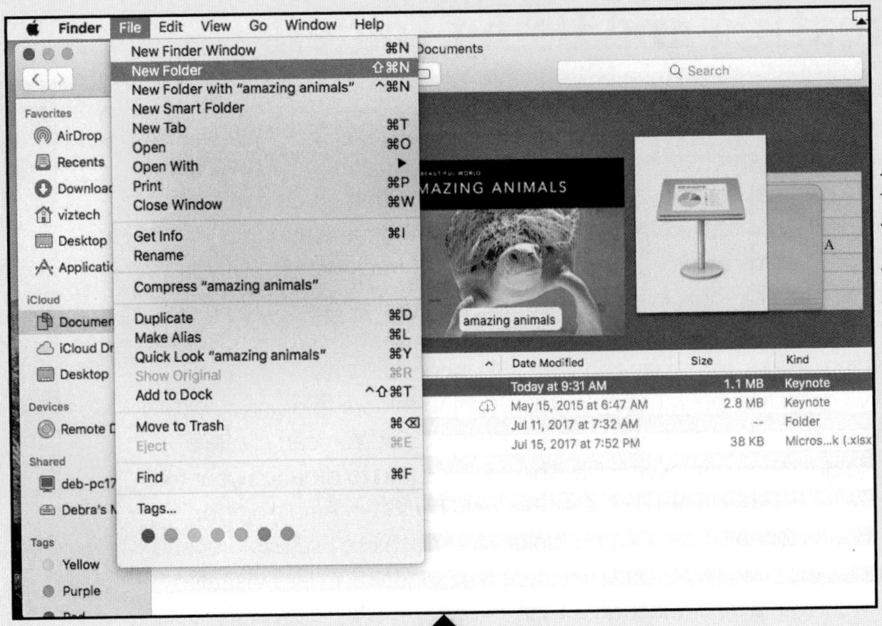

Screenshot(s) reprinted with permission from Apple Inc.; Debra Geoghan

FIGURE 3.8 Create a new folder on a Mac.

TABLE 3.1 Copying and Moving Files Using File Explorer

Method	Copy	Move
Mouse click: Click the right mouse button to display the menu.	To copy a file, right-click the file and click *Copy*. Navigate to the destination folder, right-click on it, and click *Paste*.	To move a file, right-click the file and click *Cut*. Navigate to the destination folder, right-click on it, and click *Paste*.
Mouse drag: Hold down the left mouse button while moving the file to the destination location.	To copy a file to a folder on a different disk, hold down the left mouse button and drag the file to its destination. To copy a file to a folder on the same disk, hold down the right mouse button and drag the file to its destination. Release the mouse button and click *Copy here*.	To move a file to a folder on the same disk, hold down the left mouse button and drag the file to its destination. To move a file to a folder on a different disk, hold down the right mouse button and drag the file to its destination. Release the mouse button and click *Move here*.
Keyboard shortcut: Hold down Ctrl while pressing the designated letter.	Select the file to be copied and press Ctrl + C to copy the file. Navigate to the destination location and press Ctrl + V to paste the file.	Select the file to be moved and press Ctrl + X to cut the file. Navigate to the destination location and press Ctrl + V to paste the file.

TABLE 3.2 Copying and Moving Files Using Finder

Method	Copy	Move
Mouse click: Press Ctrl and click the mouse button to display the menu.	To copy a file, press Ctrl + click and select *Copy*. Navigate to the destination folder, press Ctrl + click, and click *Paste Item*.	Follow the steps to copy a file and then drag the original file to the trash.
Mouse drag: Hold down the mouse button while moving the file to the destination location.	To copy a file to a folder on a different disk, hold down the mouse button and drag the file to its destination.	To move a file to a folder on the same disk, hold down the mouse button and drag the file to its destination.
Keyboard shortcut: Hold down Command ⌘ while pressing the designated letter.	Select the file to be copied and press Command ⌘ + C to copy the file. Navigate to the destination location and press Command ⌘ + V to paste the file.	Follow the steps to copy a file and then drag the original file to the trash.

Running Project

Using File Explorer or Finder, look at the user folder on your system. What is the user name? What subfolders are displayed for this user in addition to the Documents, Music, and Pictures folders? Take a screenshot of the user folder and paste it into your answer sheet.

3 Things You Need to Know

- Windows and macOS create a folder hierarchy for storing files.
- Each user has his or her own folder structure for storing documents, pictures, music, videos, and more.
- File Explorer in Windows and Finder in macOS are used to navigate through folders and drives.

Key Terms

cloud

File Explorer

file management

Finder

folder

hierarchy

library

path

Organize Your Files

HOW TO VIDEO

In this activity you will use File Explorer or Finder to view various file types and folders. If necessary, download the student data files from **pearsonhighered.com /viztech**. From your student data files, open *vt_ch03_howto1_ answersheet* and save it in your Chapter 3 folder as **lastname_ firstname_ch03_howto1_ answersheet**.

1 In File Explorer, navigate to the student data files for this chapter. If necessary, click **>** to expand *This PC* in the Navigation pane. Drag the *ch03_pictures* folder from the file list in the right pane to the *Pictures* folder in the Navigation pane. Drag the *ch03_music* folder to the *Music* folder. Drag the *ch03_documents* folder to the *Documents* folder.

Picture Tools   vt6_ch03_data_files

| File | Home | Share | View | Manage |

Pin to Quick access | Copy | Paste | Cut | Copy path | Paste shortcut | Move to | Copy to | Delete | Rename | New folder | New item ▾ | Easy access ▾ | Properties | Open ▾ | Edit | History | Select all | Select none | Invert selection

Clipboard   Organize   New   Open   Select

← → ∨ ↑   > OneDrive > vt6_ch03_data_files >

	Name	Date modified	Type	Size
Desktop	ch03_documents	9/10/2016 8:28 AM	File folder	
Downloads	ch03_isaac_animals	9/10/2016 8:28 AM	File folder	
Documents	ch03_music	9/10/2016 8:28 AM	File folder	
Pictures	☑ ch03_pictures	9/10/2016 8:28 AM	File folder	
Chapter 3	ch03_zoe_cupcakes	9/10/2016 8:28 AM	File folder	
OneDrive	vt_ch03_appfiles	9/10/2016 8:28 AM	File folder	
This PC	vt_ch03_CT_answersheet	9/10/2016 8:27 AM	Microsoft Word D...	18 KB
Desktop	vt_ch03_DIY2_answersheet	9/10/2016 8:27 AM	Microsoft Word D...	18 KB
Docum...	vt_ch03_ethics_answersheet	9/10/2016 8:27 AM	Microsoft Word D...	17 KB
Downl...	vt_ch03_howto1_answersheet	9/10/2016 8:27 AM	Microsoft Word D...	18 KB
Music	vt_ch03_howto1_answersheet_mac	9/10/2016 8:27 AM	Microsoft Word D...	18 KB
Pictures	vt_ch03_howto2_answersheet	9/10/2016 8:27 AM	Microsoft Word D...	17 KB
Camera Roll	vt_ch03_howto2_answersheet_mac	9/10/2016 8:27 AM	Microsoft Word D...	17 KB
Move to Pictures	3_sunset	9/10/2016 8:27 AM	TIF File	26,492 KB
Saved Pictures	vt_ch03_web_answersheet	9/10/2016 8:27 AM	Microsoft Word D...	17 KB
Videos				

2

In the Navigation pane, under This PC, click *Music*. In the file list on the right, double-click the *ch03_music* folder. If it has not been customized, the default view is Music Details. Click the *View* tab, and if necessary, in the Layout group, click *Details*. What are the headings of the columns in this view? Click the *Title* column heading. What happens to the files in the window? Click the *Name* column heading. What happens? Take a screenshot and paste it into your answer sheet.

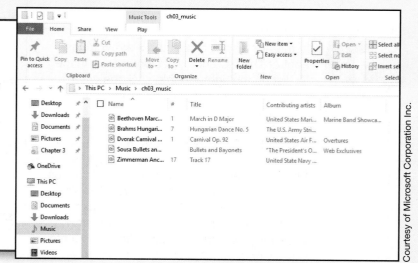

Courtesy of Microsoft Corporation Inc.

3

In the Navigation pane, click *Pictures*. In the file list on the right, double-click the *ch03_pictures* folder. The default view for this folder is Large icons. Use the View tab, if necessary, to change the view to Large icons. How is the view in this folder different from the Music folder? Take a screenshot and paste it into your answer sheet.

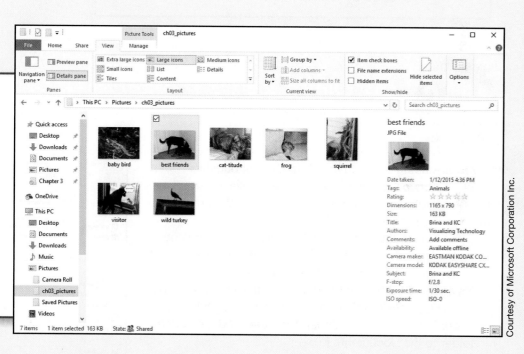

Courtesy of Microsoft Corporation Inc.

4

Click the *View* tab and in the Panes group, if necessary, select the *Details* pane. Select one image (but do not open it) and look at the Details pane. What information is found in this pane? Change the rating of the file. What other information can you change? Take a screenshot and paste it into your document.

5 In the Address bar, click the **>** arrow to the right of This PC and click *Documents*. In the file list on the right, double-click the *ch03_documents* folder. If necessary, change the view of the Documents folder to Details and turn off the Details pane. How is the Details view of this folder different from the Music Details view? On the View tab, turn on the *Preview* pane. Scroll down and select various files from this folder. What file types display their contents in the Preview pane? Take a screenshot and paste it into your document. Type your answers, including the appropriate screenshots, save your file, and submit as directed by your instructor.

Courtesy of Microsoft Corporation Inc.

MAC

If you are using a Mac: From your student data files, open *vt_ch03_howto1_answersheet_mac* and save it in your Chapter 3 folder as **lastname_firstname_ch03_howto1_answersheet_mac**.

1. Open Finder. If the Music and Pictures folders are not visible in the Sidebar, from the Finder menu, open *Preferences* and click the *Sidebar* tab to display them. Navigate to the student data files for this chapter. Drag the *ch03_pictures* folder to Pictures and the *ch03_music* folder to Music in the sidebar. Drag the *ch03_documents* folder to the Documents folder.

2. Display the contents of *ch03_music* in List view using the button on the toolbar or the View menu. What are the headings of the columns in this view? Click the *Name* column heading. What happens to the files in the window? Click the *Name* column heading again. What happens? Take a screenshot and paste it into your answer sheet.

List view

Screen shot(s) reprinted with permission from Apple Inc.

3. Display the contents of the *ch03_pictures* folder in Cover Flow view using the button on the toolbar or the View menu. How is the view in this folder different from the Music folder? Take a screenshot and paste it into your answer sheet.

4. Select one image (but do not open it). Select *Get Info* from the File menu. What information is found in this pane? What information can you change? Take a screenshot and paste it into your answer sheet. Close the Get Info pane.

5. Display the contents of the *ch03_documents* folder in Column view using the button on the toolbar or the View menu. How is the Column view of this folder different from List view? Select various files from this folder. What file types display their contents in the Preview pane? Take a screenshot and paste it into your answer sheet. Type your answers, including the appropriate screenshots, save your file, and submit as directed by your instructor.

Cover Flow view

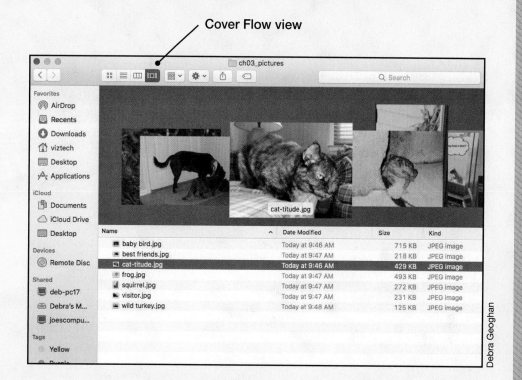

Debra Geoghan

Column view

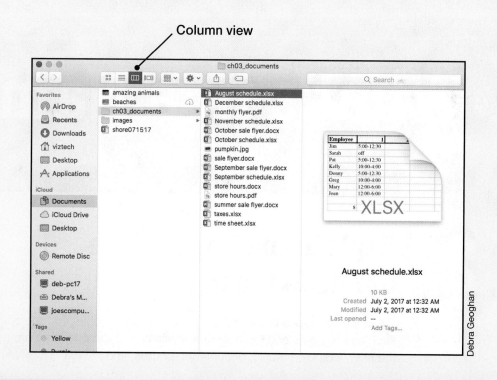

Debra Geoghan

Billion Photos/Shutterstock

What's in a Name?

2 Explain the Importance of File Extensions

There are two types of files on every computer: the ones that the computer uses to function, such as programs and the operating system, and the ones that are used and created by you, the user, including music, documents, photos, and videos.

File Names and Extensions

Every file has a **file name** that consists of a name and a file extension. The name is useful to the user and describes the contents of the file. When creating your own files, you decide the name. In the example in Figure 3.9, *ch03_homework* is the name of the file. On early PCs, file names were limited to eight characters with a three-letter extension and were often cryptic. Today, file names on Windows computers can be up to 260 characters long, including the file extension and the path to the file, and can include spaces and special characters. Table 3.3 shows illegal characters in a Windows file name. macOS file names can be up to 255 characters long, and the only illegal character is the colon (:).

TABLE 3.3 Illegal Characters in Windows File Names

Character	Description
\	Backslash
/	Forward slash
?	Question mark
:	Colon
*	Asterisk
"	Quotation marks
>	Greater than
<	Less than

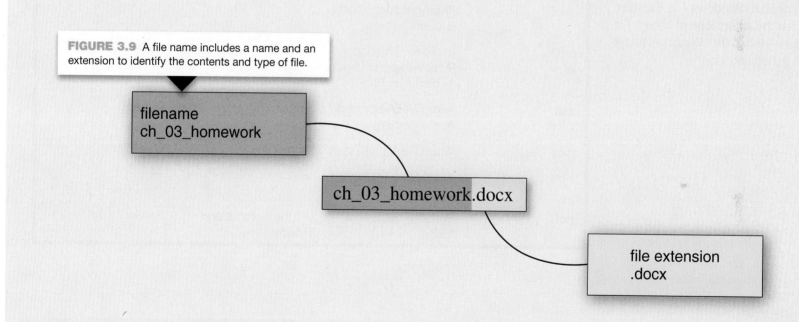

FIGURE 3.9 A file name includes a name and an extension to identify the contents and type of file.

filename
ch_03_homework

ch_03_homework.docx

file extension
.docx

The second part of the file name is the **file extension**. In this example, *.docx* is the extension. The extension is assigned by the program that's used to create the file. Microsoft Word files have the extension .docx. Windows maintains an association between a file extension and a program, so double-clicking a .docx file opens Microsoft Word. The extension helps the operating system determine the type of file. If you change the file extension of a file, you may no longer be able to open it. Table 3.4 lists some common file types and the programs associated with them. By default, Windows File Explorer hides the extensions of known file types—those that Windows has a file association for.

TABLE 3.4 Common File Extensions and Default Program Associations

Extension	Type of File	Default Program Association (Windows)	Default Program Association (macOS)
.docx	Word document	Microsoft Word	Microsoft Word
.rtf	Rich text format document	WordPad or Word	TextEdit
.pages	Pages document	—	Pages
.xlsx	Excel workbook	Excel	Excel
.pptx	PowerPoint presentation	PowerPoint	PowerPoint
.bmp	Bitmap image	Paint	Preview
.jpeg/.jpg	Image file (Joint Photographic Experts Group)	Photos	Preview
.mp3	Audio file (Moving Picture Experts Group Audio Layer III)	Windows Media Player	iTunes
.aac	Audio file (Advanced Audio Coding)	iTunes	iTunes
.mov	Video file (QuickTime)	QuickTime	QuickTime
.wmv	Video file (Windows Media Video)	Windows Media Player	—
.pdf	Portable document format	Adobe Acrobat and Reader	Preview

FIND OUT MORE

The characters \ / ? : * " > < | can't be used in a file name because they each have a special meaning in Windows. For example, the colon (:) is used to indicate the letter of a drive (such as C: for your hard drive). Use the Internet to research the remaining illegal characters. What does each symbol represent?

File Properties

Each file includes **file properties**, which provide information about the file. You can use these properties to organize, sort, and find files more easily. Some file properties, such as type, size, and date, are automatically created along with the file. Others, such as title, tags, and authors, can be added or edited by the user.

Figure 3.10 shows the properties of a file in the Details pane of File Explorer. The Details pane of the File Explorer window displays more information about a file. You can modify some of these properties, such as Title and Authors, directly in the Details pane.

When the files are displayed in the Details view, as they are in this figure, you can use the column headings to sort files by their properties. For example, clicking on the *Name* column heading lists the files in alphabetical order. The properties that display in this view depend on the type of files in the folder.

Details pane displayed

Content displayed in Details view

Details pane: document properties

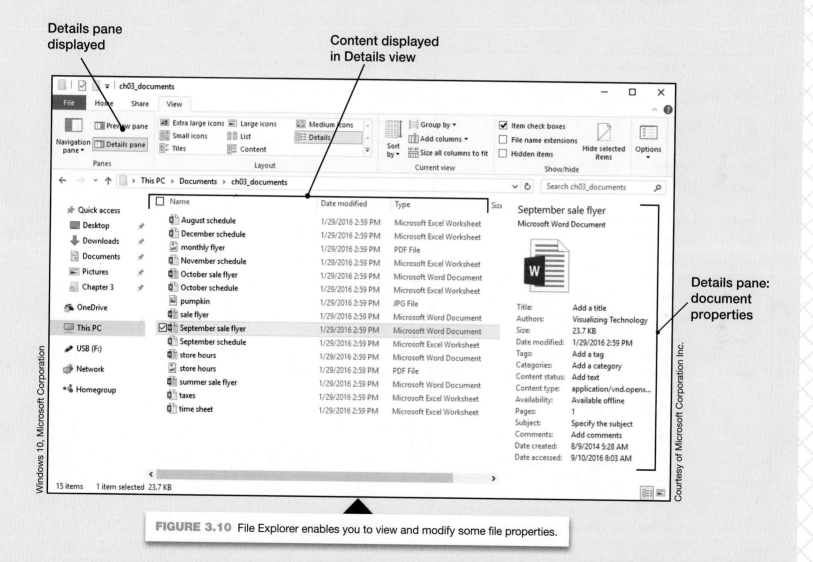

FIGURE 3.10 File Explorer enables you to view and modify some file properties.

You can view more information about a file by selecting the file in File Explorer and clicking *Properties* on the ribbon. This opens the Properties dialog box for the file. The tabs of the Properties dialog box contain a lot of information, and the tabs you see will depend on the configuration of your system and the type and location of the file or folder you are viewing. The General tab makes it easy to change the name of a file and the program that opens it. The Details tab lists information about the file, such as title, version, and author. You can change some of these properties from within this dialog box. Figure 3.11 shows these two tabs for the same file. Notice that the Details tab contains too much information to display on the page, so you need to scroll down to see the rest of it. The type of information that's displayed depends on the type of file you're viewing.

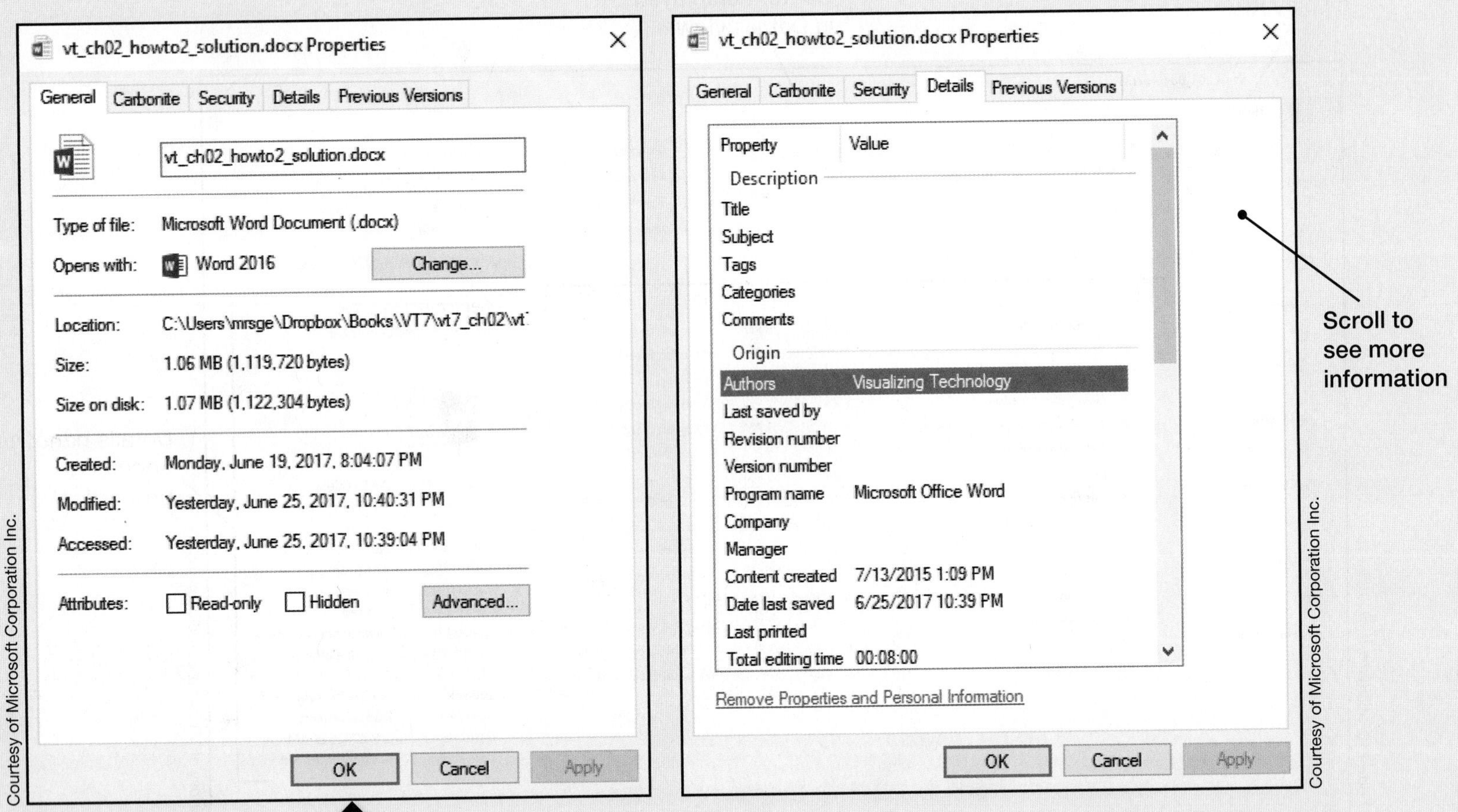

FIGURE 3.11 The Properties dialog box for a file has several tabs.

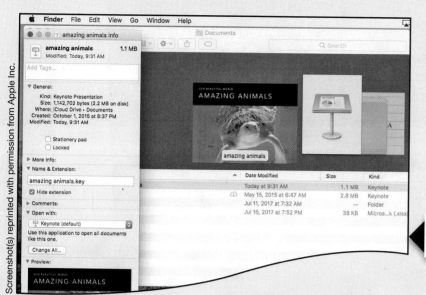

To view and modify file properties in macOS, in Finder, select the file, click *File*, and then click *Get Info*. This will open the Info pane for the file, where you can view and change some of the file properties such as the file name, sharing permissions, Spotlight comments, and the program that opens it (Figure 3.12).

File names and other properties provide you with more information about files, making them more useful and easier to manage and locate. They also save you time and give you more control over your computer systems.

FIGURE 3.12 The Info box displays file properties.

Running Project

This article discussed how to add properties to a file, but how would you remove them? Which properties can you remove? Use Windows Help and Support, macOS Spotlight, or the Internet to find the answers.

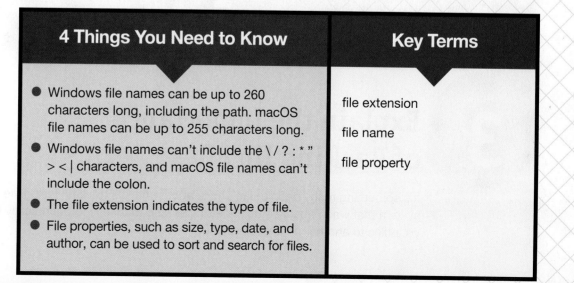

4 Things You Need to Know

- Windows file names can be up to 260 characters long, including the path. macOS file names can be up to 255 characters long.
- Windows file names can't include the \ / ? : * " > < | characters, and macOS file names can't include the colon.
- The file extension indicates the type of file.
- File properties, such as size, type, date, and author, can be used to sort and search for files.

Key Terms

file extension

file name

file property

Back It Up

3

Explain the Importance of Backing Up Files

Online Sto

It's something many people don't think about until it's too late: losing files on a computer system that wasn't backed up. One simple step to take is to periodically **back up** or copy your files to another drive or the cloud.

Windows File History

Windows includes a backup utility called File History, which is not turned on by default. You can access File History from the System and Security control panel (Figure 3.13). To use File History, you must have an external drive or network location accessible for the copies to be stored. To reduce the size of the File History saved, you can exclude specific folders or libraries.

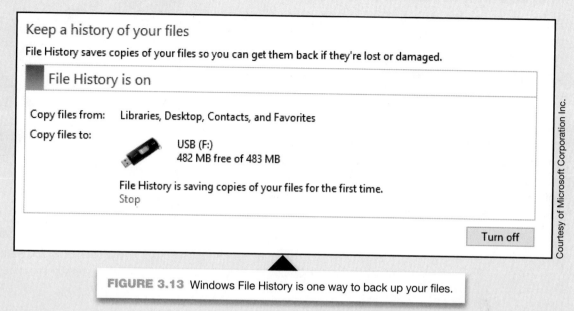

Keep a history of your files

File History saves copies of your files so you can get them back if they're lost or damaged.

File History is on

Copy files from:	Libraries, Desktop, Contacts, and Favorites
Copy files to:	USB (F:) 482 MB free of 483 MB

File History is saving copies of your files for the first time.
Stop

Turn off

Courtesy of Microsoft Corporation Inc.

FIGURE 3.13 Windows File History is one way to back up your files.

macOS Time Machine

Macs include a backup utility called Time Machine. You can open Time Machine from the Launchpad to configure it (Figure 3.14). Alternatively, you can connect a new disk, such as an external hard drive, to your Mac, and Time Machine will ask if you want to use the disk to back up your files. Time Machine keeps three types of backups: hourly backups for the previous 24 hours, daily backups for the past month, and weekly backups for all previous months. The oldest backups are deleted as the disk fills up. Time Machine backs up everything on your computer: your personal files, as well as system files, applications, and settings.

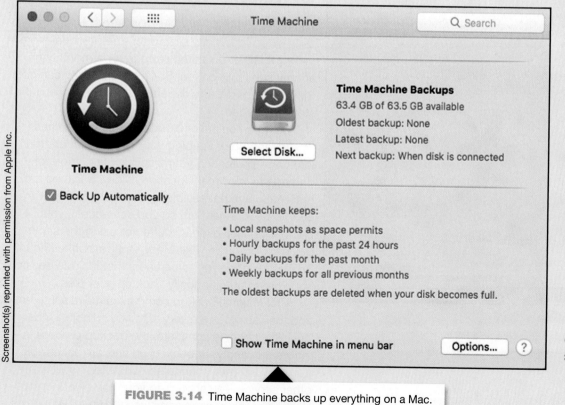

Time Machine

Time Machine

☑ Back Up Automatically

Time Machine Backups
63.4 GB of 63.5 GB available
Oldest backup: None
Latest backup: None
Next backup: When disk is connected

Select Disk...

Time Machine keeps:

• Local snapshots as space permits
• Hourly backups for the past 24 hours
• Daily backups for the past month
• Weekly backups for all previous months

The oldest backups are deleted when your disk becomes full.

☐ Show Time Machine in menu bar   Options...   ?

Screenshot(s) reprinted with permission from Apple Inc.

FIGURE 3.14 Time Machine backs up everything on a Mac.

Other Backup Software

External hard drives are an inexpensive place to back up your files (Figure 3.15). These drives often include a backup program that you can use for automatic or one-touch back-ups of your system. For example, Seagate FreeAgent external drives include Seagate Manager, and Western Digital's Passport drives include WD SmartWare. You can purchase a large-capacity external hard drive for less than $100.

Another alternative is commercial backup software. There are numerous programs on the market, including many that are free or cost less than $50. DVD-burning software, such as Roxio Creator NXT and Nero BackItUp, also includes backup features.

FIGURE 3.15 Back up to an external drive.

FIGURE 3.16 Mozy backs up files on a PC.

BACKUP to the Cloud

The use of Internet, or cloud, backup services is another option. Many sites offer free personal storage of 1 or 2 GB or unlimited storage for a monthly or annual subscription fee. Business solutions can cost thousands of dollars, depending upon the amount of storage needed.

Using an online or cloud backup service has the advantage of keeping your backups at another location—protecting your files from fire, flood, or damage to your main location. Cloud backups are automatic and accessible from any computer with an Internet connection, so you can access your backed-up files even if you're not using the same device. Companies like Mozy and Carbonite (Figure 3.16) offer plans for home users that include desktop software to automatically back up your files.

Professional backup companies make setup easy, and their services are very safe and reliable. Once the initial setup is complete, the backup process is automatic, and your backed-up files are accessible from any Internet-connected computer. As with any other service, you should do your homework before trusting online backup services with your files.

Cloud Storage

What is the difference between cloud backups and cloud storage? Cloud storage allows you to store working files in a convenient place. Although this also serves to back them up, cloud storage is generally more limited than a backup in what and how much you can store. Some popular cloud storage services include Dropbox, Google Drive, ADrive, Box, MediaFire, Amazon Drive, OneDrive, and iCloud.

When you sign up for a free Microsoft account, it includes free online storage, called **OneDrive** (Figure 3.17). If you are logged in to your Windows computer using a Microsoft account, the default save location for Microsoft Office applications is your OneDrive, and you can save to your OneDrive from other programs using the Save As dialog box. Older Windows computers, Macs, Windows Phone, iOS, and Android devices can connect to OneDrive by using a OneDrive app or the OneDrive website, so you can store files, photos, and favorites in the cloud and access and share them from any Internet-connected device. OneDrive also has the advantage of being integrated with Office Online web apps, which enable you to create and edit Microsoft Office documents in your browser.

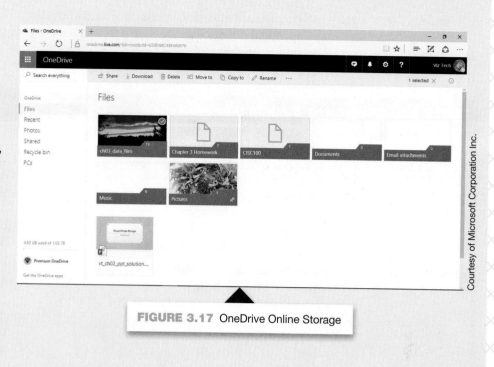

FIGURE 3.17 OneDrive Online Storage

Courtesy of Microsoft Corporation Inc.

FIGURE 3.18 iCloud can automatically back up your files and sync them with other devices.

Screenshot(s) reprinted with permission from Apple Inc.

Macs and iOS devices—iPhones and iPads—include a free online storage and sync service known as **iCloud**, and there is a version that you can download and install on your Windows computers, so you can share your files between all your devices. Your Desktop and Documents folders can be automatically synced using your iCloud drive, making the files accessible on any of your Apple devices and iCloud.com (Figure 3.18). A feature called Optimized Storage allows macOS to make more room on your computer by automatically moving infrequently used files from your computer to the cloud. iCloud uploads and stores your photos and pushes them to your Photo Stream. iCloud also includes free web versions of Pages, Numbers, and Keynote that you can use to create and edit documents.

Some mobile apps automatically upload photos to websites such as OneDrive, Dropbox, Flickr, Instagram, or Facebook. Because many people rely on the camera in their mobile devices for capturing life's important (and not-so-important) moments, as well as storing all their contacts and calendars, it is wise to regularly back up these devices.

Table 3.5 compares various types of backup solutions. No matter how you choose to back up your files, you can rest easy knowing that your files are safe and that if the inevitable hard drive failure strikes, you won't lose your important work and precious photos.

TABLE 3.5 Comparing Backup Storage Types

Storage Type	Pros	Cons
Internal hard drive	• The price per gigabyte is relatively low. • The speed of transfer is fastest. • The drive is secure inside the system unit.	• You need to open the system unit to install an internal drive. • Because it's in the same physical location as the original files, backing up to the internal hard drive doesn't keep files safe from fire, flood, or other damage.
External hard drive	• The price per gigabyte is relatively low. • The speed of transfer is fast. • The drive is easy to move and secure in another location.	• If the external hard drive is stored in another location, it must be transported back to the system location to perform a backup. • If the backup storage device is left in the same physical location as the original files, the files aren't safe from fire, flood, or other damage.
Optical drive (CD/DVD/Blu-ray)	• Media (discs) are inexpensive and easy to purchase. • Media is easy to move to store in another location. • Using new discs for each backup means the discs don't have to be returned to the system to complete future backups.	• Disc capacity is small compared to hard drives and may require several (or many) discs to complete a backup.
Network	• A shared folder or drive on another computer can be used for backup. • Placing the files on another system protects them.	• Using a network as a backup location requires some advanced setup of the network. • The network location must be available when the backup runs.
Cloud backup	• Files are stored off-site, so they're protected from fire, flood, or other damage. • Files are accessible from other devices and locations.	• Subscriptions can be expensive. • Cloud backup requires an active Internet connection. • Restoring files can be time-consuming.
Cloud storage	• Files are stored off-site, so they're protected from fire, flood, or other damage. • Files are accessible from other devices and locations.	• Storage capacity and types of files allowed may be limited.

GREEN COMPUTING
The Paperless Office

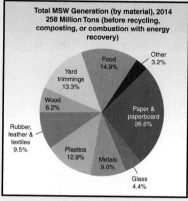

Total MSW Generation (by material), 2014
258 Million Tons (before recycling, composting, or combustion with energy recovery)

- Food 14.9%
- Other 3.2%
- Yard trimmings 13.3%
- Wood 6.2%
- Paper & paperboard 26.6%
- Rubber, leather & textiles 9.5%
- Plastics 12.9%
- Metals 9.0%
- Glass 4.4%

Source: **Courtesy of U.S. Environmental Protection Agency**

The promise of the paperless office hasn't quite become a reality. In fact, we're buried under more paper today than ever before. According to the U.S. Environmental Protection Agency (EPA), in 2014 (the most recent figures available), paper made up about 27 percent of our municipal solid waste.

The process of making paper uses water and energy in addition to trees, and it results in greenhouse gas emissions and air and water pollution. Reduce your paper usage to help the environment.

The prospect of going paperless has advantages for the environment and for your bottom line. So, how do you achieve it? The reality is that you probably can't go totally paperless, but here are a few ways to reduce your paper usage:

- Send email and make phone calls instead of sending greeting cards and letters.
- Pay your bills online and opt for paperless billing from your billers and banks.
- Don't print out electronic documents unless absolutely necessary.
- Read magazines and books in electronic formats.
- Opt out of receiving junk mail at the DMA website (**www.dmachoice.org**) and catalogs at Catalog Choice (**www.catalogchoice.org**).

Running Project

Research two online backup sites and investigate their cost, reliability, storage size, and features. Write a brief report to convince your boss of the importance of backing up files and how backups should be handled. Should the company use online storage? Explain your thoughts. In the report, be sure to describe the type and size of the business you're working for.

Viz Check—In MyLab IT, take a quick quiz covering Objectives 1–3.

4 Things You Need to Know

- You should regularly back up your important files.
- Keep your backup files in a different physical location than your working files.
- Back up (verb) is the process of creating a backup (noun).
- Cloud backup services store files using the Internet.

Key Terms

back up

iCloud

OneDrive

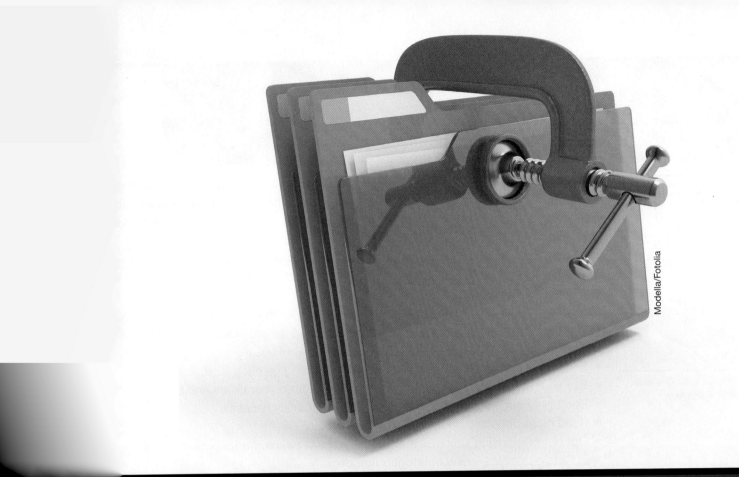

Modella/Fotolia

Shrink It

ctive

Demonstrate How to Compress Files

Some of the files used today can be rather large, especially media files such as photos, music, and videos. File **compression** is the process of making files smaller to conserve disk space and make the files easier to transfer.

Types of File Compression

An **algorithm** is a procedure for solving a problem. The compression algorithm used depends on the type of file being compressed. There are two types of file compression: lossless and lossy. **Lossless compression** takes advantage of the fact that files contain a lot of redundant information. With lossless compression, the compressed file can be decompressed with no loss of data. A lossless compression algorithm looks for the redundancy in the file and creates an encoded file using that information to remove the redundant information. When the file is decompressed, all the information from the original file is restored.

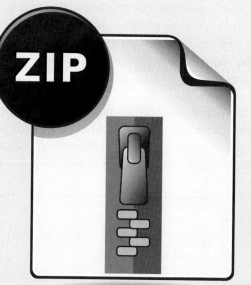

Puruan/Shutterstock

A **lossy compression** algorithm is often used on image, audio, and video files. These files contain more information than humans can detect, and that extra information can be removed from the file. An image file taken with a digital camera on its highest setting may yield a file of 5 MB to more than 50 MB in size, but the normal quality setting yields a file of 1 to 2 MB. If the file is used to create a large, high-quality print or for medical images where every detail is critical, then the high-quality information is important. Most people, however, can't tell the difference between the two when viewing them on a computer screen or printing snapshots. The highest-quality settings result in an uncompressed or minimally compressed file. BMP and TIFF images are uncompressed image file types. An image taken at a lower quality setting results in a smaller compressed file. A JPG/JPEG image is a BMP image that has been compressed using lossy compression. It's possible to compress the file after it's been taken, but once the file is compressed using lossy compression, it can't be fully restored to the uncompressed format.

Another type of file that is commonly compressed is video. Video files can be very large, making them difficult to transfer or upload or download to and from a website. YouTube accepts many video formats for upload, such as MPEG4, 3GPP, MOV, AVI, and WMV, but these files are then processed and converted to compressed formats such as Flash or HTML5 for viewing.

Working with File Compression

Windows includes the ability to compress and decompress files using the ZIP format. This is a common format that's used to send files by email or download them from the Internet. A ZIP file, known as an archive, can contain multiple files zipped together. This makes transferring multiple files easier.

To zip a file or folder using File Explorer, with the file or folder selected, click the *Share* tab and then click *Zip*. Or you can right-click on the file or folder that you want to zip, point to *Send to*, and click *Compressed (zipped) folder*. In the example shown in Figure 3.19, the *ch03_zoe_cupcakes* folder was originally 880 KB,

or 0.880 MB, and was compressed down to 731 KB, or 0.731 MB. This ZIP file can more easily be sent as an email attachment or uploaded to the web, and it takes up less space on a disk. To compress a file or folder using a Mac, in Finder, from the File menu, click *Compress*.

Windows can open and browse the files in a ZIP archive. Figure 3.20 shows the *ch03_zoe_cupcakes.zip* file and the compression ratio for each file inside it. Because each file contains different types and amounts of information, the compression ratios vary.

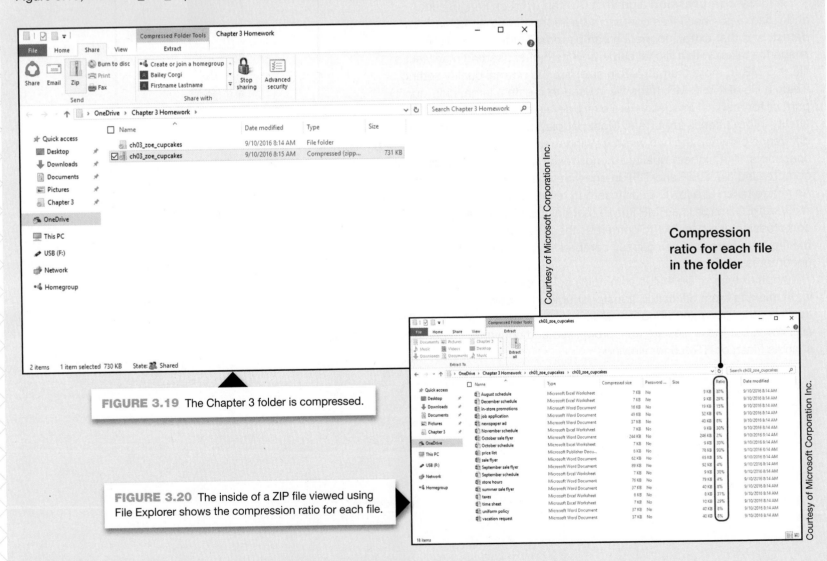

Compression ratio for each file in the folder

Courtesy of Microsoft Corporation Inc.

FIGURE 3.19 The Chapter 3 folder is compressed.

FIGURE 3.20 The inside of a ZIP file viewed using File Explorer shows the compression ratio for each file.

Windows can browse and use files inside a zipped folder, but sometimes you need to decompress, or extract, the files to work with them. In File Explorer, on the Compressed Folder Tools Extract tab, click the *Extract all* button or right-click the ZIP file and click *Extract All* (Figure 3.21). If you are using a Mac, just double-click the ZIP file to unzip it.

There are other programs that you can use to compress and decompress ZIP files, and there are other compressed formats, such as TAR and RAR, that Windows can't create or open. Some of the more popular programs available are 7-Zip, WinRAR, WinZip, and StuffIt.

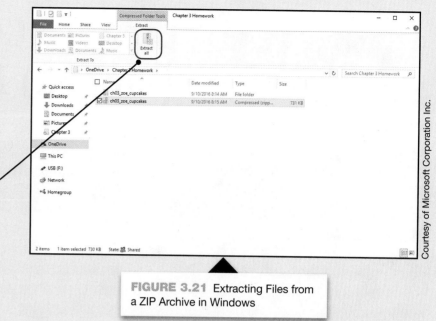

Click Extract all or right-click the zipped folder and choose Extract All

FIGURE 3.21 Extracting Files from a ZIP Archive in Windows

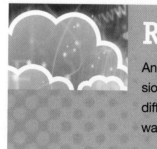

Running Project

An MP3 file is a compressed audio file that uses a lossy compression algorithm. Many audiophiles say that they can hear a noticeable difference in the quality of the sound. Use the Internet to research ways to improve the quality of MP3 files.

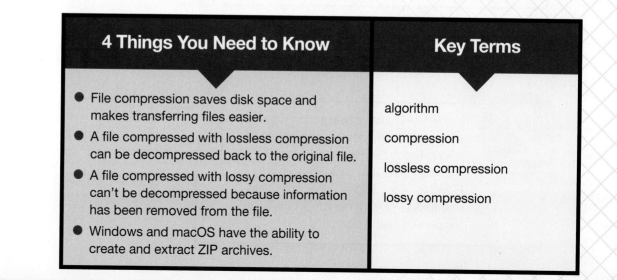

4 Things You Need to Know

- File compression saves disk space and makes transferring files easier.
- A file compressed with lossless compression can be decompressed back to the original file.
- A file compressed with lossy compression can't be decompressed because information has been removed from the file.
- Windows and macOS have the ability to create and extract ZIP archives.

Key Terms

algorithm

compression

lossless compression

lossy compression

Create a Compressed (Zipped) Folder

Essential Job Skill

HOW TO VIDEO

Have you ever tried to email a bunch of photos to a friend? If you want to send more than a couple images, you usually wind up sending multiple messages. But you can compress the files into a single zipped folder and send them all at once. In this activity, you'll compress a folder that contains several files to make it easier to email them or to submit them electronically to your teacher.

If necessary, download the student data files from **pearsonhighered .com/viztech**. From your student data files, open *vt_ch03_howto2_ answersheet* and save it in your Chapter 3 folder as **lastname_ firstname_ch03_howto2_ answersheet**.

1 Use File Explorer to navigate to the student data files for this chapter. Locate the folder *ch03_isaac_animals*. Copy this folder to your flash drive by dragging the folder to your flash drive in the Navigation pane. If you are not using a flash drive, copy the *ch03_isaac_animals* folder to your Documents folder.

2 In the File Explorer Navigation pane, click your flash drive or Documents folder. Right-click the *ch03_isaac_ animals* folder and click *Properties*. How big is the folder? How many files and folders does it contain? Close the Properties dialog box.

Courtesy of Microsoft Corporation Inc.

3 Select *ch03_isaac_animals*, click the *Share* tab, and then click *Zip* to create a zipped archive. Press Enter to accept the default file name.

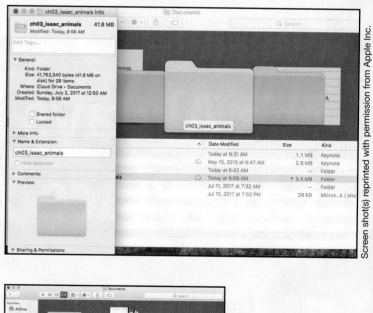

Courtesy of Microsoft Corporation Inc.

4 Right-click the compressed folder and click *Properties*. Compare the size to the original folder. Take a screenshot of the open dialog box and paste it into your answer sheet. Type up your answers, save, and submit as directed by your instructor.

If you are using a Mac: From your student data files, open *vt_ch03_howto2_answersheet_mac* and save it in your Chapter 3 folder as **lastname_firstname_ch03_howto2_ answersheet_mac**.

1. Open Finder and locate the student data files for this chapter. Copy the *ch03_isaac_animals* folder by dragging it to your flash drive. If you are not using a flash drive, copy the *ch03_isaac_animals* folder to your Documents folder.

2. Click the flash drive or Documents folder in the Sidebar and select the *ch03_isaac_animals* folder in the right pane. From the File menu, select *Get Info*. How big is the folder? How many files and folders does it contain?

3. Close the Info pane. From the File menu, select *Compress "ch03_isaac_animals"* to create a zipped archive.

4. Select the ZIP file and from the File menu, select *Get Info*. Compare the size to the original folder. Take a screenshot and paste it into your answer sheet. Type up your answers, save, and submit as directed by your instructor.

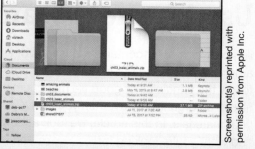

Screen shot(s) reprinted with permission from Apple Inc.

Screenshot(s) reprinted with permission from Apple Inc.

It's Always in the Last Place You Look

Use Advanced Search Options to Locate Files

A typical computer contains thousands of files, and finding what you need among them can be like looking for the proverbial needle in a haystack. If you follow the principles of good file management, create folders, and save your files in an organized way, then you'll have a much easier time keeping track of your materials. In this article, we look at how using search tools can help you find what you're looking for.

VIZ CLIP

Searching a Compute

Using Windows to Search for Files

The Windows Search feature can help you find files, settings, apps and more. There's a search box in the Settings window, every Control Panel window, and every File Explorer window. When you begin to type something in the search box, Windows immediately begins searching (Figure 3.22). Just start typing from the Start menu, or in the *Type here to search* box on the taskbar, to search apps, settings, files, and web images and video. Windows maintains an **index** that contains information about the files located on your computer. This index makes searching for files very fast. You can include unindexed locations in your search, but it causes the search to be slower. You can also ask **Cortana**—the Windows built-in personal assistant—to help you find what you are looking for.

Click *My stuff* at the bottom of the search results to launch a search of your files and apps that include that term (Figure 3.23).

In Figure 3.24, beginning a search in File Explorer with the folder for the user *Viz Tech* displayed limits the search to files and folders within that user folder. The search begins as soon as the letter *f* is typed in the Search box. The search results include files in the current location and the folders below it in the hierarchy. Search results include files with the letter *f* in file names, file properties, and file contents. You can further refine the search results by typing more letters or by adding a search filter, such as Type or Name. You can also save a search to be repeated later. If you don't find what you're looking for in your initial search, adjust your criteria.

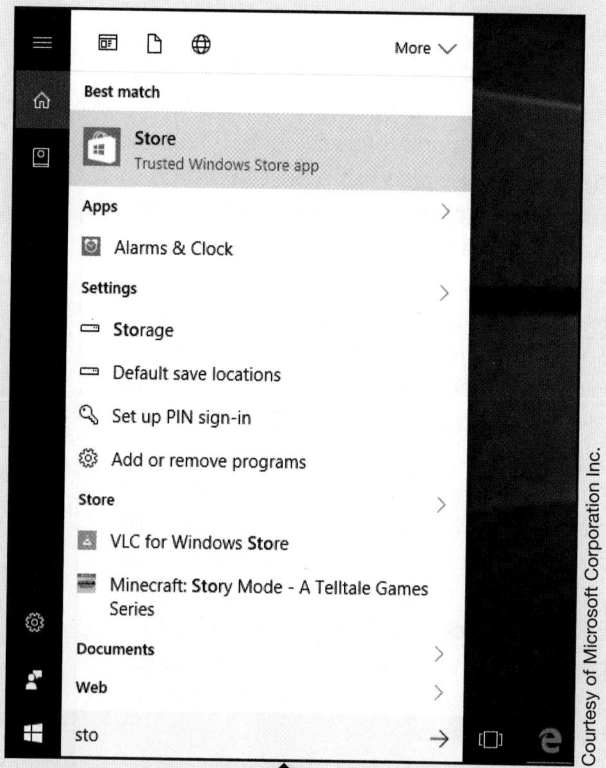

Courtesy of Microsoft Corporation Inc.

FIGURE 3.22 Windows Search locates programs and settings as well as files.

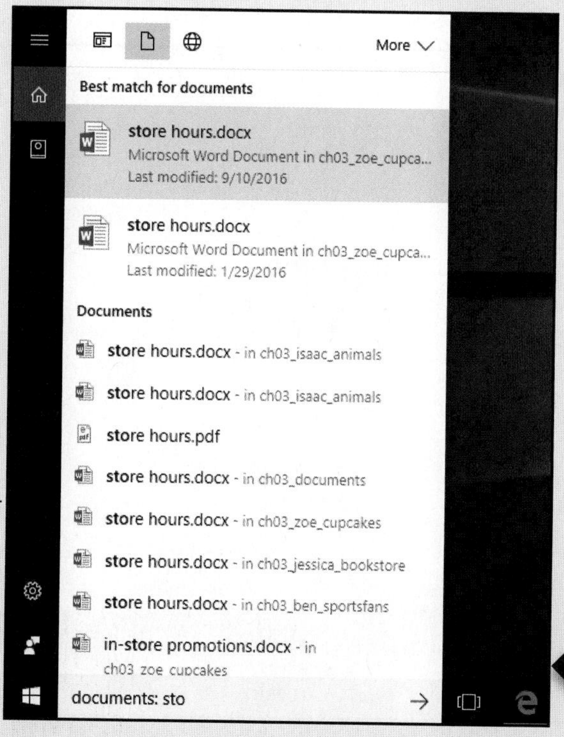

Courtesy of Microsoft Corporation Inc.

FIGURE 3.23 Click My stuff at the Bottom of the Search Results

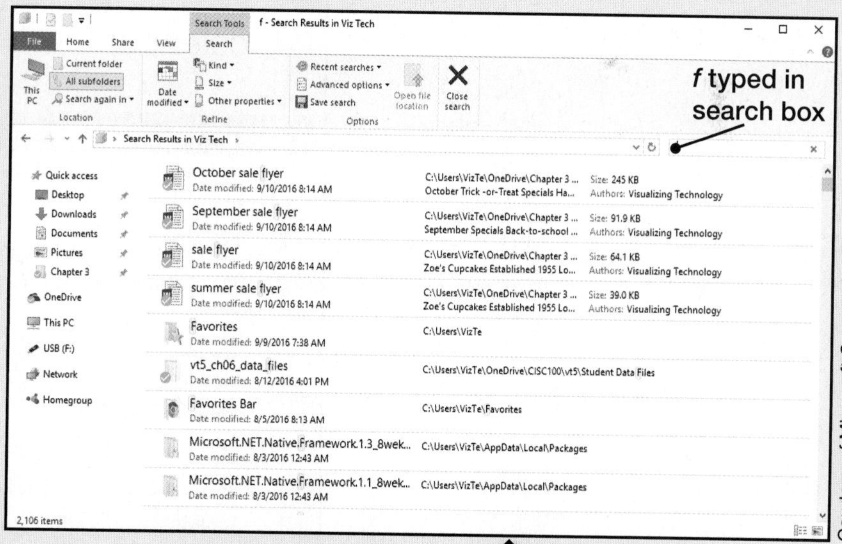

Courtesy of Microsoft Corporation Inc.

FIGURE 3.24 The search results in File Explorer show the *f* found in file names, content, and other file properties.

Searching in macOS

You can use the search field in Finder to search for files and folders (Figure 3.25), and the Help Center also has a built-in search, but the most powerful search tool in macOS is called **Spotlight**. Access Spotlight by clicking the magnifying glass on the menu bar on the upper right side of your screen. Spotlight searches applications, files and folders, contacts, and other objects on your computer (Figure 3.26), as well as displaying suggestions from the Internet, iTunes, the App Store, and locations near you. Spotlight can even provide a definition and do simple math calculations. On Macs running macOS and on iPads and iPhones running iOS you can ask Siri for help. **Siri** is an intelligent personal assistant app that enables you to speak using natural language to interact with your Apple device.

Screenshot(s) reprinted with permission from Apple Inc.

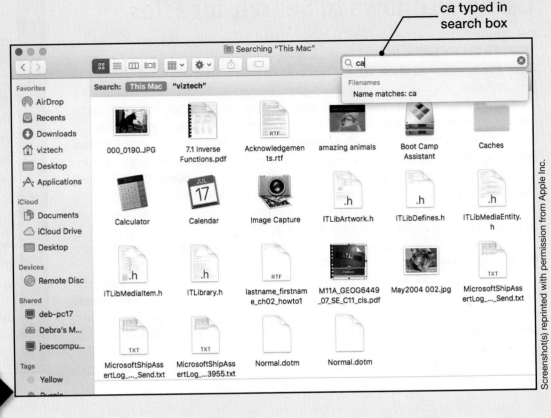

FIGURE 3.25 Search for files and folders through Finder.

Screenshot(s) reprinted with permission from Apple Inc.

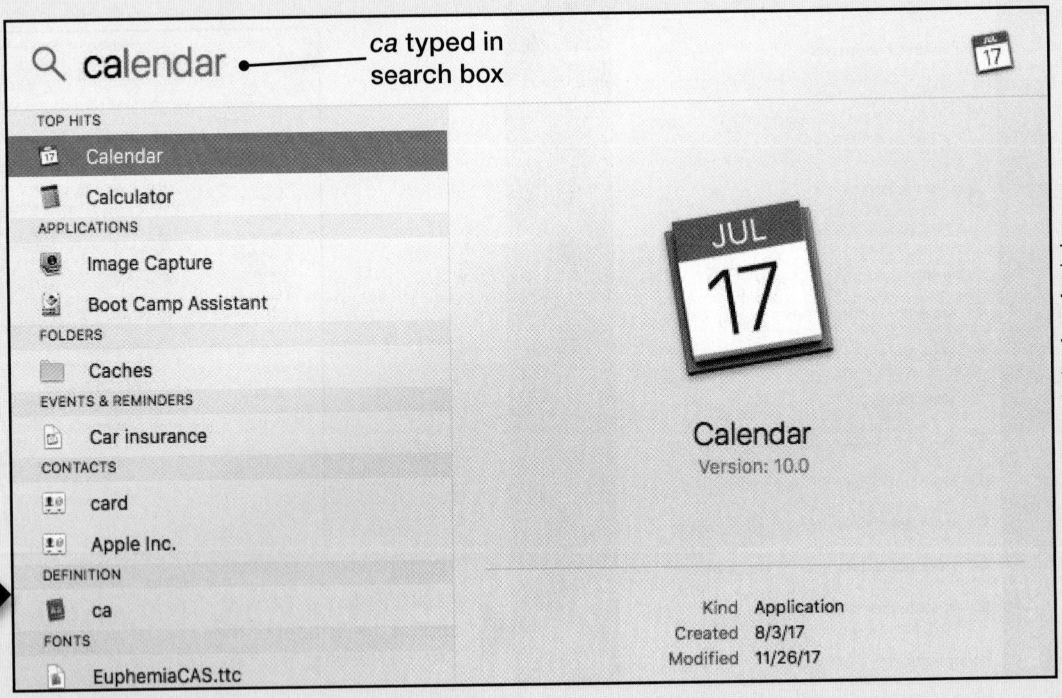

FIGURE 3.26 Spotlight searches for many types of objects on your computer.

Using Boolean Logic to Refine Searches

You can further refine your searches by using Boolean filters. George Boole was a 19th-century mathematician who created this system. There are three **Boolean operators** that define the relationships among words or groups of words: AND, OR, and NOT. Notice that they're written in all uppercase. You can use these operators to create search filters or queries in most searches, including databases and web searches. Figure 3.27 illustrates the effect of Boolean filters on the search using the terms John and Kennedy:

- **AND:** Search results must include both words: John AND Kennedy. This filter excludes files that don't include both terms.
- **OR:** Search results must include either word: John OR Kennedy. This filter includes all files that contain either or both terms.
- **NOT:** Search results must include the first term and must not include the second term: John NOT Kennedy. This filter excludes files that include the term *Kennedy*.

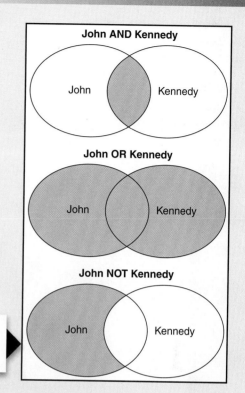

FIGURE 3.27 The shaded areas represent the search results for each Boolean filter.

Using the search feature of Windows or macOS can make locating a file or program quick and easy, saving you both time and aggravation. Good file management and searching techniques are important skills to have.

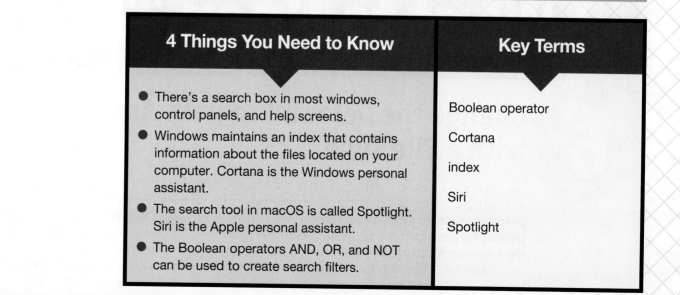

Running Project

Use the Internet to research *natural language search*. What is it, and how does it change the way you can search your computer? What are some questions you can ask Cortana or Siri?

4 Things You Need to Know

- There's a search box in most windows, control panels, and help screens.
- Windows maintains an index that contains information about the files located on your computer. Cortana is the Windows personal assistant.
- The search tool in macOS is called Spotlight. Siri is the Apple personal assistant.
- The Boolean operators AND, OR, and NOT can be used to create search filters.

Key Terms

Boolean operator

Cortana

index

Siri

Spotlight

That's Not the Program I Want to Open This File

Change the Default Program Associated with a File Type

Your operating system maintains a list of file extensions and associated **default programs** that enables it t automatically open the correct program when you click on a file. This is fine for file types that are specific to program—such as .docx for Microsoft Word and .mov for Apple QuickTime—but it can be a problem with generic file types that can be opened with several different programs. For example, the file extension .mp3 the extension for music files compressed with the MP3 lossy compression algorithm. By default, Windows associates MP3 files with the Groove Music app, but if you install another program that can play music files as iTunes or Spotify, the association may be changed.

Setting Program Defaults

In Windows you can manage default programs settings via the Default apps settings (Figure 3.28). From the Start menu, open *Settings*. In the Settings window, click *System*. Scroll down and click *Default apps*. In the right pane, scroll down and click *Set defaults by app* to open the Set Default Programs control panel window (Figure 3.29). This window enables you to view and modify the file types the program opens by default.

To restore all the program's defaults at once, click the name of the program that you want to change and then click *Set this program as default* or click *Choose defaults for this program* to modify them individually. This enables you to specify which file types should be automatically opened by this program.

If you select the *Choose defaults for this program* option, a new window opens that enables you to pick items individually. For example, Photos is the default program for displaying many types of image files, such as JPG and GIF files. If you install Adobe Photoshop Express on your computer, however, the default association for GIF files might change to the new program. You can use this dialog box to change the association back to Photos or to another program that you prefer.

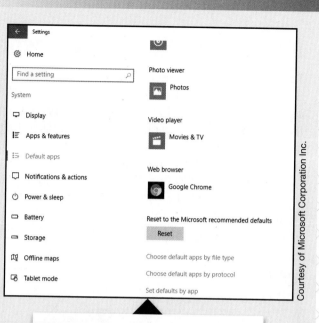

FIGURE 3.28 The Default apps settings

FIGURE 3.29 The Set Default Programs Control Panel Window for Paint

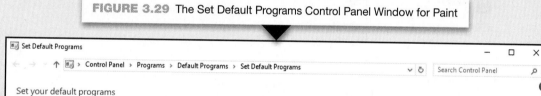

Select the program from the list to view information about the file types the program can open

Select the first option to set all the defaults, or the second option to select defaults individually

Managing File Type Associations

To manage individual file type associations, in the System Settings window, click *Default apps*, and then click *Choose default apps by file type*. Click the app or program name next to the file type you want to change and then click the new app or program (Figure 3.30). This example shows that *.bmp* files are currently associated with Photos and lists three options: Paint, Photos, and Snagit Editor. The programs you see will depend on the software installed on your system. You can also click *Look for an app in the Store* to open the Windows Store. Another way to change file type associations is to use the Default Programs

control panel window; click *Associate a file type or protocol with a program*.

Use Finder to change the program that opens a file in macOS. Open Finder and select the file. From the File menu, select *Get Info*. In the Info pane, click *Open with* and choose the proper application from the list. To make sure that every file of that type uses the new application, click the *Change All* button (Figure 3.31).

Understanding file type associations will help you avoid frustration when an association is incorrect, and it will enable you to configure your programs the way that works best for you.

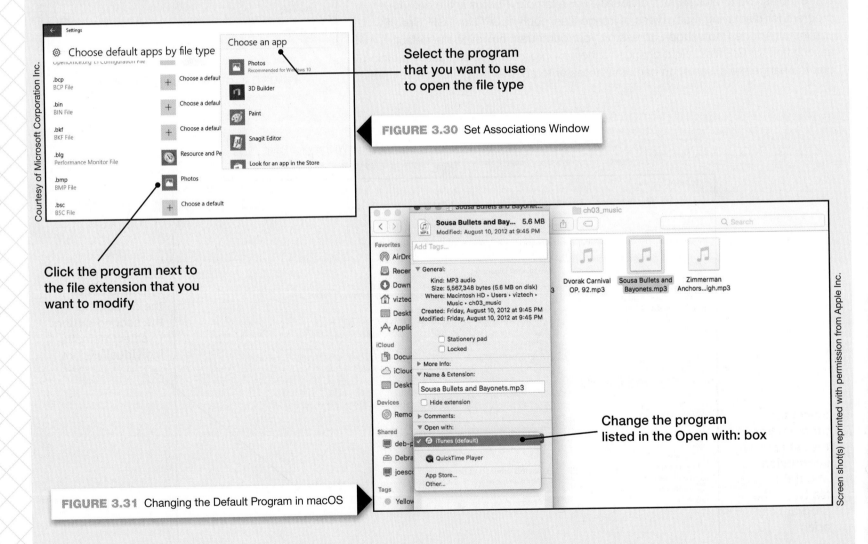

Select the program that you want to use to open the file type

FIGURE 3.30 Set Associations Window

Click the program next to the file extension that you want to modify

Courtesy of Microsoft Corporation Inc.

Change the program listed in the Open with: box

Screen shot(s) reprinted with permission from Apple Inc.

FIGURE 3.31 Changing the Default Program in macOS

CAREER SPOTLIGHT

JOBS

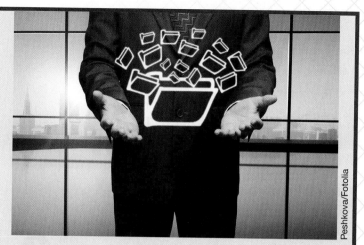

DOCUMENT CONTROL SPECIALIST A document control specialist is responsible for enterprise-wide document management systems, which enable organizations to scan, store, retrieve, share, and destroy electronic documents. The average annual income for document control specialists is between $70,000 and $100,000, depending on the industry, education, and experience. Most positions require a four-year degree and several years of experience. The largest employer of document control specialists is the U.S. government.

Peshkova/Fotolia

Running Project

Use the Set Default Programs control panel or Finder on your computer to complete this section of the project. What program is currently associated with MP3 files? What other file types can this program open by default? What other programs are installed on your computer that can open MP3 files by default? Note: If you do not have an MP3 file on your computer, use one provided with your student data files.

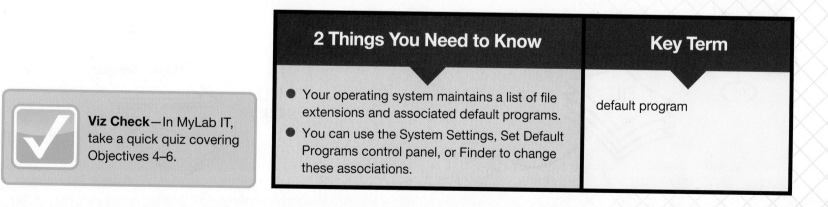

Viz Check—In MyLab IT, take a quick quiz covering Objectives 4–6.

2 Things You Need to Know

- Your operating system maintains a list of file extensions and associated default programs.
- You can use the System Settings, Set Default Programs control panel, or Finder to change these associations.

Key Term

default program

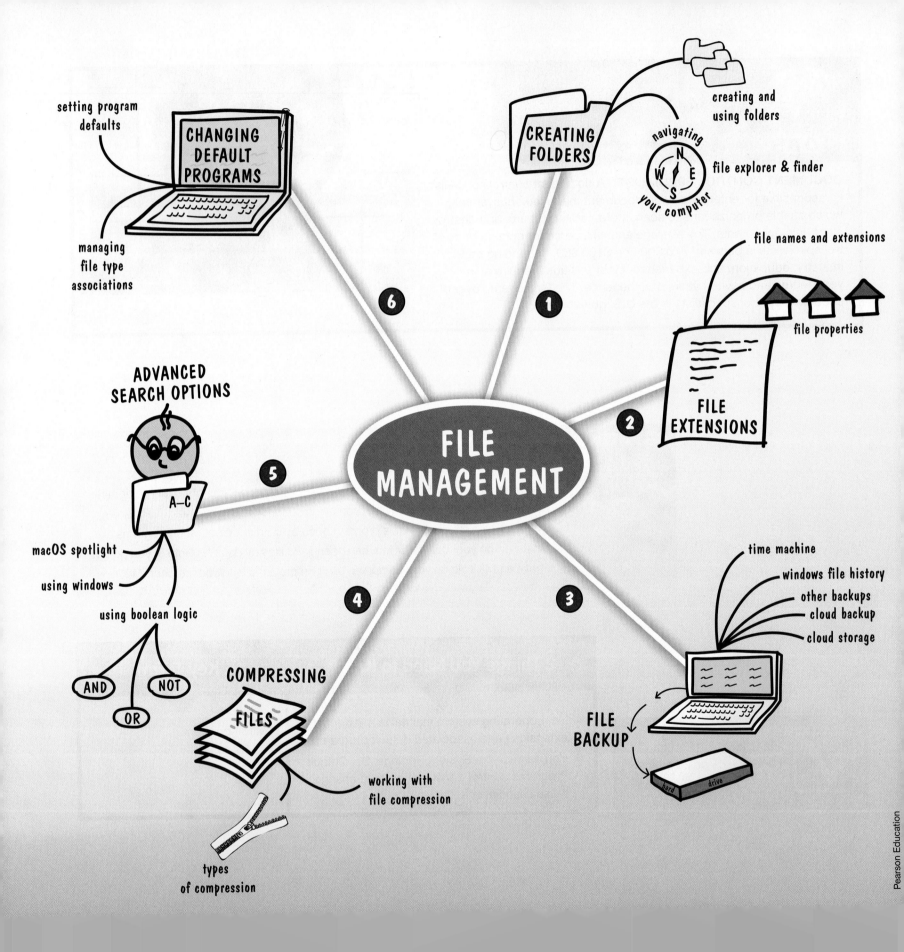

FILE MANAGEMENT

CHANGING DEFAULT PROGRAMS
setting program defaults
managing file type associations

CREATING FOLDERS
creating and using folders
navigating your computer
file explorer & finder

FILE EXTENSIONS
file names and extensions
file properties

FILE BACKUP
time machine
windows file history
other backups
cloud backup
cloud storage
hard drive

COMPRESSING FILES
working with file compression
types of compression

ADVANCED SEARCH OPTIONS
A–C
macOS spotlight
using windows
using boolean logic
AND
OR
NOT

1
2
3
4
5
6

Objectives Recap

1. Create Folders to Organize Files
2. Explain the Importance of File Extensions
3. Explain the Importance of Backing Up Files
4. Demonstrate How to Compress Files
5. Use Advanced Search Options to Locate Files
6. Change the Default Program Associated with a File Type

Key Terms

algorithm **139**	Finder **118**
back up **132**	folder **115**
Boolean operator **147**	hierarchy **115**
cloud **118**	iCloud **135**
compression **138**	index **145**
Cortana **145**	library **115**
default program **148**	lossless compression **139**
File Explorer **115**	lossy compression **139**
file extension **128**	OneDrive **135**
file management **114**	path **115**
file name **127**	Siri **146**
file property **129**	Spotlight **146**

Summary

1. Create Folders to Organize Files

Windows and macOS create a user folder hierarchy for you to use to store your files. You can create new folders in this hierarchy and in other locations, such as a flash drive or cloud storage, to organize and store your files. Windows Explorer and macOS Finder are tools you can use to work with these folders and files.

2. Explain the Importance of File Extensions

A file name consists of two parts: the name used by people to describe the contents of the file and the extension used by the operating system to identify the type of file and determine which program should be used to open it.

3. Explain the Importance of Backing Up Files

Scheduling a regular, automatic backup of important files ensures that you won't lose your files if something happens to your computer. For the greatest protection, keep the backup files in a different physical location.

4. Demonstrate How to Compress Files

Files can be compressed using several methods. An easy method on a Windows computer is to select a file or folder in File Explorer, click the *Share* tab, and then click the *Zip* button. In macOS, the *Compress* option is in the Finder File menu.

5. Use Advanced Search Options to Locate Files

Windows creates an index of files found on your computer that's used when you use search. The search tool in macOS is called Spotlight. When searching, you can add filters, such as Type and Date modified, to your search as well as use Boolean operators (AND, OR, or NOT) to further refine it. You can ask for help from Cortana in Windows or Siri on a Mac.

6. Change the Default Program Associated with a File Type

Windows provides a Default Programs control panel that can be used to modify the programs associated with specific file types. This tool allows you to control which program opens automatically when you double-click a file. The Info pane in macOS contains the *Open with* option.

Multiple Choice

Answer the multiple-choice questions below for more practice with key terms and concepts from this chapter.

1. The sequence of folders to a file or folder is known as its
   _____.
   a. Home folder
   b. library
   c. path
   d. subfolder

2. Which part of a File Explorer window contains icons for frequently used commands?
   a. Address bar
   b. File tab
   c. Quick Access Toolbar
   d. Views button

3. What tool is used to find and organize files on a Mac?
   a. File Explorer
   b. Finder
   c. Library
   d. User folder

4. Which of the following is an illegal Windows file name?
   a. hello.goodbye.hello.txt
   b. homework 11-04-17.docx
   c. homework:ch_03.xlsx
   d. make_my_day.bmp

5. Which file extension indicates an Excel workbook?
   a. .pdf
   b. .rtf
   c. .wmv
   d. .xlsx

6. The backup utility included with Windows is called_____.
   a. Carbonite
   b. File History
   c. OneDrive
   d. Time Machine

7. Which type of image uses lossy compression to reduce file size?
   a. BMP
   b. JPG
   c. MP3
   d. ZIP

8. Which search utility is included on a Mac?
   a. Explorer
   b. Cover Flow
   c. Finder
   d. Spotlight

9. Which Boolean operator excludes certain words from the search results?
   a. AND
   b. EXCLUDE
   c. OR
   d. NOT

10. What is the built-in personal assistant on a Windows computer?
   a. Explorer
   b. Cortana
   c. Siri
   d. Spotlight

True or False

Answer the following questions with *T* for true or *F* for false for more practice with key terms and concepts from this chapter.

_____ 1. Files are containers that are used to organize folders on your computer.

_____ 2. Folders within folders are also called subfolders.

_____ 3. The folder structure created by Windows is a hierarchy.

_____ 4. Windows File Explorer is a tool used to navigate the Internet.

_____ 5. You can change some of the properties of a file.

_____ 6. If you change the file extension of a file, you may be unable to open it.

_____ 7. The Finder is a tool used in macOS to work with files and folders.

_____ 8. A file compressed with a lossy compression algorithm can be decompressed to its original form.

_____ 9. The default program that opens a file can't be changed.

_____ 10. Searching using the Boolean operator OR limits the search results.

Fill in the Blank

Fill in the blanks with key terms from this chapter.

1. The processes of opening, closing, saving, naming, deleting, and organizing digital files are collectively called _____.

2. The folder structure created by Windows is a(n) _____.

3. On a Mac computer, _____ is used to find and organize files, folders, and apps.

4. The second part of the file name is the _____, which is assigned by the program that is used to create a file.

5. A(n) _____ is information about a file, such as authors, size, type, and date, which can be used to organize, sort, and find files more easily.

6. You should regularly _____ your files for ease of recovering files in case of computer damage.

7. _____ is free online storage associated with a Microsoft account.

8. Windows maintains a(n) _____ of files on your computer to speed up searching.

9. The _____ AND, OR, and NOT are used to create search filters.

10. The _____ is the program associated with a particular file type and that automatically opens when a file of that type is double-clicked.

Running Project ...

... The Finish Line

Using your answers to the previous projects' questions, write a report describing the importance of file management. Explain how to organize, protect, and manage the files you save on your computer. Save your file as **lastname_firstname_ch03_project**, and submit it to your instructor as directed.

Do It Yourself 1

In this activity you will set up folders you can use to store the work you complete in this class. This activity assumes you're using a USB flash drive to save your work for this class. If you're storing your files on your own computer, you can store them in the Documents folder. If you didn't complete the steps in the Running Project to create a class folder and a Chapter 3 folder, do so now. Open a new, blank document in your word processor.

1. In your word processor, click *File* and click *Save As*. If necessary, click *Browse*. In the Save As dialog box, in the left pane, click your flash drive. Open the class folder and the Chapter 3 folder. In the File name text field, save your work as **lastname_firstname_ch03_DIY1_answersheet**.

2. Navigate to the folder that you created for this class using File Explorer or Finder. Create new folders for each chapter in this book. Take a screenshot of the window showing these folders. Paste the screenshot into your answer sheet. Write a brief note to a friend explaining how to create a folder and why it is useful. Save your file, close your word processor, and submit the file as directed by your instructor.

Do It Yourself 2

Lossy compression is used when a BMP or TIFF file is converted into a JPG file. Most people can't tell the difference between the two when viewing them on the computer screen. From your student data files, open the file *vt_ch03_DIY2_answersheet* and save the file as **lastname_firstname_ch03_DIY2_answersheet**.

1. Open File Explorer and navigate to the data files folder for this chapter. Locate the *vt_ch03_sunset* image file. This is a photo taken with the camera's highest setting. Drag this file to your Pictures folder. Open the Pictures folder and locate the sunset file. Select the file, and if necessary, use the View tab to display the Details pane. Look at the properties in the Details pane of the window. How big is the image file? What are the dimensions of the image? What is the file type?

2. Right-click the image, point to *Open with*, and then click *Paint*. Click *File*, point to *Save As*, and then click *JPEG picture*. With the file type in the Save As dialog box as JPEG, save the file with the suggested name. In File Explorer, navigate to the location where you saved the image, and select the new .jpg version of the file. Use the Details pane to determine the new file size, dimensions, and file type. How much was the file compressed by converting it from a TIFF to a JPEG? Open the image files and look at them carefully. Compare both files. Can you tell the difference? If so, what differences do you notice? Is the JPEG file acceptable for viewing on the screen, or is the image quality too poor? Save your answers and submit the file as directed by your instructor.

If you are using a Mac:

1. Open Finder and navigate to the data files folder for this chapter. Locate the *vt_ch03_sunset* image file. This is a photo taken with the camera's highest setting. Drag this file to your Pictures folder. Open the Pictures folder and locate the sunset file. Select the file and choose *Get Info* from the File menu. How big is the image file? What are the dimensions of the image? What is the file type?

2. Double-click the file to open it in Preview or Photos. From the File menu, choose *Export*. Change the format or file type to JPEG, save the file with the suggested name. Navigate to the location where you exported the image, and select the new .jpg version of the file. In Finder, click the *File menu* and click *Get Info*. How much was the file compressed by converting it from a TIFF to a JPEG? Open the image files and look at them carefully. Compare both files. Can you tell the difference? If so, what differences do you notice? Is the JPG file acceptable for viewing on the screen, or is the image quality too poor? Save your answers and submit the file as directed by your instructor.

Critical Thinking

Your friend Zoe is starting her own cupcake business. She's overwhelmed by all the information she has to keep track of and has asked you to help her get organized. All her files are stored on one flash drive, and she needs you to sort them for her. From your student data files, open the file *vt_ch03_CT_answersheet* and save the file as **lastname_firstname_ch03_CT_answersheet**.

1. Locate the data files for this course. Copy the folder *ch03_zoe_cupcakes* to your flash drive or Documents folder. Examine the file names to determine the contents of each. Complete the table that follows. Label columns with three or four appropriate categories (such as flyers, recipes, and so on) to organize the files on the disk. In each column, list the files that belong in each category. Add columns and rows as needed to fit your organizational plan.

2. Use File Explorer or Finder to create a folder that represents each category. Move the files into the appropriate folders. Take screenshots that show the contents of each folder you create and paste these into your answer sheet. Save your file and submit it as directed by your instructor.

Flyers	Category 2	Category 3	Category 4
sale flyer			

Ethical Dilemma

Depending upon the system configuration, you may have public folders that are accessible to all users of a computer system and provide an easy way to share files among them. From your student data files, open the file *vt_ch03_ethics_answersheet* and save the file as **lastname_firstname_ch03_ethics_answersheet**.

You log into the computer in the lab at school and notice that another student has stored his or her homework assignments in the Public folder. It's the same class that you're taking, so the work could help you. What is the ethical thing to do? If the work was for a different course, what would you do? Type up your answers, save the file, and submit it as directed by your instructor.

On the Web

There are few careers today that don't require some file management skills. From your student data files, open the file *vt_ch03_web_answersheet* and save the file as **lastname_firstname_ch03_web_answersheet**.

Use the Internet to search for jobs that have file management listed as a required skill. Use at least two websites. What websites did you use? How many jobs were listed with your criteria? What were some of the industries that require this skill? Type up your answers, save the file, and submit it as directed by your instructor.

Collaboration

With your group, research the differences between two media file types and create a poster that illustrates the comparison.

Instructors: Divide the class into five groups, and assign each group one topic for this project. The topics include WMA and MP3; TIFF and JPG; MP4 and WMV; AAC and MP3; and MOV and AVI.

The Project: As a team, create a poster comparing file types. The poster should explain both the pros and cons of each file type and include examples of when it's appropriate to use them. Use at least three references. Use Google Drive or Microsoft Office to prepare your poster, and provide documentation that all team members have contributed to the project.

Outcome: Prepare a poster on your assigned topic and present it to your class. Turn in a final version of your poster named **teamname_ch03_poster** and your file showing your collaboration named **teamname_ch03_collab**. Submit your poster to your instructor as directed.

Application Project

Office 2016 Application Projects
Excel 2016: Municipal Waste

Project Description: In this Microsoft Excel project, you will format cells and a worksheet. You will create a formula and insert a header and footer. *If necessary, download the student data files from* **pearsonhighered.com/viztech**.

2014

Municipal Solid Waste Generation, Recycling, and Disposal in the United States
Facts and Figures for 2014

Material	Weight Generated	Weight Recycled	Recycling as Percent of Generation	Weight Landfilled
Paper and paperboard	68.61	44.40	64.7%	19.47
Glass	11.48	2.99	26.0%	7.04
Steel	17.69	5.84	33.0%	9.83
Aluminum	3.53	0.70	19.8%	2.36
Other nonferrous metals†	2.04	1.36	66.7%	0.63
Total metals	23.26	7.90	34.0%	12.82
Plastics	33.25	3.17	9.5%	25.1
Rubber and leather	8.21	1.44	17.5%	4.15
Textiles	16.22	2.62	16.2%	10.46
Wood	16.12	2.57	15.9%	11.01
Other materials	4.44	1.29	29.1%	2.58
Total materials in products	**181.59**	**66.38**	**36.6%**	**92.63**

Other wastes		Weight Composted	Composting as Percent of Generation	
Food, other‡	38.4	1.94	5.1%	29.31
Yard trimmings	34.5	21.08	61.1%	10.79
Miscellaneous inorganic wastes	3.97			3.19
Total other wastes	**76.87**	**23.02**	**29.9%**	**43.29**
Total municipal solid waste	258.46	89.4	34.6%	135.92

Generation, Recovery, and Discards of Materials in MSW, 2014*
(in thousands of tons and percent of generation of each material)

Source- U.S. Environmental Protection Agency (EPA)
https://www.epa.gov/sites/production/files/2016-11/documents/2014_smmfactsheet_508.pdf

lastname_firstname_ch03_excel.xlsx

Courtesy of U.S. Environmental Protection Agency

Step	Instructions
1	Start Excel. From your student data files, open the Excel file named *vt_ch03_excel.* Save the workbook as **lastname_firstname_ch03_excel**
2	Increase the width of columns B:E to 15.
3	Select the text in the range B4:E4 and set the text to wrap. Center and middle align the text in the selected range. Change the cell style to Heading 4. Copy the formatting to the range C18:D18.
4	Merge and center the text in cell A1 over columns A:E. Change the cell style to Heading 2. Merge and center the text in cell A2 over columns A:E. Change the cell style to Heading 3.
5	Change the cell style in cell A16 to Heading 4.
6	Format the range D5:D24 as percentage, 1 decimal place.
7	Delete row 7.
8	Change the cell style of the range A16:E16 to Total. Change the cell style of the range A21:E21 to Total.
9	In cell B22, create a formula to calculate the total municipal solid waste by adding the values for total materials in products and total other wastes. Copy the formula to cells C22 and E22.
10	In cell D22, create a formula to calculate the percentage of municipal waste that is recovered by dividing the weight recycled and composted by the weight generated.
11	Rename the Sheet1 tab as **2014**
12	Insert a header with the Sheet name in the center cell. Insert a footer with the file name in the left cell. Center the worksheet horizontally on the page and change the orientation to landscape. Save the workbook and close Excel. Submit the workbook as directed.

Application Project

MyLab IT
GRADER

Office 2016 Application Projects
Word 2016: Importance of File Management

Project Description: In the following Microsoft Word project, you will create a report about the importance of file management. In the project you will enter and edit text, format text, insert graphics, check spelling and grammar, and create document footers. *If necessary, download the student data files from* **pearsonhighered.com/viztech**.

File Management Primer

Have you ever saved a file on your computer and then lost it? Is your email inbox full? Is your desktop covered with icons and files? Have you downloaded a file from the Internet or email and been unable to locate it? *All of these are symptoms of poor file management.* Poor file management causes frustration, inefficiency, lost productivity, and duplication of effort. So, it is critical to practice good file management—and it's easy too.

First, get to know your folder hierarchy. Both Windows and OS X create your user folder for you—with folders for documents, pictures, music, videos, and downloads. This is a great start. It gives you logical places to put things. But if you have a lot of files or want to save them on other disks or in another structure, you'll need to do more.

Second, learn to navigate your file system. On a Windows computer, learn to use **File Explorer**. On a Mac, get friendly with **Finder**. These tools are your best friends when it comes to finding and organizing your files.

Third, organize your files into folders. Create the folders that make sense to you. Consider creating folders for each class you take, or each project you work on.

Finally, remember to use your new organization scheme. Save your files in the right place, and you will always be able to find them!

PS- I mentioned email in the first paragraph. Well guess what, same rules apply. Create folders or labels in your email program to organize your email messages—and file or delete them as soon as you have finished with them. Nothing is more satisfying at the end of the day than an empty inbox!

vt_ch03_word_solution.docx

Windows 10, Microsoft Corporation

Step	Instructions
1	Start Word. From your student data files open the file named *vt_ch03_word.* Save the document as **lastname_firstname_ch03_word**
2	Select the first line of the document and apply the Title style.
3	Format the rest of the document as Times New Roman, 12 pt.
4	In the first body paragraph, format *All of these are symptoms of poor file management.* as italic.
5	In the third body paragraph, format *File Explorer* and *Finder* as bold.
6	Place the insertion point at the end of the third body paragraph (begins with *Second*), and then press *Enter*. Insert the picture of File Explorer *vt_ch03_image1*.
7	Resize the image to a height of 2.8" and center it.
8	Use the Spelling and Grammar checker to correct the misspelling of the word *lables* to *labels* and correct the misspelling of the word *delte* to *delete*.
9	Using the Spelling and Grammar dialog box, accept the suggested correction for the grammar error *n*. Ignore all other spelling and grammar suggestions.
10	Insert the file name in the footer of the document using the File Name field. Save the document and close Word. Submit the document as directed.

CHAPTER

4

Hardware

In This Chapter

VIZ INTRO

Computers perform four tasks: input, processing, output, and storage. A computer consists of components that process data. **Hardware** refers to the physical components of a computer. After reading this chapter, you will be able to identify common input and output devices and their uses.

BrunoWeltmann/Fotolia

Objectives

1 Explain the Functions of a CPU

2 Identify the Parts of a System Unit and Motherboard

3 Compare Storage Devices

4 List and Describe Common Input Devices

5 List and Describe Essential Video and Audio Output Devices

6 Compare Various Types of Printers

7 Explain and Provide Examples of Adaptive Technology

8 Discuss Communication Devices

Running Project

In this chapter, you'll explore the key hardware components of a computer, which can be put together to create a system that fits your needs. Look for instructions as you complete each article. For most articles, there's a series of questions for you to research. At the conclusion of the chapter, submit your responses to the questions raised and present and justify your selections.

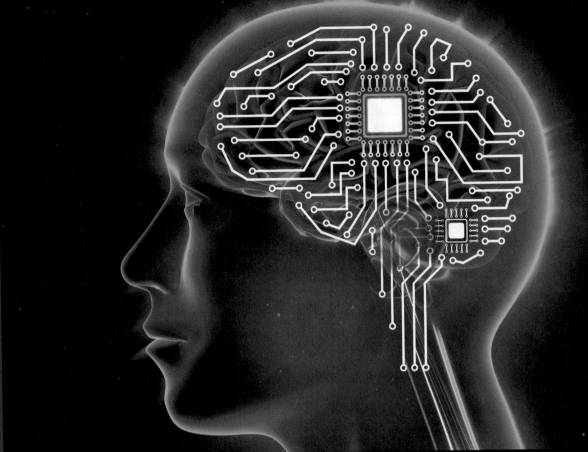

Tatiana Shepeleva/Fotolia

The CPU: The Brains of the Operation

1 Explain the Functions of a CPU

The brain of a computer is called the **central processing unit (CPU)**, or **processor**, and it is housed on the motherboard—the main circuit board of a computer (Figure 4.1). The CPU consists of two parts: the **arithmetic logic unit (ALU)** that performs arithmetic and logic (AND, OR, and NOT) calculations, and the **control unit** that manages the movement of data through the CPU. Together, these units perform three main functions: performing calculations (ALU), executing program instructions, and making decisions (control unit).

VIZ CLIP

How Processors Work

FIGURE 4.1 The central processing unit fits into the motherboard of a computer.

Instruction Cycle

The CPU utilizes the **instruction cycle**, which is also known as the fetch-and-execute cycle, or the machine cycle (Figure 4.2), to process commands. There are four steps of the instruction cycle:

- **Fetch:** An instruction is retrieved from the main memory.
- **Decode:** The control unit translates the instruction into a computer command.
- **Execute:** The ALU processes the command.
- **Store:** The results are written back to memory (stored).

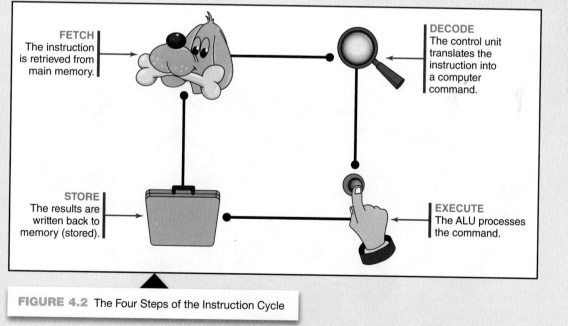

FIGURE 4.2 The Four Steps of the Instruction Cycle

CPU Performance

When you evaluate processors for performance, one of the variables to look at is **clock speed**, which is the speed at which the processor executes the cycles—today, measured in **gigahertz (GHz)**—billions of cycles per second. A 3 GHz processor performs 3 billion data cycles per second. Modern computers are capable of processing multiple instructions simultaneously rather than executing only one instruction at a time, which increases the efficiency of the processor and the performance of the computer.

MULTI-CORE AND MULTIPLE PROCESSORS

A **multi-core processor** consists of two or more processors that are integrated on a single chip. Multi-core processing increases the processing speed over single-core processors and reduces energy consumption over multiple separate processors. Dual-core and quad-core are found on most personal computers, with six- and eight-core processors on higher end machines. A video card (Figure 4.3) has its own processor called a **GPU (graphics-processing unit)**, which can contain multiple cores. The GPU reduces the processing required of the system CPU for graphics-intensive processes.

Multiple processors are found in servers, which may have anywhere from two to several hundred processors. Supercomputers are considered *massively multiprocessor* computers and may have thousands of processors, just as the massively multiplayer online game *World of Warcraft* has thousands of players.

FIGURE 4.3
This video card has a GPU hidden under the cooling fans.

Nikkytok/Shutterstock

IMPROVING PERFORMANCE: PARALLEL PROCESSING AND PIPELINING

Parallel processing distributes processing across multiple processors, or multi-core processors, (Figure 4.4), which increases computer performance when running processor-intensive programs or when running multiple programs at the same time. It is most effective when software developers write programs that can take advantage of multiple processors. Processors built by Intel implement a virtual form of parallel processing using a system called **hyper-threading**, which enables a single CPU to appear as two logical processors.

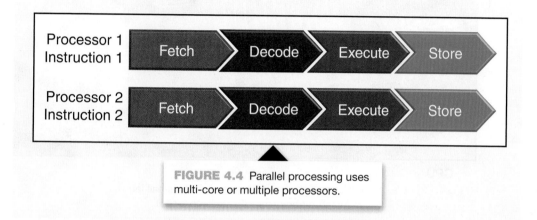

FIGURE 4.4 Parallel processing uses multi-core or multiple processors.

Pipelining is a method used by a single processor to improve performance. As soon as the first instruction has moved from the fetch stage to the decode stage, the processor fetches the next instruction (Figure 4.5). The process is like an assembly line in a factory. GPUs use a graphic pipeline to improve video performance to render 3D images.

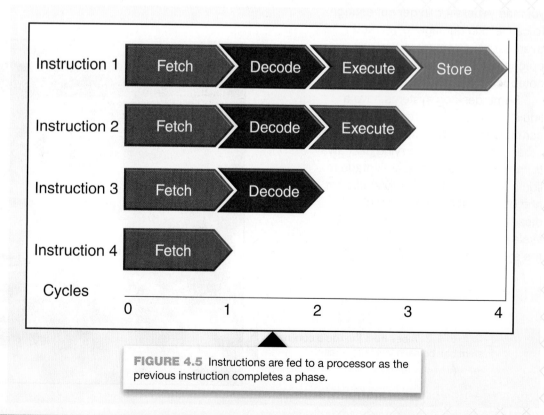

FIGURE 4.5 Instructions are fed to a processor as the previous instruction completes a phase.

COOLING SYSTEM: AIR CONDITIONING FOR THE PROCESSOR

Working quickly and using multiple processors or processing paths generates a great deal of heat. Excessive heat can damage a processor or cause it to fail, so modern computers need cooling systems for their CPUs.

To keep a processor from overheating, a cooling fan and **heat sink** are installed above the processor to dissipate the heat the processor produces (Figure 4.6). The heat sink is composed of metal or ceramic and draws heat away from the processor. In addition to the fan above the processor, most computer system units have at least one case fan to exhaust hot air and keep the entire system cool.

When using a notebook computer, you should place it on a hard surface and make sure not to block the air vents. Avoid placing a notebook on your lap, where it can get hot enough to cause skin damage to you and overheat your computer. You can purchase a USB-powered cooler for a notebook that runs hot.

Some desktop systems have a liquid cooling system that works like a car radiator by circulating liquid through tubes in the system, carrying heat away from the processor. The advantage to liquid cooling is that it's more efficient and quieter than a fan. The biggest disadvantage is that the liquid cooling system takes up much more space in the system unit (Figure 4.7).

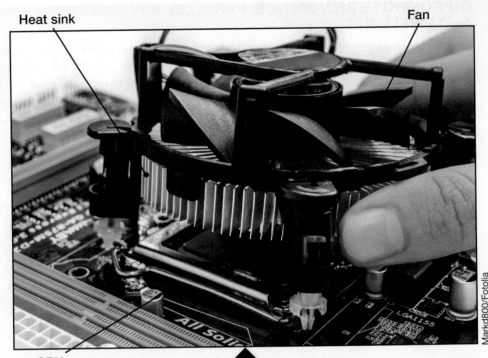

Heat sink

Fan

CPU

Markd800/Fotolia

FIGURE 4.6 A metal heat sink and a small fan are installed above the CPU to keep it cool.

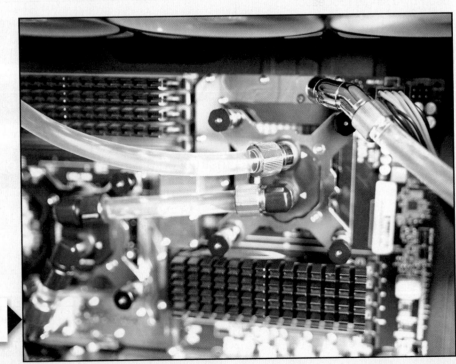

Spacedrone808/Fotolia

FIGURE 4.7 Tubes from the liquid cooling system can be seen inside this case.

FIND OUT MORE

One way to improve processor performance is to overclock the processor. This means forcing it to run at speeds higher than it was designed to perform. Use the Internet to research overclocking. How is this possible? Is it legal? Why might you consider overclocking your CPU? What are the risks? Where did you find this information?

Tehnika/Fotolia

Running Project

Use the Internet to research current processors. What companies are the two main manufacturers of processors today? What is the fastest processor available today for desktop computers? What about notebooks? Other mobile devices?

5 Things You Need to Know

- The CPU consists of the arithmetic logic unit (ALU) and the control unit.
- The four steps of the instruction cycle are fetch, decode, execute, and store.
- Modern processors use pipelining and parallel processing to improve performance.
- A multi-core processor consists of more than one processor on a single chip.
- Heat sinks, fans, and water are used to keep systems cool.

Key Terms

arithmetic logic unit (ALU)

central processing unit (CPU)

clock speed

control unit

gigahertz (GHz)

GPU (graphics-processing unit)

hardware

heat sink

hyper-threading

instruction cycle

multi-core processor

overclock

parallel processing

pipelining

processor

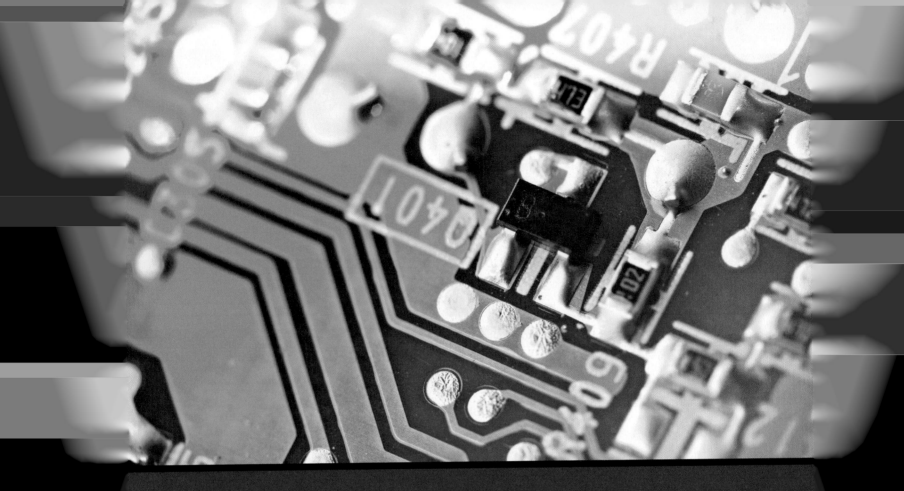

Getting to Know Your System

2 Identify the Parts of a System Unit and Motherboard

V
C

Setting Up a
Computer Sy

The **system unit** is the case that encloses and protects a computer's internal components (Figure 4.8). The components that serve the input, output, and storage functions are called **peripheral devices**. Peripherals can be external devices, or they can be integrated into the system unit.

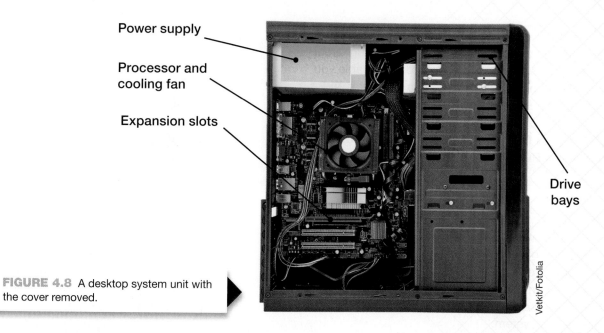

Power supply

Processor and cooling fan

Expansion slots

Drive bays

FIGURE 4.8 A desktop system unit with the cover removed.

Vetkit/Fotolia

The Motherboard

Inside the system unit is the **motherboard**—the main circuit board of a computer (Figure 4.9). In addition to housing the CPU, it contains drive controllers and interfaces, expansion slots, data buses, ports and connectors, BIOS, and memory. A motherboard may also include integrated components, such as video, sound, and network adapters. The motherboard provides a way for devices to attach to the computer.

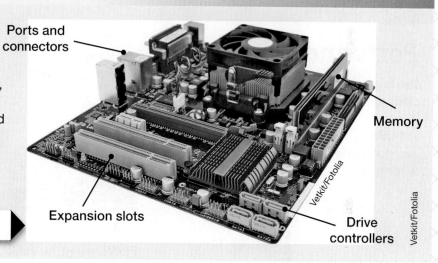

Ports and connectors

Memory

Expansion slots

Drive controllers

Vetkit/Fotolia

Vetkit/Fotolia

FIGURE 4.9 A Modern Motherboard

DRIVE CONTROLLERS AND INTERFACES

A **drive controller** on the motherboard provides a drive interface, which connects disk drives to the processor. **SATA (Serial Advanced Technology Attachment)** is the standard internal drive interface, which has replaced the legacy **EIDE (Enhanced Integrated Drive Electronics)** interface. SATA is up to three times faster than EIDE was and has smaller, thinner cables that take up less room and enable better airflow inside the system unit (Figure 4.10).

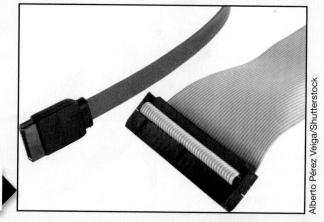

Alberto Pérez Veiga/Shutterstock

FIGURE 4.10 A SATA cable (red) takes up less room in the system unit than a legacy EIDE cable (gray).

EXPANSION CARDS

Expansion cards—also called **adapter cards**—plug directly into **expansion slots** on the motherboard and enable you to connect additional peripheral devices to a computer. Video cards, sound cards, network cards (Figure 4.11), TV tuners, and modems are common expansion cards. Most expansion cards plug into a **PCIe (PCI Express)** slot on a motherboard, replacing the older and slower **PCI (Peripheral Component Interconnect)** version.

DATA BUSES

Information flows between the components of a computer over wires on the motherboard called **data buses**. Local buses connect the internal devices on the motherboard, while external buses connect the peripheral devices to the CPU and memory of the computer. The speed of the data bus is an important factor in the performance of a system.

FIGURE 4.11 A wireless PCI adapter card can add wireless capability to a desktop computer.

Chaistock/Shutterstock

Ports and Connectors

Ports are used to connect peripheral devices to a motherboard (Figure 4.12). The most common types of general ports are USB and Thunderbolt. Bluetooth is a technology designed to connect peripherals wirelessly.

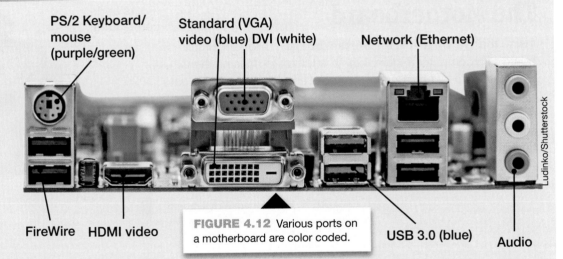

PS/2 Keyboard/ mouse (purple/green)

Standard (VGA) video (blue) DVI (white)

Network (Ethernet)

FireWire   HDMI video

FIGURE 4.12 Various ports on a motherboard are color coded.

USB 3.0 (blue)   Audio

Ludinko/Shutterstock

FIGURE 4.13 Multiple USB cables connected through a hub can share a single USB port on a computer.

Adrin Shamsudin/Fotolia

USB (Universal Serial Bus) is a standard port type that is used to connect many kinds of devices, including printers, mice, keyboards, digital cameras, mobile devices, and external drives. Most desktop computers today have six to twelve USB ports, and notebooks have two to four USB ports. Up to 127 devices can share a single USB port by using a USB hub (Figure 4.13). USB also provides power to some devices, which allows this type of connection to be used to charge a media player or smartphone and power devices such as webcams. Another advantage of USB devices is that they are **hot-swappable**, meaning they can be plugged in and unplugged without turning off the computer.

USB 1.0 was introduced in 1996 and was replaced by USB 2.0 in 2000. USB 2.0 is called Hi-Speed USB and is 40 times faster than its predecessor. The USB 3.0 SuperSpeed standard, released in 2008, is about 10 times faster than USB 2.0. This additional speed is particularly valuable for hard drives and digital video applications. The newest version, USB 3.1, released in 2013 as SuperSpeed+, is twice as fast as USB 3.0, with data transfer rates of 10 GB/s. The standard connection to the computer or hub is called USB-A. USB-B and various mini, micro, and proprietary formats are used to connect to USB devices. The USB Type-C connector, released in 2014, is a small, reversible plug that replaces both A and B type connectors (Figure 4.14).

FireWire, also known as **IEEE 1394**, was originally released by Apple in 1995. FireWire is hot-swappable and can connect up to 63 devices per port. It also allows for peer-to-peer communication between devices, without the use of a computer. The original FireWire 400 is roughly equal to USB 2.0 in speed, and FireWire 800 is twice as fast. FireWire is primarily used to connect digital video cameras, which benefit from its superior speed.

FireWire has largely been replaced by USB and the newer **Thunderbolt** technology. Thunderbolt was developed by IBM and Apple and Thunderbolt 2 is the standard on most Apple computers. It carries both PCIe and video signals on the same cable, so it can be used to connect many different types of peripherals to a computer. Thunderbolt combines two 10 Gbps channels, making it four times faster than USB 3.0 and 12 times faster than FireWire. You can connect up to six devices using one Thunderbolt connection. Figure 4.15 shows several USB and Thunderbolt ports on a computer.

Bluetooth is a short-range wireless technology that's used to connect many types of peripheral devices. It's commonly used to connect mice, keyboards, and printers to personal computers. A computer must have an adapter to communicate with Bluetooth-enabled devices. Bluetooth is also used in game consoles, such as the Nintendo Wii and Sony PlayStation 4, to connect game controllers, and in other applications, such as connecting a smartphone to a vehicle communication system.

Other ports that may be found on a computer include Ethernet ports to connect to a network, audio ports for speakers and microphones, and video ports to connect monitors and projectors. These are covered in more detail later in this chapter.

Ruslan1117/Fotolia

FIGURE 4.14 A USB-C port is ideal for thin notebook computers.

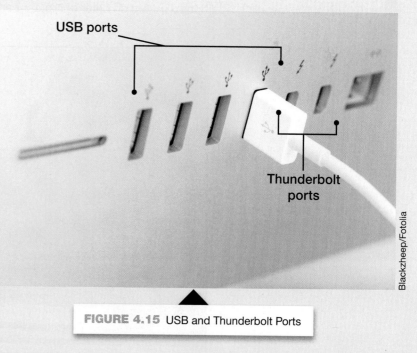

USB ports

Thunderbolt ports

Blackzheep/Fotolia

FIGURE 4.15 USB and Thunderbolt Ports

BIOS and MEMORY

Memory is temporary storage that's used by the computer to hold instructions and data. Memory is also referred to as primary storage. Memory can be volatile or nonvolatile. Volatile memory requires power—any information left in memory is lost when the power is turned off. Nonvolatile memory does not need power to keep its data.

BIOS

The **BIOS (Basic Input/Output System)** is a program stored on a chip on the motherboard that's used to start up the computer. It tests and initializes the hardware and begins to load the operating system, also known as **booting**. The BIOS chip is **ROM (read-only memory)**, a nonvolatile form of memory. On newer systems, the BIOS is stored on flash memory, which can be electrically erased and programmed. The BIOS uses settings that are stored on the **CMOS (complementary metal oxide semiconductor)** chip, which is also on the motherboard. CMOS is volatile memory and uses a small battery to provide it with power to keep the data in memory even when the computer is turned off.

RANDOM ACCESS MEMORY

The operating systems, programs, and data a computer is currently using are stored in **RAM (random access memory)**. You can think of it as your workspace. A computer that doesn't have enough RAM will be very slow and difficult to use. RAM is volatile, and any unsaved work is lost when you close a program or turn off your computer.

Memory boards are small circuit boards that contain memory chips. Most desktop memory uses a DIMM (dual in-line memory module), and notebooks use the SODIMM (small outline dual in-line memory module) configuration. There are several types of RAM available today. Older computers used SDRAM (synchronous dynamic random access memory), or DDR (double data rate) or DDR2 SDRAM. Newer computers use DDR3 or DDR4. Each type of memory is faster and more efficient than its predecessor.

RAM is fairly easy to install, and adding more memory to a computer is an inexpensive way to increase its performance (Figure 4.16). Installing additional RAM in an older computer can significantly extend its useful life.

FIGURE 4.16 Inserting RAM into a Motherboard

Noom Kittipong/Shutterstock

CACHE MEMORY

Most computers have a small amount of very fast memory that's used to store frequently accessed information close to the processor. This type of memory is called **cache memory**. Its location close to the processor greatly reduces the time it takes to access data and improves processor performance. Level 1 (L1) cache is built into the processor, and Level 2 (L2) cache is on a separate chip and takes slightly longer to access. Modern processors may have L2 cache built in and a Level 3 (L3) cache on the motherboard. Each progressive level of cache is farther from the CPU and takes longer to access.

Stocksnapper/Fotolia

Running Project

Use the Internet to research RAM. What's the fastest RAM available today for desktop computers? What about notebooks? Look at computer ads on some current retail websites. What is the average amount of RAM in desktop computers? In notebooks? What type of RAM is found in the most expensive systems?

5 Things You Need to Know

- The motherboard is the main circuit board in a computer. It provides a way for devices to attach to the computer.
- Ports and connectors attach peripheral devices to a motherboard.
- Information flows between the components of a computer over data buses.
- The BIOS is a program stored on a chip on the motherboard that's used to start up a computer.
- RAM is volatile memory that holds the operating systems, programs, and data the computer is currently using.

Key Terms

adapter card	IEEE 1394
BIOS (Basic Input/Output System)	memory
Bluetooth	motherboard
booting	PCI (Peripheral Component Interconnect)
cache memory	PCIe (PCI Express)
CMOS (complementary metal oxide semiconductor)	peripheral device
	port
data bus	RAM (random access memory)
drive controller	ROM (read-only memory)
EIDE (Enhanced Integrated Drive Electronics)	SATA (Serial Advanced Technology Attachment)
expansion card	system unit
expansion slot	Thunderbolt
FireWire	USB (Universal Serial Bus)
hot-swappable	

276

A Place for Everything

Compare Storage Devices

There are two ways to think about the storage of data: how it's physically stored on disks and how you organize the files you store. In this article, we'll look at physical storage devices. The capacity of storage has grown significantly over the past few years, as operating systems and software have gotten more sophisticated and files saved have become larger and more numerous.

SIMULATION

Hardware

Optical Discs

Optical discs are a form of removable storage and include CDs, DVDs, and Blu-ray discs. The spelling *d-i-s-c* refers to optical discs, and *d-i-s-k* refers to magnetic disks. Data is stored on optical discs using a laser to either melt the disc material or change the color of embedded dye. A laser can read the variations as binary data (Figure 4.17).

An optical disc drive is mounted in the system unit in an external drive bay, which enables you to access the drive to insert or eject discs. Optical disc drives can also be peripheral devices connected by USB or Thunderbolt. Optical discs can take several forms: read-only (ROM), recordable (+R/-R), or rewritable (+RW/-RW). The type of disc you should purchase depends on the type of drive you have. This is usually labeled on the front of the drive.

Laser

FIGURE 4.17 The data on an optical disc is read by a laser.

Tpzijl/Fotolia

CDs

A **CD (compact disc)** is the oldest type of optical disc in use today and has a storage capacity of about 700 MB. CDs are used to distribute software and music and to store photos and data, but they have been replaced by larger-capacity DVDs to distribute movies and some software.

DVDs

A **digital video disc** or **digital versatile disc**, more commonly known as a **DVD**, has the same physical dimensions as a CD but stores more than six times as much data. Single-layer (SL) DVDs can hold about 4.7 GB of information. Double-layer (DL) DVDs have a second layer to store data and can hold about 8.5 GB. DVDs are used to distribute movies and larger software programs.

BLU-RAY

A **Blu-ray disc (BD)** is an optical disc with about five times the capacity of a DVD. Blu-ray uses a violet laser, which enables information to be stored at a greater density than the red laser used in DVDs. The single-layer disc capacity is 25 GB, the double-layer disc capacity is 50 GB, and the triple layer capacity is 100 GB. Because of this larger storage capacity, Blu-ray is used for high-definition video and data storage. Table 4.1 provides a comparison of the storage capacities of various optical media.

TABLE 4.1 Comparison of the Capacities of Optical Disc Formats

Optical Disc	Capacity	Number of 3.5 MB Photos	Video	High-Definition Video
CD-ROM	700 MB	200	35 minutes	—
DVD, single layer	4.7 GB	1,343	2 hours	—
DVD, dual layer	8.5 GB	2,429	4 hours	—
Blu-ray, single layer	25 GB	7,143	—	4.5 hours
Blu-ray, dual layer	50 GB	14,286	—	9 hours
Blu-ray, triple layer	100 GB	28,572	—	18 hours

Flash Memory

Flash memory is a nonvolatile form of memory that can be electrically erased and programmed. Unlike optical and magnetic storage, flash memory is non-mechanical. Because it has no moving parts, flash memory is resistant to shock and very durable, making it ideal in devices that are mobile. It is used in solid-state drives, flash drives, memory cards, and mobile devices.

SSD DRIVES

Because there are no moving parts, a **solid-state drive (SSD)** is fast, quiet, and sturdy (Figure 4.18). SSDs are used in small electronic devices, such as media players, as well as in notebooks and desktops. Solid-state drives can use the same controllers as hard drives and can be either internal or external. Because SSDs are more expensive than similar-capacity hard drives, they are used primarily where speed and durability are necessary. SSDs are standard in many notebook computers because they are small, fast, and light.

Scanrail/Fotolia

FIGURE 4.18 An Assortment of SSD Drives

FLASH DRIVES AND MEMORY CARDS

Sometimes called key drives, thumb drives, or jump drives, **flash drives** are small, portable, solid-state drives that can hold up to 1 TB of information, although the largest capacities are very expensive. Flash drives connect to a computer via a USB port and come in a variety of shapes and sizes (Figure 4.19). Flash drives are also used as internal storage in tablets and mobile devices.

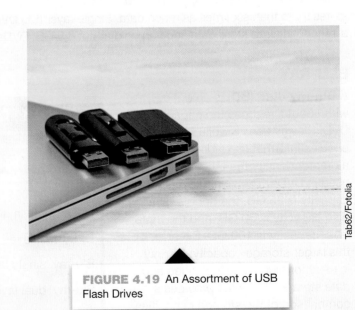
Tab62/Fotolia

FIGURE 4.19 An Assortment of USB Flash Drives

You can expand the storage of smartphones, digital cameras, and other devices with **memory cards**—a storage medium that uses flash memory to store data. The type of memory card you use is dependent upon the device (Figure 4.20). The most common formats include Secure Digital (SD), microSD and miniSD cards, CompactFlash (CF), Memory Stick (MS), and Extreme Digital xD-Picture Card (xD). Card readers are used to transfer data, such as photos and music, between a card and a computer or printer. Personal computers and photo printers may have built-in card readers, or you can use USB card readers on computers that don't have them.

FIGURE 4.20 Various Memory Cards

Sergey Ryzhov/Fotolia

Hard Drives

A **hard drive** is the primary mass-storage device in most computers. Hard drives are a form of nonvolatile storage; when the computer is powered off, the data isn't lost. The primary hard drive holds the operating system, programs, and data files. Hard drives are measured in hundreds of gigabytes or terabytes and can hold hundreds of thousands of files. They are sometimes called hard disks or hard disk drives.

Hard drives store data magnetically on metal platters. The platters are stacked, and read/write heads move across the surface of the platters, reading data and writing it to memory (Figure 4.21). The drives spin at up to 15,000 revolutions per minute, allowing for very fast data transfer.

Hard drives can be either internal or external. Internal drives are located inside the system unit in an internal drive bay and are not accessible from the outside. An external drive may be attached as a peripheral device using a USB, Thunderbolt, or FireWire connection. The advantages of external drives are that they can be installed without opening the system unit and can be easily moved to another computer.

A common desktop configuration includes both an SSD drive and a hard drive installed—the faster SSD drive is used to boot the system, while the larger but less expensive hard drive is used for storage of data.

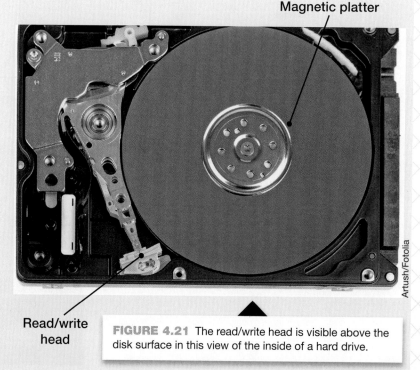

Magnetic platter

Read/write head

Artush/Fotolia

FIGURE 4.21 The read/write head is visible above the disk surface in this view of the inside of a hard drive.

Disconnecting an External Drive

Removable drives that connect to your computer via USB, such as flash drives or external hard drives, need special steps to be disconnected from a computer. It is important to be sure that your operating system has finished writing to a drive before you remove it, to prevent data from becoming corrupted. Open File Explorer, with *This PC* selected, right-click the drive, and then click *Eject* (Figure 4.22a). Once Windows has finished with the device, you will see a message that tells you it is safe to remove the device. Alternatively, in the Notification area of the taskbar, click the icon to *Safely Remove Hardware and Eject Media*, and then click to eject the appropriate item (Figure 4.22b).

Courtesy of Microsoft Corporation Inc.

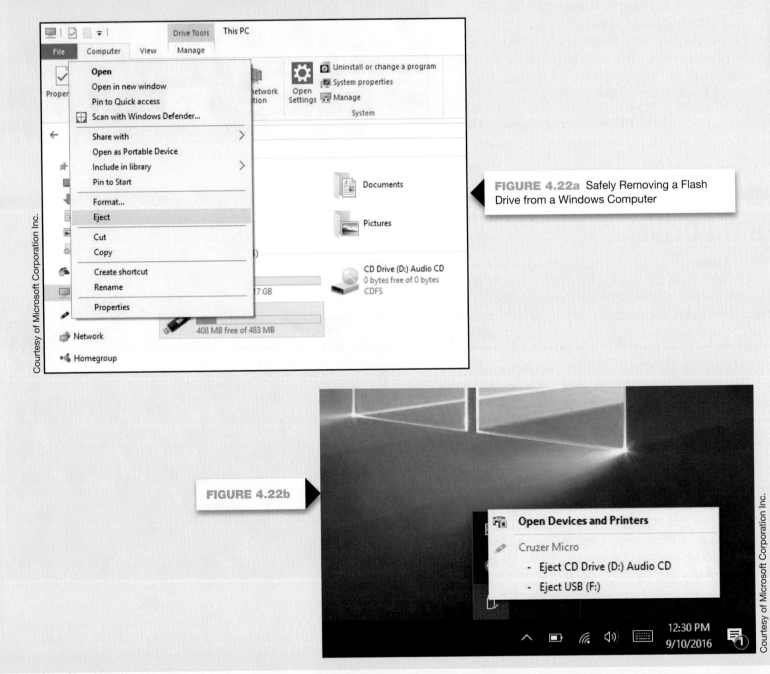

FIGURE 4.22a Safely Removing a Flash Drive from a Windows Computer

FIGURE 4.22b

Courtesy of Microsoft Corporation Inc.

Sun 10:07 AM Visualizing Technology

Open

Eject "Flash Drive"

Get Info
Rename
Duplicate
Make Alias
Quick Look "Flash Drive"

Copy "Flash Drive"

Clean Up Selection
Show View Options

Tags...

Folder Actions Setup...

Screen shot(s) reprinted with permission from Apple Inc.

FIGURE 4.22c Ejecting a Flash Drive from a Mac

If you are using a Mac, drag the drive from the desktop to the trash to eject it, or press Ctrl + click and choose *Eject* from the shortcut menu (Figure 4.22c), or click the *Eject* button next to the drive's icon in the Navigation pane of Finder.

Running Project

Look at computer ads on some current retail websites. What is the average size of a hard drive in desktop computers? In note-books? What about SSD drives? What type of optical disc drive is found in most desktops? Notebooks? What type and capacity of storage is found in most tablets? Think about your needs. What types of storage do you need and how much? Can you easily add more storage later?

4 Things You Need to Know

- Lasers read the data on optical discs (CDs, DVDs, and Blu-ray discs).
- Hard drives store data magnetically on metal platters.
- Flash memory can be electrically erased and programmed.
- It's important to properly eject a disk to prevent data corruption.

Key Terms

Blu-ray disc (BD)

CD (compact disc)

DVD (digital video disc/digital versatile disc)

flash drive

flash memory

hard drive

memory card

optical disc

solid-state drive (SSD)

Assess Your Computer Hardware

Digital Literacy Skill

HOW TO VIDEO

Computer performance is affected by many things. In this activity, you'll learn a little bit about your own computer. Your operating system can provide many details about your computer's hardware through a variety of built-in utilities. If necessary, download the student data files from **pearsonhighered.com/viztech**. From your student data files, open the *vt_ch04_howto1_answersheet* file and save the file as **lastname_firstname_ch04_howto1_answersheet**.

1 Open File Explorer. If necessary, in the Navigation pane click *This PC*, and then on the Computer tab of the ribbon, click *System properties*. **Another Way**—right-click *This PC* and then click *Properties*.

2 In the middle of the screen, under System, is the information about your processor and memory. What type of processor do you have? What is its clock speed? How much RAM do you have?

System — □ ×

← → ∨ ↑ 🖳 › Control Panel › System and Security › System   ∨ ᶜ   Search Control Panel   🔎

Control Panel Home

View basic information about your computer

Device Manager
Remote settings
System protection
Advanced system settings

Windows edition

Windows 10 Home
© 2016 Microsoft Corporation. All rights reserved.

Windows 10

System

Processor: Intel(R) Celeron(R) CPU 1007U @ 1.50GHz   1.50 GHz
Installed memory (RAM): 2.00 GB (1.89 GB usable)
System type: 64-bit Operating System, x64-based processor
Pen and Touch: Touch Support with 10 Touch Points

Computer name, domain, and workgroup settings

Computer name: Tablet   🛡Change settings
Full computer name: Tablet
Computer description:
Workgroup: WORKGROUP

Windows activation

Windows is activated   Read the Microsoft Software License Terms

Product ID: 00326-10000-00000-AA498   🛡Change product key

See also

Security and Maintenance

3 Click the back arrow and return to the File Explorer window. If necessary, click *This PC*. List all the devices and drives that are displayed in the right pane. Include any additional information, such as size and free space, for each.

Courtesy of Microsoft Corporation Inc.

4 Type your answers, save the file, and submit it as directed by your instructor.

If you are using a Mac:
From your student data files, open the *vt_ch04_howto1_answersheet_mac* file and save the file as **lastname_firstname_ch04_howto1_answersheet_mac**.

1. Click the *Apple* menu, click *About This Mac*.
2. On the Overview tab you'll find information about your processor and memory. What type of processor do you have? What is its clock speed? How much RAM do you have?
3. Click the *Storage* tab. List all disks that are displayed. Include any additional information, such as size and free space, for each.
4. Type your answers, save the file, and submit it as directed by your instructor.

Screen shot(s) reprinted with permission from Apple Inc.

Jinning Li/Shutterstock

What Goes In...

ctive

List and Describe Common Input Devices

An **input device** is a device that's used to enter data into a computer system. The type of input device you use depends on many factors, including the type of data to be input, the type of computer the input device is connected to, and the application you're using.

Keyboards

The primary input device to enter text is a **keyboard** that consists of alphabet keys, numeric keys, and other specialized keys. A keyboard translates keystrokes into a signal a computer understands. The most common type of keyboard is the standard QWERTY format, so called because *Q-W-E-R-T-Y* are the first alphabetic keys on the keyboard. The QWERTY design was originally developed by Christopher Sholes in 1873 to reduce the number of key jams on a mechanical typewriter, which can occur when adjacent keys on the keyboard are pressed quickly and interfere with each other. It's an inefficient typing layout that's not necessary on electronic keyboards. We have become so accustomed to the QWERTY layout that even virtual keyboards use it.

In addition to the alphabet and number keys, most standard keyboards have specialized keys (Figure 4.23). Some keys, such as [Esc] and the Function keys, have specific actions associated with them. Other keys, such as [Ctrl], [Alt], and [Shift], are modifiers and are pressed in conjunction with other keys. Toggle keys, such as [CapsLock] and [NumLock], turn a feature on or off when pressed. Full-sized keyboards contain 101 or 104 keys; notebook computer keyboards are smaller and may not include a separate numeric keypad.

FIND OUT MORE

Numerous standard keystroke combinations can be used to perform common tasks. For example, [Ctrl] + [X] cuts a selected item, [Ctrl] + [C] copies a selected item, and [Ctrl] + [V] pastes the copied or cut item. Research useful keystroke shortcuts that can be used with your favorite program and present them in a table. Which program did you research? Where did you find your information? Are there any keystroke shortcuts you already use? Is there a way to create your own keystroke shortcuts in this program? If so, what additional tasks would you create them for?

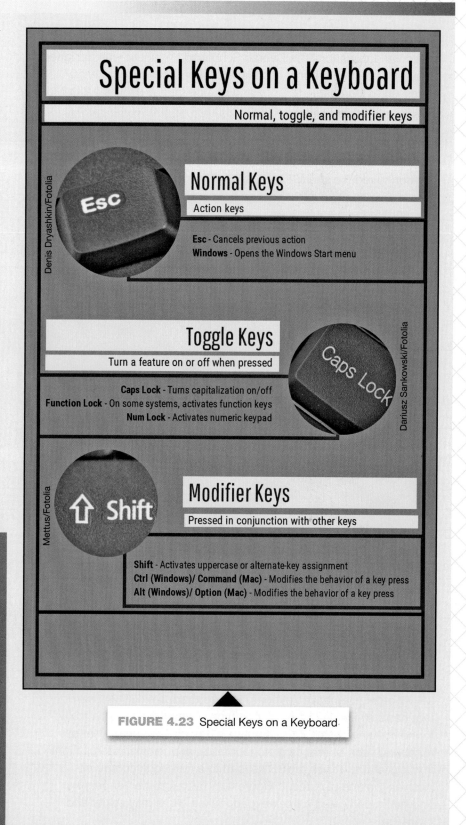

FIGURE 4.23 Special Keys on a Keyboard

Keyboards can also have alternate layouts or be customized for a particular application. The Dvorak Simplified Keyboard was designed to put the most commonly used letters where they're more easily accessed to increase efficiency and reduce fatigue (Figure 4.24). Most modern operating systems include support for the Dvorak layout, but it's not been widely adopted.

Ergonomic keyboards are full-sized keyboards that have a curved shape and are designed to position the wrists in a more natural position to reduce strain (Figure 4.25). They may look funny, but many people who spend a lot of time on the computer rely on ergonomic keyboards to prevent injuries.

QWERTY Keyboard

DVORAK Keyboard

FIGURE 4.24 The QWERTY Keyboard Layout (top) and the Dvorak Keyboard Layout (bottom)

Creativa Images/Shutterstock

FIGURE 4.25 The curved shape of an ergonomic keyboard reduces wrist strain.

FIGURE 4.26 A USB keypad can be attached to a notebook computer.

Roman A. Kozlov/Fotolia

Another alternative keyboard is a **keypad**, a small keyboard that has a limited set of keys. This type of input device is typically found in point-of-sale (POS) terminals. People who enter a lot of numbers, such as teachers, accountants, and telemarketers, might find it useful to attach a USB keypad to a notebook computer, such as the one pictured in Figure 4.26. Many computer gamers find that a dedicated game keypad makes game play easier and more fun.

The Mouse and Other Pointing Devices

Pointing devices, such as mice and touchpads, are input devices that enable a user to interact with objects by moving a pointer, also called a cursor, on the computer screen. They enable you to point and click instead of typing text commands.

Szasz-Fabian Jozsef/Fotolia

MOUSE AND TOUCHPAD

A **mouse** may include one or more buttons and a scroll wheel and works by moving across a smooth surface to signal movement of the pointer. Modern optical mice detect motion by bouncing light from a red LED (light-emitting diode) off the surface below it.

Most notebook computers include a built-in **touchpad** (also called a track pad) instead of a mouse (Figure 4.27). With this device, you move a finger across the touch-sensitive surface, and the computer detects and translates your motion. Touchpads also have buttons that function like mouse buttons and special areas that enable you to quickly scroll through documents, webpages, and images.

Aperturesound/Fotolia

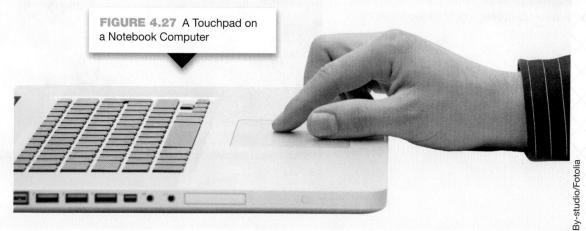

FIGURE 4.27 A Touchpad on a Notebook Computer

By-studio/Fotolia

TOUCH INPUT

Tablets, graphic design tablets (Figure 4.28), cell phones, handheld game consoles, and other devices have **touchscreens** that can accept input from a finger or a stylus. A **stylus** is a special pen-like input tool. Resistive touchscreens sense pressure and can be used with a finger or an ordinary stylus. A capacitive screen senses the conductive properties of an object such as your finger or a specially designed conductive stylus. Interactive whiteboards are large interactive displays used in classrooms and businesses. They have touch-sensitive surfaces and enable the user to control the computer from the screen as well as capture what's written on the screen with special pens.

Jacob Lund/Fotolia

FIGURE 4.28 A graphic design tablet with a stylus is a specialized input device used in graphic arts, CAD (computer-aided design), and other applications.

Digital Cameras and Webcams

Digital cameras can capture still images or video. The cameras can be built in, directly connected to a computer by USB or FireWire cable, or transfer files to the computer via a removable flash card or wireless transfer. **Webcams** are specialized video cameras that provide visual input for online communication, such as web conferencing or video chatting, as shown in Figure 4.29.

FIGURE 4.29 Video Chatting Using a Tablet Webcam

ArtFamily/Fotolia

Scanners

Scanners have many uses, from archiving old documents to organizing libraries to assisting law enforcement. The use of **scanners** increases the speed and accuracy of data entry and converts information into a digital format that can be saved, copied, and manipulated.

OPTICAL SCANNERS

You can convert a photo or document into a digital file by using an optical scanner. Flatbed scanners are the most common type of optical scanner used in homes and offices. You place the document or photo you wish to scan on a glass screen, and the scanner head moves underneath the glass to convert the image to a digital file. Business card readers and photo scanners typically have a sheet-feed format that moves the page to be scanned and keeps the scanner head stationary. Handheld scanners such as bar code readers are small and portable (Figure 4.30).

Many retail stores and magazines include **QR (Quick Response) codes**, two-dimensional bar codes, in ads and on merchandise tags that the shopper can scan to learn more about the item. Using a code scanner app on a smartphone, a shopper can scan an item to learn more about the item, including which store or website has the lowest price. Website analytics can track webpages accessed from QR codes, providing useful information to the retailer about its shoppers.

QR and bar codes are used to share information in digital business cards and to ensure packages are delivered to the correct address. A mobile boarding pass includes traveler and flight information encoded in a QR or bar code that can be scanned by an attendant at the gate (Figure 4.31).

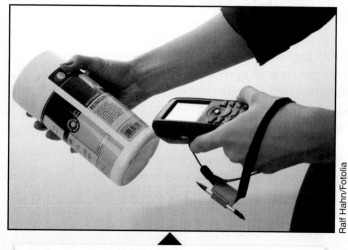

FIGURE 4.30 A bar code reader quickly scans the label, saving time and reducing data entry errors.

FIGURE 4.31 A QR code on this mobile boarding pass eliminates the need to print out the pass.

RFID SCANNERS, MAGNETIC STRIP READERS, AND NEAR FIELD COMMUNICATION

An RFID scanner can read the information in an **RFID tag**, which contains a tiny antenna for receiving and sending a radio-frequency signal. RFID (radio-frequency identification) is used in inventory tracking, electronic toll collection, and passports.

Another common scanner is a magnetic strip reader, which can read information encoded in the magnetic strip on a plastic card, such as a driver's license, gift card, library card, credit card, or hotel door key.

Near field communication (NFC) is a technology that enables devices to share data with each other by touching them together or bringing them within a few centimeters of each other. Interaction is possible between two NFC-enabled devices or between an NFC device and an NFC tag. For example, a tablet can be configured to use a wireless printer by tapping an NFC tag that has the configuration encoded in it. NFC is used in contactless card reading transactions (Figure 4.32).

FIGURE 4.32 NFC is used in a contactless card reading system.

AA+W/Fotolia

Bloomicon/Fotolia

FIGURE 4.33 A fingerprint scanner built into a smartphone can be used for added security.

BIOMETRIC SCANNERS

Used in banks to identify patrons, in theme parks to ensure that tickets aren't transferred to other guests, and in corporate security systems, **biometric scanners** measure human characteristics such as fingerprints and eye retinas. Some notebook computers and smartphones use a fingerprint scanner to authenticate a user (Figure 4.33).

Microphones and Game Controllers

Common input devices include microphones, game controllers, and joysticks. **Microphones** convert sound into digital signals and are used to chat in real time, as part of voice-recognition applications, for playing video games, and for dictating text. They are often integrated into notebook computers and headsets or can be connected via USB or to the microphone port on a sound card.

Game controllers enable you to interact with video games (Figure 4.34). Game controllers include steering wheels, tennis rackets, guns, musical instruments, and pressure-sensitive mats. A **joystick**, which is mounted on a base, consists of a stick, buttons, and sometimes a trigger. Typically used as a game controller, especially in flight-simulator games, a joystick also may be used for such tasks as controlling robotic machinery in a factory.

Production Perig/Fotolia

FIGURE 4.34 Game controllers and headsets are used to interact with video games.

Running Project

A mouse or touchpad and keyboard are standard input devices. Think about how you might use your computer in the future. What other input devices might you need? Pick at least one additional input device and research current models and costs. Which model would you choose, and why?

4 Things You Need to Know

- The mouse and keyboard are the most common input devices.
- Digital cameras and webcams input images and video.
- Scanners convert information into a digital format.
- Microphones are audio input devices.

Key Terms

biometric scanner	near field communication (NFC)
game controller	QR (Quick Response) code
input device	RFID tag
joystick	scanner
keyboard	stylus
keypad	touchpad
microphone	touchscreen
mouse	webcam

 Viz Check—In MyLab IT, take a quick quiz covering Objectives 1–4.

. . . Must Come Out

List and Describe Essential Video and Audio Output Devices

Processed information is returned to you through **output devices**. Computer output comes in two basic forms: tangible and intangible. In this article, we look at intangible outputs: video and audio. Video and audio output has changed computers from simply being calculators of data to being an integral part of education and entertainment experiences.

Video Output Devices

What you see on your computer screen is video output. There are a variety of video output devices that provide visual output to the user. The most popular types of monitors and projectors come in many different sizes, technologies, and price ranges. Modern operating systems support multiple monitor configurations, enabling you to work on two or more screens at once.

MONITORS

Similar to television screens, **monitors** work by lighting up **pixels**—short for picture elements—on the screen. Each pixel contains three colors: red, green, and blue (RGB). All colors can be created by varying the intensities of the three colors. Display **resolution** indicates the number of horizontal pixels by vertical pixels, such as 1280×1024 or 1920×1080. The higher the resolution, the sharper the image. The size of a monitor is measured diagonally across the screen.

Older **CRT monitors** and televisions use a cathode ray tube to excite phosphor particles coating the glass TV screen to light up the pixels. CRT monitors are big and use a lot of energy, and have been replaced by smaller and more energy-efficient flat-panel monitors (Figure 4.35). CRT monitors are considered **legacy technology**, which is old technology that's still used alongside its more modern replacement because it still works and is cost-effective. Modern computers have flat-panel displays, which create bright, crisp images without using traditional picture tubes.

FIGURE 4.35 An LCD monitor is much thinner than a CRT monitor of the same screen size.

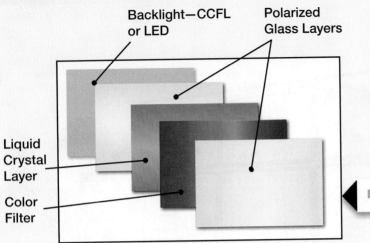

Backlight—CCFL or LED

Polarized Glass Layers

Liquid Crystal Layer

Color Filter

LCD (liquid crystal display) panels are found on most desktop and notebook computers. They consist of two layers of glass that are glued together with a layer of liquid crystals between them (Figure 4.36). When electricity is passed through the individual crystals, it causes them to pass or block light to create an image. LCDs do not give off any light, so they need to be backlit by a light source, either CCFLs (cold cathode fluorescent lamps) or LEDs. The LED versions are thinner and more energy efficient, but they're also more expensive.

FIGURE 4.36 A Simplified Diagram of an LCD Panel

The newest technology in monitors is **OLED (organic light-emitting diode)**, composed of extremely thin panels of organic molecules sandwiched between two electrodes. These monitors can be very thin and even bendable (Figure 4.37). OLEDs use very little energy and are more energy efficient than LCDs, but OLED monitors are just beginning to become available and cost significantly more than LCDs. OLED technology has a way to go before prices drop enough to make them practical for most consumers. AMOLED (active-matrix OLED) screens can be found in some mobile devices. AMOLED screens are sharper and have a wider viewing angle than LCDs, making them ideal for watching video and sports.

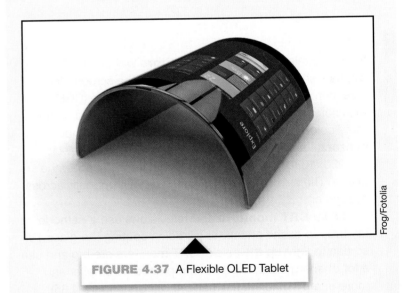

Frog/Fotolia

FIGURE 4.37 A Flexible OLED Tablet

PROJECTORS

When making a presentation or sharing media with a group in such places as classrooms, conference rooms, and home theaters, **projectors** are more practical than monitors because they produce larger output (Figure 4.38). They can be classified as video projectors, which are used in home media centers to display movies on a wall or screen, and data projectors, which are designed for presentations in a business or classroom setting. The two primary projector technologies are DLP and LCD.

DLP (digital light-processing) projectors have hundreds of thousands of tiny swiveling mirrors that are used to create an image. They produce high-contrast images with deep blacks but are limited by having weaker reds and yellows. The most portable projectors on the market today are DLP projectors, which weigh less than 3 pounds. DLPs also are very popular home theater projectors because of the higher contrast and deeper blacks that they produce.

LCD projectors pass light through a prism that divides the light into three beams—red, green, and blue—which are then passed through an LCD screen. These projectors display richer colors but produce poorer contrast and washed-out blacks. LCDs tend to have sharper images than DLPs and are better in bright rooms, making them ideal for presentations in conferences and classrooms.

FIGURE 4.38 Using a Projector to Give a Presentation

Each technology has distinct advantages and disadvantages. The choice between them depends on many factors, including the primary use, the room the projector is in, portability, and cost.

FIGURE 4.39 This video card has HDMI, VGA, and DVI ports to connect a variety of monitors.

VIDEO CARDS

The data signal and connection for a monitor or projector are provided by a **video card**, also called a graphic accelerator or display adapter. Modern video cards contain their own memory, known as VRAM (video RAM), and a graphics-processing unit (GPU) in order to produce the best and fastest images. **VGA (video graphics array)** is a legacy analog standard used by CRT monitors and projectors. The **DVI (digital visual interface)** standard was released in 1999 to replace the analog VGA standard. It has been the standard video port found on video cards; but HDMI and DisplayPort have largely replaced it on newer systems. The DVI port provides a digital connection for flat-panel displays, data projectors, TVs, and DVD players. **HDMI (High-Definition Multimedia Interface)** is a digital port that can transmit both audio and video signals. It is the standard connection for high-definition TVs, video game consoles, and other media devices. The video card in Figure 4.39 has both DVI and HDMI ports. **DisplayPort** is a digital video interface designed to replace DVI and VGA. It is sometimes implemented in the Mini DisplayPort format, which is ideal for smaller notebook bodies. A video card may also include input ports to connect a TV tuner or another video device to the system.

Westend61 Premium/Shutterstock

Audio Output Devices

Audio output can be anything from your favorite song to sound effects in a video game to an email alert chime. The sound can be heard through speakers or headphones.

SPEAKERS AND HEADPHONES

Speakers and **headphones** convert digital signals from a computer or media player into sound. Speakers may be integrated into notebook computers or monitors or connected via USB or to the speaker ports on a sound card. Typical desktop speaker systems include two or three speakers (Figure 4.40), but speaker systems designed for gaming or home theater uses include as many as eight speakers and can cost hundreds of dollars.

Headphones come in several different sizes and styles, ranging from tiny earbuds that fit inside your ear to full-size headphones that completely cover your outer ear. High-quality headphones can cost hundreds of dollars and incorporate up to eight speakers in the design. Noise-canceling headphones reduce the effect of ambient noise and are especially useful in noisy environments, such as airplanes. Headphones can plug into the headphone or speaker port of a computer or mobile device, the headphone port on a speaker, or a USB port, and they can connect wirelessly via Bluetooth. Headphones that also include a microphone are called headsets.

JackF/Fotolia

FIGURE 4.40 External Speakers

SOUND CARDS

A **sound card** provides audio connections for both input devices (microphones and musical instruments) and output devices (speakers and headphones). Sound cards can be integrated into the motherboard—onboard—or connected through expansion cards (Figure 4.41) or external USB or FireWire ports. High-end sound cards support surround sound, have connections for up to eight speakers, and include a digital optical port for connecting to a home entertainment system.

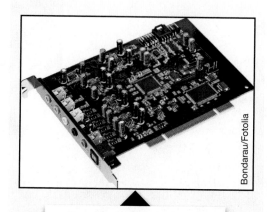

Bondarau/Fotolia

FIGURE 4.41 A Sound Card

Running Project

If you were going to purchase a new desktop computer today, one decision you would have to make is what type and size of monitor to get. Think about the room you would put the system in and what you might use it for. Would you be watching movies on the screen? Is the room really bright? Does the screen need to be large enough for several people to view at once? Do you need, or want, multiple monitors? Using the answers to these questions, determine the type and size of monitor(s) you would need. Use the Internet to compare several models and select the one that best fits your needs.

5 Things You Need to Know

- Most personal and notebook computers have LCD monitors.
- Resolution is the number of horizontal pixels by the number of vertical pixels on a screen.
- The two types of video projectors are DLP and LCD.
- Video cards connect monitors and projectors to a computer.
- Speakers and headphones are audio output devices that connect to a sound card.

Key Terms

CRT monitor	monitor
DisplayPort	OLED (organic light-emitting diode)
DLP (digital light-processing) projector	output device
DVI (digital visual interface)	pixel
HDMI (High-Definition Multimedia Interface)	projector
	resolution
headphones	sound card
LCD (liquid crystal display)	speakers
LCD projector	video card
legacy technology	VGA (video graphics array)

Pick a Printer

Compare Various Types of Printers

Tangible output—hard copies of documents and photos and 3D objects—are produced by
printers. There are printers that generate everything from photos to blueprints to ID cards.
The type of printer you choose depends on many things, including the type and size of
output you need, cost, and size.

Photo Printers, Inkjets, and Dye-Sublimation Printers

A **photo printer** is a printer designed to print high-quality photos on special photo paper. Photo printers can be inkjet printers that use special ink cartridges or dye-sublimation printers, which produce lab-quality prints. Some photo printers connect directly to a digital camera or read data from a memory card. Many newer cameras and cell phones connect to printers through Wi-Fi or Bluetooth (Figure 4.42).

The most common personal printers are **inkjet printers**, which work by spraying droplets of ink onto paper. Some printers use one ink cartridge; others may use two, three, four, or even more. The standard ink colors are cyan, magenta, yellow, and key (black), abbreviated as **CMYK**. Printers mix these colors to form every color (Figure 4.43). The black ink is usually in a separate cartridge because black is used for printing text and often runs out before the other colors. Inkjets are inexpensive to purchase, but the cost of ink can quickly add up. When purchasing a printer, you should factor in the cost of ink, which is responsible for a large portion of the cost per page.

Dye-sublimation printers, or dye-sub printers, use heat to turn solid dye into a gas that's transferred to special paper. The dye comes on a three- or four-color ribbon that prints a single color at a time. After all colors have been printed, the print is then coated with a clear protective layer to produce high-quality photos that last longer than those printed on an inkjet printer. Dye-subs aren't general-purpose printers—they're limited to printing photos and some specialty items, such as ID badges and medical scans.

FIGURE 4.42 You can print directly from a digital camera or smartphone connected by Wi-Fi or USB cable to a compatible printer.

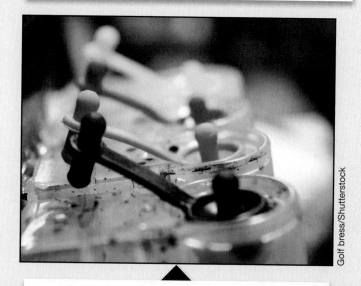

FIGURE 4.43 CMYK (cyan, magenta, yellow, black) are the colors used by inkjet and dye-sublimation printers.

Thermal and 3D Printers

The receipts you receive from gas pumps, ATMs, and many cash registers are printed by **thermal printers**. They create an image by heating specially coated heat-sensitive paper, which changes color where the heat is applied. Because a thermal printed receipt will fade over time, you should scan it if you'll need the receipt later. Thermal printers can print in one or two colors and can also be used to print bar codes, postage, and labels (Figure 4.44).

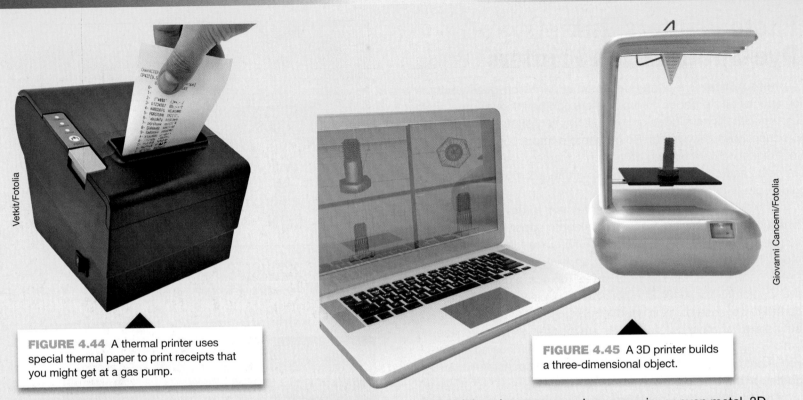

FIGURE 4.44 A thermal printer uses special thermal paper to print receipts that you might get at a gas pump.

FIGURE 4.45 A 3D printer builds a three-dimensional object.

Vetkit/Fotolia

Giovanni Cancemi/Fotolia

Three-dimensional (3D) printers can create objects such as prototypes and models (Figure 4.45). A digital image can be created by scanning an object or can be designed using computer software. The 3D printer creates the model by building layers of material such as paper, polymers, resin, or even metal. 3D printing has many interesting uses, such as dental and medical imaging and prosthetics, paleontology, architecture, and creating sculptures and jewelry.

Laser Printers, Plotters, and Multifunction Devices

The most common type of office printer is a **laser printer** (Figure 4.46). Laser printers produce the sharpest text at a lower cost per page than inkjet printers. Although they initially cost more than inkjets, the lower cost per page makes them less expensive for high-volume printing. Laser printers use a laser beam to draw an image on a drum. The image is electrostatically charged and attracts a dry ink called toner. The drum is then rolled over paper, and the toner is deposited on the paper. Finally, the paper is heated and pressure is applied, bonding the ink to it.

FIGURE 4.46 Laser printers are commonly found in offices.

Amakar/Fotolia

FIGURE 4.47 A Large Format Printer

To produce very large printouts, such as blueprints, posters, and maps, **plotters** use one or more pens to draw an image on a roll of paper. Large inkjet and laser printers have mostly replaced pen plotters (Figure 4.47).

Also known as all-in-one printers, **multifunction devices** are laser or inkjet printers that have built-in scanners and sometimes fax capabilities (Figure 4.48). They can also be used as copy machines and eliminate the need for several different devices, saving both space and money. The disadvantage to using an all-in-one device is that if it needs to be repaired, all of its functions are unavailable.

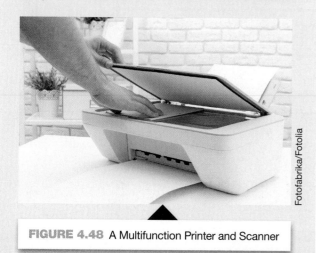

FIGURE 4.48 A Multifunction Printer and Scanner

Running Project

What type of printer will you need? Think about the types of documents you'll print. Will you need to print mostly text? Do you print a lot of photos? Do you want to be able to connect your camera or memory card directly to the printer? Do you want to be able to scan and fax? Will your printouts get wet? Do they need to last a long time? Using the answers to these questions, decide which type of printer is right for you. Use the Internet to compare several models and select the one that best fits your needs.

4 Things You Need to Know

- The most common personal printer is an inkjet printer.
- The most common office printer is a laser printer.
- Dye-subs, thermal printers, and plotters are specialized printers.
- Three-dimensional (3D) printers can create objects such as prototypes and models.

Key Terms

CMYK

dye-sublimation printer

inkjet printer

laser printer

multifunction device

photo printer

plotter

thermal printer

three-dimensional (3D) printer

How To? Reduce Energy Consumption Using Power Settings

Essential Job Skill

HOW TO VIDEO

Windows and macOS provide several ways to reduce the energy consumption of your computer. In this activity, you'll examine the power settings on your computer.

From your student data files, open the file *vt_ch04_howto2_answersheet* and save the file as **lastname_firstname_ch04_howto2_answersheet**.

1 Open File Explorer, if necessary, click *This PC*, and then, on the Computer tab, click *Open Settings*.

2 Click *System* and then click *Power & sleep*, and click *Additional power settings*. What power plans are available on your system? This may vary depending on your computer manufacturer.

Power Options

Control Panel › Hardware and Sound › Power Options

Search Control

Control Panel Home
Choose what the power buttons do
Choose what closing the lid does
Create a power plan
Choose when to turn off the display
Change when the computer sleeps

Choose or customize a power plan

A power plan is a collection of hardware and system settings (like display brightness, sleep, etc.) that manages how your computer uses power. Tell me more about power plans

Plans shown on the battery meter

◉ Balanced (recommended)   Change plan settings
Automatically balances performance with energy consumption on capable hardware.

○ Power saver   Change plan settings
Saves energy by reducing your computer's performance where possible.

Show additional plans

Courtesy of Microsoft Corporation Inc.

3 Which power plan is your computer currently using? Click *Change plan settings* for the selected plan. What are the settings to turn off the display and put the computer to sleep? If this is a notebook computer, how do the settings differ when plugged in versus on battery? Are these settings appropriate for the way you use your computer?

Change settings for the plan: Balanced
Choose the sleep and display settings that you want your computer to use.

	On battery	Plugged in
Turn off the display:	5 minutes	10 minutes
Put the computer to sleep:	15 minutes	30 minutes
Adjust plan brightness:		

Change advanced power settings

Restore default settings for this plan

Courtesy of Microsoft Corporation Inc.

4 Click *Change advanced power settings*. Scroll down to and expand *Power buttons and lid*. What happens when you close the lid of your computer (if this is a notebook)? When you press the Power button? When you press the Sleep button?

Change settings for the plan: Balanced
Choose the sleep and display settings that you want your computer to use.

	On battery	Plugged in
Turn off the display:	5 minutes	
Put the computer to sleep:	15 minutes	
Adjust plan brightness:		

Change advanced power settings

Restore default settings for this plan

Power Options ? ✕

Advanced settings

Select the power plan that you want to customize, and then choose settings that reflect how you want your computer to manage power.

Balanced [Active]

⊟ Hard disk
  ⊟ Turn off hard disk after
    On battery (Minutes): 10
    Plugged in: 20 Minutes
⊞ Internet Explorer
⊞ Desktop background settings
⊞ Wireless Adapter Settings
⊞ Sleep
⊞ USB settings
⊞ Intel(R) Graphics Settings
⊞ Power buttons and lid

Restore plan defaults

OK   Cancel   Apply

Courtesy of Microsoft Corporation Inc.

5 Use the Internet or Windows Help to learn about *sleep* and *hibernation*. What is the difference between the two, and what purpose do they serve? Type your answers in the answer sheet, save the file, and submit it as directed by your instructor.

If you are using a Mac:

1. From the Apple menu or dock, open *System Preferences*.
2. Click *Energy Saver*. What power settings are available on your system?
3. What are your settings to put the computer and display to sleep? If this is a notebook computer, how do the settings differ when plugged in (Power Adapter) versus on battery? Are these settings appropriate for the way you use your computer?

Screen shot(s) reprinted with permission from Apple Inc.

4. Click the Help button at the bottom right of the window—this opens the Help screen for Energy Saver preferences. Are there any settings in this list that are not available on your computer? What is Power Nap? Is it enabled on your system?
5. Use the Internet to learn about *Sleep*, *Safe Sleep*, and *Standby Mode*. What is the difference between them, and what purpose do they serve? Type your answers in the answer sheet, save the file, and submit it as directed by your instructor.

Energy Saver

Q Search

Battery   Power Adapter

Computer sleep:

1 min   15 min   1 hr   3 hrs Never

Display sleep:

1 min   15 min   1 hr   3 hrs Never

☑ Put hard disks to sleep when possible
☑ Wake for Wi-Fi network access
☑ Enable Power Nap while plugged into a power adapter
While sleeping, your Mac can back up using Time Machine and periodically check for new email, calendar, and other iCloud updates

Battery is charged.

Restore Defaults

☑ Show battery status in menu bar

Schedule... ?

Screen shot(s) reprinted with permission from Apple Inc.

Adaptation: Making Technology Work for You

Explain and Provide Examples of Adaptive Technology

The Americans with Disabilities Act (ADA) of 1990 requires employers with 15 or more employees "to make a reasonable accommodation to the known disability of a qualified applicant or employee if it would not impose an 'undue hardship' on the operation of the employer's business. Reasonable accommodations are adjustments or modifications provided by an employer to enable people with disabilities to enjoy equal employment opportunities."

Adaptive Technology

As a result of the ADA, many hardware and software vendors have developed new technologies. Businesses benefit by gaining the skills and talents of employees with disabilities.

Also called assistive technology, **adaptive technology** is used by individuals with disabilities to interact with technology—both hardware and software. In many cases, everyday input and output devices can be adapted to the user. For example, a computer monitor screen image can be enlarged for a visually impaired user, and a hearing-impaired user might have lights flash when an audio signal sounds. Modern operating systems include accessibility settings that can easily be changed. While adaptive technology can make technology more accessible for individuals with disabilities, it also benefits those without disabilities. Enlarging the screen, touch-sensitive surfaces, easy-to-read buttons, and other accommodations make accessing technology easier for everybody.

ADAPTIVE INPUT DEVICES

Alternate input devices include Braille-writing devices, eye-driven keyboards, and keyboards that have locator dots on commonly used keys or large-print key labels. Onscreen keyboards can be typed on using a pointing device or a touchscreen. Such devices are being used in many public locations, such as libraries, schools, and polling places (Figure 4.49). Trackballs, head wands, mouth sticks, and joysticks are all alternatives to the standard mouse.

Voice-recognition software enables you to verbally control a computer and dictate text. Dragon NaturallySpeaking and Dragon for Mac are two of the most popular voice-recognition programs, and Windows and macOS include built-in speech recognition. Software settings, such as Sticky Keys and Mouse Keys, adapt a standard keyboard for users with limited fine-motor control and enable the user to use arrow keys on the keyboard to move the pointer.

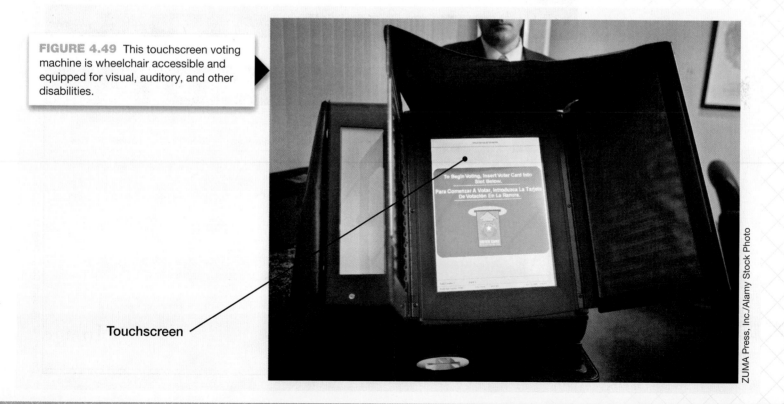

FIGURE 4.49 This touchscreen voting machine is wheelchair accessible and equipped for visual, auditory, and other disabilities.

Touchscreen

ZUMA Press, Inc./Alamy Stock Photo

ADAPTIVE OUTPUT DEVICES

Standard monitors can be adapted by magnifying the screen (Figure 4.50) and adjusting color and contrast settings. Speech synthesis screen-reader software and audio alerts aid visually and learning-disabled users, while closed captions and visual notifications, such as flashing lights, aid those with auditory disabilities.

Braille embossers are special printers that translate text to Braille. They're impact printers that create dots in special heavy paper that can be read by touch by visually impaired users. A Braille computer display (Figure 4.51) has movable pins that enable a blind person to read text output.

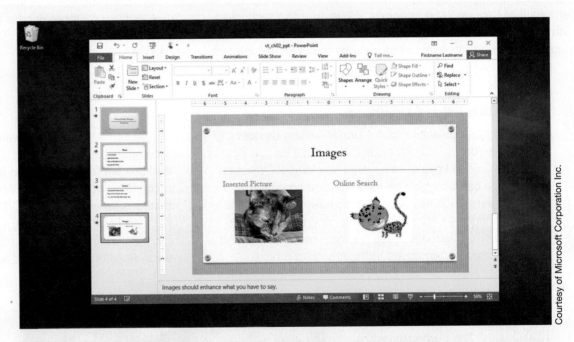

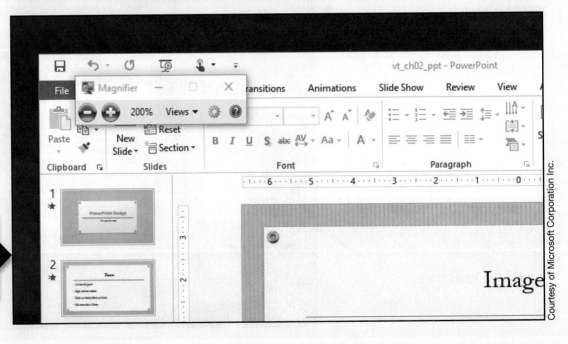

FIGURE 4.50 Windows includes Magnifier, a screen magnification program that can be used to enlarge portions of the screen, as it has in this PowerPoint presentation.

Courtesy of Microsoft Corporation Inc.

FIGURE 4.51 A blind person reads on a Braille display.

Elypse/Fotolia

Running Project

If you were going to purchase a new desktop computer today, are there any adaptive technology devices that you would include to meet the current or future needs of any of the users of this computer?

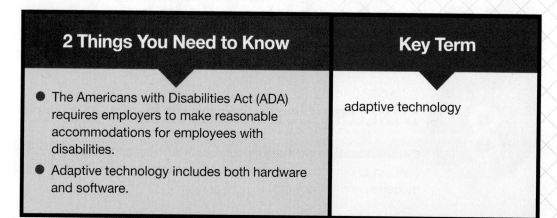

2 Things You Need to Know

- The Americans with Disabilities Act (ADA) requires employers to make reasonable accommodations for employees with disabilities.
- Adaptive technology includes both hardware and software.

Key Term

adaptive technology

Communicate, Communicate, Communicate

3 Discuss Communication Devices

Communication devices function as both input and output devices and enable you to connect to other devices on a network or to the Internet. These include network adapters, modems, and fax devices.

Network Adapters

Used to establish a connection with a network, a **network adapter**, also called a **network interface card (NIC)**, may be an onboard expansion card or USB device and may be wired or wireless. Wired cards are sometimes referred to as Ethernet cards and have a port that resembles a telephone jack as shown in Figure 4.52, while wireless cards are used to connect to Wi-Fi networks.

Gresei/Fotolia

FIGURE 4.52 An Ethernet cable can plug into the onboard network adapter on a notebook computer.

Modems and Fax Devices

An analog **modem** connects a computer to a telephone line and is most often used for dial-up Internet access. Modem is short for *mo*dulator-*dem*odulator. A modem modulates digital data into an analog signal that can be transmitted over a phone line and, on the receiving end, demodulates the analog signal back into digital data. Traditional analog modems have largely been replaced with newer, faster ways to connect to the Internet.

A cable modem is a special type of modem that connects to the cable system instead of a telephone line to provide fast Internet access. Digital subscriber line (DSL) modems, which are used to provide broadband services, aren't really modems at all because the DSL line is already digital, and there's no need to modulate the signal to analog.

A fax device can be a stand-alone fax machine (Figure 4.53), part of a multifunction device, or built into a modem. A fax (or facsimile) device works by scanning a document and converting it into a digital format that can then be transmitted over telephone lines to a receiving fax device, which then outputs the document.

Communication devices enable you to connect your computers to other devices in your own home and to the world, providing you with access to resources that just a few short years ago were unimaginable.

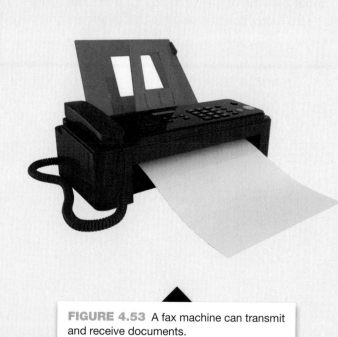

Nerthuz/Fotolia

FIGURE 4.53 A fax machine can transmit and receive documents.

CAREER SPOTLIGHT

COMPUTER SALES AND SUPPORT   Computer sales is a good career choice for a person who has excellent communication and technical skills. Salespeople must be able to help customers find the right computer based on their needs and explain the features of a system in lay terms. Many companies offer their employees on-the-job training in this field, but a background in computers, including the CompTIA A+ certification, an industry certification for computer technicians, is helpful.

If you like helping people, have strong communication skills, and are good with computers, a computer technician position might be a good career for you. Companies such as Geek Squad send technicians out to homes and businesses to troubleshoot and repair computer systems. This is hands-on work that may involve travel and working nights and weekends. A+ certification is usually the minimum requirement at the entry-level positions in this field. Much of the training in this field takes place on the job.

Even if you're not looking for a technical career, understanding how computer hardware works and being able to make decisions about the hardware purchases you might make will help you be a better consumer and enable you to succeed in many different careers. For example, an office worker might need to make decisions about the type of printer to buy, or a teacher might need help choosing the type of projector to install in a classroom. Very few careers today don't involve the use of some computer technology.

Vikulin/Shutterstock

GREEN COMPUTING
Shop Smart

The efficient and eco-friendly use of computers and other electronics is called *green computing*. Green computing is good for the environment, but it also saves money, making it a win–win proposition.

Environmental Protection Agency

Choose Energy Star–rated devices. Energy Star (**energystar.gov**) is a rating system that's awarded to devices that use an average of 25–30 percent less energy than comparable devices. Saving energy saves money and reduces greenhouse gas emissions that contribute to global warming.

Green Electronics Council EPEAT®

The Green Electronics Council has a program called the EPEAT (Electronic Product Environmental Assessment Tool; **epeat.net**) that can help you choose systems with environmentally friendly designs. The assessment is based on industry standards and ranks the devices as bronze, silver, or gold, depending on the number of environmental performance criteria they meet.

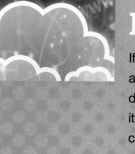

Running Project

If you were going to purchase a new desktop computer today, think about the location for this computer. What type of communication devices do you need to connect this system to the Internet? Will it connect to a network? Is it wired or wireless? Do you need fax capabilities?

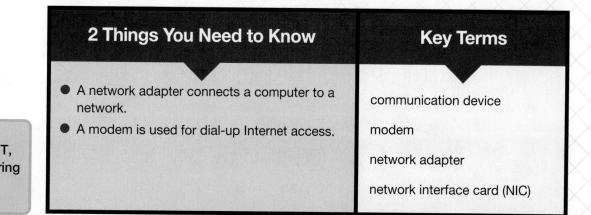

Viz Check—In MyLab IT, take a quick quiz covering Objectives 5–8.

2 Things You Need to Know

- A network adapter connects a computer to a network.
- A modem is used for dial-up Internet access.

Key Terms

communication device

modem

network adapter

network interface card (NIC)

THE CPU

instruction cycle

1 → 2 → 3 → 4

CPU performance

cooling system

network adapter

fax

modem

COMMUNICATION DEVICES

press enter

output

ADAPTIVE TECHNOLOGY

input

press enter

motherboard

DVD RW

CD Rom

SYSTEM UNIT

memory

8

1

7

2

HARDWARE

6

3

optical discs

solid state

hard drive

A·C

STORAGE

plotters

3D

inkjet

photo

multitouch

laser

dye sublimation

PRINTERS

5

4

OUTPUT

INPUT

audio

video

digital cameras and webcams

scanners

mouse

keyboard

microphone

speakers

headphones

monitor

Projector

Objectives Recap

1. Explain the Functions of a CPU
2. Identify the Parts of a System Unit and Motherboard
3. Compare Storage Devices
4. List and Describe Common Input Devices
5. List and Describe Essential Video and Audio Output Devices
6. Compare Various Types of Printers
7. Explain and Provide Examples of Adaptive Technology
8. Discuss Communication Devices

Key Terms

Summary

1. Explain the Functions of a CPU

The CPU is the brain of the computer and consists of the control unit and arithmetic logic unit. It processes data through the instruction cycle: fetch, decode, execute, and store. Features such as parallel processing, pipelining, and multi-core processing increase the CPU's ability to process multiple instructions at the same time.

2. Identify the Parts of a System Unit and Motherboard

The system unit is the case that houses the power supply, motherboard, processor (CPU), heat sink and cooling fan, and memory of a computer. It also has drive bays to hold the storage devices and openings for peripheral devices to connect to expansion cards on the motherboard. The motherboard is the main circuit board of a computer. In addition to housing the CPU, it contains drive controllers and interfaces, expansion slots, data buses, ports and connectors, BIOS, and memory. A motherboard may also include integrated peripherals, such as video, sound, and network cards.

3. Compare Storage Devices

Optical discs are removable and include CDs, DVDs, and Blu-ray discs. They range in capacity from 700 MB to 100 GB and are used to distribute music, programs, and movies as well as to archive data. Flash memory is a non-mechanical form of storage found in solid-state drives (SSDs), flash drives, memory cards, personal media players, and notebooks. Hard disks are a form of magnetic storage that can be mounted in the system unit or connected via USB, Thunderbolt, or FireWire cable. They have the largest capacities of any current storage device and hold the operating systems, programs, and data on the computer.

4. List and Describe Common Input Devices

Input devices include keyboards and keypads for entering text; pointing devices, such as the mouse, touchpad, stylus, and touch-sensitive screens that move the cursor on the screen; cameras and webcams for video input; optical scanners, RFID scanners, magnetic strip readers, and biometric scanners that read data and convert it into digital form; near field communication (NFC) devices that can share data among devices by bringing them near each other; microphones that convert sound into digital signals; and video game controllers and joysticks to interact with games and other software programs.

5. List and Describe Essential Video and Audio Output Devices

The most common output devices are monitors and projectors attached to video cards that produce video output; printers that produce hard copies; and speakers and headphones attached to sound cards that produce audio output.

6. Compare Various Types of Printers

The most common personal printer is the inkjet, which works by spraying droplets of ink onto paper. Dye-sublimation printers use heat to turn solid dye into a gas that's then transferred to special paper to primarily produce photos. Photo printers can be either inkjet or dye-sublimation printers. Thermal printers use special heat-sensitive paper to produce receipts, postage, and bar code labels. Three-dimensional (3D) printers can create objects such as prototypes and models. Plotters produce very large printouts, such as blueprints, posters, and maps. Laser printers produce the sharpest text at a much lower cost per page than inkjet printers. A multifunction device combines a printer with a scanner and sometimes a fax machine.

7. Explain and Provide Examples of Adaptive Technology

Adaptive technology enables users with a variety of disabilities to access technology through special hardware and software. Input devices include head wands, mouth sticks, voice-recognition software, and onscreen keyboards. Output devices include Braille embossers, screen readers, and enlarged screens.

8. Discuss Communication Devices

Communication devices serve as both input and output devices and include network adapters, modems, and fax devices. A network adapter connects a computer to a network. A modem connects a computer to a telephone line for dial-up Internet access. The cable and DSL modems are special modems that enable access to high-speed Internet. Fax devices, which can be stand-alone fax machines, part of a multifunction device, or built into a modem, scan and convert a document into a digital form that can be transmitted over telephone lines.

Multiple Choice

Answer the multiple-choice questions below for more practice with key terms and concepts from this chapter.

1. The _____ is part of the processor that manages the movement of data through the CPU.
   a. arithmetic logic unit
   b. control unit ← *(selected)*
   c. data bus
   d. peripheral device

2. A(n) _____ is a processor found on a video card.
   a. arithmetic logic unit (ALU)
   b. CMOS
   c. GPU (Graphics-Processing Unit) ← *(selected)*
   d. multi-core processor

3. A(n) _____ is a wire on a motherboard over which information flows.
   a. adapter card
   b. data bus ← *(selected)*
   c. expansion slot
   d. USB hub

4. Which is a volatile form of memory that holds the operating system, programs, and data the computer is currently using?
   a. Flash
   b. CMOS
   c. RAM ← *(selected)*
   d. ROM

5. Data is stored on _____ using a laser to either melt the disc material or change the color of embedded dye.
   a. flash drives
   b. hard drives
   c. optical discs ← *(selected)*
   d. SSDs

6. A(n) _____ is an input device typically found on a notebook computer instead of a mouse.
   a. joystick
   b. stylus
   c. scroll wheel
   d. touchpad ← *(selected)*

7. _____ measure human characteristics such as fingerprints and eye retinas.
   a. Biometric scanners ← *(selected)*
   b. Near field communications
   c. Optical scanners
   d. QR codes

8. Which type of monitor is composed of extremely thin panels of organic molecules sandwiched between two electrodes?
   a. CRT
   b. LCD
   c. OLED ← *(selected)*
   d. LED

9. Which type of printer produces the highest quality photos?
   a. Laser
   b. Dye-sublimation ← *(selected)*
   c. Inkjet
   d. Thermal

10. _____ are used to connect a computer to a telephone line for dial-up Internet access.
    a. Analog signals
    b. Modems ← *(selected)*
    c. Network interface cards
    d. Wi-Fi adapters

True or False

Answer the following questions with *T* for true or *F* for false for more practice with key terms and concepts from this chapter.

_____ 1. Hyper-threading requires multiple processors or cores.

_____ 2. The terms *CPU* and *system unit* mean the same thing.

_____ 3. Bluetooth is a short-range, wireless technology used to connect peripheral devices to a computer.

_____ 4. Read only memory (ROM) loses the information stored in it when power is turned off.

_____ 5. SSDs store data magnetically.

_____ 6. Hard drives store data optically on metal platters.

_____ 7. QWERTY keyboards were designed to improve ergonomics.

_____ 8. LCD monitors consist of two layers of glass that are glued together with a layer of liquid crystals between them.

_____ 9. Adaptive technology includes the hardware and software used by individuals with disabilities to interact with technology.

_____ 10. Digital signals are superior to analog signals because they don't have to be converted for use by computers and other digital devices.

Fill in the Blank

Fill in the blanks with key terms from this chapter.

1. A computer's clock speed is measured in _____.

2. The _____ performs arithmetic (addition and subtraction) and logic (AND, OR, and NOT) calculations, and the _____ manages the movement of data through the CPU.

3. To keep the processor from overheating, a(n) _____ and cooling fan are installed above the processor to dissipate the heat the processor produces.

4. _____ enable you to connect additional peripheral devices to a computer.

5. _____ is a standard port type that is used to connect many kinds of devices.

6. The _____ is a program stored on a chip on the motherboard that is used to start up the computer.

7. The operating systems, programs, and data a computer is currently using are stored in _____.

8. A(n) _____ monitor is composed of extremely thin panels of organic molecules sandwiched between two electrodes.

9. _____ printers create objects such as prototypes and models.

10. A(n) _____ is used to connect a computer to a computer network.

Running Project . . .

. . . The Finish Line

Use your answers to the previous sections of the Running Project to determine what you would need in a desktop system. Look at computer ads on some current retail websites and select a computer system that meets your needs. Pick a system in the $300–600 price range. Does it include everything you need? What's missing? What additional features does it have that you will find useful? Does it have extras that you could do without? Is it fairly priced? What features would you get if you spent more money? What would you lose if you spent less? Justify why the system you chose is a good choice for you.

Write a report describing your selection and responding to the questions raised. Save your file as **lastname_firstname_ch04_project** and submit it to your instructor as directed.

Do It Yourself 1

Color calibration helps you set your monitor to display colors as accurately as possible. You may need to supply an administrator password to complete some steps in this exercise. If you can't adjust the settings, read each screen for information only. From your student data files, open the file *vt_ch04_DIY1_answersheet* and save the file as **lastname_firstname_ch04_DIY1_answersheet**.

1. From the Windows 10 Search bar, type **calibrate** and click *Calibrate display color* from the search results. What is display color calibration? How does it work? Follow the directions on the next several screens to adjust your color.

   If you are using a Mac:

   1. From the dock, open *System Preferences*, click *Displays*, click the *Color* tab, and then click *Calibrate*.

   2. Use the information on each screen or search the Internet to answer the following questions. What is gamma? What does brightness adjustment control? What is contrast? How does color balance work? Type your answers in the answer sheet, save the file, and submit it as directed by your instructor.

Do It Yourself 2

Windows and macOS provide several ways to adjust accessibility settings of your computer. In this activity, you'll examine these settings on your computer. From your student data files, open the file *vt_ch04_DIY2_answersheet* and save the file as **lastname_firstname_ch04_DIY2_answersheet**.

1. Open File Explorer, in the Navigation pane, click *This PC*, and on the Computer tab, click *Open Settings*. Click *Ease of Access*.

2. Click each tab and read the description and settings for each. What is the Narrator? Click *Keyboard*. What are Sticky Keys, Toggle Keys, and Filter Keys? Click *Mouse*. What are Mouse keys?

   If you are using a Mac:

   1. From the Apple menu or dock, open *System Preferences* and click *Accessibility* to examine the settings.

   2. Click each tab and read the description and settings for each. What is the VoiceOver? Click *Keyboard*. What are Sticky Keys and Slow Keys? Click *Mouse* (or *Mouse and Trackpad*). What are Mouse Keys?

3. Type your answers in the answer sheet, save the file, and submit it as directed by your instructor.

File Management

Windows and macOS include a Downloads folder for each user. From your student data files, open the file *vt_ch04_FM_answersheet* and save the file as **lastname_firstname_ch04_FM_answersheet**.

1. Open File Explorer or Finder and click *Downloads*. Are there any files in this folder? If so, what types of files are they? Search Windows Help or Spotlight or use the Internet to learn about the Downloads folder. What is the purpose of the Downloads folder? Type up your answers, save the file, and submit the assignment as directed by your instructor.

Critical Thinking

You are a member of a student club on campus that is in need of a new computer to keep records, produce newsletters, etc. It needs to run Microsoft Office 2016 and needs wireless network access. Because you're the computer expert in the group, you have been given the job of choosing a computer that meets the club's needs. Determine other requirements based upon the type of club (your choice). You have $500 to spend. From your student data files, open the file *vt_ch04_CT_answersheet* and save the file as **lastname_firstname_ch04_CT_answersheet**.

Evaluate three computer choices from current newspaper ads or websites and compare them with respect to the club's requirements. Complete the following table, comparing the features of each computer. Explain your recommendation in a two- to three-paragraph summary. Which computer should the club buy and why? What other peripherals and software will they need to purchase? Also recommend necessary peripherals, including a monitor and printer. Remember, your budget is fixed, so you can't exceed $500. Save your file, and submit both your table and summary as directed by your instructor.

	Computer 1	Computer 2	Computer 3
Website or store			
Brand			
Model			
Price			
Processor type			
Processor speed			
Memory type			
Memory amount			
Hard drive capacity			
Additional equipment/ features			
Additional purchases required/ recommended			

Ethical Dilemma

The Americans with Disabilities Act (**ada.gov**) requires businesses with 15 or more employees to provide reasonable accommodation for all employees who have—or who have a record of having—a disability. A disability is any condition that limits one or more major life activities. From your student data files, open the file *vt_ch04_ethics_answersheet* and save the file as **lastname_firstname_ch04_ethics_answersheet**.

Should small businesses be required to provide adaptive technology to all employees, regardless of cost? Should they have to provide the technology the employee wants? Or can they choose other methods of addressing the issue of concern? What if the disability becomes so great that it causes the business financial hardship? Is the business then legally required to provide accommodation? What is the moral responsibility? Type your answers, save the file, and submit it as directed by your instructor.

On the Web

The EPEAT website provides information to help you "evaluate, compare and select electronic products based on their environmental attributes." From your student data files, open the file *vt_ch04_web_answersheet* and save the file as **lastname_firstname_ch04_web_answersheet** and visit the site **www.epeat.net** to answer the following questions:

1. What manufacturers participate in the program? How is it funded? Is there any conflict of interest?

2. What types of devices are included in the system? How are they placed into the registry?

3. What testing do they undergo? What are the environmental performance criteria the devices must meet?

Type your answers, save the file, and submit it as directed by your instructor.

Collaboration

Instructors: Divide the class into small groups, and assign each group one topic for this project. The topics include motherboards, processors, storage devices, input devices, and output devices.

The Project: As a team, prepare a multimedia presentation for your assigned topic. The presentation should explain your hardware category and compare different types of devices in that category. Use at least three references, only one of which may be this text. Use Google Docs or Microsoft Office to plan the presentation, and provide documentation that all team members have contributed to the project.

Outcome: Prepare a multimedia presentation on your assigned topic in PowerPoint or another tool approved by your instructor, and present it to your class. The presentation may be no longer than 3 minutes and should contain five to seven slides. On the first slide, be sure to include the name of your presentation and a list of all team members. Turn in a final version of your presentation named **teamname_ch04_presentation** and your file showing your collaboration named **teamname_ch04_collab** and submit your presentation to your instructor as directed.

Application Project

MyLab IT
GRADER

Office 2016 Application Projects
Word 2016: Ergonomics

Project Description: *You have been asked to write an article on ergonomics. You will need to change alignment, line and paragraph spacing, margins, and lists and edit the header and footer. You will also find and replace text, create and modify a footnote, and use the Format Painter. If necessary, download the student data files from* **pearsonhighered.com/viztech**.

Ergonomics

January 2, 2018

Welcome back to a new year. I am excited to get started. We have a lot of work to do this year and some exciting new projects underway. One important task we have to do this year is evaluating our safety practices. To that end, we have compiled this informative tip sheet on ergonomics. Please take a few moments to review the important safety tips included in this tip sheet.

SAVE YOUR EYESIGHT

How many hours a day do you spend in front of your computer? Don't forget to include the hours at home! The average person spends at least several hours a day in front of a video screen. This can cause eyestrain- in fact there is a name for it—video terminal syndrome or VTS. So what can you do about it?

- ✓ Proper monitor placement
- ✓ Good lighting
- ✓ Prescription eyewear if needed[1]
- ✓ Take a break—at least 5 minutes for every hour
- ✓ Exercise your eyes

BACK AND NECK PAIN

Sitting at a desk all day can literally be a pain in the neck. Setting up your workstation properly can help you avoid painful neck and back pain. Here are some recommendations for avoiding neck and back pain.

- ✓ Set monitor height so you are looking straight ahead or slightly up—not down
- ✓ Adjust chair height so feet are flat or slightly elevated—not dangling
- ✓ Sit up straight- your mom had it right, proper posture is important
- ✓ Take frequent breaks—get up and move around

WRISTS AND HANDS

If you spend a lot of time using the keyboard and mouse, you could be bothered by repetitive stress injuries. To avoid these painful conditions, follow these suggestions.

---
[1] May be covered under your health insurance benefits.

2

- ✓ Make sure keyboard and mouse are set at a proper height—if necessary get an adjustable drawer or shelf
- ✓ Use an ergonomic keyboard
- ✓ Grip mouse loosely
- ✓ Use gel wrist rests
- ✓ Rest elbows on chair arms

As you can see, with proper ergonomics you can avoid many discomforts. Here's to a healthy and productive new year!

 Sally Mosley—CEO

Step	Instructions
1	Start Word. From your student data files, open the Word file *vt_ch04_word*. Save the file as **lastname_firstname_ch04_word**
2	Change the left and right margins of the document to 1.0".
3	Center the first two paragraphs (title and date).
4	Change the line spacing of the entire document to 1.5 lines. Change the paragraph spacing of the entire document to 6 pt after.
5	Center the heading *Save Your Eyesight*.
6	Using the Format Painter, apply the formatting from the heading *Save Your Eyesight* to the headings *Back and Neck Pain* and *Wrists and Hands*.
7	Use the Find and Replace dialog box to search for and replace all instances of the word *report* with **tip sheet** There should be two replacements.
8	In the *Save Your Eyesight* section, format the list beginning *Proper monitor placement* and ending *Exercise your eyes* as a bulleted list using check mark bullets.
9	In the *Back and Neck Pain* section, format the list beginning *Set monitor height* and ending *Take frequent breaks* as a bulleted list using check mark bullets.
10	In the *Wrists and Hands* section, format the list beginning *Make sure keyboard and mouse are set a proper height* and ending *Rest elbows on chair arms* as a bulleted list using check mark bullets.
11	In the document header, add a page number using the Plain Number 2 style at the Top of Page. In the footer, add the File Name field using the default format. Ensure the header and footer are not displayed on the first page.
12	In the *Save Your Eyesight* section, in the bulleted list, insert a footnote immediately following the text *Prescription eyewear if needed* reading **May be covered under your health insurance benefits.** (include the period).
13	Use the Spelling and Grammar dialog box to correct the misspelling of the word *imporatn* to *important*. Ignore all other spelling and grammar suggestions.
14	Place the insertion point at the beginning of the last line of the document—before Sally. Insert the picture *vt_ch04_image1*. Change text wrapping to Square.
15	Save the file and close Word. Submit the document as directed.

Application Project

Office 2016 Application Projects
PowerPoint 2016: Comparing Printers

Project Description: *In this project, you will create a presentation about printers. In creating this presentation you will apply design, font, and color themes. You will also change font colors, bullet symbols, and slide layout. If necessary, download the student data files from* **pearsonhighered.com/viztech**.

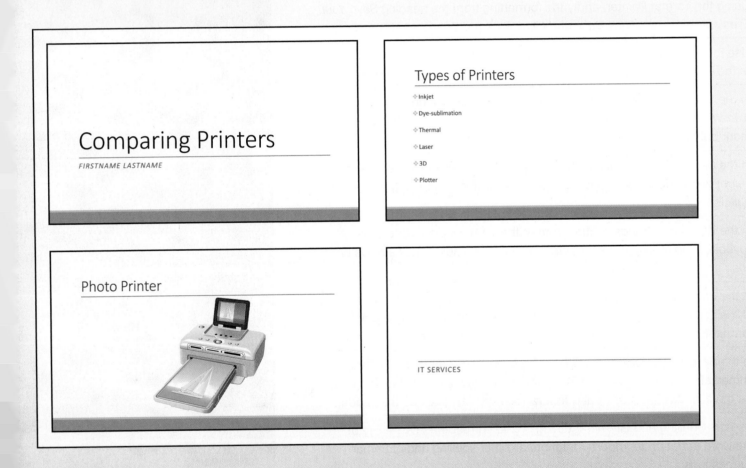

Step	Instructions
1	Start PowerPoint. From your student data files, open the file *vt_ch04_ppt*. Save the presentation as **lastname_firstname_ch04_ppt**
2	Apply the Retrospect theme to the presentation. From the Variant gallery, apply the green variant to the presentation.
3	On Slide 1, using your own name, type **Firstname Lastname** in the subtitle placeholder. Apply bold and italic formatting to the subtitle text.
4	On Slide 2, type **Types of Printers** in the title placeholder.
5	On Slide 2, change the bullets to Star Bullets and change the line spacing of the bullets to 1.5.
6	On Slide 3, insert the image *vt_ch04_image2* in the content placeholder. Apply the Metal Frame picture style to the image.
7	On Slide 1, copy the title text, *Comparing Printers*. On Slide 4, paste the copied text into the title placeholder using the destination theme.
8	Change the layout of Slide 4 to Section Header.
9	On Slide 4, type **IT Services** in the content placeholder. Change the font color of the title text, *Comparing Printers*, to Black, Background 1 (under Theme Colors).
10	Insert the page number and the footer **Firstname Lastname** on the notes and handouts pages for all slides in the presentation. View the presentation in Slide Show view from beginning to end, and then return to Normal view.
11	Save the presentation and close PowerPoint. Submit the presentation as directed.

Production Perig/Shutterstock

System Software

BrunoWeltmann/Fotolia

In This Chapter

VIZ INTRO

A computer is a programmable machine that converts raw data into useful information. Programming is what makes a computer different from a toaster. In this chapter, we look at the system software used to make computers run smoothly and securely. When you have finished this chapter you will be able to recognize and use the features of various operating systems.

Objectives

1 Explain What an Operating System Does

2 Compare Desktop Operating Systems

3 Configure a Desktop Operating System

4 Compare Specialized Operating Systems

5 Compare the Most Common Network Operating Systems

6 List and Explain Important Utility Software

7 Troubleshoot Common Computer Problems

Running Project

In this chapter, you'll learn about different kinds of system software. Look for instructions as you complete each article. For most, there's a series of questions for you to research. At the conclusion of the chapter, you'll submit your responses to the questions raised.

Maradon 333/Shutterstock

Who's the Boss?

1 Explain What an Operating System Does

VIZ CLIP

Installing
Hardware
Device Drivers

Application software is software that performs a useful task for the user. Software that makes the computer run is **system software**. The **operating system (OS)** is the most important type of system software because it provides the user with the interface to communicate with the hardware and other software on the computer and manages system resources. Without an operating system, a personal computer is unusable.

Provides User Interface

The **user interface** is the part of the operating system that you see and interact with. Modern operating systems, such as Microsoft Windows, Linux, and macOS, have a **graphical user interface (GUI)**. A GUI enables you to point to and click on graphic objects such as icons and buttons to initiate commands. Older operating systems had a command-line interface, which required you to type out all commands. If you look at the interface on most personal computers, you'll see that they have a lot in common. Figure 5.1 shows how the interface has changed from command-line to GUI in Microsoft operating systems. This change made PCs more user friendly, which helped them increase in popularity. A similar evolution occurred in the Apple systems.

FIGURE 5.1 The user interface of the Microsoft operating system has evolved from the MS-DOS command-line (bottom right), to the Windows 10 GUI (top).

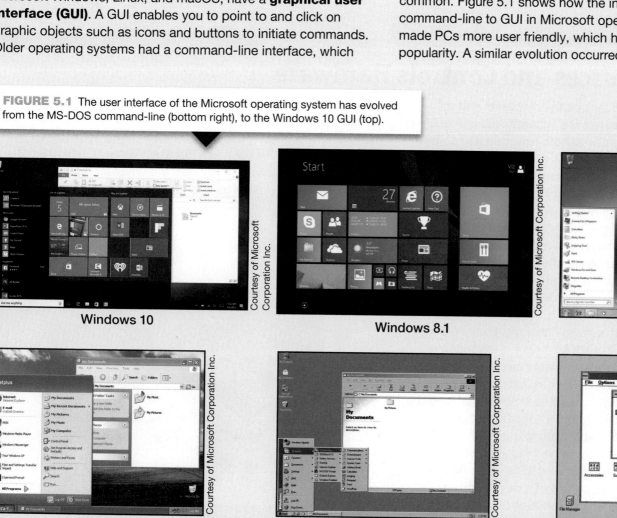

Windows 10

Windows 8.1

Windows 7

Courtesy of Microsoft Corporation Inc.

Windows XP

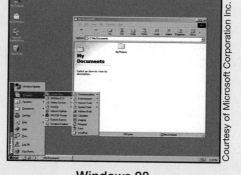

Windows 98

Windows 3.1

Courtesy of Microsoft Corporation Inc.

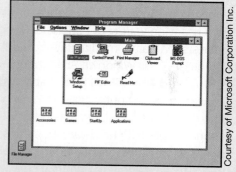

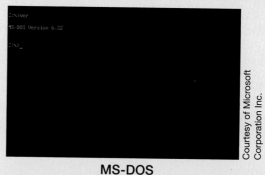

```
C:\>ver

MS-DOS Version 6.22

C:\>_
```

MS-DOS

Courtesy of Microsoft Corporation Inc.

All user interfaces serve the same basic function: to allow the user to control the computer. If you want to play a game, for example, you navigate to the icon for the game and click on it to begin. The clicking tells the computer to open the file—in this case, to run the game. The procedure to open a Word document is the same. These tasks require the OS user interface. GUIs use icons, menus, dialog boxes, and windows, and often there are multiple ways to perform the same task.

Manages Resources and Controls Hardware

The resources on your system include the processor and the memory. The operating system has the important job of managing how these resources are allocated to both hardware and software. The OS makes sure that each process is allocated its own memory and manages the instructions that are sent to the processor. Modern operating systems support **multitasking**, which is the ability to do more than one task at a time. A single processor can't actually do more than one thing at a time but switches between the tasks so quickly that it's transparent to the user. Each running application is assigned its own area of memory and is prevented from accessing the memory area of other programs. This prevents a program crash from affecting other processes running in other areas of memory.

The OS manages and controls the hardware. Early PCs were simple devices that had limited hardware: a keyboard, a monochrome monitor, a disk drive, and not much else. Today, there is a wide variety of peripheral devices, including printers, scanners, cameras, media players, video and sound cards, and storage devices. Windows 95 introduced a feature known as **Plug and Play (PnP)** that enables you to easily add new hardware to a computer system. When you plug in a new piece of hardware, the OS detects it and helps you set it up. An OS communicates with hardware by means of a **device driver** that acts as a translator, enhancing the capabilities of the operating system by enabling it to communicate with hardware. If it were not for device drivers, there would be no way for you to install new hardware on your system. When you first connect the hardware, Windows detects it and informs you that it's installing the device

driver software. If Windows cannot locate the device driver, it asks you for permission to search the web or instructs you to insert the manufacturer's disc. The message *Device driver software installed successfully* indicates your new hardware is now ready to use. In Figure 5.2, Windows has installed the driver for the attached smartphone and asks the user to choose how the device is configured.

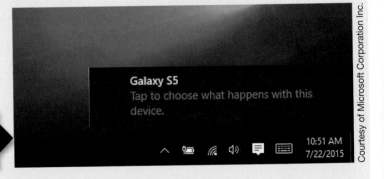

Galaxy S5
Tap to choose what happens with this device.

10:51 AM
7/22/2015

FIGURE 5.2 After the operating system installs a device such as this phone, it notifies you of the status of the device or asks you to choose what happens next.

Interacts with Software

When you look at the system requirements to install software, you'll see a list of supported operating systems. The OS on a computer interacts directly with the software you install, giving the software access to resources it needs to run. This happens through the use of an **application programming interface (API)**, which allows the application to request services—such as printing or saving a file—from the operating system. An API lets a computer programmer write a program that will run on computers with different hardware configurations by sending such service requests to the OS to handle. Figure 5.3 shows Microsoft Word using the API to request save services from Windows. Different applications use a common Windows dialog box to save files.

An operating system manages interactions between the user, the software, and the hardware of a computer. These critical functions make the computer more user friendly, flexible, and expandable. The OS is the most important software on the computer because without it the computer won't run at all.

FIGURE 5.3 Programs use the application programming interface (API) to save files.

Courtesy of Microsoft Corporation Inc.

Running Project

What operating system is on your computer? To check on a Windows computer, open File Explorer, if necessary click *This PC*, and on the ribbon, click *System Properties*. To check a Mac, open the About This Mac window from the Apple menu. Is your OS the latest version? If you have not upgraded yet, why not?

4 Things You Need to Know

- A GUI allows you to point and click to control your computer.
- The OS manages the system resources: processing and memory.
- PnP allows you to add new hardware easily.
- Application software communicates with the OS through an API.

Key Terms

application programming interface (API)

device driver

graphical user interface (GUI)

multitasking

operating system (OS)

Plug and Play (PnP)

system software

user interface

Digital Literacy Skill

Keep Your Desktop OS Up to Date

HOW TO VIDEO

One of the most important things you can do to protect your system is to keep your software up to date. Some programs will check automatically and prompt you when a new version or update is available. In this activity you will examine your update settings. It's important to set the utility up correctly and monitor it to be sure that your updates are being installed. (Note: The IT department at your school may have disabled these settings through group policies.) Complete each step, and compare your screen to the figures that accompany each step. If necessary, download student data files from **pearsonhighered.com/viztech**. From your student data files, open the *vt_ch05_howto1_answersheet* file and save the file as **lastname_firstname_ch05_howto1_answersheet**.

1 On a Windows 10 computer, click the *Start* button and click *Settings*. Click *Update & security*. (For Windows 8, open the Settings charm, click *Change PC settings*, and then click *Update and recovery*.) Take a screenshot of the Windows Update screen and paste it in your document. If necessary, click *Check for updates*. How many updates are available on your system? When was the most recent check for updates?

← Settings   — □ ×

⚙ Home

Find a setting 🔍

Update & security

🔄 Windows Update

🛡 Windows Defender

⤒ Backup

🔧 Troubleshoot

🕑 Recovery

⊘ Activation

📍 Find My Device

🎚 For developers

👤 Windows Insider Program

Windows Update

Update status

Updates are available.
• Definition Update for Windows Defender - KB2267602 (Definition 1.247.739.0)
• Update for Microsoft Office 2016 (KB3213549) 64-Bit Edition
• Update for Microsoft Project 2016 (KB3203476) 64-Bit Edition
• Update for Skype for Business 2016 (KB3213548) 64-Bit Edition
• Update for Microsoft Access 2016 (KB3191926) 64-Bit Edition

Downloading updates 32%

Update history

Update settings

We'll automatically download and install updates, except on metered connections (where charges may apply). In that case, we'll automatically download only those updates required to keep Windows running smoothly.

Courtesy of Microsoft Corporation Inc.

2 On a Windows 10 computer, scroll down and under Update settings, click *Advanced options* (for Windows 8, click *Choose how updates get installed*) to verify that you're getting the updates you need. How is your computer configured to handle updates? What types of updates are included? Click the checkboxes for the other options you want. Microsoft Update will also get you updates for other Microsoft products, such as Office. (On a Windows 8 computer, click the back arrow to return to the Windows Update window.)

3 Click the back arrow and then click *Update history.* Take a screenshot of this window and paste it into your answer sheet. Close the Settings window, save your file, and submit it as directed by your instructor.

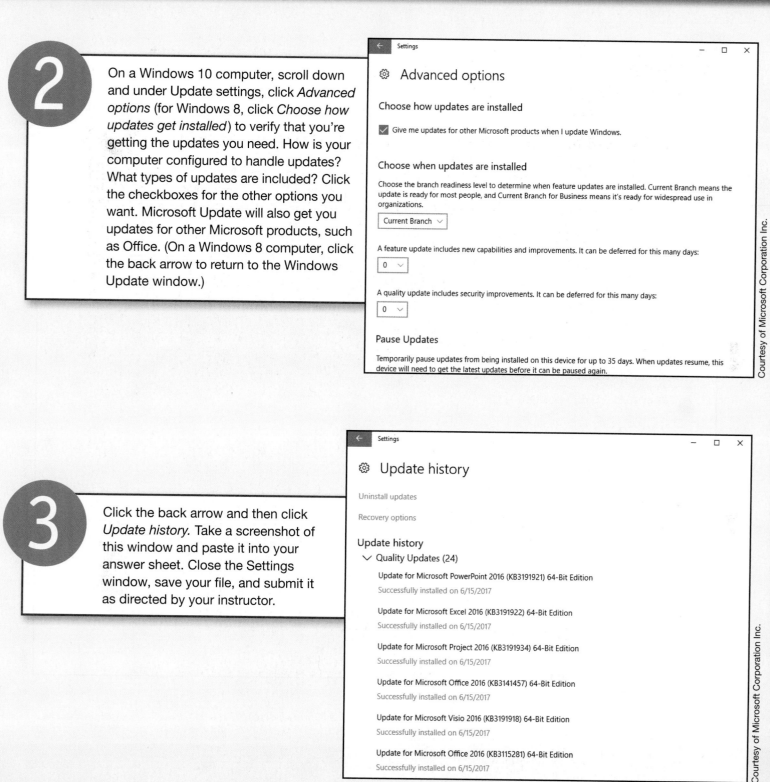

Courtesy of Microsoft Corporation Inc.

If you are using a Mac: From your student data files, open the *vt_ch05_howto1_answersheet_mac* file and save the file as **lastname_firstname_ch05_howto1_answersheet_mac**.

1. Open the Apple menu and click *App Store.* If necessary, wait for macOS to check for updates. Click the *Updates* tab, take a screenshot of this window, and paste it into your answer sheet. How many updates are available? What, if any, updates were installed in the last 30 days? Close the App Store window.

● ● ●	★ Featured	▦ Top Charts	🗂 Categories	🏷 Purchased	⬇ Updates	Q Search

< >

No Updates Available

Updates Installed in the Last 30 Days

macOS High Sierra 10.13.2 Developer Beta
Version 4
Installed Nov 26, 2017   This update is recommended for all users.

Keynote
Apple
Version 7.3.1   This update contains stability and performance improvements.
Installed Nov 11, 2017

Pages
Apple
Version 6.3.1   This update contains stability and performance improvements.
Installed Nov 11, 2017

Numbers
Apple
Version 4.3.1   This update contains stability and performance improvements.
Installed Nov 11, 2017

iMovie
Apple   • Improves overall stability
Version 10.1.8

2. Open System Preferences and click *App Store*. Take a screenshot of this window and paste it into your document. How frequently does your computer check for updates? When was the last check? Save your file, and submit it as directed by your instructor.

Screen shot(s) reprinted with permission from Apple Inc.

Screen shot(s) reprinted with permission from Apple Inc.

OPERATING SYSTEM

Desktop Operating Systems

ctive

2

Compare Desktop Operating Systems

There are many different operating systems. The operating system used on a personal computer is referred to as a desktop OS—even if it is a notebook computer.

Windows

The most common desktop operating system is **Microsoft Windows**. Figure 5.4 shows a timeline of the release of successive versions of Windows desktop operating systems. At the time of this writing, the current version is Windows 10, although you'll still find many computers running previous versions of Windows, notably Windows 7 or 8.1. About 90 percent of personal computers are running a version of Windows. Sales of Windows XP ended in 2008, and Microsoft support for Windows XP ended in 2014, leaving older systems without patches or updates for any newly discovered problems. Windows Vista was released in 2006 but was met with much resistance from both the public and business customers. The hardware requirements to install Vista were much more stringent than those for XP, so it would not run on many older systems. In addition,

software and device driver compatibility were problematic when Vista was first released, adding to the cost of upgrading. Windows 7 was greeted much more favorably, and both home and business users who were still using XP began to upgrade to it. In 2012, Microsoft released Windows 8, updated to Windows 8.1 in 2013. Windows 10 was released in 2015 as a free upgrade for Windows 7 and 8 systems. Windows 10 Creators Update was released in 2017.

Each release of Windows added new features and security measures and was designed to be easier to use, more secure, and able to incorporate new technologies. Moving from one version of Windows to the next usually requires a fairly small learning curve, and users adapt quickly to the changes. Some important features added with each version follow:

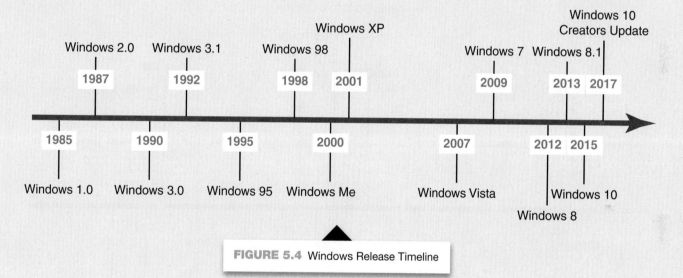

FIGURE 5.4 Windows Release Timeline

- Windows 95 introduced Plug and Play (PnP), enhanced support for CD-ROMs, and the right mouse click.
- Windows 98 included Internet Explorer, better PnP support, and more multimedia features.
- Windows XP introduced a new interface, automatic updates, easier networking and Internet connectivity, and increased reliability.
- Windows Vista introduced a new interface; gadgets; enhanced networking, entertainment, and accessibility features.
- Windows 7 included a redesigned taskbar, new ways to manipulate windows, Remote Media Streaming, and Windows Touch multi-touch technology.
- Windows 8 introduced a totally new interface, which uses a Start Screen with Live Tiles instead of a Start menu to access applications.
- Windows 10 restores the Start button that users missed with Windows 8, while keeping the Live Tiles from the Start screen. A new browser, Edge, replaces the tired Internet Explorer. A virtual assistant—Cortana—a feature on Windows phones, is now part of the desktop OS. Screenshots in this book use Windows 10.

macOS

In 1984, Apple introduced its first Macintosh computer, which had a GUI interface. The OS at the time was called Mac System Software. New versions and updates that improved stability and hardware support were released between 1984 and 1991. Figure 5.5 shows a timeline of Mac releases.

- System 7 was released in 1991 with an updated GUI, multitasking support, built-in networking, better hardware and memory management, and new applications. Beginning with version 7.6, the name was changed to Mac OS.
- Mac OS 8 was released in 1997 and included a new interface; a better file system, searching, and Internet browsing.
- Mac OS 9 had improved wireless networking support, a better search tool, and the ability to be updated over the Internet. Mac OS 9 is referred to today as Mac Classic.

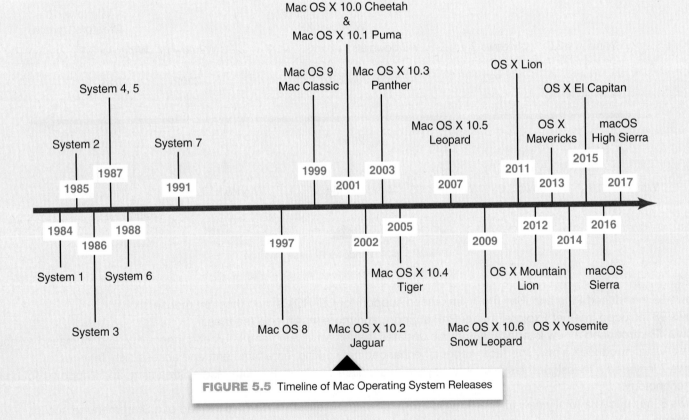

FIGURE 5.5 Timeline of Mac Operating System Releases

The **OS X** operating system was first released in 2001 as Mac OS X 10.0, also called Cheetah. This OS wasn't an updated version of the classic Mac OS but an entirely new operating system based on Unix. Early versions of OS X included a Mac OS 9 emulation to run older applications. Cheetah integrated iMovie and iTunes. Each new version included more integrated applications for email, chat, Internet, and multimedia. In 2016, Apple changed the name to **macOS** and released Sierra. Screenshots in this book use High Sierra (Figure 5.6). macOS High Sierra was released in 2017.

ETHICS

Early versions of Mac operating systems only ran on Mac hardware with PowerPC processors, but modern Macs now use Intel processors just like many PCs. With a bit of tweaking, it's possible to get some versions of the macOS to run on a non-Mac PC. *Hackintosh* is the name given to a PC that's been modified so macOS can be run on it. The question is, is it legal? Is it ethical? What are the restrictions on the macOS EULA? Why do people do it? Would you?

FIGURE 5.6 macOS High Sierra

Screen shot(s) reprinted with permission from Apple Inc.

Linux

Unlike Windows and Mac, Linux doesn't refer to a single operating system but rather many different versions or distributions that use the same kernel, or core OS: Linux. **Linux** was first developed in 1991 by Linus Torvalds, then a graduate student at the University of Helsinki. It was designed to be similar to **Unix**—a multiuser OS developed in the 1970s that is still used on servers and some specialized workstations. Unlike Unix, however, Linux is **open source**—the code is publicly available, and developers around the world have created hundreds of Linux distributions (distros) with all kinds of features. Distros include the OS, various utilities, and software applications, such as web browsers, games, entertainment software, and an office suite. One popular personal version of Linux is Fedora, shown in Figure 5.7. Most Linux distros come with a GUI that's similar to Windows or macOS, and users can easily navigate through the system.

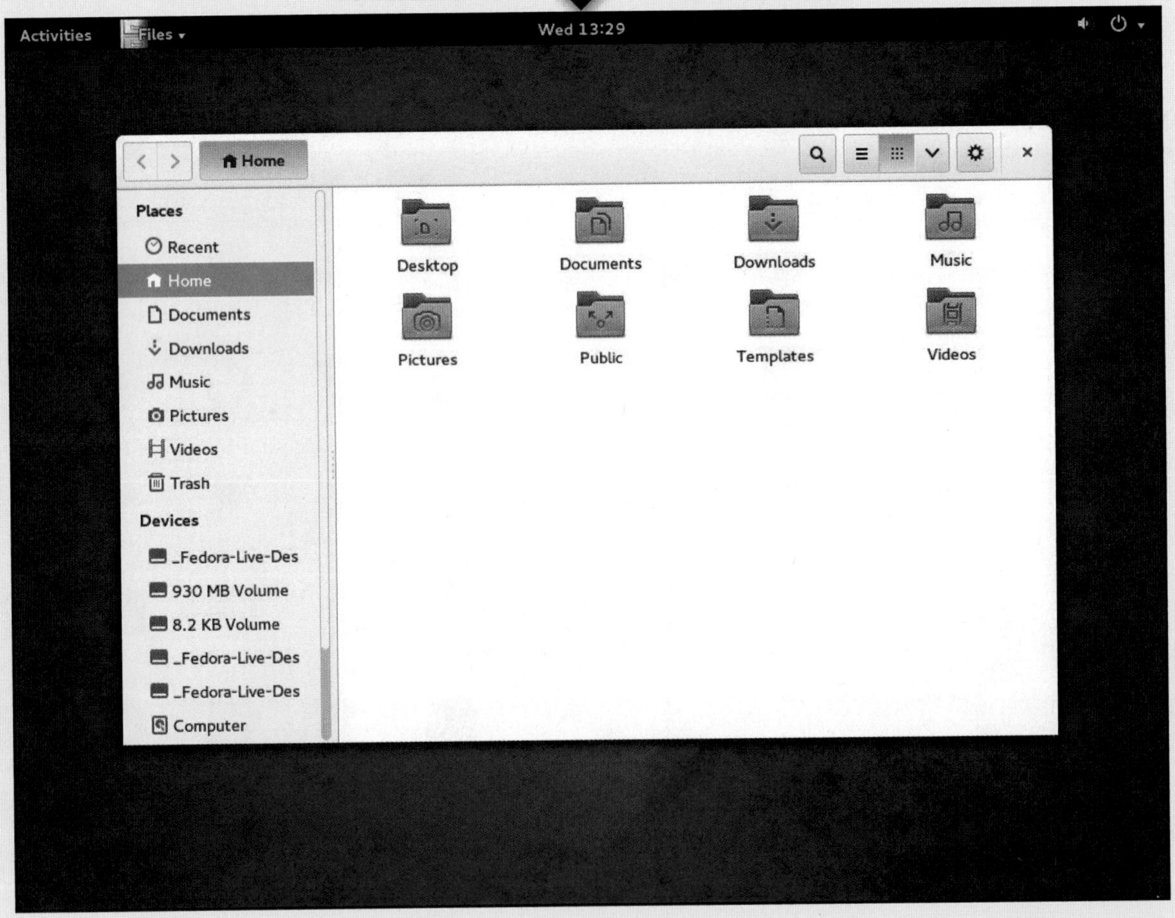

FIGURE 5.7 The Fedora desktop features a GUI that's easy to navigate for most users.

The Fedora® Project, Red Hat, Inc.

Linux desktops make up a very small percentage of personal computers, but the number is growing. Linux has found a niche in the subnotebook market. On machines with limited memory and processing power, Linux excels. In 2011, several manufacturers began shipping Chromebooks that run the Chrome OS—a Linux distro released by Google. These notebooks are designed to work best when connected to the Internet and rely on web apps and cloud storage rather than traditional software. In businesses, Linux has a less than 2 percent market share of desktop computers, but it has a larger share of the server market. Red Hat Enterprise Linux is the world's leading open source application platform.

PSL Images/Alamy Stock Photo

Beta Software

When new software is being developed, it is often released in a preview or **beta version**—a pre-release version that is provided to some users and developers to preview and test before the final version is released. Beta and other early releases of software should only be used for testing, as they are often incomplete, unstable, and buggy.

Running Project

Microsoft Windows is the primary desktop operating system installed on new personal computers, but not every consumer is happy with that choice. Some manufacturers sell Linux computers such as Chromebooks. Use the Internet to research the versions of Linux currently available preinstalled on new computers. Write a two- to three-paragraph essay summarizing your findings, which applications are included, the cost, and any other details you deem important.

4 Things You Need to Know

- Microsoft Windows is the primary OS installed on PCs.
- macOS is the proprietary Mac OS.
- Linux is an open source kernel OS that's distributed as part of many versions or distros.
- Unix is a multiuser OS developed in the 1970s that is still used on servers and some specialized workstations.

Key Terms

beta version

Linux

macOS

Microsoft Windows

open source

OS X

Unix

MODUS OPERANDI

Make Your OS Work for You

Configure a Desktop Operating System

A desktop operating system has features that you can configure to make your system more secure, efficient, and personalized. On a Windows 10 computer, the settings can be changed through the Settings app, the Control Panel, or the Action Center. On a Windows 8.1 computer, the settings can be changed through PC settings, the Control Panel, or the Settings charm. In macOS, most settings are changed through System Preferences.

Configuring Your OS

The Windows 10 **Settings window** enables you to change many common settings on your system (Figure 5.8). It helps you to configure user accounts, privacy settings, and accessibility settings. You can add and remove hardware devices and customize time and date and language settings.

- System: configure displays and power and sleep settings; get more information about your PC
- Devices: configure Bluetooth settings, mouse and keyboard settings, and printers
- Network & Internet: change network, Wi-Fi, and workplace VPN settings
- Personalization: configure how Windows looks
- Accounts: configure, add, and remove user accounts
- Time & language: set time and language settings
- Ease of Access: set accessibility settings
- Privacy: change privacy and location settings
- Update & security: configure Windows Update, backup, and recovery options

The **Control Panel** gives you access to even more options to configure, monitor, or troubleshoot settings, hardware, and software (Figure 5.9). To access Control Panel, right-click the Start button or use Windows search. Most of the settings in the Settings window are also accessible in Control Panel, as well as many more advanced settings. The programs that make up Control Panel are sometimes called **control panel applets**. Some third-party

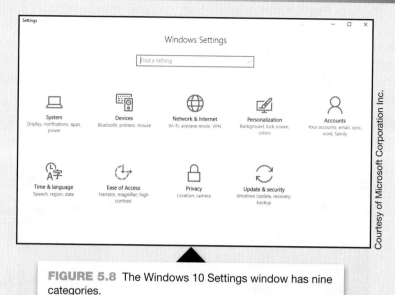

FIGURE 5.8 The Windows 10 Settings window has nine categories.

Courtesy of Microsoft Corporation Inc.

programs and computer manufacturers may add applets to the Control Panel. If you are not sure which tool to use to change a setting, type a keyword or phrase into the Search on the taskbar or Control Panel window. The default view of Control Panel is by category, which groups the applets into the following categories:

- System and Security: computer status, backups, troubleshooting applets
- Network and Internet: network, sharing, and Internet settings
- Hardware and Sound: devices and printers, and other hardware settings
- Programs: install, uninstall, and configure software
- User Accounts: add, remove, and configure user accounts and set up parental controls
- Appearance and Personalization: change desktop and display settings.
- Clock, Language, and Region: change language and input settings, set date and time.
- Ease of Access: set accessibility settings.

In the notification area, on the far right end of the taskbar, click the Notification icon to open the Action Center. There are system messages, buttons to change a few settings and to open All Settings. The settings available depend upon your system. The system in Figure 5.10 is a touchscreen notebook computer, and has settings including Tablet mode, Location services, Airplane mode, and Battery saver, all of which are important for a notebook user. A desktop computer would not have these same options.

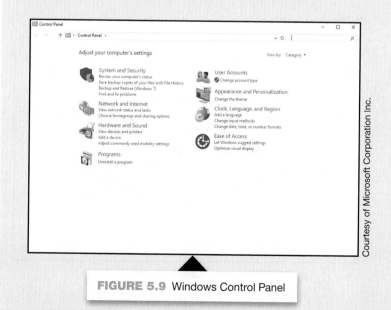

FIGURE 5.9 Windows Control Panel

Courtesy of Microsoft Corporation Inc.

System Preferences in macOS are grouped into rows (Figure 5.11). You can configure hardware settings, manage user accounts, and customize the way your computer looks and responds. Some third-party applications may install items in the System Preferences that can be used to configure the settings for that application. The System Preferences are accessed through the Apple menu or by clicking the icon on the dock.

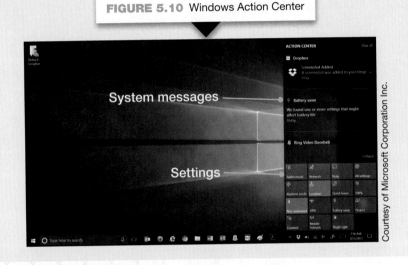

FIGURE 5.10 Windows Action Center

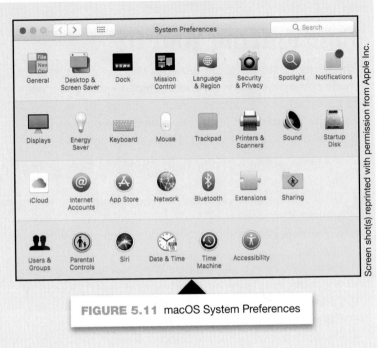

FIGURE 5.11 macOS System Preferences

User Accounts

Create a separate **user account** for each person that shares a device, which grants each user access to the system and enables you to keep your files private and set restrictions on what other users can do. Windows and macOS user accounts have several layers of security built into them. There are four types of user accounts:

- Standard account—for everyday computing; can modify settings that affect the user account only.
- Child account—a Windows standard account that has Family Safety turned on by default. On a Mac this is called Managed. Not available in every version of Windows.
- Administrator account—for making global changes, installing software, configuring settings, and completing other tasks; called Admin on a Mac.
- Guest account—for users who need temporary access to a system. This account is off by default. Not available in every version of Windows.

You can change the type of account on a Windows computer through Account Settings (Figure 5.12). When you create an account on a Windows computer, you have the option to use your email address linked to your Microsoft account or to create a local user. Either account type can be set up as an administrator or a standard user. Using your Microsoft account links you to cloud resources and syncs settings across systems. A Mac account can be linked to an Apple ID, which is necessary to make purchases from the App Store and use iCloud services. Figure 5.13 shows several Mac user accounts.

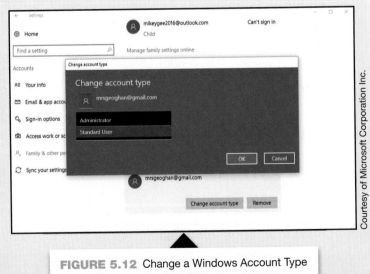

FIGURE 5.12 Change a Windows Account Type

Figure 5.13 Mac Users & Groups window showing:

Users & Groups

Current User
Visualizing Technol...
Admin

Other Users
Firstname Lastname
Standard
Guest User
Off

Password | Login Items

Visualizing Technology   Change Password...

Contacts Card: Open...
☑ Allow user to administer this computer
☐ Enable parental controls   Open Parental Controls...

Login Options
+ −

🔒 Click the lock to make changes.

Screen shot(s) reprinted with permission from Apple Inc.

It's good practice to create a standard user account for your day-to-day tasks and use the administrator account only when necessary. Tasks that require administrator-level permission—such as installing a new program—will prompt you for administrator credentials. In a business, only the IT staff should have administrator rights to a computer. Computer settings can be controlled by the IT staff through the use of group policies, which can be configured for a local computer or through a network domain.

FIGURE 5.13 A Mac with Admin, Standard, and Guest Accounts

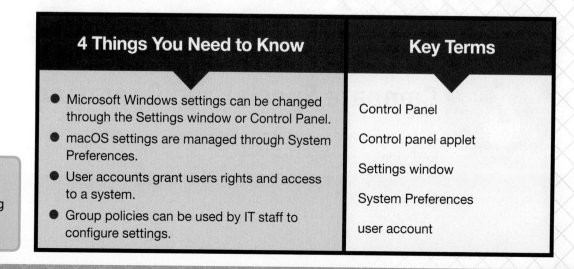

Running Project

Use the Internet to research group policies on a Windows computer. What types of settings can be controlled? What is the advantage of using group policies over allowing users to modify their own settings?

Viz Check—In MyLab IT, take a quick quiz covering Objectives 1–3.

4 Things You Need to Know

- Microsoft Windows settings can be changed through the Settings window or Control Panel.
- macOS settings are managed through System Preferences.
- User accounts grant users rights and access to a system.
- Group policies can be used by IT staff to configure settings.

Key Terms

Control Panel

Control panel applet

Settings window

System Preferences

user account

Garagestock/Shutterstock

Something Special for You

Compare Specialized Operating Systems

So far, we've discussed operating systems that run on personal computers. Other devices have specialized operating systems, including embedded and mobile operating systems.

Embedded Operating Systems

Devices such as ATMs, GPS devices, video game consoles, ultrasound machines, and communication and entertainment systems in automobiles run **embedded operating systems** (Figure 5.14). Because they have very specialized and limited functions, embedded operating systems can be very small and are able to run on simple hardware.

The Windows Embedded OS has been around since 1996. It can be found on many devices from set-top cable boxes and GPS devices to complex industrial automation controllers and medical devices. The advantage to using an embedded version of Windows is that users recognize the familiar interface.

Mobile devices such as smartphones and tablets run embedded **mobile operating systems**. These are more full-featured than the versions on devices such as GPS and cable boxes. Mobile versions of Windows can be found on many smartphones. The iPhone, iPad, and iPod touch run **iOS**, a scaled-down version of macOS that uses direct manipulation and multi-gesture touch such as swipe, tap, and pinch to control it. **Android** is an embedded version of Linux that runs on many phones and tablets. These small operating systems have familiar interfaces and features, including touch-screen support, email, and web browsers. As people have become more dependent upon mobile devices, these mobile OSs have become more full-featured and easier to use. The newer versions of desktop operating systems have even begun to look more like their mobile cousins.

FIGURE 5.14 A GPS unit runs an embedded OS.

The most popular mobile operating systems are illustrated in Figure 5.15. The market changes quite rapidly as new technologies are released. As technology becomes more mobile, smaller, faster, and less tethered to the desk, alternative operating systems become an important way to interface with your files and applications. Developers know this and strive to create the best interfaces—ones you can learn to use easily and quickly come to depend upon.

FIGURE 5.15 Smartphone Operating Systems

OS Version	Features	
Apple iOS	Proprietary; found only on Apple devices such as iPad, iPod touch, Apple TV, and iPhones	 Duncan Selby/Alamy Stock Photo
Google Android	Linux kernel, found on devices from many companies including this Samsung Galaxy S7	 Pawan Kumar/Alamy Stock Photo
Microsoft Windows	Windows mobile version, found on devices from many companies including this Nokia Lumia 900	 StancaSanda/Alamy Stock Photo

CAREER SPOTLIGHT

JOBS

HELPDESK An entry-level IT job that requires good OS skills is a computer support specialist working at a helpdesk. Helpdesk specialists are the folks you speak with when you call, chat, or email for tech support. Computer support specialists assist people with computer problems— both hardware and software related. As you can imagine, a good foundation in operating systems is a must. Helpdesk technicians typically have an associate's degree or certifications such as CompTIA A+. According to the U.S. Bureau of Labor Statistics, by 2024, the demand for helpdesk jobs will increase by 12 percent.

Andy Dean/Fotolia

Running Project

What's the mobile OS on your favorite handheld device? What are some of the features that you like about it? Are there any features that are missing? What features do you use the most? Did you select your device because of the OS?

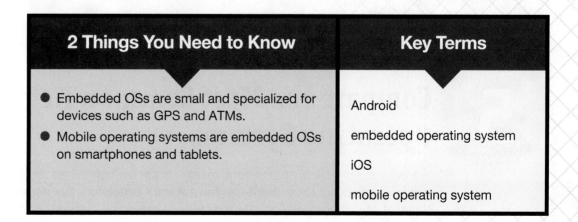

2 Things You Need to Know

- Embedded OSs are small and specialized for devices such as GPS and ATMs.
- Mobile operating systems are embedded OSs on smartphones and tablets.

Key Terms

Android

embedded operating system

iOS

mobile operating system

Massimo_g/Fotolia

The NOS Knows

Compare the Most Common Network Operating Systems

In a business or school environment, a network **server** centralizes resources, storage, and security in a **client–server network**, a network that has at least one server at its center. Users log in to the network instead of their local computers and are granted access to resources based on that login. Servers run a specialized operating system called a network operating system.

SIMULATION

System Software

What is an NOS?

A **network operating system (NOS)** is a multiuser operating system that controls the software and hardware running on a network. The NOS allows multiple computers—**clients**—to communicate with the server and each other to share resources, run applications, and send messages. The NOS provides services such as file and print services, communication services, Internet and email services, and backup and database services to the client computers. Table 5.1 details the most common network operating systems.

TABLE 5.1 Comparing Modern Network Operating Systems

Network (NOS)	Current Version	Comments
Windows Server: First released as Windows NT in 1993	Windows Server 2016	Scalable; found on many corporate networks; available in versions from Small Business edition to Enterprise and Datacenter editions.
Linux: Linux kernel is part of many different distros	Some of the most popular server versions used in business are Red Hat Enterprise Linux and Novell SUSE.	It's impossible to know how many Linux servers are currently installed because many versions can be downloaded and installed for free and without registration.
Unix: The oldest NOS	Unix itself is not an OS but a set of standards that are used to create a Unix OS.	Found on servers from HP, IBM, and Sun.
Apache Web Server	Apache Web Server is one of the most widely used NOS found on web servers.	Apache can run on Unix, Linux, or Windows servers.
Novell	Novell Open Enterprise Server 2015	Novell was a leader in business servers throughout the 1980s and 1990s with its Netware products but has moved to open source products.

Your school network is most likely a client–server network. When you log in to the network, you're given access to certain resources, such as printers and file storage. Figure 5.16 shows the Windows login screen from a Windows 10 computer for the VIZTECH network. When the user name and password are entered correctly, the user is granted access to network resources on the VIZTECH network.

Courtesy of Microsoft Corporation Inc.

FIGURE 5.16 Windows Login Screen for the VIZTECH Client–Server Network

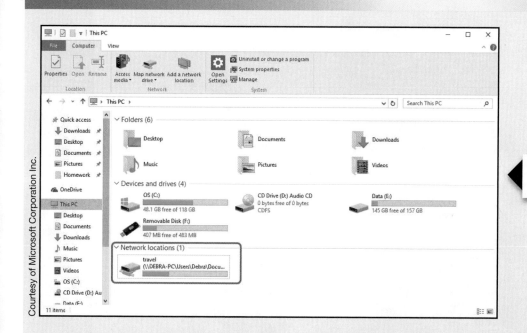

Courtesy of Microsoft Corporation Inc.

FIGURE 5.17 This Windows client has access to a drive on another computer in the network.

Centralized resources and security make a network operating system indispensable in a business setting. When a client logs in to a network, the appropriate resources appear in the client's environment. In Figure 5.17, you can see a network drive that appears in the File Explorer window of a Windows client.

At home, the network you set up is a **peer-to-peer network (P2P)** that doesn't require an NOS. Although your personal operating system has networking features, the files and services that are shared between your devices aren't centralized. An NOS provides important security and resource management in a business environment. Without an NOS, businesses would have to rely on P2P networks, which are not practical for more than a few computers.

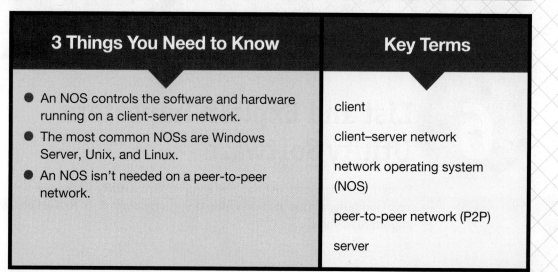

Running Project

The one area of NOS usage that can be easily monitored is activity on web servers. These are the servers that serve up web pages when you go to a URL, such as **amazon.com**. Netcraft does a monthly survey of web servers. Go to **news.netcraft.com/archives/category/web-server-survey/** and look at the most recent month. What are the three most popular web servers for this month? How much has the list changed in the past month? Are there any servers not mentioned in this chapter?

3 Things You Need to Know

- An NOS controls the software and hardware running on a client-server network.
- The most common NOSs are Windows Server, Unix, and Linux.
- An NOS isn't needed on a peer-to-peer network.

Key Terms

client

client–server network

network operating system (NOS)

peer-to-peer network (P2P)

server

Utilities You Should Use

List and Explain Important Utility Software

System software isn't just the operating system. **Utility software** helps you maintain your computer and is also considered system software. In this article, we look at some important utilities.

Using Disk
Utility Softw

Why Use Disk Utilities?

It's important to keep your disks healthy to keep your system running efficiently and to protect the files stored on them. **Formatting** a disk prepares it to store files by dividing it into tracks and sectors and setting up the file system. When a hard disk is first formatted, a set of concentric circles called tracks are created. The disk is then divided up like a pie into sectors (Figure 5.18). The files you save to your disk are stored in **clusters**, which consist of one or more sectors. This physical, low-level formatting occurs when the disk is manufactured. Think of this like a library full of empty bookshelves. The second part of formatting a disk is called high-level formatting. High-level formatting sets up the **file system** of the disk. You can think of it like a library catalog. When you save files to your disk, the file system keeps track of what you saved and where you saved it. The file system used on hard disks in Windows is the NTFS file system. External disks or those from older versions of Windows may be formatted with the FAT file system. The older Mac OS X file system is HFS+, and the macOS file system is called Apple File System—APFS, which is designed to work optimally with SSD drives.

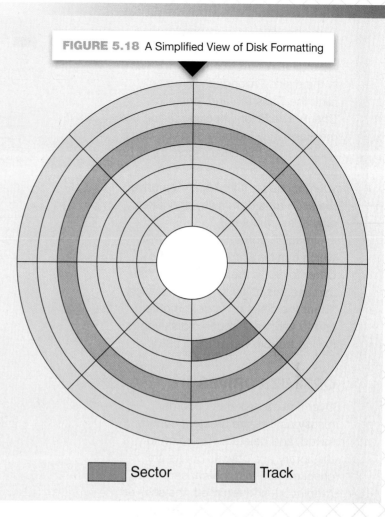

FIGURE 5.18 A Simplified View of Disk Formatting

▢ Sector   ▢ Track

Utilities for Disk Health

Windows includes several disk utilities to help you maintain your disks: Check Disk, Optimize Drives, and Disk Cleanup. To open these tools, open the File Explorer, This PC window, and then right-click the disk you want to work with. Click *Properties* to open the Properties dialog box for the disk. Some of these utilities can also be accessed through the Drive Tools tab on the ribbon.

Romolo Tavani/Fotolia

DISK CHECKING

Disk-checking utilities monitor the health of the file system on a disk. To check a disk for errors in Windows, in the disk's Properties dialog box, click the *Tools* tab and then click *Check*. The Error Checking dialog box message may indicate that you don't need to scan this drive (Figure 5.19), but it allows you to run the scan anyway if you choose to. If you scan the drive, the scan runs right away and takes only a few minutes.

macOS comes with Disk Utility, which can be accessed from the *Other* folder in the Launchpad. You can use this utility to get information about the disks on your computer and to verify and repair a disk you're having trouble with (Figure 5.20).

OPTIMIZE DRIVES

Over time, a disk can become messy as files are created, edited, saved, and deleted. Returning to the library analogy, as books are checked out, lost, purchased, misplaced, and returned, the shelves can become disorganized and require someone to periodically go through and clean them up. In addition to being unorganized, files that are fragmented are broken into small pieces that are stored in nonadjacent or noncontiguous clusters on the disk. This is referred to as **file fragmentation**. A disk **defragmenter** is a utility that rearranges the fragmented files on your disk to improve efficiency. You should not manually run a defragmenter on a solid-state disk (SSD) as it will shorten the life of the disk, and because the files are not stored on SSDs in the same way they are on mechanical disks, defragmenting isn't necessary.

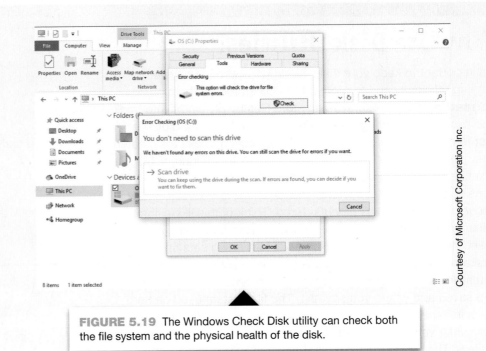

Courtesy of Microsoft Corporation Inc.

FIGURE 5.19 The Windows Check Disk utility can check both the file system and the physical health of the disk.

Screen shot(s) reprinted with permission from Apple Inc.

FIGURE 5.20 The macOS Disk Utility

The Windows Optimize Drives utility optimizes and defragments hard drives automatically on a weekly basis, and optimizes SSD drives monthly. You can also run it manually if you need to. Microsoft recommends that you defragment a drive that's more than 10 percent fragmented. Figure 5.21 shows the Optimize Drives utility. Like the Disk Check utility, the Optimize Drives utility can be accessed from the Tools tab of the disk's Properties dialog box.

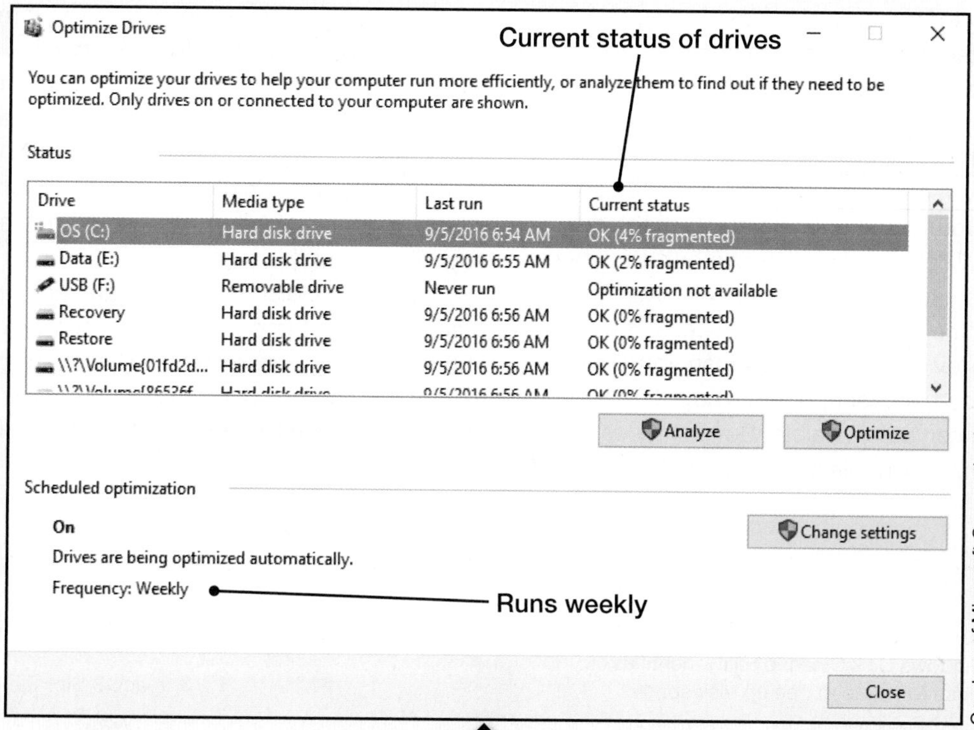

Courtesy of Microsoft Corporation Inc.

FIGURE 5.21 The Windows Optimize Drives utility is scheduled to run automatically.

FIND OUT MORE

Is defragmenting a hard disk really necessary? Some people say no. Use the Internet to research the controversy. Do you agree with the contention? Why or why not? What webpages did you find supporting this argument? What credentials does the author have that make you trust the information you found? Make sure you're using recent information.

The (OS X) HFS+ and (macOS) APFS file systems have safeguards against fragmentation, and Macs rarely need to be defragmented. Macs do not include a defragmenter utility, although there are third-party tools you can use.

DISK CLEANUP

Back to the library—over time, books become damaged, old, outdated, duplicated, and obsolete. A librarian will go through the stacks of books and remove those books. A disk cleanup utility looks for files that can be safely deleted to free up disk space so you have more space to store your files and to help keep your system running efficiently. The Windows Disk Cleanup utility is found on the General tab of the disk's Properties dialog box. Click the *Disk Cleanup* button to begin. Figure 5.22 shows the result of running the Windows Disk Cleanup utility. During the first part of the process, the disk is analyzed and you can review the results. When you click on any of the file types listed, a description displays to help you decide which files you can safely delete. Several types of files are checked by default, and in this example, the total amount

of disk space that would be gained is a meager 95.2 MB. Choosing to delete the Recycle bin files would free up another 7.22 MB of space. To proceed with the cleanup, click OK.

Macs have daily, weekly, and monthly maintenance routines that run automatically, so you normally don't need to do any other disk cleanup of your own. You should regularly delete unneeded files and empty the Trash to keep your disk clutter free. To view and manage the files stored on your Mac, from the Apple menu, open About This Mac. On the storage tab, click Manage. The Storage Management utility (Figure 5.23) displays the types of files on your system and several ways to optimize storage on your device. Since newer Mac notebooks include small SSD drives, macOS optimizes storage by automatically moving infrequently used files to the cloud. You can customize these settings and manually optimize your files using this tool.

The utilities discussed here are included with Windows and Mac; however, there are also third-party tools available. The important thing is to remember to use them. Like changing the oil in your car and checking the tire pressure, regular maintenance of your computer will keep it running more efficiently and help it last longer.

FIGURE 5.22 The Windows Disk Cleanup utility identifies files that you might choose to delete to free up disk space.

FIGURE 5.23 macOS Storage Management

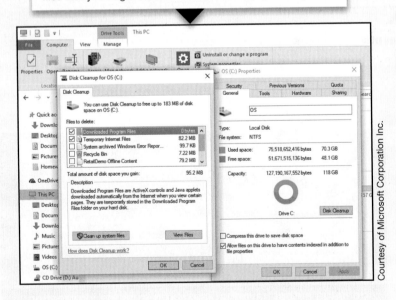

Courtesy of Microsoft Corporation Inc.

Screen shot(s) reprinted with permission from Apple Inc.

Security Software

Security software such as firewalls, antivirus software, and antispyware software is also considered utility software. **Firewall** software blocks unauthorized access to a computer. Both Windows and macOS include a software firewall, although you have to manually enable it on a Mac.

Malware is a computer program that's designed to be harmful or malicious, such as a virus, worm, or spyware. An **antivirus program** protects against viruses, Trojan horses, worms, and spyware. **Antispyware software** prevents adware and spyware infections. Windows includes Windows Defender to protect against viruses and spyware (Figure 5.24).

A security suite is a package of security software that includes a combination of features such as antivirus, firewall, and privacy protection. If you connect your computer to the outside world, it is important to protect it with good security software. Malicious attacks are common and difficult to avoid without using good security software and practicing smart computing.

Courtesy of Microsoft Corporation Inc.

FIGURE 5.24 Windows Defender scans your system for malware.

Running Project

Open the disk properties for your primary hard drive (C). What's the disk file system? What is the capacity of the drive, and how much disk space is used? If you are using a Windows computer, on the Tools tab, click *Optimize* to start the Optimize Drives utility. When was the disk last defragmented? What percentage of the disk is currently fragmented?

4 Things You Need to Know

- Utility software helps you maintain your computer.
- You format a disk to prepare it to hold data.
- Files that are broken up and stored in noncontiguous clusters are considered to be fragmented.
- NTFS is the file system used on Windows-formatted hard drives. HFS+ and APFS are the file systems used on Macs.

Key Terms

antispyware software

antivirus program

cluster

defragmenter

file fragmentation

file system

firewall

formatting

malware

utility software

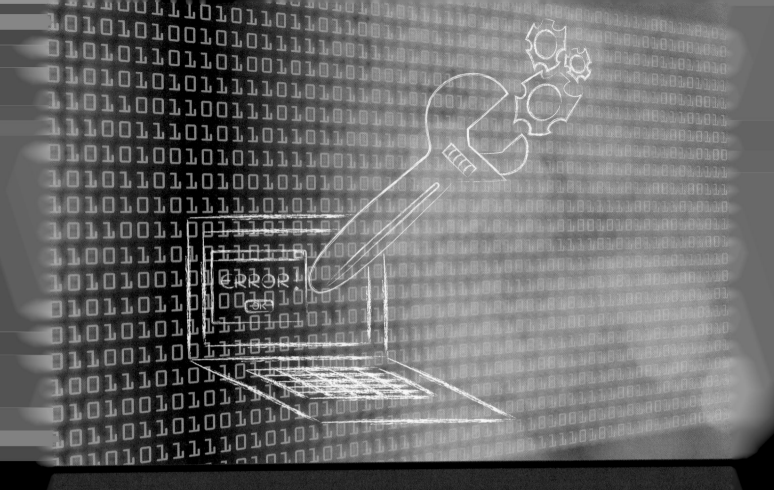

Troubleshooting and Maintenance

ctive

7

Troubleshoot Common Computer Problems

Developing a systematic, consistent approach to troubleshooting and system maintenance can prevent or quickly resolve many problems.

Basic Troubleshooting Methods

Complex problems may still require assistance from tech support, but by performing the first-level troubleshooting tasks first, you can resolve or rule out common problems before seeking help. Most computer users can perform basic troubleshooting by following these steps:

1. **Reboot the system:** This fixes many issues when a program or system is frozen or stuck. Reboot, or restart, the system to clear problems from memory and reload software.

2. **Check connections:** Even if connections appear sound, a loose cable or plug can cause problems. Unplug or disconnect suspicious cables and reconnect them. When possible, try a different cable, outlet, or port.

3. **Ask what has changed:** Has the system been updated recently? A new program installed or additional hardware connected? Rolling back these changes can often fix the problem. Windows includes built-in system protection that consists of options to restore or reset your system. By using **System Restore** you can return the system to a previous state saved as a restore point. This is commonly used if the installation of an update, a driver, or an application caused a problem. There are three options when you choose to reset: *Keep my files* removes your apps and settings, but keeps your personal files. *Remove everything* removes all of your personal files, apps, and settings. *Restore factory settings* removes your personal files, apps, and settings, and reinstalls the original version of Windows.

4. **Search online:** Most manufacturers and software companies provide online resources such as forums and knowledge bases where you can find help from other users and company experts.

5. **Run troubleshooters:** Windows includes a number of troubleshooters that you can run to detect and fix problems such as network connectivity or printing issues. Access these from the Troubleshooting Control Panel or Settings as shown in Figure 5.25.

6. **Check the Task Manager:** View the processes that are running on a Windows computer. This tool can help you troubleshoot system performance and stop a running process that is causing trouble. To access Task Manager, from the desktop, right-click the taskbar, and then click *Task Manager*. Along with other troubleshooting utilities, use this tool with caution.

On a Mac, from the Apple menu open the About this Mac window and click the Support tab for help (Figure 5.26).

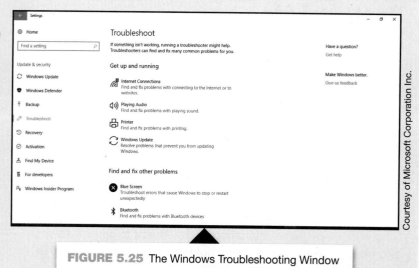

FIGURE 5.25 The Windows Troubleshooting Window

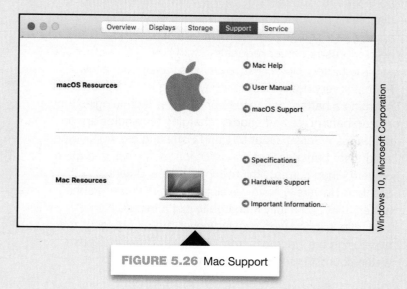

FIGURE 5.26 Mac Support

Saving Energy and Extending Battery Life

Notebook computers, tablets, and smartphones are typically used heavily by their owners, which can quickly deplete a battery's charge. Here are two simple things you can do to extend the battery life of your devices:

First, turn off features that you are not using, such as **location services**, which determines your location by using GPS or wireless networks (Figure 5.27). Location services are useful, even necessary, for some programs—such as mapping, but when not needed, can be turned off to save battery life. Many mobile apps regularly poll your location services to offer you appropriate information. For example, RetailMeNot and Key Ring will determine your location and alert you to current sales and offers in the area. If you are not interested in shopping, this is a needless drain on your system.

Second, put your mobile device in power saving mode, which will extend your battery life by reducing the frequency of power-hungry requests such as email and social network notifications. You can put your system in airplane mode to disable all network adapters. This allows you to use local apps, like reading a book on your device, without using any network resources or requests.

The battery life of mobile devices varies from a few hours for very heavy use, to a day or two for lighter use. Fully charging a battery can take hours. Newer technologies that extend battery life and shorten charging to minutes are on the horizon. Scientists at MIT and Samsung are working on solid-state batteries that are safer, longer lasting, and more powerful than current lithium-ion batteries. Scientists at Stanford University have developed an aluminum-graphite battery that could fully recharge in just a minute. Other innovations in the works include over-the-air charging and even using the electricity from your skin. Other ideas use water, sound, or solar charging methods.

Radeboj11/Fotolia

Courtesy of Microsoft Corporation Inc.

FIGURE 5.27 Location Settings on a Windows 10 Notebook

Configuring Hardware

A common cause of hardware problems is an out-of-date or missing device driver. To update a driver on your system, open the **Device Manager**—this tool enables you to view and configure the settings of your system devices. Double-click a device in the list to open the device Properties dialog box. As a standard user, you can view the settings, but you must be an administrator to make changes. Click the Drivers tab, as shown in Figure 5.28, to view the current installed driver and options to update, roll back, disable, or uninstall the current driver.

Occasionally, a device driver causes system problems and must be uninstalled. If the system can boot normally, use the Device Manager to uninstall, or roll back, the driver. If the system cannot boot normally, Windows can be booted into **Safe Mode**—a special diagnostic mode that starts Windows without most device drivers for troubleshooting the system.

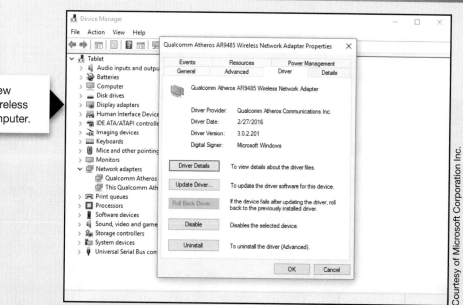

FIGURE 5.28 View the driver for the wireless adapter on this computer.

Courtesy of Microsoft Corporation Inc.

Running Project

Open the Device Manager on a Windows computer. Expand several sections and review the devices installed on your system. Open the Network adapters section. How many of these devices do you have? Double-click the first device in the list to open the Properties dialog box. Click the Driver tab. Who is the publisher of the driver? What is the driver date? Is the driver digitally signed? Use the Internet to find out why it is important to have digitally signed drivers. Close all windows without making any changes.

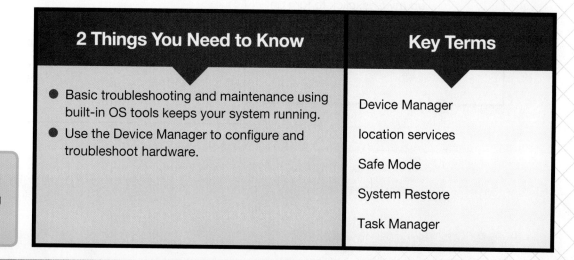
Viz Check—In MyLab IT, take a quick quiz covering Objectives 4–7.

Back Up Important Files

HOW TO VIDEO

Backing up your important files allows you to recover them if something happens to your system. You can use a third-party tool or the built-in tools in your operating system to do this. In this activity, you will use File History or Time Machine to back up your files. You will need a flash drive or access to another external or network drive to complete this activity. (Note: Security settings may prevent you from performing these steps in the lab.) If necessary, download student data files from **pearsonhighered.com/viztech**.

From your student data files, open the *vt_ch05_howto2_answersheet* file and save the file as **lastname_firstname_ch05_howto2_answersheet**.

1 Insert your flash drive into your system. Click the *Start* button and click *Settings*. Click *Update & security*. In the left navigation pane, click *Backup*. If necessary, under *Automatically back up my files*, click to turn on File History. If necessary, click *Add a drive* and navigate to your flash drive.

Settings

Select a drive

USB (F:)
235 MB free of 483 MB

Back up using File History

Back up your files to another drive and restore them if the originals are lost, damaged, or deleted.

+ Add a drive

More options

Looking for an older backup?

If you created a backup using the Windows 7 Backup and Restore tool, it'll still work in Windows 10.

Go to Backup and Restore (Windows 7)

Courtesy of Microsoft Corporation Inc.

2 Click *More options*. What folders are listed under *Back up these folders*? Paste a screenshot of this window in your answer sheet.

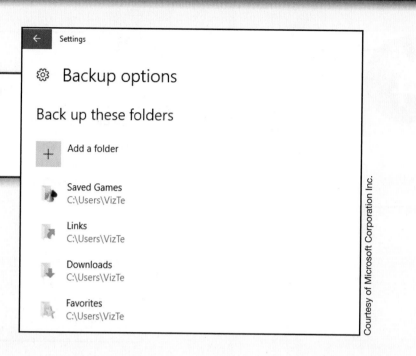

Courtesy of Microsoft Corporation Inc.

3 Are there any items listed under *Exclude folders*? Click *Add a folder*. In the Select Folder window, click *Videos*, and then click *Choose this folder*. This excludes the Video library from your backup. Paste a screenshot of this window in your answer sheet. Click *Cancel*.

Courtesy of Microsoft Corporation Inc.

4

How often are files saved? How long are they kept? Change the *Back up my files setting* to *Every 10 minutes* and the *Keep my backups* to *Until space is needed*. Take a screenshot of this window and paste into your answer sheet. Click *Cancel*.

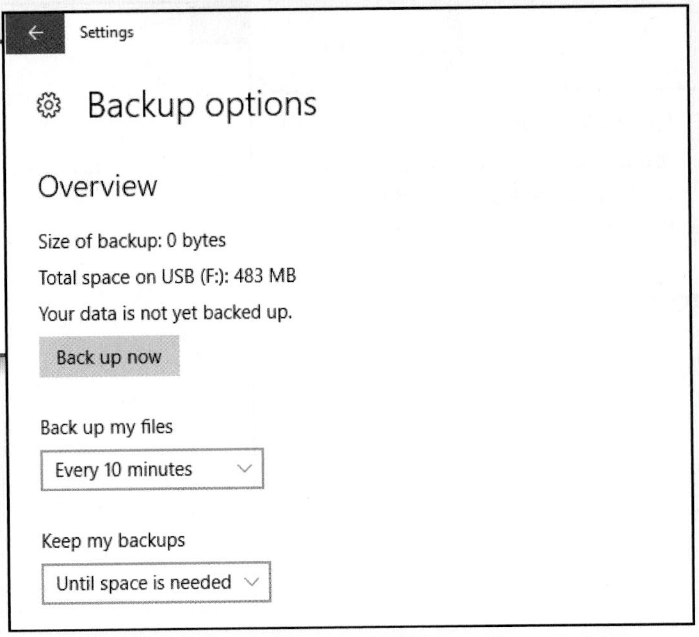

← Settings

⚙ Backup options

Overview

Size of backup: 0 bytes

Total space on USB (F:): 483 MB

Your data is not yet backed up.

Back up now

Back up my files

Every 10 minutes ⌄

Keep my backups

Until space is needed ⌄

Courtesy of Microsoft Corporation Inc.

5

If File History was off when you began this exercise, click to turn it off. Remember to safely remove your flash drive from the system. Save your answer sheet and submit as directed.

If you are using a Mac: Time Machine is the backup utility in macOS. For this activity, you will need a flash drive. Be careful when performing this exercise—do not erase your disk when prompted unless it can be safely erased. From your student data files, open the *vt_ch05_howto2_answersheet_mac* file and save the file as **lastname_firstname_ch05_howto2_answersheet_mac**.

1. Insert your flash drive into your system. Open System Preferences and click *Time Machine.* In the Time Machine window, what disk is selected as your Backup Disk? Is Time Machine on? If it is off, click *ON.* If you are asked to erase your disk, click Cancel. Paste a screenshot of this window in your answer sheet.

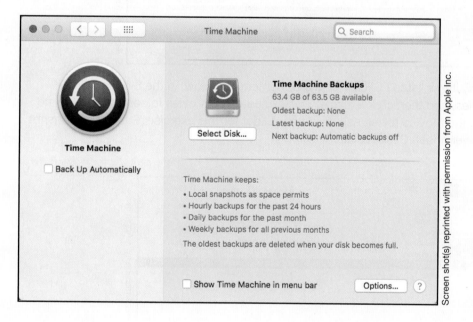

2. Click *Select Backup Disk*. What options are listed on your system? Paste a screenshot of this window in your answer sheet. Click *Cancel*.

Screen shot(s) reprinted with permission from Apple Inc.

3. Click *Options*. Are there any items listed? Click **+**. In the Documents window, in the Sidebar, click your user name, click *Movies*, and then click *Exclude*. This excludes the Movies folder from your Time Machine. If you do not see the Movies folder, select another folder for this exercise. Paste a screenshot of this window in your answer sheet. Click *Cancel*.

Screen shot(s) reprinted with permission from Apple Inc.

4. How frequently does Time Machine back up your files? How long does it keep the backup copies? If Time Machine was off when you began this exercise, click *OFF* to restore that setting. If necessary, remove your flash drive from the system. Save your answer sheet and submit as directed.

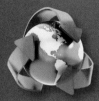

GREEN COMPUTING
Power Management

Did you know that you could cut the energy used by your computer in half, saving between $25 and $75 a year in energy costs, by using its power management features? That would save more than lowering your home thermostat by 2 degrees or replacing six regular light bulbs with compact fluorescents (CFLs). Putting your computer into a low-power mode can save on home cooling costs and even prolong the life of your notebook battery.

Energy Star power management features are standard in both Windows and macOS operating systems. Activating these settings is easy and saves both money and resources. The EPA recommends setting computers to sleep or hibernate after 30 to 60 minutes of inactivity. To save even more, set monitors to sleep after 5 to 20 minutes of inactivity. And don't use screensavers—they actually increase energy use.

Courtesy of Microsoft Corporation Inc.

Screen shot(s) reprinted with permission from Apple Inc.

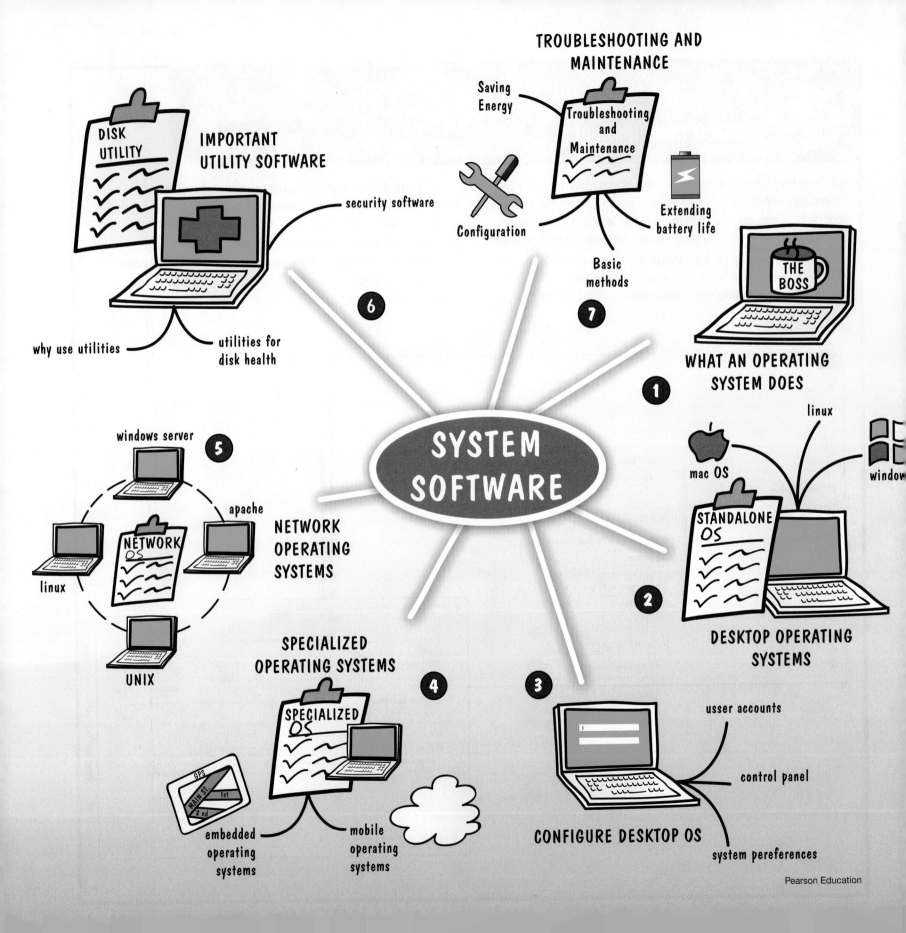

TROUBLESHOOTING AND MAINTENANCE

IMPORTANT UTILITY SOFTWARE

DISK UTILITY

security software

Saving Energy

Troubleshooting and Maintenance

Extending battery life

Configuration

Basic methods

why use utilities

utilities for disk health

7

6

THE BOSS

WHAT AN OPERATING SYSTEM DOES

1

SYSTEM SOFTWARE

linux

mac OS

window

STANDALONE OS

2

DESKTOP OPERATING SYSTEMS

windows server

5

apache

NETWORK OS

NETWORK OPERATING SYSTEMS

linux

UNIX

SPECIALIZED OPERATING SYSTEMS

4

3

SPECIALIZED OS

GPS
MAIN ST.
1st
2 nd

embedded operating systems

mobile operating systems

CONFIGURE DESKTOP OS

usser accounts

control panel

system pereferences

Pearson Education

Objectives Recap

1. Explain What an Operating System Does
2. Compare Desktop Operating Systems
3. Configure a Desktop Operating System
4. Compare Specialized Operating Systems
5. Compare the Most Common Network Operating Systems
6. List and Explain Important Utility Software
7. Troubleshoot Common Computer Problems

Key Terms

Android **247**
antispyware software **259**
antivirus program **259**
application programming
   interface (API) **231**
beta version **241**
client **251**
client–server network **250**
cluster **255**
Control Panel **243**
control panel applet **243**
defragmenter **256**
device driver **230**
Device Manager **263**
embedded operating
   system **247**
file fragmentation **256**
file system **255**
firewall **259**
formatting **255**
graphical user interface
   (GUI) **229**
iOS **247**
Linux **240**

location services **262**
macOS **239**
malware **259**
Microsoft Windows **237**
mobile operating system **247**
multitasking **230**
network operating system
   (NOS) **251**
open source **240**
operating system (OS) **228**
OS X **239**
peer-to-peer (P2P) network **253**
Plug and Play (PnP) **230**
Safe Mode **263**
server **250**
Settings window **243**
System Preferences **244**
System Restore **261**
system software **228**
Task Manager **261**
Unix **240**
user account **244**
user interface **229**
utility software **254**

Summary

1. **Explain What an Operating System Does**

   The operating system (OS) is the most important type of system software because it provides the user with the interface to communicate with the hardware and other software on the computer. The OS also manages the allocation of memory and processing resources to both hardware and software, manages and controls hardware using Plug and Play and device drivers, and provides services to applications through the use of an application programming interface (API).

2. **Compare Desktop Operating Systems**

   The three most common desktop operating systems are Microsoft Windows, macOS, and Linux. Windows has been around since 1985 and is installed on over 90 percent of personal computers. The Mac OS has been around since the first Mac computer was released in 1984—the version released in 2017 is called macOS High Sierra. Linux was first released in 1991 and is the OS kernel for hundreds of different distributions (distros) that come bundled with utilities and applications.

3. **Configure a Desktop Operating System**

   Windows settings can be configured through the Settings window and Control Panel. macOS settings are configured through System Preferences. A user account grants users access and rights to a system and keeps each user's files private.

4. **Compare Specialized Operating Systems**

   Embedded operating systems run on devices such as ATMs, GPS devices, video game consoles, ultrasound machines, and communication and entertainment systems. Because they have specialized and limited functions, these operating systems can be very small and run on simpler hardware.

   A mobile operating system such as Windows Phone, iOS, or Android runs on devices such as smartphones and tablets and is more full-featured than other embedded OSs.

5. **Compare the Most Common Network Operating Systems**

   A network operating system (NOS) is a multiuser operating system that controls the software and hardware running on a network. It allows multiple client computers to communicate with the server and each other as well as to share resources, run applications, and send messages. An NOS centralizes resources and security and provides services such as file and print services, communication services, Internet and email services, and backup and database services. Most servers run some version of Windows server, Linux, or Unix. Apache Web Server is the most widely used NOS found on web servers.

Summary continues on the next page

Summary *continued*

6. List and Explain Important Utility Software

Windows includes several disk utilities to help you maintain your disks: Check Disk, Optimize Drives, and Disk Cleanup. Disk-checking utilities monitor the health of the file system on a disk. macOS includes Disk Utility to verify and repair disk problems. A defragmenter is a utility that rearranges fragmented files on your disk to improve efficiency. Security software such as firewalls, antivirus software, and antispyware software is also considered utility software.

7. Troubleshoot Common Computer Problems

You should develop basic troubleshooting and maintenance skills to keep your system running. Windows has built-in troubleshooting and other tools—such as Device Manager and Task Manager—to help you.

Multiple Choice

Answer the multiple-choice questions below for more practice with key terms and concepts from this chapter.

1. Which is a function of an operating system?
   a. Browse the Internet
   b. Edit images
   c. Protect against malware
   d. Manage hardware

2. What software enables an OS to communicate with hardware?
   a. Application programming interface
   b. Device driver
   c. Graphical user interface
   d. Plug and Play

3. _____ enables you to easily add new hardware to a computer system.
   a. Graphical user interface
   b. Multitasking
   c. NOS
   d. Plug and Play

4. Which operating system is a multiuser OS developed in the 1970s, primarily used on servers and some specialized workstations?
   a. Microsoft Windows
   b. macOS
   c. Linux
   d. Unix

5. Which Windows feature allows you to change, configure, monitor, or troubleshoot most system settings, hardware, and software?
   a. Application programming interface (API)
   b. Control Panel
   c. Settings charm
   d. System Preferences

6. Which operating system is a mobile Linux operating system?
   a. Android
   b. BlackBerry OS
   c. iOS
   d. Windows Phone

7. Which is a popular NOS found on web servers?
   a. Apache
   b. Novell Linux
   c. Red Hat
   d. Windows 10

8. _____ keeps track of files that are saved and where they're stored on the disk.
   a. Defragmenting
   b. Disk cleanup
   c. File system
   d. Formatting

9. Which Windows utility should you use to reorganize the files on your disk to improve efficiency?
   a. Disk Checker
   b. Disk Cleanup
   c. Disk Properties
   d. Optimize Drives

10. Which Windows utility should you use to view processing running on your system?
    a. Device Manager
    b. File History
    c. Task Manager
    d. System Preferences

True or False

Answer the following questions with *T* for true or *F* for false for more practice with key terms and concepts from this chapter.

_____ 1. You can use a computer without an operating system installed.

_____ 2. The user interacts with the operating system through the use of a GUI.

_____ 3. The OS communicates with software applications via an application programming interface (API).

_____ 4. A mobile operating system that runs on Apple mobile devices is iOS.

_____ 5. You should use a guest account for everyday computing.

_____ 6. An NOS centralizes resources and security and provides services such as file and print services to servers.

_____ 7. The file system used on hard disks in Windows is the NTFS file system.

_____ 8. Malware is a computer program that's designed to prevent viruses.

_____ 9. Disk-checking utilities monitor the health of the file system on a disk.

_____ 10. Location services use only GPS to determine your device location.

Fill in the Blank

Fill in the blanks with key terms from this chapter.

1. A(n) _____ acts as a translator, enhancing the capabilities of the operating system by enabling it to communicate with hardware.

2. _____ is the ability to do more than one task at a time.

3. Sierra is a version of _____.

4. Chrome and Fedora are popular distros of _____.

5. A(n) _____ is security software that protects against viruses, Trojan horses, worms, and spyware.

6. The programs that make up the _____ are sometimes called applets.

7. The OS in a smartphone or tablet is referred to as a(n) _____.

8. A(n) _____ is a network in which each computer is considered equal.

9. A(n) _____ is one or more sectors on a disk where data is stored.

10. The _____ enables you to view and configure the settings of your system devices.

Running Project...

...The Finish Line

Use your answers from the previous sections of the running project. Assume that you just bought a new computer with no software on it. What operating system and version would you install? Select one utility that you consider indispensable. Which program did you pick and why?

Write a report describing your selections and responding to the questions raised. Save your file as **lastname_firstname_ch05_project** and submit it to your instructor as directed.

Do It Yourself 1

Utility software is important to protect and maintain your computer. In this activity, you'll examine your computer to determine what type of utility software is installed on it and if it's properly protected. From your student data files, open the file *vt_ch05_DIY1_answersheet* and save the file as **lastname_firstname_ch05_DIY1_answersheet**.

Open the Control Panel, click *System and Security,* and then click *Security and Maintenance* (Windows 8, click *Action Center).* If necessary, click the arrow to open the Security section. What is your status for each category? Are there any important notices? What software is reported for virus protection? Take a screenshot of the Security section and paste it into your answer sheet.

If necessary, click the arrow to open the Maintenance section. What is your status for each category? Are there any important notices? Take a screenshot of the Maintenance section and paste it into your answer sheet. Type your answers in your answer sheet, save your file, and submit your work as directed by your instructor.

If you are using a Mac:

From the Launchpad, open the *Other* folder. Take a screenshot of the Other folder and paste it into your answer sheet. Explore the Activity Monitor, AirPort Utility, and System Information utilities. Use Help to look up each of these utilities. What is the purpose of each of these? Type your answers in your answer sheet, save your file, and submit your work as directed by your instructor.

Do It Yourself 2

In this exercise, you'll perform a disk check on your flash drive. From your student data files, open the file *vt_ch05_DIY2_answersheet* and save the file as **lastname_firstname_ch05_DIY2_answersheet**.

1. Insert your flash drive into the computer. If necessary, wait until Windows finishes installing drivers. Close any windows that open automatically. Open File Explorer. Right-click on your flash drive, and click *Properties*. What file system is on the disk? What is the capacity, and how much free space is on the disk? Take a screenshot of the Properties dialog box, and paste it into your answer sheet.

2. Click the *Tools* tab and click *Check*. When the scan is finished, take a screenshot of the results and paste it into your answer sheet. Type your answers in your answer sheet, save the file, and submit your work as directed by your instructor.

If you are using a Mac:

1. Insert the flash drive into the computer. Open the Disk Utility from Launchpad, Other folder. Select the flash drive from the left pane of the Disk Utility. What file system is on the disk? What's the capacity, and how much free space is on the disk? Take a screenshot and paste it into your answer sheet.

2. If necessary, click the *First Aid* tab and click *Verify Disk*. Make sure *Show details* is checked. When the scan is finished, take a screenshot of the results and paste it into your answer sheet. Type your answers in your answer sheet, save the file, and submit your work as directed by your instructor.

File Management

Utility software such as disk defragmenters and cleanup utilities help you keep your computer running efficiently. In this activity, you'll use the Windows Disk Cleanup utility to examine some of the files on your computer. From your student data files, open the file *vt_ch05_FM_answersheet* and save the file as **lastname_firstname_ch05_FM_answersheet**.

1. Open File Explorer, and if necessary, click *This PC*. What items are listed under Devices and drives? Right-click the *C:* drive, and click *Properties*. What is the capacity of the disk? How much free space is currently available?

2. Click the *Disk Cleanup* button. Allow the Disk Cleanup utility to analyze your system. When it's finished, take a screenshot of this dialog box and paste it into your answer sheet. Note: This process may take several minutes to complete.

3. Click on each of the categories of files listed, and read the descriptions in the bottom of the dialog box. What types of files are included in Downloaded Program Files and Temporary Internet Files? What are Temporary Files, and is it safe to delete them? What other categories of files are listed? Which ones have check marks next to them? How much space could you free up if you cleaned up all the files found? Type your answers in your answer sheet, including the screenshot from step 2. Save your file and submit it as directed by your instructor.

If you are using a Mac:

From the Apple menu, open *About This Mac*. Click the *Storage* tab and then click *Manage*. Under Recommendations, click each category and review the items and suggestions for optimizing storage. How does macOS optimize photos? Select the largest category on your system and take a screenshot of the window. Paste the screenshot into your answer sheet, type up your answers, save your file, and submit it as directed by your instructor.

Critical Thinking

Your school is still running Windows 8.1 in the computer lab. It's considering upgrading to Windows 10. As a user of the computer lab, you've been asked to give some input into the decision process. From your student data files, open the file *vt_ch05_CT_answersheet* and save the file as **lastname_firstname_ch05_CT_answersheet**.

Use the Internet to research the improvements in Windows 10 over Windows 8.1. What are the improvements you feel are the most important? Do they require any special hardware or software to be installed? Do you recommend the school upgrade the computer lab? Give two reasons supporting your recommendation. Type up your answers, save the file, and submit your assignment as directed by your instructor.

Ethical Dilemma

Miriam works at a small company and was just passed over for a promotion, which was given to a new employee, Bill, because he has a certification. Bill let it slip that he easily passed the test because he paid $50 for a study guide that had all the test answers in it. From your student data files, open the file *vt_ch05_ethics_answersheet* and save the file as **lastname_firstname_ch05_ethics_answersheet**.

Miriam is frustrated. She has experience with the company, but Bill got the job because he has the certification. What should she do? Should she report Bill to her employer? To the certification testing center? Borrow the questions and take the exam herself? What would you do? Because this has been a common issue in the past, the certification tests have become stricter and more difficult to cheat on, but it still happens. Use the Internet to find out the penalty for cheating on one of the current IT industry exams. Type your answers in your answer sheet, save the file, and submit it as directed by your instructor.

On the Web

In this activity, you'll compare the hardware requirements for different versions of Windows. From your student data files, open the file *vt_ch05_web_answersheet* and save the file as **lastname_firstname_ch05_web_answersheet**.

Use the Internet to research the hardware requirements for each of the following versions of Windows:

- Windows XP
- Windows Vista
- Windows 7
- Windows 8.1
- Windows 10

Choose the original release and the Home (or Home Premium) version, and complete the table below. What websites did you use to locate this information? Save the file and submit your work as directed by your instructor.

Windows Version	Year Released	Minimum Processor	Minimum Memory	Minimum Free Disk Space	Optical Disc Type	Other Requirements
Windows XP						
Windows Vista						
Windows 7						
Windows 8						
Windows 10						

Collaboration

Instructors: Divide the class into groups of three to five members, and assign each group one topic for this project. The topics include Windows 10, macOS High Sierra, and Fedora Linux. For larger classes, assign multiple groups the same operating system.

The Project: As a team, prepare a commercial that includes an explanation of your assigned operating system and special features that aren't included in this book. Use at least three references. Use Google Drive or Microsoft Office to prepare your presentation and provide documentation that all team members have contributed to the project.

Outcome: Prepare a commercial on your assigned topic. The presentation may be no longer than 2 minutes. You may record it or perform it live for your class. On the first page of your written outline, be sure to include the name of your commercial and a list of all team members. Turn in a final version of your outline and script named **teamname_ch05_collab** and submit your project to your instructor as directed.

Application Project

Office 2016 Application Projects
PowerPoint 2016: Should You Upgrade Your OS?

Project Description: In this project, you will create a presentation about upgrading your operating system. In creating this presentation, you will apply design, font, and color themes. You will also change font colors, bullet symbols, and slide layout. If necessary, download student data files from **pearsonhighered.com/viztech**.

PowerPoint 2016, Microsoft Corporation

Step	Instructions
1	Start PowerPoint. From your student data files, open the PowerPoint file *vt_ch05_ppt* Save the presentation as **lastname_firstname_ch05_ppt**
2	Apply the Ion theme, purple variant, to the presentation.
3	On Slide 1, using your name, type **Firstname Lastname** in the subtitle placeholder.
4	On Slide 2, type **Will it Run?** in the title placeholder. On Slide 2, change the bullet style to Arrow Bullets, and change the line spacing of the bullets to double.
5	On Slide 3, change the title to **Check Hardware and Software**
6	On Slide 3, insert the image *vt_ch05_image1* in the content placeholder. Apply the Reflected Perspective Right picture style to the image and change the picture height to 4".
7	Change the layout of Slide 4 to Two Content.
8	On Slide 4, in the left pane, type the following four list items. **Pros**, **Latest features**, **Modern interface**, **Security**
9	On Slide 4, in the right pane, type the following four list items. **Cons**, **Hardware requirements**, **Software compatibility**, **Learning curve**
10	On Slide 4, select the last three items in each list, and use the Increase List level button to indent them.
11	Insert a new Title and Content slide after Slide 4.
12	On Slide 5, in the title placeholder, type **For More Information** In the content placeholder, type **Contact IT Services** and change the bullet to None.
13	Insert the page number and the footer **Firstname Lastname** on the notes and handouts pages for all slides in the presentation.
14	Apply the Cover slide transition to all slides, with a duration of 2.00. View the presentation in Slide Show view from beginning to end, and then return to Normal view.
15	Save the presentation and close PowerPoint. Submit the presentation as directed.

Application Project

Office 2016 Application Projects
Excel 2016: Worldwide Smartphone Sales

Project Description: Data is collected every year comparing worldwide shipments of computers and mobile devices. In this project, using the data for 2014, you will format cells and use functions and an absolute cell reference in a formula. You will also create and format a pie chart. If necessary, download student data files from **pearsonhighered.com/viztech**.

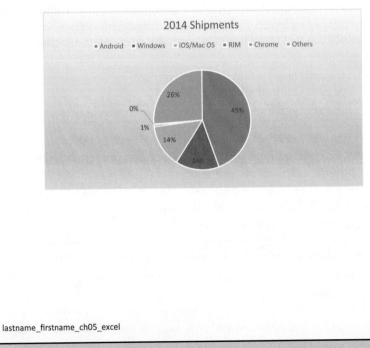

2014

Worldwide Device Shipments by Operating System		
(Thousands of Units)		
Operating System	2014	Market Share
Android	1,102,572	44.6%
Windows	359,855	14.5%
iOS/Mac OS	344,206	13.9%
RIM	15,416	0.6%
Chrome	4,793	0.2%
Others	647,572	26.2%
Total	2,474,414	

2014 Shipments

lastname_firstname_ch05_excel

Step	Instructions
1	Start Excel. From your student data files, open the Excel file *vt_ch05_excel*. Save the workbook as **lastname_firstname_ch05_excel**
2	Set the width of columns A, B, and C to **20**. Set the height of row 1 to **40**.
3	Merge and center the text in cell A1 over columns A:C. Apply the cell style Heading 1. Merge and center the text in A2 over columns A:C. Apply the cell style Heading 2.
4	Select the range A3:C3 and center and middle align the text in the selected range.
5	In cell A10, type **Total** In cell B10, use the SUM function to calculate the 2014 shipments.
6	In cell C4, create a formula using an absolute cell reference to calculate the Market Share of Android. Copy the formula in cell C4 down to C5:C9. Apply the Percent number format. Display 1 decimal place.
7	Select the range A10:C10 and apply the Total cell style.
8	Select the range A4:B9 and insert the Recommended pie chart. Move the chart so that its upper left corner aligns with the upper left corner of cell A13.
9	Change the layout of the chart to Layout 2. Change the chart title to **2014 Shipments**
10	Format the chart area with the default gradient fill.
11	Insert a header with the Sheet name in the center cell. Insert a footer with the file name in the left cell. Return to Normal View.
12	Change the orientation of Sheet 1 to Portrait. Center the worksheet horizontally and vertically on the page.
13	Rename Sheet 1 as **2014**
14	Ensure that the worksheets are correctly named and placed in the following order in the workbook: 2014, Source. Save the workbook and close Excel. Submit the workbook as directed.

Digital Devices and Multimedia

In This Chapter

VIZ INTRO

Digital devices, such as digital cameras, smartphones, and tablets, have become essential tools. **Multimedia**, which is the integration of text, graphics, video, animation, and sound, describes the type of content you view and create with these devices. In this chapter, we discuss digital devices and multimedia content and how we use them every day. After completing this chapter, you will be able to recognize different types of media and select and use various hardware and software to create and play multimedia files.

BrunoWeltmann/Fotolia

Objectives

1 Explain the Features of Digital Cameras

2 Compare Methods for Transferring Images from a Digital Camera

3 Identify Several Ways to Edit and Print Photos

4 Recognize Important Audio File Types

5 Describe Several Ways to Create Videos

6 Compare Portable Media Players, Tablets, and Smartphones

Running Project

In this chapter, you'll explore how to select and use digital devices and share multimedia content that you create. Look for instructions as you complete each article. For most articles, there is a series of questions for you to research. At the conclusion of the chapter, you'll submit your responses to the questions raised.

Digital Camera Basics

Explain the Features of Digital Cameras

In this article we look at the different types of digital cameras on the market, the features that distinguish them, and how to use them to capture memories. You don't even need to have a computer to use a digital camera.

Photo and
Resolutio

Key Features

Choosing a digital camera can be bewildering with all of the choices available. Three important features that can help you sort it all out are resolution, storage type, and lenses.

FIGURE 6.1 The dimensions of an image can be expressed in pixels.

Courtesy of Microsoft Corporation Inc.

Dimensions
4,032 x 3,024 pixels

RESOLUTION

The quality of the images that a camera can take is determined by the **resolution**—the measure of the number of pixels in an image, expressed in megapixels. When you view a picture file in File Explorer or Finder, the picture dimension is listed in pixels. The resolution can be calculated by multiplying the length by the width of the image in pixels. The image in Figure 6.1 has the dimensions 4,032 × 3,024 pixels, so it has a resolution of 12,192,768 pixels, or about 12 megapixels. Another way to measure resolution is in dots per inch (dpi). An image that is 300 pixels wide will have 300 dots (pixels) across, whether the screen or print is 3 inches or 30 inches wide. If the image dimension is large but the dpi is small, the pixels become visible.

The higher the resolution, the more detail in the image and the larger the prints you can make before the image quality suffers. Table 6.1 lists the best resolutions to use for various photo print sizes. Images that will only be viewed on a computer screen can be taken at a lower resolution than those intended for photo-quality prints. This is important because resolution also affects file size—the higher the resolution, the larger the file. A very-high-resolution image is not appropriate for use on a webpage because larger files take longer to load onto the screen. File size also impacts storage. An image file taken with a digital camera on its highest setting can yield a file of more than 25 MB in size, while the lower quality setting yields a file of 1 to 2 MB. Many cameras enable you to select the image quality before you take a picture. Setting the camera to take lower-resolution pictures will allow you to fit more pictures on your camera or memory card.

TABLE 6.1 Image Resolution for Photo-Quality Prints

Resolution	Photo-Quality Print Size (in inches)
1–2 megapixels	Up to 4 × 6
2–3 megapixels	Up to 5 × 7
4–5 megapixels	Up to 8 × 10
6–7 megapixels	Up to 11 × 14
8 megapixels	Up to 16 × 20
10 megapixels	Up to 20 × 30

Pearson Education, Inc.

STORAGE

Digital cameras can store images internally or on removable memory cards. The internal memory on most cameras is relatively small compared to the capacity of removable media. The type of card you choose depends on the camera. Flash memory cards come in capacities up to 2 TB in size, depending on the type of card. Memory cards are relatively inexpensive, so you might want to carry multiple cards with your camera. They can be read by most computers and photo printers, or you can bring the memory card to a local store to have the pictures printed. Once the images have been printed, saved to your computer, or uploaded to the web, the memory card can be erased and reused.

SomTaste/Shutterstock

LENSES

To focus a camera, you adjust the **focal length**—the distance at which subjects in front of the lens are in sharp focus—by changing or moving the lens. Many cameras are **autofocusing**—when you point the camera at a subject, the camera adjusts the focal length by using a small motor to move the lens in or out. If you snap the shutter too quickly, the camera may not have time to properly focus the image, resulting in a blurry photo. A **fixed-focus** camera has a stationary lens with a preset focal length that focuses well on objects within a specific distance.

Most digital cameras can **zoom** in or out before you take a picture, making objects appear closer or farther away. Zoom can be either optical or digital, and some cameras combine both. Optical zoom uses a zoom lens to change the focal length of the camera. Low-end digital cameras have an optical zoom of 3×–5×, while more advanced cameras may have 20×–24× zoom or more. Cameras may have a macro or close focus setting for taking pictures of objects that are very close. A **telephoto lens** enables you to zoom in on an object. A **wide-angle lens** gives you a wider view, which makes the objects appear farther away, much like taking a step backward does. A wide-angle lens is useful for shooting images such as panoramas or landscapes.

Digital zoom crops the image and enlarges a portion of it, resulting in a zoomed image of lower quality because the dpi of the image doesn't change. Total zoom on a camera is determined by multiplying its optical zoom by its digital zoom. A camera with a 3× optical zoom and a 10× digital zoom has a total zoom of 30×. Because digital zoom lowers the image quality, it's better to rely on optical zoom when taking a picture. You can use software to crop and enlarge the image later (Figure 6.2).

Debra Geoghan

Debra Geoghan

FIGURE 6.2 These images illustrate how zoom can make the subject appear closer.

Types of Digital Cameras

Digital cameras range from disposable cameras you can buy in a convenience store for a few dollars to high-performance professional quality cameras that can cost thousands of dollars. Most fall somewhere in between the two. Your smartphone has the advantage of always being in your pocket, and many smartphones have high-quality digital cameras built in, but taking lots of pictures can quickly use up your battery and built-in storage. There is an expression that says "the best camera is the one you have with you". Choosing the camera that is right for you will depend on a number of factors, including the types of pictures you plan to take, ease of use, and cost.

POINT-AND-SHOOT

Point-and-shoot cameras are the simplest, least expensive type of digital camera, and they have the fewest features. You can purchase one for under $20 or spend hundreds of dollars for a more sophisticated camera. The most basic cameras have fixed focus, may not have a flash, and may suffer from noticeable **shutter lag**— the time between pressing the button and the camera snapping the picture. When your subject is smiling and waiting for the flash to go off, several seconds can seem like a long time, and shutter lag can cause you to miss that action shot.

FIGURE 6.3 Point-and-Shoot Cameras Compared

Point-and-Shoot Digital Cameras

Basic Point-and-Shoot

Small size, inexpensive, easy to use

Good for snapshots, especially outdoors and web/email
1–16 megapixels
Low-resolution video, may be used as a webcam, may not have a flash
Usually has little optical zoom, fixed focus

lofoto/Shutterstock

Advanced Point-and-Shoot

Better pictures, more control and features

Good for snapshots, portraits, enlargements, and web/email
18–24 megapixels and up
May capture short video clips, special effects, manually controlled settings, image stabilization, burst mode, little or no shutter lag
Up to 24× optical and additional digital zoom, autofocus

Xixinxing/Fotolia

Single-use disposable cameras are basic point-and-shoot cameras that can be purchased in many retail stores and at tourist spots such as monuments, theme parks, and hotels. These are great to carry on trips, send to school with your kids, and put out on tables at weddings and other celebrations for the guests to take pictures.

Advanced point-and-shoot cameras are moderate in price and features. Although still easy to use, they include better zoom, macro functions, auto focus, and special effects. Most also include the ability to capture video and may have special features such as **image stabilization**, which compensates for camera shake to take sharper images, and **burst mode**, which enables you to take several pictures in quick succession by holding down the shutter button. They may also include some more professional features, such as the ability to adjust speed and exposure settings. Most point-and-shoot cameras don't have a viewfinder to help you frame your image. They rely instead on an LCD screen. Most of the time an LCD screen works fine, but a true viewfinder does a better job of framing a shot. Figure 6.3 compares features of different types of point-and-shoot cameras.

MIRRORLESS COMPACT SYSTEM CAMERAS

Also known as superzooms, **compact system cameras (CSC)** are advanced point-and-shoot cameras that have interchangeable lenses (Figure 6.4), some manual controls, 10× to 26× optical zoom lenses, and the ability to capture HD video. CSCs are also known as **mirrorless cameras**, because unlike DSLRs, they do not use a mirror to bounce light up from the lens to a viewfinder. This is one of the key differences between CSCs and DSLRs and makes CSCs smaller and lighter than DSLRs. CSCs can produce better images than point-and-shoots. Other features include hot-shoe and accessory ports to attach an external flash, microphone, or viewfinder. Priced from about $300 to $2,000, these cameras are more expensive than most point-and-shoot cameras, but they're less expensive than most DSLRs.

FIGURE 6.4 A Compact System Camera with Interchangeable Lenses

Lourens Smak/Alamy Stock Photo

DIGITAL SINGLE-LENS REFLEX (DSLR) CAMERAS

If you want maximum control or a more traditional type of camera, then opt for a **digital single-lens reflex (DSLR) camera**, which uses interchangeable lenses, can be manually focused, and gives you more control than either point-and-shoots or CSCs (Figure 6.5). With DSLRs, you can change the lens, which can cost hundreds or even thousands of dollars, to get the exact zoom you need. You can attach a hot-shoe flash, and you can manually adjust focus and exposure. DSLRs use a mirror that enables you to see the image you're about to shoot through a viewfinder, allowing you to create artistic images that autofocusing point-and-shoots can't. Most DSLRs also include an LCD that you can use to review your images as soon as you shoot them. There is almost no shutter lag, so DSLRs are the best type of digital camera for shooting action shots. Most DSLRs can shoot HD video. All this comes at a steep cost—from $600 to $5,000, plus hundreds or thousands of dollars for additional lenses.

FIGURE 6.5 A DSLR Camera with Various Lenses and Hot-Shoe Flash

Sergio Martinez/Fotolia

Halfpoint/Fotolia

Running Project

Use the Internet to research digital cameras. What is the highest resolution available today in point-and-shoot cameras? CSCs? DSLRs? Choose one point-and-shoot, one CSC, and one DSLR camera with the same resolution. How do they compare in terms of price, features, and reviews? What other factors affect the price?

5 Things You Need to Know

- Resolution determines the quality of the print you can make and the size of the image file.
- Optical zoom is better than digital zoom for image quality.
- Point-and-shoot cameras are the easiest to use.
- CSCs blend the ease of use of point-and-shoot with some of the control and quality of a DSLR.
- DSLRs take the best pictures and cost the most.

Key Terms

autofocus	mirrorless camera
burst mode	multimedia
compact system camera (CSC)	point-and-shoot camera
digital single-lens reflex (DSLR) camera	resolution
	shutter lag
fixed-focus	telephoto lens
focal length	wide-angle lens
image stabilization	zoom

Expressiovisual/Fotolia

Bridging the Gap: Transferring Photos

2 Compare Methods for Transferring Images from a Digital Camera

You take photos for many reasons—to remember a special occasion, a vacation, friends and family members, and pets—and for more practical reasons, such as documenting an accident or how to take apart (and put back together) a car engine. Once the pictures have been transferred to your computer or the cloud, they can be saved, edited, printed, and shared.

Memory Cards

If your camera uses a memory card to store images, you can take the card out of the camera and put it in a card reader attached to your computer. Many computers have a card reader built in, or you can purchase a removable card reader that plugs into a USB port. When you put the memory card into the reader, Windows will detect it, and it will appear in the File Explorer window under Devices and drives (Figure 6.6). You can copy, move, and delete the pictures just as you would any other type of file, and you can add and edit some file properties, such as tags. **Tagging** images or files with keywords makes it easier to organize and search for them. If you are using a Mac, the memory card will appear as a disk on your desktop, and you can simply open it and copy the images over to your computer (Figure 6.7), or the Photos app may open and give you the option to import the images.

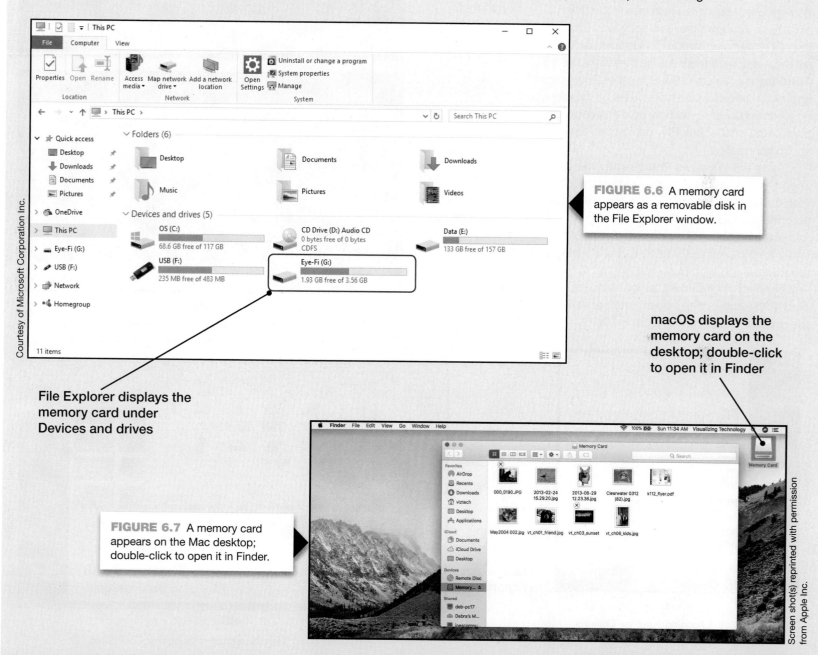

FIGURE 6.6 A memory card appears as a removable disk in the File Explorer window.

File Explorer displays the memory card under Devices and drives

macOS displays the memory card on the desktop; double-click to open it in Finder

FIGURE 6.7 A memory card appears on the Mac desktop; double-click to open it in Finder.

Connecting via Cable

Digital cameras may have a USB, or less commonly a Thunderbolt or a FireWire connection that can be used to connect a camera directly to a computer. This requires device drivers in order for the computer to be able to talk to the camera. The driver may be installed through software that comes with your camera or through the operating system. When you first connect a new removable drive or camera, Windows may prompt you to *Choose what to do with this device*. This is how you can set the AutoPlay settings for the device (Figure 6.8). **AutoPlay** is a feature of Windows that launches an application based on the type of files on the media. So when you insert a memory card that contains photos and videos, AutoPlay could open the Photos app to import them.

Using the Windows Photos app, you can import your pictures directly from your camera to your computer (Figure 6.9). The app will create a new folder inside your Pictures folder and copy the selected pictures into it. The folder will be named based on the date of the transfer so you can find your pictures easily later. If you are using a Mac, you can use the Photos app to import your photos to your computer. Once you connect your camera to your Mac, or insert your memory card, if the app doesn't open automatically, you can start it from the dock or Launchpad (Figure 6.10).

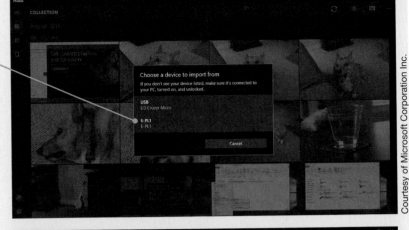

1. Connect your camera or insert your memory card and select the device that contains your pictures

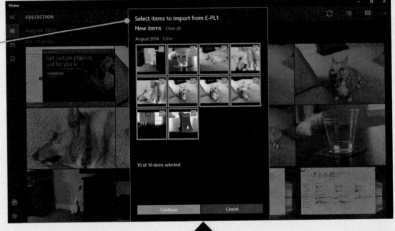

2. Select images to be imported.

Courtesy of Microsoft Corporation Inc.

FIGURE 6.9 Importing Images Using the Windows Photos App

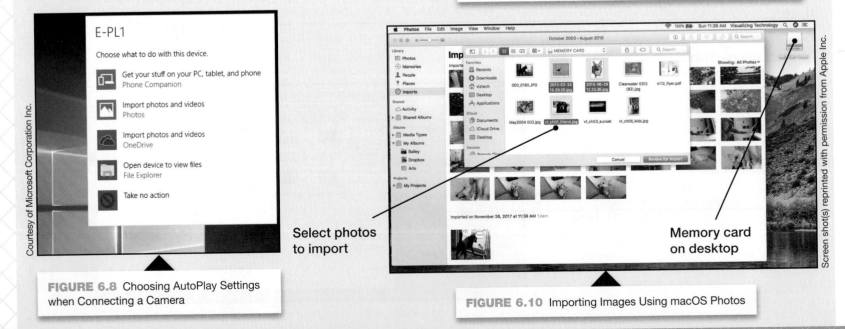

Select photos to import

Memory card on desktop

Screen shot(s) reprinted with permission from Apple Inc.

Courtesy of Microsoft Corporation Inc.

FIGURE 6.8 Choosing AutoPlay Settings when Connecting a Camera

FIGURE 6.10 Importing Images Using macOS Photos

Wireless and Cloud Transfer

Wireless-enabled digital cameras and smartphones can transfer photos using Wi-Fi wireless technology, enabling you to connect to a computer network and save photos to your computer or print photos without cables or card readers. For cameras that don't have wireless built into them, several companies make Wi-Fi–enabled SD memory cards that are compatible with thousands of camera models. If you are in range of the stored network, your images will automatically fly to your computer or mobile device.

Cameras built into smartphones and tablets can use either 4G or Wi-Fi to wirelessly transfer photos. Many mobile apps enable you to configure this to happen automatically, sending your pictures to the cloud so they are accessible on all of your devices. There is even a wedding app that guests can use to share all the photos they take with the happy couple.

Instagram, Dropbox, Photobucket, Facebook, OneDrive, and Google Photos are commonly used apps that work on multiple platforms. **iOS devices**, mobile devices made by Apple (iPad, iPhone, iPod), use iCloud (Figure 6.11), which can sync your data among multiple devices—including a Mac or Windows PC.

Screen shot(s) reprinted with permission from Apple Inc.

FIGURE 6.11 From an iPad you can email, message, tweet a photo, or use iCloud to sync a photo to all your devices.

Running Project

Do any of the cameras you researched in the last section include wireless capabilities? If so, how fast can they transfer images? What are the limitations? If the cameras didn't include wireless, look up the current Eye-Fi card. Is your camera compatible with the card? How much will it cost to purchase the card? Find a similar-model camera that includes wireless. How does the price compare to adding the Eye-Fi card instead?

3 Things You Need to Know

- Memory cards can be transported from camera to computer.
- USB, Thunderbolt, and FireWire cables connect a camera directly to a computer.
- Wireless transfer uses a Wi-Fi or cellular network to transfer photos to your computer or the cloud.

Key Terms

AutoPlay

iOS device

Tagging

REDPIXEL/Fotolia

A Picture Is Worth a Thousand Words

Identify Several Ways to Edit and Print Photos

The beauty of digital photography is what you can do with the images after you transfer them from your camera. With film photography, unless you invest in expensive darkroom equipment, you are limited to choosing the size and finish of your prints and maybe ordering double prints to share with someone else; cropping a photo means taking a pair of scissors to it. Today, anyone can create amazing-looking photos by using a home computer and free or inexpensive software.

Editing Photos

One of the biggest advantages of digital photography over film is the ability to edit images. This can mean doing something as simple as cropping out unwanted parts of the image or removing red-eye, as advanced as using sophisticated software to create works of art, or anything in between. You can add a variety of special effects to photographic images, as well as remove blemishes, adjust colors, and save images in a variety of file formats.

EDITING SOFTWARE

Photo editing software is available in simple, free programs to very sophisticated and expensive professional programs. Older versions of Windows include the ability to edit your pictures using the Windows Photo Gallery, but Windows no longer includes this feature. The Windows Photos app gives you some limited ability to edit photos. Macs include Photos (Figure 6.12). These programs also integrate online photo sharing.

ONLINE EDITING

Many online photo services, such as Google Photos (Figure 6.13), Shutterfly, and Flickr, include basic editing tools with options such as cropping, resizing, and red-eye removal. Editing options also often include special effects like making the picture look black-and-white and adding special borders.

Debra Geoghan

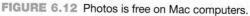
FIGURE 6.12 Photos is free on Mac computers.

Google and the Google logo are registered trademarks of Google Inc., used with permission.

FIGURE 6.13 Online photo editing tools enable you to edit your images without installing software on your computer.

IMAGE FILE FORMATS AND COMPRESSION

Several different file formats are used for digital photos. Point-and-shoot cameras normally take JPEG images, but higher-end cameras may also be able to take higher-quality images using TIFF or other formats. Table 6.2 lists some common graphic file formats.

Lossless compression takes advantage of the fact that files contain a lot of redundant information, and it creates an encoded file by removing redundant information. When a file is decompressed, all the information from the original file is restored. A TIFF image compressed with lossless compression can be decompressed with no loss of data. A JPG/JPEG image is compressed using lossy compression. The **lossy compression** algorithm removes information that humans can't normally detect. It's possible to compress an image after it's been taken, but once the file is compressed using lossy compression, it can't be fully restored to the original format.

TABLE 6.2 Important Image File Types

Format	File Extension	Description
Joint Photographic Experts Group	JPEG or JPG	• Can store up to 16.7 million colors • Uses lossy compression to reduce file size
Windows Bitmap	BMP	• A standard graphic format originally developed for Microsoft Windows • Compression is optional, resulting in large file size
Tagged Image File Format	TIFF or TIF	• A lossless graphic format, often with no compression applied, resulting in large file size
RAW	Camera manufacturers have proprietary file formats, such as NEF (Nikon) or CRW/CR2 (Canon)	• Raw images are not processed by the camera and must be processed by software in order to be used

Printing and Sharing Photos

The cost of creating prints of your photos varies depending on the paper, ink, and type of printer you use. Photo printers can be inkjet printers that use special ink cartridges or dye-sublimation printers, which produce lab-quality prints. Less expensive prints using regular ink and paper have a lower quality and shorter lifespan. At home, printing can cost 50 to 70 cents per print.

FIGURE 6.14 Wireless Printing from a Smartphone

Rasulov/Fotolia

CAMERA TO PRINTER

Photo printers today can read directly from memory cards or connect using Wi-Fi as shown in Figure 6.14. You can use a small, portable printer to print photos on the spot. You may also be able to do some limited editing on either the camera or printer before you print.

KIOSKS

Photo kiosks in retail stores have built-in editing capabilities and are very easy to use. These kiosks enable you to print only the pictures you want and fine-tune your images without needing to use your own computer. You can connect your camera or you can insert a memory card into the kiosk. Kiosks can even print photos you have stored in the cloud or on websites like Facebook. These prints typically cost between 15 and 59 cents per print.

ONLINE PRINTING AND SHARING

Websites like Shutterfly are personal image-sharing sites. Their main goal is to get you to buy prints and other merchandise they offer. The advantage to using these sites is that you can share your photos with your friends and family members, who can order the items they want. The prints can be mailed or picked up at local retail partners. Companies like Walgreens and Walmart enable you to upload your pictures at home and pick up the prints in a store. Standard prints from these sites cost about 15 cents each.

Flickr (Figure 6.15) is an online photo-sharing community owned by Yahoo. Flickr has millions of users and millions of images in its vast repository. When you upload images to Flickr, you are able to tag them with keywords that you define. The tags link your images to other Flickr images with the same tags, and though you can choose to keep your pictures private, the majority of the images on Flickr are publicly available. Another feature is **geotagging**, which allows you to add location information to your digital photos.

Yahoo Inc.

FIGURE 6.15
The Author's Photostream on Flickr

Flickr also allows you to control how other people can legally use your pictures by applying **Creative Commons (CC) licensing** (Figure 6.16). According to the Creative Commons website, Creative Commons "tools give everyone from individual creators to large companies and institutions a simple, standardized way to grant copyright permissions to their creative work. The Creative Commons licenses enable people to easily change their copyright terms from the default of 'all rights reserved' to 'some rights reserved.'" You can visit the Creative Commons website to learn more about how it works. You can search Flickr for images that have CC licensing applied. Another feature of Flickr is The Commons. There are dozens of institutions participating in The Commons, a project that is designed to make publicly held photography collections accessible to everyone. This is a great resource to use when you need an image for a school project. Images in The Commons have no known copyright.

Creative Commons (**creativecommons.org**) is a project that has been developed as a way to increase sharing and collaboration by specifying how images and other materials can be used. One of the first institutions to embrace this idea was the Smithsonian Institution, which made hundreds of images available on Flickr under Creative Commons. Visit **flickr.com/photos/smithsonian** to see them.

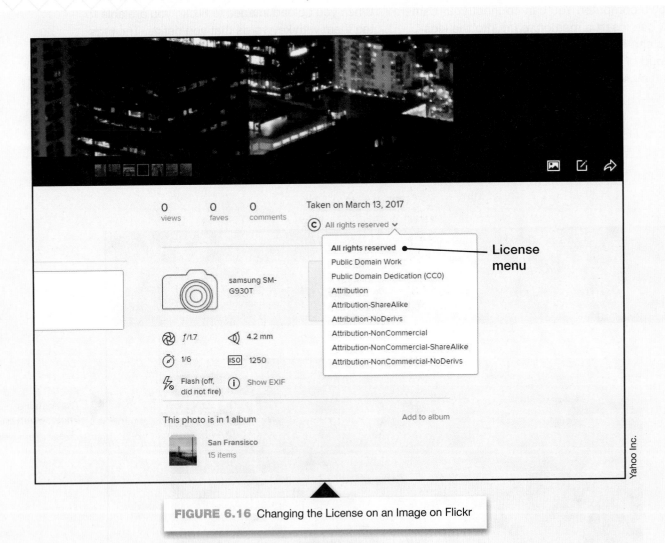

FIGURE 6.16 Changing the License on an Image on Flickr

George Dolgikh/Fotolia

For years, whenever I celebrated a special occasion with family and friends, I would take my film to the store to be developed—always ordering a second set of prints so I could share them. It was expensive, it would take at least a day or two to get back, and often there were several (okay, many) prints that were just awful, and I would throw them away. There was no way to decide ahead of time which prints I wanted; I had to pay for them all. Not anymore—now, if I take a lousy picture, I can review it right on my camera, and if needed, delete it and reshoot. When I get home, I download the pictures to my computer, crop and enhance them, upload them to Facebook, Instagram, or Google Photos, and share away. That process is so much easier and faster—and much less expensive—because I do not print all the pictures and instead view and share them online.

> **Viz Check**—In MyLab IT, take a quick quiz covering Objectives 1–3.

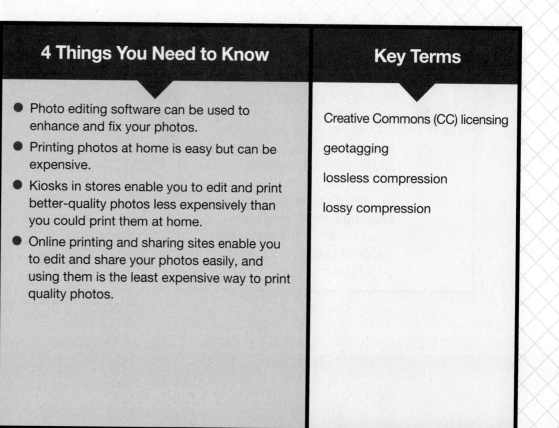

Running Project

Use the Internet to compare the cost and quality of photo prints from several home photo printers, online services, and local retailers in your area. Create a chart comparing them. Include the following information: cost per print, sizes, finish types, expected lifespan of prints, water resistance, and any other details you think might be important. When might you choose to use each of these methods for prints?

4 Things You Need to Know

- Photo editing software can be used to enhance and fix your photos.
- Printing photos at home is easy but can be expensive.
- Kiosks in stores enable you to edit and print better-quality photos less expensively than you could print them at home.
- Online printing and sharing sites enable you to edit and share your photos easily, and using them is the least expensive way to print quality photos.

Key Terms

Creative Commons (CC) licensing

geotagging

lossless compression

lossy compression

Edit a Photo Using the Windows Photos or macOS Photos App

HOW TO VIDEO

In this exercise you will perform some basic editing on a photo using the Windows Photos app or the macOS Photos app. If you do not have this app, use another program such as Windows Photo Gallery or iPhoto. If necessary, download the student data files from **pearsonhighered.com /viztech**.

1 Open File Explorer. Locate the student data files for this chapter. Right-click the file *vt_ch06_kids* and click *Copy*. Navigate to the folder where you save your work and then on the Home tab of the ribbon, click *Paste*. Right-click the file, click *Rename,* type **lastname_ firstname_ch06_howto1** and press Enter. Right-click the new file, point to *Open with*, and then click *Photos*.

Courtesy of Microsoft Corporation Inc.

2 Click the *Edit* button on the menu bar. With *Basic fixes* selected on the left, click *Enhance* on the right. (Windows 8: Right-click to display the menu bar, click *Edit*. With *Auto fix* selected on the left, click the third option on the right. Click *Basic fixes*.) Click the *Red eye* tool and click each eye to clean up the eyes.

Courtesy of Microsoft Corporation Inc.

3 Click *Crop*. On the menu bar, click the *Aspect ratio* button, and then click *5 x 7*. Drag and resize the grid to crop the image so that the boys make up most of the image. Drag the image to the center of the grid and then click *Apply*.

Courtesy of Microsoft Corporation Inc.

4 On the left, click *Color*, and then on the right, click *Temperature*. Use the arrow keys on your keyboard to adjust the temperature to *15*.

Courtesy of Microsoft Corporation Inc.

5 On the left, click *Light*, and then on the right, click *Contrast*. Use the arrow keys on your keyboard to adjust the contrast to *25*. Click *Shadows*. Use the arrow keys on your keyboard to adjust the shadows to *–25*. Click *Save*. Close Photos and submit your image as directed by your instructor.

Courtesy of Microsoft Corporation Inc.

If you are using Photos on a Mac:

1. Open Finder. Locate the student data files for this chapter. Press ⌨Ctrl + click the file *vt_ch06_kids,* and click *Copy "vt_ch06_kids.jpg".* Navigate to the folder where you save your work and then press ⌨Command ⌘ + ⌨V. Click the file one time, press ⌨Return, type **lastname_firstname_ch06_howto1** and press ⌨Return. Open Photos. From the File menu, click *Import*. Browse to the location of your files for this chapter, click the image *lastname_firstname_ch06_howto1*, and then click *Review for Import*. Double-click the image, click the *Image* menu, and then click *Show Edit Tools*.

Screen shot(s) reprinted with permission from Apple Inc.; Debra Geoghan

2. In the right pane, if necessary, click *Enhance*. Click the *Red-eye* tool, if necessary, drag the Size slider to the bottom (smallest) size, and then click each eye to clean up the eyes.

3. Above the image, click *Crop*, click *Aspect*, and click *5:7*. Drag and resize the grid to crop the image so that the boys make up most of the image. Drag the image to the center of the grid Return

4. Click *Adjust*. To the right of *Color*, click *Auto*.
5. Click the Options arrow below *Light* Drag the *Contrast* slider to 0.25. Drag the Shadows slider to −0.25.

6. Click *Done*. Click *File*, point to *Export*, and then click *Export 1 Photo*. In the dialog box, click *Export*. If necessary, navigate to your chapter folder and then click *Export*. Close Photos and submit your image as directed by your instructor.

Kentoh/Fotolia

Making Sense of Sound

4 Recognize Important Audio File Types

From listening to songs on a mobile device, to using speech to control computers and video games, to receiving alerts about new email and text messages, sound plays an important role in the multimedia experience. In this article we'll examine the differences between several audio file types and compare various media player programs and speech-recognition programs.

Audio File Types

When multimedia files are stored on your computer, they can take up large amounts of storage space. To use the space on your hard drive efficiently and improve file transfer speeds over the Internet, multimedia software reduces file size by using codecs, short for compression/decompression. **Codecs** are compression algorithms that reduce the size of digital media files. Without the use of codecs, downloads would take much longer than they do now because the files would be significantly larger. There are hundreds of codecs, but you probably use only a few of them on a regular basis. Common audio codecs include MP3 and AAC.

Sound files contain digitized data in the form of recorded live sounds or music, which are saved in one of several standardized sound formats. These formats specify how sounds should be digitally represented and commonly include some type of data compression. A common music file format is **MP3 (MPEG-1 Audio Layer 3)**. The MP3 codec creates files that are compressed, enabling them to maintain excellent quality while being reasonably small. When you rip a CD, you transfer your music files to your computer and convert them to a compressed format such as MP3 or AAC. The files on an audio CD are very large, which is why there are usually only 10–12 songs per disc. An MP3 file is about one-tenth the size of a CD audio file. There is, however, a trade-off between file size and quality: The smaller MP3 files are not the same quality as the original audio files. MP3 files have the file extension .mp3.

The default file type used by Apple's iTunes software is **AAC (advanced audio coding)**, which compresses a file in a manner similar to MP3. The AAC codec creates files that are somewhat higher quality than MP3 files, and support for it is growing on other devices, such as the Sony PlayStation 4, Nintendo Wii, and many smartphones and media players.

There are several other common audio file types, including Windows Media Audio (WMA) files and MIDI files, which are synthesized digital media files you might hear as a soundtrack to a video game.

Ra2 studio/Fotolia

Digital rights management (DRM) is a technology that is applied to digital media files, such as music, eBooks, and videos, to impose restrictions on the use of these files. This may mean that you cannot transfer the file from one device to another or make a backup copy, or that you will only be able to access the file for a limited amount of time. The companies that apply DRM to media files argue that it is necessary to protect the copyright holder. The Digital Millennium Copyright Act (DMCA) made it illegal to remove DRM from protected files. Opponents of DRM argue that it not only prevents copyright infringement but also restricts other lawful uses of the media.

Media Software

Media software is used to organize and play multimedia files such as music, videos, and podcasts. You can rip your music CDs to your computer; organize your songs into playlists for working out, driving, or dancing; and find new music that you might like by using the online store feature. You can watch a movie trailer, a professor's lecture, or a music video. The content available to you grows daily.

iTunes is a program from Apple that you can use to organize your music, videos, and other media files. If you have an iOS device, then you use iTunes to transfer music and other media files from your computer to your device. You can use iTunes to shop for new music, find podcasts to subscribe to, rip your music CDs to your computer, and watch movies. **Podcasts** are prerecorded radio- and TV-like shows you can download and listen to or watch any time. There are thousands of podcasts you can subscribe to. Your instructors may even have podcasts of their class lectures. Figure 6.17 shows the iTunes podcasts page for US House of Representatives. With iCloud, items purchased using iTunes will automatically sync to all your registered devices and computers.

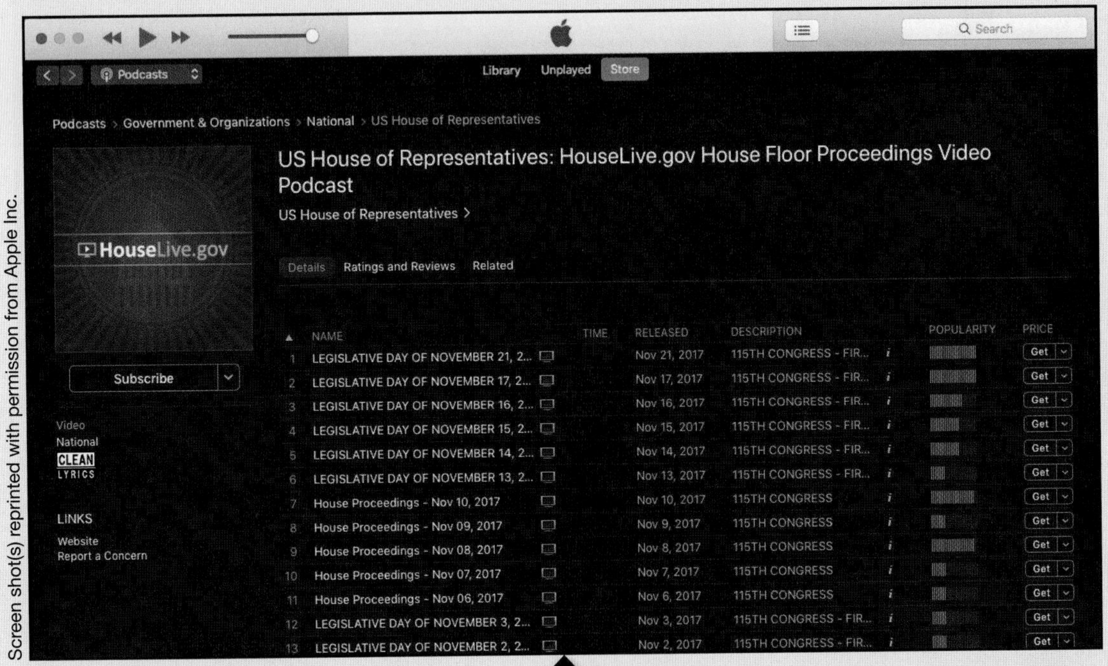

Screen shot(s) reprinted with permission from Apple Inc.

FIGURE 6.17 US House of Representatives House Floor Proceedings Podcasts in iTunes

Windows Media Player is a legacy product included with Windows, and like iTunes, it can be used to organize and play all your media files, find media on the web to purchase and download, rip CDs, and transfer your media files to your media player (unless it's an iOS device). Windows Media Player has the ability to stream media files to computers and other devices on your home network. You can also use it to burn CDs of your music. Although you can still find it on a Windows 10 computer in the Windows Accessories folder, Media Player has been replaced with Groove Music (Figure 6.18).

Connecting your music to the cloud enables you to listen to your favorite songs on any device that has an Internet connection. There are a lot of music services out there—some that incorporate your own tracks and others that don't. Many radio stations stream live over the Internet. In fact, some radio stations broadcast exclusively over the Internet.

With a Pandora account, you can listen on a game console, Blu-ray player, computer, Internet-enabled TV, set-top box, or mobile device. You create stations by selecting songs or artists that you like. Pandora has a massive collection of music that has been analyzed and classified by musician-analysts. You can refine the results you get by giving each track a thumbs up or thumbs down. Pandora also displays the lyrics for many songs, so you can sing along to your favorite tunes. Spotify (Figure 6.19) uses both the music on your devices and millions of tracks stored in the cloud. It enables you to share playlists and recommend tracks to your friends. Spotify has a radio feature that can automatically create stations for you based on both your music collection and your most frequently played tracks.

Other music services include Amazon Prime, Google Play, and Apple Music. Most services have free, ad-supported plans and premium subscriptions that eliminate ads and include more features. Connections to Facebook, Twitter, and other services make sharing and listening to music a social experience. Using one of these services allows you some control over the songs you listen to—unlike with a normal radio broadcast. If you like to create and share your own music or listen to tracks from independent musicians, check out SoundCloud.

IanDagnall Computing/Alamy Stock Photo

FIGURE 6.19 Spotify uses both your local music files as well as those shared online by others.

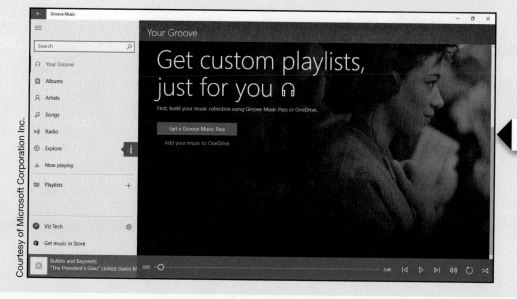

Courtesy of Microsoft Corporation Inc.

FIGURE 6.18 Groove Music App

Speech Recognition

Speech recognition, also known as voice recognition, is a feature that enables you to use a device by speaking commands. It can be used to automatically provide customer service through a call center, dial a cell phone, dictate a term paper, or control your vehicle navigation system. Speech recognition enables you to use a computer or mobile device without a keyboard. Windows, macOS, iOS, and Android all have built-in speech recognition, and there are also third-party speech-recognition programs and apps.

Personal digital assistant apps are voice-activated: macOS and iOS include Siri, Android devices include Google Now, and Windows phones and Windows 10 include Cortana. These intelligent apps enable you to speak using natural language to interact with them. For example, you can ask what the weather is, where the closest gas station is, and the score of last night's game. With the desktop versions of Siri and Cortana, you can also search for items on your computer. They can use information from your contacts, music library, calendars, reminders, and other interactions to make recommendations and perform other actions. A few things they can do include: launching apps, providing weather forecasts, reading and editing your calendar, setting reminders and alarms, making calls, sending messages and emails, playing and recognizing music, and performing a web search. Amazon's Echo is a stand-alone voice-controlled device with a more limited feature set.

Sound is an important component of multimedia content. Speech recognition enables you to interact with your systems by using voice commands, making for easy access and increasing safety. The use of compression enables you to convert your music collection into digital files that are small enough to enable you to carry thousands of songs on a media player or smartphone while still maintaining high-quality sound. Media player software gives you control over how and what you listen to. How many songs do you have on your playlist?

OK smartphone, find nearest coffee shop.

WavebreakMediaMicro/Fotolia

FIND OUT MORE

Use the Internet to find a list of Internet radio stations. How many did you find? Which of them have you used? Are any of your favorite local stations broadcasting over the Internet? Do you listen to them online?

ETHICS

Cameron purchased an eBook to use for his physics course at school. He downloaded the book to his desktop computer, intending to transfer it to his tablet to take it to class with him. To his surprise, the DRM protection on the file prevented him from reading it on any device other than the computer he originally downloaded the file to. Because he can't bring his computer to class, Cameron sees no way to bring the eBook to school. His friend Abbie has a solution—a free program that can strip the DRM from the file, making a new copy that Cameron can easily transfer to his tablet. Cameron takes her advice, makes a copy of the book, and brings it to class with him. Cameron feels that this is okay because he paid for the book and should be able to read it on any device he owns.

Was stripping the DRM rights from the book legal? Was it ethical? Was Cameron justified in what he did? Did he have any other alternatives?

Running Project

Use Windows Help and Support or the Mac Help Center to research speech recognition. What are three ways you can use speech recognition on your computer? What advantages can you see to using this feature? What disadvantages? Think about your interactions with technology every day and give an example of speech recognition that you use.

5 Things You Need to Know

- MP3 and AAC are the most common music file types.
- Digital rights management imposes restrictions on the use of DRM-protected media files.
- Media programs organize and play multimedia files.
- Streaming media services allow you to listen to music on any Internet-connected device.
- Speech recognition enables you to interact with your systems by using voice commands.

Key Terms

AAC (advanced audio coding)

codec

digital rights management (DRM)

MP3 (MPEG-1 Audio Layer 3)

podcast

speech recognition

Lights, Camera, Action

Objective 5

Describe Several Ways to Create Videos

It's estimated that more than one-third of all Internet traffic is video, and that number continues to rise. Creating, viewing, and sharing video is not very different from handling any other media, except that video files tend to be larger and require more storage and bandwidth. To ensure the best accessibility for your videos, they should contain **captions** that display the text of the audio in a video. A caption file is a specially formatted text file that includes the captions and the timing of the captions in the video.

Watching
on Your O...
Terms

Videoconferencing, Webcasting, and Streaming Video

Webcams are specialized video cameras that provide visual input for online communication. They can be used in live video chat sessions through an app such as FaceTime or Skype, or through more sophisticated videoconferencing software (Figure 6.20).

Webcams enable you to have virtual meetings with people in different cities, connect classrooms on different campuses, collaborate on projects with others in real time, or say goodnight to your family when you are far away. Such two-way interactions require both locations to have webcams and software setups that allow them to communicate with each other. Webcams are relatively inexpensive and come built in to most tablets, smartphones, and notebook computers.

Broadcasting on the web, or **webcasting**, can be used to monitor a child in daycare, stream a live performance or lecture, check out the waves on your favorite surfing beach, or watch a live feed from the International Space Station (Figure 6.21). Webcasting is not interactive—it's a one-way process. The broadcast, known as a video stream, can be live or prerecorded. **Streaming** media begins to play immediately as it is being received and does not require the whole file to be downloaded to your device first.

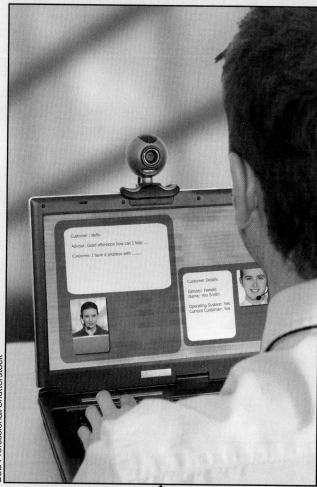

ESB Professional/Shutterstock

FIGURE 6.20 Online customer support is one application of live video chat.

FIGURE 6.21 Live video from the International Space Station can be viewed at **www.nasa.gov/multimedia/nasatv/iss_ustream.html**.

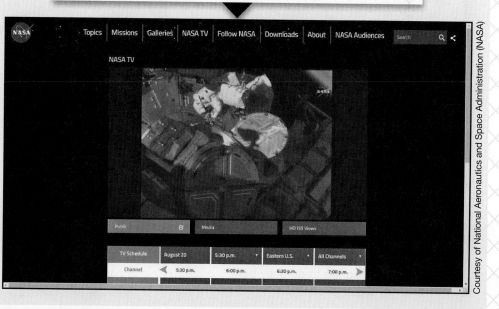

Courtesy of National Aeronautics and Space Administration (NASA)

Streaming video services such as Amazon Prime, Netflix, Hulu, and Crunchyroll (anime), as well as many television networks, stream commercial television and movie content. Some content is available for free, some requires a subscription, and some services allow you to pay for individual shows. Streaming video services allow you to time- and place-shift—deciding when and where to watch your favorite shows and movies—and include apps that let you stream content to your game consoles, smart TVs, and mobile devices (Figure 6.22). These services enable you to binge-watch multiple episodes or seasons of current and older programs. They also have some original content that can't be seen anywhere else. Each service has different content, and choosing the right service depends on the types of programming you prefer.

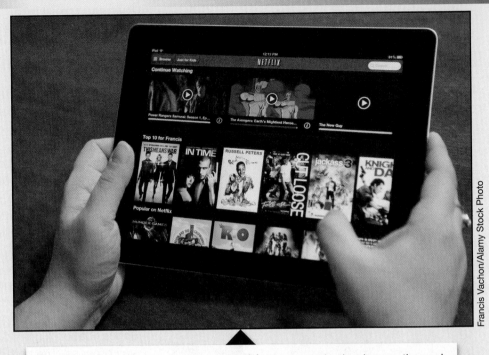

FIGURE 6.22 Netflix streaming video service lets you take the show on the road.

VIDEO CAMERAS

You can use a webcam to record video, but if you want to record something that is not right in front of your computer, you need a video camera. Most digital cameras and smartphones include a video mode, but for the best quality, you may want a stand-alone video camera. A digital video camera enables you to record video that can be easily uploaded to your computer, where it can be edited, stored, and shared. The features of video cameras—megapixels, storage, zoom—are similar to those of regular digital cameras, and the more money you spend, the more features you get. Some video cameras are small, lightweight, and durable. They enable you to record your activities from your perspective. Rugged video cameras, such as the GoPro, are designed to go anywhere, even under water (Figure 6.23)!

FIGURE 6.23 A video camera can record the action anywhere it occurs.

An important thing to consider when buying a digital video camera is the media it uses. Some video cameras have a built-in hard drive or flash memory and do not use any removable media. Although this is convenient, it also means that once the internal drive is full, you'll need a computer nearby to upload the video to before you can record any more. Another option is a camera that uses flash memory cards. Memory cards come in large capacities, are relatively inexpensive, and can be easily reused. In addition, it is easy to carry several with you. Cost, convenience, and the amount of storage you need will all affect your decision.

SCREEN CAPTURE

There are several ways to create videos. **Screen capture** software tools enable you to create a video of what happens on your computer screen. This is a handy way to create a how-to video or to capture a video of a problem you are having. You don't need a camera to do it. Macs include QuickTime, which has a built-in screen recorder function.

Windows 10 includes a tool called the Game Bar, which is part of the Game DVR feature in the Xbox app. The tool is designed to record your PC game play, but can also be used to record other screen activities. **Machinima**, the art of creating videos using screens captured from video games, is one creative use of screen capture software.

Sharing Video

As with photos, many people create videos intending to share them. This can mean using an online service or burning the video onto a DVD or Blu-ray disc. Regardless of how you decide to share your video, you may want to do some editing before you share it.

VIDEO EDITING

Video editing software, like photo editing software, comes in a variety of forms. Video editing software ranges from free online services such as YouTube, to free programs including Windows Movie Maker and Apple iMovie, to very expensive professional-quality programs such as Adobe Premiere and Sony Vegas. All video editing software will capture, edit, and export video. Most programs allow you to add features like captions, credits and titles, fades between scenes, and music. The software enables you to share your video by burning it to DVD or uploading it to the web. If you want more than the free programs offer but don't want to spend hundreds of dollars for professional software, programs in the $50 to $200 range, such as Adobe Premiere Elements or Corel VideoStudio, may have all the features you need. DVD authoring is a feature of most video editing software. Basic programs have design templates you can use to create attractive titles and menus and enable you to burn your creation to a DVD that can be played in any DVD player.

Maksym Yemelyanov/Fotolia

YOUTUBE

YouTube (Figure 6.24) is the most popular video-sharing site on the Internet. Some photo sites and social media sites—including Facebook, allow you to upload video, too. According to YouTube, 48 hours of video are uploaded every minute, resulting in nearly 8 years of content uploaded every day. The quality ranges from awful cell phone videos to professionally created music videos, movie trailers, and full-length programs. You can upload your videos to YouTube and other video-sharing sites and share them with friends and family—or the world. You can create channels to group and share videos about a similar topic. I have created a YouTube channel for each of the classes I teach, and I subscribe to channels other people have created with videos that I am interested in.

In 1888, Thomas Edison filed a caveat with the U.S. Patent Office describing his plan to invent a motion picture camera that would "do for the eye what the phonograph does for the ear." In 1892, he opened a motion picture production studio to create motion pictures. One of the first motion pictures made there was called "Fred Ott's Sneeze," a recording of an Edison employee sneezing for the camera. You can watch the clip on YouTube today. Little could Edison have imagined the impact that video would have on society a century later.

FIGURE 6.24 YouTube Video of the Author

FIND OUT MORE

In 2009, broadcast television was converted to digital TV (DTV). Older televisions now require a DTV converter box to convert the digital TV signal into an analog signal the TV can display. Why was the switch made? Was it strictly an economic decision, or does it benefit society in some ways? What are the advantages of DTV over analog TV? Try checking dtv.gov for answers.

CAREER SPOTLIGHT

JOBS

Healthcare

Nyul/Fotolia

The use of technology has become commonplace in many healthcare careers. Many medical schools and nursing programs now require their students to learn to use handheld devices, which give them instant access to vast amounts of clinical information in one small mobile device. These devices can be loaded with drug and diagnostics manuals, calculators, and other medical reference materials. They can also be used for patient tracking, ordering laboratory tests, and even billing. Handheld devices and other computing technology have changed the way healthcare providers practice medicine. Using digital technologies is a critical skill for practitioners to have.

Running Project

Use the Internet to research digital video cameras. Select a model in the same price range as the point-and-shoot camera you researched earlier. Compare the video capabilities of the two cameras. What features does a dedicated video camera have that the point-and-shoot camera does not? Is the video camera capable of taking still images? How do still images taken with a video camera compare to those taken with a point-and-shoot camera? Do you think it is worth the money to purchase both types of camera? Explain your answer.

4 Things You Need to Know

- Webcams enable you to videoconference with others.
- Webcasting is broadcasting on the web.
- Screen capture software records what happens on your computer screen.
- YouTube is the most popular video-sharing site on the web.

Key Terms

caption	streaming
machinima	webcam
screen capture	webcasting

Create a Screen Capture Video Using Screencast-O-Matic

Essential Job Skill

HOW TO VIDEO

In this activity, you will use the web tool Screencast-O-Matic (SOM) to create a screen capture video. Screencast-O-Matic can run in your browser if you have the Java plugin installed, but many systems and browsers do not support Java. If you do not have Java, you can download and run the Recorder launcher instead. Another option is to download and install the full SOM app on your system. You will create a free account for this activity. If necessary, download the student data files from **pearsonhighered.com/viztech**. From your student data files, open the *vt_ch06_howto2_answersheet* file and save the file as **lastname_firstname_ch06_howto2_answersheet**.

1 From the student data files for this chapter, open the PowerPoint file *vt_ch06_presentation*. Leave the presentation open and open your browser.

2 Go to **screencast-o-matic.com** and click *Sign Up*. Create a new Screencast-O-Matic account using your email address, open your email program and click the link to finish signing up. Create a password, agree to the Terms of Service, and create your account.

3 Click *Start Recorder*. If necessary, click Get recorder launcher!. Save the installer to your computer, and then, depending on your browser, click the file or click Run and install the launcher. After you have installed the launcher, click *Ok* to return to SOM. Click *Start Recorder*. Minimize the browser window so that you can see the SOM frame over PowerPoint.

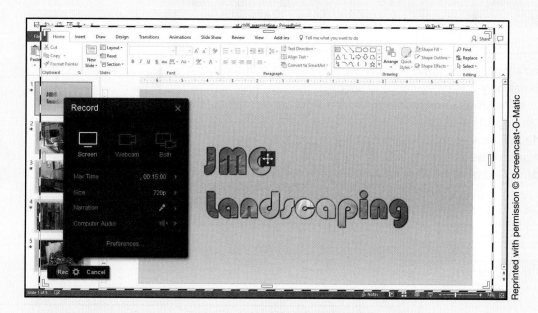

Reprinted with permission © Screencast-O-Matic

NOTE: If you are unable to run the browser-based version of Screencast-O-Matic because of browser security, you can download and install the SOM app instead.

4 On the SOM toolbar, click the size button and select *Fullscreen*. Start the PowerPoint slideshow. Click the red record button on the SOM toolbar to begin recording.

NOTE: If you are using a microphone, you will record your voice-over for this presentation. If you do not have a mic, you can still read the voice-over prompts out loud to practice.

5 Read and record the following script, keeping in mind that the slides will automatically advance after 8–10 seconds:

Title slide (JMG Landscaping): We are JMG Landscaping, family owned and operated since 1985.

Slide 2: Beautiful patio furniture and gazebos to make your outdoor spaces as inviting as your indoor rooms.

Slide 3: Decks, in wood or newer high-tech materials, last a lifetime.

Slide 4: Cedar fences age with grace.

Slide 5: Hardscaping with stone and other materials creates walls, gardens, pathways, and more.

6 Press Alt + P to pause the recording and then click *Done*. Click *Upload to Screencast-O-Matic*.

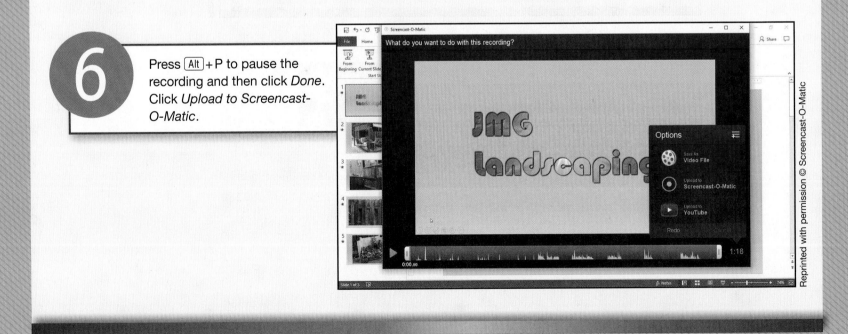

7 Change the title to **Firstname Lastname VT Project** and in the description, type **JMG promo**. Click *Captions*, click *Add New*. Click *Choose Text File*, navigate to the student data files, and upload the *vt_ch06_captions.txt* file.

8 Click the *Play* button to preview your video in the SOM window. Take a screenshot of this page and paste it into your answer sheet. Click *Publish*. Click *Copy Link*, paste it into your answer sheet, and submit to your instructor as directed. Click *Done* and close your browser.

You have created a video that can be shared on popular video hosting websites, embedded in your own website, or shared via other media. Purchasing a premium subscription to the SOM service will enable you to create longer videos and includes editing features that will help you make your video more professional—for example, editing out any mistakes you made when reading the script.

Rawpixel.com/Fotolia

Technology on the Move

6

Compare Portable Media Players, Tablets, and Smartphones

Digital mobile devices enable you to take technology everywhere you go. These mobile devices range from small, inexpensive MP3 players to multifunction smartphones and tablets costing hundreds of dollars. Apple's release of the iPod in 2001 changed the way we listen to music forever, and smartphones and tablets are changing how we watch videos, share photos, and much more.

SIMULATION

Digital Devices and Multimedia

Analog vs. Digital

The terms *analog* and *digital* are used throughout this textbook. The difference is in the way the data is encoded and transmitted (Figure 6.25). Analog devices convert data signals into continuous electronic waves or pulses; analog devices, such as telephones and legacy CRT monitors, translate the electronic pulses back into audio and video signals. In **digital devices**, the audio or video data is represented by a series of 0s and 1s. Digital signals can carry more data and are less prone to interference than analog signals.

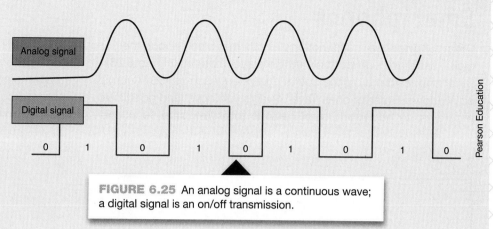

Analog signal

Digital signal

0 1 0 1 0 1 0 1 0

Pearson Education

FIGURE 6.25 An analog signal is a continuous wave; a digital signal is an on/off transmission.

Portable Media Players

Today **MP3 players**, or **portable media players**, allow you to carry thousands of songs and podcasts, and perhaps photos, videos, and games, with you, so you can access them wherever you are. You can plug portable media players into your computer, your home stereo, and even your car. Tablets and smartphones have built-in media players, and many people choose not to have a separate media device at all. But there are times when you might find it convenient to have a media player—for example, on a plane, in the gym, or by the pool. Playing music and videos on your phone can use a lot of battery life, so using a separate device can help you stay connected longer.

The simplest MP3 players, like the iPod shuffle and SanDisk Sansa Clip Jam, have flash memory capacities from 2 GB to 8 GB, start at under $40, and have limited features. Midrange flash media players, with capacities ranging from 8 GB to 32 GB, can hold up to two days' worth of music and may have more features, such as video and photo support. Because they use flash memory, they have no moving parts, which makes them ideal for high-impact activities like jogging. Higher-end media players, such as the iPod touch and iPod nano, can hold many days' worth of music, video, and photos on flash memory or hard drives up to 160 GB in size. These players also have other features like built-in games and Internet access.

Smartphones

Smartphones are multifunction devices that blend phone, personal digital assistant, and portable media player features (Figure 6.26). Smartphones run a mobile operating system such as iOS, Android, or Windows. Smartphones have the ability to download additional programs, called **mobile applications (mobile apps)**, to extend their capabilities, making them convergence devices. The 4G—or fourth generation—cellular networks offered by major carriers have data transfer speeds that rival those of home connections. Such improved connection speeds enable you to watch TV, video chat, and play online games from your phone.

FIGURE 6.26 Mobile devices have the ability to download apps to extend their capabilities.

Boris Lehner/Alamy Stock Photo

Tablets

A **tablet** falls somewhere between a notebook computer and a smartphone. These handheld devices can be multifunctional devices or dedicated e-readers and cost from under $100 to nearly $1,000. Many tablets run a mobile operating system: iOS, Android, or Windows. Other tablets run a full version of Windows. Tablets have an LCD screen, a fairly long battery life, built-in Wi-Fi, and

IanDagnall Computing/Alamy Stock Photo

possibly 3G or 4G cellular connectivity, making them great for travel. Tablets come with a variety of mobile apps preinstalled. Out of the box, you can surf the web, send and receive email, watch videos, and much more. The coolest part is the vast collection of apps that you can download to your device—many for free or very little cost. At the time of this writing, the iOS App Store (Figure 6.27) and the Google Play Store (Android) each had more than 1 million apps.

FIGURE 6.27 Apple's iOS App Store has more than 1 million apps.

E-READERS

E-readers are a special class of tablets that are designed specifically for reading books, magazines, and other publications. Dedicated e-readers are lightweight, inexpensive devices that can hold thousands of books (Figure 6.28). Through a wireless connection, users can browse an electronic bookstore and download a new book in seconds. Some libraries also lend eBooks, and many textbooks come in eBook form that can be read on a computer or e-reader.

Some e-readers use e-ink, including the Kindle Paperwhite and Nook GlowLight Plus. E-ink technology creates a screen that is most like the experience of reading an actual book and extends battery life for as long as two months. The screen can easily be read, even in the brightest conditions—like on the beach—but as with a paper book, you need a book light to read in bed at night because e-ink readers are not backlit. Some e-ink readers have a built-in book light. Other e-readers have an LCD screen. An LCD screen is backlit, and the brightness can be adjusted so you can read in bed at night—but the glossy screen is subject to glare and is harder to read in a brightly lit location, and battery life is shortened.

FIGURE 6.28 With an e-reader, you can hold dozens of books in the palm of your hand.

Melpomene/Shutterstock

The two main e-reader tablets available are the Amazon Kindle and the Barnes & Noble Nook. Both come in several versions and cost anywhere from $79 to $379, depending on the features you choose. The Kindle Fire HD and the Samsung Galaxy Tab E NOOK are full-fledged tablet computers. As prices have come down, the lines have blurred between the devices, but for someone who really just wants a lightweight, inexpensive device to read and store a library collection, a dedicated e-reader is still a smart choice.

For many people, mobile devices have become a part of everyday life. Even the simplest cell phone is likely to have a built-in camera, the ability to send and receive text messages via Short Message Service (SMS) and multimedia text messages via Multimedia Messaging Service (MMS), and perhaps a game or two. Many people find that they are so plugged in that they can never really relax. Sometimes it makes sense to just turn off your mobile devices. Hey, leave a message. Beep.

FIND OUT MORE

There are lots of places on the web to find free eBooks. Some notable resources include the Google Books Library Project, Project Gutenberg, and the Online Computer Library Center. Choose one of these resources to research. When and why was it established? What types of books and other materials are included? Are there any partner institutions or projects? How can you access the materials? Where did you find this information?

GREEN COMPUTING
E-Waste

The amount of **e-waste** (electronic waste) generated every year is staggering. Old computers, cell phones, TVs, and other electronic devices make up e-waste, some of which is considered hazardous. A CRT monitor can contain more than 8 pounds of lead, and by Environmental Protection Agency (EPA) regulations cannot be disposed of in a landfill. eCycling, or recycling electronics, is one way to reduce the amount of e-waste and hazardous materials that end up in landfills, as well as to cut down the cost of hauling it away. The EPA provides information on its website about eCycling in your community (**epa.gov/recycle/electronics-donation-and-recycling**).

You can also dispose of e-waste in an altruistic manner by donating working electronics to worthwhile charities. Your donations of working electronics not only help reduce e-waste but also benefit the recipients.

Sharon Day/Shutterstock

Running Project

Use the Internet to research the newest smartphones. Select two models you would like to purchase. Create a table comparing their features. Include the following information: cost, carrier, contract length, camera type, media player, video, games, Internet, email, mobile operating system, and any other information you think is important. How do the devices stack up? Write up a summary explaining which one you would buy and why.

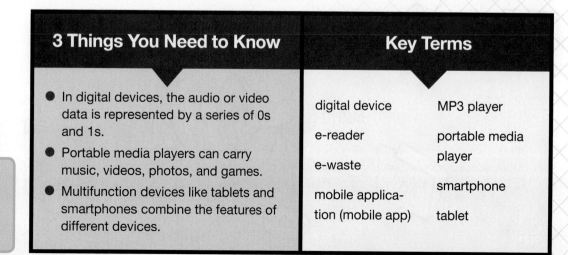

3 Things You Need to Know

- In digital devices, the audio or video data is represented by a series of 0s and 1s.
- Portable media players can carry music, videos, photos, and games.
- Multifunction devices like tablets and smartphones combine the features of different devices.

Key Terms

digital device	MP3 player
e-reader	portable media player
e-waste	
mobile application (mobile app)	smartphone
	tablet

Viz Check—In MyLab IT, take a quick quiz covering Objectives 4–6.

smartphones

portable media devices

DIGITAL CAMERAS

features

zoom lens 2x

zoom lens 4x

types

point-and-shoot

compact system

DSLR

TRANSFERRING PHOTOS TO YOUR COMPUTER

memory cards

4 GB

tablets

e-readers

DIGITAL MOBILE DEVICES

USB & firewire

1

2

6

cloud

wireless

DIGITAL MEDIA DEVICES

5

3

You Tube

VIDEO

video camera

4

EDITING, PRINTING AND SHARING PHOTOS

editing

screen capture

webcam

AUDIO

file types .mp3 .acc

media & software

speech

recognition

online

Objectives Recap

1. Explain the Features of Digital Cameras
2. Compare Methods for Transferring Images from a Digital Camera
3. Identify Several Ways to Edit and Print Photos
4. Recognize Important Audio File Types
5. Describe Several Ways to Create Videos
6. Compare Portable Media Players, Tablets, and Smartphones

Key Terms

AAC (advanced audio coding) **305**
autofocus **284**
AutoPlay **290**
burst mode **285**
caption **310**
codec **305**
compact system camera (CSC) **286**
Creative Commons (CC) licensing **296**
digital device **321**
digital rights management (DRM) **306**
digital single-lens-reflex (DSLR) camera **286**
e-reader **323**
e-waste **309**
fixed-focus **284**
focal length **284**
geotagging **295**
image stabilization **285**
iOS device **291**
lossless compression **294**
lossy compression **294**

machinima **313**
mirrorless camera **286**
mobile application (mobile app) **322**
MP3 (MPEG-1 Audio Layer 3) **305**
MP3 player **321**
multimedia **281**
podcast **306**
point-and-shoot camera **285**
portable media player **321**
resolution **283**
screen capture **313**
shutter lag **285**
smartphone **322**
speech recognition **308**
streaming **311**
tablet **322**
tagging **289**
telephoto lens **284**
webcam **311**
webcasting **311**
wide-angle lens **284**
zoom **284**

Summary

1. **Explain the Features of Digital Cameras**

   The three types of digital cameras are: point-and-shoot, compact system/mirrorless, and DSLR. Each type is progressively more expensive and complex. Resolution is the measure of pixels in an image, and higher-resolution cameras can take higher-quality pictures. Storage includes internal camera storage as well as flash memory cards. Zoom and lenses are important features that can make an object appear closer or farther away.

2. **Compare Methods for Transferring Images from a Digital Camera**

   Flash memory cards can be removed from a camera and plugged directly into a card reader in a computer or a kiosk in a store. Most cameras can also be connected to a computer via USB, Thunderbolt, or FireWire cable. Some cameras include Wi-Fi or can use a Wi-Fi-enabled SD card. The images can be copied to a disc, the cloud, or a computer or made into prints.

3. **Identify Several Ways to Edit and Print Photos**

   At home, you can print photos by first transferring the images to a computer or by directly connecting a printer and camera. In-store kiosks can read most memory card types or access images on the Internet, and online services allow you to upload images to be printed that can be mailed home or picked up at a local retailer.

4. **Recognize Important Audio File Types**

   Codecs are compression algorithms that reduce the size of digital media files. The most common audio codecs include MP3, which is the most common format for music files, and AAC, which is primarily used by Apple iTunes. Another common audio file is a MIDI file, which is often used for synthesized music in video games.

5. **Describe Several Ways to Create Videos**

   Screen capture software is used to create a video of what is happening on a computer screen, but video cameras are needed to record action away from the screen. You can use a webcam to stream a live feed or to have a real-time video conference.

6. **Compare Portable Media Players, Tablets, and Smartphones**

   Portable media players are small, handheld devices that play music, video, and photos and may also have games, Internet access, and other features. Tablet devices are multifunction devices that fall somewhere between notebook computers and smartphones and include built-in apps as well as the ability to download others. Smartphones are cell phones with PDA functions and portable media players built in. Smartphones can extend their capabilities with mobile apps and are true convergence devices.

Multiple Choice

Answer the multiple-choice questions below for more practice with key terms and concepts from this chapter.

1. Which term describes the number of pixels in an image?
   a. Codec
   b. Focal length
   c. Resolution
   d. Zoom

2. Which type of camera has a lens with a preset focal length that focuses well on objects within a specific distance?
   a. Autofocusing
   b. Fixed-focus
   c. Macro
   d. Optical zoom

3. Which type of lens would be best for shooting a beach scene?
   a. Digital zoom
   b. Macro
   c. Telephoto
   d. Wide-angle

4. Which type of camera uses a mirror?
   a. Compact system camera (CSC)
   b. Digital single-lens reflex (DSLR)
   c. Point-and-shoot
   d. Smartphone

5. What feature of Windows launches an application based on the type of files on the media?
   a. AutoPlay
   b. Codec
   c. Device drivers
   d. Tagging

6. Which file format must be processed by software in order to be used?
   a. BMP
   b. JPG
   c. RAW
   d. TIF

7. Which codec is the default audio file type used by Apple iTunes?
   a. AAC
   b. MIDI
   c. MP3
   d. WMA

8. Which tool enables you to create a video of what happens on your computer screen?
   a. Machinima
   b. Screen capture software
   c. Streaming
   d. Webcam

9. Why might you carry a tablet instead of a notebook?
   a. Longer battery life
   b. To listen to music
   c. To take pictures
   d. All of the above

10. Which e-reader technology makes a screen that is easy to read and extends battery life?
   a. Backlight
   b. E-ink
   c. HD
   d. LCD

True or False

Answer the following questions with *T* for true or *F* for false for more practice with key terms and concepts from this chapter.

_____ 1. Multimedia is the integration of text, graphics, video, animation, and sound.

_____ 2. Resolution is the measure of the number of pixels in an image.

_____ 3. Autofocus cameras automatically adjust the focal length by using a small motor to move the lens in or out.

_____ 4. Digital zoom is better than optical zoom.

_____ 5. Point-and-shoot cameras use interchangeable lenses and can cost thousands of dollars.

_____ 6. Tagging images or files with keywords makes it easier to organize and search for them.

_____ 7. Once an image is compressed using a lossy compression it can't be fully restored to the original format.

_____ 8. Geotagging allows you to add location information to your digital photos.

_____ 9. The MP3 codec creates files that are higher quality than AAC files.

_____ 10. Machinima is a prerecorded radio- and TV-like show that you can download and listen to or watch any time.

Fill in the Blank

Fill in the blanks using the words from the key terms.

1. _____ is the measure of the number of pixels in an image and is expressed in megapixels.

2. The _____ is the distance at which subjects in front of the lens are in sharp focus.

3. A(n) _____ is an algorithm that reduces the size of digital media files.

4. _____ use a mirror that enables you to see the image you're about to shoot through a view finder.

5. A(n) _____ is a prerecorded radio- and TV-like show that you can download and listen to or watch any time.

6. The _____ compression algorithm removes information that humans can't normally detect.

7. You can change copyright terms on your work by applying _____.

8. _____ is a technology that is applied to digital media files, such as music, eBooks, and videos, to impose restrictions on the use of these files.

9. _____ media, such as video or audio, begins to play immediately as it is being received and does not require the whole file to be downloaded to your computer first.

10. A(n) _____ can be downloaded to extend the functionality of a mobile device.

Running Project ...

... The Finish Line

In this chapter you researched a number of digital devices. Think about the career you are planning to pursue. What is one such device that would be important in your career? Using your answers to the previous sections of the Running Project, write a report describing your selections and responding to the questions raised. Save your file as **lastname_firstname_ch06_project** and submit it to your instructor as directed.

Do It Yourself 1

Purchasing a smartphone can be a difficult task, as there are many different models to choose from. In this exercise, you will research several smartphones and determine which is right for you. For this exercise, the cellular provider should not be a factor that you consider. From your student data files, open the file *vt_ch06_DIY1_answersheet* and save the file as **lastname_firstname_ch06_DIY1_answersheet**.

Use the Internet to research three smartphones. Complete the following chart. Write up a summary of your findings. Which device is the best choice for you and why? If you had more money, would your choice change? Save your file and submit your work as directed by your instructor.

	Phone 1	Phone 2	Phone 3	Comments
Smartphone model				
Price				
Mobile operating system				
Wireless connectivity				
Memory capacity				
Expandability				
Included apps				
Additional app availability				
Special features				
Website where you found your information				

Do It Yourself 2

In this activity, you will use iTunes to locate podcasts. If you are unable to use iTunes, then use the website **stitcher.com**. From your student data files, open the file *vt_ch06_DIY2_answersheet* and save the file as **lastname_firstname_ch06_DIY2_answersheet**.

1. Open iTunes. Click *Go to the iTunes Store*. (*Note*: Your college may have disabled the iTunes store on your campus.) On the menu bar, click the *Podcasts* arrow. List three categories where you would find shows to help you with this course.

2. Click the Categories arrow and then click the *Technology* link. Scroll down to What's Hot and then click *See All*. Browse through some of the featured shows. Select one that interests you and watch it. What show did you pick and why? Is there a Subscribe button on the show page? If so, what options are listed for subscribing to the show? Take a screenshot to capture the page and paste it into your answer sheet. Type your answers and include the screenshot. Save the file and submit your work as directed by your instructor.

File Management

Files stored on your computer have properties attached to them that make searching for and organizing files easier. In this exercise, you will examine and modify the properties of an image file. From your student data files, open the file *vt_ch06_FM_answersheet* and save the file as **lastname_firstname_ch06_FM_answersheet**.

1. Use File Explorer to locate the data files for this chapter. Open the image file *vt_ch06_tags* and save a copy to the folder where you save your work for this class as **lastname_firstname_ch06_tags**.

2. In File Explorer, navigate to the folder where you save your work for this class. Select, but do not open, the file *lastname_firstname_ch06_tags*. Click the *View* tab, and then, if necessary, click the *Details* pane. Click *Add a tag* in the Details pane and type **logo** and then click *Save*. Take a screenshot of this window and paste it into your answer sheet.

3. On the Home tab of the ribbon, in the Open group, click *Properties*. Click the *Details* tab and compare the properties visible to those in the Details pane of File Explorer. Point to each property in the dialog box. Which properties can you change?

4. Add your name as the author and **VT Chapter 6** as the title. Take a screenshot and paste it into your answer sheet. Save your image file and answer sheet and submit both as directed by your instructor.

Critical Thinking

You are excited about the idea of using the cloud to stream your entertainment, but before you begin, you need to do some home-work to decide what the best option is for you. From your student data files, open the file *vt_ch06_CT_answersheet* and save the file as **lastname_firstname_ch06_CT_answersheet**.

Use the Internet to research three video-streaming services, such as Netflix, Amazon Instant Video, Crunchyroll, or Hulu Plus. If you are a TV subscriber, be sure to include your TV provider as one of the services to compare. What are the basic features of each? Do they require any special hardware or software to be installed? What is the difference between their free, ad-supported service and premium paid subscription? Is it worth the price? Examine your own computer. Does it have all of the hardware you will need? If not, what will you need to purchase? What about your mobile devices?

Write up a summary that includes the answers to these questions. Save the file and submit your assignment as directed by your instructor.

Ethical Dilemma

Anna received some music CDs of her favorite band for her birth-day. She likes to listen to her music on her smartphone, so she ripped the music to her computer and transferred the songs to her phone. Because she no longer needs the CDs to listen to her music, her roommate Monica suggested that she sell them on eBay. This would free up some space in their cramped apartment and generate some much needed cash. From your student data files, open the file *vt_ch06_ethics_answersheet* and save the file as **lastname_firstname_ch06_ethics_answersheet**.

Anna wonders if this is ok. Is it ethical to sell the CDs and still keep the music? Is it legal? Because Anna and Monica share a computer, is it ok for both of them to transfer the music files to their smartphones? Write up a one-page summary that includes the answers to the questions above. Save the file and submit it as directed by your instructor.

On the Web

Webcams have become common tools for scientists to use to mon-itor animals, weather conditions, and even volcanoes. From your student data files, open the file *vt_ch06_web_answersheet* and save the file as **lastname_firstname_ch06_web_answersheet**.

Search the web for a webcam that is streaming a live feed of a place you would like to visit. Choose a webcam that is sponsored by a reputable organization. Visit the site, take a screenshot of the webcam feed, and paste it into your answer sheet. Are there any other webcam feeds on the same site? What is the address of the webcam you chose? What location is being observed? What organization sponsors the webcam? How did you locate it?

Type your answers in your answer sheet, save the file, and submit your file as directed by your instructor.

Collaboration

In this project you will create your own video podcast. You'll need a video camera and video editing software such as Windows Movie Maker or iMovie to complete this project.

Instructors: Divide the class into small groups of two to four students. The topic for each group is a smartphone or tablet that is used by a member of the group.

The Project: As a team, prepare a video podcast that includes an explanation of your chosen device, favorite features, and a demonstration of how to send and receive email using the device. Write a script for a two- to five-minute presentation. Choose a format that best suits your group. For example, it can be a news magazine, talk show, game show, or any other format you'd like to use. Use at least three references. Use Google Drive or Microsoft Office to prepare the presentation and provide documentation that all team members have contributed to the project.

Outcome: Prepare a video podcast on your assigned topic. Submit a copy of the script. Save the file as **teamname_ch06_collab** and be sure to include the name of your podcast and a listing of all team members on the first page. The podcast will be two to five minutes in length and uploaded to YouTube. It requires participation from everyone in the group. Save the final project as **teamname_ch06_podcast** and submit it as directed by your instructor.

Application Project

MyLab IT
GRADER

Office 2016 Application Projects
Excel 2016: Worldwide Digital Camera Sales

Project Description: In this project, you will analyze the global digital camera sales from 2014 to 2016. You will format cells and use a function, and you will create and format a column and a pie chart. *If necessary, download the student data files from* **pearsonhighered.com/viztech**.

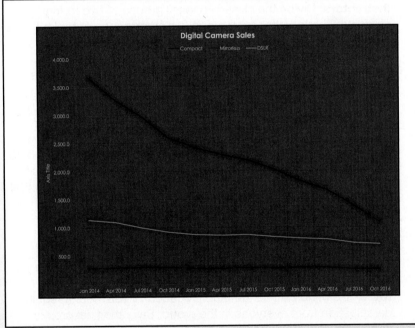

http://promuser.com/markets/2016/global-digital-camera-market-report-november-2016

Digital Camera Sales

Global Digital Camera Unit Trend (K) by Type - 2014 to 2016

Camera Type	Jan 2014	Apr 2014	Jul 2014	Oct 2014	Jan 2015	Apr 2015	Jul 2015	Oct 2015	Jan 2016	Apr 2016	Jul 2016	Oct 2016
Compact	3,672.0	3,276.0	2,976.0	2,599.0	2,424.0	2,295.0	2,201.0	2,035.0	1,826.0	1,665.0	1,381.0	1,082.0
Mirrorless	278.0	284.0	293.0	290.0	271.0	267.0	279.0	276.0	282.0	281.0	252.0	253.0
DSLR	1,139.0	1,099.0	1,000.0	921.0	876.0	862.0	872.0	832.0	803.0	784.0	719.0	696.0
All-types	**5,089**	**4,659**	**4,269**	**3,810**	**3,571**	**3,424**	**3,352**	**3,143**	**2,911**	**2,730**	**2,352**	**2,031**

vt_ch06_excel_solution.xlsx

Step	Instructions
1	Start Excel. From your student data files, open the Excel file *vt_ch06_excel.* Save the workbook as **lastname_firstname_ch06_excel**
2	Apply the Slice theme to the workbook.
3	Merge and center the text in cell A7 over columns A:M. Increase the font size to 14 pt. Middle align the text, and change the row height to 65.
4	Select the range A8:M8, increase font size to 12 pt., and set the text to wrap in the cells. Center and middle align the text in the selected range.
5	In cell B12, use the SUM function to calculate the digital still camera sales for January 2014. Copy the formula over the range C12:M12.
6	Change the cell style of B16 to Comma [0] and Total. Apply the Comma cell style to the range B9:M11. Decrease the decimals displayed to 1.
7	Select the range A8:M11 and insert the Recommended Stacked Column chart. Move the chart so that its upper left corner aligns with the upper left corner of cell C15.
8	Format the column chart with Chart Style 10. Change the chart title to **Digital Camera Sales**
9	Select the range A8:M11 and insert the Recommended Line chart. Move the chart to a new sheet named **Sales Chart**
10	Change the layout of the line chart to Layout 1. Change the title to **Digital Camera Sales** Format the chart with the chart Style 9.
11	On the 2014–2016 sheet, insert the text **Digital Camera Sales** as WordArt using Fill – Dark Blue, Accent 1, Shadow. Move the WordArt so that its upper left corner aligns with the upper left corner of cell A1.
12	Change the scaling of the 2014–2016 worksheet so the width will fit to one page. Center the 2014–2016 worksheet horizontally on the page. Change the orientation to Landscape.
13	Ensure that the worksheets are correctly named and placed in the following order in the workbook: Sales Chart, 2014–2016. Save the workbook and close Excel. Submit the workbook as directed.

Application Project

MyLab IT
GRADER

Office 2016 Application Projects
Word 2016: Making the Most of Your Cellphone Camera

Project Description: You have been asked to write an article on digital cameras. You will need to change alignment, line and paragraph spacing, margins, and lists and edit the header and footer. You will also find and replace text, create and modify a footnote, and use the Format Painter. *If necessary, download the student data files from* **pearsonhighered.com/viztech**.

Make the Most Out of Your Mobile Camera

July 21, 2018

With the summer season in full swing, our digital cameras are getting a full workout. The cameras built into our smartphones are always with us—allowing us to capture those special moments. But what to do with the images we capture? Fear not my friends. We are going to look at some amazingly easy ways to really make those photos something special to share.

Android Devices

One of the coolest features of an Android phone is the ease of sharing media. The list of ways you can share depends upon the apps you have on your smartphone, but at minimum you can send an email or SMS message.

Some of the apps that you can use to share images are:

- Email or Messaging
- Facebook or Instagram
- Twitter[1]

Let's get started. Once you've taken the picture that you want to share, there are just a few easy steps you need to do.

1. Open the Gallery
2. Select the photo you want to share
3. If necessary, tap the photo to display the Share option
4. Tap the Share icon to open the Share menu
5. Select the service you want to use to share the photo
6. Follow the service screens directions to enter any log in or recipient information

That's it!

---
[1] Some services require separate account setup.

vt_ch06_word_solution.docx

---

iOS Devices

Apple's iOS on the iPhone and iPad also has pretty slick sharing capabilities. As with the Android devices, the list of sharing options will vary depending upon the services and apps on your iOS device.

Some of the choices on an iOS device include:

- Email
- Assign to contact
- Tweet

So here are the steps using an iPad.

1. Open the Photo app
2. Select the photo you want to share
3. Tap the Options icon in the upper right hand corner
4. Select the service you want to use to share the photo
5. Follow the service screens directions to enter any log in or recipient information

vt_ch06_word_solution.docx

As you can see, sharing your photos instantly has never been easier. So snap away and be sure to share the best and funniest photos with us on Instagram. Use the hashtag #viztech.

Step	Instructions
1	Start Word. From your student data files, open the Word file *vt_ch06_word*. Save the file as **lastname_firstname_ch06_word**
2	Change the left and right margins of the document to 1.25". Change the line spacing of the entire document to 1.5 lines. Change the paragraph spacing (before and after) of the entire document to Auto.
3	Center the heading *Android Devices*. Using the Format Painter, apply the formatting from the heading *Android Devices* to the heading *iOS Devices*.
4	Use the Find and Replace dialog box to search for and replace all instances of the word *cellphone* with **smartphone** There should be two replacements.
5	In the Android Devices section, format the list beginning *Email* and ending *Twitter* as a bulleted list using solid round bullets. Increase the left indent of the bulleted list to 0.5".
6	In the Android Devices section, format the list beginning *Open the Gallery* and ending *Follow the service screens* as a numbered list using the 1., 2., 3. format. Increase the left indent of the numbered list to 0.5".
7	In the iOS Devices section, format the list beginning *Email* and ending *Tweet* as a bulleted list using solid round bullets. Increase the left indent of the bulleted list to 0.5".
8	In the iOS Devices section, format the list beginning *Open the Photo app* and ending *Follow the service screens* as a numbered list using the 1., 2., 3. format. Increase the left indent of the numbered list to 0.5".
9	In the document header, add a page number using the Plain Number 2 style at the Top of Page. In the footer, add the FileName field using the default format. Ensure the header and footer are not displayed on the first page.
10	In the Android Devices section, in the bulleted list, insert a footnote immediately following the text *Twitter* reading **Some services require separate account setup.** (Include the period.)
11	Use the Spelling and Grammar dialog box to correct the misspelling of the word *lsit* to *list*. Ignore all other spelling and grammar suggestions.
12	Place the insertion point after last line of the Android Devices section (That's it!). Press Enter and insert the picture *vt_ch06_image1*. Center align the image and change the image height to 3 inches.
13	Place the insertion point at the beginning of the last paragraph ("As you can see …"). Press Enter, move the insertion point up to the new blank line, and insert the picture *vt_ch06_image2*. Center align the image and change the image height to 3 inches.
14	Save the file and close Word. Submit the document as directed.

Cybrain

Cybrain/Fotolia

The Internet

In This Chapter

VIZ INTRO

The Internet is such an integral part of our everyday lives that you may already know a lot about it. But there's so much to know that most people only scratch the surface. After reading this chapter you'll understand the wide variety of tools and information at your fingertips and why you need to be fluent in the tools and language of the Internet in order to be an educated consumer, a better student, and a valuable employee.

BrunoWeltmann/Fotolia

Objectives

1 Recognize the Importance of the Internet

2 Compare Types of Internet Connections

3 Compare Popular Web Browsers

4 Demonstrate How to Navigate the Web

5 Discuss How to Evaluate the Credibility of Information Found on the Web

Running Project

In this chapter, you'll learn about the Internet. Look for project instructions as you complete each article. For most articles, there's a series of questions for you to research. At the conclusion of the chapter, you'll submit your responses to the questions raised.

BillionPhotos.com/Fotolia

Internet Timeline

1 Recognize the Importance of the Internet

There is an urban myth that Al Gore invented the Internet. Al Gore didn't invent the Internet, but early on, he recognized its potential and, as a congressman and vice president, promoted its development through legislation. In 2005, he received a Webby Lifetime Achievement Award for his contributions (**webbyawards.com**). He was one of the first politicians to see the potential of the Internet, but it actually started much earlier.

How It All Got Started

In 1957, the Soviet Union launched the first space satellite, *Sputnik*. The United States and the Soviet Union were, at the time, engaged in a political conflict—the Cold War—and the launch of *Sputnik* led to fears that the United States was falling behind in the technology race. In 1958, President Eisenhower created the Advanced Research Projects Agency (ARPA) to jumpstart U.S. technology for the military. One of ARPA's early projects was to create a "Galactic Network" that would connect smaller networks around the world.

The Internet started as a U.S. Department of Defense ARPA project in the 1960s to design a communications system that had multiple pathways through which information could travel, so that losing one part of the system (for example, in a nuclear strike) wouldn't cripple the whole thing. It took about 10 years to develop the technology. The original system, called **ARPANET**, connected four sites (Figure 7.1): The University of California—Los Angeles (UCLA), the Stanford Research Institute (SRI), the University of California—Santa Barbara (UCSB), and the University of Utah.

In 1979, the National Science Foundation (NSF) began developing CSNET—the Computer Science Network, which was brought online in 1981 to connect the computer science departments at universities using the ARPANET technology. In the mid-1980s, the NSF created NSFNET, giving other academic disciplines access to supercomputing centers and connecting smaller networks together. By the late 1980s, NSFNET was the primary **Internet backbone**—the high-speed connection between networks. In 1995, NSF decommissioned the NSF backbone, the Internet backbone was privatized, and the first five large **Network Access Points (NAPs)** that made up the new backbone were established in Chicago, New Jersey, San Francisco, San Jose, and Washington, D.C. Today, the backbone of the Internet is composed of numerous **Internet Exchange Points** around the world.

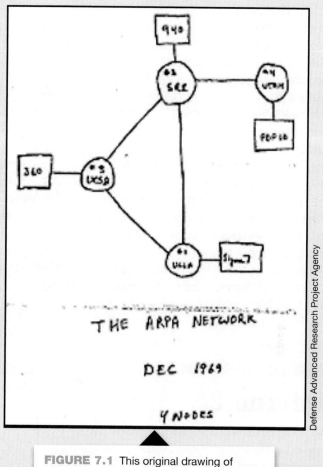

Defense Advanced Research Project Agency

FIGURE 7.1 This original drawing of ARPANET shows the first four sites at UCLA, SRI, UCSB, and the University of Utah.

World Wide Web

Many people use the terms *Internet* and *World Wide Web* interchangeably, but they are two different things. The **Internet**, or just *net*, is the physical entity—a network of computer networks. The **World Wide Web**, or just *web*, is just one way that information moves on the Internet. Email, instant messaging, file sharing, and making calls via **VoIP (Voice**

over IP) are other ways that you might use the Internet.

In 1991, Tim Berners-Lee and CERN (European Organization for Nuclear Research) released the hypertext system known as the World Wide Web. The web is made up of **hypertext**, which is text that contains links to other text or objects such as images. Hypertext enables you to

navigate through pieces of information by clicking the links, or **hyperlinks**, that connect them. The milestone of having a million Internet nodes—networks or web servers—was reached in 1992, and commercial sites, such as Pizza Hut, began to appear. The first White House website was launched in 1994.

In 1993, a group of graduate students led by Marc Andreessen released the Mosaic point-and-click graphical browser for the web, which later became Netscape Navigator—the dominant web browser in the 1990s. A **web browser** is a program that interprets HTML to display webpages. These events helped create a user-friendly Internet. A few years later, Microsoft released Windows 95 and Internet Explorer, which made personal computers easier to use and more popular. Around that time, existing online service companies such as AOL and CompuServe began offering Internet access to subscribers. As personal computers dropped in price and became more powerful, the Internet grew at an incredible rate, and the widespread use of mobile devices such as tablets and smartphones has put Internet access in the hands of even more people. Figure 7.2, from the ITU World Telecommunication/ICT Indicators database, shows the global growth of Internet use from 2005 to 2016, divided into Developed and Developing countries.

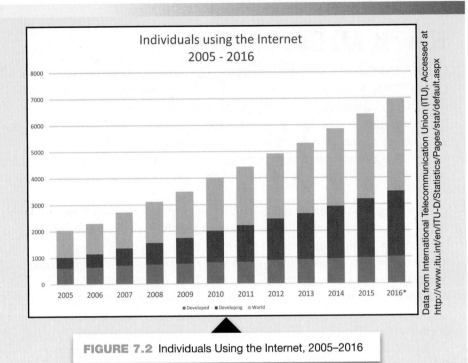

Data from International Telecommunication Union (ITU). Accessed at http://www.itu.int/en/ITU-D/Statistics/Pages/stat/default.aspx

FIGURE 7.2 Individuals Using the Internet, 2005–2016

Internet2

The original uses of the Internet—research and education—have been overtaken by commercial and social uses. Even as bandwidth and the Internet infrastructure have increased, educational and research institutions have been unable to access the speed and resources they need, and so the Internet2 project was born. **Internet2** is a second Internet, designed for education, research, and collaboration, very much like the original Internet—only faster. In 1995, when NSFNET was decommissioned, a small part of it was retained just for research. Called the Very High Speed Backbone Network Service (vBNS), it later evolved into the Internet2 project. Although the Internet is composed of a mix of older telephone cables and newer fiber optics, the Internet2 backbone is all fiber. The data travels much faster and is less prone to corruption.

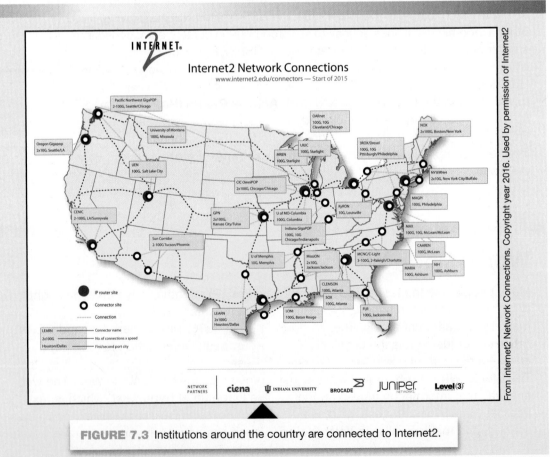

FIGURE 7.3 Institutions around the country are connected to Internet2.

Membership in Internet2 is limited to colleges, universities, other educational institutions, museums and art galleries, libraries, hospitals, and other organizations that work with them. It's a pretty small group, and that's one of the reasons it's so fast. Collaboration, streaming video, and web conferencing are just some of the applications that benefit from the faster speed. Figure 7.3 shows the Internet2 Connectors map. A connector site provides an Internet2 connection and other network services to regional participant institutions.

Running Project

Does your school participate in the Internet2 project? Ask your librarian or instructor. If yes, what features does your school use? Where is your Internet2 connector? If your college does not use Internet2, find out why not.

4 Things You Need to Know

- ARPANET was the original Internet.
- The Internet is the physical network; the web is just one way data moves on the Internet.
- Hypertext is used to navigate the World Wide Web by using hyperlinks.
- Internet2 is a second Internet, designed for education, research, and collaboration.

Key Terms

ARPANET

hyperlink

hypertext

Internet

Internet backbone

Internet Exchange Point

Internet2

Network Access Point (NAP)

VoIP (Voice over IP)

web browser

World Wide Web

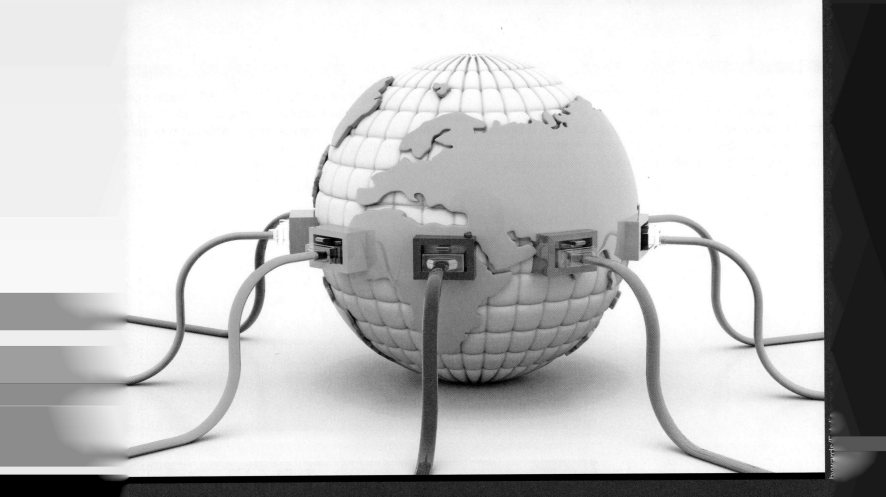

Get Connected

ctive

2 Compare Types of Internet Connections

There are many different ways to get on the Internet. **Internet service providers (ISPs)** are companies that offer Internet access. The options available to you depend on where you live and how much you have to spend.

SIMULATION

The Internet

How Do You Get Connected?

A good place to find local ISPs is by searching the web. If you don't have access at home, most schools and libraries offer free access. Search for a list of ISPs that offer service in your area; there are many websites that compare services and prices for you.

Ask yourself what you need, based on how you use the Internet. Do you just check email and look up recipes? If so, a slower, less expensive connection might work for you. If you work from home, play games, share photos, or watch videos, you'll need a faster connection. **Bandwidth**—the data transfer rate of a network—is measured in kilobits per second (Kbps), megabits per second (Mbps), or gigabits per second (Gbps). Advertised rates are maximum download speeds, but the actual rate can fluctuate and may often be much lower. Some types of Internet access deliver lower upload speeds, also called asynchronous connections. Figure 7.4, from the FCC, compares the bandwidths needed for various uses.

Household Broadband Guide

	Light Use	Moderate Use	High Use
	(Basic functions only: email, web surfing, basic streaming video)	(Basic functions plus *one* high-demand application: streaming HD, video conferencing, OR online gaming)	(Basic functions plus *more than one* high demand application running at the same time)
(e.g., laptop, tablet, or game console)	Basic	Basic	Medium
2 users or devices at a time	Basic	Basic	Medium/Advanced
3 users or devices at a time	Basic	Basic/Medium	Advanced
4 users or devices at a time	Basic/Medium	Medium	Advanced

Basic Service = 1 to 2 Mbps
Medium Service = 6 to 15 Mbps
Advanced Service = More than 15 Mbps

FIGURE 7.4 FCC Household Broadband Guide

DIAL-UP

The least expensive type of connection is usually **dial-up**. With a dial-up connection, you use your regular phone lines to connect to the Internet. Plans range from about $10 to $30 per month. This might be a good back-up plan to have in case your normal connection becomes unavailable. For some people, especially those in rural areas, a dial-up connection may be the only option available. Dial-up maxes out at 56 Kbps, and it can be very slow, especially if you're trying to download a file or watch a video. Another drawback is that the connection ties up your phone line while you're online. Aging phone lines were not designed to carry data, so they do a poor job of it, and dial-up is almost obsolete.

Blackday/Fotolia

BROADBAND

To get more speed than with dial-up, you have several options: cable, DSL, fiber-optic, and wireless technologies. The Federal Communications Commission (FCC) defines **broadband** as anything over 25 Mbps. Availability, speed, and costs vary depending on where you live. You'll have to do some research to get the best price and service. Figure 7.5 compares the download speeds of popular residential Internet connection types.

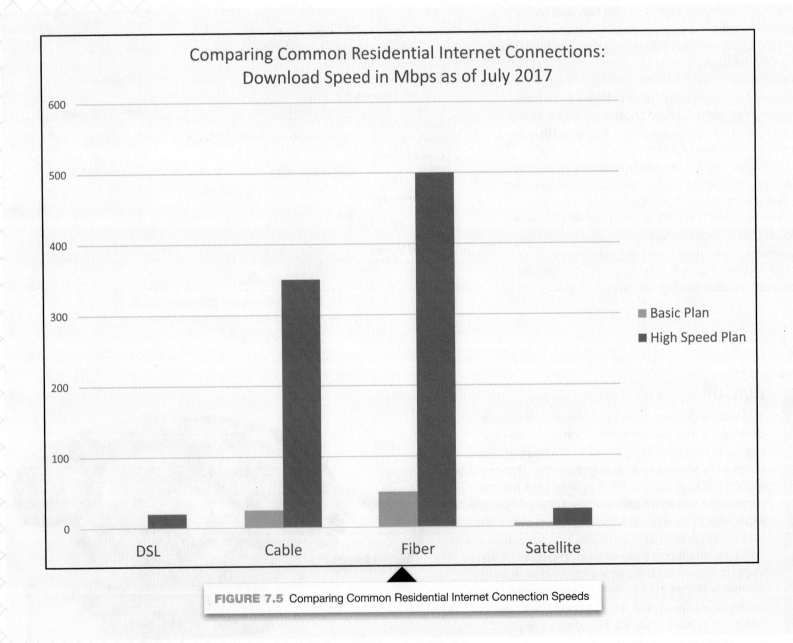

FIGURE 7.5 Comparing Common Residential Internet Connection Speeds

Cable Internet access is offered by your cable TV provider and uses the same wires to carry both signals. Some cable companies also offer digital phone service. This requires older cable systems to be upgraded, so it's not available everywhere. Residential cable speeds range from 1–2,000 Mbps (2 Gbps) but are typically 25–350 Mbps. One potential drawback to using cable Internet access is that you share the cable, and therefore bandwidth, with your neighbors. This could negatively impact your Internet speed if many neighbors are online at the same time.

DSL (digital subscriber line) technologies use telephone lines to carry digital signals. Unlike your normal phone line that's designed to carry analog signals (sound), DSL lines are designed to carry digital signals and are much faster than ordinary telephone lines. DSL averages speeds of 512 Kbps to 20 Mbps, which is slower than cable; and by the FCC definition of 25Mbps, not technically broadband. One of the biggest problems with DSL is its distance limitations. You must be within 3 miles of the DSL service provider's facilities. The further away you are, the slower your connection will be. Aging phone lines can also significantly slow down DSL.

Fiber-to-the-home (FTTH), also known as fiber-to-the-premises, is one of the fastest of the broadband alternatives, with top speeds of 940 Mbps—although most companies offer rates only of up to 500 Mbps. FTTH can carry Internet, TV, and phone calls to your home over fiber-optic cable and is available in limited areas—those where the fiber-optic cable has been installed. In the United States, the primary FTTH service is Verizon **FiOS (Fiber Optic Service)**. Google Fiber, which is currently available in limited markets, offers speeds of 1–10 Gbps (10,000 Mbps). Unlike cable and DSL lines, which many people already have, FTTH requires a contractor to lay a fiber-optic conduit directly to the home, which can be costly and can involve digging up your lawn.

WIRELESS

What if you live in a rural or remote area without cable, DSL, or fiber access? What about if you're on the road? There are several wireless alternatives available, too. These options include mobile cellular access, Wi-Fi, and satellite.

Mobile Internet access enables you to connect to the Internet using the cellular network standards 3G (third generation) and 4G (fourth generation). 4G is faster and includes **WiMAX Mobile Internet** and **LTE (Long-Term Evolution)** technologies. The signals are transmitted by a series of cellular towers; thus, coverage can be spotty in some places. Coverage maps that are available on the carrier's websites, or sites such as OpenSignal (Figure 7.6), enable you to verify whether coverage exists where you need it before you make a commitment.

Coverage map created by OpenSignal using real-world, on-device measurements to analyse subscriber experience. More information at OpenSignal.com

FIGURE 7.6 Cellular maps show mobile network coverage.

Several companies are developing mobile technologies for fifth-generation networks that will provide data transmission up to several hundred times faster than the current 4G technology. The new 5G networks will transmit data up to 1 Gbps, which exceeds the wired broadband speeds currently available to most consumers. The 5G networks will transmit large amounts of data over long distances, using a wide band of frequencies. With such speeds, you will be able to download a full-length high-definition movie in seconds; video streaming will be seamless, with no lagging; and online games will be played in real time. Samsung expects to begin implementing 5G in 2018.

Although you may think about 3G/4G in terms of mobile devices, mobile Internet can be used on a personal computer with a special network adapter. Special modems make 4G available at home, too. In some cases, a smartphone can serve as a wireless access point to share the connection with other devices via wireless or USB tethering. So you could use your smartphone to provide Internet access to your notebook when traveling. Several automobile makers have incorporated 4G into their entertainment and navigation systems. Top mobile Internet speeds are considered broadband and rival wired broadband service.

Satellite Internet access is a more global and more expensive option than the others mentioned so far. Satellite service speeds are comparable to those of DSL. You need a clear view of the southern sky, where the communication satellites are positioned in geosynchronous orbit 22,000 miles above Earth, and weather conditions can affect your service. Geosynchronous satellites match the earth's rotation, and so remain above the same spot on earth. You would probably consider satellite only if there were no other options available where you live. Over the next few years, several new satellites are scheduled to be launched, which will increase the availability and speed of satellite Internet.

Wi-Fi uses radio waves to provide wireless high-speed network connections. It is the type of wireless networking you may have set up in your home or office. **Municipal Wi-Fi** is offered in some cities and towns. Wi-Fi **hotspots** are wireless access points that are available in many public locations, such as airports, schools, hotels, and restaurants, either free or for a fee (Figure 7.7).

FIGURE 7.7 You can find Wi-Fi hotspots in many public spaces.

CONNECTING WITHOUT A COMPUTER

Smartphones, tablets, video game consoles, and media players can connect to the Internet via cellular or Wi-Fi networks. Some e-readers include free cellular Internet access or use Wi-Fi to shop for and download books and to access other resources. These devices generally have small screens and limited keyboards, which can make using them difficult. However, mobile devices are becoming more powerful and easier to use, and many people rely on them as their primary Internet access devices. According to the ITU (www.itu.int /ict), as of 2016, 95 percent of the global population live in areas covered by mobile networks.

Satellite phones connect to satellites instead of cellular towers, making them useful in places where cell service is lacking, such as remote locations. They need a clear view of the sky and don't work well indoors. Satellite phones and satellite phone services are very expensive.

Oleksii Akhrimenko/Fotolia

Access for All

According to the Pew Research Center, in 2015, 85 percent of adults in the United States were Internet users, and 70 percent of adults had home broadband access. For those who don't have broadband at home, cost and inaccessibility are often cited as the reasons. The 2015 Broadband Progress Report concluded that 17 percent of the U.S. population lack access to advanced broadband—broadband exceeding 25 Mbps download service. Of course, some people just aren't interested—they don't find any need to have Internet access at home. But for the rest of us, not having a good Internet connection just isn't an option.

FIND OUT MORE

The Open Internet Transparency Rule is an ambitious plan to ensure that all Americans have access to fast, affordable Internet access. Go to fcc.gov to find out why the U.S. government considers this so important. Explain the Open Internet Transparency Rule.

Running Project

Use the Internet to research the current state of satellite Internet access. Have the newest satellites been deployed? What services and speeds are available, and what do they cost? Is satellite Internet access a viable option where you live?

4 Things You Need to Know

- Dial-up is the slowest type of Internet access.
- Broadband Internet access includes cable, DSL, FTTH, satellite, and cellular 3G/4G.
- Satellite and cellular access are options for those without a computer.
- The type of Internet access you choose largely depends on where you live.

Key Terms

bandwidth

broadband

cable Internet access

dial-up

DSL (digital subscriber line)

fiber-to-the-home (FTTH)

FiOS (Fiber Optic Service)

hotspot

Internet service provider (ISP)

LTE (Long-Term Evolution)

municipal Wi-Fi

satellite Internet access

Wi-Fi

WiMAX Mobile Internet

Female photographer/Fotolia

Surf's Up

Compare Popular Web Browsers

Some people use the Internet strictly for email, others for schoolwork, and still others for watching videos. Some folks visit specific websites regularly, while others like to surf and explore. Regardless of how you use the web, you need the right tools to access it and enjoy the content.

VIZ CLIP

HTML

Browsers

Most information on the web is in the form of basic **webpages**, which are written in **HTML (Hypertext Markup Language)**—the authoring language that defines the structure of a webpage. Mosaic, released in 1993, was the first web browser—a program that interprets HTML to display webpages. Mosaic eventually became Netscape Navigator, which dominated the market until Microsoft got in the game. Google Chrome, Internet Explorer, Mozilla Firefox, Microsoft Edge, and Apple Safari are the most widely used browsers for personal computers today, but there are numerous alternatives. Many people simply use the browser that comes preinstalled on their device, but using an alternate browser, or even multiple browsers, allows you to use the best browser for each application. Some websites, tools, and technologies are optimized or better supported by specific browsers, so you may find it helpful to have more than one browser installed on your system.

INTERNET EXPLORER AND MICROSOFT EDGE

First released in 1995, Internet Explorer (IE) is included with Windows, so there's no special download needed. Windows 8.1 includes two versions of IE: a full-screen app and a desktop version. Windows 10 includes the desktop version of IE 11 hidden in the Windows Accessories folder of the Start menu, and a new browser—Microsoft Edge—which has replaced IE as the default browser. Figure 7.8 shows some important features of Edge.

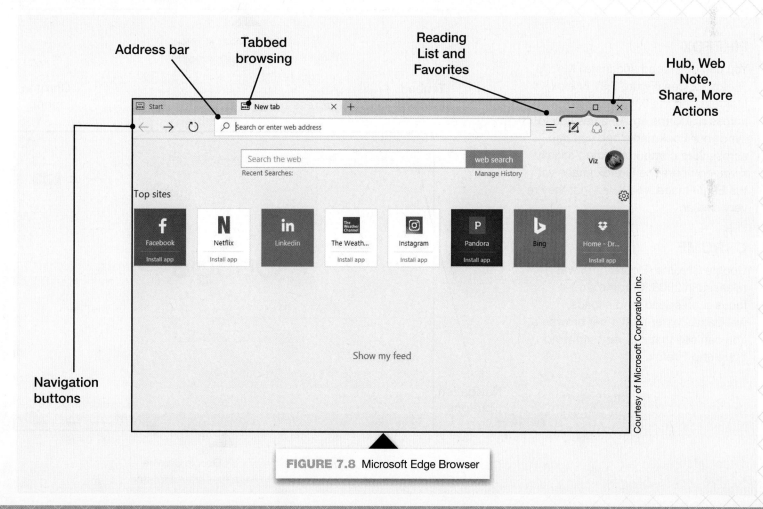

FIGURE 7.8 Microsoft Edge Browser

Courtesy of Microsoft Corporation Inc.

Some important features of Edge and Internet Explorer are:

- **Navigation buttons:** Provide a means to navigate back and forward through browsed webpages.
- **Address bar:** Contains the web address of the current webpage. You can also search the web from the address bar without having to go to a search provider's website first.
- **Favorites:** Enables you to save web addresses, giving you easy access to your favorite websites. Favorites are sometimes called bookmarks.
- **Tabbed browsing:** Enables you to have multiple webpages open in tabs.

FIREFOX

You can download and install Mozilla Firefox for free (Figure 7.9). Firefox, first released in 2004, is available across platforms and enables you to sync your bookmarks and settings across your computers automatically. If you compare the Firefox image with the Edge image, you'll see that they're very similar.

CHROME

Google Chrome (Figure 7.10) was released in 2008. Chrome's main focus is on speed, and it loads webpages faster than other browsers. You can see that it is very similar to Edge and Firefox.

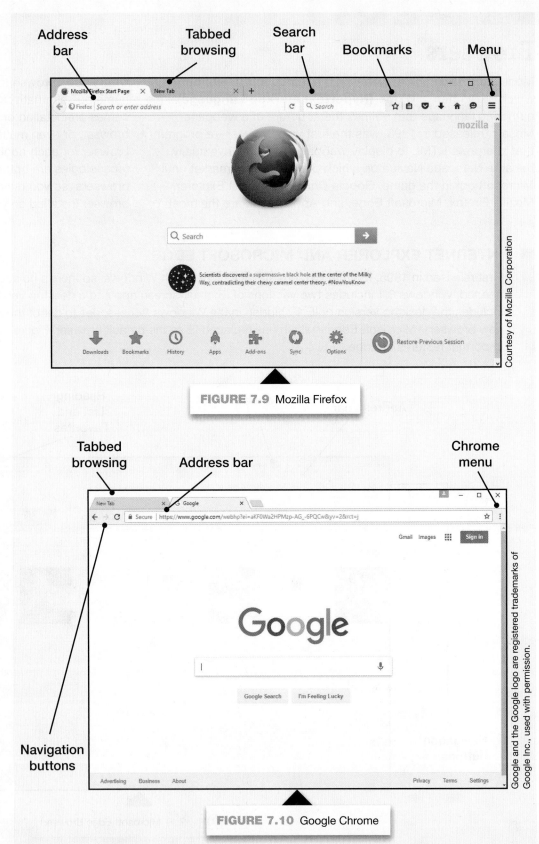

FIGURE 7.9 Mozilla Firefox

FIGURE 7.10 Google Chrome

Courtesy of Mozilla Corporation

Google and the Google logo are registered trademarks of Google Inc., used with permission.

SAFARI

Safari (Figure 7.11) is the most popular web browser for Macs. It comes bundled with macOS. The mobile version of Safari—the default on iOS devices—has almost 60 percent of the mobile browser market.

MOBILE BROWSERS

Small-screen devices, such as tablets, e-readers, and smartphones, use **mobile browsers**, which are optimized for small screens. Firefox, Chrome, Safari, and Opera all come in mobile versions. Other mobile browsers are proprietary—such as the Kindle and Android browsers. Most websites today can be accessed with a mobile browser, and many websites offer alternative pages that are optimized to be viewed with a mobile browser. Figure 7.12 shows the iPad version of Safari.

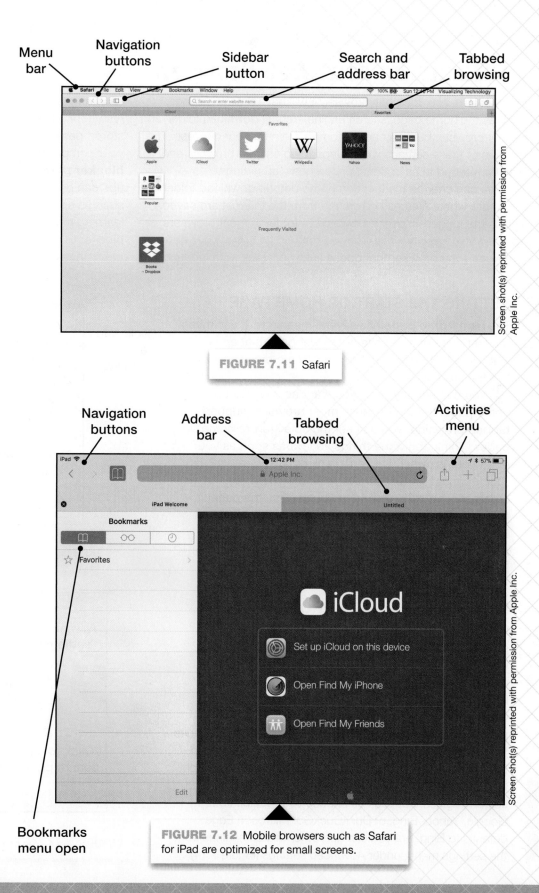

FIGURE 7.11 Safari

FIGURE 7.12 Mobile browsers such as Safari for iPad are optimized for small screens.

Configuring Your Web Browser

The first time you open any browser, it will have default settings, such as the home page, search engine, default download folder, and default browser, but you can customize them for your own use. The location of these settings varies depending on your browser, and may be referred to as options, preferences, or settings.

You can change the location of the default download folder—the folder where files you download from the Internet are saved. This is the logged-in user's Downloads folder in most browsers. You can also specify which browser should be set as your **default browser**—the browser that opens links you click from locations such as your desktop, email messages, and links in documents. Also configure the security and privacy settings, history settings, stored passwords, and how **cookies**—small text files placed on your computer by websites that you visit—are handled. A **pop-up blocker** prevents webpages from opening a new window. Pop-ups can be used for advertising, but also for other useful purposes, such as opening a quiz or external video from your classroom learning management system—LMS. You can configure a pop-up blocker to allow pop-ups from specific sites—such as your school or business—while blocking pop-ups for all other sites.

SETTING THE START OR HOME PAGE

The term **home page** has several meanings. It can mean the first page of a website or the webpage that appears when you first open your browser. Some browsers call this the start page.

You can set any page you want as your start or home page. In fact, because most browsers support tabbed browsing, you can set multiple start or home pages. Think about the things you do as soon as you open your browser. Do you check email? Weather? Stock prices? Traffic? Knowing where you most commonly go online will help you choose the page(s) that open when you start your browser. The Microsoft Edge default is a news feed that you can customize. In the settings for Edge, you can change what page(s) Edge opens with (Figure 7.13).

SETTING THE SEARCH PROVIDERS

When you type a search term in the address bar or search box of your browser, what search engine is used? By default, the **search engine**—a website that provides search capabilities on the web—will be the one that your browser, computer manufacturer, or ISP chose, but as with your start page, you can modify this to your own preferences. Firefox defaults to Yahoo, and Chrome defaults to Google, and both allow you to add to or modify this. In Firefox, you can change the search engine for each search right from the search bar. Safari does not allow you to add search engines, but you can choose your default from Google, Yahoo, Bing, or DuckDuckGo. Microsoft Edge defaults to Bing, but you can add other search engines from the settings menu, under *Advanced settings* (Figure 7.14).

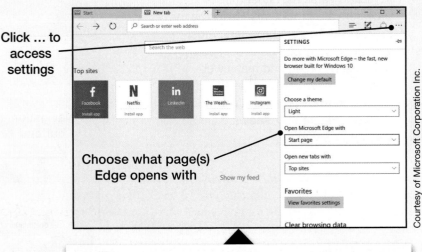

Click ... to access settings

Choose what page(s) Edge opens with

Courtesy of Microsoft Corporation Inc.

FIGURE 7.13 Edge settings let you choose what page(s) open.

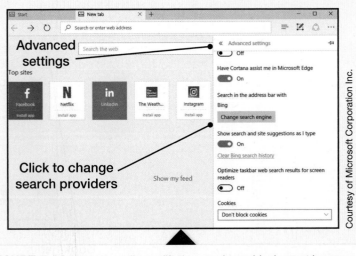

Advanced settings

Click to change search providers

Courtesy of Microsoft Corporation Inc.

FIGURE 7.14 You can easily modify the search provider in most browsers.

Add-Ons, Plug-Ins, and Toolbars

You can extend the functionality of your web browser by installing extensions—add-ons, plug-ins, and toolbars. The distinction between the terms *add-on* and *plug-in* varies by browser. A **plug-in** is a third-party program, such as Adobe Reader. An **add-on** is created for a specific browser to add features to it. Some popular add-ons capture video from the web, block ads, and connect to maps and shopping. A word of warning, though: Add-ons and plug-ins need to be updated regularly, as they can present security risks when they're not properly patched. Adding a **browser toolbar** to your browser gives you quick access to the features of the application that installed it—but be wary of toolbars that come bundled with software you install. Toolbars can be a source of malware and may slow down your browsing.

Plug-in software, such as Adobe Flash Player, Microsoft Silverlight, and Oracle Java, helps your browser display the multimedia-rich, interactive, dynamic content that's increasingly common on the Internet. Many plug-ins are being replaced with newer, safer options such as HTML5. If your school uses an online learning management system or other tools, you might need to install specific plug-ins on your computer. Modern browsers may restrict some plug-ins from running, and you may find you can't access certain websites with your browser of choice. Figure 7.15 shows the Extensions settings in Edge. From this window, you can discover new extensions and disable or remove those that you don't want.

Viz Check—In MyLab IT, take a quick quiz covering Objectives 1–3.

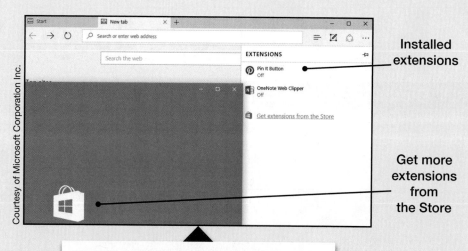

Courtesy of Microsoft Corporation Inc.

Installed extensions

Get more extensions from the Store

FIGURE 7.15 Managing Edge Extensions

Running Project

Research the versions and market shares of the top five web browsers. What is the market share of each desktop version? What about mobile versions? Are there any browsers in the current list that are not mentioned in this text?

4 Things You Need to Know

- The most popular web browsers are Google Chrome, Internet Explorer, Mozilla Firefox, Microsoft Edge, and Apple Safari.
- Mobile browsers are optimized for the small screens of mobile devices.
- You can customize the home page and other settings in most browsers.
- Add-ons and plug-ins extend the functionality of web browsers.

Key Terms

add-on

cookie

default browser

home page

HTML (Hypertext Markup Language)

mobile browser

plug-in

pop-up blocker

search engine

web browser

webpage

Use Google Drive

Digital Literacy Skill

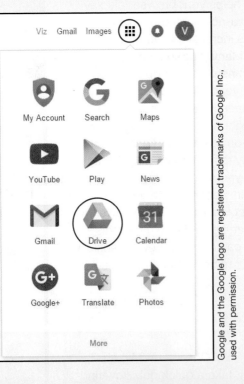

HOW TO VIDEO

Google provides free online storage, called Google Drive, and applications that you can use to create and share many types of documents. If you do not have a Google account, on the Google home page, click *Sign in*, click *Create an account*, and create a new account for this exercise. You can delete it when you have finished the exercise, or you can keep it as an extra account.

Using Google Drive is an easy way to create and share documents with others. There is no software to purchase or install; the Google Drive applications run right from your browser. Google Drive is an example of SaaS (software-as-a-service). It doesn't matter if you have a PC and your friend has a Mac. Collaboration with Google Drive is easy, and you can work on files together even if you are not in the same location.

1 Go to **Google.com** and sign in to your Google account. Click the *Apps* menu icon at the top of the screen and then click *Drive*.

Viz Gmail Images

My Account   Search   Maps

YouTube   Play   News

Gmail   Drive   Calendar

Google+   Translate   Photos

More

Google and the Google logo are registered trademarks of Google Inc., used with permission.

2 On the **Google Drive** page, you can see the files you have created and shared, and you can see files others have shared with you. To create a new file, click the *NEW* button and choose the type of file you want to create. Click *Google Docs*.

3 The word processing tool includes standard formatting options and is easy to use. Enter the following text in the document, pressing Enter after each sentence.

A simple Google document can be shared and used as an easy collaboration tool, no installation required!
The toolbar includes standard formatting options, including font styles and alignment.
You can add elements such as links, images, and lists.
There is a built-in spell checker.
You can share your file with others by clicking the blue Share button.

Untitled document

File Edit View Insert Format Tools Table Add-ons Help   All changes saved in Drive

A simple Google document can be shared and used as an easy collaboration tool, no
installation required!
The toolbar includes standard formatting options, including font styles and alignment.
You can add elements such as links, images, and lists.
There is a built-in spell checker.
You can share your file with others by clicking the blue Share button.

4 Google automatically saves your file as *Untitled document*, so you need to rename the file. Above the menu bar, click *Untitled document* and then change the file name to **lastname_firstname_ch07_howto1**.

5 If possible, work with a classmate on this part of the activity. Click the *Share* button and, in the *Share with others* box, enter an email address to share the file with your classmate. Click *Send*.

Share with others   Get shareable link

People

Enter names or email addresses...

Done   Advanced

6

Close the browser tab to close the file and return to **Google Drive**. Take a screenshot of the file list and then open the shared file. If you are working with a classmate, you should both open the same shared file. If you are working alone, open the file you created for this exercise. Paste the screenshot at the end of the document.

A list of people working on the document displays in the upper right corner, and you can see their edits in real time. Open the list to view and chat with collaborators in the current session. At the end of the document, each collaborator should type a sentence about the topic and include his or her own name. From the File menu, choose *See revision history* to see each revision of the document.

You can download the file into many popular formats, such as a Microsoft Office format, by clicking *Download as* on the File menu. Submit as directed by your instructor.

BillionPhotos.com/Fotolia

Navigating the Net

Demonstrate How to Navigate the Web

Congratulations—you're connected. Now what? There's so much information out there, it can be overwhelming. How do you know where to start? How do you find what you're looking for?

VIZ
CLIP

Smart Searching

Web Addresses

There are two ways to move around the web. You can type in the **URL (uniform resource locator)** or address of the website you want to visit—such as **http://www.google.com**—or you can follow hyperlinks embedded in webpages from one place to the next. A URL consists of several parts, including the protocol, domain name, and top-level domain. A **website** consists of one or more webpages, all located in the same place. The home page of a website is the main, or starting, page. It's the page you see when you type in the web address for a site.

http://www.google.com

http is the protocol that tells your computer what type of page you're looking at. This is almost always http (a webpage) but can be other protocols such as https (a secure webpage) or ftp (file transfer protocol). It is so likely to be http that you can leave out this part of the address when you type it.

http://www.google.com

The *www* represents the computer on the *google* domain and is called the third-level domain, or subdomain. It is common to name the computer *www*, so this part of the URL is also often omitted. In this textbook, the *http://www* part of a URL is generally omitted.

http://www.google.com

The **domain name**, also called the second-level domain, represents a company or product name and makes the address easy to remember. In this example, *google* is the domain name.

http://www.google.com

.com is the **top-level domain (TLD)** and represents the type of website you're visiting. Generic TLDs, or gTLDs, can be sponsored (sTLD), meaning they are restricted to specific purposes defined by the sponsor organization, such as .edu (educational institutions) and .gov (government). Common unsponsored gTLDs, which do not have restrictions, are .com, .org, and .net, as well as many newer ones, such as .biz and .info. Websites outside the United States have a country code TLD, or ccTLD, such as .ca (Canada) or .uk (United Kingdom).

When you visit other pages on a website, the URL will have an additional part after the TLD that indicates the location of the webpage on the web server. For example, to view the Facebook page about this textbook, you can type **facebook.com /visualizingtechnology**.

ICANN (Internet Corporation for Assigned Names and Numbers) coordinates the Internet naming system. Computers on the Internet are assigned **IP (Internet Protocol) addresses**. An IP address is a unique numeric address assigned to each node on a network.

http://www.google.com

IP addresses are composed of numbers, which can be hard for a person to remember, so the DNS system was developed. **DNS (Domain Name System)** enables you to use a friendly name like google.com instead of an IP address like 74.125.224.72 to contact a website. DNS works like a telephone directory. When you enter a URL in your browser, your computer requests the IP address of the computer. Your DNS server, which is probably provided by your ISP, locates the IP address information and sends it back to your computer, which then uses it to address your request (Figure 7.16).

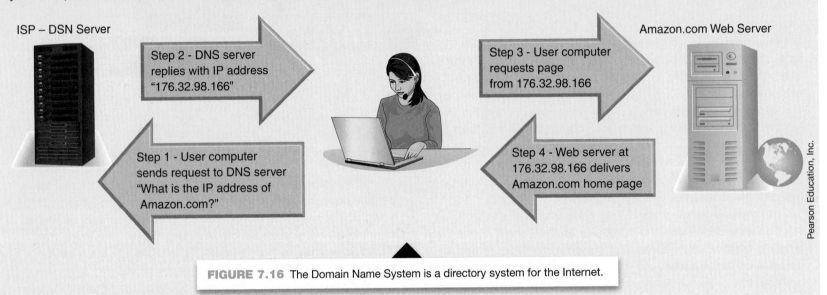

ISP – DSN Server

Step 2 - DNS server replies with IP address "176.32.98.166"

Step 1 - User computer sends request to DNS server "What is the IP address of Amazon.com?"

Step 3 - User computer requests page from 176.32.98.166

Step 4 - Web server at 176.32.98.166 delivers Amazon.com home page

Amazon.com Web Server

Pearson Education, Inc.

FIGURE 7.16 The Domain Name System is a directory system for the Internet.

FIND OUT MORE

Check out the iana.org website and click *Database of Top Level Domains* to view the current list of TLDs. What are some of the gTLDs in the list that are less common? What is the difference between a ccTLD and a gTLD?

ETHICS

In the early days of the web, it was common practice to buy up domain names to resell them. Speculators would buy domain names that they anticipated would be worth a lot of money. This practice is known as *cybersquatting*. Intentionally buying a domain name that's the same as a trademark another company owns (for example, Avon or Hertz, which were both victims) for the purpose of selling it to the trademark owner at a profit is a trademark infringement, but what about something that's not trademarked but still recognizable—like a catchphrase or a person's name?

Smart Searching

When did *google* become a verb? The verb *google*—to use the Google search engine to obtain information about (as a person) on the World Wide Web—was added to the Merriam-Webster Dictionary in 2006. With billions of webpages on the Internet, how do you begin to find what you're looking for, and when you do find it, how can you trust it? Searching for information on the Internet is a crucial skill in today's world. Although it may seem that everything you want to know is on Google, Google covers only part of the Internet. Also, when you type the words *dog care* in a search page such as Google, you'll get millions of results, or hits. So, the first part of the puzzle is knowing how to ask the right question.

Suppose you want to learn about the eagle you saw nesting in a building on the news. You go to **google.com** and type the word *eagles* in the search box. Performing that search on Google displayed 200 million hits on the day of this writing. Because the web is constantly changing, if you perform the same search today, your numbers will be different. Also, if your browser or device is using location services, your results might be location specific. Because the search was performed from a computer in Philadelphia, the Philadelphia Eagles football team is near the top of the results. If you live in Denver, the results might be different (unless it happens to be football season).

So where do you start? A good approach is to look at the first few hits and see if what you want is there. If not, think about a better way to ask the question. To narrow down the results, you can add some more keywords to the search. The first few hits using the word *eagles* got the football team and the rock band. You need to be more specific in your query if you're really interested in the kind of eagles that fly! You can do this by adding more terms to your search, such as *birds*, *raptors*, or *bald*. To get narrower search results, you can use the advanced search tool to filter the results. You can add or exclude terms as well as specify a language and date, among other things. The advanced search options are fairly common among search sites. Using Google, click the *Options* button (Figure 7.17) to access the Advanced search screen.

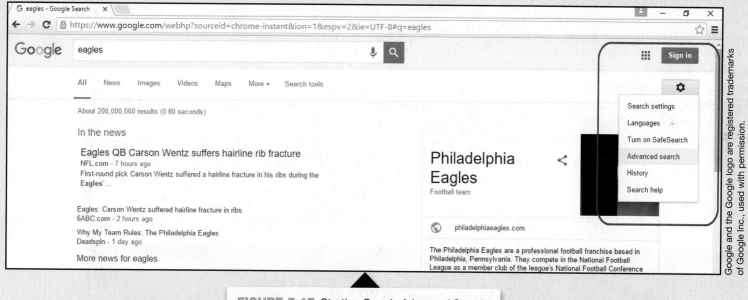

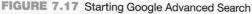

FIGURE 7.17 Starting Google Advanced Search

Google and the Google logo are registered trademarks of Google Inc., used with permission.

You can use **Boolean operators** to refine your search. A Boolean operator defines the relationship between words or groups of words and is used to create a search filter. There are three Boolean operators: AND, OR, NOT. Using AND to join two words results in pages that include both words—so the number of hits is lower. Joining two words with an OR means that either word can be present—so the number of hits is much larger. Using NOT is exclusive, which means the results must include the first word but cannot include the second word. Figure 7.18 shows the eagles search using various Boolean operators.

Search engines are huge databases. They send out software called spiders, or bots, to crawl the web and gather information, which is then indexed. Because the web is dynamic and constantly changing, this method helps the search engine stay up to date. Some search engines also accept submissions, and others use both methods to gather information. There are even **metasearch engines** that search other search engines. There may be differences in the ways the information is classified and categorized by different search engines. There are so many places to search for information that it can be hard to figure out where to start. Contrary to popular belief, Google doesn't track the entire web, so it's wise to become familiar with at least a couple other search tools you can use.

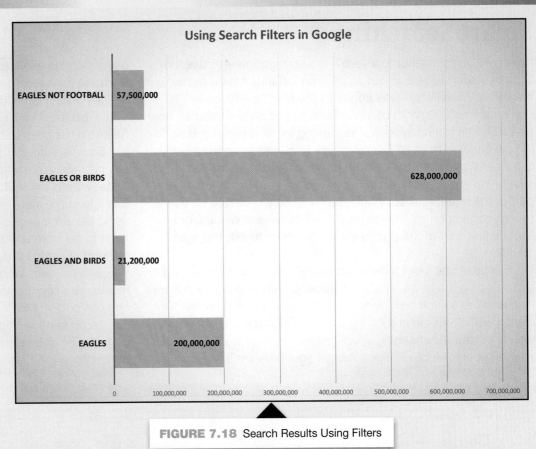

FIGURE 7.18 Search Results Using Filters

FIND OUT MORE

Did you ever wonder what your favorite website used to look like? The Internet Archive Wayback Machine can show you. Go to archive.org and enter the address of the website you want to see. The archives go back only to 1996, so you can't see the original Pizza Hut or White House site, but you can see the 1996 versions. Type in the address of your school's website and click *Take Me Back*. Click on several available dates to see how the site has changed over time. Try a few other sites that you visit regularly.

CAREER SPOTLIGHT

Roman Samborskyi/Shutterstock

WEB DESIGNER A person who decides how a website will look is called a web designer. For a simple website, the web designer may also be the person who creates the website. If you have ever created your own webpage, then you were the designer.

Today, it's pretty easy to create a basic website. There are software programs, templates, and websites such as Squarespace and Wix that can help you make something quickly and easily. A professional web designer, however, goes beyond the basics and creates designs that are customized and branded for a business. A web designer needs to have a good understanding of the capabilities of the web to design an interesting, dynamic, and professional site. Some web designers are self-taught; others have degrees in graphic arts, computer science, e-business, or marketing.

Running Project

Think Google, Bing, and Yahoo! are the only search engines around? Try googling *search engine* to see how many you get. How many of them have you used in the past? Select two that look interesting and search for the name of your local sports team on each. Did you get the same results? How were the results different? Read the About section of the search tool to determine how content is added. You can usually find this link at the bottom of a webpage. What are some of the unique features of each?

5 Things You Need to Know

- A web address is also known as a URL.
- gTLDs include .com, .edu, .gov, and so on. ccTLDs are country codes.
- DNS enables you to use URLs instead of IP addresses to access websites.
- Every node on the Internet has a unique IP address.
- Search engines are websites that provide search capabilities on the web.

Key Terms

Boolean operator

DNS (Domain Name System)

domain name

IP (Internet Protocol) address

metasearch engine

top-level domain (TLD)

URL (uniform resource locator)

website

How To? Create a Website Using Wix

HOW TO VIDEO

A small business or organization can use free or low-cost services to create a professional-looking website that provides customers with important information. In this project, you will use Wix to create a free website for JMG Landscaping. One advantage to using a website tool like Wix is the availability of premade templates that provide you with a professional layout and look without requiring you to build something from scratch. To use Wix, you can log in with your Facebook or Google account, or you can create a new Wix account using your email address. Note: The figures in this activity were taken using Google Chrome. If you use a different browser, your screens may differ slightly.

If necessary, download the student data files from **pearsonhighered.com/viztech**. From your student data files, open the *vt_howto2_answersheet* file and save the file as **lastname_firstname_howto2_answersheet**.

1 Go to **wix.com**, click *Sign In*, and log in or click *Sign Up* to create a new Wix account. On the *What kind of website do you want to create?* page, click *Business*. Click *Start with Wix Editor*. Click *Blank Templates*.

Used by permission of Wix.com

2 On the *Pick the website template you love* page, point to *Strip Header Layout* and click *Edit*. (Note: If this template is not available, select an appropriate template to use instead.)

Used by permission of Wix.com

3 If an introductory video displays, watch and then close the video. On the menu bar at the top of the page, click *Save*. In the Choose a domain to save your site box, in the Get a Free Wix.com domain box, type **jmglandscapes** and click *Save & Continue*. Click *Done*. On the Home page, click the *NAME OF SITE* box, click *Edit Text*, and with the text selected, press Delete and type **JMG Landscaping**. If necessary, close the Text Settings panel. Click the background image placeholder at the top of the screen, click *Change Strip Background*, and then on the *Strip Background* panel that displays, click *Image*.

4 In the *Choose an Image for Your Background* dialog box, click *Upload Images*. Browse to the student data files for this project and open the *banner* folder.

5 In the Open dialog box, drag to select all four images in the folder and then click *Open*. When the images have finished uploading, click *Done*. In the *Add Images* window, select the yellow flowers image *vt_banner02*, and then click *Change Background*. Close the Strip Background panel.

6 In the middle of the page, under the *I'm a paragraph* section, click the image placeholder, click *Change Image*. In the *Choose an Image* dialog box, click the picture of the red and yellow flowers, and then click *Choose Image*. Above the inserted image, click *Settings*. Scroll down to *Image Text*. Add the *Alt text* **Fall Color** and change the tooltip of the image to **Fall Mums**. Close the Image Settings panel.

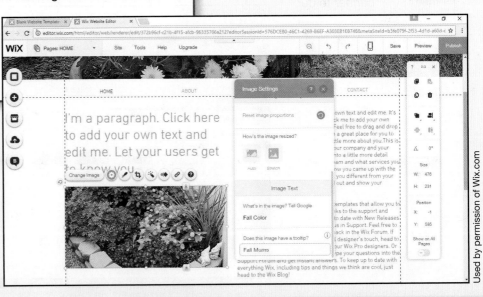

Used by permission of Wix.com

Used by permission of Wix.com

Alt text is a text description of an image that makes the website more accessible for visitors who use screen readers to read the content.

7 Scroll to the bottom of the page, click the image placeholder and change the image to the *vt_banner04.jpg* image. Change the *Alt text* and *tooltip* to **Rock Garden**.

8 Scroll to the top of the page. Click in the text box that begins with *I'm a paragraph*. Click *Edit Text*. With the text selected, press *Delete*, and type **Quality Landscaping**. Select all of the text and change the font size to **72 px** in the *Text Settings* panel. Click the *B* to make the text bold. Close the *Text Settings* panel.

Used by permission of Wix.com

9 Click the paragraph text box on the right. Click *Edit Text*. With the text selected, press *Delete*. In the blank box, type **We are JMG Landscaping, family-owned and operated since 1985.** (include the period). Select all of the text and change the font size to **24 px** in the *Text Settings* panel. Drag to select the text *JMG Landscaping* and click the *B* button to apply bold. Close the *Text Settings* panel. On the Wix menu on the top left, click the *+* to add an element. With *Add Text* selected, scroll down to *Titles*. Drag the *Story Title* element below the paragraph of text on your page. Click *Edit Text* and type **Making Beautiful Outdoor Spaces**. Select the new line of the text and change the font size to **44 px**. Close the *Text Settings* panel. Click outside the textbox to deselect it, and take a screenshot and paste it into your answer sheet.

These text boxes should contain important keywords and phrases that customers would use when searching for you.

10 Scroll to the bottom of the page. In the footer, click any of the social network icons to select the *Social Bar*, and then click *Set Social Links*. Click the *Facebook* icon, click in the textbox that contains the link, and change the URL to **http://www.facebook.com /visualizingtechnology** click *Done*, and then click *Done*.

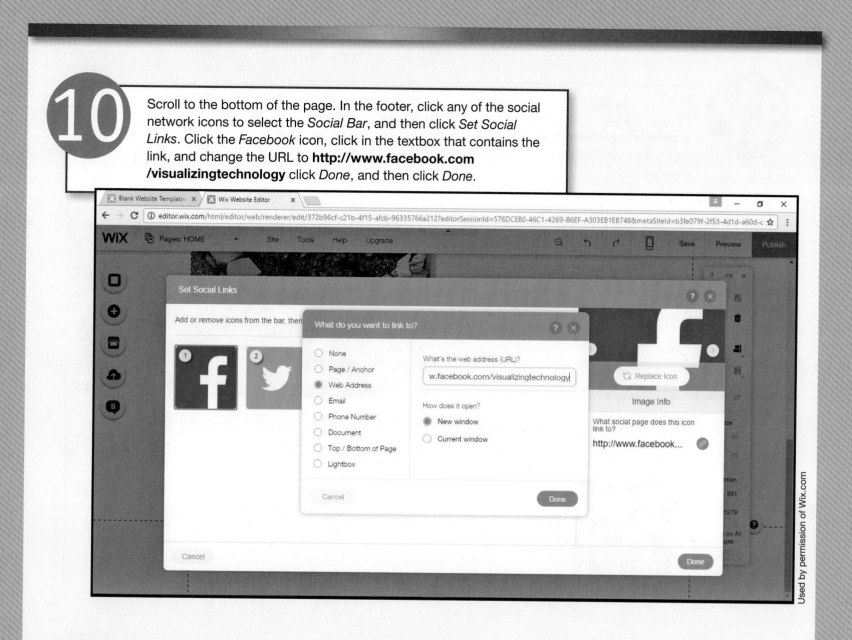

11 Click the *Pages* menu at the top of the page, and then click *About*. The banner at the top of the page does not change, but the content below the banner changes to the *About* page. Close the *Pages* panel. Click the image placeholder in the middle of the page, click *Change Image*, click the *vt_banner03* image, and then click *Choose Image*.

12

In the text box on the right, change the title to **Landscaping**. Change the paragraph text in the *Landscaping* section to **Fences, stonework, gardens, and more.** (include the period). Change the font size of the paragraph text to **20 px** and then close the *Text Settings* panel.

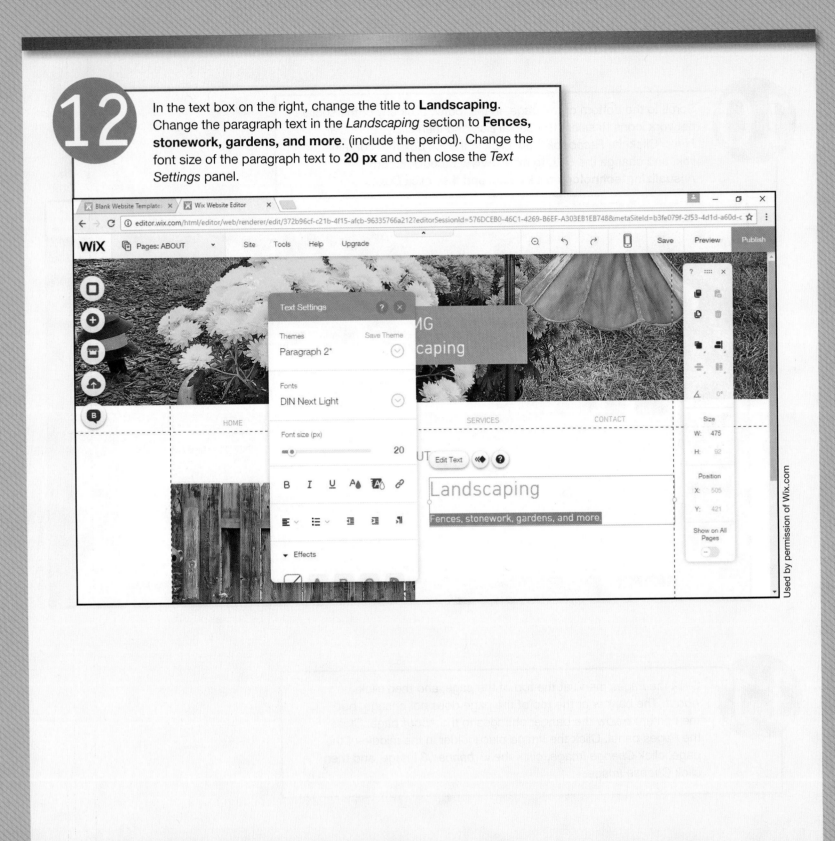

13

At the top of the page, click *Save*, click *Done*, and then click *Preview*. Test that everything is working correctly, click *Back to Editor*, and edit if necessary, and then click *Publish*. In the *Congratulations* pop-up, copy the URL of your website, paste it into your answer sheet, and submit to your instructor as directed.

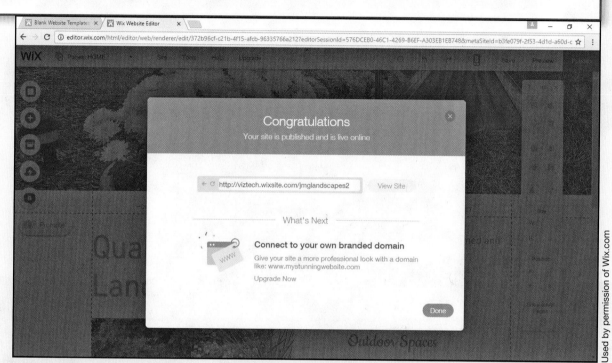

Used by permission of Wix.com

Your URL is your brand name. Using the default URL from Wix is fine for building and testing your page, but a real business or organization should register a domain name, such as **jmglandscaping.net.** To register a domain name, you can upgrade your Wix account to a premium plan which includes a voucher for a one-year domain name registration for free, or use a domain name registrar, such as **GoDaddy.com** or **register.com**. Your registered domain name URL belongs to you, not the service that you use to register it. You can easily connect a domain name purchased elsewhere to your Wix website, by following the instructions provided on the Wix platform or via Wix Help Center articles.

Would I Lie to You?

ctive
5

Discuss How to Evaluate the Credibility of Information Found on the Web

So, now that you have millions of hits, how do you know what to believe? The Internet is full of **user-generated content**—content that has been written by everyday users. Although there's a lot of wonderful content out there, anyone can say almost anything on the Internet. You need to be able to evaluate the information you find. There are many clues to look for when deciding whether a website is one that you can trust. Here are just a few.

Who Wrote It?

Do you believe everything you hear? Or everything you read? Do you evaluate the credentials of the people that you take advice from? How do con artists scam so many people into investing their money with them? They are convincing, and nobody questions the results until it is too late—even if what is promised is too good to be true. Be a skeptic when evaluating information that you find on the Internet.

Look at the URL. Ask yourself: Is it an sTLD like .edu or .gov, or a general one like .com? Take a look at **fda.gov** and **fda.com** and compare them. The .com version isn't the Food and Drug Administration website. On the **fda.com** website, at the top of the page in small type you will see, "Food and Drug Assistance; Resources for Industry and Consumers." Because most people are in the habit of typing *.com* rather than *.gov*, it's easy to end up at a site you didn't intend to visit. Some organizations go so far as to own both domains so you can't make that mistake—for example, you can reach the U.S. Postal Service website by typing either **usps.com** or **usps.gov**. When you enter the .gov URL you are automatically redirected to the .com site. A restricted TLD such as .edu or .gov gives some authority to a site, but even that's not a guarantee that the author is credible.

For more information, read the home page and About Us page, and look for the credentials of the author or organization. Check out the Contact page. Is there contact information? Ask yourself if there are any conflicts of interest or obvious biases. How up to date is the website? You can usually find this information at the bottom of the home page (Figure 7.19). Not being able to find any of this information should raise a red flag.

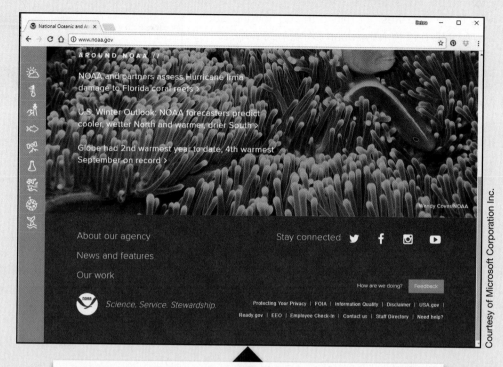

Courtesy of Microsoft Corporation Inc.

FIGURE 7.19 Find important information at the bottom of a webpage to help identify who wrote it.

Stick to well-known sources for important information. For example, if you're looking up health advice, try websites of trustworthy authorities, such as WebMD and the American Cancer Society. A URL such as **skipyourselfhealthy.info** may not be trustworthy. Then again, it might, but you'll need to do a bit of research before you can be sure. Take a look at other sites. Does the information you've found match what you can find on other sites that cover the same topics? Does it make sense? This is really key: If it's too good to be true, it probably is.

A good search tool to use when doing scholarly research is Google Scholar (**scholar.google.com**) to search for articles, theses, books, abstracts, and court opinions (Figure 7.20). Also check with your school library to see which databases and resources you have access to as a student.

FIGURE 7.20 Google Scholar

What About the Design?

Look at the design of the site, including its sophistication, grammar, and spelling. What impression do you get from the site? Don't be fooled: A well-designed and well-executed site can still have bad information, and a poorly designed site might have really good information. Pop culture websites like The Onion, America's Finest News Source (Figure 7.21), may be very well designed but are certainly not valid news sources.

Critically evaluating the information that you find on a website is a skill that takes time to master. It may not be a big deal if you believe a website that says you should eat tofu to make your hair grow (although it probably won't work), but if you follow online advice to invest all your money, and it turns out to be a scam, then it will be a huge deal.

FIGURE 7.21 theonion.com Website

GREEN COMPUTING
Telecommuting to Save

As I write this, I'm sitting in my home office in my sweat pants. I'm one of the millions of Americans who telecommute at least part-time. I go to campus a few days a week to teach classes, but I also teach many online classes, especially in the summer, which allows me to work from home. Although there are lots of arguments for and against telecommuting, there's no denying the positive impact it

UBER IMAGES/Fotolia

can have on the environment. It saves me a few days' worth of gas, which really adds up. It's better for the environment to keep my car off the road, and it's better for my wallet, too.

Not every job lends itself to telecommuting, but according to one study, if just 50 percent of the people who could work from home did so just half of the time, in the United States we would:
- Save over $650 billion a year
- Reduce greenhouse gas emission by the equivalent of taking 9 million cars off the road
- Reduce oil imports by 37 percent

Businesses that encourage telecommuting can also save on real estate expenses. Having fewer employees onsite means smaller office space requirements and lower utility bills.

Running Project

Compare these two websites: **choosemyplate.gov** and **foodpyramid.com**. Use the guidelines discussed in this article to evaluate and compare the two. Pay special attention to the About Us section on each site.

4 Things You Need to Know	Key Term
● User-generated content means anybody can create content on the web.	user-generated content
● Use the home page, contact information, and About pages of a website to look for credentials of the author or organization.	
● Sponsored TLDs are restricted and include .gov and .edu. They add some credibility to the content.	
● Good website design doesn't guarantee credible website content.	

Viz Check—In MyLab IT, take a quick quiz covering Objectives 4–5.

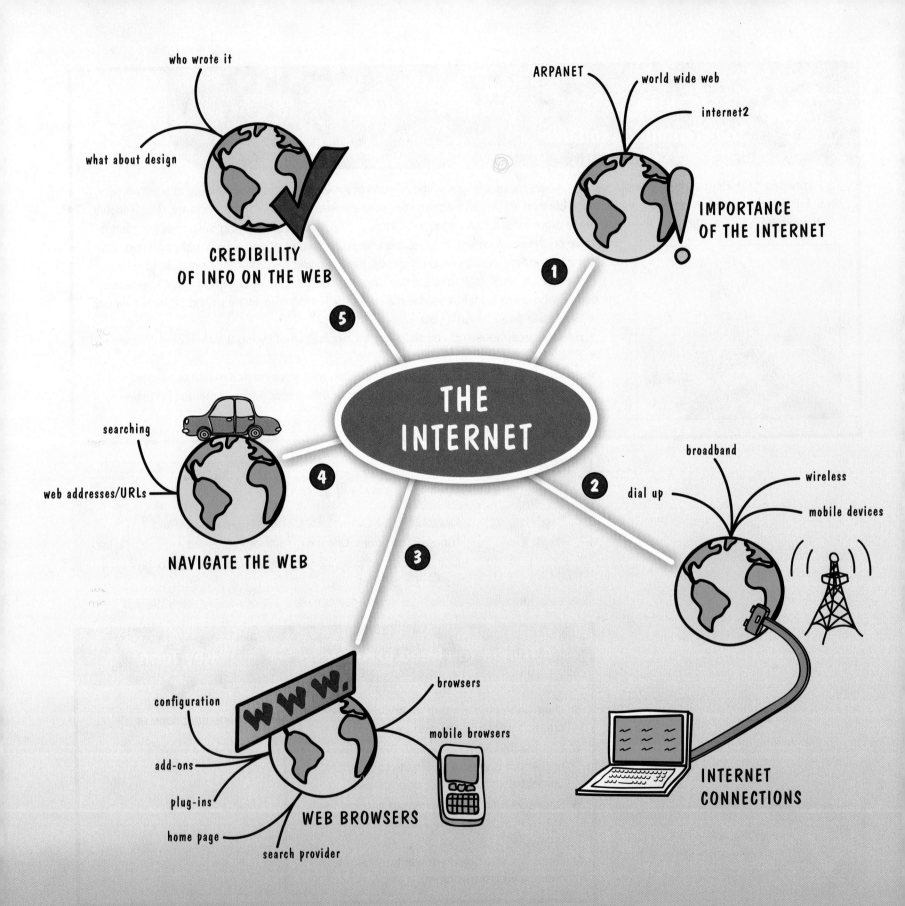

Objectives Recap

1. Recognize the Importance of the Internet
2. Compare Types of Internet Connections
3. Compare Popular Web Browsers
4. Demonstrate How to Navigate the Web
5. Discuss How to Evaluate the Credibility of Information Found on the Web

Key Terms

add-on **353**
ARPANET **339**
bandwidth **343**
Boolean operator **362**
broadband **344**
browser toolbar **353**
cable Internet access **345**
cookie **352**
default browser **352**
dial-up **343**
DNS (Domain Name System) **360**
domain name **359**
DSL (digital subscriber line) **345**
fiber-to-the-home (FTTH) **345**
FiOS (Fiber Optic Service) **345**
home page **352**
hotspot **346**
HTML (hypertext markup language) **349**
hyperlink **339**
hypertext **339**
Internet **339**
Internet backbone **339**
Internet Exchange Points **339**

Internet service provider (ISP) **342**
Internet2 **340**
IP (Internet protocol) address **359**
LTE (Long Term Evolution) **345**
metasearch engine **362**
mobile browser **351**
municipal Wi-Fi **346**
Network Access Point (NAP) **339**
plug-in **353**
pop-up blocker **352**
satellite Internet access **346**
search engine **352**
top-level domain (TLD) **359**
URL (uniform resource locator) **359**
user-generated content **372**
VoIP (Voice over IP) **339**
web browser **340**
webpage **349**
website **359**
Wi-Fi **346**
WiMAX Mobile Internet **345**
World Wide Web **339**

Summary

1. **Recognize the Importance of the Internet**

   Since its invention in 1969, the Internet has grown to over 3 billion users. It's now an integral part of research, education, commerce, and communication for people around the world. The Internet2 project is a second Internet that's limited to educational and research institutions.

2. **Compare Types of Internet Connections**

   Dial-up Internet uses regular telephone lines to access the Internet and is very slow. Broadband connections provide speeds of at least 25 Mbps and include cable, DSL, and fiber. Cable is provided by the same company that provides you with cable TV and uses the same lines for both services. DSL (digital subscriber line) uses digital telephone lines to provide Internet access. DSL is slower than cable and is affected by the distance from the telephone company switch. Fiber-to-the-home (FTTH) delivers Internet access over fiber-optic cable. Wireless Internet access includes municipal Wi-Fi, satellite, and 3G/4G cellular service.

3. **Compare Popular Web Browsers**

   The most popular web browsers are Google Chrome, Internet Explorer, Mozilla Firefox, Microsoft Edge, and Apple Safari. Mobile browsers are optimized for small-screen devices, such as smartphones and tablets.

4. **Demonstrate How to Navigate the Web**

   A web address or URL (uniform resource locator) can be broken down into protocol, TLD (top-level domain), and domain name. URLs can be typed in or embedded into a webpage as a hyperlink that you can click on. When you type a URL in your browser, your computer sends a DNS (Domain Name System) request to find the IP (Internet protocol) address of the website. You can search for information using search engines—huge databases that index webpages.

5. **Discuss How to Evaluate the Credibility of Information Found on the Web**

   Be skeptical. Look at the URL for restricted TLDs such as .gov and .edu. Read the About Us page and other website information to view the author's credentials. Look for professional design and writing style. Finally, verify information using other sources.

Multiple Choice

Answer the multiple-choice questions below for more practice with key terms and concepts from this chapter.

1. Hypertext enables you to navigate through pieces of information by clicking the _____ that connect them.
   a. hyperlinks
   b. Network Access Points
   c. Internet Exchange Points
   d. Connectors

2. A _____ is a program that interprets HTML to display webpages.
   a. hyperlink
   b. URL
   c. web browser
   d. VoIP

3. _____ is the data transfer rate of a network: measured in kilobits per second (Kbps), megabits per second (Mbps), or gigabits per second (Gbps).
   a. Bandwidth
   b. Broadband
   c. LTE
   d. WiMAX

4. Which technology uses fiber-optic cable to carry digital signals to your home?
   a. Cable
   b. DSL
   c. FTTH
   d. Wi-Fi

5. Which is the default browser on Windows 10 computers?
   a. Chrome
   b. Internet Explorer
   c. Safari
   d. Edge

6. A(n) _____ is optimized for a small-screen device.
   a. add-on
   b. toolbar
   c. mobile browser
   d. tab

7. Examples of sponsored TLDs (top-level domains) are:
   a. .gov and .edu
   b. .org and .net
   c. .tv and .biz
   d. .ca and .af

8. What enables you to type a URL in your browser instead of an IP address to reach a website?
   a. DNS (Domain Name System)
   b. Hypertext
   c. ICANN
   d. TLD (top-level domain)

9. A _____ is used to create a search filter.
   a. Boolean operator
   b. bot
   c. metasearch
   d. spider

10. Check the _____ on a website for the credentials of the author or organization.
    a. About Us page
    b. Contact page
    c. Home page
    d. All the above

True or False

Answer the following questions with *T* for true or *F* for false for more practice with key terms and concepts from this chapter.

_____ 1. The web was developed in 1991 by the Advanced Research Projects Agency (ARPA).

_____ 2. The web is just one way that information moves on the Internet.

_____ 3. Membership in Internet2 is limited to colleges, universities, other educational institutions, museums and art galleries, libraries, hospitals, and other organizations that work with them.

_____ 4. Internet Exchange Points are companies that offer Internet access.

_____ 5. With WiMAX Mobile Internet, you connect to the Internet using cellular networks that provide 4G service.

_____ 6. Most information on the web is in the form of basic HTML webpages.

_____ 7. Microsoft HTML5 is a popular web browser.

_____ 8. It's necessary to type **http://** when entering a URL in your browser.

_____ 9. Every device on the Internet must have a unique IP address.

_____ 10. Much of the Internet consists of user-generated content that should be critically evaluated.

Fill in the Blank

Fill in the blanks with key terms from this chapter.

1. The backbone of the Internet is composed of numerous _____ around the world.

2. The _____ is the part of the Internet that uses hypertext to connect pieces of information.

3. _____ is a service that allows phone calls to be transmitted over the Internet instead of over traditional phone lines.

4. _____ is a network designed for education, research, and collaboration.

5. Internet access that exceeds 25 Mbps is considered _____.

6. _____ uses radio waves to provide wireless high-speed network connections.

7. _____ is a description of an image that makes a website more accessible for visitors who use screen readers to read the content.

8. A(n) _____ is a small text file placed on a computer when you visit a website that helps the website identify you when you return.

9. A(n) _____, or web address, consists of three main parts: the protocol, domain name, and top-level domain.

10. A(n) _____ is a unique numeric address assigned to each node on a network.

Running Project ...

... The Finish Line

Use your answers to the previous sections of the project to answer the following questions. Why is the Internet important to you, and why is it important to be knowledgeable about it? Write a report describing how you use the Internet in your daily life and respond to the questions raised. Save your file as **lastname_firstname_ch07 project** and submit it to your instructor as directed.

Do It Yourself 1

The actual Internet access speed that you get is rarely as high as your ISP advertises. In this activity, you'll use an online speed test to measure your speed. From your student data files, open the file *vt_ch07_DIY1_answersheet* and save the file as **lastname_ firstname_ch07_DIY1_answersheet**.

Close anything that uses Internet access, such as your email or instant messaging programs. Open your browser and using your favorite search engine, search for **broadband speed test**. From your search results, run three speed tests on your connection using three different test services. Because results can fluctuate, run your test at least twice on each service. Is there a significant difference? Take a screenshot of the results screen for each of your tests and paste them into your answer sheet. What type of Internet connection do you have? How do the results compare to your expected speeds? Type your answers in your answer sheet, save the file, and submit as directed by your instructor.

Do It Yourself 2

In this activity, you will perform a search using Google and refine your search using advanced options. From your student data files, open the file *vt_ch07_DIY2_answersheet* and save the file as **last-name_firstname_ch07_DIY2_answersheet**.

1. Open your browser and go to **google.com**. In the search box, type **rose** and press Enter. Take a screenshot of this page and paste it into your answer sheet. How many results did you get? What type of information is displayed in the first page of results?

2. Add the word **red** before rose and press Enter. How does this affect the results?

3. Click the *Options* icon at the top right of the screen, and then click *Advanced search*. In the *none of these words* box, type **king** to exclude it from the search. Press Enter. How are the results affected? Take a screenshot of the results, and paste it into your answer sheet. Type your answers in your answer sheet, save the file, and submit it as directed by your instructor.

File Management

Saving information from the web can be tricky. In this exercise you will save a webpage in various formats and compare them using Google Chrome. From your student data files, open the file *vt_ch07_FM_answersheet* and save the file as **lastname_ firstname_ch07_FM_answersheet**.

1. Open Chrome and go to your school's home page. Click the Chrome menu, point to *More tools,* and then click *Save page as*. What is the default Save as type? Save the page as Home1 using the default file format. Be sure to note where you save the page.

2. Repeat the procedure and save the page using the other Save as file type, changing the name to **Home2**. What other file types are available?

3. Close your browser and open the folder that contains the saved files. Open each file by double-clicking it. What application opens each format? Compare how the page appears. What other files/objects are saved? Which format do you think is the best way to save this file and why?

4. Type your answers in your answer sheet, save the file, and submit as directed by your instructor.

Critical Thinking

In this exercise you will consider the Internet options available where you live. From your student data files, open the file *vt_ch07_CT_answersheet* and save the file as **lastname_firstname_ch07_CT_answersheet**.

Use the Internet to determine which broadband services are available where you live. Create a chart comparing prices and features. What questions should you ask to help you choose? Write up a summary of the services available and the questions you would ask each company. Type your answers in your answer sheet, save the file, and submit as directed by your instructor.

Ethical Dilemma

Use the Internet to research laws regarding parking and selling unused URLs. From your student data files, open the file *vt_ch07_ethics_answersheet* and save the file as **lastname_firstname_ch07_ethics_answersheet**.

Is it legal to grab up domains and park them? Is it ethical? What about changing the TLD of a well-known website (**nasa.com**, for example)? With new TLDs being implemented, such as .biz, .bargain, and .tv, should all related domain names be protected? Suppose you purchase a domain name for your own use, and it turns out that a company wants to buy it from you? Is it legal to sell it to them? At a profit? Type your answers in your answer sheet, save the file, and submit as directed by your instructor.

On the Web

Many websites will allow you to personalize the content that you see. Choose one of the following websites: NetVibes, My Yahoo!, or ProtoPage. In this exercise you will create a personalized web portal page that brings information from various sources together onto one page. From your student data files, open the file *vt_ch07_web_answersheet* and save the file as **lastname_firstname_ch07_web_answersheet**.

If necessary, create an account on your chosen website and log in. (This might be a good time to use a secondary email account created just for such purposes.) What personalization and customizations are available to you? Create your personal page on the site. What items did you choose to modify, add, or delete? Type your answers, take a screenshot of your customized page, and paste it in your answer sheet. Save the file and submit it as directed by your instructor.

Collaboration

Instructors: Divide the class into five groups, and assign each group one browser for this project. The topics include Internet Explorer, Edge, Firefox, Chrome, and Safari.

The Project: As a team, prepare a multimedia commercial for your assigned browser. The presentation should be designed to convince a consumer to use the browser. Use at least three references. Use Google Drive or Microsoft Office to prepare your presentation and provide documentation that all team members have contributed to the project.

Outcome: Prepare a multimedia presentation or video on your assigned topic and present it to your class. The presentation should be 2–3 minutes long. Be sure to include the name of your presentation and a list of all team members. Turn in a final version of your presentation named **teamname_ch07_presentation** and your file showing your collaboration named **teamname_ch07_collab** and submit your presentation to your instructor as directed.

Application Project

Office 2016 Application Projects
Word 2016: Cellular Internet Service

Project Description: You have been asked to write an article on cellular Internet service. You will need to change alignment, line and paragraph spacing, margins, and lists and edit the header and footer. You will also find and replace text, create and modify a footnote, and use the Format Painter. If necessary, download student data files from **pearsonhighered.com/viztech**.

Cellular Internet

First-generation, or 1G, cellular telephone technology was analog. It was introduced in the 1980s and was replaced by the digital 2G or second-generation in the early 90s. 2G not only carried voice signals, but also data such as text messages and email.

Third-generation, or 3G, access was launched in 2001 and was the first cellular technology that offered reasonably fast data transfer speeds.[1] Smartphones became increasingly popular and more websites began to support mobile access.

The first 4G networks began appearing in 2009 and offer even faster data rates.

- **1G** - introduced 1979- Speed 28- 56 kbps
- **2G** - introduced 1991- Speed 56-384 kbps
- **3G** - introduced 2001- Speed At least 200 kbps
- **4G** - introduced 2009- Speed 1 Gbps for stationary and 100 Mbps for mobile operation

Boris Lehner/Alamy

---

[1] Some earlier technologies were referred to as 2.5G and 2.75G.

lastname_firstname_ch07_word

Step	Instructions
1	Start Word. Download and open the Word file named *vt_ch07_word*. Save the file as **lastname_firstname_ch07_word**
2	Change the left and right margins of the document to 1.25".
3	Change the line spacing of the entire document to 2.0 lines. Change the paragraph spacing (before and after) of the entire document to 6.0 points.
4	Apply the Title style and center the heading *Cellular Internet*.
5	Use the Find and Replace dialog box to search for and replace all instances of the word *wireless* with **cellular** There should be two replacements.
6	In the paragraph that begins *1G,* apply bold and underline formatting to the text *1G.* Using the Format Painter, apply the formatting from the text *1G* to the text *2G, 3G,* and *4G* in the three lines that follow.
7	Select the last four lines and format as a bulleted list using solid square bullets.
8	In the paragraph that begins *Third-generation*, insert a footnote immediately following the period following the text *data transfer speeds,* reading **Some earlier technologies were referred to as 2.5G and 2.75G.** (include the period).
9	Move the insertion point to the end of the document, press Enter twice, and insert the picture *vt_ch07_image1*.
10	Resize the image to a height of 2.5". Position in Bottom Center with Square Text Wrapping. Apply the Double Frame, Black Picture Style.
11	Use the Spelling and Grammar dialog box to correct the misspelling of the word *genaration* to *generation*. Ignore any other spelling and grammar suggestions.
12	In the document footer, add the FileName field using the default format.
13	Save the file and close Word. Submit the document as directed.

Application Project

Office 2016 Application Projects
PowerPoint 2016: Internet Services

Project Description: In this project, you will create a presentation about Internet services. In this presentation you will apply design, font, and color themes. You will also change font colors, bullet symbols, and slide layout. If necessary, download student data files from **pearsonhighered.com/viztech**.

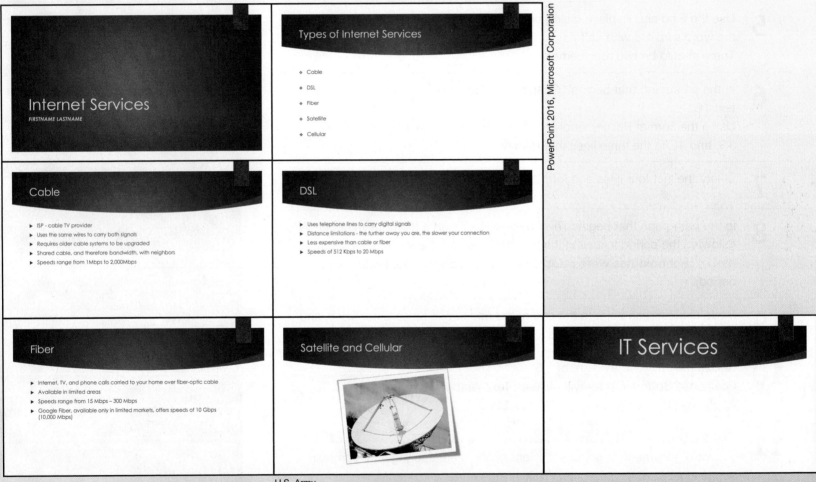

U.S. Army

Step	Instructions
1	Start PowerPoint. Download and open the file named *vt_ch07_ppt*. Save the presentation as lastname_firstname_ch07_ppt
2	Apply the Ion Boardroom theme, green variant, to the presentation.
3	On Slide 1, in the subtitle placeholder, using your name, type **Firstname Lastname** Apply bold and italic formatting to the subtitle text.
4	On Slide 2, in the title placeholder, type **Types of Internet Services** In the content placeholder, enter the following five bullet points: **Cable** **DSL** **Fiber** **Satellite** **Cellular**
5	On Slide 2, change the bullet style to Star bullets and set the line spacing to 2.0.
6	On Slide 3, in the title placeholder, type **Cable** On Slide 4, in the title placeholder, type **DSL** On Slide 5, in the title placeholder, type **Fiber**
7	Insert two new Title and Content slides after Slide 5. On Slide 6, in the title placeholder, type **Satellite and Cellular**
8	On Slide 6, in the content placeholder, insert the downloaded image *vt_ch07_image2*. Apply the Rotated, White picture style to the image.
9	Change the layout of Slide 7 to Title Only.
10	On Slide 7, in the title placeholder, type **IT Services** Center the title and change the font size to 72.
11	Apply the Split transition to all slides with a duration of 2.00.
12	Insert the page number and the footer **Firstname Lastname** on the notes and handouts pages for all slides in the presentation. View the presentation in Slide Show view from beginning to end, and then return to Normal view.
13	Save the presentation and close PowerPoint. Submit the presentation as directed.

Rawpixel/Fotolia

Communicating and Sharing: The Social Web

In This Chapter

VIZ INTRO

The first thing I do every morning is check my email and the notifications on my smartphone. Then, when I get into my office, I open the browser on my computer. I have multiple start page tabs, which include my email, calendar, social media feeds, and feeds from my favorite blogs and news and sports websites. In just a few minutes, I can find out everything I need to start my day. Online communication is an integral part of my life—and probably yours, too. When you have finished this chapter, you'll have an understanding of the world of online communication and the impact it has on society.

Objectives

1 Compare Different Forms of Synchronous Online Communication

2 Compare Different Forms of Asynchronous Online Communication

3 Discuss the Impact of Social Media in Society

4 Locate User-Generated Content in the Form of a Blog or Podcast

5 Discuss How Wikis and Other Social Media Sites Rely on the Wisdom of the Crowd

6 Explain the Influence of Social Media on E-commerce

7 Compare Social Media and Other Online Technologies Used in Business

Running Project

In this project, you'll explore online communication. Look for instructions as you complete each article. For most articles, there's a series of questions for you to research. At the conclusion of the chapter, you'll submit your responses to the questions raised.

BrunoWeltmann/Fotolia

Dangubic/Fotolia

Talk to Me

1 Compare Different Forms of Synchronous Online Communication

Want to talk to someone right now? That's what chat and instant messaging allow you to do. The term **synchronous online communication** means communication that happens in real time, with two or more people online at the same time. Face-to-face conversations and telephone calls are examples of synchronous communication. Online synchronous communication tools let you communicate in real time on the web.

Chat and IM

Online **chat** enables you to talk to multiple people at the same time. **Instant messaging** or **IM** is real-time communication between two or more participants over the Internet. The terms chat and IM are often used interchangeably.

Traditional chat rooms are text-based and persistent, and users come and go, often not knowing each other. To access client-based chats, you need to install client software. Some IM programs allow you to create group chats. You can find chat rooms that are geared toward common interests, such as travel or cooking, or more general chats for people who just want to talk.

Some chats are moderated, which means a moderator screens all content; others are not moderated, and anything goes.

Social media sites such as Facebook and Google Hangouts also enable you to chat with others. Using chat is perfect for a class discussion or getting a group of family members together to plan a reunion. And if you're on the go, you can use mobile versions of these tools—so you can start a chat while you're in front of your computer and then continue the conversation from your smartphone or tablet when you're not.

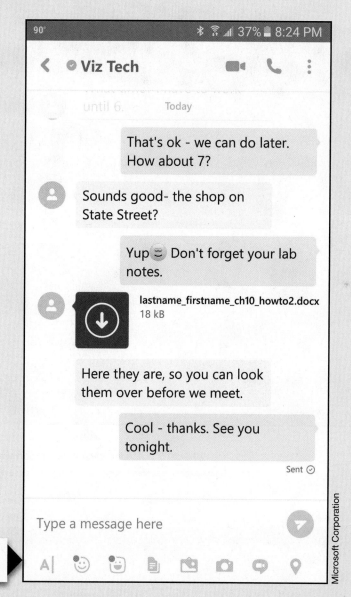

FIGURE 8.1 Using Skype to Chat with a Classmate

Microsoft Corporation

Instant messaging sessions can be web-based, but some require client software or mobile apps that must be installed on your computer or mobile device, such as Skype (Figure 8.1) and Facebook Messenger. Some apps allow you to collaborate by sending files and sharing screens. Many businesses find IM and chat to be useful tools for holding meetings and providing customer support (Figure 8.2).

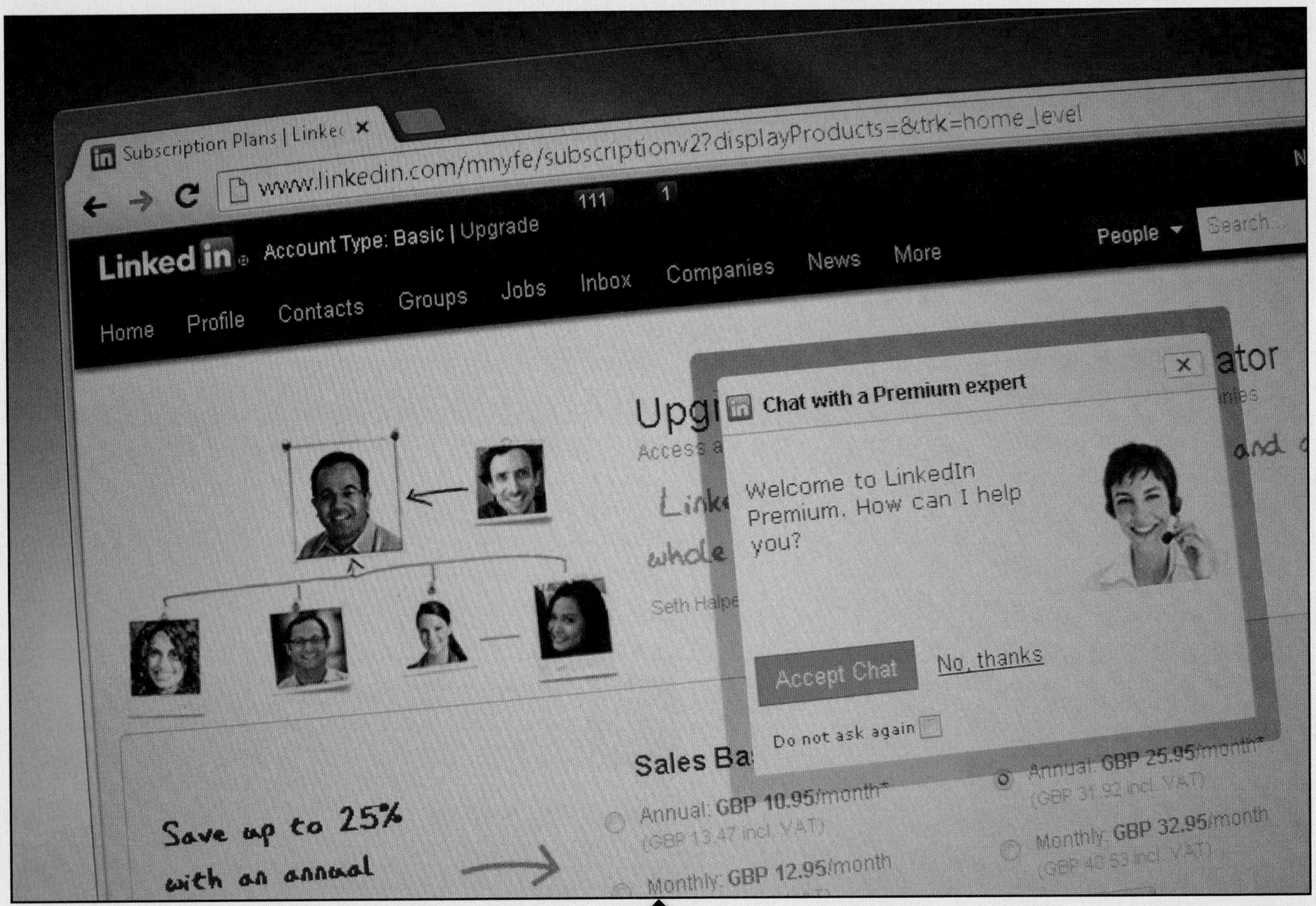

Web Pix/Alamy Stock Photo

FIGURE 8.2 LinkedIn offers support via chat.

FIGURE 8.3 VoIP helps people keep in touch using the Internet.

VoIP

You can make voice and video calls (Figure 8.3) using **VoIP (Voice over IP)**, which enables calls to be transmitted over the Internet instead of via traditional phone lines or cellular towers. You can make calls from your computer or mobile device from anywhere you have Internet access, even if you don't have phone service. If you have broadband Internet access, your Internet service provider may offer VoIP phone service. Apple FaceTime, which is built into macOS and iOS, enables you to make video calls to other FaceTime users. In addition to the chat function, Skype, which is available across platforms and devices, enables you to place calls to other Skype users for free or to regular phones for a small fee. FaceTime can use your cellular network to place calls. Using FaceTime or Skype to talk to friends and family members who are in other countries can save a lot of money over traditional telephone calls. My cousin, who lives in Australia, talks regularly with his family here in the United States, and his children are able to keep in touch with their faraway grandparents.

Running Project

Use the Internet to research chat and IM rules for business. Create a list of five rules you consider most important.

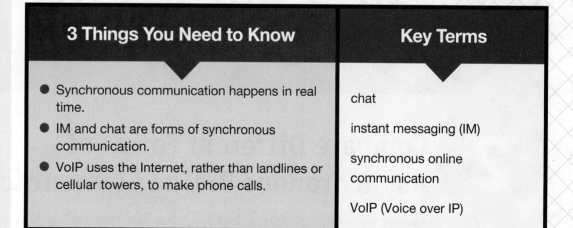

3 Things You Need to Know

- Synchronous communication happens in real time.
- IM and chat are forms of synchronous communication.
- VoIP uses the Internet, rather than landlines or cellular towers, to make phone calls.

Key Terms

chat

instant messaging (IM)

synchronous online communication

VoIP (Voice over IP)

Ra2 studio/Fotolia

Leave a Message

Compare Different Forms of Asynchronous Online Communication

SIMULATION

Communicating and Sharing

Asynchronous forms of communication don't require the participants to be online at the same time. Like leaving a voicemail or sending a letter, **asynchronous online communication** technology lets you send a message that the receiver can access later.

How do You Read and Send Email?

The Internet was designed for communicating and sharing. One of the first applications was email, which quickly became the most widely used Internet application. **Email** is a system of sending electronic messages using store-and-forward technology. That means an email server holds your messages until you request them. So someone can send you an email message even if you're not online at the time. Even if you prefer other forms of communication for your personal contacts, using email to communicate is an essential business skill.

There are two ways to access email: using an email client on a device or reading it online through a webmail interface. When you use an email client, such as Outlook, the email server sends you a copy of the message. The client then makes the message available to read even after you disconnect from the Internet. If you configure your client to leave a copy of the message on the email server, then you will still be able to access the messages from a webmail interface. The advantage to using a webmail interface is that your email is available to you from anywhere—home, school, vacation, or work—whenever you're online (Figure 8.4).

Whether you use an email client or webmail interface, you can configure it to filter out spam or junk mail, create folders and filters to sort and save messages, and archive old messages in case you ever need to retrieve them. When you delete an email message, most email clients will move the message to a trash or deleted folder, where you can recover it or empty the trash to permanently delete it.

It makes sense to have multiple email accounts, which enables you to keep your private, work, and school communication separate. Think about the impression you'd make if you sent a job inquiry from cutiepie_cupcake@gmail.com. You might have one account just for shopping websites, another for friends and family, and yet another at school. Your ISP will provide you with at least one email account. Your employer or school may provide you with another. There are also many places for free email accounts, such as Yahoo!, Google, and Outlook.com. The advantage to using an email account not tied to your ISP is that you will not lose your email account if you change your ISP.

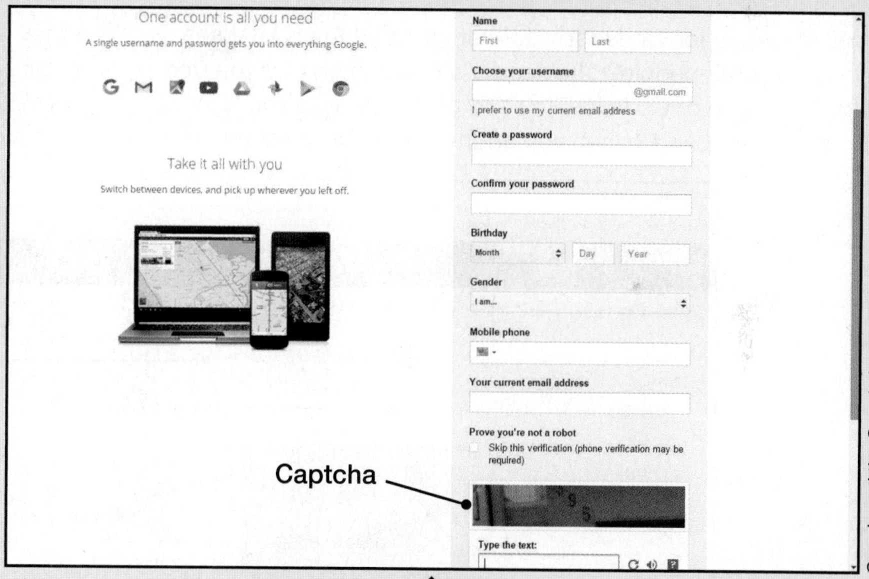

When creating a new account, you might be required to use a **captcha (Completely Automated Public Turing Test to Tell Computers and Humans Apart)**—a series of letters and numbers that are distorted in some way so that they are difficult for automated software to read but relatively easy for humans to read

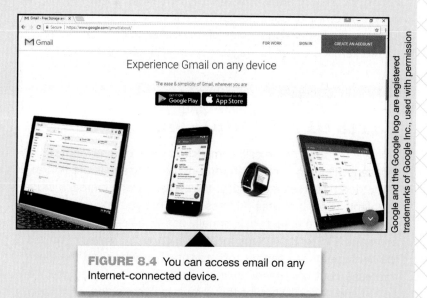

FIGURE 8.4 You can access email on any Internet-connected device.

Captcha

FIGURE 8.5 Creating a Free Google.com Email Account

Google and the Google logo are registered trademarks of Google Inc., used with permission

(Figure 8.5). Captchas are used to prevent automated software from creating online accounts. Free email accounts are often linked to other services, such as online storage.

To access your new Google account, log in to the Google website and click the Gmail link. New email messages are in your

Inbox. You can read a message by double-clicking it. One very important thing to remember about email is that it's not secure. As it travels from your computer over the Internet, it can be read by hackers along the way. Copies of the message exist on servers and routers it crosses on its journey, and those copies can be retrieved long after you've deleted the message from your inbox. Your email provider might scan your messages to deliver you targeted advertising, and your employer or school network administrator might also read your email. A good analogy is to think of email as a postcard, not a letter in a sealed envelope.

Parts of an Email Message

Figure 8.6 shows some of the important parts of a new email message. The most important part of the message is the address. If you don't address it correctly, the message will not reach its recipient. There are three address fields that you can use: To, Cc, and Bcc. To is the field you normally use when sending an email to someone. Cc, which stands for *carbon copy* or *courtesy copy*, is the field you use to send a copy to someone who's not the main addressee but who needs to know about a conversation. It's like an FYI and generally means that a reply isn't expected. Functionally, there's no real difference in the way the message is sent or received. *Bcc*, however, has an important difference. Did you ever have an email message forwarded to you that included the addresses of dozens of other people? The sender should have used the *Bcc* field, not the *To* or *Cc* fields, to send that message. The *B* in Bcc stands for *blind*. When you address an email message to several people, using the *Bcc* field keeps the addresses in that field private.

Use the **Subject line** of an email message to give the recipient a clear idea of the content of the message. This can be read in most email programs without opening the message. The body of the message should contain the remainder of the information. The body of the message in Figure 8.6 includes some formatted text, an image, and two **emojis**—small images that represent facial expressions, common objects, and people and animals. Not all email programs will let you format text or include images, and not everybody will be able to view those elements. You must use an email program that is configured to read HTML email messages in order for those elements to be visible. An email program that is configured to view only text email messages will only see the text in this message.

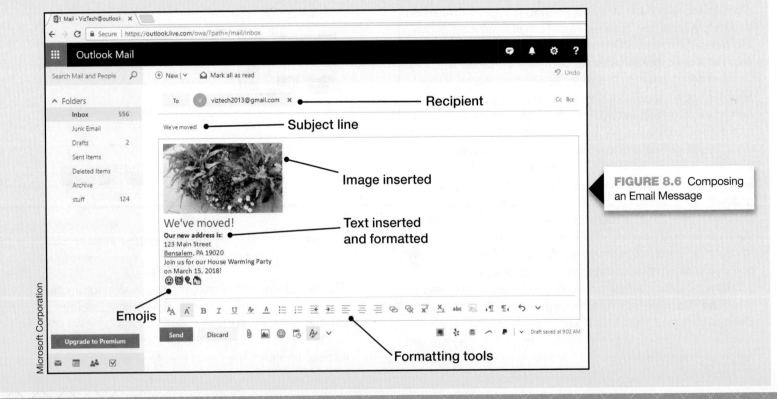

FIGURE 8.6 Composing an Email Message

Microsoft Corporation

An email **signature line** is a block of text that's automatically put at the end of a message you compose. It can be a very simple message that just includes your name, or it can contain more contact information and perhaps a privacy statement. You need to create a signature and enable it in your email settings for the signature to appear on your email messages.

When you receive an email message, you can reply to the message or forward it to someone else (Figure 8.7). When you choose Reply, your response is sent back to the original sender. When you choose Reply all (or Reply to All), the response is sent to all the addressees in the To and Cc lines of the original message as well as the original sender. Think carefully before you use this option. Do you really want everyone to receive your reply? The subject line for a reply will include Re: before the original subject. If you want to send the message to someone else, then you should use the Forward option, which allows you to select new addresses and puts Fw: before the subject.

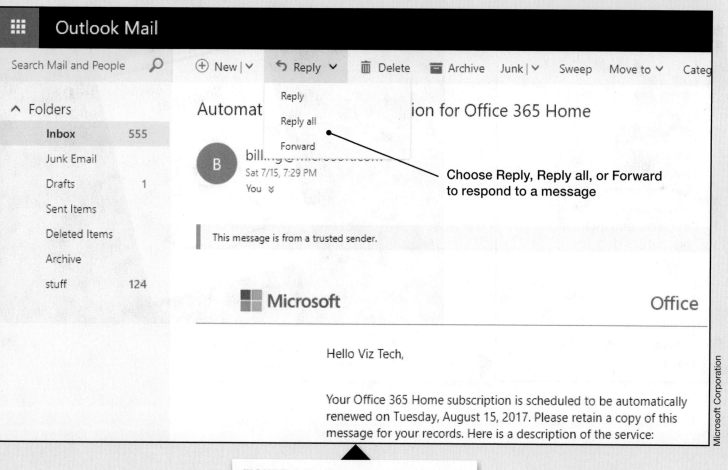

FIGURE 8.7 Replying to an Email Message

Text and Multimedia Messaging

A popular form of asynchronous communication is **text messaging**. Using the **Short Message Service (SMS)**, you can send brief electronic messages between mobile devices. Messages that include multimedia such as images or videos use the Multimedia Messaging Service (MMS). Most mobile devices include a built-in messaging app. Figure 8.8 shows a conversation on an Android smartphone. Snapchat—a multimedia messaging app that you can download to your mobile device—allows you to send a photo or short video message to specific recipients (Figure 8.9). Once the message is opened, it is viewable for a brief amount of time (1–10 seconds) that the sender specifies and then disappears from the recipient's device. Snapchat stories allow you to string together multiple snaps you have posted in a 24-hour period to create a video that persists for up to 24 hours. You can share your Snapchat stories with specific people or with everyone.

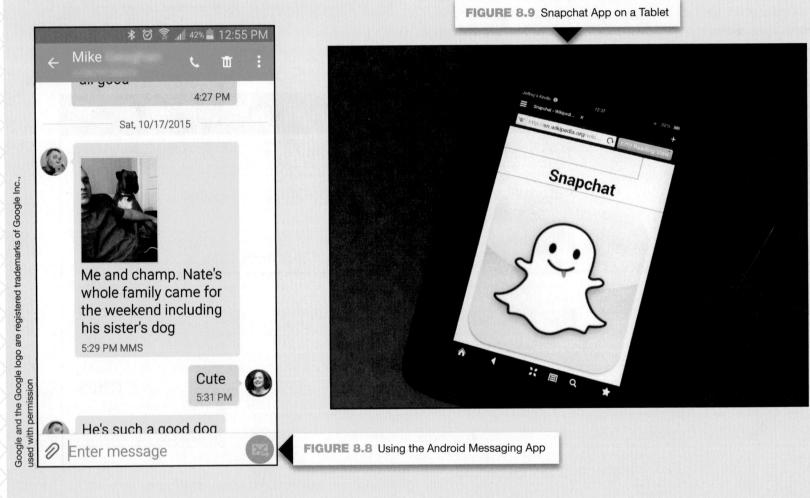

FIGURE 8.9 Snapchat App on a Tablet

FIGURE 8.8 Using the Android Messaging App

Google and the Google logo are registered trademarks of Google Inc., used with permission

Jeffrey Blackler/Alamy Stock Photo

Forums and Discussion Boards

Forums, also known as discussion boards or message boards, were one of the first forms of social media. They're conversations much like chat but not in real time. There are forums for people with common interests, such as sports, pets, video games, or travel. Many technology and product websites include forums, which may be used as a support system, such as the Google forums shown in Figure 8.10. Some websites refer to a forum as a community.

Participants post comments and questions, usually about a particular topic or problem, and other participants respond. Each conversation is called a thread, and the responses are called posts. Forums are great places to get help with problems, ask for advice, or just communicate with folks with similar interests. Threads can be searched and read long after the initial conversation has ended. Most forums are moderated and require you to create an account before you're allowed to post.

The advantage to using email or a forum over chat or IM is that the conversations have a longer life span. You can save email messages indefinitely, as long as you have the storage space, and forums can persist for years after a thread is started. These tools have become critical ways to communicate in all types of businesses.

FIGURE 8.10 Google hosts dozens of forums about Google products.

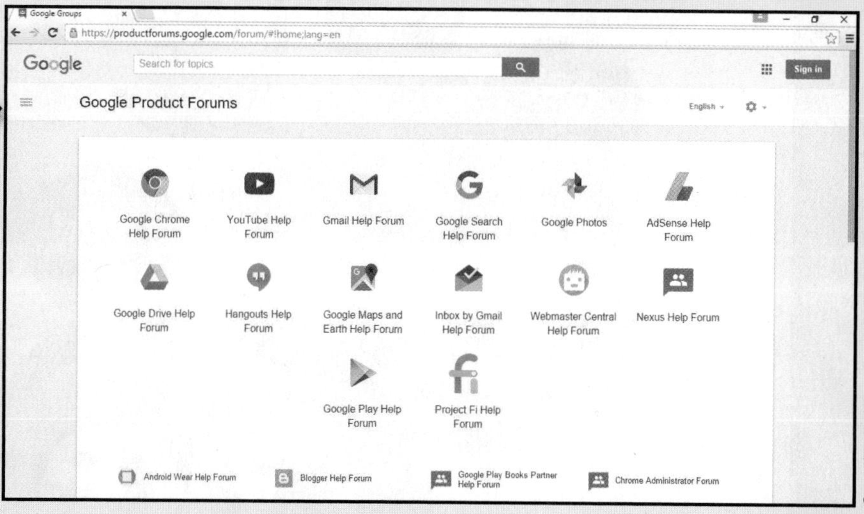

Google and the Google logo are registered trademarks of Google Inc., used with permission.

Running Project

Visit **tripadvisor.com/forum**. Select a destination that you have visited in the past. Read some of the threads. Select a thread that you would like to reply to. Do you agree with the replies posted? Would you find them helpful if you were deciding to visit this location?

5 Things You Need to Know

- With asynchronous communication you don't need to be online when someone sends a message to you.
- Email is not necessarily private.
- A captcha ensures that a person and not a machine is creating an account.
- Text messaging and multimedia messaging send electronic messages between mobile devices.
- Forums are online discussion boards.

Key Terms

asynchronous online communication

captcha (Completely Automated Public Turing Test to Tell Computers and Humans Apart)

email

emoji

forum

Short Message Service (SMS)

signature line

subject line

text messaging

There's a Place for Everyone ...

Discuss the Impact of Social Media in Society

Forums and email are old technologies, having been around almost as long as the Internet itself. Recently, newer technologies have emerged. In the first few years of the web most people were consumers of information, but now much of the content on the web is user generated. The tools that allow users to create content are sometimes called **Web 2.0** tools and have changed the way people communicate and collaborate on the web.

Social Media

Collectively, the websites that use these tools—which enable you to create content, connect, network, and share—are called **social media**. As ordinary users create more content, what's important, interesting, or relevant is no longer decided by a few experts or journalists sitting around a table, but by the crowd of participants. An Internet **meme** is a funny image or catchphrase, often of celebrity or pop culture reference, that is spread by Internet users across social media (Figure 8.11). The concept of the **second screen**, using a computer or mobile device while watching television to interact with other viewers or view enhanced content, has changed TV watching from a passive experience to an active, social experience.

If you have friends who tag you in their photos, even if your profile is private, you may be sharing more than you want to. Be sure to use the security and privacy settings to keep your private life private, and consider creating a second public profile on a professional social network. Many employers will expect you to be technically literate and to use social networking tools, so not having a professional online presence could be a disadvantage.

It's Hump Day!

Evitaz/Fotolia

FIGURE 8.11 A Funny Meme

SOCIAL NETWORK SITES

Social networks such as Facebook and LinkedIn are online communities that combine many of the features of the other online tools. Social networks enable you to chat in real time and to post messages for all to see or to send a personal message similar to an email. Some focus on business, and others are language-specific or location-specific. Social networking enables you to keep in touch with old friends and make new ones.

The Whole Earth 'Lectronic Link, or The Well, is an online community that launched in 1985. The first social network sites began in the late 1990s; now there are hundreds of social networking sites. Neo is a popular, internal social network used by schools and businesses. Internal social networks provide a common location to store information, discuss ideas, collaborate, and share insights.

Currently, the largest site is Facebook, which was launched in 2004 for Harvard students and in 2006 for everyone else. On Facebook, you can create a profile that includes some personal information, pictures, and interests, and then you can connect with other Facebook users or friends. You can also join groups within the network that interest you. For some people, the most important part of

Petroudny/Fotolia

using a social network is the number of "friends" they have, but for others, it is a way to stay in touch with people. Many companies use Facebook to connect with customers and to offer special discounts and other perks for those that click the Like button associated with the company.

LinkedIn is a professional social networking site where you can find past and present colleagues and classmates, connect with appropriate people when seeking a new job or business opportunity, or get answers from industry experts. Figure 8.12 shows the author's LinkedIn profile viewed in the LinkedIn mobile app. There are no games or applications, no place to post photos except on the standard profile image, and there is no chat. People to whom you are linked are referred to as connections rather than friends. LinkedIn—or other business social networks that relate to your field of interest—should be part of your personal brand.

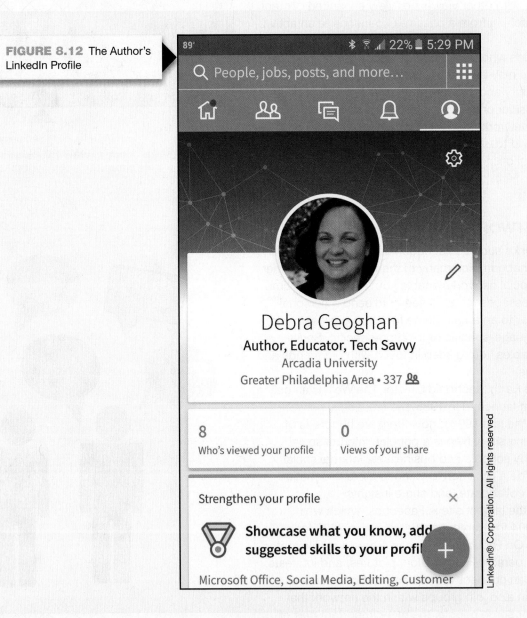

FIGURE 8.12 The Author's LinkedIn Profile

VIRTUAL WORLDS

Virtual communities, such as Second Life and Webkinz, and **massively multiplayer online role-playing games (MMORPG)**, such as World of Warcraft and The Elder Scrolls: Online, enable you to interact online with people in real time using an **avatar**, or virtual body (Figure 8.13). Some schools offer virtual classes in Second Life. You can visit virtual art galleries, memorials and museums, castles and ruins, and cities—both real and fictional, and many businesses and professional societies. Go back in time and join others around the radio as you listen to old radio shows, or travel to a distant world. Virtual worlds and multiplayer games can have pretty high system requirements and require fairly new and powerful systems.

FIGURE 8.13 Avatars interact in a virtual world.

Social Video, Image, and Music Sites

Social sharing sites, such as YouTube, Flickr, and SoundCloud, enable anyone to create and share media. These sites are outside of social networks, although you can often share content between the networks. One of the key features of these sites is the ability to tag items. Tagging makes the sharing even more social, as users tag not just their own creations but also those of others.

VIDEO

YouTube is the largest online video-hosting site in the world. It's also social in the sense that you can subscribe to other users' channels, send messages, and recommend videos. A **viral video** (Figure 8.14) is a video that becomes extremely popular because of recommendations and social sharing. Other video-sharing sites include CollegeHumor, Vimeo, TeacherTube, and Facebook and Flickr. Streaming sites like Hulu and Netflix don't host user-created content but are still social in that they keep track of the popularity of videos and have users review and discuss the videos.

Web Pix/Alamy Stock Photo

FIGURE 8.14 "Charlie bit my finger — again!" has been viewed millions of times.

IMAGES

Flickr is one of the largest image-sharing sites (Figure 8.15). With a free account, you can post up to 1 terabyte of images—that's more than 500,000 images. You can mark your pictures as private or make them public. You can adjust the copyright to allow others to use your images legally, and tag them with keywords and geographic information so people can search for things that interest them. Other popular photo-sharing sites include Facebook and Google Photos. Instagram and other mobile apps allow you to take and edit photos on your mobile device and upload them to the web automatically. You can also comment on and share images that you like and add location information to them.

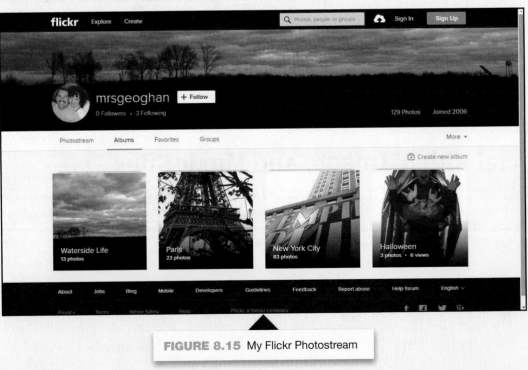

Courtesy of Yahoo

FIGURE 8.15 My Flickr Photostream

MUSIC

What is more social than music? There are lots of places on the web to find music, but if you want a social experience, you can create an account on a site such as Spotify (Figure 8.16) or Pandora, which recommend music to you based on what you listen to and what your friends are listening to. You can follow friends to see what they like, and mark tracks, which will help you get recommendations. The more you listen to and mark tracks, the more recommendations you will get. Both Pandora and Spotify are available in free and subscription versions. You can stream from the website or by using an app on a mobile device or in some vehicles. Other popular music services include Amazon Prime Music and Apple Music, both of which require a subscription.

If you like to make and share your own music, you can use a website like SoundCloud (**soundcloud.com**). Using a browser or mobile app, you can upload sound files that you have created and share them with the community. Users can follow their favorites and comment and share new finds. Artists can communicate directly with their fans, and musicians can collaborate with each other, even if they are many miles apart.

FIGURE 8.16 You can use the Spotify app on many different devices.

IanDagnall Computing/Alamy Stock Photo

Presenting Yourself Online

Think about your online identity or **digital footprint**—all the information that someone can find out about you by searching the web, including social networking sites and online gaming. This includes both content that you post and content posted by others. A cyberbully, disgruntled employee, unhappy customer, or former partner might post negative, untrue, or unflattering information about you. While you have little control over what others post, you can and should carefully curate what you post. Remember that after something has been posted on the web, it is almost impossible to completely get rid of it. Suppose you were a prospective employer. Would you hire someone who has compromising pictures online?

Separating your personal online identity and professional online identity enables you to share and enjoy yourself while still presenting a professional appearance to employers, clients, and others in your professional network. You can use an alias for your personal identity to keep it independent from your professional one. Keep your privacy settings high on your personal accounts and choose your friends and followers carefully.

You need to develop your own brand and be sure that anything that is publically viewable fits into that brand. Your brand is something you should create and manage to make the best impression. The information that appears at the top of the search results when someone Googles your name should highlight your skills and achievements. The content you share, Tweets you post, and social media connections you make are all part of your brand.

One of the best ways to improve search results for your name is to build a website or set up a blog using Blogger or WordPress. You can create your own website where you post your resume, list your achievements, highlight awards, and write a short bio. Add new content to your site regularly so that it does not become out of date. You can buy a domain from Hover.com or GoDaddy. Try to buy your own name, or something closely related such as your last name and field. Everyone knows Bill Nye the Science Guy!

Your public social media profiles should be complete and present you in the best light possible. Use high-quality professional photography for your profile pictures. Regularly interacting with others and sharing their content will increase your visibility. The more active you are on social media, the better.

Finally, Google yourself regularly to see how others see you, and what they say about you.

Simeonvd/Fotolia

Puhhha/Fotolia

GREEN COMPUTING
Raising Social Awareness

How much paper mail do you receive every week? And how much of it do you actually read? The cost of a direct-mail campaign is huge, and many people simply toss into the trash what they see as junk mail anyway, so the costs are also large in terms of the environment. SMM isn't just for businesses; it can also be used to raise awareness of important issues.

Debra Geoghan

Not long ago, thousands of people began posting videos of themselves dumping ice water over their heads and challenging others to do the same. The ALS Ice Bucket Challenge went viral and, as a result, the ALS foundation received millions of dollars in donations—and many people who had known nothing about ALS before learned about the disease. So a simple act of social networking resulted in raising money and also raising social awareness without printing a single piece of paper. In 2016, the ALS foundation announced a major breakthrough as a direct result of the campaign.

Running Project

Imagine that you're a job applicant. Search the web and major social networks to see what your prospective employers would find. Log out of your social networking sites to see how an outsider would view you. How is your brand? Would you hire yourself? Was it easy to find things that you would rather keep private?

4 Things You Need to Know

- Social networks are online communities where people connect with each other.
- Video-, image-, and music-sharing sites allow users to post their creations on the web for others to see and use.
- Tagging creates a way to search for content on social websites.
- You should carefully curate your digital footprint.

Key Terms

avatar	second screen
digital footprint	social media
massively multiplayer online role-playing game (MMORPG)	social network
	viral video
meme	Web 2.0

Viz Check—
In MyLab IT, take a quick quiz covering Objectives 1–3.

Digital Literacy Skill

Create a LinkedIn Profile

HOW TO VIDEO

In this exercise, you will create an account on LinkedIn. Many companies use LinkedIn as a recruiting tool. Because this is a business network, you should use a professional email address, not a cute nickname. If you don't have an appropriate email address to use, this would be a good time to create one. You will be required to confirm your email address before you can successfully complete your LinkedIn sign-up. You should also post a professional photo. Many school career centers can help with this. No selfies—have someone else take the photo for you. If necessary, download the student data files from **pearsonhighered. com/viztech**. From your student data files, open the *vt_ch08_ howto1_answersheet* file and save the file as **lastname_firstname_ ch08_howto1_answersheet**.

1 Open your browser and go to **linkedin.com**. On the home page, type your name and email address and create a password. Click *Join now*.

Be great at what you do

Get started - it's free.

First name

Janet

Last name

Kazen

Email

vizualizingtechnology@gmail.com

Password (6 or more characters)

••••••••

By clicking Join now, you agree to the LinkedIn User Agreement, Privacy Policy, and Cookie Policy.

Join now

2 Verify your location, and then click *Next*. Create your professional profile by completing the information on the next screen. Select *Student* and complete your school and dates attended information, and then click *Next*. On the What are you most interested in? screen, click *Not sure yet. I'm open!*

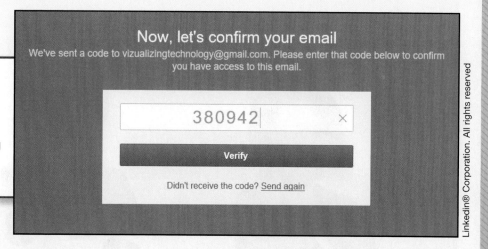

What are you most interested in?
We'll use this info to personalize your experience. (Don't worry, we'll keep it private.)

Finding a job	>
Keeping in touch with my contacts	>
Building my professional network	>
Staying up-to-date with my industry	>
Not sure yet. I'm open!	>

3 Open your email program and click the link in the confirmation email to confirm your email address and activate your LinkedIn account. Skip importing your address book (you can do this later if you choose).

Now, let's confirm your email
We've sent a code to vizualizingtechnology@gmail.com. Please enter that code below to confirm you have access to this email.

380942 ×

Verify

Didn't receive the code? Send again

4 If you know anyone in the list of suggested contacts, select them to add to your network, or click *Skip*. Add a photo to your profile. This should be a clear, professional head-shot. Adjust to make sure you're looking your best, and then click *Save*. Click *Continue*. Remember that potential employers may view this profile, so make it professional and appealing. Some schools offer professional services, or you can ask a friend to take a few pictures of you to choose from. Try to avoid using a selfie!

5 On the Get the app pages, do not enter your phone number, and click *Next*. You can download the app later to your mobile devices if you want to.

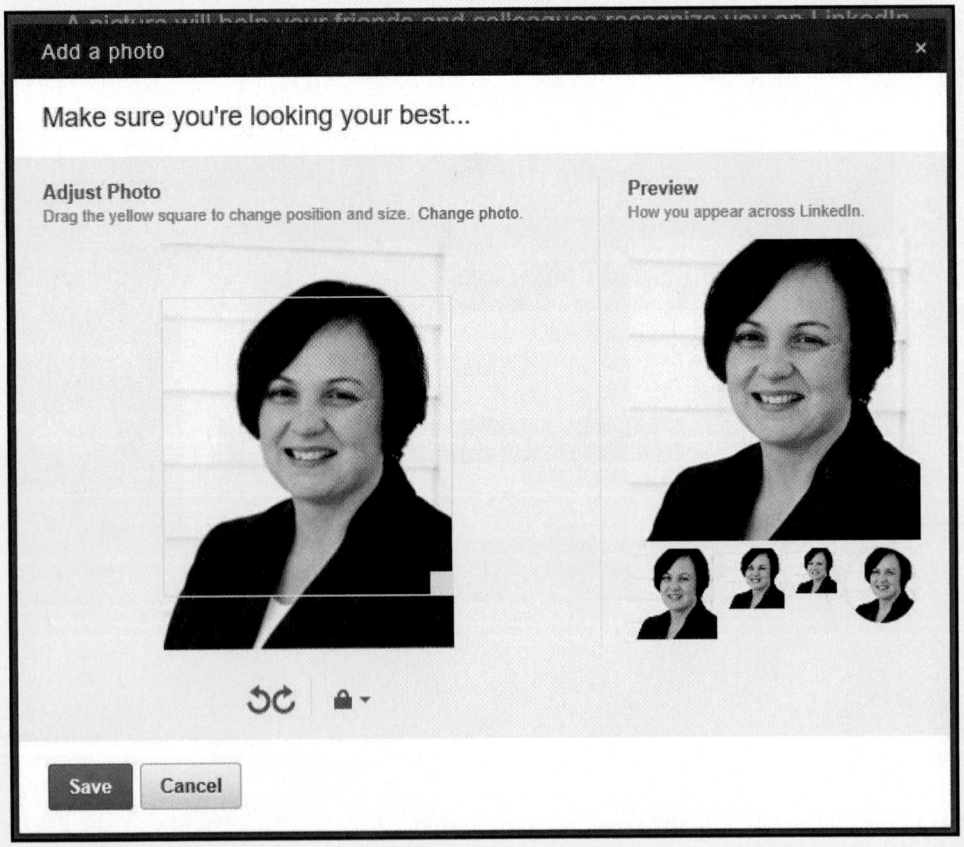

Add a photo ✕

Make sure you're looking your best...

Adjust Photo
Drag the yellow square to change position and size. Change photo.

Preview
How you appear across LinkedIn.

Save Cancel

6 Use the Profile Strength box to improve your profile by adding work experience and industry. Add a few items under *Skills*, including skills that you have gained from taking this course, and write a brief summary. Edit your education information—including expected date of graduation and degrees and or certifications earned.

7 Take a screenshot of your finished profile and paste it into your answer sheet. Copy the URL and paste into your answer sheet. Save your file and submit it as directed by your instructor.

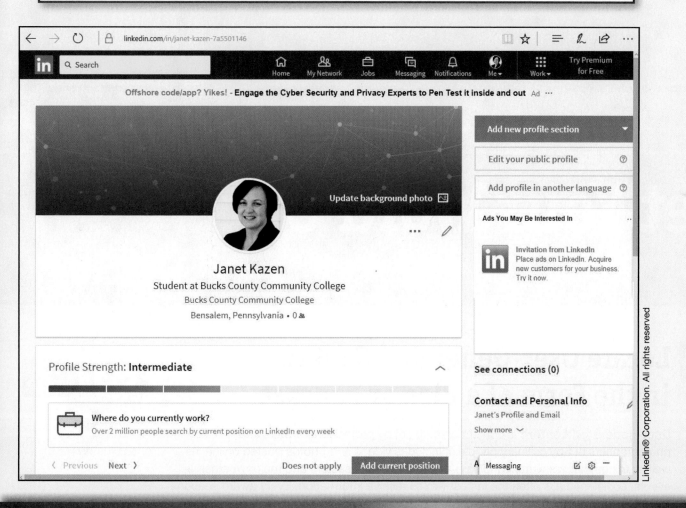

Get Your Word Out

ective

Locate User-Generated Content in the Form of a Blog or Podcast

V
C

Microbloggi
with Twitter

User-generated content is content created not by professional writers and photographers but by ordinary people. It includes videos and photos posted online, as well as things that are written and said. During national disasters and major weather events, social media is often the fastest way to receive information. Every award season, major sporting event, election, and breaking news story sets the social media world abuzz.

Blogs

A **blog**, or weblog, is an online journal that anyone can set up using simple blog tools to write about whatever they like. Blogs are a running commentary—with posts coming frequently (or not so frequently). The difference between just creating a webpage and writing a blog is that a blog can be interactive—your readers can post comments about your blog posts.

There are many prolific bloggers, and some even earn a living by blogging. Some organizations have multi-author blogs, in which multiple authors blog at a common site, rather than have each blogger use his or her own address. Many bloggers link to other related blogs. There are millions of blogs in the **blogosphere**—all the blogs on the web and the connections among them. Two of the most popular blog sites are WordPress (Figure 8.17) and Blogger. Both of these sites allow you to create an account and blog for free.

A more social form of blogging in which posts are typically limited to a relatively small number of characters and users post updates frequently is called **microblogging**. Twitter and Tumblr are the most popular microblogging sites.

Twitter posts are called **Tweets** and are limited to 140 characters (Figure 8.18). Instead of friends, Twitter users have followers. A **hashtag** is a word or phrase preceded by a # symbol that is used to organize and make your Tweets searchable. You can link your Twitter account to your Facebook account, so that your Tweets will also appear in your Facebook feed. Unlike most other social networks, you don't have to ask for permission to follow someone on Twitter—although they can block you or create restricted accounts. Twitter describes itself with the words *It's what's happening*. You can post photos, text, links, videos, and music. You can link your Tumblr account to your Twitter account, so that your posts appear on both sites.

FIGURE 8.17 You can use Wordpress.com to create a blog.

Twitter, Tweet and Twitter Bird Logo are trademarks of Twitter, Inc. or its affiliates

Tweet text

Hashtag

Tweet actions

Deb Geoghan @DebGeoghan · 18m
Another gorgeous fall day in #BucksCounty - the beautiful and mighty Delaware river in #Bensalem PA.

FIGURE 8.18 Tweets contain up to 140 characters, hashtags, and images.

Podcasts

A **podcast** is a digital media file of a prerecorded radio- or TV-like show that's distributed over the web to be downloaded and played on a computer or portable media player. Podcasts allow both time shifting (listening on your own schedule) and location shifting (taking it with you).

You can find and play podcasts by using a **podcast client** or media player program, such as iTunes, and download single episodes or subscribe to a podcast that's part of a series. There are hundreds of thousands of podcasts available. A few places to search for podcasts are YouTube, iTunes, **podcasts.com,** and **stitcher.com.** Many U.S. government agencies, such as the National Oceanic and Atmospheric Administration (NOAA), produce regular podcasts that you can listen to using a podcast client or directly from their websites, using your browser (Figure 8.19).

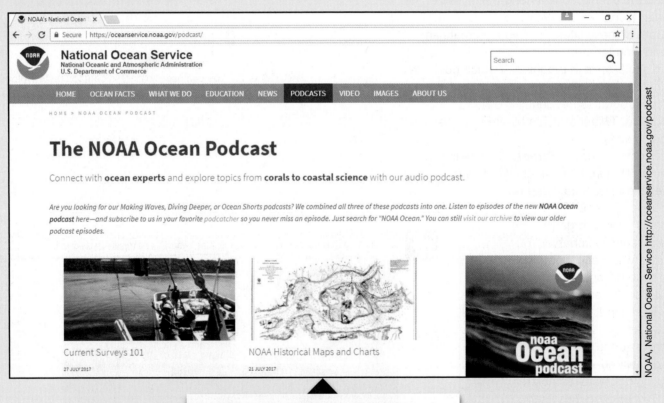

FIGURE 8.19 National Ocean Service Podcasts

NOAA, National Ocean Service http://oceanservice.noaa.gov/podcast

RSS

So, how do you keep up with all your favorite websites? **RSS (Really Simple Syndication)**, also called *Rich Site Summary*, is a format used for distributing web feeds that change frequently—for example, blogs, podcasts, and news. RSS saves you time by sending you updates on the sites you subscribe to. Subscribing to the RSS feeds of your favorite blogs, podcasts, and other websites brings the information right to you. You need a feed reader—also called a news reader app—such as feedly or Flipboard (Figure 8.20). To subscribe to an RSS feed, you just click the orange RSS icon at the top of the page or search from within your feed reader app. Although many people have stopped using RSS feeds in favor of getting their news from social media sites, the advantage of RSS is that the news comes to you—rather than you going out to find it. You're less likely to miss something that way.

FIGURE 8.20 Flipboard on a Smartphone

Iain Masterton/Alamy Stock Photo

Crowdfunding

A social way to get investors for your start-up project or to fund social and charitable projects is **crowdfunding**, which raises money from multiple small investors rather than a few large investors. It also replaces the need to take out a traditional loan. On websites such as **gofundme.com**, **kickstarter.com**, and **indiegogo.com** you can set up campaigns to seek out investors for your project. Or, you can search for interesting projects to support. Often, the investors receive something in return, such as early access to a game or movie, a discounted price for a product, or a t-shirt. **DonorsChoose.org** is a site where public school teachers can set up projects that you can help fund for their classrooms.

leekris/Fotolia

Running Project

Search for a podcast at **podcasts.com** about a topic that interests you. Find out as much as you can about the podcast and its creators. Listen to or watch an episode and write a short summary of the contents. Did you enjoy it? Would you subscribe to it? Would you recommend it to a friend? Do you feel this is a good way to get this information? Explain your answers.

5 Things You Need to Know

- Anybody can create a blog to talk about almost anything.
- A microblog site restricts posts to a limited number of characters.
- Podcasts are radio- or TV-like shows that you can download and listen to or watch anytime.
- You can subscribe to the RSS feeds of blogs, podcasts, and other sites to be notified of new content.
- Crowdfunding raises money from many small investors to fund a project.

Key Terms

blog (weblog)	podcast client
blogosphere	RSS (Really Simple Syndication)
crowdfunding	
hashtag	Tweet
microblogging	user-generated content
podcast	

How To? Essential Job Skill

Create a Blog with Blogger

HOW TO VIDEO

A blog is an online journal that you can easily set up using simple blog tools. In it you can talk about whatever you like. Blogs can be interactive, allowing readers to post comments about blog posts. One website for creating free blogs is **Blogger.com**. To use Blogger, you need to have a Google account. If necessary, download the student data files from **pearsonhighered.com/viztech**. From your student data files, open the *vt_ch08_howto2_answersheet* file and save the file as **lastname_firstname_ch08_howto2_answersheet**.

1 Go to **Google.com**. Click the *App* menu, click *More*, and then click *Blogger*. If necessary, click *Blogger Profile*, and then click *Continue to Blogger*.

google.com

Gmail   Images

Google+   Translate   Photos

Shopping   Wallet   Finance

Docs   Books   Blogger

Contacts   Hangouts   Keep

Even more from Google

Google

Google Search   I'm Feeling Lucky

2 Click *Create New Blog*. On the Create a new blog screen, enter a blog title and address (type the address you want to use and Blogger will add .blogspot.com to the end) and choose a template. Try to select something that is easy to remember (and spell). You want it to be easy for people to find your blog. Choose a template that visually complements the style and content of your blog. Don't worry—you can change or customize it later. Take a screenshot of this window and paste it into your answer sheet. Click *Create blog!* If necessary, on the Google Domains dialog box, click *No thanks.*

Blogs List › Create a new blog   ✕

Title   We've Moved!

Address   bayleesdoghouse.blogspot.com   ✓

                                        This blog address is available.

Theme   Notable   Simple   Dynamic Views

             Picture Window   Awesome Inc.   Watermark

             Ethereal   Travel

                        You can browse many more themes and customize your blog later.

                                              Create blog!   Cancel

3 You now have a blog. Click the orange *New post* button to begin. The Post screen is where you compose and format your blog postings. Use the formatting toolbar to format your text. Include a title using the Heading Style, center align, and insert an image or video clip in your post.

4 Under Post settings, click *Labels* and type at least one label (tag) to help your readers find posts that are related, and then click *Done*. Click *Options* and allow comments (the default), and then click *Done*.

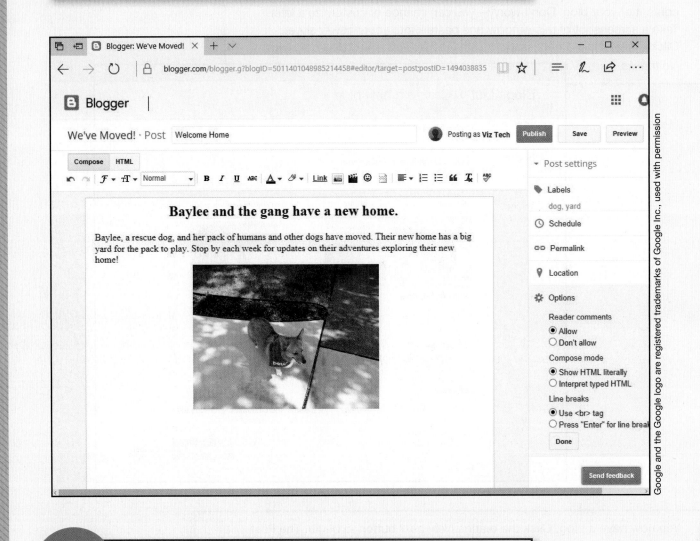

5 Click *Preview* to view your blog post. Close the Preview tab. Make any edits, and then when you are satisfied with your post, click *Publish*. Share on Google+ if you so choose.

6 Click *View blog* to view your finished product. Explain the steps you took to create your blog and include the URL of your blog and a screenshot of the finished blog in your answer sheet. Save the file and submit it as directed by your instructor.

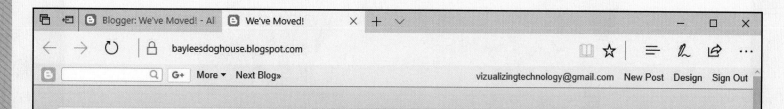

| Blogger: We've Moved! - Al | We've Moved! | × | + |

← → ↻ | 🔒 bayleesdoghouse.blogspot.com

Q | G+ More ▾ Next Blog»

vizualizingtechnology@gmail.com New Post Design Sign Out

We've Moved!

SATURDAY, JULY 29, 2017

Welcome Home

BAYLEE AND THE GANG HAVE A NEW HOME.

Baylee, a rescue dog, and her pack of humans and other dogs have moved. Their new home has a big yard for the pack to play. Stop by each week for updates on their adventures exploring their new home!

Posted by Viz Tech at 11:52 AM   No comments: ✏ M🅱 t f ⓟ G+

Labels: dog, yard

ABOUT ME
🅱 **Viz Tech**

View my complete profile

BLOG ARCHIVE
▼ 2017 (1)
  ▼ July (1)
    Welcome Home

The Wisdom of the Crow

Discuss How Wikis and Other Social Media Sites Rely on the Wisdom of the Crowd

One of the most interesting aspects of the social uses of the web is the reliance on the wisdom of the crowd, or **crowdsourcing**—obtaining the collective opinion of a crowd of people rather than the individual opinion of an expert.

Sites such as Digg, reddit, and Slashdot allow users to share content and webpages they find interesting. **Wikis** are websites that allow users to edit content, even if it was written by someone else. Review sites such as Yelp and TripAdvisor give you both a voice and a place to get advice and recommendations from other folks. Waze is a mapping app that is 100% user-generated content, with real-time traffic and route information. Relying on the wisdom of the crowd is much like asking your friends, family, and coworkers for advice. Did you enjoy the movie? Where should I go for the best ice cream? How do you change the oil in your car? Everybody's an expert in something, and the web makes it easier for us to find and share that expertise with each other. But just a word of caution: With anything you read on the web, you should be critical in your evaluation of the credibility and reliability of its author.

Soloviova Liudmyla/Fotolia

Wikis

Wikis differ from blogs and podcasts in that they're designed for collaboration—not just posting responses to another post but actually editing the content. The most well-known wiki is Wikipedia (Figure 8.21), which is a massive free encyclopedia that is written by—anyone. How can you trust something that anyone can edit? Well, that's part of the design. The idea is that if many people are involved in a wiki, then the person (or people) who knows the right information will (eventually) be the one to write or edit it. There are people that deliberately vandalize Wikipedia articles with incorrect information, so always verify the information you read. In less than 15 years, Wikipedia grew to over 5 million articles in English alone. Wikipedia is a great place to start but is generally frowned upon for use as a primary source in academic research.

Wikipedia is the most well-known wiki, but it's not the only one. Wikis abound and are often used as a way for communities to develop instructions. For example, wikiHow (Figure 8.22) is a website that contains how-to articles on thousands of topics. You can read, write, or edit an existing wikiHow article or request that someone else write one if you can't find what you're looking for.

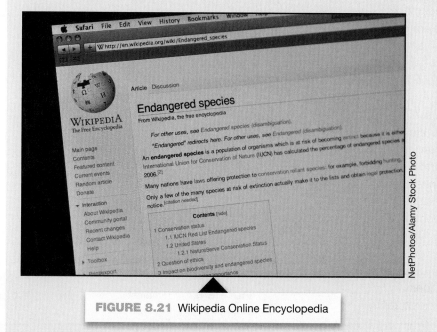

NetPhotos/Alamy Stock Photo

FIGURE 8.21 Wikipedia Online Encyclopedia

webpics/Alamy Stock Photo

FIGURE 8.22 wikiHow has thousands of articles.

Social Review Sites

Social review sites such as TripAdvisor let users review hotels, movies, games, books, and other products and services. Yelp allows users to review local businesses and places with physical addresses such as parks. Figure 8.23 shows a Yelp map of Times Square restaurants on the iPad app. The reviews are from regular people, not expert food critics, and can help you decide where to eat. You can use the Yelp app on a mobile device to get information when you are right in the area.

FIGURE 8.23 Searching for a Place to Eat in Times Square Using the Yelp App on an iPad

Social Bookmarking and News Sites

Social bookmarking sites allow you to save and share your bookmarks or favorites online. Pinterest allows you to create virtual cork boards around topics of interest and pin webpages to them (Figure 8.24). You can share your boards with others, and you can follow other people to see what they have pinned. StumbleUpon discovers websites based on your interests. When you sign up, you indicate topics that interest you. Then, as you visit websites, you can click the *StumbleUpon* button to be taken to a similar site. You can click *I like this* to improve the selection of pages you stumble onto. Delicious allows you to not only save and share your bookmarks online but also search the bookmarks of others. It's a great way to quickly find out what other people find interesting and important right now. The links are organized into topics, or tags, to make it easier for you to find links. You can click the *Follow* button if you have a Delicious account, but you don't need an account to browse Delicious.

    Social news sites are different from traditional mass media news sites in that at least some of the content is submitted by users. Social news is interactive in a way that traditional media isn't. It's like having millions of friends sharing their finds with you. Content that's submitted more frequently or gets the most votes is promoted to the front page.

FIGURE 8.24 Pinterest

Three of the most popular social news sites are reddit, Digg, and Slashdot. Digg doesn't publish content but allows the community to submit content they discover on the web and puts it in one place for everyone to see and to discuss. reddit (Figure 8.25) allows community members to submit content and to vote that content up or down, as well as discuss it. reddit is organized into categories called subreddits. Celebrities often participate in AMA—ask me anything—interviews on reddit. Slashdot, which focuses primarily on technology topics, produces some content but also accepts submissions from its readers. Whatever your interests, there's probably a social news site for you.

FIGURE 8.25 reddit

IanDagnall Computing/Alamy Stock Photo

ETHICS

Some people create multiple accounts on social bookmarking and news sites so they can promote their own content. For example, a blogger might create several accounts on Digg and use each one to Digg a blog post, artificially raising its popularity on Digg and driving more traffic to it. This violates the Digg terms of use. But what if the blogger had all his friends and family members create accounts and Digg his post? Is it ethical? Does it violate the terms of use? Is it fair to other bloggers?

Running Project

Go to the Wikipedia article "Reliability of Wikipedia" at **wikipedia.org/wiki/Reliability_of_Wikipedia**. How does Wikipedia ensure that the content is correct? What procedures are in place to remove or correct mistakes? How does Wikipedia compare to other online sources of information?

3 Things You Need to Know

- Social media relies on the wisdom of the crowd rather than that of an expert.
- Anybody can edit a wiki.
- Social bookmarking and news sites help users find content that others recommend.

Key Terms

crowdsourcing

social bookmarking site

social news site

social review site

wiki

E-Commerce

ctive

5 Explain the Influence of Social Media on E-commerce

Businesses use social media sites to provide support and interaction to customers. **Social media marketing (SMM)** is the practice of using social media sites to sell products and services.

Types of E-Commerce

E-commerce is doing business on the web and consists of three categories—B2B, B2C, and C2C—where *B* stands for *business* and *C* stands for *consumer*.

B2B, or business-to-business, services are those that one business provides another, for example, website hosting, website design, and payment services such as PayPal (Figure 8.26). B2B services allow smaller companies to have a web presence or store without needing to have the in-house expertise or expense. A small business is able to have a professional-looking website and a sophisticated shopping cart system because of B2B services it purchases from other companies.

B2C, or business-to-consumer, is the most familiar form of e-commerce. Amazon.com, Overstock.com, and most other retailers sell their goods and services online. Many small businesses sell exclusively online, eliminating the overhead of running a brick-and-mortar store and increasing their reach to customers outside the area, as shown in Figure 8.27. This form of e-commerce has grown exponentially since Pizza Hut began offering pizza ordering on its website in 1994. B2C companies leverage social media to help customers find out about their products.

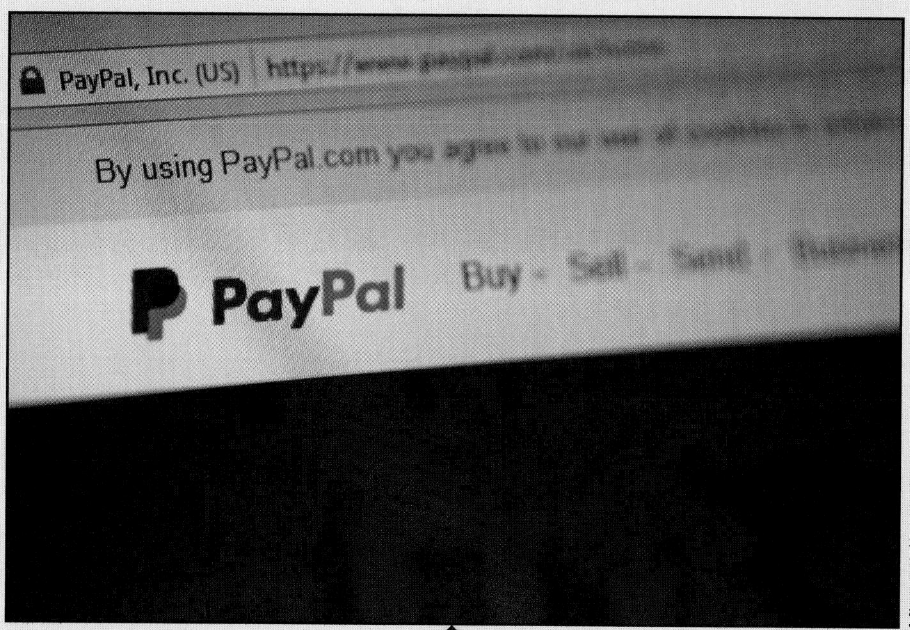

Migstock/Alamy Stock Photo

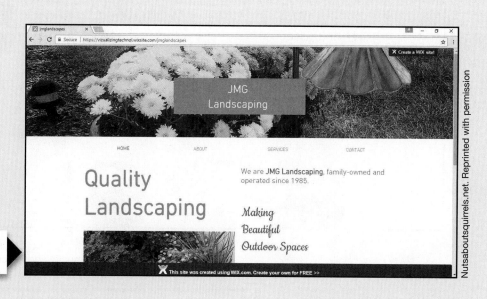

FIGURE 8.26 PayPal provides payment services for small companies that want a web presence.

Nutsaboutsquirrels.net. Reprinted with permission

FIGURE 8.27 A small business can use the web to reach customers.

The third form of e-commerce is C2C, or consumer-to-consumer. Websites such as eBay and Craigslist have created a global yard sale, where you can find, sell, or trade virtually anything. eBay (Figure 8.28) has a seller rating system that helps ensure honest transactions and a community that includes discussion boards, groups, and chats. An unscrupulous seller will quickly get a bad reputation, and a top-rated seller will see more sales as a result.

Airbnb is a community marketplace for accommodation rentals. It allows you to list your home for rent or find a rental anywhere in the world. Airbnb's standards and expectations help keep the transactions safe. Ride-sharing services Uber and Lyft are also considered C2C services.

FIGURE 8.28 The eBay community adds social media to the world's largest C2C site.

How Safe Is My Money?

E-commerce on the web requires you to hand over some sensitive information. So is it okay to shop online? Yes, but just as you wouldn't leave your doors unlocked, you need to be sure that you're shopping wisely. Shop at well-known sites or use third-party payment sites such as PayPal or Amazon Payments to protect credit card information. Many credit cards have the ability to create a temporary account number to use for online transactions.

Make sure you're on a secure website when completing transactions. Look at your browser's address bar. If the URL begins with *https*, then the site is using **Secure Sockets Layer (SSL)** security—a protocol that encrypts information before it is sent across the Internet. You'll also notice a padlock icon that indicates a secure site. Clicking on the padlock will open a security report about the website. And don't forget to regularly monitor all credit card transactions to look out for fraud.

Sending payments between friends is easy using PayPal or Venmo (which incidentally is now owned by PayPal), SquareCash, or Google Wallet. These services offer a secure way of splitting the bill without cash.

Ollyy/Shutterstock

Running Project

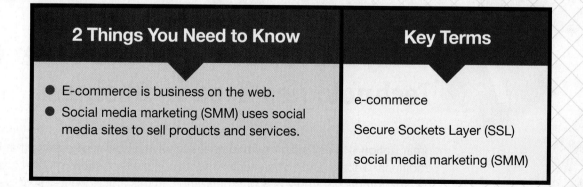

Visit **Amazon.com**. What are two ways that Amazon uses social media marketing? Can you find any other ways? How is this experience different from shopping in a store?

2 Things You Need to Know

- E-commerce is business on the web.
- Social media marketing (SMM) uses social media sites to sell products and services.

Key Terms

e-commerce

Secure Sockets Layer (SSL)

social media marketing (SMM)

Aey/Fotolia

Online Tools for Busines

Objective 7

Compare Social Media and Other Online Technologies Used in Business

When customers go looking for a company or service, they turn to the web. A successful organization in today's digital world needs to have an online presence that includes both a traditional website and social media. There are dozens of social media sites that you could use to promote your business or organization. In this article we'll look at just a few of them.

Collaborating
with Office

Facebook Pages

Unlike a Facebook profile, which is linked to a person, a Facebook Page is used to promote an organization, a product, or a service. A Facebook Page can have more than one administrator, so you can share the responsibilities among several people or departments. The Facebook Page for this textbook can be found at **facebook.com/visualizingtechnology**. A Page is public, so it can be viewed by anyone, even those who are not logged in to Facebook.

To create a Facebook Page, you need a personal Facebook account. Facebook's Terms of Service permit you to have only one personal Facebook account, but you can create multiple Facebook Pages. So, for example, a college representative might create a page for each department, club, or office. Once you are logged in to your personal account, the option *Create Page* can be found in the menu options. You can choose from several page categories (Figure 8.29). A page for a business or an organization will have

FIGURE 8.29 Create a Page Categories

NetPhotos3/Alamy Stock Photo

different features than a page for a person or cause. When you create a page, read the Facebook Pages terms carefully. Customize your page with a profile picture and header image that represents your brand.

A Facebook Page has an Insights section that allows you to view page activity and engagement. You can also pay for ads to promote your Facebook Page or website. The key to successful use of any social media tool is to keep it up to date and relevant to your customers. A Facebook Page shouldn't just be a static webpage. Use it to interact with and engage your customers and use it to post interesting updates, specials, and links to relevant information. Check out what other companies are doing on their pages. Try typing **facebook.com/** followed by a brand, an organization, or a company name.

Twitter

Unlike Facebook, Twitter has only one type of account, and you do not have to create a personal account first. So you can use Twitter to engage your customers and members even if you don't use Twitter personally. Visit **business.twitter.com** for information about ways that businesses use Twitter and tools and advice to help you target and engage followers. You can use Twitter to advertise specials, reward loyal customers with discounts, and share your mission and achievements. Share positive messages and include links, images, and videos. Use hashtags to organize and make your Tweets searchable, and respond to customers when they tweet you or retweet your messages. You can set up a Twitter ad campaign, which helps you target your Tweets to drive traffic to your website and gain new customers. You pay a fee when users follow your account or retweet, favorite, reply, or click on your promoted Tweet.

Customize your profile with a photo, header, bio, and website link and start tweeting. Figure 8.30 shows a Twitter account created for this book, **twitter.com/VizTech4,** with a profile photo, header image, and #myfirsttweet. I used the same images from the book's Facebook Page to keep the brand consistent. You can link your Twitter feed to other accounts like Facebook, and you can embed your feed in your website or blog, so the content you post on Twitter also displays in the other media as well.

FIGURE 8.30 Customize Your Twitter Profile Page

Search Engines

Creating social media profiles and websites using your brand is an important step, but most people start by using a search engine to find you. You want your site to appear on the first page of the search results. You should create a local business page on each of the three largest search engines: Google, Bing, and Yahoo! (Figure 8.31). Doing this is free, and such a page enables you to post basic information such as your hours, contact information, location, and website. In fact, the page might already exist, and you simply need to claim it as yours. Make sure that your business is correctly categorized and that everything is correct. Google allows users to review businesses, but Bing and Yahoo! rely on Yelp reviews—so you might also want to list your business on Yelp.

Search engine optimization (SEO) is used to make a website easier to find by both people and software that indexes the web and to increase the webpage ranking in search engine results. SEO is most often associated with using keywords and key phrases in the webpage content and code, but this is only one part of SEO. The quality and quantity of content on a site; the number of images, videos, and external links; the social media presence; as well as the number of visitors that click on the link to a site in the search engine results all factor into search engine rankings.

FIGURE 8.31 A Local Business Page on Yahoo!

Courtesy of Yahoo

Digital Communication Tools

The immediacy of our digital communications has in some ways changed our expectations and behavior. In the past, it was unusual to contact someone outside of normal business hours. Today, it is common to expect answers to email and text messages in the evenings and on the weekends. An employer that provides a smartphone to an employee might expect that employee to be available outside of work. These expectations and responsibilities should be clear to both parties. The nature of the business might require someone to be on call at all times. A company with global connections needs to consider the business hours of other locations. A web conference with someone located half way around the world will require at least one party to be online during odd hours. When it is noon in Tokyo, it is 10:00 PM the previous day in New York. It is still good manners and business practice to limit these interruptions whenever possible.

ONLINE COLLABORATION TECHNOLOGIES

Collaboration can go beyond simply exchanging email messages or chatting on the phone. When the collaborators are not in the same location, online tools can enhance this collaboration. Google Apps for Work is a suite of tools to communicate, store, and collaborate. **SharePoint** is a Microsoft technology that enables employees in an organization to access information across organizational and geographic boundaries. Organizations use Microsoft SharePoint to create websites to use as a secure place to store, organize, share, and access information from almost any device. A team site (Figure 8.32) is used by a group of collaborators, such as a department or committee. You can access your SharePoint sites when you sign in to Office 365, or your organization's corporate intranet site. With a SharePoint site, you can share a common document library, and work with others on the same document and at the same time. You can share documents with people inside your organization, and share documents and sites with people outside your organization.

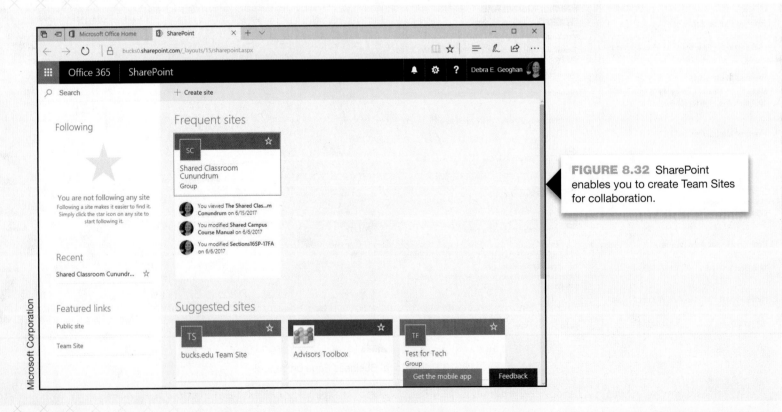

FIGURE 8.32 SharePoint enables you to create Team Sites for collaboration.

Microsoft Corporation

Slack is a team communication and collaboration tool. Teams organize conversations and projects into channels, which can be public and accessible by all team members, or private and accessible only by invited members. You might use Slack to collaborate with a team of classmates working on a group project. With Slack you can share files by dragging and dropping them into the app or connecting to Dropbox, Box, or Google Drive. Everything you do in Slack is archived and searchable. Figure 8.33 shows Slack on a desktop and on two mobile devices. Because Slack integrates with your other apps, it provides a single place to work and communicate. Even if you are not online, you can configure Slack to send you notifications.

FIGURE 8.33 Slack is available for multiple devices.

CONFERENCING WITH DIGITAL TOOLS

Collaborating and conferencing in real-time using digital tools enable teams to work together, even when in different locations. Choose the right tool for the task. For example, save the cost of travel by interviewing potential employees via Skype or Facetime. Provide client support and offer online presentations or webinars with web conferencing software such as WebEx or GoToMeeting to present to a group, ensuring everyone is on the same virtual page. For simple discussions, a voice call may be all that is needed—or add video by using a tool such as Skype, FaceTime, or Google Hangouts. These tools enable collaborators to log in from anywhere and view the same screen. As the leader of a presentation or conference, you can share your own screen or pass control over to another participant to share theirs. Using a screen sharing program, you can display your computer screen and make it visible to others. This is a common way to collaborate on a project, enabling everyone to be looking at the same thing at the same time. Figure 8.34 shows screen sharing using Skype. In this example, a teacher is sharing a presentation with her students.

Be aware of your intended audience and collaborators. Verify that everyone has the necessary technology and skills to use it, and do a practice run-through ahead of time to be sure everything works correctly.

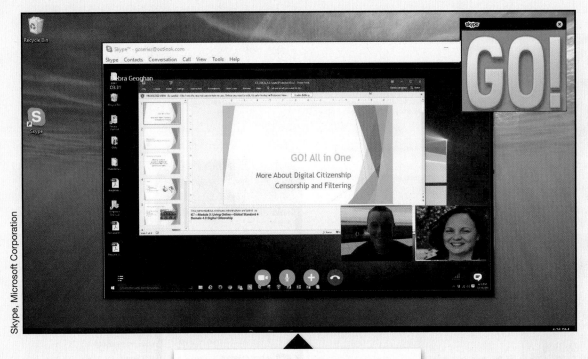

Skype, Microsoft Corporation

FIGURE 8.34 Sharing a Screen with Skype

FIND OUT MORE

Virtual Meetings

According to Merriam-Webster, **virtual reality** is "an artificial world that consists of images and sounds created by a computer and that is affected by the actions of a person who is experiencing it." In the movie Kingsman: The Secret Service, there were only two people physically in the room, but when they put on special glasses, they could see the other participants. Virtual reality meetings are not just science fiction. By placing multiple people in the same virtual reality setting, a virtual meeting room can be created. You will be able to interact with other people's avatars, which can be made to look as realistic as you want them to. The technology is still fairly new, but it won't be long before a web conference can be replaced with a VR meeting room. Use the Internet to research the current state of virtual meetings.

Stuart Miles/Fotolia

BLOGGER Although many blogs are personal in nature and earn the writer no compensation, some folks are professional bloggers. These bloggers may be paid by a company to blog about a product or provide news or reviews, and their blogs are usually part of a bigger website. Some professional bloggers use their blogs to drive customers to their other products. Successful bloggers monetize the content on their sites in several ways, including placing ads and links to other sites. A professional blog may earn money by using Google AdSense to place ads and links on it. It takes a lot of time and work to write a good blog and even more to make money doing it.

Running Project

Select a local business that you regularly patronize or are interested in learning about, and search the web for evidence of online brand marketing. Does this business have a presence on Facebook, Google, Yahoo!, and Twitter? How easy is it for a potential customer to locate information about the business? What advice would you give to this business to improve its online presence?

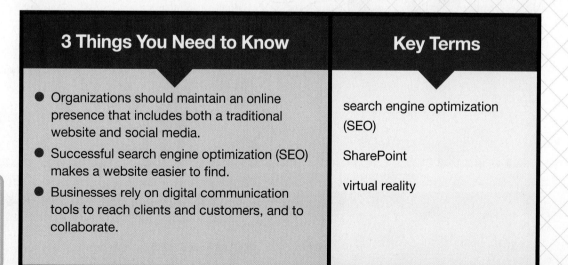

3 Things You Need to Know

- Organizations should maintain an online presence that includes both a traditional website and social media.
- Successful search engine optimization (SEO) makes a website easier to find.
- Businesses rely on digital communication tools to reach clients and customers, and to collaborate.

Key Terms

search engine optimization (SEO)

SharePoint

virtual reality

Viz Check—In MyLab IT, take a quick quiz covering Objectives 4–7.

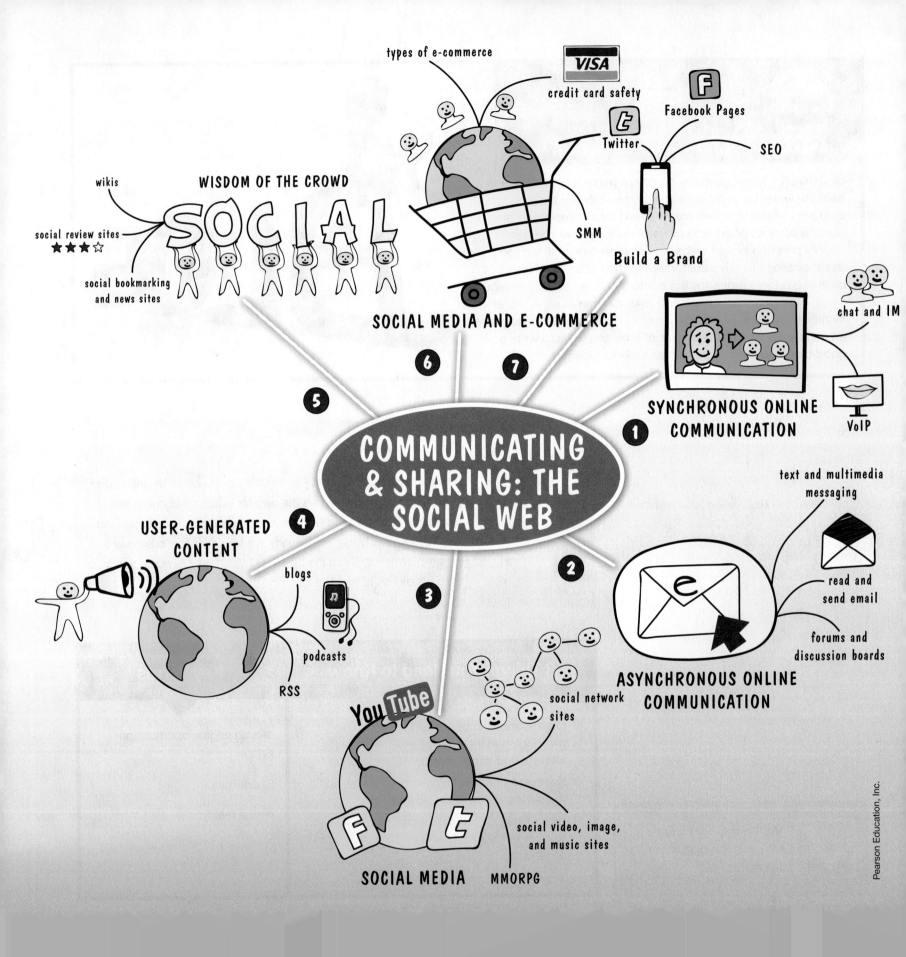

types of e-commerce

VISA

credit card safety

Facebook Pages

Twitter

SEO

wikis

WISDOM OF THE CROWD

SOCIAL

social review sites
★★★☆

SMM

social bookmarking
and news sites

Build a Brand

SOCIAL MEDIA AND E-COMMERCE

chat and IM

5

6

7

SYNCHRONOUS ONLINE
COMMUNICATION

VoIP

1

COMMUNICATING
& SHARING: THE
SOCIAL WEB

text and multimedia
messaging

USER-GENERATED
CONTENT

4

blogs

2

read and
send email

podcasts

3

RSS

forums and
discussion boards

social network
sites

ASYNCHRONOUS ONLINE
COMMUNICATION

You Tube

f t

social video, image,
and music sites

SOCIAL MEDIA   MMORPG

Objectives Recap

1. Compare Different Forms of Synchronous Online Communication
2. Compare Different Forms of Asynchronous Online Communication
3. Discuss the Impact of Social Media in Society
4. Locate User-Generated Content in the Form of a Blog or Podcast
5. Discuss How Wikis and Other Social Media Sites Rely on the Wisdom of the Crowd
6. Explain the Influence of Social Media on E-commerce
7. Compare Social Media and Other Online Technologies Used in Business

Key Terms

Summary

1. Compare Different Forms of Synchronous Online Communication

Synchronous communication happens in real time. Chat usually involves more than two people having a conversation in a chat room and is usually text based. Instant messaging is similar to chat, but the conversation is between only two people. The terms *IM* and *chat* are often used interchangeably. VoIP service uses the Internet to place voice and video phone calls.

2. Compare Different Forms of Asynchronous Online Communication

Email is an asynchronous, store-and-forward technology. You shouldn't expect that your email is private. You can access email by using webmail or a desktop email program. Use the To, Cc, and Bcc fields to address your messages and the subject line to tell the receiver what the message is about.

3. Discuss the Impact of Social Media in Society

Social networking and sharing allow you to keep in touch, create content, share ideas, and benefit from the expertise of others. You no longer need to rely on experts for news or advice.

4. Locate User-Generated Content in the Form of a Blog or Podcast

Blogs can be created on websites such as Blogger and WordPress. Podcasts can be found using a podcast client or by searching websites such as YouTube or podcasts.com. RSS feeds push frequently updated content to subscribers.

5. Discuss How Wikis and Other Social Media Sites Rely on the Wisdom of the Crowd

Wikis are unique because anyone can edit their content. Many types of social websites, including wikis, rely on the wisdom of the crowd rather than experts. Social review sites let users review hotels, movies, games, books, and other products and services; social bookmarking sites allow you to save and share your bookmarks or favorites online; and social news sites are different from traditional media news sites in that at least some of the content is submitted by users.

Summary continues on the next page

Summary *continued*

6. Explain the Influence of Social Media on E-commerce

Businesses leverage social media through social media marketing strategies such as contests, fan pages, and review sites. B2B (business-to-business), B2C (business-to-consumer), and C2C (consumer-to-consumer) are three forms of e-commerce.

7. Compare Social Media and Other Online Technologies Used in Business

A successful organization in today's digital world needs to have an online presence that includes both a traditional website and social media, and local business pages on search engines. Search engine optimization (SEO) is used to make a website easier to find by both people and software that indexes the web and to increase the webpage ranking in search engine results. Businesses use online tools to store, share, and collaborate.

Multiple Choice

Answer the multiple-choice questions below for more practice with key terms and concepts from this chapter.

1. Which form of online communication happens in real time?
   a. Blog
   b. IM
   c. Email
   d. Forums

2. Which technology enables calls to be transmitted over the Internet instead of via traditional phone lines or cellular towers?
   a. Instant messaging
   b. Forums
   c. Message boards
   d. VoIP

3. A(n) _____ is a small image that represents facial expressions, common objects, and people and animals.
   a. emoji
   b. meme
   c. avatar
   d. hashtag

4. Websites that enable you to create content, connect, network, and share are called _____.
   a. asynchronous
   b. MMORPG
   c. social media
   d. viral

5. A funny image or catchphrase, often of celebrity or pop culture reference, that is spread by Internet users across social media is called a(n):
   a. emoji
   b. meme
   c. avatar
   d. MMORPG

6. The social web relies on _____, obtaining the collective opinion of a crowd of people rather than the individual opinion of an expert.
   a. chat
   b. crowdsourcing
   c. forums
   d. RSS

7. Which type of social media site are Twitter and Tumblr?
   a. Bookmarking
   b. Forum
   c. Microblog
   d. Wiki

8. What is a digital media file of a prerecorded radio- or TV-like show that's distributed over the web?
   a. Captcha
   b. Podcast
   c. SMS
   d. RSS

9. _____ is the practice of using social media sites to sell products and services.
   a. B2B
   b. SEO
   c. SMM
   d. Twitter

10. Which is a protocol that encrypts data before it is sent across the Internet?
    a. SEO
    b. SMM
    c. SMS
    d. SSL

True or False

Answer the following questions with *T* for true or *F* for false for more practice with key terms and concepts from this chapter.

_____ **1.** Chat is a service that allows phone calls to be transmitted over the Internet instead of traditional phone lines.

_____ **2.** Email is private and cannot be read by others.

_____ **3.** Using the Short Message Service (SMS), you can send brief electronic messages between mobile devices.

_____ **4.** Social media enables users to create user-generated content, connect, network, and share.

_____ **5.** A viral video spreads computer viruses.

_____ **6.** User-generated content includes videos and photos posted online but not what is written and said.

_____ **7.** E-commerce is doing business on the web.

_____ **8.** Like a wiki, a blog usually has many authors.

_____ **9.** Crowdsourcing means obtaining the collective opinion of a crowd of people rather than the individual opinion of an expert.

_____ **10.** SharePoint enables employees in an organization to access information across organizational and geographic boundaries.

Fill in the Blank

Fill in the blanks with key terms from this chapter.

1. _____ online communication happens in real time.

2. A(n) _____ is a series of letters and numbers that are distorted in some way so that they are difficult for automated software to read but relatively easy for humans to read.

3. Tools called _____ are used to communicate and collaborate on the web and enable you to be a creator, not just a consumer, of content.

4. Your _____ is all the information that someone could find out about you by searching the web, including social networking sites.

5. A(n) _____ is an online journal.

6. The _____ consists of all the blogs on the web and the connections between them.

7. A(n) _____ is a digital media file of a prerecorded radio- or TV-like show that's distributed over the web.

8. A(n) _____ is a website that allows users to edit content, even if it was written by someone else.

9. A(n) _____ is a word or phrase preceded by a # symbol that is used to organize and make tweets searchable.

10. _____ is used to make a website easier to find by both people and software that indexes the web and to increase the webpage ranking in search engine results.

Running Project ...

... The Finish Line

Use your answers from the previous sections of the chapter project to discuss the impact of social networking on society. How has it changed the way we keep in touch with others? Do business? How has it personally changed the way you connect with others? Write a report responding to the questions raised throughout the chapter. Save your file as **lastname_firstname_ch08_project** and submit it to your instructor as directed.

Do It Yourself 1

Instant messaging and chatting are important tools businesses use to provide services to customers. Some schools also offer virtual advisors and librarians that you can chat with live online. From your student data files, open the file *vt_ch08_DIY1_answersheet* and save the file as **lastname_firstname_ch08_DIY1_answersheet**.

If your school or local library offers this service, use it to ask about the success of this service. Take a screenshot of your conversation and paste it into your answer sheet. If you don't have a local library that uses chat or IM, use the Internet to find another library that does. Have you ever used this type of service in researching a topic? What type of help can this particular library chat service provide? What are the hours the service is available? What other online resources does the library offer? Type up your answers, save the file, and submit your work as directed by your instructor.

Do It Yourself 2

Many websites require you to provide an email address to register and use the site. In this activity, you will create a free Yahoo! email account. From your student data files, open the file *vt_ch08_DIY2_answersheet* and save the file as **lastname_firstname_ch08_DIY2_answersheet**.

1. Go to **yahoo.com** and if you're already logged in to Yahoo!, click your name and sign out. Click *Sign in* and then click *Sign up*. Fill in the form. Type a simple, 5 letter word or name as a password. What is the message you see? Try adding characters and numbers until the password is accepted. How many characters were required? Click *Continue*.

2. After you successfully create your account you will be sent a text message with an account key. Verify your account and then click *Let's Get Started*. On the Yahoo! homepage, in the menu on the left, click *More*, and then click *More on Yahoo*. Click *My Yahoo*. On the Welcome page, click *Get started*. Choose a theme, choose a layout, and choose at least three interests. Which options did you choose? Click *Show my page*. Take a screenshot of your profile page, paste the image into your answer sheet, and save and submit your file as directed by your instructor.

File Management

Social sharing sites allow you to put your videos and images online. To help organize this content, these sites use social tagging. For this activity, you'll create tags for a group of images. From your student files, open the file *vt_ch08_FM_answersheet* and save the file as **lastname_firstname_ch08_FM_answersheet**.

1. Using File Explorer or Finder, navigate to the student data files for this chapter. Look at the 21 images in the *vt_ch08_file_management* folder. In your answer sheet, for each image, list at least two tags that you would use to tag the file. Try to use the same tags for multiple files.

Image	Tag 1	Tag 2

2. Go to the Flickr website and search for the three tags that you used the most often in your table. Do you find images that are similar to the ones you tagged? Do you think you did a good job of tagging them? Take a screenshot of one of the images you found and paste it into your answer sheet. Save your file and submit it as directed by your instructor.

Critical Thinking

Social networks are often criticized in the media for their privacy settings. In this exercise you will examine the privacy policy of Facebook to determine the appropriate settings to use for your own profile. You do not need to have a Facebook account to do this exercise. From your student data files, open the file *vt_ch08_CT_answersheet* and save the file as **lastname_firstname_ch08_CT_answersheet**.

Go to **www.facebook.com/about/basics**. Read through the various topics on this page. How does Facebook protect your privacy? What are the default privacy settings, and do you think they do a good job protecting you? If you have a Facebook account, have you set your privacy settings to keep your personal information protected? When was the last time you checked and updated them? Have the terms of service changed since you first joined this network? Type your answers in your answer sheet, save your answer sheet, and submit it as directed by your instructor.

Ethical Dilemma

Your digital footprint says a lot about you, but not everything is true or accurate. When you're a student, you may not think about the impact your digital life will have on future employment. Potential employers may search the web looking for information on job applicants. From your student data files, open the file *vt_ch08_ethics_answersheet* and save the file as **lastname_firstname_ch08_ethics_answersheet**.

Is it ethical for a potential employer to use the Internet this way? Is it legal? What if an angry ex-partner posted some things pretending to be you? How might this affect your chances for employment? Do you think it's okay to post things that make you look good, even if they're not true? Use the Internet to look up Internet defamation. Look up the definitions of *libel* and *slander*. How do they differ? What are the legal consequences of each? Type up your answers, save the file, and submit your work as directed by your instructor.

On the Web

Using social news sites is a great way to find out what other people think is important. From your student data files, open the file *vt_ch08_web_answersheet* and save the file as **lastname_firstname_ch08_web_answersheet**.

Visit Slashdot, reddit, or Digg. What are some of the recent stories? How do these compare to the headlines today in traditional mass media? Select two stories that you think are interesting or important and write a short summary of each. Why did you select these stories? Type up your answers, save the file, and submit your answer sheet as directed by your instructor.

Collaboration

With a group of three to five students, research the history of social networks and create a timeline showing five to seven important milestones of this development.

Instructors: Divide the class into groups of three to five students.

The Project: As a team, research the history of social networks. Create a timeline showing five to seven important milestones of social networks. Use at least three references. Use Google Drive or Microsoft Office to prepare your research and provide documentation that all team members have contributed to the project.

Outcome: Use a free online timeline generator, a drawing program, a word processor, or a presentation tool to create your timeline and present it to your class. The presentation may be no longer than 3 minutes and should contain five to seven milestones. Turn in a final version of your presentation named **teamname_ch08_timeline** and your file showing your collaboration named **teamname_ch08_collab**. Be sure to include the name of your presentation and a listing of all team members. Submit your presentation to your instructor as directed.

Application Project

Office 2016 Application Projects
PowerPoint 2016: Browsers

Project Description: In this project, you will create a presentation about desktop browsers. In this presentation, you will apply design and color themes. You will also insert and format a chart and apply animations to objects on your slides, as well as transitions between slides. *If necessary, download student data files from* **pearsonhighered.com/viztech**.

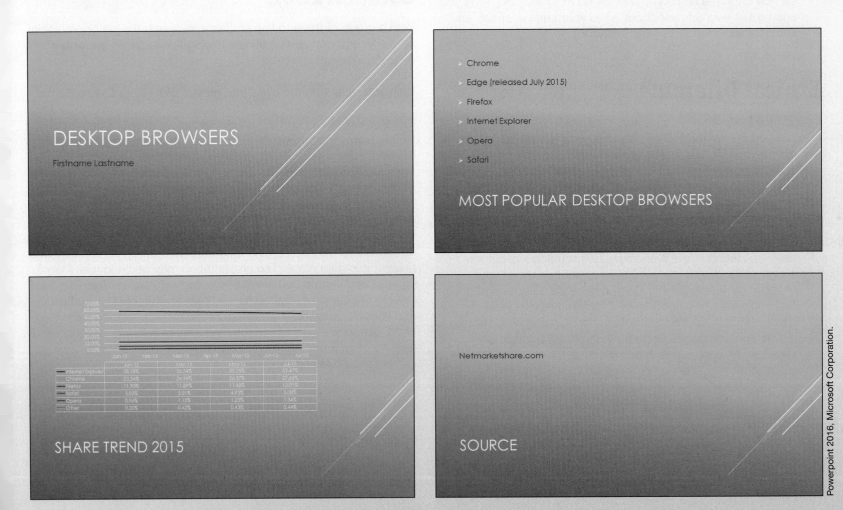

Step	Instructions
1	Start PowerPoint. From your student data files, open *vt_ch08_ppt* Save the file as **lastname_firstname_ch08_ppt**
2	Apply the Slice theme, green variant, to the presentation.
3	On Slide 1, using your name, type **Firstname Lastname** in the subtitle placeholder.
4	On Slide 2, change the bullets to Arrow bullets and set the line spacing to 1.5.
5	Apply the Appear animation and set a duration of 00.50 to the bulleted list on Slide 2.
6	On Slide 3 in the title placeholder, type **SHARE TREND 2015-2016**
7	On Slide 3, in the content placeholder, add a line chart. In the range A1:G5 enter the following data to create the chart:

Month	Chrome	Internet Explorer	Firefox	Edge	Safari	Other
September 2015	29.86%	49.19%	11.46%	2.41%	5.08%	2.00%
December 2015	32.33%	46.32%	12.13%	2.79%	4.49%	1.95%
March 2016	39.09%	39.10%	10.54%	4.32%	4.87%	2.09%
June 2016	48.65%	31.65%	7.98%	5.09%	4.64%	1.99%

Step	Instructions
8	Change the chart to Layout 5. Delete the Chart Title and Axis Title.
9	Insert a new Title and Content slide after Slide 3. On Slide 4, in the title placeholder, type **SOURCE** In the content placeholder, type **Netmarketshare.com** and remove the bullet.
10	Apply the Split transition to all slides in the presentation.
11	Insert the footer **Firstname Lastname**, using your name, on the notes and handout pages for all slides in the presentation. View the presentation in Slide Show, view from beginning to end, and then return to Normal view.
12	Save the presentation and close PowerPoint. Submit the presentation as directed.

Application Project

MyLab IT
GRADER

Office 2016 Application Projects
Excel 2016: Broadband Internet Growth

Project Description: In this project, using data from the World Bank, you will format a spreadsheet and create and format a chart showing broadband growth from 2000 to 2015. *If necessary, download student data files from* **pearsonhighered.com/viztech**.

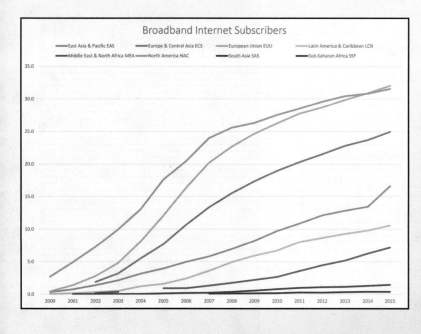

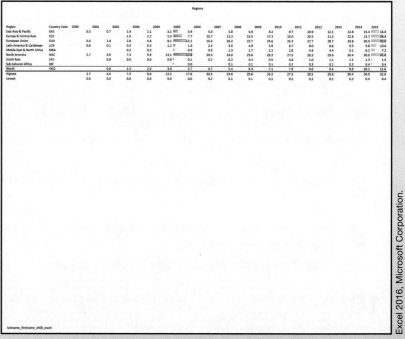

Excel 2016, Microsoft Corporation.

Step	Instructions
1	Start Excel. From your student data files, open the Excel file *vt_ch08_excel* Save the file as **lastname_firstname_ch08_excel**
2	On the Regions sheet, select the range C2:R10. Apply the Number Format to the selected range. Decrease the decimals displayed to 1.
3	Select A1:R1 and apply the Heading 4 cell style.
4	Adjust the widths of columns A and B to fit the contents.
5	Select A10:R10 and apply a Top and Double Bottom Border to the range.
6	In cell A11, type **Highest** In cell A12, type **Lowest**
7	In cell C11, use a function to calculate the highest number of broadband subscriptions in the range C2:C9; do not include the world data. Copy the formula from C11:R11.
8	In cell C12, use a function to calculate the lowest number of broadband subscriptions in the range C2:C9. Copy the formula from C12:R12.
9	Select the range A1:R9 and insert a line chart. Move the chart to a new sheet named **Line Chart** Format the chart Style 8.
10	Change the chart title to **Broadband Internet Subscribers**
11	On the Regions sheet, apply the Gradient Blue Data Bar conditional formatting to the range H2:H9 and apply the Gradient Orange Data Bar conditional formatting to the range R2:R9.
12	Change the orientation of the Regions worksheet to Landscape. Adjust the Scale option to change the Width to 1 page.
13	Insert a header with the sheet name in the center cell. Insert a footer with the file name in the left cell. Return to Normal view.
14	Ensure that the worksheets are correctly named and placed in the following order in the workbook: Line Chart, Regions, Source. Save the workbook and then exit Excel. Submit the workbook as directed.

CHAPTER
9

Networks and Communication

In This Chapter

VIZ INTRO

The Internet is the largest computer network in the world, but it is actually a network of networks. On a much smaller scale, most of the computers that you use at school and in the workplace are part of a network, and you likely also have a network at home. When you have finished this chapter, you'll be able to identify and use different kinds of computer networks.

BrunoWeltmann/Fotolia

Objectives

1 Discuss the Importance of Computer Networks

2 Compare Different Types of LANs and WANs

3 List and Describe the Hardware Used in Both Wired and Wireless Networks

4 List and Describe Network Software and Protocols

5 Explain How to Protect a Network

Running Project

In this chapter, you'll learn about computer networks and communication. Look for instructions as you complete each article. For most articles, there is a series of questions for you to research. At the conclusion of this chapter, you'll submit your responses to the questions raised.

From Sneakernet to Hotspots

Discuss the Importance of Computer Networks

A **computer network** is two or more computers that share resources. **Network resources** can be software, hardware, or files. Computer networks can save you both time and money and make it easier to work, increasing productivity. Before computers were connected in networks, moving files between them involved physically putting them on a disk and carrying the disk to the new machine. This is wistfully referred to by some as *sneakernet*.

Peer-to-Peer Networks

In a **peer-to-peer (P2P) network**, such as the one shown in Figure 9.1, all computers are considered equal—each device can share its resources with every other device, and there's no centralized authority. The computers might, for example, share music files and a printer, and although they can share an Internet connection, they don't have to connect to the Internet at all. Computers in a P2P network belong to a **workgroup**. P2Ps don't require a specialized NOS (network operating system). Desktop and mobile operating systems include the networking features to set up and join a P2P network. Most P2P networks are found in homes or small businesses.

P2Ps are easy to set up and configure and provide basic file and print sharing. For example, if you have a printer in your house that's connected to your desktop computer, you can easily share the printer with your notebook computer through your home network. The drawback to this type of setup is that the computer that's sharing a resource must be turned on for the other computers in the network to access its resources—if your desktop computer is turned off or in sleep mode, then the printer will be unavailable to other computers on the network.

Windows Network and Sharing Center enables you to view and configure your network settings (Figure 9.2). When you add a new computer to your home and turn it on, Windows will automatically detect the other devices that are already on your network. In File Explorer, in the Navigation pane, click *Network* to view the devices on your network. Figure 9.3 shows a mixed home network consisting of both Windows and Mac computers, printers, a scanner, and a router. Other devices that you can have on a home network include Smart TVs, tablets, smartphones, and video game consoles.

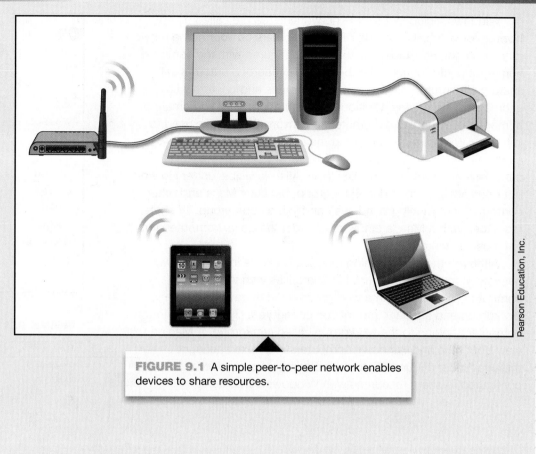

Pearson Education, Inc.

FIGURE 9.1 A simple peer-to-peer network enables devices to share resources.

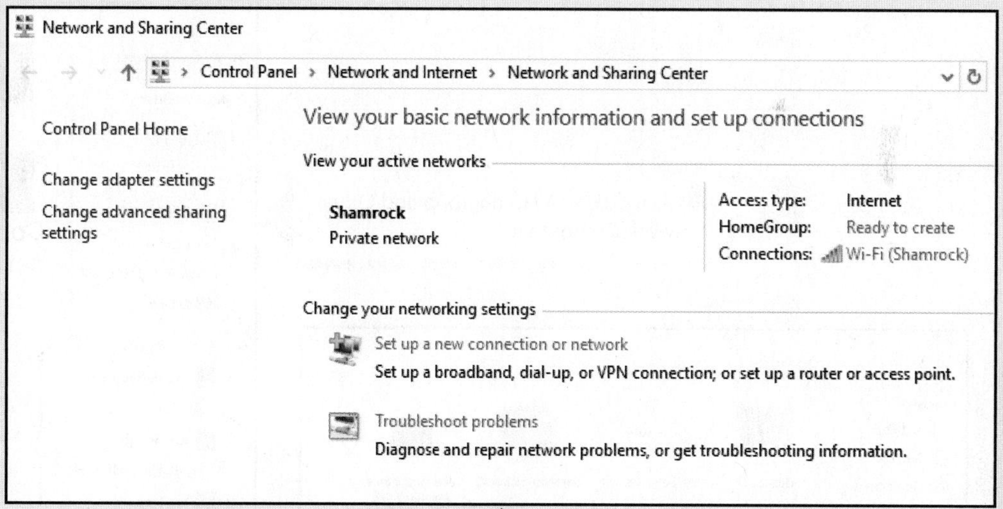

Network and Sharing Center

← → ↑ ▦ > Control Panel > Network and Internet > Network and Sharing Center   ∨ ↻

Control Panel Home

Change adapter settings

Change advanced sharing settings

View your basic network information and set up connections

View your active networks

Shamrock
Private network

Access type: Internet
HomeGroup: Ready to create
Connections: ⧏ Wi-Fi (Shamrock)

Change your networking settings

Set up a new connection or network
Set up a broadband, dial-up, or VPN connection; or set up a router or access point.

Troubleshoot problems
Diagnose and repair network problems, or get troubleshooting information.

Microsoft Corporation

FIGURE 9.2 Windows Network and Sharing Center

Windows includes a simple networking feature called a **homegroup**, which consists of the computers on your home network running Windows 7 or higher that are configured with the same homegroup information. Members of a homegroup automatically share their picture, music, and video libraries and printers with each other without any additional configuration. After you create a homegroup, Windows will create a password that can be used to join other Windows computers to the homegroup. In Figure 9.4, you can see a homegroup in the File Explorer window. In the Navigation pane, my MacBook laptop—DEBRAS-AIR—is visible under Network but does not appear under Homegroup, because Macs and other computers not running Windows can't join a homegroup. To share resources with a Mac, a Linux, or an older Windows computer, you must use a workgroup.

Although the Mac, running macOS, is visible in the Windows network, it must be configured to share files with Windows computers. Computers in a workgroup need to have the same workgroup and account information configured. By default, Windows computers belong to the workgroup called *workgroup*. A Mac can view both Mac and Windows computers in a mixed network through Finder (Figure 9.5), but Mac computers need to be configured to share resources with Windows computers.

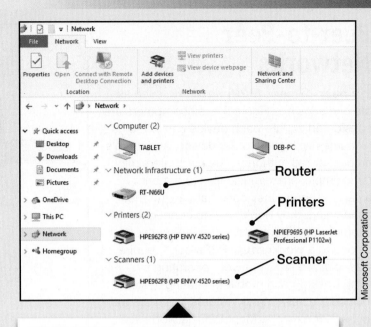

FIGURE 9.3 The File Explorer Network Window

FIGURE 9.4 A Homegroup and Other Network Computers

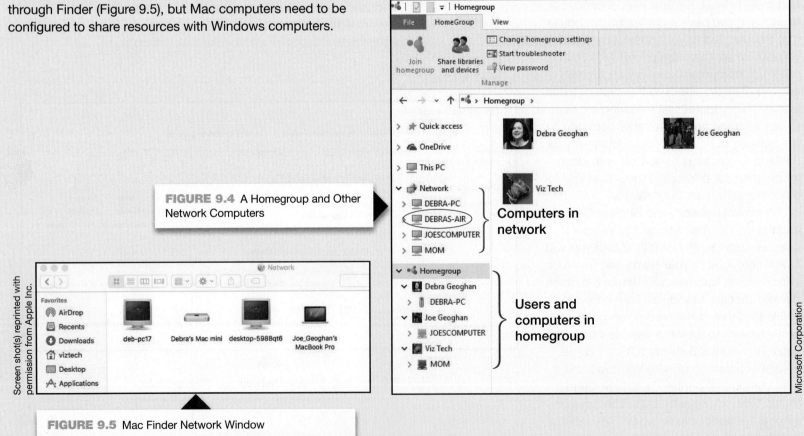

FIGURE 9.5 Mac Finder Network Window

Client–Server Networks

P2P networks are suitable for homes and very small businesses, but they have two major drawbacks. They're limited to a small number of devices, and they provide no centralization of resources and security. In most business settings, a more common configuration is a **client–server network**—a network that has at least one server at its center (Figure 9.6).

A **server** is a multiuser computer system that runs a network operating system (NOS) and provides services—such as Internet access, email, or file and print services—to client systems. The personal computers and other devices that connect to the server are called **clients**. Server computers range from very small to massive enterprise-level systems that serve hundreds of thousands of clients. The server provides a way to centralize the network management, resources, and security. In a client–server network, users log in to the network instead of to their local computers and are granted access to resources based on their logins.

Ranjith ravindran/Shutterstock

Running Project

Select a computer network that you use (school, home, or work). Is it a P2P or client–server network? How do you connect to it? What resources do you access or share on this network?

3 Things You Need to Know

- A computer network is two or more computers that share resources, such as software, hardware, or files.
- A peer-to-peer (P2P) network is a network in which all computers belong to the same workgroup and are considered equal.
- A client–server network is a network that has at least one server at its center that provides centralized management, resources, and security.

Key Terms

client

client–server network

computer network

homegroup

network resource

peer-to-peer (P2P) network

server

workgroup

Examine Network and Sharing Settings

Digital Literacy Skill

HOW TO VIDEO

In this activity, you'll examine your current network settings and share resources on your network. (Note that in a school network, security settings may prevent you from being able to perform parts of this exercise.) If necessary, download student data files from **pearsonhighered.com/viztech**. From your student data files, open the *vt_ch09_howto1_answersheet* file and save the file as **lastname_firstname_ch09_howto1_answersheet**.

1 From the Windows desktop, right-click the network icon on the taskbar and click *Open Network and Sharing Center*. Take note of the Connections listed in the right pane. In the left pane, click *Change adapter settings*. How many network connections do you have on this computer? Which ones are connected? Take a screenshot and paste it into your answer sheet.

Network Connections

Control Panel > Network and Internet > Network Connections >

Organize ▼

Ethernet
Network cable unplugged
This Qualcomm Atheros network ...

Wi-Fi
Shamrock
Qualcomm Atheros AR9485 Wirel...

Microsoft Corporation

2 Locate the connection that you are currently using and double-click it to open the status window. Is this connection wired or wireless? What speed is the connection? Click the *Details* button. What is the IPv4 address of this connection? What other information can you locate here? Take a screenshot and paste it into your answer sheet. Close the open dialog boxes and windows.

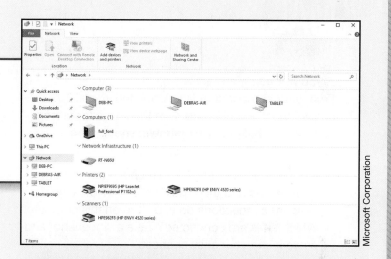

3 Open File Explorer and click *Network* in the Navigation pane. List the other devices in your network. What resources do you access or share from or with these devices? Take a screenshot and paste it into your answer sheet. Close File Explorer.

4 Right-click the desktop, point to *New*, and click *Folder*. Name the folder **myshare**. Right-click the *myshare* folder and point to *Share with*. Is the folder shared with anyone?

5 Click *Specific people* to open the File Sharing control panel window. Click the down arrow next to Add. Who can you share this folder with? Choose *Everyone* and click *Add*. By default, what permissions are granted to Everyone? Take a screenshot and paste it into your document. Click *Cancel* and then delete the folder. Save your answer sheet, including screenshots, and submit as directed.

Microsoft Corporation

If you are using a Mac:
From your student data files, open the *vt_ch09_howto1_answersheet_mac* file and save the file as **lastname_firstname_ch09_howto1_answersheet_mac**.

1. From the Dock or the Apple menu, open *System Preferences* and then click *Network*. How many network connections do you have on this computer? Which ones are connected? Take a screenshot and paste it into your answer sheet.

2. If necessary, click the connection that you are currently using. Is this connection wired or wireless? Click *Advanced*. Click and review each tab. What is the IP address of this connection? What other information can you locate here? Take a screenshot of the TCP/IP settings and paste it into your answer sheet. Close the Network window.

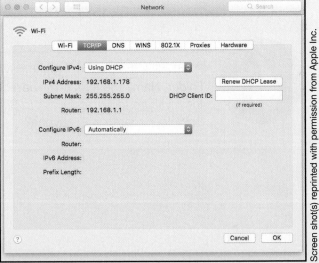

Screen shot(s) reprinted with permission from Apple Inc.

Screen shot(s) reprinted with permission from Apple Inc.

3. Open Finder. Click the *Go* menu, then click *Network*. List the other devices in your network. What resources do you access or share from or with these devices? Take a screenshot and paste it into your answer sheet.

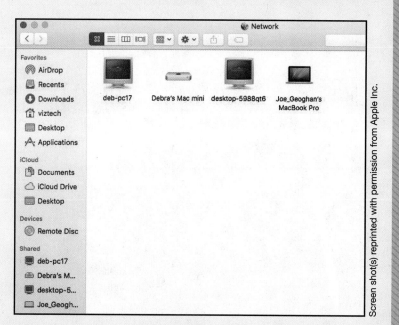

Screen shot(s) reprinted with permission from Apple Inc.

4. In Finder, click *Desktop*. Click *File*, click *New Folder*, and name the new folder **myshare**. Return to the System Preferences window and click *Sharing*. What services are you sharing? If necessary, check *File Sharing*. What folders are shared?

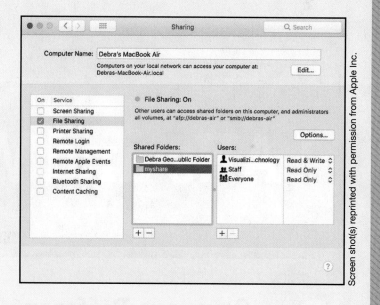

Screen shot(s) reprinted with permission from Apple Inc.

5. Click *Options* and, if necessary, select *Share files and folders using SMB* to make your shares accessible to Windows computers on your network. Click *Done*. In the Sharing window, under Folders, click the + sign, navigate to your new folder, and then click *Add* to share your new folder. Take a screenshot and paste it into your answer sheet. Close the Sharing window and close File Explorer. If you have a Windows computer on the same network, see if you can access your Mac files from it. Save your file, including screenshots, and submit it as directed.

Tomasz Zajda/Fotolia

LANs and WANs

Compare Different Types of LANs and WANs

Networks come in many different shapes and sizes. In this article, we discuss some of the most common types of networks found in both homes and businesses.

SIMULATION

Networks

Small Networks

A **local area network (LAN)** is a network in which all connected devices or nodes are located in the same physical location. On a small scale, a home network is a LAN. In a business, a LAN might consist of a single room, a floor, a building, or an entire campus. A home LAN is probably a peer-to-peer network, but a business LAN is more likely to be a client–server network that consists of computers, printers, and servers as well as the network hardware that connects them. Devices on a LAN are connected using switches (Figure 9.7) or wireless access points.

A small network that consists of devices connected by **Bluetooth**—a technology that connects peripherals wirelessly at short ranges—is referred to as a **personal area network (PAN)**. Bluetooth has a very limited range of only about 10 to 100 meters (30 to 300 feet). Bluetooth is designed to be easy to use, enabling devices to talk to each other securely over short distances. Each device in a PAN can connect to up to seven other devices at a time. Some common devices that use Bluetooth include mice, keyboards, interactive whiteboards, headsets, smartphones, cameras, media players, video game consoles, speakers, automobiles, and printers (Figure 9.8). Bluetooth is an important Internet of things technology.

A LAN that uses Wi-Fi to transmit data is known as a **wireless LAN (WLAN)**. Wi-Fi uses radio waves to provide wireless, high-speed network connections; it has a much larger range, higher speeds, and better security, and it supports more devices than Bluetooth, but it is also more expensive and complicated to set up.

Stanisic Vladimir/Fotolia

FIGURE 9.7 A switch connects clients to a LAN.

Dean Bertoncelj/shutterstock

FIGURE 9.8 A Personal Area Network Using Bluetooth Devices: Mouse, Keyboard, Headset

LAN Topologies

Standards—specifications that have been defined by an industry organization—ensure that equipment made by different companies work together. The **Ethernet** standard defines the way data is transmitted over a local area network. A home LAN uses the same Ethernet standards and equipment used in larger business networks.

Network data transmission speed is measured in bits per second. Ethernet networks transmit signals over twisted-pair cable, fiber-optic cable, and Wi-Fi, at data transmission speeds of 10 Mbps to 10 Gbps. Most home networks use 100 Mbps or 1 Gbps Ethernet—also called Gigabit Ethernet. The maximum speed depends on the type of media and capability of the network hardware on the LAN.

The devices, or nodes, on the LAN can be connected in three physical layouts: bus, ring, or star **topology** (Figure 9.9). In a bus topology, the nodes are all connected via a single cable. The data travels back and forth along the cable, which is terminated at both ends. In a ring topology, the devices are connected to a single cable, but the ends of the cable are connected in a circle, and the data travels around the circle in one direction. Both buses and rings are simple networks that were popular in the past; you are not likely to find a pure bus or ring network today. Modern LANs use a physical star topology—or a hybrid star–ring or star–bus topology. In a star topology, every node on the network is attached to a central device such as a switch or wireless access point. This connection device allows nodes to be easily added, removed, or moved without disrupting the network.

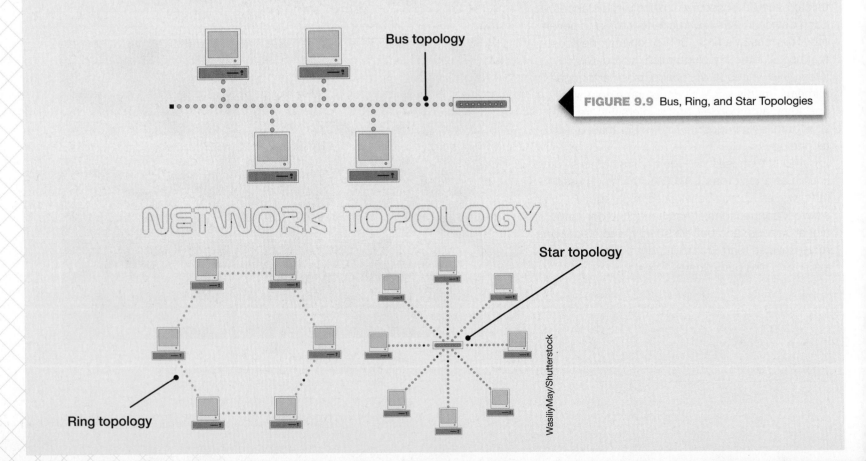

Bus topology

FIGURE 9.9 Bus, Ring, and Star Topologies

NETWORK TOPOLOGY

Star topology

Ring topology

WasiliyMay/Shutterstock

Large Networks

A **wide area network (WAN)** is a network that spans multiple locations and connects multiple LANs over dedicated communication lines using **routers**—devices that connect two or more networks together. A college that has multiple campuses uses WAN connections between them. WAN technologies are much more expensive than LAN technologies. At home, the WAN you connect to is the Internet, and the port on your router that connects to the modem may be labeled the *WAN* or *Internet* port, distinguishing it from the LAN ports your other devices connect to (Figure 9.10).

Denis Dryashkin/Fotolia

FIGURE 9.10 A Home Router with a WAN Port Labeled Internet

What if you need to connect to your work network from home or while on the road? Because you're located in a different location, you must use a WAN connection to access your work network. It isn't practical for a business to provide its employees dedicated WAN lines for every offsite location. Instead, companies use a special type of connection called a **virtual private network (VPN)**. A VPN creates a private network through the public network—the Internet—allowing a remote user to access a LAN securely without needing a dedicated line (Figure 9.11). VPNs use encryption to ensure that data is secure as it travels through the public network. This is much less expensive and more practical for businesses than providing a dedicated line to each remote employee.

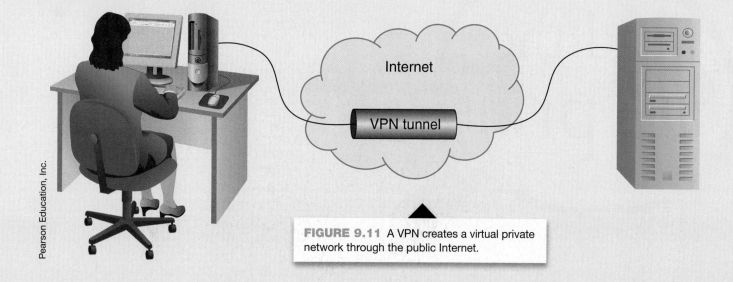

Pearson Education, Inc.

FIGURE 9.11 A VPN creates a virtual private network through the public Internet.

Somewhere between a LAN and a WAN is an enterprise network. In a business that is large and has many computers to manage, there may be multiple LANs located in the same location. These LANs are connected to each other using routers—technically making them WANs. This hybrid is sometimes called a **campus area network (CAN)**.

Companies that have massive amounts of information to move and store may have a **storage area network (SAN)** between the data storage devices and the servers on a network, making the data accessible to all servers in the SAN. Users are not part of the SAN but are able to access the information stored in the SAN through the LAN servers.

A network that covers a single geographic area is called a **metropolitan area network (MAN)**.

Cellular networks use cell towers to transmit voice and data over large distances. Modern 4G networks have speeds that make these networks a practical way for people on the move to connect to network resources, including the Internet and corporate VPNs, from almost anywhere in the world. Accessing resources using a smartphone or cellular-enabled tablet can quickly use all of your allotted data and increase your cost. When shopping for cellular phone carriers, compare the cost of data and choose a plan that gives you enough data for your normal usage. Some basic plans include only 1 Gb of data a month—enough for casual email users, but if you spend a lot of time on the Internet, play games online, stream videos, or engage in other heavy uses, you should look for plans with at least 5 Gb or more. Unlimited plans often throttle, or slow, your speed after you reach a certain threshold. The data limits are found in the fine print on your cellular contract.

read the fine print

IQoncept/Shutterstock

Scanrail/Fotolia

CAREER SPOTLIGHT

JOBS

ESB Professional/Shutterstock

NETWORK ADMINISTRATOR You'll find computer networks in every type of business, and knowing how to access network resources is a critical skill for most employees.

A **network administrator** is the person responsible for managing the hardware and software on a network. The job may also include troubleshooting and security. Although not required, a two- or four-year college degree is helpful in this field, as are certifications. According to Salary.com, the average salary for a person in this field with two to five years' experience is about $64,000. As with any technical field, you should expect to continue your training to keep up with the changes in technology. An entry-level person may be called a network technician rather than an administrator.

Because networks and connectivity are critical for most businesses, experts in making networks secure and reliable will always be in demand. The *Occupational Outlook Handbook* at **bls.gov/ooh** predicts that network-related jobs will grow faster than the average for all occupations over the next decade, so considering a career in this field might be a good choice for you.

Running Project

Make a list of networks that you use regularly. Include home, cellular, work, and school networks. Label each as a LAN, WAN, or one of the other network types described in this article. List the devices you use to connect to each. What resources do you access?

5 Things You Need to Know

- A local area network (LAN) is a network that has all its nodes located in the same physical location.
- Wireless network types include Bluetooth personal area networks (PANs), Wi-Fi wireless LANs (WLANs), and cellular networks.
- Ethernet is the standard that defines the way data is transmitted over a LAN. Topology describes the physical layout of a network.
- A wide area network (WAN) is a network that spans multiple locations and connects multiple LANs.
- A VPN creates a private network through the public network (Internet).

Key Terms

Bluetooth	router
campus area network (CAN)	standard
cellular network	storage area network (SAN)
Ethernet	
local area network (LAN)	topology
metropolitan area network (MAN)	virtual private network (VPN)
network administrator	wide area network (WAN)
personal area network (PAN)	wireless LAN (WLAN)

Silvano Rebai/Fotolia

Network Hardware

Objective

3

List and Describe the Hardware Used in Both Wired and Wireless Networks

Every network has two major components: hardware to create the physical connections between devices and software to configure the resources and security. In this article, we look at the hardware needed to create different types of networks.

VIZ CLIP

Home
Networking
Hardware

Network Adapters

The hardware needed to set up a peer-to-peer network is much less complicated than what is needed in a client-server network. The simplest P2P network can consist of two devices sharing files by using a wireless connection or a single cable. For example, you can beam data from your smartphone directly to your colleague's phone, or transfer music from your computer to your media player through a USB cable. Connecting larger home networks with many types of devices requires additional hardware.

Each device that connects to a network must have some type of **network adapter**—a communication device used to establish a connection with a network. Most desktop and many notebook computers today come with a built-in Ethernet adapter. This type of connection, called an RJ-45 port, looks like a large phone jack (Figure 9.12). The cable used for this type of connection is called twisted-pair, Ethernet cable, Cat-5e, or Cat-6. Depending on the size of the network you're connecting to, the other end of the cable might plug into a wall jack or a port on a switch, a router, or a modem. Many devices have built-in wireless adapters, but for those that don't, a USB adapter is an easy fix (Figure 9.13).

The advantages to using a wired network connection include speed, location, and security. Wired Ethernet connections use Fast Ethernet at 100 Mbps, or Gigabit Ethernet at 1,000 megabits per second. No wireless technology can currently reach the 1 Gbps speed, but Wi-Fi and cellular networks can equal or exceed the 100 Mbps speed, and in 2017 the first certified WiGig (short-range, high speed) devices were scheduled to be released. A wired connection is less subject to interference and can travel long distances without slowing. Buildings and other structures can slow or even prevent a wireless connection from working. Finally, a wired connection is more secure than a wireless connection, especially if the wireless connection is not configured with strong security settings.

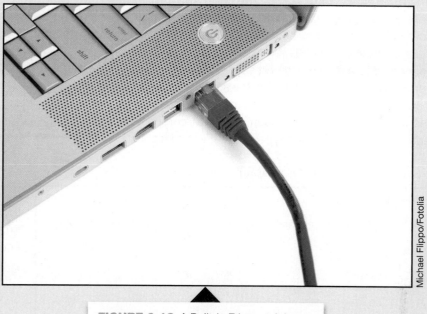

Michael Flippo/Fotolia

FIGURE 9.12 A Built-in Ethernet Adapter Connected to an Ethernet Cable

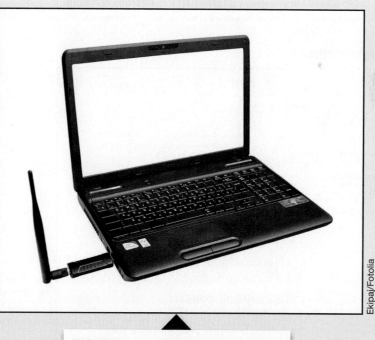

Ekipaj/Fotolia

FIGURE 9.13 A USB Wireless Adapter

There are several types of wireless network adapters. The Wi-Fi networks found in homes and public hotspots use the **IEEE 802.11** standards. The Wi-Fi Alliance certifies wireless devices to ensure interoperability. Most notebook computers and mobile devices come with a built-in wireless adapter, and a USB wireless adapter can easily be connected to a desktop, smart TV, or game console that does not have one built in. Wireless printers can be connected directly to a network, eliminating the need to be shared from an individual computer. Table 9.1 compares the speeds of the most common types of Wi-Fi connections.

TABLE 9.1 A Comparison of Wi-Fi Standards

802.11 Standard	Maximum Speed	Date Introduced
802.11b	11 Mbps	1999
802.11g	54 Mbps	2003
802.11n	300 Mbps–600 Mbps	2009
802.11ac	1.3–6.9 Gbps	2012
802.11ad (WiGig)	up to 8Gbps	2016

Debra Geoghan

Ethernet adapter

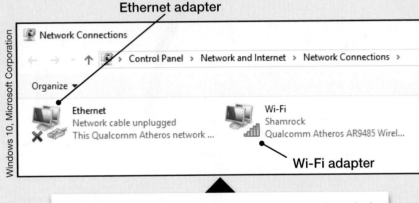

Windows 10, Microsoft Corporation

Wi-Fi adapter

FIGURE 9.14 This Network Connections window shows both wired and wireless network adapters on this Windows computer.

Wi-Fi wireless adapter

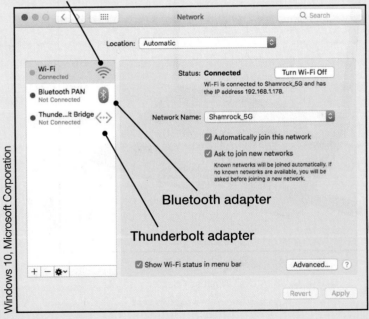

Windows 10, Microsoft Corporation

Bluetooth adapter

Thunderbolt adapter

When two wireless devices connect to each other directly, they create an **ad hoc network**. In an **infrastructure wireless network**, devices connect through a wireless access point. At home, a wireless access point is built into your wireless router.

A 3G or 4G adapter can be built into a mobile device or can be connected by USB to a computer, allowing you to use a cellular network for network access.

To view the network adapters that are installed on your Windows computer, right-click the network icon on the taskbar and click *Open Network and Sharing Center*. In the left pane, click *Change adapter settings*. This opens the Network Connections window, which lists all the network adapters on the machine and the status of each. From here, you can manage your connections. The computer in Figure 9.14 has both a wired Ethernet adapter and a wireless Wi-Fi adapter. Computers can have multiple types of network adapters, and you might also find Bluetooth or cellular adapters listed in this window. To view the network adapters on a Mac, open System Preferences from the Dock or Apple menu and then click *Network*. The Mac in Figure 9.15 has three adapters: Wi-Fi, Bluetooth, and Thunderbolt Bridge—which lets two Macs communicate through the Thunderbolt port.

FIGURE 9.15 This Network window shows the network adapters on a Mac.

Network Connectivity Hardware

Creating networks with many resources and devices requires some additional hardware. The first device on a network is usually the device that connects to the Internet. If you are using a dial-up connection, this is an analog **modem**—short for modulator-demodulator. Cable and DSL have special digital modems, and fiber networks use **optical network terminals (ONTs)**. You can connect your computer directly to a modem or an ONT, but you can share the connection with other devices more easily with some basic network hardware.

A business network consists of routers, switches, wireless access points, and firewalls. A router connects two or more networks together—for example, your home network and the Internet. It uses address information to correctly route the data packets it receives. In a home network, the router is a convergence device that serves several functions: It shares the Internet connection, provides IP addresses to the other devices on the network, and, if configured correctly, provides security for your network.

Routers make up the backbone of the Internet and are responsible for sending data packets along the correct route to their destination (Figure 9.16). If you think of the Internet as a map of highways, you'll realize that there are many different ways to get from one place to another. When you plan a trip, you take not only the distances into consideration but also traffic congestion and construction. You might make a detour if you run into a problem along the way. The shortest route is not always the fastest route. Routers serve the same function, routing data packets around traffic, collisions, and other impediments.

Router

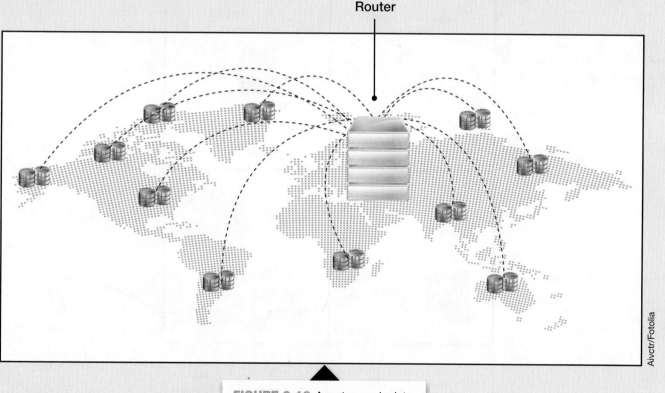

Aivctr/Fotolia

FIGURE 9.16 A router sends data packets to their destinations.

A home router also includes a built-in **switch**—a device that connects multiple devices on a LAN—and can also serve as a **wireless access point (WAP)**—a device that allows wireless devices to join a network. Switches are sometimes referred to as hubs, which they have largely replaced. Within the network, a switch uses address information to send data packets only to the port that the appropriate device is connected to. To set up a Wi-Fi network, you need a wireless access point—a large wireless network may have many WAPs installed, but one or two WAPs can usually provide enough coverage in a home network. Figure 9.17 shows a home network that includes both wired and wireless devices.

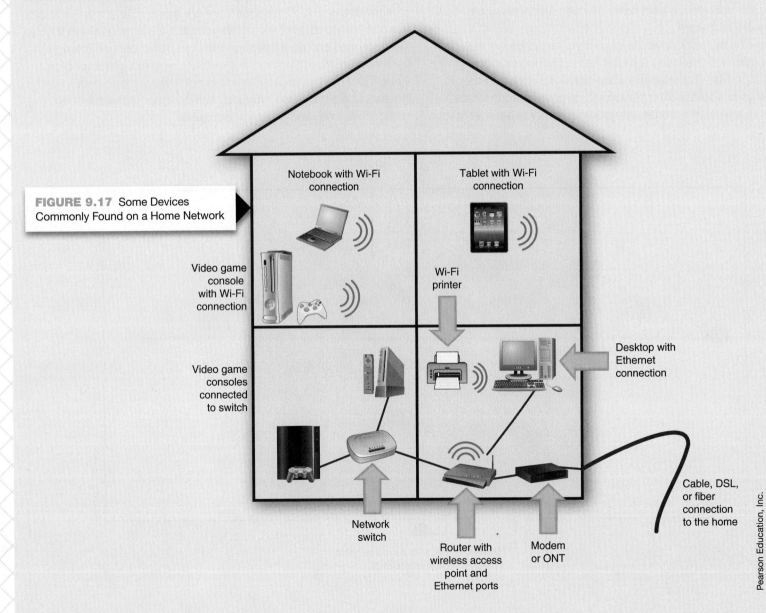

FIGURE 9.17 Some Devices Commonly Found on a Home Network

Notebook with Wi-Fi connection

Tablet with Wi-Fi connection

Video game console with Wi-Fi connection

Wi-Fi printer

Video game consoles connected to switch

Desktop with Ethernet connection

Network switch

Router with wireless access point and Ethernet ports

Modem or ONT

Cable, DSL, or fiber connection to the home

Pearson Education, Inc.

A **firewall** blocks unauthorized access to a network. There are both software firewalls, such as the one included with your operating system, and hardware firewalls. A hardware firewall may be part of a router or a stand-alone device as shown in Figure 9.18. Firewalls can check both outgoing and incoming data packets and can be configured with filters to allow or deny various kinds of traffic based on IP address, protocol type, domain name, or other criteria. For example, a firewall might block access to certain websites or deny Internet access to certain computers during certain hours. Incoming packets that try to access restricted data will be denied access to the network.

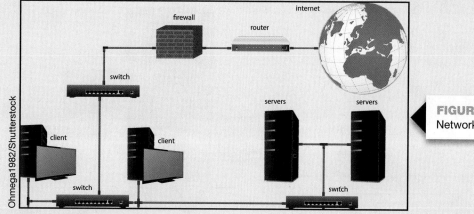

FIGURE 9.18
Network Diagram

Ohmega1982/Shutterstock

Running Project

Network security is everybody's job. What are some steps you can take to help protect the network? What should you do if you discover someone has learned your password? What are three ways an employee might inadvertently compromise the security of a company network?

VizCheck—In MyLab IT, take a quick quiz covering Objectives 1–3.

4 Things You Need to Know

- Each device that connects to a network must have a network adapter.
- The first device on a network connects to the Internet and is a modem or an optical network terminal (ONT).
- A router connects two or more networks together; switches and wireless access points connect multiple devices on a network.
- A firewall blocks unauthorized access to a network.

Key Terms

ad hoc network

firewall

IEEE 802.11

infrastructure wireless network

modem

network adapter

optical network terminal (ONT)

switch

wireless access point (WAP)

Hywards/Shutterstock

Software and Protocols

Objective

4 List and Describe Network Software and Protocols

VIZ CLIP

Network hardware allows devices to physically connect to each other, but software and protocols enable them to communicate with and understand each other. In this article, we look at network operating systems, communication software, and protocols that make a network work.

Connecting to a Public Wi-Fi Hotspot

Peer-to-Peer Network Software

No special software is required to create a simple peer-to-peer network. When Windows is installed on a computer, it includes a feature called Client for Microsoft Networks, which allows it to remotely access files and printers on a Microsoft network. To verify that the Client for Microsoft Networks is installed on your computer, open the Network and Sharing Center from the taskbar, click *Change adapter settings* in the left pane, right-click the active adapter, and click *Properties* to open the properties dialog box for the connection (Figure 9.19).

Using the workgroup feature of Windows allows you to share and remotely access files on a Windows network. macOS includes Windows File Sharing, and its network discovery tool should locate your Windows computers automatically in Finder. To configure Windows File Sharing (SMB) on a Mac, open System Preferences, click *Sharing*, select *File Sharing*, and then click *Options* (Figure 9.20). If your network consists of computers running the same OS, the computers are able to detect and share resources with each other with little or no configuration on your part.

Microsoft Corporation

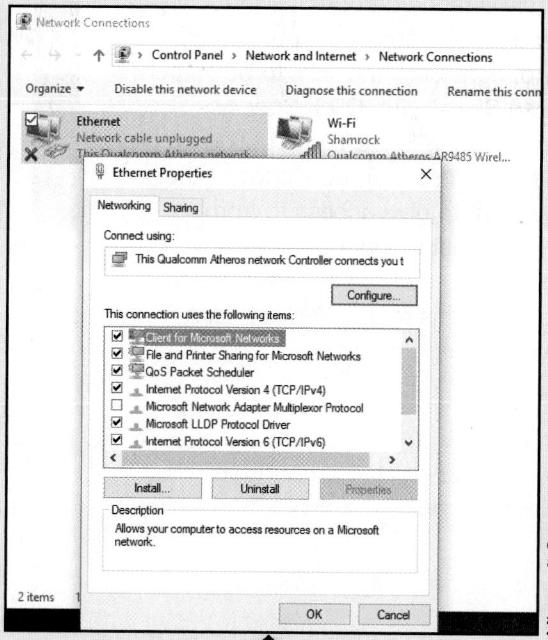

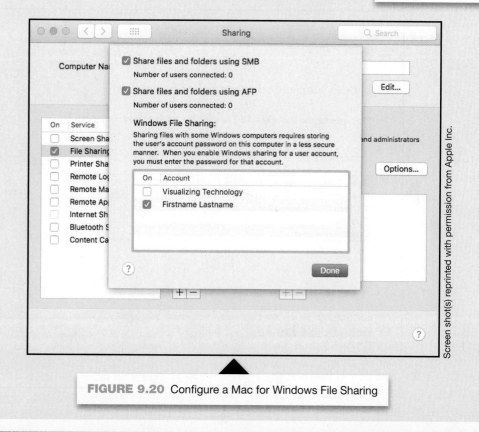

FIGURE 9.19 The Ethernet Properties dialog box shows the Client for Microsoft Networks installed.

Screen shot(s) reprinted with permission from Apple Inc.

FIGURE 9.20 Configure a Mac for Windows File Sharing

To share a resource from a Windows computer with computers in your workgroup, right-click the item to be shared and choose *Share with*. Click *Specific people* to open the File Sharing dialog box. In the File Sharing dialog box, choose the users you want to give access to from the drop-down list box and click *Add* (Figure 9.21). You can grant read or read/write access to this folder. You can also remove users from this list.

Microsoft Corporation

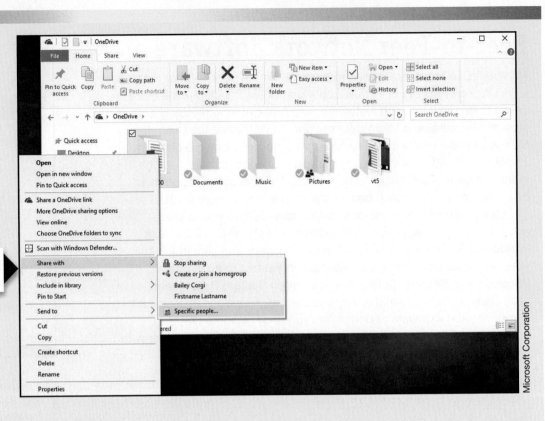

FIGURE 9.21a Right-click and select *Share with* to grant access to your files.

Microsoft Corporation

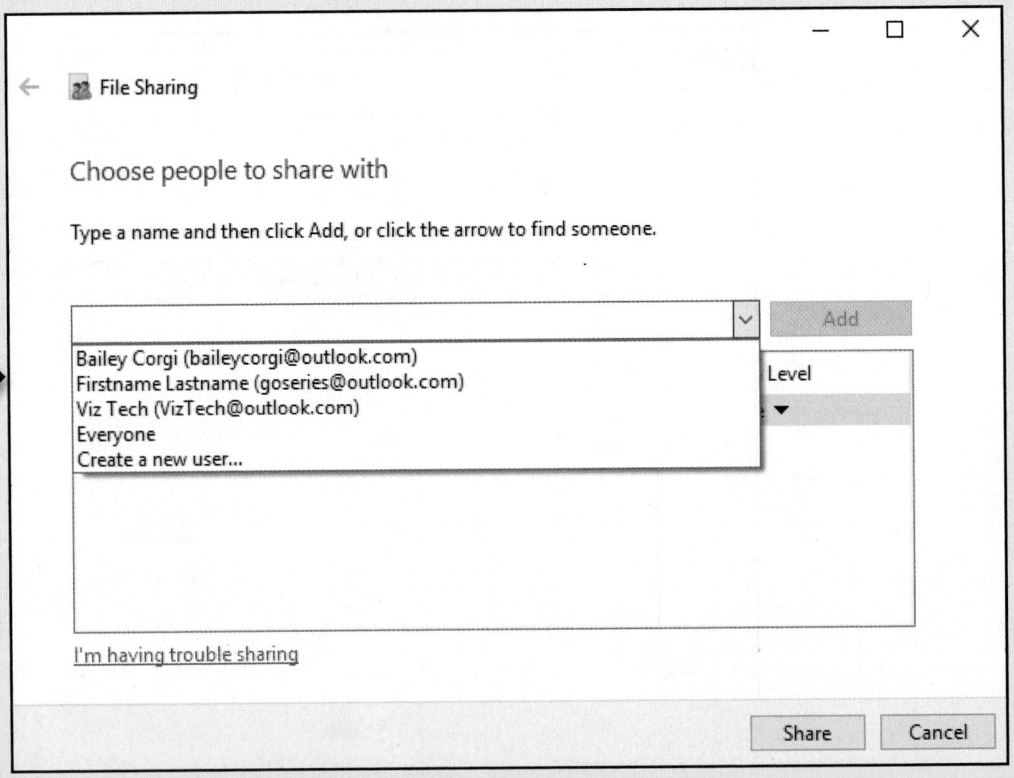

FIGURE 9.21b Choose the users and permission in the File Sharing dialog box.

With two Macs, using a macOS feature called AirDrop is an easy way to wirelessly share files. Simply open Finder and click the *AirDrop* folder on both computers. Once you see each other in your AirDrop folders, you can drag and drop files to share them (Figure 9.22). There is no configuration or password necessary to use AirDrop, and once the file has been accepted, the connection is broken.

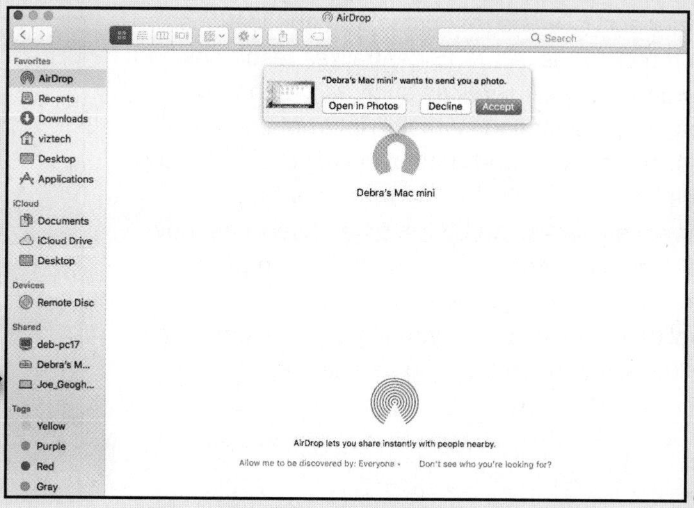

FIGURE 9.22 AirDrop easily shares files between Macs.

Client–Server Network Software

As the name implies, both client software and server software are needed on a client–server network. The client software makes requests, and the server software fulfills them (Figure 9.23). In a network where the servers run the Microsoft Server NOS, Windows clients don't need any special client software for basic file and print services. Instead, they use the same Client for Microsoft Networks used in peer-to-peer networks to connect to the servers. A **domain** is a network composed of a group of clients and servers under the control of one central security database on a special server called the domain controller. You log in to the domain to have access to all the servers in the domain—in a network with multiple servers, you don't need to log in to each one individually. The domain security database includes your user information—who you are, what your password is, and what your access and restrictions are.

For many types of servers, special client software is needed. When you use your web browser to access your email, the browser serves as an email client. The browser can also act as an FTP client when you download a file, a database client when you access your bank transactions, and an HTTP client when you access a webpage. Other client software you may use includes VPN software, desktop email programs, instant messaging/chat programs, and mobile banking apps.

Server software is also known as a **network operating system (NOS)**—a specialized operating system that controls the software and hardware on a network. It enables multiple client devices to communicate with the server and

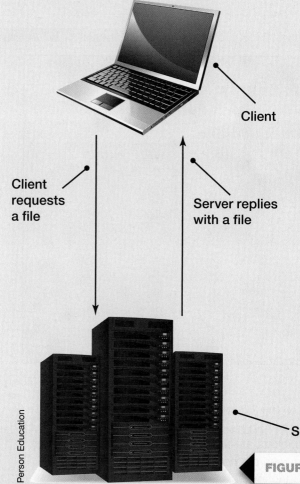

Client

Client requests a file

Server replies with a file

Server

Person Education

FIGURE 9.23 A Client Request to a Server

each other and to share resources, run applications, and send messages. An NOS centralizes resources and security and provides services such as file and print services, communication services, Internet and email services, and backup and database services to the client computers.

Servers are classified by the type of services they provide. Some common services are file and print services, email, database, web, chat, audio/video, and applications. Whenever you log in to a website (Figure 9.24), you're connecting to a server.

FIGURE 9.24 Using a Web Browser as a Client

Network Protocols

Protocols define the rules for communication between devices—how data is formatted, transmitted, received, and acknowledged. Without protocols, devices could be physically connected and still unable to communicate.

Think about a meeting between two people. When you walk into the meeting, you greet the other person, perhaps shake hands, and exchange names. Mutually agreed-upon protocols determine how you begin the conversation. Network protocols also define how a conversation between devices begins, which ensures that both are ready to communicate and agree on how to proceed. During the meeting, you also follow rules: what to say, how to say it, what language to speak, and what's appropriate and what's not. Protocols define how devices converse in much the same way. Finally, at the end of your meeting, you stand up, shake hands, say goodbye, and depart; similarly, protocols define the method to end an electronic conversation.

Although there are hundreds of different protocols, the most important ones belong to the **TCP/IP protocol stack**. This is a suite of protocols that define everything from how to transfer files (FTP) and webpages (HTTP) to sending (SMTP) and receiving (POP) email. **TCP** stands for **Transmission Control Protocol**, and it's responsible for ensuring that data packets are transmitted reliably. **IP**, or **Internet Protocol**, is responsible for addressing and routing packets to their destinations. Both pieces are needed for data to move between devices. Figure 9.25 lists some of the important protocols in the TCP/IP stack and their functions.

✓ Network Protocols

 **Transmission Control Protocol**
TCP
Ensuring that data packets are transmitted reliably

 Internet Protocol
IP
Addressing and routing packets to their destination

 **Hypertext Transfer Protocol**
HTTP
Requesting and delivering webpages

 **File Transfer Protocol**
FTP
Transferring files between computers

Post Office Protocol
Receiving email

 **Simple Mail Transfer Protocol**
POP/ SMTP
Sending email

Dynamic Host Configuration Protocol

 **DHCP**
Requesting and receiving IP addresses from a DHCP server

FIGURE 9.25 TCP/IP Protocols

The TCP/IP protocol stack runs on the Internet, and because of this, it's also the protocol stack that runs on most LANs. TCP/IP is the default protocol stack installed on Windows, Mac, and Linux computers, and it's what allows them to communicate with each other easily. Figure 9.26 shows the properties for the Ethernet adapter. You can see that both TCP/IPv6 and TCP/IPv4 are installed. TCP/IP version 4 is used on the Internet and most LANs. Although many older devices don't support TCP/IP version 6, it is currently being implemented and will eventually replace version 4 altogether. By default, Windows computers are set to obtain an IP address automatically, using DHCP (Dynamic Host Configuration Protocol). An **IP address** is a unique numeric address assigned to each node on a network. The computer sends out a DHCP request that's answered by a DHCP server—most likely your router at

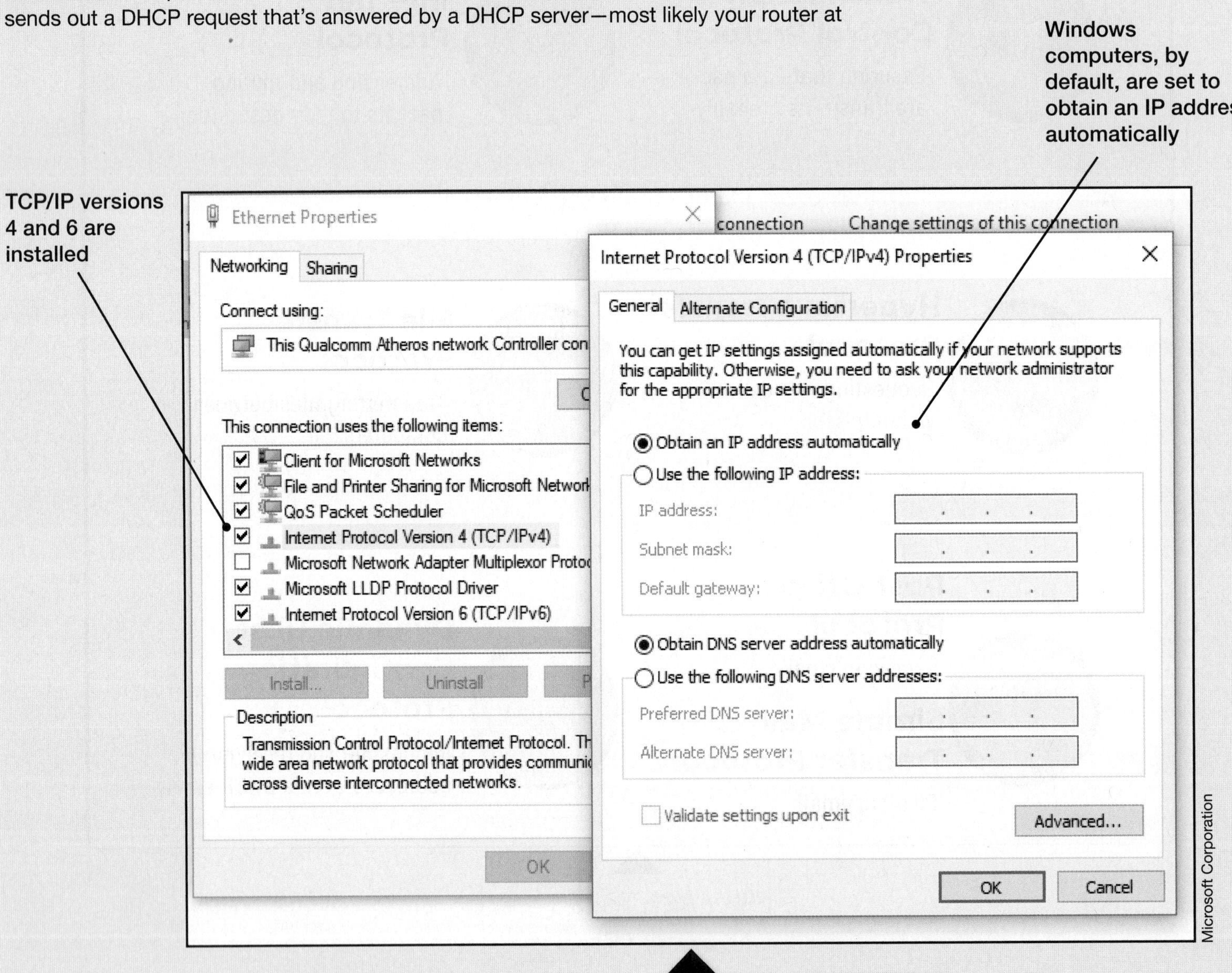

Windows computers, by default, are set to obtain an IP address automatically

TCP/IP versions 4 and 6 are installed

FIGURE 9.26 Windows computers are set to use DHCP to obtain an IP address.

Microsoft Corporation

home. Every computer on the network must have a unique IP address. This automatic configuration makes it easy to create a home network.

As with any computer system, the hardware of a network is useless without the software to make it work. In a network, that software also includes protocols to define the rules of communication. Together, the hardware, software, and protocols allow devices to share resources securely, efficiently, and (hopefully) easily.

Running Project

Make a list of the networks you use. Include home, cellular, work, and school networks. List the software clients that you use to connect to each. What resources do you access? Do you use different clients to access different resources?

5 Things You Need to Know

- Computers in a peer-to-peer network are able to detect and share resources with each other with little or no configuration.
- A domain is a network composed of a group of clients and servers under the control of the domain controller.
- Client devices log in to a server and request access to resources.
- Server software enables clients to communicate with the server to share resources, run applications, and send messages.
- Protocols define the rules for communication between devices. TCP/IP is the protocol stack that runs on the Internet and on most LANs.

Key Terms

domain

IP (Internet Protocol)

IP address

network administrator

network operating system (NOS)

protocol

TCP (Transmission Control Protocol)

TCP/IP protocol stack

Check Your System Security Software

Essential Job Skill

HOW TO VIDEO

Security software is important for protecting your computer from malicious attacks. In this activity, you'll examine your computer to determine what type of security software is installed on it and whether your computer is properly protected. From your student data files, open the file *vt_ch09_howto2_answersheet* and save the file as **lastname_firstname_ch09_howto2_answersheet**.

1 Right-click the Start button and click *Control Panel* or type **control panel** in Windows Search. If necessary, change to View by Category. Under *System and Security*, click *Review your computer's status*. If necessary, click the arrow to open the *Security* section. What information is located here? What is your status for each category? Are there any important notices? What software is reported for virus protection?

2 If necessary, click the arrow to open the *Maintenance* section. What's your status for each category? Are there any important notices? Take a screenshot of the *Security and Maintenance* window (Windows 8.1 Action Center) and paste it into your answer sheet.

Security and Maintenance

Control Panel › System and Security › Security and Maintenance

Search Control Panel

Control Panel Home

Change Security and Maintenance settings

Change User Account Control settings

Change Windows SmartScreen settings

View archived messages

Review recent messages and resolve problems

Security and Maintenance has detected one or more issues for you to review.

Security

Windows Defender needs to scan your computer

Scanning on a regular basis helps improve the security of your computer.

Scan now

Maintenance

Finish installing device software

One or more devices connected to your PC needs additional software to work properly.

Turn off messages about Device software

Install

If you don't see your problem listed, try one of these:

Troubleshooting
Find and fix problems

Recovery
Refresh your PC without affecting your files, or reset it and start over.

See also

File History

Windows Program Compatibility Troubleshooter

Microsoft Corporation

3 In the navigation pane on the left, click *Change Security and Maintenance settings* (Windows 8.1: click *Change Action Center settings*). Take a screenshot of the settings window and paste it into your answer sheet. Click *OK*.

Turn messages on or off

For each selected item, Windows will check for problems and send you a message if problems are found.
How does Security and Maintenance check for problems?

Security messages

- ☑ Windows Update
- ☑ Internet security settings
- ☑ Network firewall
- ☑ Microsoft account
- ☑ Windows activation

- ☑ Spyware and unwanted software protection
- ☑ User Account Control
- ☑ Virus protection
- ☑ SmartScreen

Maintenance messages

- ☑ Windows Backup
- ☑ Automatic Maintenance
- ☑ Drive status
- ☑ Device software
- ☑ Startup apps

- ☑ Windows Troubleshooting
- ☑ HomeGroup
- ☑ File History
- ☑ Storage Spaces
- ☑ Work Folders

[OK] [Cancel]

Microsoft Corporation

4 In the navigation pane on the left, click *Change Windows SmartScreen settings*. How does SmartScreen protect you? Take a screenshot of the SmartScreen dialog box and paste it into your answer sheet. Close any open windows and dialog boxes. Type your answers in your answer sheet, save the file, and submit your work as directed by your instructor.

⊞ Windows SmartScreen   ✕

What do you want to do with unrecognized apps?

Windows SmartScreen can help keep your PC safer by warning you before running unrecognized apps and files downloaded from the Internet.

- ● Warn before running an unrecognized app
- ○ Don't do anything (turn off Windows SmartScreen)

[OK] [Cancel]

Some info is sent to Microsoft about files and apps you run on this PC.
Privacy statement

Microsoft Corporation

If you are using a Mac, from your student data files, open the file *vt_ch09_howto2_answersheet _mac* and save the file as **lastname_firstname_ch09_howto2_answersheet_mac**.

1. Open *System Preferences* and then click *Security & Privacy*. Examine the *General tab* and record your settings for each section. Take a screenshot of the General tab and paste it into your answer sheet.

2. If necessary, click to unlock the padlock and type your password to unlock Security & Privacy preferences. Click *Advanced*. What settings display? Close the Advanced window.

3. Examine the Privacy tab and record your settings for each section. How do Location Services affect your privacy? Do you have any apps configured to use location services? Take a screenshot of the Privacy tab and paste it into your answer sheet. Close the Security & Privacy window.

4. Close any open windows and dialog boxes. Type your answers in your answer sheet. Save your file and submit your work as directed by your instructor.

GREEN COMPUTING:
Server Virtualization

Technically, the term *server* refers to the server software on a computer, not to the hardware it runs on. So a network server computer might actually run mail server, web server, and file and print server software. The advantage to this is that a single physical computer can be several different servers at once. Server computers are high-end, with fast processors and lots of storage. Sometimes, the computer's capabilities aren't fully utilized, and its processors are idle much of the time. Virtualization takes advantage of such unused resources. A common configuration would be running both a Microsoft Exchange email server and an Apache web server on the same computer. Each virtual server runs in its own space; the virtual servers share the hardware but do not interact with each other in any way. To the client, they appear to be separate servers.

Server virtualization is a big component of cloud computing. A company that offers IaaS (Infrastructure as a Service) provides access to servers through the Internet. An IaaS company can set up virtual servers for many small companies on a large enterprise server. This saves money and reduces the amount of hardware needed and e-waste created for each business. Keeping servers in one location can also save on cooling and electricity costs.

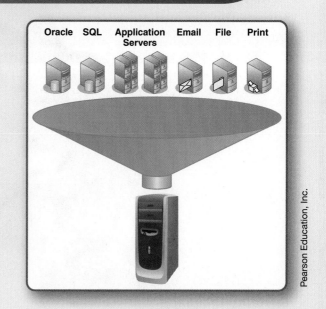

Pearson Education, Inc.

Zinkevych/Fotolia

Protecting Your Network

Explain How to Protect a Network

Not long ago, network security was a concern only to network administrators; today, with networks everywhere, it has become everyone's problem. Just as you use layers of security at home—fences, door locks, alarm systems, and even guard dogs—the same approach should be used with network security.

Layer 1: The Fence

The first layer of defense is the hardware at the access point to the network. A firewall blocks unauthorized access to a network (Figure 9.27). There are both software firewalls and hardware firewalls. The firewall examines the data packets as they enter or leave the network and will deny access to traffic based on rules that the network administrator defines. It also shields the network computers from direct access to the Internet, hiding them from hackers looking for an easy target.

A firewall can be configured with filters to allow or deny various kinds of traffic. Filters can be based on IP address, protocol type, domain names, and other criteria. For example, a firewall might block access to certain websites or deny Internet access to specific computers during certain hours. Incoming packets that try to access restricted data will be denied access to the network.

At home, you should use a router between your computers and the Internet. The router provides several important security functions. First, the router acts like a firewall. The default setup of most home routers has this feature enabled, and you can customize it by using the router utility. For example, you might restrict the time of day that a computer can access the Internet or define which sites can or cannot be accessed. You might need to customize your router to allow certain applications through—especially if you like to play online games. The router faces the public network—the Internet— and has a public IP address that it uses to communicate with the network. Inside your house, the router supplies each device with a private IP address that is only valid on your private network. To the outside world, only the router is visible, so it shields the other devices. The devices inside your network can communicate with each other directly, but any outside communication must go through the router.

A wireless router also provides a wireless access point to your network. This can be a potential security risk if it is not properly secured. Use the router setup utility to change the **service set identifier** or **SSID**, or wireless network name, and enable and configure wireless encryption, as shown in Figure 9.28. **Wireless encryption** adds security to a wireless network by encrypting transmitted data. **Wi-Fi Protected Setup—WPS** is a way to automatically configure devices to connect to a network by using a button, a personal identification number—PIN—or a USB key. By using this method, you do not need to manually type the network name and wireless security passphrases. You should use the strongest form of wireless encryption that is supported by the devices and operating systems on your network. In addition, you can disable the broadcast of the SSID, preventing the network from being visible to devices not already configured to use it. This requires extra configuration of the devices that connect to the network but adds another layer of security.

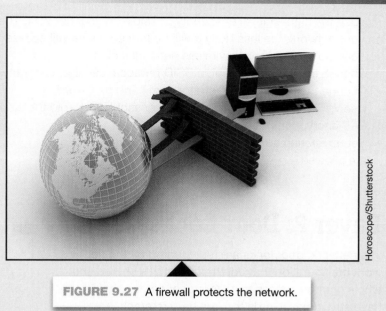

FIGURE 9.27 A firewall protects the network.

Horoscope/Shutterstock

FIGURE 9.28 Enter the security key or press the button on the router to use Wi-Fi Protected Setup to join this network.

Microsoft Corporation

Use the highest level of security possible on your network. The harder it is to find and guess the settings on your network, the less likely it will be that someone will access it without your permission. Some things that you can do to secure your wireless network include:

- Change the SSID and disable SSID broadcast so that your network is not visible to others.
- Change the default administrator name and password.
- Use WPA2 encryption and a difficult passphrase. Avoid the older and less secure WEP and EAP encryption options.
- Set up filtering so that only devices in the list are allowed.

Layer 2: Door Locks

In a network, door locks are represented by the network configuration that determines what's shared and who's granted access to it. Your user names should have strong passwords that are hard to crack, and users should be granted access only to what they need. Using no passwords or using passwords that are easy to guess—such as birthdays or pets' names—is equivalent to leaving your doors unlocked.

Windows (Figure 9.29) and macOS (Figure 9.30) enable you to create standard users or administrators, and they also include parental controls for child accounts. For normal use, it is best to use a standard user account, which has less access to change system and security settings. An administrator account should be used only when necessary and should be protected by a strong password. In a business environment, only IT staff should have administrator accounts on computers.

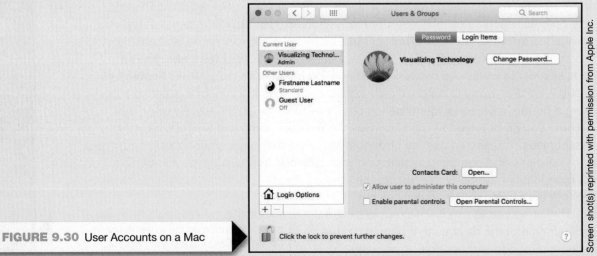

FIGURE 9.29 User Accounts on a Windows Computer

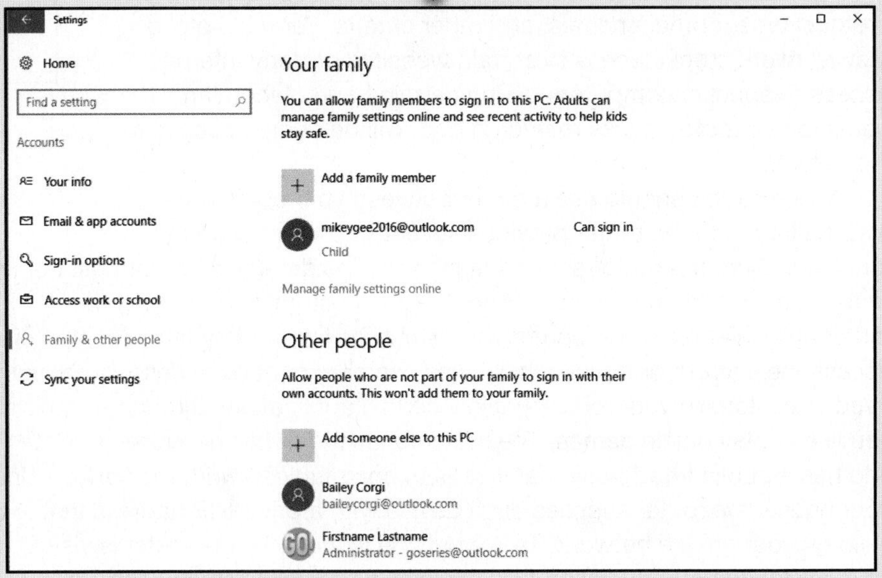

Microsoft Corporation

FIGURE 9.30 User Accounts on a Mac

Screen shot(s) reprinted with permission from Apple Inc.

Layer 3: Alarm Systems

The alarm system on a computer network includes software-based firewalls and security software on the individual computers on the network. **Antispyware software** prevents and removes adware and spyware infections. **Antivirus programs** protect against many forms of **malware**—software with malicious intent—including viruses, Trojan horses, worms, and spyware. **Windows Defender** is built-in antimalware software that protects against computer viruses and other malware on a Windows computer (Figure 9.31). Your individual computers should be protected by software firewalls such as those included with Windows or macOS. If an intruder somehow breaches your network, software will detect and prevent unauthorized actions.

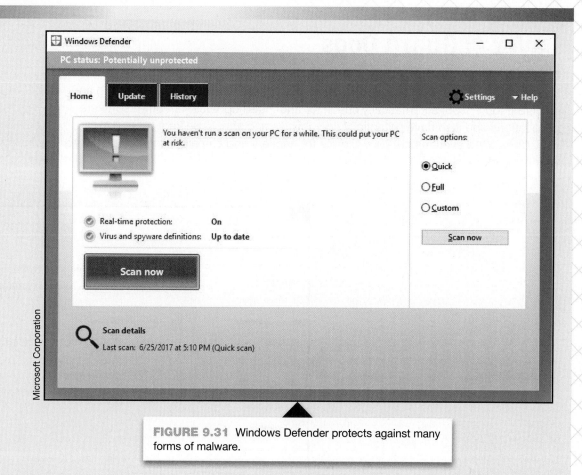

Microsoft Corporation

FIGURE 9.31 Windows Defender protects against many forms of malware.

Joe Gough/Fotolia

FIND OUT MORE

Password Security
Some security experts argue that forcing users to change password frequently, and to use complex passwords, in fact makes them less secure. Use the Internet to find out why this is so.

Layer 4: Guard Dogs

The network administrator—on a home network, that's you—needs to be diligent in keeping the systems on the network up to date and secure. Windows (Figure 9.32) and macOS (Figure 9.33) automatically check for and install updates, but other software applications can also have potential vulnerabilities and should be kept up to date as well. Unpatched systems are easy targets for hackers and can allow them access into your network.

Adisak Panongram/Shutterstock

FIGURE 9.32 Windows Update Window

Settings

- Home

Find a setting

Update & security

- Windows Update
- Windows Defender
- Backup
- Recovery
- Activation
- Find My Device
- For developers
- Windows Insider Program

Update status

Updates are available.

• Update for Adobe Flash Player for Windows 10 Version 1607 for x64-based Systems (KB3189031).

• Cumulative Update for Windows 10 Version 1607 for x64-based Systems (KB3176938).

Downloading updates 4%

Update history

Update settings

Available updates will be downloaded and installed automatically, except over metered connections (where charges may apply).

Change active hours

Restart options

Advanced options

Looking for info on the latest updates?
Learn more

Microsoft Corporation

Featured   Top Charts   Categories   Purchased   Updates

Q Search

No Updates Available

Updates Installed in the Last 30 Days

macOS High Sierra 10.13.2 Developer Beta
Version 4
Installed Nov 26, 2017   This update is recommended for all users.

Keynote
Apple
Version 7.3.1
Installed Nov 11, 2017   This update contains stability and performance improvements.

Pages
Apple
Version 6.3.1
Installed Nov 11, 2017   This update contains stability and performance improvements.

Numbers
Apple
Version 4.3.1
Installed Nov 11, 2017   This update contains stability and performance improvements.

iMovie
Apple
Version 10.1.8   • Improves overall stability

Screen shot(s) reprinted with permission from Apple Inc.

FIGURE 9.33 macOS Update Window

ETHICS

The term **piggybacking** means using an open wireless network to access the Internet without permission. Many times, people intentionally use open wireless access. If an access point is left unsecured, they figure, "Why not?" In some places, it's illegal to use a network without authorization, but many statutes—if they exist at all—are vague. It's difficult to detect when someone is piggybacking. Still, it's unethical to use someone's connection without his or her knowledge.

To make things more confusing, some free hotspots—such as in cafes and hotels—might be accessible beyond the premises. So, a person sitting in a car parked on the street might be able to access the coffee shop hotspot intended for patrons of the shop.

The practice of **wardriving**—driving around and locating open wireless access points—is closely related. There are communities on the Internet where wardrivers post maps of the open networks they find, along with free software that makes it easy to locate wireless networks. Wardrivers don't actually access the wireless networks, so the practice isn't illegal—but is it ethical?

Running Project

Think about the user names and passwords you use on the computer networks that you use most often—such as school and work networks. Are there strong password rules you must follow? How often do you change your passwords? When was the last time you changed them?

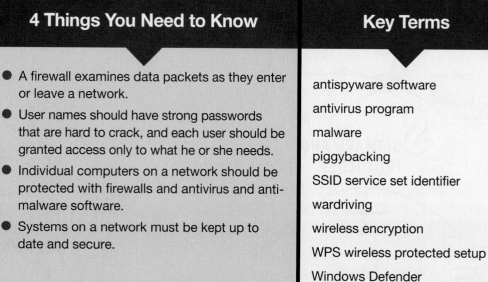

4 Things You Need to Know

- A firewall examines data packets as they enter or leave a network.
- User names should have strong passwords that are hard to crack, and each user should be granted access only to what he or she needs.
- Individual computers on a network should be protected with firewalls and antivirus and anti-malware software.
- Systems on a network must be kept up to date and secure.

Key Terms

antispyware software

antivirus program

malware

piggybacking

SSID service set identifier

wardriving

wireless encryption

WPS wireless protected setup

Windows Defender

VizCheck—In MyLab IT, take a quick quiz covering Objectives 4–5.

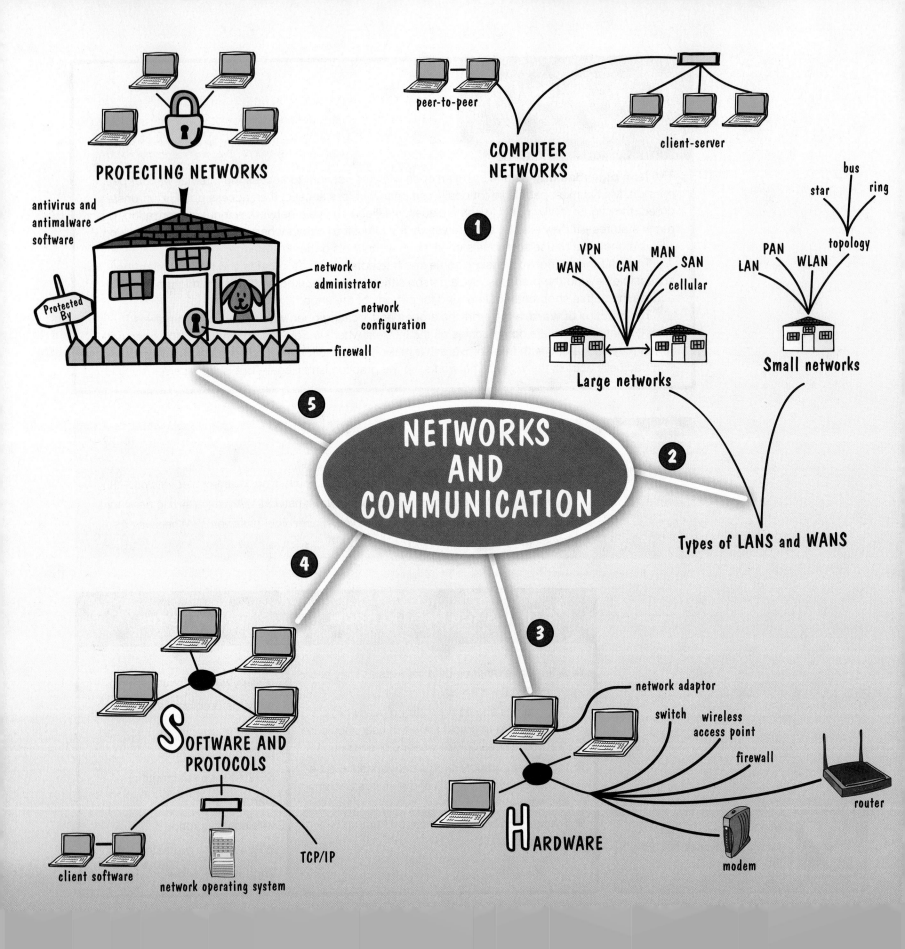

Objectives Recap

1. Discuss the Importance of Computer Networks
2. Compare Different Types of LANs and WANs
3. List and Describe the Hardware Used in Both Wired and Wireless Networks
4. List and Describe Network Software and Protocols
5. Explain How to Protect a Network

Key Terms

Summary

1. **Discuss the Importance of Computer Networks**

   A computer network is two or more computers that share resources: software, hardware, or files. Computer networks save us both time and money and make it easier to work, increasing productivity. A peer-to-peer (P2P) network is a network in which all computers are members of a workgroup and are considered equal. A client–server network is a network that has at least one server at its center and provides a way to centralize the network management, resources, and security.

2. **Compare Different Types of LANs and WANs**

   A local area network (LAN) is a network that has all nodes located in the same physical location. Devices on a LAN are connected using switches. A wireless LAN (WLAN) uses Wi-Fi to transmit data, and a personal area network (PAN) uses Bluetooth. Ethernet defines the way data is transmitted over a local area network, and topology is the physical layout of a network. A wide area network (WAN) is a network that spans multiple locations and connects multiple LANs over dedicated lines using routers. A VPN creates an encrypted private network through the public network (Internet), allowing remote users to access a LAN securely without dedicated lines. A campus area network (CAN) connects multiple LANs located in the same location. A network that covers a single geographic area is called a metropolitan area network (MAN). A storage area network (SAN) connects data storage devices and servers on a network. Cellular networks use 3G and 4G cell towers to transmit voice and data.

3. **List and Describe the Hardware Used in Both Wired and Wireless Networks**

   Each device that connects to a network must have a network adapter. The first device on a network is the device that connects to the Internet: a modem or an optical network terminal (ONT). A business network consists of routers, switches, wireless access points, and firewalls. A home router serves all these functions. A router is a device that connects two or more networks together. It uses address information to correctly route the data packets it receives. A switch is a device that connects multiple devices on a LAN. A wireless access point (WAP) is a device that allows wireless devices to join a network. A firewall is a device that blocks unauthorized access to a network.

4. **List and Describe Network Software and Protocols**

   Clients log in to a server and request access to resources. A web browser can act as an FTP client, a database client, and an HTTP client. Other client software you may use includes VPN software, desktop email programs, instant messaging or chat programs, and mobile banking apps. Server software—also known as a network operating system (NOS)—is a multiuser operating system

Summary continues on the next page

Summary *continued*

that controls the software and hardware on a network. Protocols define the rules for communication among devices and determine how data is formatted, transmitted, received, and acknowledged. The most important protocols belong to the TCP/IP protocol stack and define everything from how to transfer files (FTP) and webpages (HTTP) to sending (SMTP) and receiving (POP) email. TCP stands for Transmission Control Protocol, and it's responsible for ensuring that data packets are transmitted reliably. IP stands for Internet Protocol, and it's responsible for addressing and routing packets to their destination.

5. Explain How to Protect a Network

Use a layered approach to security. Protect the access point to your network with a firewall. Ensure correct network configuration—that is, what is shared and who is granted access to it. Secure individual computers with software-based firewalls as well as antivirus and antimalware software. Be diligent in keeping the systems on the network up to date and secure.

Multiple Choice

Answer the multiple-choice questions below for more practice with key terms and concepts from this chapter.

1. Computers in a peer-to-peer network belong to a _____.
   a. client-server group
   b. domain
   c. personal area network
   d. workgroup

2. A _____ is a multiuser computer system that runs a network operating system (NOS).
   a. client
   b. node
   c. server
   d. workgroup

3. In which topology is every node on the network attached to a central device such as a switch or wireless access point?
   a. Bus
   b. Ring
   c. Star
   d. Hybrid

4. Which type of network creates a private network through the public network (Internet)?
   a. LAN
   b. MAN
   c. WAN
   d. VPN

5. The device needed to connect a LAN to a fiber network is called a(n) _____.
   a. access point
   b. modem
   c. optical network terminal
   d. router

6. A(n) _____ is created when two wireless devices connect to each other directly.
   a. ad hoc network
   b. infrastructure wireless network
   c. personal area network (PAN)
   d. virtual private network (VPN)

7. A(n) _____ blocks unauthorized access to a network.
   a. modem
   b. firewall
   c. ONT
   d. switch

8. Which type of network consists of a group of clients and servers under the control of one central security database?
   a. Domain
   b. Homegroup
   c. IEEE 802.11
   d. Workgroup

9. Which protocol is responsible for receiving email?
   a. IP
   b. POP
   c. SMTP
   d. TCP

10. The _____ is also known as the wireless network name.
   a. domain
   b. homegroup
   c. service set identifier
   d. wireless access point

True or False

Answer the following questions with *T* for true or *F* for false for more practice with key terms and concepts from this chapter.

_____ 1. In a peer-to-peer network, all computers are considered equal.

_____ 2. It's not possible to share files between computers running Windows and macOS.

_____ 3. Most LANs are configured in a physical bus topology.

_____ 4. A metropolitan area network (MAN) is a small network that consists of devices connected by Bluetooth.

_____ 5. Computers can have more than one network adapter.

_____ 6. When devices connect through a wireless access point, they form an infrastructure wireless network.

_____ 7. A firewall is a device that connects two or more networks together.

_____ 8. You must install special software to create a peer-to-peer network.

_____ 9. TCP/IP is the protocol responsible for ensuring that data packets are transmitted reliably on a network.

_____ 10. Using an open wireless network to access the Internet without permission is called piggybacking.

Fill in the Blank

Fill in the blanks with key terms from this chapter.

1. _____ include the software, hardware, and files that are shared in a network.

2. In a(n) _____ network, all computers are considered equal.

3. A(n) _____ computer connects to, or requests services from, another computer called a server.

4. In a(n) _____, devices connect through a wireless access point.

5. _____ ensure that equipment that is made by different companies will be able to work together.

6. _____ is the most commonly used standard on local area networks.

7. A(n) _____ is a device that connects two or more networks together.

8. A(n) _____ is a communication device used to establish a connection with a network.

9. _____ define the rules for communication between devices.

10. The protocol responsible for addressing and routing packets to their destination is _____.

V

Running Project ...

... The Finish Line

Assume that you just moved into a new apartment with several roommates. Use your answers to the previous sections of the project to help decide the best type of network setup to use so you can all share an Internet connection and printer as well as stream media files. Describe the hardware and software requirements for your setup. What other devices might you also connect to the network? Write a report describing your selections and responding to the questions raised throughout the chapter. Save your file as **lastname_firstname_ch09_project** and submit it to your instructor as directed.

Do It Yourself 1

Network security is an important topic for all network users to understand. In this exercise, you will create a mind map to illustrate network security. A mind map is a visual outline. More information about using mind maps can be found in Appendix B. From your student data files, open the file *vt_ch09_DIY1_answersheet* and save the file as **lastname_firstname_ch09_DIY1_answersheet**.

Use an online mind mapper tool such as MindMeister (**mindmeister.com**) or Mindomo (**mindomo.com**) to create a mind map that visualizes network security. Your map should have three or four major branches, and each branch should have at least two leaves. When you are finished your map, take a screenshot of this window and paste it into your answer sheet, or, if available, export your mind map as a PNG or JPG file. Save the file and submit the assignment as directed by your instructor.

Do It Yourself 2

In this exercise, you'll examine a network you use and the devices that are part of it. There is no answer sheet for this assignment; you will create your own file.

Use a program such as MS Paint, Visio, PowerPoint, or Prezi to create a diagram of a network you use. If you don't have a home network, you may draw a friend's network or one you work on at school or work. Label the computers and other devices, including printers, game consoles, media devices, and routers. Save the file as **lastname_firstname_ch09_DIY2** and submit it as directed by your instructor.

File Management

In this activity, you'll examine sharing settings on your computer. From your student data files, open the file *vt_ch09_FM_answersheet* and save the file as **lastname_firstname_ch09_FM_answersheet**.

1. Open File Explorer. In the Navigation pane, click *Network*. Are there any items listed under Network? If so, what are they? NOTE—you may need to turn on Network Discovery to view the network. (On a Mac, use Finder; on the Go menu, click Network.) Take a screenshot of this window and paste it into your answer sheet.

2. Search Google for *Map network drive*. What's the purpose of mapping a drive?

3. Open File Explorer, click *This PC*, and then, on the Computer tab, point to *Map network drive*. To what places can you create shortcuts? Type your answers in your answer sheet, include the screenshot, save the file, and submit the assignment as directed by your instructor.

Critical Thinking

You work for a small accounting office. Your boss wants to ensure that everyone in the office knows the basics of keeping the office network secure. There is no answer sheet for this assignment; you will create your own file.

Use the Internet and the information you learned in this chapter to create a list of five rules that employees should follow to ensure the security of the office computers. Use a word processor or drawing software to create a poster that can be displayed in the office to remind the employees of these rules. Save the file as **lastname_firstname_ch09_ct** and submit your work as directed by your instructor.

Ethical Dilemma

From your student data files, open the file *vt_ch09_ethics_answersheet* and save the file as **lastname_firstname_ch09_ethics_answersheet**.

A help desk technician received a call from an upset customer, Samantha. Samantha had been accessing the Internet at home with her tablet for months but was suddenly unable to connect. The technician asked her some questions to help her troubleshoot the problem. Did she try turning off her router and turning it back on? No—she didn't have a router. What about a wireless access point? No—she didn't have one of those either. Did she call her ISP for help? You guessed it—she didn't have one of those either! After some more questions, the technician finally realized that Samantha had been piggybacking her neighbor's wireless network.

Samantha was very upset to have lost her Internet connection, and a few days later, when her neighbor returned from vacation, it was restored. Her neighbor was unaware that Samantha had been using the connection. Is it acceptable for Samantha to continue to use her neighbor's network now that she understands what she's doing? Look up the laws where you live. Is it legal? Is it ethical? Would you do it? Type your answers in your answer sheet, save the file, and submit it as directed by your instructor.

On the Web

IPv6 is designed to replace IPv4. In this exercise, you will learn more about each IP version and why the change is important. From your student data files, open the file *vt_ch09_web_answersheet* and save the file as **lastname_firstname_ch09_web_answersheet**.

Go to the Internet Society website, **internetsociety.org**, and search for IPv6. What are some of the advantages of switching to IPv6? What was World IPv6 Day, and what were the results? How does the number of IPv6 addresses compare to the number of IPv4 addresses? Type your answers in your answer sheet, save the file, and submit it as directed by your instructor.

Collaboration

Instructors: Divide the class into small groups and provide each group with a large piece of paper or poster board or access to computers.

The Project: As a team, prepare a Venn diagram that compares the features of peer-to-peer and client-server networks. Use at least three references. Use Google Drive or Microsoft Office to prepare your research and provide documentation that all team members have contributed to the project.

Outcome: Prepare a Venn diagram using a large piece of paper or a computer drawing program. The diagram must have at least four items in each of the three areas of the diagram. Present your findings to the class. Be sure to include a listing of all team members. Turn in your diagram named **teamname_ch09_collab**. Submit your presentation to your instructor as directed.

Application Project

Office 2016 Application Projects
Excel 2016: Mobile Cellular Subscriptions

Project Description: In this project, using data from the World Bank, you will format and summarize a large spreadsheet showing mobile cellular subscription growth from 2000 to 2014. *If necessary, download the student data files from* **pearsonhighered.com/viztech**.

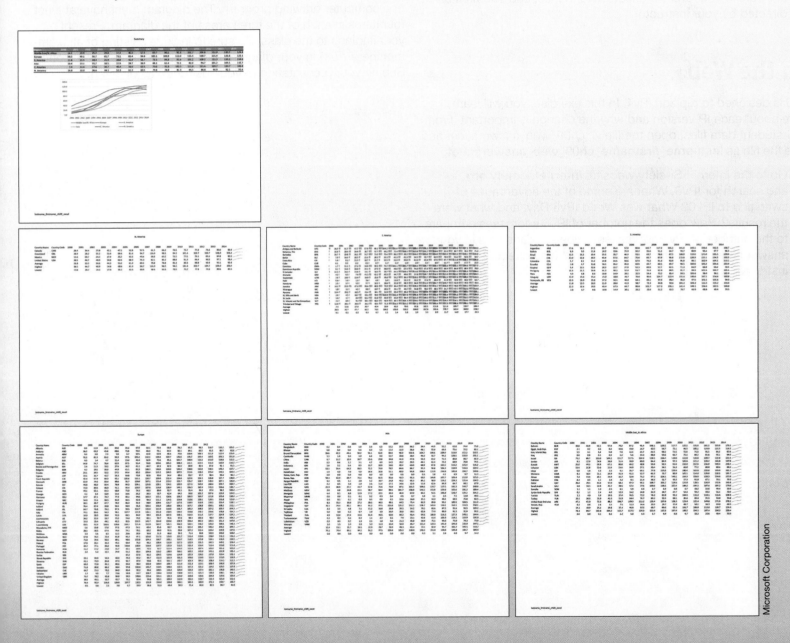

Step	Instructions
1	Start Excel. From your student data files, open the Excel file *vt_ch09_excel*. Save the file as **lastname_firstname_ch09_excel**
2	Insert a header with the sheet name in the center cell. Insert a footer with the file name in the left cell. Return to Normal view.
3	On the N. America sheet, select the range C2:Q5. Apply the Number Format to the selected range and decrease the decimals displayed to 1.
4	In cell C6, use the AVERAGE function to average the values in the range C2:C5. Copy the formula from C6:Q6.
5	In cell C7, use a function to calculate the highest number of cellular subscriptions of the range C2:C5. Copy the formula from C7:Q7.
6	In cell C8, use a function to calculate the lowest number of cellular subscriptions of the range C2:C5. Copy the formula from C8:Q8.
7	In the range R2:R5, using the data range C2:Q5, insert line Sparklines. Apply Sparkline Style Accent 2 (no dark or light).
8	Copy the Average row C6:Q6 from the N. America sheet. Use the Paste link function to paste it into row 2 of the Summary sheet. Repeat the process to copy the average row for the remaining regions on the Summary sheet.
9	On the Summary sheet, format the values B2:P7 with the Number Format and decrease the decimals displayed to 1.
10	Select the range A1:P7 and insert the recommended line chart. Move the chart so the top left corner is in the top left corner of cell B10. Format the chart Style 4. Remove the chart Title.
11	On the Summary worksheet, format the data in the range A1:P7 as a table with headers using Table Style Medium 16. Sort the 2014 column from the largest to the smallest value.
12	On the C. America sheet, apply the Gradient Light Blue Data Bar conditional formatting (under Gradient Fill) to the range C2:Q21.
13	On the Europe sheet, click cell A2, and then freeze the panes of the worksheet so that when you scroll down, the headings in row 1 remain visible.
14	Select all worksheets. Prepare the worksheets for printing by changing the orientation to Landscape. Adjust the Scale option to change the Width to 1 page. Ungroup the worksheets and hide the Source worksheet.
15	Ensure that the worksheets are correctly named and placed in the following order in the workbook: Summary, N. America, C. America, S. America, Europe, Asia, Middle East, N. Africa. Save the workbook and close Excel. Submit the workbook as directed.

Application Project

Office 2016 Application Projects
Word 2016: Secure Passwords

Project Description: In this project, you will format a document with columns, outline and shade text, create and apply styles, work with images and SmartArt graphics, and insert and format a table. *If necessary, download the student data files from* **pearsonhighered.com/viztech**.

Creating a Secure Password

We are all responsible for system security!

Password Policy

IT Services provides you with security and tech support for all school systems. In order to ensure the security of college resources, all users are required to create a secure password that must be changed at the start of each semester.

No dictionary words

Mixed case letters

Numbers

Creating Your Password

Here are some guidelines for creating (and remembering) a secure password. You must use a combination of letters and numbers. You must use at least one uppercase and one lowercase letter. Your password must be between 8-12 characters. Try using a combination of words that you can easily remember, but that someone else cannot easily guess. So don't use your kid's name (or your pet's, spouse's...) Everybody knows who your favorite sports team is (because you wear the team shirt to class every day). Instead, go for less obvious choices. One idea: pick a famous song lyric and use the first letter of each word. So, for example, Mary Had a Little Lamb becomes MHaLL. Mix up the case and add a few numbers and you have MhAlL345.

Tech	Extension
Sue	X5421
Charlie	X5422

For help with your password or other security questions, contact IT Services. (702) 555-1234.

vt_ch09_word_solution.docx

Step	Instructions
1	Start Word. From your student data files, open *vt_ch09_word*. Save the file as **lastname_firstname_ch09_word**
2	To the title of the document, *Creating a Secure Password*, apply the Title style and apply the Fill – Blue, Accent 1, Shadow text effect. Center the title and change the font size to 36.
3	To the text *We are all responsible for system security!* apply the Heading 1 style and center align.
4	Select the subtitle *Password Policy* and all the remaining text in the document. Modify the selected text so that it displays in two columns.
5	Immediately to the left of the subtitle *Creating Your Password*, insert a column break.
6	Position the insertion point at the end of the paragraph that begins *Here are some guidelines...* Insert a 2x3 table. Apply the Grid Table 6 Colorful - Accent 3 table style. Enter the following in the table: **Tech** **Extension** Sue X5421 Charlie X5422
7	Center align the subtitle *Password Policy* and change the font size to 22. Change the font color of the selected text to Green, Accent 6, Lighter 40% and format as bold.
8	Create a new style based on the formatting of the subtitle *Password Policy*. Name the style **Password** Apply the Password style to the subtitle *Creating Your Password*.
9	Position the insertion point immediately to the left of the paragraph beginning *IT Services*. Insert the image *vt_ch09_image1* from your student data files.
10	With the image selected, change the text wrapping to tight. Resize the image height to 1.5 inches, lock aspect ratio.
11	Add a box border to the paragraph beginning *For help with your password* and then change the shading to Green, Accent 6, Lighter 80%.
12	Position the insertion point at the end of the paragraph that begins *IT Services provides* in the first column. Insert a SmartArt graphic using the Vertical Box List style from the List category.
13	Increase the height of the graphic to 3.5 inches. Apply the Intense Effect style to the SmartArt graphic. Change color to Colorful Range - Accent Colors 5 to 6.
14	Display the text pane for the SmartArt graphic and insert the following text as the three bullet items and then close the text pane: **No dictionary words** **Mixed case letters** **Numbers**
15	Insert the file name in the footer. Save the document and close Word. Submit the document as directed.

CHAPTER

10

Security and Privacy

In This Chapter

 **VIZ INTRO**

Do you leave your doors unlocked? Do you let strangers into your home? Do you hand out business cards with your Social Security number on them? Of course not. You take steps to protect your security and privacy in the real world, and it's just as important to do so in the electronic world. When you have finished this chapter, you will recognize some of the threats we all face and how you can protect yourself in this digital age.

BrunoWeltmann/Fotolia

Objectives

1 **Recognize Different Types of Cybercrime**

2 **Differentiate between Various Types of Malware**

3 **Explain How to Secure a Computer**

4 **Practice Safe Computing**

5 **Discuss Laws Related to Computer Security and Privacy**

Running Project

In this project, you'll explore security and privacy. Look for instructions as you complete each article. For most articles, there's a series of questions for you to research. At the conclusion of the chapter, you'll submit your responses to the questions raised.

SWEviL/Shutterstock

Cybercrime: They Are Out to Get You

ctive

Recognize Different Types of Cybercrime

The term **cybercrime** means criminal activity on the Internet. Most of the crimes now perpetrated online existed in some form long before computers came along, but technology has made them easier to commit and more widespread.

SIMULATION
Security

Personal Cybercrime

Personal cybercrime is perpetrated against individuals, as opposed to businesses and other organizations. These are crimes that affect you directly and range from harassment to identity theft. The more you know about these threats, the better you can protect yourself.

HARASSMENT

Cyberbullying and cyber-stalking fall into the category of harassment. **Cyberbullying** usually refers to exchanges between minors, but between adults, it is called **cyber-harassment**. Harassers use email, text messages, IMs, and social networks to embarrass, threaten, or torment someone—often because of their gender, race, religion, nationality, or sexual orientation. Unlike traditional schoolyard bullying, cyberbullying follows a child beyond the schoolyard and beyond the school day. **Cyber-stalking** is more serious in nature, with the stalker demonstrating a pattern of harassment that poses a credible threat of harm.

PHISHING AND PHARMING

Phishing uses email messages or IMs that appear to be from those you do business with, such as your bank, social network, auction site, online payment processor, or IT administrator.

Phishing messages are designed to trick you into revealing personal information, such as user names and passwords for your accounts.

Pharming redirects you to a phony website by hijacking the domain name of a company or poisoning the DNS server references to a site, which is like having the wrong phone number listed in the phonebook. Both phishing and pharming are effective because their messages appear to be from legitimate sources. Figure 10.1 shows a phishing email message that appears to be from a credit union. If you look closely, you can see signs that it is fake. The email address of the sender is a *gmail.com* address—not from the bank's domain, a link is provided asking you to verify your account information, and there are spelling errors. When in doubt, call or visit the website of the company before responding to any inquiries rather than replying to or clicking links in an email message. Legitimate companies never ask for personal information or passwords in email messages.

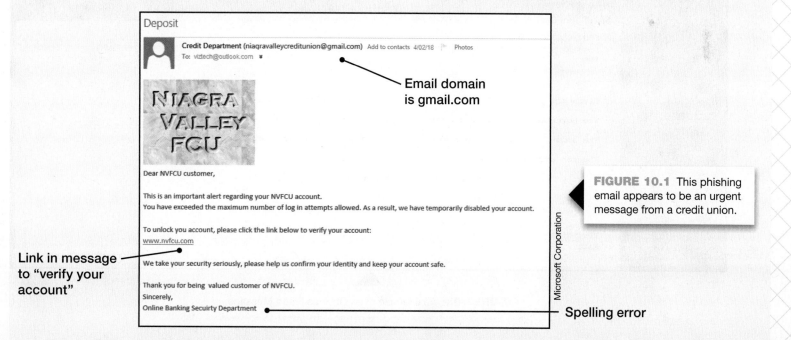

FIGURE 10.1 This phishing email appears to be an urgent message from a credit union.

SOCIAL NETWORK ATTACKS

Social networks are vulnerable to many types of attacks. Because you are "friends" with other users, you tend to trust what they post and send you, and it is easy to be fooled into clicking on something malicious. Some common attacks include:

- Adware and other malware
- Email messages or other notifications that appear to be from the site administrator, asking for your password or threatening to suspend your account
- Phishing and "Please send money" scams that can fool you into downloading malware or sending money

- **Clickjacking**, in which clicking on a link allows malware to post unwanted links on your page
- **Clickbait**, a link that teases you with just enough information to get you to click the link, driving traffic to a webpage
- **Sharebaiting**, when users share posts, often without actually clicking them first, which can lead you to believe the links are safe

You can read more on Facebook security at **facebook.com/ help/security**. (You can read this information without having an account or being logged in.)

FRAUD

Successful **computer fraud** schemes convince a victim to voluntarily and knowingly give money or property to another person. Some of the most well-known computer fraud schemes on the Internet involve email messages claiming that you have won a lottery or inherited money. Figure 10.2 shows a message claiming the recipient is entitled to money for school. Although

most people are wise enough to ignore messages as obvious as this one, the pleas are often more personal and believable, perhaps appearing to be from a friend or relative in trouble, and many people fall victim to the scams. Such a scam can also occur on social networks when a cybercriminal hacks into an account, or creates a new account with the same name and profile picture, and sends messages to the user's friends asking for help.

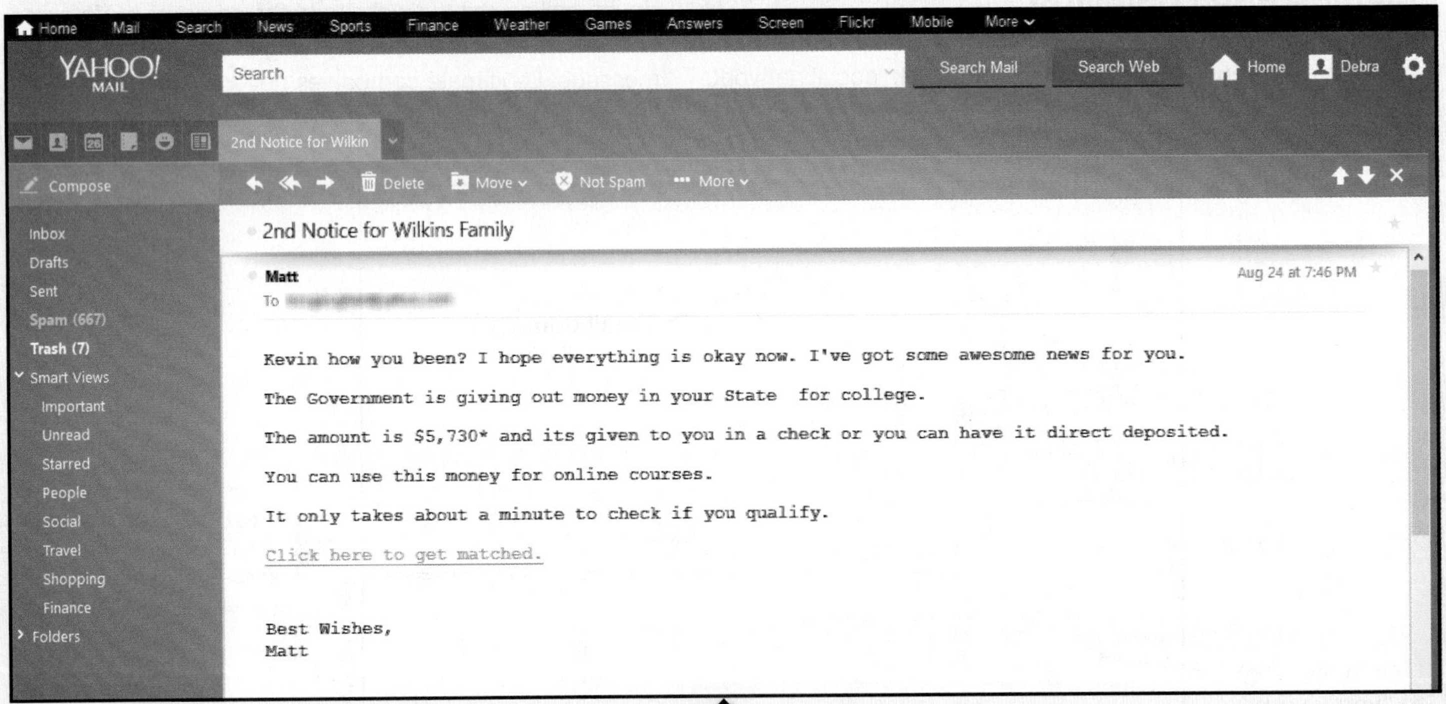

FIGURE 10.2 An Example of an Obvious Fraud Message

Auction fraud is a common type of cybercrime that occurs when you purchase something from an online auction site. This can take many forms, including non-delivery of the item, bait-and-switch, excessive fees, counterfeit goods, and **shill bidding** — fake bidding by the seller or an accomplice to drive up the price of an auction item. Sadly, many victims of computer fraud lose thousands of dollars that can never be recovered. Shopping on sites such as Amazon or eBay, which have seller rating systems, can help prevent auction fraud. Sellers that have a bad reputation will be evident in poor ratings. Stick with sellers with lots of high ratings.

IDENTITY THEFT

Identity theft occurs when someone fraudulently uses your name, Social Security number, or bank or credit card number. The thief may purchase items, open new accounts, or commit a crime using your identity. Using phishing and pharming, password-stealing software, and **keyloggers** — programs or devices that capture what is typed on a keyboard — criminals can obtain enough personal information to wreak havoc on you. Victims of identity theft can spend several years and thousands of dollars clearing up the mess. Companies that claim to protect you from identity theft have sprung up, but what they really do are things you can and should do yourself, including the following:

- Monitor your bank and credit card statements, carefully checking each charge every month. Also, watch for charges on your phone bills.
- Check your account online between statements and set up alerts for charges that exceed a certain amount or are used outside of your home area.
- Monitor your credit report. By law, you're entitled to one free credit report per year from each of the three major credit reporting companies. Instead of requesting them all at once, space them out every four months to keep an eye out for suspicious activity throughout the year. Make sure to use the correct website — **annualcreditreport.com** — many other sites that offer "free" reports actually charge you for expensive credit monitoring services.
- If you suspect you might be a victim of identity theft, immediately place a fraud alert on your credit reports.
- Protect your personal information. Be smart about the information you share and with whom you share it.

If you decide to purchase identity theft protection, you should compare products and services carefully and be sure that you're getting services that are right for you. Also check with your homeowners' or renters' insurance for available coverage.

Zimmytws/Shutterstock

Cybercrime against Organizations

Hacking is the act of gaining unauthorized access to a computer system or network. Hackers can be categorized as white-hat, gray-hat, or black-hat, depending on their motivation and the results of their hacking. White-hat hackers' motivation is to find security holes in a system for the purpose of preventing future hacking. They are security experts paid to hack systems, and they're sometimes called *sneakers*. Black-hat hackers hack into systems for malicious purposes, such as theft or vandalism. They are sometimes referred to as *crackers*. Gray-hat hackers fall somewhere in between. They hack into systems illegally but not with malicious intent. A gray-hat hacker might break into a system to prove that he or she can, or to expose a system's vulnerability. Although it's possible to hack into an individual's computer, the more valuable targets are large companies and government agencies. **Hacktivism**, such as that committed by Anonymous (Figure 10.3) and Shadow Brokers, is hacking to make a political statement.

A **data breach** occurs when sensitive data is stolen or viewed by someone who is not authorized to do so. Massive data breaches in the past few years, including those at Target, Home Depot, Dropbox, and iCloud, have exposed the personal information of millions of accounts. In just the first half of 2017, over 800 data breaches were reported by the Identity Theft Resource Center, with an estimated 16 million records exposed. Internet extortion occurs when a hacker takes control of a database and threatens to release sensitive information unless a ransom is paid.

An unlawful attack on computers or networks done to intimidate a government or its people for a political or social agenda is known as **cyber-terrorism**. Although many terrorist groups use technology such as the Internet and email to do business, cyber-terrorism is more than just using computers as a tool. Cyber-terrorists attack information systems to cause harm. A study by the Center for Strategic and International Studies estimates the cybercrime cost to the global economy is at least $400 billion dollars annually. Between 2013 and 2016, there were roughly 100 significant attacks on "government agencies, defense and high tech companies, or economic crimes with losses of more than a million dollars." U.S. Cyber Command reports that the Pentagon systems are attacked 250,000 times an hour — 6 million times a day! The attacks come from ordinary hackers, criminal enterprises, and foreign intelligence agents.

FIGURE 10.3 The group Anonymous, whose members appear in public wearing masks, uses hacktivism to make a political statement.

Stephen Barnes/Alamy Stock Photo

Though the majority of cyber-terror attacks are unsuccessful and unreported, experts agree the threat is growing. Government agencies spend millions of dollars on protecting themselves. Potential targets include the financial sector; infrastructure, such as communications, utilities, and transportation; and hospitals. A successful attack on such a target could cost millions of dollars and cause major problems — even loss of life. In March 2013, a cyber-attack on the websites of major South Korean banks and TV broadcasters wiped out data from the hard drives of more than 32,000 computers.

FIND OUT MORE

Research the hacktivist group Anonymous. Who are they? What do they stand for? What are some of their most recent exploits? How effective have they been?

Running Project

What steps should you take to prevent identity theft? How have you implemented these in your activities? Are there other things you should be doing? Has identity theft happened to you or someone you know? If so, describe what happened.

5 Things You Need to Know

- Cybercrime is criminal activity on the Internet.
- Harassment, phishing, pharming, fraud, and identity theft are forms of cybercrime against individuals.
- Hackers gain unauthorized access to computer systems or networks.
- A data breach exposes sensitive data to unauthorized eyes.
- Cyber-terrorism attacks have political or social agendas.

Key Terms

clickbait

clickjacking

computer fraud

cyberbullying

cybercrime

cyber-harassment

cyber-stalking

cyber-terrorism

data breach

hacking

hacktivism

identity theft

keylogger

pharming

phishing

sharebaiting

shill bidding

Digital Literacy Skill

Configure Secure Browser Settings Using Google Chrome

HOW TO VIDEO

Web browsers come with security features and settings to help protect your computer as you browse the web. In this activity, you will examine and configure these settings in Google Chrome. If you do not have Chrome installed, you can download it for free from **google.com/chrome**. If necessary, download the student data files from **pearsonhighered.com/viztech**. From your student data files, open the *vt_ch10_howto1_answersheet* file and save the file as **lastname_firstname_ch10_howto1_answersheet**.

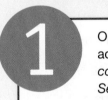

1 Open Chrome. To the right of the address bar, click *Customize and control Google Chrome*. Click *Settings*.

New tab	Ctrl+T
New window	Ctrl+N
New incognito window	Ctrl+Shift+N
History	▶
Downloads	Ctrl+J
Bookmarks	▶
Zoom	− 100% + ⛶
Print...	Ctrl+P
Cast...	
Find...	Ctrl+F
More tools	▶
Edit	Cut	Copy	Paste
Settings	
Help	▶
Exit	Ctrl+Shift+Q

Google and the Google logo are registered trademarks of Google Inc., used with permission.

Customize and control Google Chrome

2

On the Settings tab, under On startup, what page(s) are configured to display?

Settings ×

← → C ⌂ chrome://settings

Chrome

History
Extensions
Settings

About

Settings

Search settings

Sign in

Sign in to get your bookmarks, history, passwords and other settings on all your devices. You'll also automatically be signed in to your Google services. Learn more

Sign in to Chrome

On startup

○ Open the New Tab page
○ Continue where you left off
○ Open a specific page or set of pages. Set pages

Appearance

Get themes   Reset to default theme

☐ Show Home button
☐ Always show the bookmarks bar

Search

Set which search engine is used when searching from the omnibox.

Google ▼   Manage search engines...

People

👤 Person 1 (current)

Google and the Google logo are registered trademarks of Google Inc., used with permission.

3

Scroll down and click *Show advanced settings*. Under Privacy, what web services are enabled? Click *Clear browsing data*. What options are available, and which options are checked? Click *Learn more* and read the Help page. If you were going to delete some of these objects, which would you choose, and why? Close the Help page. Click *Cancel* in the Clear browsing data dialog box.

Clear browsing data ×

Obliterate the following items from: the past hour ▼

☑ Browsing history – 6 items

☑ Download history

☑ Cookies and other site and plugin data

☑ Cached images and files – less than 291 MB

☐ Passwords

☐ Autofill form data

☐ Hosted app data

☐ Content licenses

Clear browsing data   Cancel

ⓘ Some settings that may reflect browsing habits will not be cleared. Learn more

Google and the Google logo are registered trademarks of Google Inc., used with permission.

4 Under Privacy, click *Content settings*. What settings are selected under Cookies, Images, JavaScript, Handlers, Plugins, Pop-ups, and Location? Under Pop-ups, click *Manage exceptions*. Are there any websites in this dialog box? If it's not already listed, in the [*.]example.com box, type **pearsoned.com** Be sure *Allow* is selected under *Behavior*, take a screenshot of this window, and paste it into your answer sheet. Click *Done*. Use the Internet to answer the following: What is a pop-up? What are two reasons to allow pop-ups? Why should you block them?

Pop-up exceptions   ✕

Hostname pattern   **Behavior**

[*.]example.com   Allow   ▼

Learn more   Done

5 In the Content settings dialog box, under Plugins, click *Manage individual plugins*. What plugins are installed? Are any disabled? Take a screenshot of this window and paste it into your document. Close any open tabs and dialog boxes. Type up your answers and submit your file as directed by your instructor.

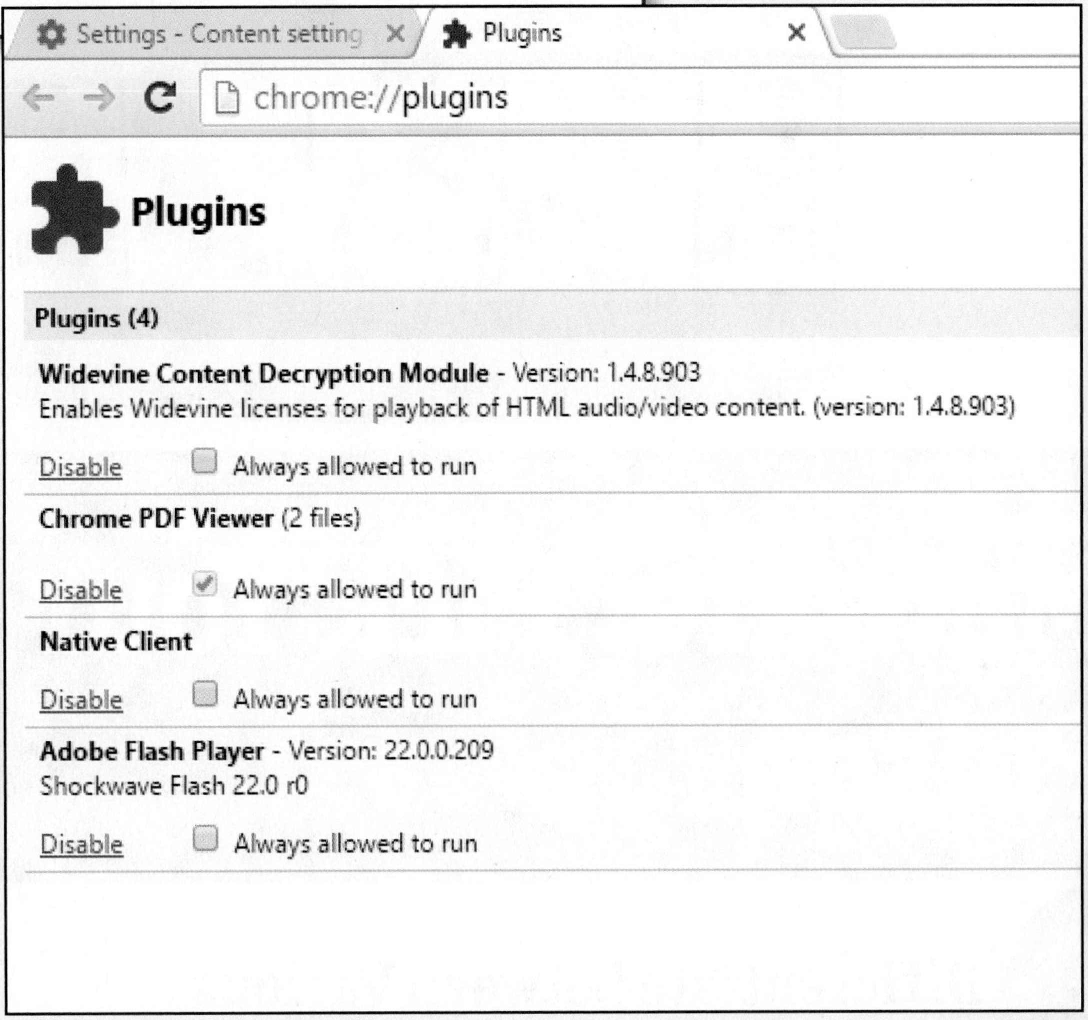

Settings - Content setting ✕ / 🧩 Plugins ✕

← → C 🗋 chrome://plugins

🧩 Plugins

Plugins (4)

Widevine Content Decryption Module - Version: 1.4.8.903
Enables Widevine licenses for playback of HTML audio/video content. (version: 1.4.8.903)

Disable ☐ Always allowed to run

Chrome PDF Viewer (2 files)

Disable ☑ Always allowed to run

Native Client

Disable ☐ Always allowed to run

Adobe Flash Player - Version: 22.0.0.209
Shockwave Flash 22.0 r0

Disable ☐ Always allowed to run

Destina/Fotolia

Malware: Pick Your Poison

Differentiate between Various Types of Malware

The term **malware** — short for *malicious software* — includes many different types of programs that are designed to be harmful. Protecting your computer from malware can be a difficult task. In this article, we discuss some of the most common types of malware.

Spotting S
and Email
Fraud

Spam and Cookies

Sending mass, unsolicited emails is called **spamming**, and the messages themselves are called **spam**, or junk mail. Spamming is popular because it's easy and very inexpensive to do—no paper to print, no envelopes to stuff, and no postage. The same things that make email a good thing for all of us make it good for spammers. There are other forms of spam too: IM spam (spim), fax spam, and text message spam, to name a few. Although spam may seem to be just a nuisance, it costs businesses millions of dollars each year. It's estimated that more than 80 percent of all email messages are abusive in some way. That includes not just ads but also phishing messages and malware. Figure 10.4 shows a sample of spam messages received over just a few days.

FIGURE 10.4 Spam in a Web Email Account

Many websites put a small text file called a **cookie** on your computer when you visit them. The cookie helps the website identify you when you return. Whenever you visit a site and click *Remember me* or *Keep me logged in*, you agree to allow the website to put a cookie on your computer. Your personal information, such as your credit card number, isn't stored in the cookie. These cookies can personalize the website, making for a better customer experience. When you return to shop again, the site recognizes you because there's a cookie on your computer (Figure 10.5). But sometimes cookies are installed without your choosing them, notably by advertisers. These cookies are used to track the websites and pages you visit to better target the ads you see. Although cookies are useful, they could be used to collect information that you don't want to share. Modern browsers include protection against potentially harmful or invasive cookies.

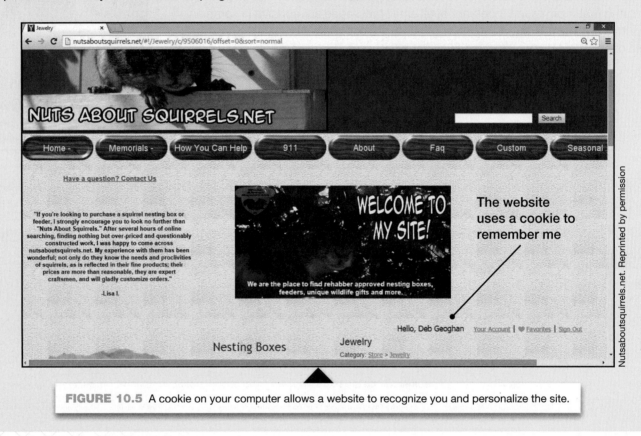

The website uses a cookie to remember me

FIGURE 10.5 A cookie on your computer allows a website to recognize you and personalize the site.

Adware and Spyware

One of the most annoying forms of malware you can get on your computer is called adware. **Adware**, as its name implies, shows you ads—usually in the form of pop-ups or banner ads on websites or in software. Adware can use CPU cycles and Internet bandwidth and, as a result, greatly reduce your computer's performance.

Spyware is a form of malware that secretly gathers personal information about you. The information is sent to a third party that may use it for anything from targeted advertisements to identity theft. Spyware is usually installed inadvertently by a user who clicks on a pop-up or installs a freeware program that includes a tracking feature. The information about the tracking feature might be buried in the license agreement that many people simply accept without reading or understanding. Sometimes, you can choose not to install these extra features by simply unchecking them in the installer. A common type of spyware infection is a **browser hijacker**, which changes your home page and redirects you to other websites. Spyware can be very difficult to remove and can cause your security programs to stop running.

Viruses, Worms, Trojans, and Rootkits

A computer **virus** is a program that replicates itself and infects computers. A virus needs a host file to travel on, such as a game. The attack, also known as the **payload**, may corrupt or delete files, or it may erase an entire disk. A virus might use the email program on an infected computer to send out copies of itself and infect other machines. Virus hoaxes are common in email messages. Although not a true virus, a hoax can trick a user into harmful behavior, such as searching for and deleting files that the computer actually needs. Another danger of hoaxes is that, like the boy who cried wolf, it's easy to get desensitized and ignore a real virus alert when it does occur. You can check to see if a message is a hoax at **Snopes.com** (Figure 10.6) or **hoax-slayer.com**. In this era of fake news, it is wise to fact-check information before sharing or acting on it.

A **logic bomb** behaves like a virus in that it performs a malicious act, such as deleting files, but unlike a virus, it doesn't spread to other machines. A logic bomb attacks when certain conditions are met, such as when an employee's name is removed from a database. Logic bombs are often used by disgruntled IT employees. When the trigger is a specific date and time, such as April Fools' Day or Friday the 13th, a logic bomb may be called a **time bomb**. A virus may have logic bomb characteristics and can lay dormant on a system until certain conditions are met.

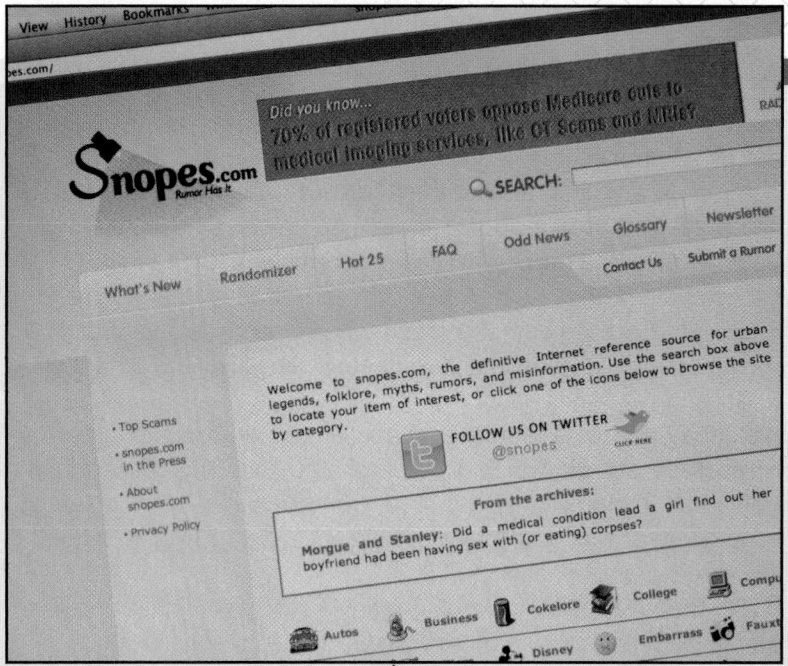

FIGURE 10.6 Snopes.com is a reliable place to check for hoaxes.

A **worm**, like a virus, is self-replicating, but it doesn't need a host to travel. Worms travel over networks, including the Internet. Once a system on a network is infected, the worm scans the network for other vulnerable machines to infect and spreads over the network connections without any human intervention. In 2017, the WannaCry ransomware outbreak was spread by an Internet worm.

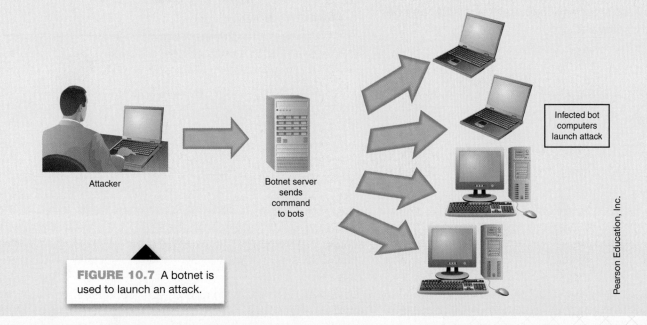

Attacker

Botnet server sends command to bots

Infected bot computers launch attack

FIGURE 10.7 A botnet is used to launch an attack.

Pearson Education, Inc.

On April 1, 2009, millions of email spam messages were sent out by computers infected with the Conficker worm. These computers were part of a massive **botnet** — a network of infected computer **zombies**, or **bots**, that are controlled by a master (Figure 10.7). The message was an advertisement for a fake antispyware program that, when installed, infected many more machines. Sending out fake security notifications is one of the most common ways to infect computers. The ability to control millions of machines has the potential to cause real harm. A botnet could be used to send out spam and viruses or to launch a **denial-of-service attack**, which is perpetrated by sending out so much traffic that it cripples a server or network. Denial-of-service attacks have taken down many major websites, including Twitter, Yahoo!, CNN, eBay, and Amazon.

A **Trojan horse**, or simply Trojan, is a program that appears to be a legitimate program but is actually something malicious. A Trojan might install adware, a toolbar, or a keylogger, or it might open a backdoor to allow remote access to the system. A famous example of a Trojan is the Sinowal Trojan horse, which criminals used to steal more than 500,000 banking passwords and credit card numbers over a period of three years.

A computer program that captures information a user enters on a keyboard is called a keylogger. A keylogger may be installed as a Trojan and reside unnoticed on an infected machine. When a user enters user names and passwords or credit card numbers, the keylogger gathers that information. Some people install keyloggers on their own computers to monitor the activity of other users. There are also hardware keyloggers — USB devices that plug in between the keyboard and computer. They are small and inconspicuous and can't be detected by security software.

Ransomware is malware that prevents you from using your computer until you pay a fine or fee. In lock screen ransomware, a fake security violation that appears to be from a law enforcement agency locks your computer screen. The lock screen message claims that your computer has been locked because of illegal activity and that you must pay a fine to unlock your system. Once you pay the fine, a code is sent that enables you to unlock your system. Encryption ransomware encrypts files on your system and requires you to pay a fee to get the decryption key. In May 2017, the WannaCry ransomware attack infected hundreds of thousands of computers world-wide, demanding payment by anonymous

FIGURE 10.8 Ransomware

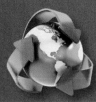

GREEN COMPUTING
Botnets

How do security and privacy relate to green computing? If you leave your computer turned on but idle, you expect it to go into sleep mode. If your computer becomes infected with malware and becomes part of a botnet, then it may be using energy even when you think it's in sleep mode. Imagine the amount of energy that's consumed by the thousands of compromised systems all over the world that are part of botnets. So keep your machine clean and secure, to help ensure that it's not part of a botnet, and when you know you'll be away from it for long periods of time, turn it off.

TAlex/Fotolia

bitcoin — an anonymous, digital, encrypted currency. Fake antivirus warnings are another form of ransomware. Clicking on a security warning installs a fake antivirus software on your computer, which then requires you to pay to remove it. Of course, if you pay the ransom, you are relying on the criminal to help you restore your system (Figure 10.8).

A **rootkit** is a set of programs that enables someone to gain control over a computer system while hiding the fact that the computer has been compromised. A rootkit can be almost impossible to detect and also allows the machine to become further infected by masking the behavior of other malware.

More than 1 million computer viruses and other malware have been identified. You can check the current state of malware threats by visiting websites such as **home.mcafee.com /virusinfo/global-virus-map**. Understanding the threats your computer faces is the first step in preventing these programs from infecting your machine.

Running Project

Visit the U.S. Computer Emergency Readiness Team website at **us-cert.gov/ncas/tips**. Click the *Guidelines for Publishing Information Online* link and read about it. Write a two- to three-paragraph summary of the tip. Which of these suggestions do you follow? Are there any that you disagree with?

5 Things You Need to Know

- Malware is the term for harmful and malicious software.
- Spam is a common way to distribute malware.
- Spyware secretly gathers personal information about you.
- Viruses, worms, Trojans, ransomware, and rootkits are the most dangerous types of malware.
- Malware may damage your system or make it part of a botnet that attacks other systems.

Key Terms

adware	ransomware
bitcoin	rootkit
bot	spam
botnet	spamming
browser hijacker	spyware
cookie	time bomb
denial-of-service attack	Trojan horse
logic bomb	virus
malware	worm
payload	zombie

Adempercem/Fotolia

Shields Up!

3

Explain How to Secure a Computer

Protecting your computer from intrusion or infection can be a daunting task. In this article, we discuss important steps to keep your system secure. Because there are so many kinds of malware that can infect your computer, it takes a multilevel approach to safeguard your system.

Software

Most of the time, a machine becomes infected because of software exploits, lack of security software, or unpatched programs. One of the most common ways to get a malware infection on a computer is by downloading it. This might be in the form of a Trojan that you think is a game or useful app, or it might occur when you open an email attachment. A **drive-by download** happens when you visit a website that installs a program in the background without your knowledge.

A **firewall** is a hardware device that blocks unauthorized access to your network, but a software firewall — such as the one that comes with Windows — also blocks access to an individual machine. It's a good idea to use both forms to protect your systems. The Windows firewall monitors both outgoing and incoming network requests and protects you from local network threats as well as those from the Internet. It's turned on by default and can be used with a hardware firewall, such as one in a home router. You shouldn't run another software firewall at the same time because they can conflict with each other, causing connectivity issues. A software firewall blocks connections to programs that aren't on an allowed list of programs. The first time a new program tries to access the network, the software firewall asks you whether to allow or block access. In this way, the firewall program learns which programs should be allowed access and denies access to any unauthorized programs — such as a backdoor Trojan. Figure 10.9 shows the Windows firewall default settings. macOS has a built-in firewall, but it is turned off by default. Use Security & Privacy preferences to turn it on.

Antivirus programs provide protection against more than just viruses; they also protect against threats such as Trojans, worms, and spyware. To search for known malware, antivirus programs use signature checking — scanning files on your computer, looking for items found in a virus definition file. Outdated definition files leave a machine vulnerable to attack. Most antivirus software also uses heuristic methods, such as monitoring your machine for suspicious activity, to catch new malware that is not in the definition files. Good antivirus programs can cost from nothing to $100 or more, depending on the features included in the package you choose. Some very good free programs include AVG Free and Avast. Windows includes Windows Defender (Figure 10.10), an antivirus and antispyware program that performs both real-time protection and system scanning. Real-time protection monitors your system for suspicious behavior such as a program trying to change your home page or other Windows settings. It's important to have only one antivirus program running on your machine because multiple programs will interfere with each other and slow your computer's performance.

Most good antivirus programs also protect against spyware and other malware. **Antispyware software** prevents adware and spyware software from installing itself on your computer and can be used to clean an infected machine. Some good stand-alone — and free — antispyware programs for personal use include Ad-Aware, Spybot, and Malwarebytes Anti-Malware.

Help protect your PC with Windows Firewall

Windows Firewall can help prevent hackers or malicious software from gaining access to your PC through the Internet or a network.

Private networks	Connected
Networks at home or work where you know and trust the people and devices on the network	
Windows Firewall state:	On
Incoming connections:	Block all connections to apps that are not on the list of allowed apps
Active private networks:	Shamrock
Notification state:	Notify me when Windows Firewall blocks a new app

Guest or public networks	Not connected
Networks in public places such as airports or coffee shops	
Windows Firewall state:	On
Incoming connections:	Block all connections to apps that are not on the list of allowed apps
Active public networks:	None
Notification state:	Notify me when Windows Firewall blocks a new app

FIGURE 10.9 The Windows Firewall Control Panel

Security suites are packages of security software that include a combination of features such as antivirus, firewall, and privacy protection. The advantage to using a suite is that you get complete protection; the downsides are that they can be expensive and they may use a lot of system resources. The main complaint many people have is that they decrease system performance. This may not be a big deal if you have a fast machine with lots of system resources, but if you have an older, slower machine, the effects could be quite noticeable.

Macs come preconfigured to provide protection against malicious software and security threats, and there are far fewer threats to Macs to begin with, so many Mac users don't install additional security software on their computers. File quarantine, found in macOS applications that download files from the Internet (Safari, Messages, iChat, and Mail), checks for known malware when you try to open a downloaded file. Although attacks are less common on Macs than on Windows computers, Macs can still be targeted. In 2012, more than 700,000 Macs were infected with a Trojan called Flashback via a Java vulnerability. The infected systems became part of a massive botnet. In 2017, Fruitfly and OSX.Dok malware infected Mac computers. Using the Security & Privacy preferences (Figure 10.11), you can further secure your Mac by requiring passwords, enabling the firewall, and turning off location services. Businesses that have both Mac and Windows computers should consider adding another layer of security to prevent the Macs from becoming hosts that spread malware to Windows systems.

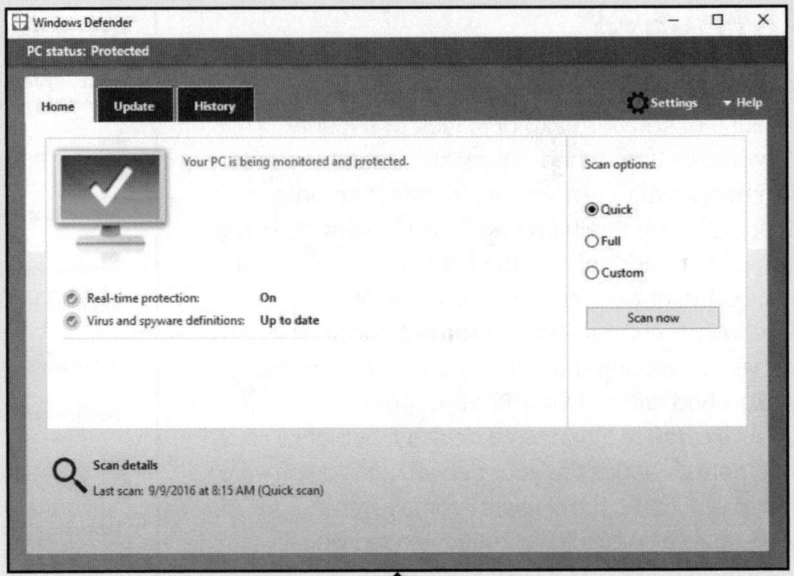

Windown Defender, Windows 10, Microsoft Corporation

FIGURE 10.10 Windows Defender protects against many forms of malware.

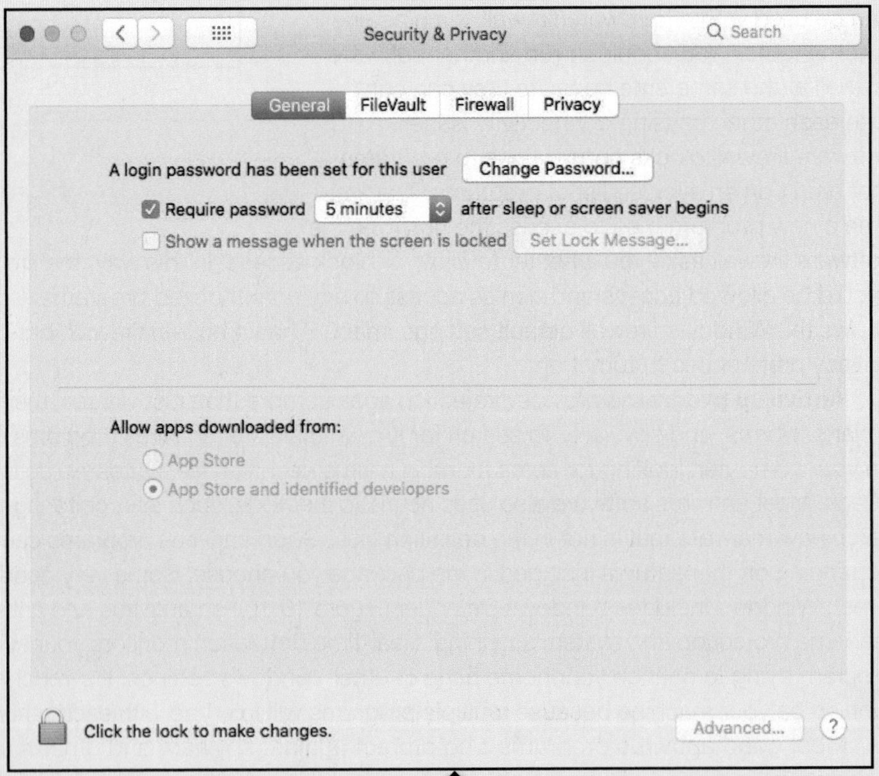

Screenshot(s) reprinted with permission from Apple Inc.

FIGURE 10.11 Mac Security & Privacy Preferences

Hardware

At home, you should use a router between your computers and the Internet. A **router** (Figure 10.12) is a device that connects two or more networks together — for example, your home network and the Internet. A router provides several important security functions. First, a home router acts like a firewall, preventing unauthorized access to your network. The default setup of most home routers has this feature enabled, and you can customize it by using the router utility. For example, you might set restrictions on the type of traffic that can access your network, restrict the time of day that a computer can access the Internet, or define which sites can or cannot be accessed. You might need to customize your router to allow certain applications through — especially if you like to play online games.

Another important security feature of a router is called **network address translation (NAT)**. The router connects you to the public network — the Internet–and has a public IP address that it uses to communicate with the network, but inside your house, the router supplies each device with a private IP address that's valid only on your private network. To the outside world, only the router is visible, so it shields the rest of your devices. The devices inside your network can communicate with each other directly, but any outside communication must go through the router.

A wireless router has all the features described but also provides a wireless access point to your network. This can be a potential security risk if it's not properly secured. Use the router setup utility to change the **SSID (service set identifier)**, or wireless network name, and enable and configure wireless encryption. And be sure to change the default login name and password on the router itself. When setting up a wireless network, you should put security at the top of your list. Older routers came with no encryption configured and a default user name and password that anyone could find on the Internet. Newer routers come preconfigured with security in place.

Wireless encryption adds security to a wireless network by encrypting transmitted data. Use the strongest form of wireless encryption that's supported by the devices and operating systems on your network. WPA2-PSK (Wi-Fi Protected Access 2 — Pre-Shared Key) is designed for use on home networks and is the

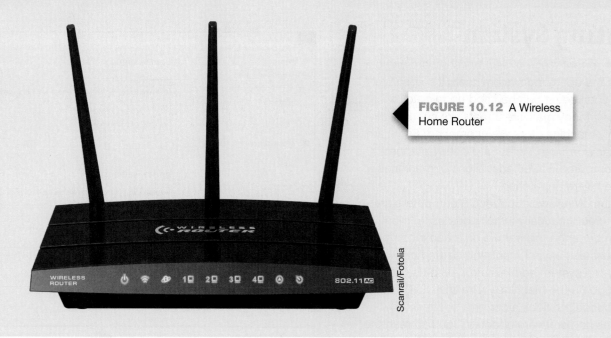

FIGURE 10.12 A Wireless Home Router

Scanrail/Fotolia

recommended encryption or security mode to use on your home router. Avoid the older and less secure WEP and EAP encryption options. Using **Wi-Fi Protected Setup (WPS)** is a way to set up a secure wireless home network. Routers with WPS use a push button, personal identification number (PIN), or USB key to automatically configure devices to connect to your network. Using this method, you don't need to manually type (or remember) the network name (SSID) and wireless security passphrases (Figure 10.13).

You should strive to use the highest level of security on your network, even though configuring all your devices can be tricky. The harder it is to find and guess the settings on your network, the less likely it will be that someone will access it without your permission. These are some things that you can do to secure your network:

- Change the SSID and disable SSID broadcast so that your network is not visible to others.
- Change the default administrator name and password.
- Use wireless encryption and a difficult passphrase.
- Set up filtering so that only devices in the list are allowed.

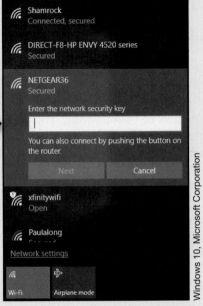

FIGURE 10.13 Enter the security key or press the button on the router to use Wi-Fi Protected Setup to join this network.

Windows 10, Microsoft Corporation

Operating System

The most important piece of security software on your computer is the operating system itself. It's absolutely critical that you keep it patched and up to date (Figure 10.14). Many malware threats are capable of infecting only machines that are unpatched. For example, the Conficker worm can't infect a properly patched Windows computer; it infected millions of machines because they were unpatched.

By default, Windows and macOS computers are configured to automatically install updates. In most cases, you shouldn't change this setting on a home computer. In a school or business environment, this setting may be changed by the system administrator, who uses another method to update the machines. The US-CERT Current Activity webpage provides a current list of security vulnerabilities and software updates. You can read the updates at **us-cert.gov/ncas/current-activity**.

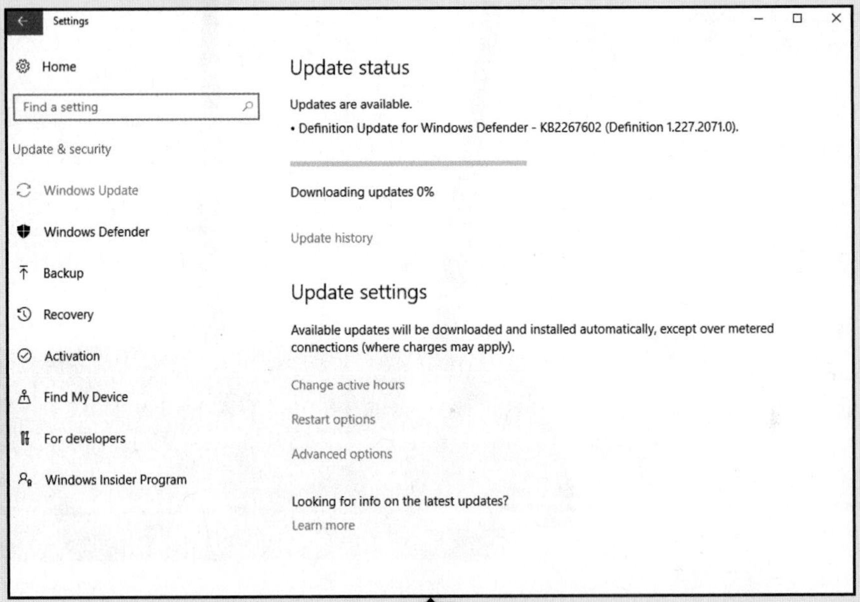

Windows 10, Microsoft Corporation

FIGURE 10.14 Windows 10 Update Settings

You can access the Windows Action Center through the Control Panel to verify that your computer is adequately protected. Figure 10.15 shows a computer that isn't protected because the firewall is turned off. There's a button to click to easily correct the problem.

Properly protecting your computer systems requires you to be diligent and proactive, installing and maintaining security software and monitoring it for important messages. Even with the best protection, it's possible to get an infection on your machine, but without protection, it's almost a certainty that you will.

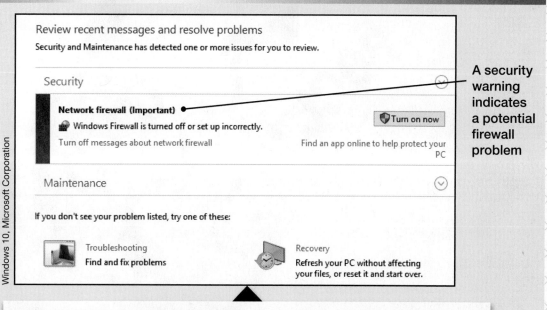

Windows 10, Microsoft Corporation

Review recent messages and resolve problems

Security and Maintenance has detected one or more issues for you to review.

Security

Network firewall (Important)
Windows Firewall is turned off or set up incorrectly.
Turn off messages about network firewall

Turn on now

Find an app online to help protect your PC

A security warning indicates a potential firewall problem

Maintenance

If you don't see your problem listed, try one of these:

Troubleshooting
Find and fix problems

Recovery
Refresh your PC without affecting your files, or reset it and start over.

FIGURE 10.15 The Action Center notifies you and helps resolve potential security problems.

Running Project

Use the Internet to find out what might happen if you use the Windows firewall and another software firewall at the same time.

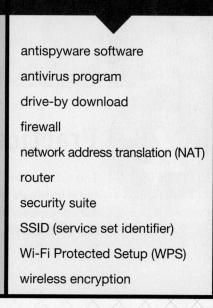

5 Things You Need to Know

- A software firewall blocks access to an individual machine.
- Antivirus programs protect against viruses, Trojans, worms, and some spyware.
- Antispyware software prevents and cleans adware and spyware infections.
- Network address translation shields your computers from the public network (Internet).
- Use the strongest form of wireless encryption that's supported by your network.

Key Terms

antispyware software

antivirus program

drive-by download

firewall

network address translation (NAT)

router

security suite

SSID (service set identifier)

Wi-Fi Protected Setup (WPS)

wireless encryption

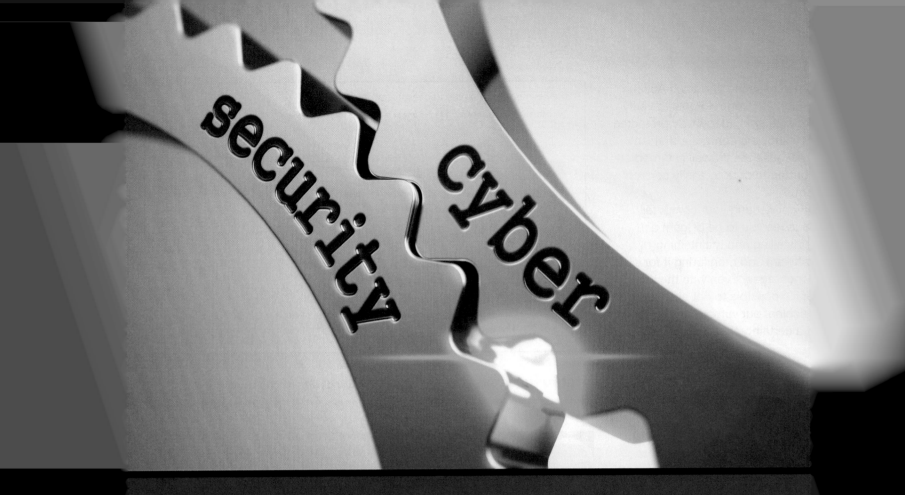

An Ounce of Prevention

Practice Safe Computing

The list of online threats grows daily in size and danger. The only way to be truly safe is to unplug your computer and never connect it to a network — especially the Internet — but because this isn't practical for most computer users, practicing safe computing is critical to protecting your system and your personal information.

Setting Parental Controls

User Accounts

Windows and macOS user accounts have several layers of security built into them. Parental controls allow you to put limits on your children's user accounts. Of course, if the child knows the administrator password, he or she can easily change these settings. Figure 10.16 shows several accounts set up on a Windows desktop.

There are three types of accounts:

- Standard account — for everyday computing. A standard account with Family Safety turned on by default can be set up for a child.
- Administrator account — for making changes, installing software, configuring settings, and completing other tasks; called Admin on a Mac.
- Guest account — for users who need temporary access to a system; this account is off by default.

When you create an account on a Windows computer, you have the option to use your email address linked to your Microsoft account or to create a local user. Either account type can be set up as an administrator or a standard user. Using your Microsoft account links you to your cloud resources, such as OneDrive and Office Online.

It's a good idea to create a standard user account for your day-to-day tasks and use the administrator account only when

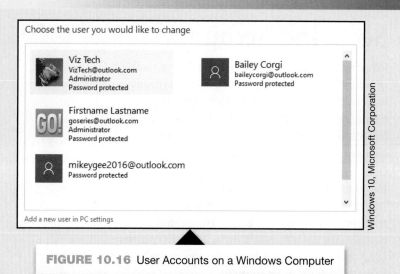

FIGURE 10.16 User Accounts on a Windows Computer

necessary. Tasks that require administrator-level permission, such as installing a new program, will prompt you for administrator credentials. Also, on a Windows computer, **User Account Control (UAC)** will notify you before changes are made to your computer (Figure 10.17). Though this may seem like a nuisance, it prevents malware from making changes to your system without your knowledge. It's important to always read the message in the UAC box before clicking Yes. Some malware infects computers by tricking users into clicking fake Windows notification boxes. macOS will prompt for your administrator password before installing or updating software or changing settings that affect all users (Figure 10.18).

FIGURE 10.17 User Account Control requests administrator credentials to install or update software.

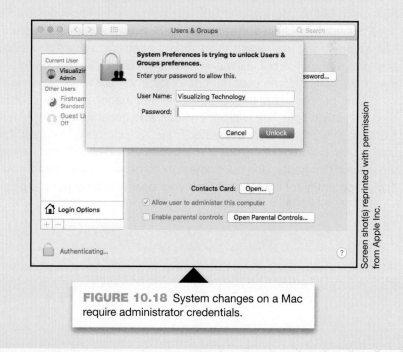

FIGURE 10.18 System changes on a Mac require administrator credentials.

Securing Accounts

What's the password on your computer user account? Is it your pet's name, your birthday, your middle name, or something else that someone who knows you could easily guess? Is it written on a sticky note and affixed to your monitor or hidden under your keyboard? Most people have multiple accounts that they need to log in to, with numerous user names and passwords to remember, so it's not a surprise that they try to make it easier by making passwords easy to recall. How well you protect your accounts goes a long way toward protecting the information they contain.

To make matters worse, different systems have different rules for acceptable passwords. The more places you have accounts, the more complicated it gets. Many people use the same password on multiple accounts, but this makes them less secure. If a hacker manages to get the password to your email account, he or she may also have just gotten the password to your bank account. And it's pretty easy for someone to get your password. Don't think so? Ask Sarah Palin. In 2008, when she was a vice presidential candidate, her personal Yahoo! email account was hacked by a college kid. He reset her password by correctly answering her security questions. The security questions on most sites are things that are easy to find out about a person: high school mascot, mother's maiden name, favorite color, birth date. In Palin's case, she's a public figure, so the information was pretty much common knowledge, but how much of this information could be found on your Facebook profile?

Password-cracking software can crack even the strongest passwords that are six to eight characters long in a matter of minutes. Still, using strong passwords is an important step to secure your accounts. A deadbolt on your door could be thwarted by someone breaking the door in but will make less determined thieves look for easier targets. A strong password works in much the same way. Figure 10.19 lists some important rules to remember when creating strong passwords.

Some people prefer to use a password manager, such as RoboForm or LastPass, to store passwords rather than try to remember them all individually. These programs can also generate passwords that are more secure than the passwords people normally create because they're randomly generated. macOS includes a feature called *Keychain* that encrypts and stores your user names and passwords in one place, syncs them across your devices, and makes them accessible through a master password. If you choose to use a password manager, do your homework to be sure the program you choose is very secure and that your passwords are safe. There is always potential for someone to find your passwords by using a password-stealing program easily found online.

Creating Strong Passwords

Use a mixture of upper- and lowercase letters, and at least one number

uPLo

!@#$

Use at least eight characters, with at least one special character

Don't use any words that can be found in a dictionary and don't use anything personally identifiable

Always change default passwords and use different passwords for different accounts

FIGURE 10.19 Rules for Creating Strong Passwords

Many computers come with fingerprint scanners, which add an additional layer of security in terms of gaining access to your computer and enable you to bypass entering a password. Biometric scanners that measure human characteristics, such as fingerprints, retinal patterns, or voice patterns, can replace the need to enter passwords. Requiring a magnetic card swipe is another way that businesses control access. You may have seen an example of this when you returned an item to a store. To allow a transaction that takes money out of a cash register, the clerk often needs to swipe an ID card to complete the transaction. Only users with the authority to reverse a transaction, such as a manager, are able to do so.

When you create a new account (Figure 10.20), you're asked for a lot of information to help identify you. Think about your answers carefully so they are hard for someone to guess but do not give away too much personal information. Select questions that are hard for other people to answer, and use good passwords, following the rules of the site.

When you create an account on a website that requires registration, such as a forum, don't use the same password that you use for other websites that need more security. It also makes sense to have an alternate email account to use just for website registrations. This will help keep the amount of spam down in your regular email account, and if it gets too bad, you can always delete the account without losing your personal contacts. Although it may be fine to have your passwords to such sites saved in your browser, don't have your browser save your passwords to websites such as bank and credit card companies. Storing secure passwords in a browser leaves them open to potential hackers and other users of your computer.

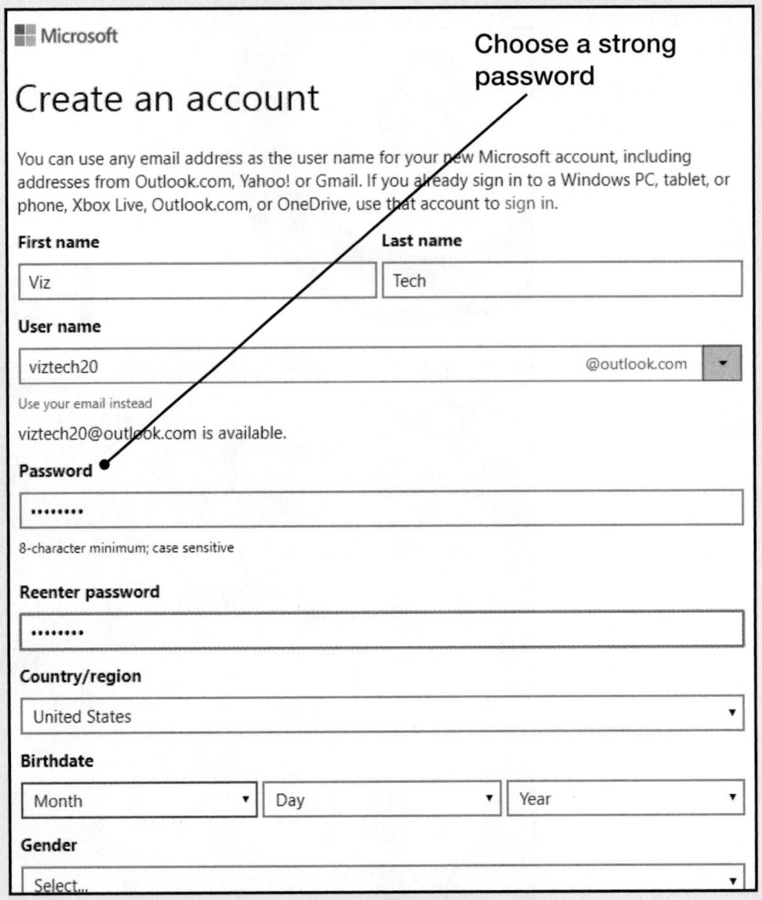

Microsoft

Create an account

You can use any email address as the user name for your new Microsoft account, including addresses from Outlook.com, Yahoo! or Gmail. If you already sign in to a Windows PC, tablet, or phone, Xbox Live, Outlook.com, or OneDrive, use that account to sign in.

First name
Viz

Last name
Tech

User name
viztech20   @outlook.com

Use your email instead

viztech20@outlook.com is available.

Choose a strong password

Password
•••••••

8-character minimum; case sensitive

Reenter password
•••••••

Country/region
United States

Birthdate
Month   Day   Year

Gender
Select...

Courtesy of Yahoo

FIGURE 10.20 Registering for a new account requires you to create a password and answer security questions.

FIGURE 10.21 This site uses encryption to safeguard the information you send.

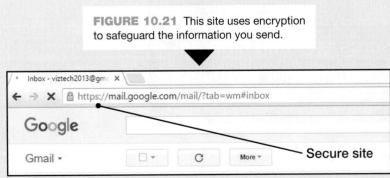

Secure site

Google and the Google logo are registered trademarks of Google Inc., used with permission.

Encryption

Any time you send information across a network, there's potential for someone to intercept it. **Encryption** converts unencrypted, plain text into code called **ciphertext**. To read encrypted information, you must have a key to decrypt it. This prevents a thief from being able to read the information. When you log in to a website, be sure that you're using a secure connection. Verify that the address bar of your browser shows *https*, which indicates that the site is using encryption (Figure 10.21). This ensures that your information is safe to send. If the connection uses regular *http*, then your information is sent in plain text.

File and drive encryption secure the data in your files. Windows includes Encrypting File System (EFS), which enables you to encrypt individual files, and BitLocker, which encrypts the entire drive. You can use BitLocker To Go to encrypt removable drives. macOS has a feature called FileVault, which, when turned on, encrypts the contents of your hard disk.

Safely Installing Software

The process of installing software copies files to the computer, may alter system settings, and may create new folders. The process might require you to enter administrator credentials to proceed. To protect yourself from downloading problems, you should download only from reliable sources. All the major app stores have checks in place to ensure that the software they offer is safe. Carefully read the license, terms of use, and each screen of the setup as you install; deselect any optional features that you don't want, such as toolbars and other helper apps. Also carefully read any request for permissions to use features such as your location, which can affect your privacy (Figure 10.22). If you have antimalware software running with real-time scanning, it should check the file for you, or you can manually scan it. macOS has a feature called Gatekeeper that checks for a digital Developer ID from Apple. Gatekeeper blocks software that doesn't have this ID from installing.

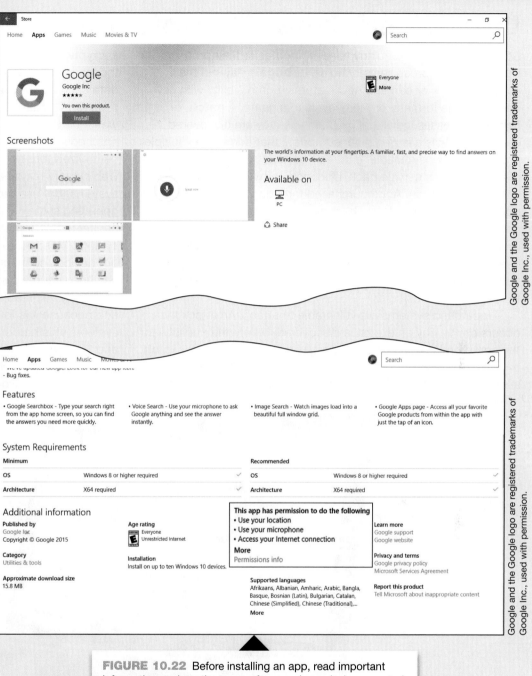

Google and the Google logo are registered trademarks of Google Inc., used with permission.

FIGURE 10.22 Before installing an app, read important information such as the terms of use and permissions granted.

Updating and Uninstalling Software

Software publishers regularly release updates to their programs. Updates can address security holes, or **bugs** — flaws in the programming — or can add new features, compatibility with new devices or file formats, or more levels to a game. A **patch**, or **hotfix**, addresses individual problems as they are discovered. A **service pack** is a larger, planned update that addresses multiple problems or adds multiple features. Previous patches and hotfixes are included in a service pack. Updating software requires an Internet connection. Apps purchased through an app store can be updated through the store. Other programs require files to be downloaded from the web. You can configure software to check for updates automatically, or you can search for updates yourself. In a business environment, computers are generally not set to update software automatically because updates are centrally managed by the IT department.

Unpatched systems are vulnerable to attack. An attack that occurs on the day an exploit is discovered, before the publisher of the compromised software can fix it, is called a **zero-day exploit**. In 2014, two massive software bugs left millions of systems vulnerable to attacks. The Heartbleed bug is a flaw in an online encryption tool called OpenSSL that is used by hundreds of thousands of web servers. Heartbleed enables a hacker to access data such as user names and passwords located in the memory of a server. The flaw was not discovered for two years, but once it was found, a patch was quickly released. Once a web server is patched and users change their passwords, the threat is neutralized, but several months after its discovery, thousands of web servers remained unpatched. The Shellshock flaw affects systems that use the Unix Bash shell — a component of many operating systems, including Linux and macOS. The flaw allows a hacker to run commands on, and take control of, an unpatched system. Most personal computers are protected behind a firewall, but devices connected directly to the Internet, such as web servers, security cameras, smart appliances, and routers, are especially vulnerable. The flaw was undiscovered for over 20 years, and because it is found on so many different devices and operating systems, it is harder to patch than Heartbleed. Both Heartbleed and Shellshock demonstrate the importance of keeping a system up to date and patched, as well as securing your online accounts with unique passwords.

Nerthuz/Fotolia

When a program is no longer needed on your computer, you should uninstall it, using the proper uninstaller, to ensure that all files and settings are correctly removed. Troubleshooting computer problems sometimes involves uninstalling and reinstalling software or updates. To view or uninstall a program on a Windows computer, open File Explorer, in the Navigation pane click *This PC*, and then, on the Compute tab, click *Uninstall or change a program*. In the Programs and Features window (Figure 10.23), click the program that you want to uninstall and then click either the *Uninstall* or *Uninstall/Change* button that appears above the programs list. The options available will vary depending on the program. To uninstall a program from the Start menu, right-click the app and then click *Uninstall*. To uninstall a program on a Mac, if no uninstaller is provided, simply drag the program from the Applications folder in Finder to the trash.

FIGURE 10.23 The Windows Programs and Features window is used to uninstall software.

Acceptable Use Policies

Many businesses and schools have an **acceptable use policy (AUP)** that computer and network users must abide by. Although you might find them restrictive and annoying, from a business perspective, AUPs force users to practice safe computing and prevent a lot of potential problems from affecting the systems. The restrictions of an AUP depend on the type of business and the type of information you need access to. In a highly secure business, the AUP would likely prohibit all personal use of systems, including checking email, shopping online, using social networks, and playing online games. All these activities could potentially lead to malware being introduced into the system.

It's a good idea to have a personal AUP in place, too. It doesn't need to be a formal document, but all the users of your computers and home network should follow safe computing guidelines. It's a lot easier to prevent damage than it is to fix it. Figure 10.24 illustrates a simple home AUP.

Personal Acceptable Use Policy

Some basic rules for safe computing

Email

Be smart when reading email: Open attachments only if they're expected and you know exactly where they came from. Be sure your antivirus software scans them before you open them.

Websites

Be cautious about the information you enter on websites, and look for *https* encrypted pages.

Scams

Be wary of phishing and fraud scams and delete any suspicious email right away.

FIGURE 10.24 Personal Acceptable Use Policy

ETHICS

When criminals use encryption to hide their illegal activities, law enforcement officials often need to crack the codes. The U.S. government has tried to require encryption companies to provide them with a backdoor key that would enable them to unlock anything that uses the encryption. Thus far, they've been unsuccessful in making this happen and have been forced to use brute-force methods to try to guess criminals' passwords. Over the years, there have been allegations that the National Security Agency (NSA) has embedded a back-door into various versions of encryption and random number generators used to create encryption algorithms.

In 2010, even after a year of attempts, the U.S. government was unable to crack the password of a Brazilian banker who had been seized by Brazilian authorities. Should the government have the right to require a company to provide the government with the key to unlock such types of evidence? What if such a key also enables the government to decrypt any other information that's encoded with the same key — such as yours? What if the encryption hides suspected terrorism information? Or the hard drive of a suspected pedophile? Does your answer depend on the type of crime?

Running Project

Visit **staysafeonline.org/teach-online-safety/higher-education**. Use the advice from this website to craft an AUP for your college classmates.

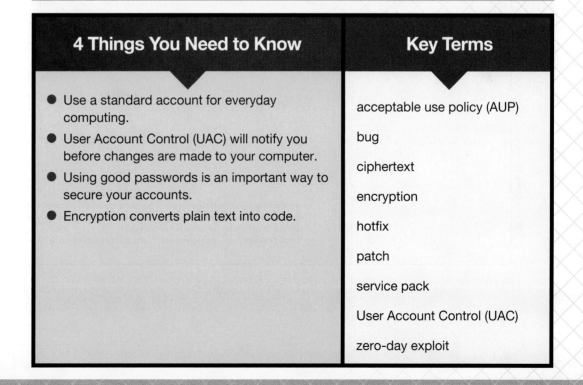

4 Things You Need to Know	Key Terms
● Use a standard account for everyday computing.	acceptable use policy (AUP)
● User Account Control (UAC) will notify you before changes are made to your computer.	bug
	ciphertext
● Using good passwords is an important way to secure your accounts.	encryption
	hotfix
● Encryption converts plain text into code.	patch
	service pack
	User Account Control (UAC)
	zero-day exploit

Secure a Microsoft Word Document

HOW TO VIDEO

Microsoft Office allows you to set different levels of protection on your documents. In this activity, you will secure your document with a password and restrict editing.

1 Open a new, blank Word document; type your name and date in the file; and save it as **lastname_firstname_ch10_howto2**. Type the following bulleted list, pressing Enter after each point:

- Mark as Final makes the file read-only and lets readers know the document is the final version.
- Encrypt with Password uses encryption to protect the document. Once the correct password is entered, the document can be viewed and edited.
- Restrict Editing allows you to control which parts of the document can be edited.

Word 2016, Windows 10, Microsoft Corporation

lastname_firstname_ch10_howto02 - Word

File   Home   Insert   Design   Layout   References   Mailings   Review   View   Add-Ins   Tell me what you want to do...   Viz Tech   Share

Calibri (Body)   11

B I U abc x₂ x²

Clipboard   Font   Paragraph   Styles   Editing

AaBbCcDc AaBbCcDc AaBbCc AaBbCcD AaB AaBbCcD
¶ Normal   ¶ No Spac... Heading 1 Heading 2 Title Subtitle

- Mark as Final makes the file read-only and lets readers know the document is the final version.
- Encrypt with Password uses encryption to protect the document. Once the correct password is entered, the document can be viewed and edited.
- Restrict Editing allows you to control which parts of the document can be edited.

2

Press Enter. Click the *File* tab, click *Protect Document*, and then click *Encrypt with Password*. In the Encrypt Document dialog box, type the password **password1** and then click *OK*. Reenter the password and click *OK* again. Word will now require the password to open this document.

lastname_firstnam

⊖

Info
New
Open
Save
Save As
Print
Share
Export
Close

Account
Options
Feedback

Info

lastname_firstname_ch10_howto02

Documents » Homework » vt

Protect Document

🔒 A password is required to open this document.

Protect Document ▾

Inspect Document

Before publishing this file, be aware that it contains:
■ Document properties and author's name

Check for Issues ▾

Manage Document

Check in, check out, and recover unsaved changes.
🗋 There are no unsaved changes.

Manage Document ▾

Word 2016, Windows 10, Microsoft Corporation

3

Save and close your document and then reopen it. When prompted for a password, enter **password1** and take a screenshot of this prompt, then click *OK*. Paste your screenshot into your document below the bulleted list. Click the File tab, click *Protect Document*, click *Encrypt with Password*, delete the symbols in the password box, and then click *OK* to remove the encryption.

Password	?	×

Enter password to open file
C:\...\Documents\Homework\vt\lastname_firstname_ch10_howto02.docx

●●●●●●●●●|

OK   Cancel

Word 2016, Windows 10, Microsoft Corporation

4 On the File tab, click *Protect Document*, and then click *Restrict Editing*. In the Restrict Editing pane, check the *Allow only this type of editing in the document* box, and if necessary select *No changes (Read only)*.

5 Check to make sure that your document is correct and complete and then click the *Yes, Start Enforcing Protection* button. Verify that Password is selected and type **password2** twice in the dialog box. Word will now require the password to edit this document.

6 Try to edit your document to verify that your protection was enforced. What happened? Click *Stop Protection* and enter **password2** in the dialog. Below the screenshot in your document, type **I can edit after I click Stop Protection**. Save your file and submit as directed by your instructor.

Restrict Editing

1. Formatting restrictions

☐ Limit formatting to a selection of styles

Settings...

2. Editing restrictions

☑ Allow only this type of editing in the document:

[No changes (Read only) ▼]

Exceptions (optional)

Select parts of the document and choose users who are allowed to freely edit them.

Groups:

☐ Everyone

👥 More users...

3. Start enforcement

Are you ready to apply these settings? (You can turn them off later)

[Yes, Start Enforcing Protection]

Word 2016, Windows 10, Microsoft Corporation

- Mark as Final makes the file read-only and lets readers know the document is the final version.
- Encrypt with Password uses encryption to protect the document. Once the correct password is entered, the document can be viewed and edited.
- Restrict Editing allows you to control which parts of the document can be edited.

I can edit after I click Stop Protection.

Word 2016, Windows 10, Microsoft Corporation

If you are using a Mac:

1. Open a new, blank Word document; type your name and date in the file; and save it as **lastname_firstname_ch10_howto2**. Type the following bulleted list, pressing Enter after each point:

   - Set a password to open this document: Once the correct password is entered, the document can be viewed and edited.
   - Set a password to modify this document: A password is required to edit, but not to view the document.
   - Read-only recommended: When the file is opened, a message gives the option to open the file as read-only.

2. Press Enter. Click the *Review* tab and click *Protect Document*. Under Security, in the *Set a password to open this document* box, type **password1** and then click *OK*. Reenter the password and click *OK* again. Word will now require the password to open this document.

Screen shot(s) reprinted with permission from Apple Inc.

3. Save and close your document and then reopen it. When prompted for a password, enter **password1** and take a screenshot of this prompt, then click *OK*. Paste your screenshot into your document below the bulleted list.

4. Click the *Review* tab, and click *Protect Document*. Under Security, in the *Set a password to open this document* box, delete the symbols in the password box to remove the protection. Under Security, in the *Set a password to modify this document* box, type **password2** and then click *OK*. Reenter the password and click *OK* again. Word will now require the password to edit this document. Save and close your document, and then reopen it. In the Password dialog box, do not enter a password. Click *Read Only*.

5. Try to edit your document to verify that it is protected. What happened? Close and reopen your document, and enter **password2** in the dialog box. Below the image, type **I can edit after I enter the correct password**. Click the *Review* tab, click *Protect*, and click *Protect Document*. Under Security, in the *Set a password to modify this document* box, delete the symbols in the password box and then click *OK* to remove the protection. Save your file and submit it as directed by your instructor.

Firstname Lastname
November 26, 2017

- Set a password to open this document: Once the correct password is entered, the document can be viewed and edited.
- Set a password to modify this document: A password is required to edit, but not to view the document.
- Read-only recommended: When the file is opened, a message gives the option to open the file as read-only.

Password

Enter the password to open this file:

https://d.docs.live.net/1c160a109ed2e3f0/Documents/lastname_firstname_ch10_howto2.docx

●●●●●●●●●

Cancel   OK

I can edit after I enter the correct password.

The Law Is on Your Side

Discuss Laws Related to Computer Security and Privacy

Because computer crimes are so closely related to ordinary crime, many laws that already exist also apply to computer crimes. For example, theft and fraud are illegal whether a computer is used or not. However, cybercrime has also created new crimes that aren't covered by existing laws, and over the past two decades, the United States has enacted several important laws.

The Enforcers

Because the types of crimes are so varied, there's no single authority that's responsible for investigating cybercrime. The federal agencies that investigate cybercrime include the Federal Bureau of Investigation (FBI); the U.S. Secret Service; the U.S. Immigration and Customs Enforcement; the U.S. Postal Inspection Service; the Bureau of Alcohol, Tobacco, Firearms and Explosives (ATF); and the U.S. Department of Justice Computer Crime and Intellectual Property Section (CCIPS). Numerous local agencies and task forces also exist. To make it easier for victims to report cybercrimes, the **Internet Crime Complaint Center (IC3)** provides a website — **ic3.gov** — where you can file a report. The IC3 will then process your complaint and forward it to the appropriate agency. The IC3 website has valuable information about cybersecurity and how to protect yourself (Figure 10.25).

Current Laws

In 1986, recognizing the growth and potential of cybercrime, the U.S. Congress passed the Computer Fraud and Abuse Act, making it a crime to access classified information. Amendments between 1988 and 2008 added additional cybercrimes, including theft of property as a part of a fraud scheme; intentionally altering, damaging, or destroying data belonging to others; distribution of malicious code; denial-of-service attacks; and trafficking in passwords and other personal information. The USA PATRIOT Act antiterrorism legislation in 2001 and the Cyber Security Enhancement Act (part of the Homeland Security Act) in 2002 included many provisions for fighting cybercrime. In 2012, a simulated cyber-attack on New York City's power supply was used to help gain Senate support for the Cybersecurity Act of 2012, which was later defeated.

One of the things that make it difficult to catch cyber criminals is that many of them attack from outside the United States. Countries around the world have been trying to create a united system to fight cybercrime. The Convention on Cybercrime is a treaty drafted by the Council of Europe and signed by more than 40 countries, including the United States, Canada, and Japan, but to date, there has been little progress in stemming the tide of cybercrime.

FIND OUT MORE

Visit ic3.gov and click *Internet Crime Prevention Tips*. Read several of the categories to evaluate your risks. How well did you do? Are there steps that you should be taking to better protect yourself?

Who Is Danny/Shutterstock

FBI FRAUD ALERT

IF YOU ANSWER "YES" TO ANY OF THE FOLLOWING QUESTIONS, YOU MAY BE GETTING

SCAMMED!

Are you about to cash a check from an item you sold on the Internet, such as a car, boat, jewelry, etc?

❖ Is it the result of communicating with someone by email?

❖ Did it arrive via an overnight delivery service?

❖ Is it from a business or individual account that is different from the person buying your item or product?

❖ Is the amount for more than the item's selling price?

Are you sending money overseas?

❖ Did you win an international lottery you didn't enter?

❖ Have you been asked to pay money to receive an inheritance from another country?

❖ Are you receiving a commission for accepting money transfers through your bank and/or PayPal account?

To report an online crime, go to:

www.IC3.gov

DON'T BE A VICTIM OF IDENTITY THEFT!

FIGURE 10.25 The IC3 provides information and assistance.

Federal Bureau of Investigation

CAREER SPOTLIGHT

JOBS

IT SECURITY IT security is a great field to consider if you have an interest in technology and like to solve problems. According to the *Occupational Outlook Handbook*, "the responsibilities of computer security specialists have increased in recent years as cyber-attacks have become more sophisticated." Employment prospects are good, with IT security and related occupations expected to grow much faster than average. Upper-level positions require several years of experience, at least a bachelor's degree, and industry certifications, but there are also entry-level positions that have less demanding requirements.

In 2015, **CNNMoney** ranked forensic PC analyst and computer security specialist among the top 50 Best Jobs in America, with a projected 10-year job growth rate of 37% and a median annual salary of $110,000.

Den Rise/Shutterstock

Running Project

The Cybersecurity Act of 2012 was defeated in 2012. What was the opposition argument against this bill? Have any other cybercrime laws been passed since then?

 Viz Check—From either the Companion Website or MyLab IT, take a quick quiz covering Objectives 4–5.

3 Things You Need to Know

- Existing laws (such as theft and fraud laws) apply to cybercrime.
- The Internet Crime Complaint Center (IC3) is the place to file a cybercrime report.
- Because many attacks originate from outside the United States, international cooperation is needed.

Key Term

Internet Crime Complaint Center (IC3)

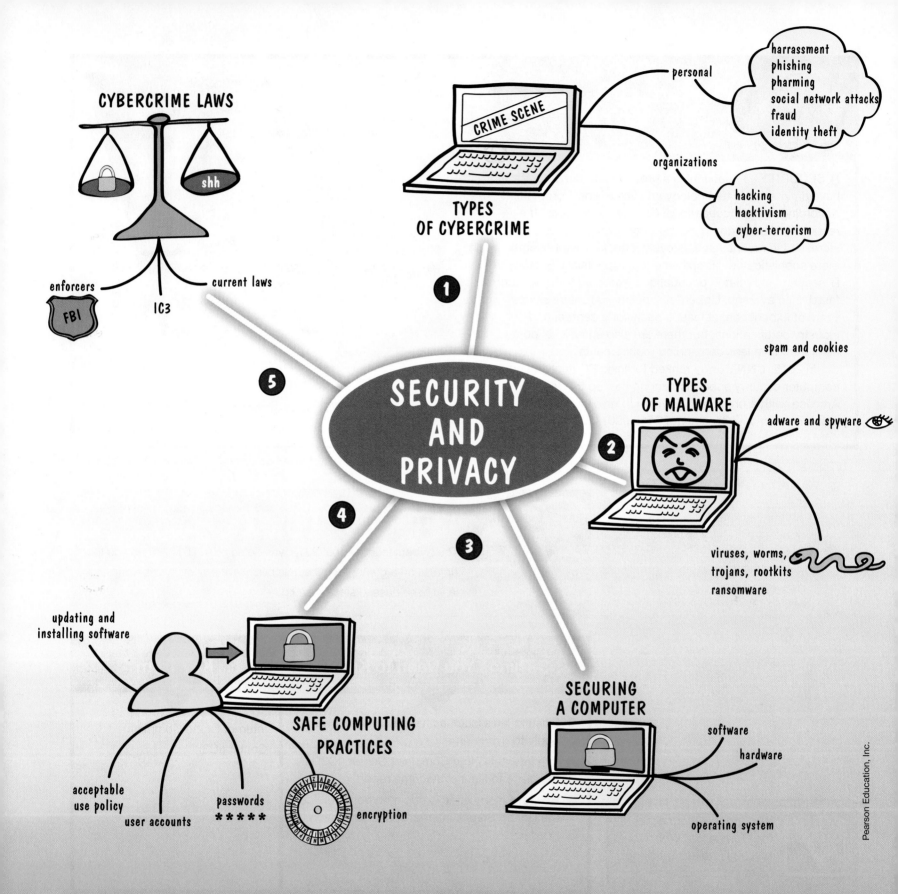

CYBERCRIME LAWS

enforcers
FBI
IC3
current laws

TYPES OF CYBERCRIME

CRIME SCENE

personal
harrassment
phishing
pharming
social network attacks
fraud
identity theft

organizations
hacking
hacktivism
cyber-terrorism

SECURITY AND PRIVACY

1
2
3
4
5

TYPES OF MALWARE

spam and cookies
adware and spyware
viruses, worms, trojans, rootkits ransomware

SAFE COMPUTING PRACTICES

updating and installing software
acceptable use policy
user accounts
passwords *****
encryption

SECURING A COMPUTER

software
hardware
operating system

Pearson Education, Inc.

Objectives Recap

1. Recognize Different Types of Cybercrime
2. Differentiate between Various Types of Malware
3. Explain How to Secure a Computer
4. Practice Safe Computing
5. Discuss Laws Related to Computer Security and Privacy

Key Terms

acceptable use policy (AUP) **525**
adware **508**
antispyware software **513**
antivirus program **513**
bitcoin **511**
bot **510**
botnet **510**
browser hijacker **508**
bug **524**
ciphertext **522**
clickbait **498**
clickjacking **498**
computer fraud **498**
cookie **508**
cyberbullying **497**
cybercrime **496**
cyber-harassment **497**
cyber-stalking **497**
cyber-terrorism **500**
data breach **500**
denial-of-service attack **510**
drive-by download **513**
encryption **522**
firewall **513**
hacking **500**
hacktivism **500**

hotfix **524**
identity theft **499**
Internet Crime Complaint Center (IC3) **535**
keylogger **499**
logic bomb **509**
malware **506**
network address translation (NAT) **515**
patch **524**
payload **509**
pharming **497**
phishing **497**
ransomware **510**
rootkit **511**
router **515**
security suite **514**
service pack **524**
sharebaiting **498**
shill bidding **499**
spam **507**
spamming **507**
spyware **508**
SSID (service set identifier) **515**
time bomb **509**
Trojan horse **510**

User Account Control (UAC) **519**
virus **509**
Wi-Fi Protected Setup (WPS) **516**

wireless encryption **515**
worm **509**
zero-day exploit **524**
zombie **510**

Summary

1. **Recognize Different Types of Cybercrime**

   Cybercrime is any crime that happens via the Internet. Cybercrime against individuals includes cyberbullying, cyber-harassment, cyber-stalking, phishing, pharming, fraud, social network attacks, and identity theft. Cybercrime against organizations includes hacking and cyberterrorism.

2. **Differentiate between Various Types of Malware**

   Malware is malicious software. It ranges from spam, cookies, and adware to spyware, viruses, worms, Trojans, rootkits, and ransomware. Most malware carries a payload that causes harm to your system or causes your system to attack others.

3. **Explain How to Secure a Computer**

   Software to secure a system includes firewall, antivirus, and antispyware programs. It's also critical to keep operating systems and other software up to date. Hardware protection includes a router with firewall functions, network address translation (NAT), and wireless encryption. Using Wi-Fi Protected Setup (WPS) is a way to set up a secure wireless home network.

4. **Practice Safe Computing**

   Standard user accounts should be used for normal computing, and administrator accounts should be used only when needed. Passwords should be strong and should be changed frequently. Accounts that require more security should not share a password with less secure accounts. Encryption should be used to transmit data securely, and acceptable use policies should outline permitted activities. Software should be updated regularly and uninstalled when no longer needed.

5. **Discuss Laws Related to Computer Security and Privacy**

   The Internet Crime Complaint Center accepts victim reports and sends them to the proper authorities. Normal theft and fraud laws apply to cybercrime. Federal laws that cover cybercrime include the Computer Fraud and Abuse Act, the USA PATRIOT Act, and the Homeland Security Act. International agreements are also in place to fight cybercrime.

Multiple Choice

Answer the multiple-choice questions below for more practice with key terms and concepts from this chapter.

1. A serious form of personal cybercrime with the perpetrator demonstrating a pattern of harassment and posing a credible threat of harm is _____.
   a. cyberbullying
   b. identity theft
   c. cyber-stalking
   d. cyber-terrorism

2. _____ redirects you to a phony website even if you type the correct address into your browser.
   a. botnet
   b. pharming
   c. phishing
   d. spam

3. _____ occurs when someone fraudulently uses your name, Social Security number, or bank or credit card number.
   a. A botnet
   b. Computer fraud
   c. A denial-of-service attack
   d. Identity theft

4. _____ is an unlawful attack against computers or networks that's done to intimidate a government or its people for a political or social agenda.
   a. A botnet
   b. Cyber-terrorism
   c. Denial-of-service attack
   d. Hacktivism

5. _____ occurs when sensitive data is stolen or viewed by someone who is not authorized to do so.
   a. A data breach
   b. Computer fraud
   c. Identity theft
   d. Spyware

6. A _____ is a form of malware that changes your home page and redirects you to other websites.
   a. denial-of-service attack
   b. browser hijacker
   c. time bomb
   d. virus

7. A _____ sends out so much traffic that it could cripple a server or network.
   a. botnet
   b. denial-of-service attack
   c. Trojan horse
   d. worm

8. A(n) _____ captures information a user enters on a keyboard.
   a. anti-malware program
   b. firewall
   c. keylogger
   d. WPS

9. _____ is a security feature of a router that shields the devices on a private network from the public network (the Internet).
   a. Acceptable use policy (AUP)
   b. Encryption
   c. User Account Control (UAC)
   d. Network address translation (NAT)

10. Which password is the strongest?
    a. mypassword
    b. myPwa0rd
    c. password
    d. pwa05r5d

True or False

Answer the following questions with *T* for true or *F* for false for more practice with key terms and concepts from this chapter.

_____ 1. Cyber-harassment between two minors is known as cyber-terrorism.

_____ 2. Clickjacking is a link that teases you with just enough information to get you to click the link, driving traffic to a webpage.

_____ 3. On auction websites, one should be wary of shill bidding — fake bidding by the seller or an accomplice to drive up the price of an auction item.

_____ 4. Ransomware prevents you from using your computer until you pay a fine or fee.

_____ 5. A worm needs a host file, such as a game, to travel on.

_____ 6. A rootkit is a set of programs that allows someone to gain control over a computer system while hiding the fact that the computer has been compromised.

_____ 7. You shouldn't run a hardware and software firewall at the same time because they can conflict with each other, causing connectivity issues.

_____ 8. The SSID (service set identifier) shields the devices on your network from the outside world.

_____ 9. A service pack is a large planned update that addresses multiple problems or adds multiple features and includes previous patches and hotfixes.

_____ 10. The Internet Crime Complaint Center (IC3) provides a website for victims to report cybercrimes.

Fill in the Blank

Fill in the blanks with key terms from this chapter.

1. _____ occurs when someone fraudulently uses your name, Social Security number, or bank or credit card number.

2. _____ is any computer program that's designed to be harmful or malicious.

3. _____ is the process of converting unencrypted plain text into code, called ciphertext.

4. A(n) _____ appears to be a legitimate program but is actually something malicious instead.

5. A(n) _____ is a small text file placed on a computer when you visit a website that helps the website identify you when you return.

6. _____ is an anonymous, digital, encrypted currency.

7. _____ adds security to a wireless network by encoding the transmitted data.

8. An attack that occurs on the day an exploit is discovered, before the publisher can fix it, is called a(n) _____.

9. Businesses and schools require computer users to abide by a(n) _____.

10. The _____ processes cybercrime complaints and forwards them to the appropriate agency.

Running Project ...

... The Finish Line

Use your answers from the previous sections of the chapter project to discuss the impact of cybercrime on society. How has it changed the way we keep in touch with others? How has it affected the way we conduct business? How has it changed the way you, personally, conduct yourself online?

Write a report responding to the questions raised throughout the chapter. Save your file as **lastname_firstname_ch10_project** and submit it to your instructor as directed.

Do It Yourself 1

Visit your college website and search for your school's privacy policy. How does your college protect your private information? What is the Family Educational Rights and Privacy Act (FERPA)?

Do It Yourself 2

The amount of information that someone can find out about you may be surprising. In this activity, you'll investigate yourself. From your student data files, open the file *vt_ch10_DIY2_answersheet* and save the file as **lastname_firstname_ch10_DIY2_answersheet**.

1. Google yourself. Try different variations of your name. Did you find any information about yourself? Do you have a common name that gives you lots of results or an uncommon one that nets you fewer? If you had no luck, try using your parents' names.

2. Now try a few more websites. Choose any two–if you have an account on any of these sites, make sure you're logged out: **zabasearch.com**, **spokeo.com**, **pipl.com**, **anywho.com/ whitepages**, **addresses.com**. Did you find any information about yourself (or your parents)? Was it correct? Is there a way to have the entry removed from the site?

3. Take screenshots of the results pages of your searches. Use an editing tool to obscure any information that you don't wish to submit. Type your answers, paste the screenshots in your answer sheet, save the file, and submit as directed by your instructor.

File Management

One of the most common ways to spread malware is by email attachment. It's important to recognize the types of attachments that potentially contain malware. From your student data files, open the file *vt_ch10_FM_answersheet* and save the file as **lastname_firstname_ch10_FM_answersheet**.

> Go to **support.office.com** and, in the search box, type **Blocked attachments in Outlook 2016**.

> What are some of the file types that are blocked by Outlook? Why are they blocked? What should you do if you need to send someone a blocked file type? Type your answers in your answer sheet, save the file, and submit as directed by your instructor.

Critical Thinking

From your student data files, open the file *vt_ch10_CT_answersheet* and save the file as **lastname_firstname_ch10_CT_answersheet**.

1. Think about the ways you and your family use your home computers and network. Who are the users of computers in your family? For what purpose(s) does each family member use computers? What type of accounts do they each have? Are the accounts password protected?

2. Think about the ways each person uses the computer. What are the most likely threats that their usage leaves them vulnerable to? Why?

3. What security software is installed on your computer(s)? How effective has it been in protecting your system? Have you or your family members ever had a virus or other malware infection?

4. Create a family AUP with three to five rules that everyone should follow. Are there different rules for different users?

5. Type your answers in your answer sheet, save the file, and submit it as directed by your instructor.

Ethical Dilemma

There's a fine line between white-hat and gray-hat hackers and between gray-hats and black-hats. If a gray-hat hacker breaches a system and posts a warning to the site administrator about the vulnerabilities, the intent isn't malicious. From your student data files, open the file *vt_ch10_ethics_answersheet* and save the file as **lastname_firstname_ch10_ethics_answersheet**.

It's illegal to hack into a system without authorization, but is it ethical for a gray-hat to hack into a system if the intent is to help it become more secure? Some experts consider gray-hat hackers an essential part of securing the Internet because they often expose vulnerabilities before they're discovered by the security community. What do you consider the dividing line? Type your answers in your answer sheet, save the file, and submit your work as directed by your instructor.

On the Web

There are hundreds of known malware threats. Visit the websites of two antivirus software vendors, such as McAfee (**mcafee.com**), Norton (**norton.com**), TrendMicro (**trendmicro.com**), or Panda (**pandasecurity.com**). From your student data files, open the file *vt_ch10_web_answersheet* and save the file as **lastname_firstname_ch10_web_answersheet**.

What websites did you use? What's the current threat level? Of the top threats, how many can be classified as viruses? Worms? Trojans? How many of them were discovered today? In the past week? How many are at least one year old? Are the threats and threat levels the same on both sites? Type your answers in your answer sheet, save the file, and submit your work as directed by your instructor.

Collaboration

Instructors: Divide the class into groups of three to five students and approve the topics the teams propose.

The Project: Each team is to prepare a public service announcement that teaches your community about a current cyber-threat. You may use any multimedia tool that you're comfortable with. Here are just a few ideas:

- Create a video. You can write a script and cast your group members in it.
- Use an online presentation tool, such as Google Docs, Prezi, or Microsoft Sway.
- Use a screen capture tool, such as Jing.

Don't be limited by the above suggestions; pay attention to both the content and the delivery method.

Outcome: Record the public service announcement using the script you've written. The announcement should be one or two minutes long. Save this video as **teamname_ch10_project** and turn in a final text version of your script named **teamname_ch10_script** showing your collaboration. Be sure to include the name of your presentation and a list of all team members. Submit your presentation to your instructor as directed.

Application Project

MyLab IT
GRADER

Office 2016 Application Projects
Word 2016: Security Certifications

Project Description: In this project, you will format a document with columns, outline and shade text, apply styles, and work with clip art and SmartArt graphics. If necessary, download the student data files from **pearsonhighered.com/viztech**.

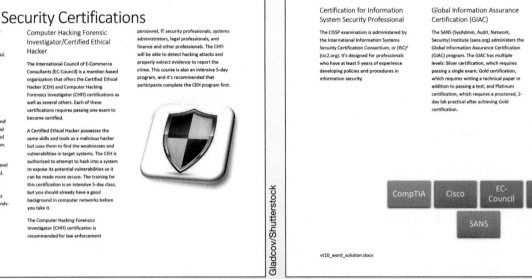

Gladcov/Shutterstock

Word 2013, Windows 8.1, Microsoft Corporation

Step	Instructions
1	Start Word. From your student files, open the file *vt_ch10_word*. Save the file as **lastname_firstname_ch10_word**
2	Change the orientation of the document to landscape.
3	Apply the Title style to *Security Certifications*. Center the title and change the font size to 36 point.
4	Select all of the text except the title. Modify the selected text so that it displays in three columns.
5	Apply the Subtitle style to the four subtitles: CompTIA and Cisco Certifications Computer Hacking Forensic Investigator/Certified Ethical Hacker Certification for Information System Security Professional Global Information Assurance Certification (GIAC)
6	Insert a column break immediately to the left of each of the following three subtitles: Computer Hacking Forensic Investigator/Certified Ethical Hacker Certification for Information System Security Professional Global Information Assurance Certification (GIAC)
7	Move the insertion point to the end of the third column on the first page and press Enter. Search for an online image using the phrase **security badge** and then insert an image of a gold and black security badge into the document, or use the image included with your student files with the file name *vt_ch10_image1*.
8	Apply the Bevel Perspective picture style to the graphic. Resize the image height to 2.5 inches.
9	Move the insertion point to the end of the document and press Enter. Insert a SmartArt graphic using the Basic Block List style from the List category.
10	Use the Position button to move the SmartArt graphic in the bottom center of the page with square text wrapping and then increase the width of the graphic to 6 inches.
11	Apply the Intense Effect style to the SmartArt graphic. Change color to Colorful Range - Accent Colors 2 to 3.
12	Display the text pane for the SmartArt graphic and insert the following text as the five bottom bullets (in this order), and then close the text pane: **CompTIA, Cisco, EC-Council, (ISC)2, SANS**
13	Insert the file name in the footer, save and close the document, and then exit Word. Submit the document as directed.

Application Project

Office 2016 Application Projects
PowerPoint 2016: User Accounts

Project Description: In this project, you will create a presentation about Windows user accounts. In creating this presentation, you will apply design and color themes. You will also insert and format a table and apply animations to objects on your slides, and transitions between slides. If necessary, download the student data files from **pearsonhighered.com/viztech**.

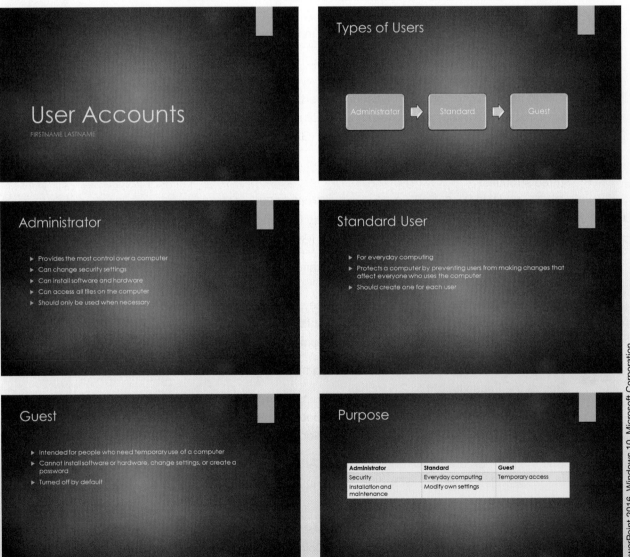

Step	Instructions
1	Start PowerPoint. From your student file, open the file *vt_ch10_ppt*. Save the file as lastname_firstname_ch10_ppt
2	On Slide 1, in the subtitle placeholder, enter your name, using the format Firstname Lastname
3	Apply the Ion theme, blue variant, to the presentation.
4	On Slide 2, convert the bulleted list in the content placeholder to Basic Process SmartArt graphic.
5	Change the SmartArt style to Cartoon Effect.
6	On Slide 3 in the content placeholder, add the following five bullets: • Provides the most control over a computer • Can change security settings • Can install software and hardware • Can access all files on the computer • Should only be used when necessary
7	On Slide 4, in the content placeholder, add the following three bullets: • For everyday computing • Protects a computer by preventing users from making changes that affect everyone who uses the computer • Should create one for each user
8	Apply the Fly In animation with the From Left Effect Option and a duration of 01.50 to the bullet list on Slides 3, 4, and 5.
9	Insert a new slide after Slide 5. Add the title Purpose
10	In the content pane, add this 3 × 3 table:

Administrator	Standard	Guest
Security	Everyday computing	Temporary access
Installation and maintenance	Modify own settings	

Step	Instructions
11	Change the table style to Medium Style 4 - Accent 1 and align it with the middle of the slide.
12	Apply the Fade transition to all slides in the presentation.
13	Insert the page number and the footer Firstname Lastname on the notes and handouts pages for all slides in the presentation. View the presentation in Slide Show View from beginning to end and then return to Normal view.
14	Save the presentation and close PowerPoint. Submit the presentation as directed.

CHAPTER

11

Databases

In This Chapter

VIZ INTRO

We live in the Information Age. The amount of information we all deal with every day can be overwhelming, and it's growing exponentially every year. A database enables you to organize, sort, filter, and query the data in it and find useful information. When you finish this chapter, you'll understand electronic databases—what they are, how they're created, and what they're used for.

BrunoWeltmann/Fotolia

Objectives

1 Identify the Parts of a Database

2 Compare the Four Types of Databases

3 Explain Database Management Systems

4 Discuss Important Types of Information Systems

5 List Examples of Databases Used in Law Enforcement and Research

Running Project

In this chapter, you'll learn about databases. Look for project instructions as you complete each article. For most articles, there's a series of questions for you to research. At the conclusion of the chapter, you'll submit your responses to the questions raised.

Robynmac/Fotolia

Karenkh/Fotolia

| Produce | Health & Beauty | Dairy | Frozen Food | Snack & Sweets |

Coupon

Database Basics

Objective

Identify the Parts of a Database

SIMULATION
Databases

I have a coupon organizer that I use to sort my coupons. It's a small folder that has divider labels: *Produce*, *Health and Beauty*, *Meat*, *Dairy*, *Frozen Food*, *Snacks and Sweets*, *Household*, and *Pets*. When I clip my coupons, I place them in the appropriate sections so they're easy to find when I'm in the store. The system works pretty well—until I get an item like ice cream. Is it Frozen Food, Dairy, or Snacks and Sweets?

Tables, Fields, and Records

A **database** is a collection of information that's organized in a useful way. The coupon organizer is a simple database that works reasonably well for the narrow type of information stored in it. An electronic version of the coupon organizer would give me more ways to manage my coupons. I wouldn't be limited to a single category for my ice cream. I could search for coupons from a particular manufacturer or sort them by expiration date, and I could create custom shopping lists based on the coupons I have. In fact, today many of my coupons are digital, not paper, and the stores where I shop allow me to keep everything in my digital wallet or mobile app.

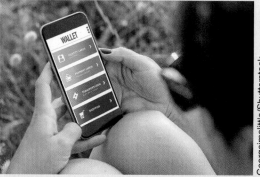

A **table** is a database object in which data is stored, arranged in rows and columns. The simplest databases consist of a single table—such as a contact address list—but a database can also have multiple tables. The tables can be distinct, or they can be related by common information. The database in Figure 11.1 consists of two tables, as well as several other database objects that are used to manipulate, sort, query, and present the data. You'll explore this database throughout this chapter.

The two tables in this database are named *Expenses* and *Vehicles*. Each column in a table is known as a **field**. A field is a single piece of information in a record within a database. In the *Vehicles* table (Figure 11.2), the fields include *ID*, *Make*, *Model*, *Year*, *Color*, and so on. Each row is called a **record** and contains the information for a single entity—a person, a place, a thing, an event, or an idea—in the database. This table has five records in it, each representing a different vehicle. All five records have the same

Two tables:
Vehicles and Expenses

Other database objects
include queries, forms,
and reports

ID	Vehicle	Service Description	Service Date	Mileage
1	2012 Toyota Tacoma	CAP	6/18/2012	2
2	2012 Toyota Tacoma	INSPECTION	6/24/2013	17,1
3	2012 Toyota Tacoma	INSPECTION	6/21/2014	25,8
4	2012 Toyota Tacoma	INSPECTION	6/26/2015	
6	2005 Honda Civic	TIRES	8/2/2008	33,4
7	2012 Toyota Tacoma	TIRES	10/11/2015	45,3
8	2012 Toyota Tacoma	TIRES ALIGNED	10/18/2015	46,1
9	2012 Toyota Tacoma	BRAKE PADS	6/22/2013	52,0
11	2005 Honda Civic	REAR BRAKES	6/30/2009	
13	2012 Toyota Tacoma	V-BELT AND FILTER	9/19/2014	
18	2005 Honda Civic	REPAIRED HOLE IN DOOR INTERIOR	9/7/2005	
19	2005 Honda Civic	REPLACED REAR BRAKES AND ROTORS	9/30/2005	2,7
20	2005 Honda Civic	REPLACED PASS MIRROR	10/21/2005	3,0
21	2005 Honda Civic	REPLACED BRAKE PADS	11/9/2005	4,4
22	2005 Honda Civic	ROUTINE MAINTENANCE AND OIL CHANGE	2/6/2006	7,3
23	2005 Honda Civic	INSPECTION AND OIL CHANGE	7/10/2006	13,0
24	2005 Honda Civic	INSPECTION	7/28/2008	35,3

Navigation pane items:
Vehicle Mainten...
Search...
Vehicles and Expenses
Expenses Table
Vehicles Table
Expenses Query
Expense Details Form
Expenses List Form
Future Expenses Form
Vehicle Details Form
Future Expenses Report
Past Expenses Subreport
Vehicle Details Report
Supporting Objects
Unassigned Objects

Ribbon tabs: File Home Create External Data Database Tools Fields Table   Tell me what you want to do

FIGURE 11.1 An Access Database with Many Database Objects

Georgejmclittle/Shutterstock

Access 2016, Windows 10, Microsoft Corporation

fields, but the data, or field values, vary. For example, in two of the records, the *Make* fields contain the same field value (Honda), but the *Model*, *Year*, and other field values are different. The special field in a record that uniquely identifies the record in the table is called the **primary key**, or ID. The primary key in this example is an index number, but it could be a student ID, Social Security number, order number, or any other unique identifier associated with the record. Using a table is an easy way to look at small amounts of information, but it's not the best way to look at large amounts of data. Even in this small example, several fields are cut off and not displayed on the right.

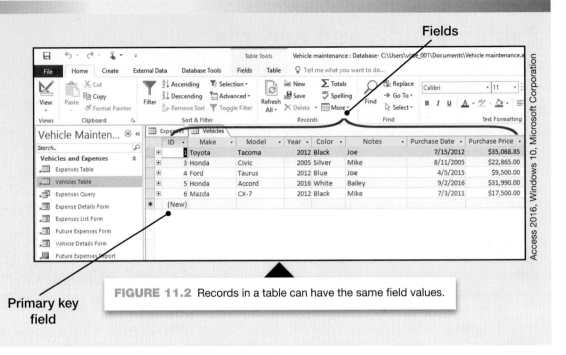

Fields

Primary key field

Access 2016, Windows 10, Microsoft Corporation

FIGURE 11.2 Records in a table can have the same field values.

Forms, Queries, and Reports

The tables contain all the data, but other database objects are used to manage the information. Forms, reports, and queries are some of the ways you can interact with a table and use the data contained in it in constructive ways.

Forms serve two purposes: They make data entry easier, and they make it easier to look at specific information on the screen. Figure 11.3 shows a form called *Vehicle Details*. It shows a single record in an easy-to-view layout. Compare the form in Figure 11.3 to the same record in the table in Figure 11.2. All the fields for this record are visible in the form, unlike in the table, where some fields are cut off.

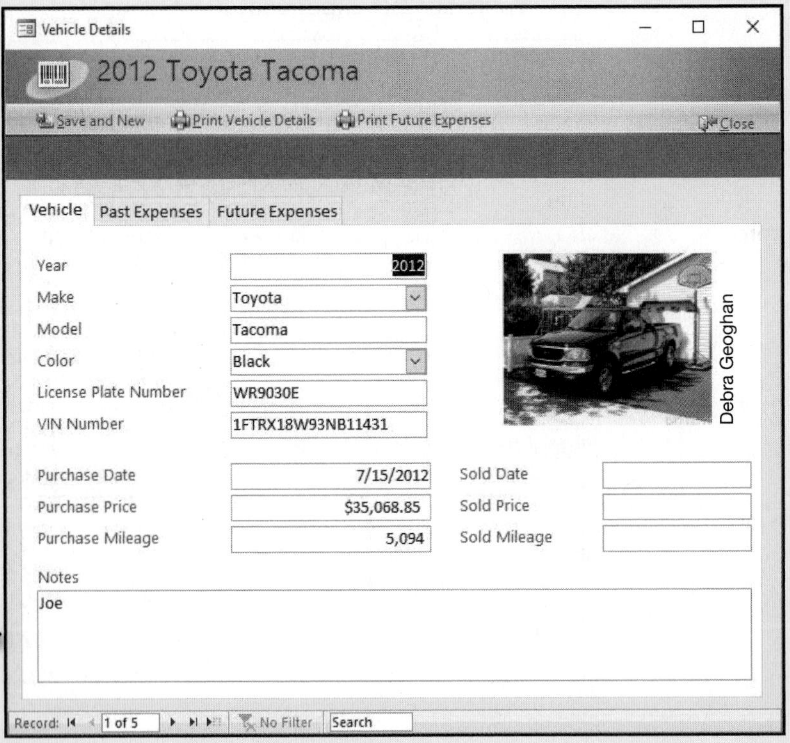

FIGURE 11.3 This form shows a single record.

Geoghan, Debra (Photo of truck); Access 2016, Windows 10, Microsoft Corporation

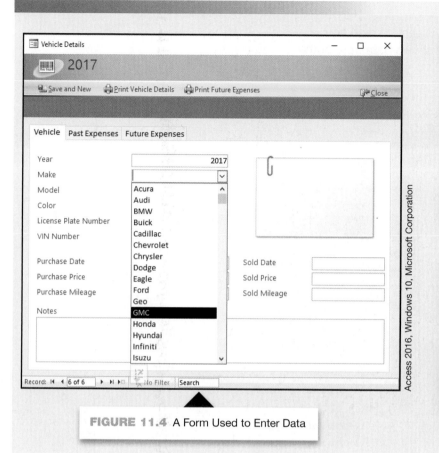

FIGURE 11.4 A Form Used to Enter Data

A form also makes it easier to enter a new record into a database. In Figure 11.4, a new record has been created, and data is being entered. Forms can be created so they match the layout of a paper form. Data entry errors can be reduced by including drop-down lists for fields such as the car make in this example.

In a large database, you often need to pull out information to answer a question. A **query** retrieves specific data from one or more tables. You use a query to ask a question. In Figure 11.5, the question asked is: "What are the expenses for the 2012 Toyota Tacoma?" The query results are presented in a new datasheet.

Vehicle	Service Description	Cost
2012 Toyota Tacom	CAP	$996.40
2012 Toyota Tacoma	INSPECTION	$84.69
2012 Toyota Tacoma	INSPECTION	$84.69
2012 Toyota Tacoma	INSPECTION	$84.69
2012 Toyota Tacoma	TIRES	$839.69
2012 Toyota Tacoma	TIRES ALIGNED	$0.00
2012 Toyota Tacoma	BRAKE PADS	$70.28
2012 Toyota Tacoma	V-BELT AND FILTER	$71.13
2012 Toyota Tacoma	OIL CHANGE	$60.00
		$0.00

FIGURE 11.5 The Results of a Query

A **report** displays data from a table or a query in a format that is easy to read and print. In Figure 11.6, the professional-looking *Vehicle Details* report shows data from both the *Expenses* and *Vehicles* tables.

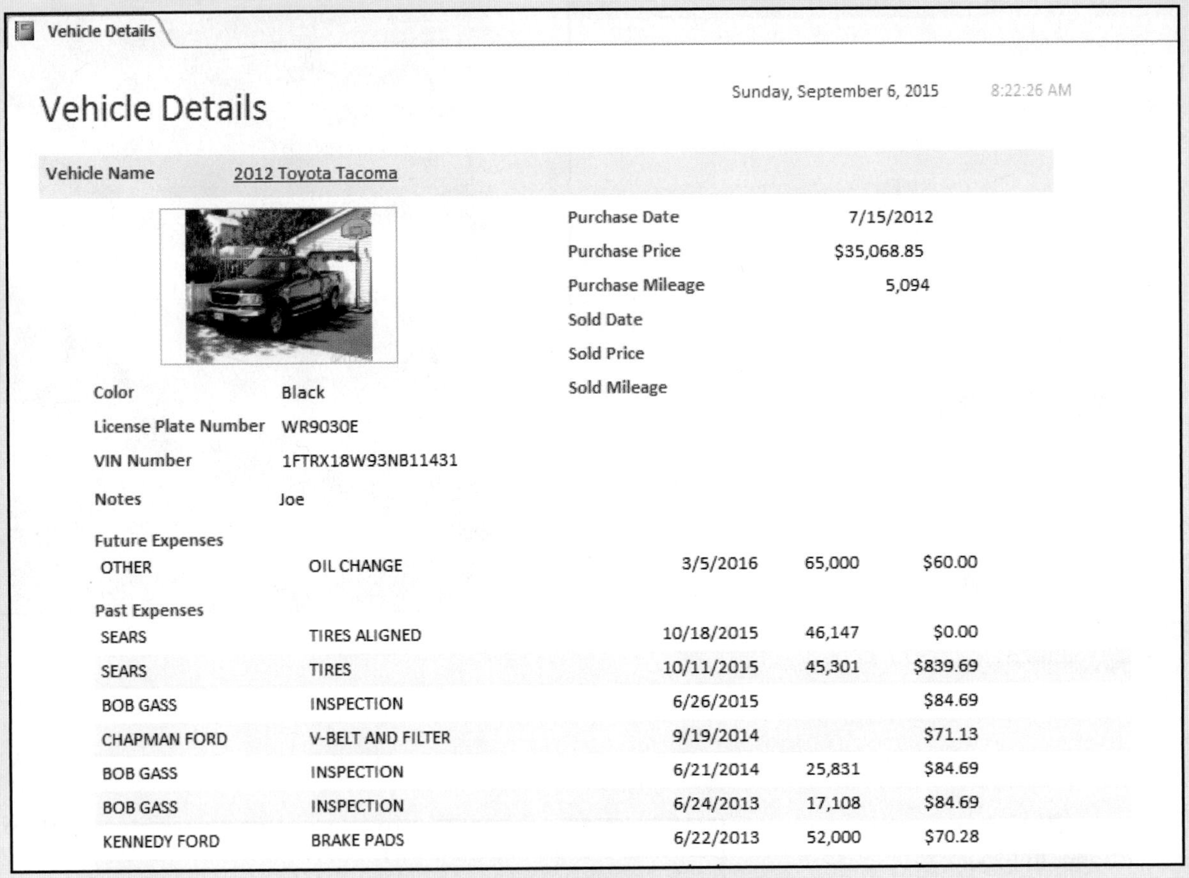

Vehicle Details

Vehicle Details

Sunday, September 6, 2015   8:22:26 AM

| Vehicle Name | 2012 Toyota Tacoma | | | |

		Purchase Date	7/15/2012
		Purchase Price	$35,068.85
		Purchase Mileage	5,094
		Sold Date	
		Sold Price	
Color	Black	Sold Mileage	
License Plate Number	WR9030E		
VIN Number	1FTRX18W93NB11431		
Notes	Joe		

Future Expenses

| OTHER | OIL CHANGE | 3/5/2016 | 65,000 | $60.00 |

Past Expenses

SEARS	TIRES ALIGNED	10/18/2015	46,147	$0.00
SEARS	TIRES	10/11/2015	45,301	$839.69
BOB GASS	INSPECTION	6/26/2015		$84.69
CHAPMAN FORD	V-BELT AND FILTER	9/19/2014		$71.13
BOB GASS	INSPECTION	6/21/2014	25,831	$84.69
BOB GASS	INSPECTION	6/24/2013	17,108	$84.69
KENNEDY FORD	BRAKE PADS	6/22/2013	52,000	$70.28

FIGURE 11.6 A Professional-Looking Report

Access 2016, Windows 10, Microsoft Corporation

GREEN COMPUTING

Green Datacenters

All the computing power required to maintain large databases uses a lot of energy and has a large impact on the environment. The energy costs for a business with large datacenters can be staggering. A **datacenter**—sometimes called a server farm—is a facility designed to house a company's servers and other equipment in a secure and controlled environment.

A green datacenter's mechanical, lighting, electrical, and computer systems are designed for maximum energy efficiency and minimum environmental impact. Green datacenters can

Billion Photos/Shutterstock

be certified by the U.S. Green Building Council (USGBC). Many companies look for datacenter locations with cheaper energy in order to lower power costs. In 2006, Google moved its datacenters

to rural Oregon, which has cheap, renewable hydroelectric energy, and according to Google, each of its datacenters uses about half the energy required in a typical datacenter. Locations near wind farms, hydroelectric plants, and geothermal plants are good places to build new datacenters. Building green also involves other steps, such as low-emission building materials, sustainable landscaping, recycling, and the use of alternative energy technologies, such as heat pumps and evaporative cooling.

- Redesign cooling system. Channel heat away from servers, seal leaks, and use high-efficiency cooling units.
- Scale back equipment. Use smaller and more energy-efficient systems.
- Consolidate and virtualize. Move equipment to one central location, and consolidate equipment to fewer, more efficient machines.
- Use Energy Star–rated appliances, computers, and servers.

Running Project

Design a table for a simple database that you might use to organize your video or music collection. Include at least five fields. Use a Word table or Excel worksheet for your design, and complete at least two records.

4 Things You Need to Know

- A database is a collection of related information.
- A table is a database object in which data is stored. It's arranged in rows (records) and columns (fields).
- The primary key uniquely identifies a record in a table.
- Use forms, reports, and queries to interact with table data.

Key Terms

database	query
datacenter	record
field	report
form	table
primary key	

Rawpixel/Shutterstock

A Database for Every Purpose

Compare the Four Types of Databases

Databases can be very simple or very complex. Different database models store and access data differently. The appropriate model to use depends on the type of data stored in the database and the way in which the data will be used and accessed.

VIZ
CLIP

Relationships

Flat Databases

The simplest form of database is a **flat database**, which consists of a single list of items. It can be a list or table in a document or a spreadsheet. Any time you make a to-do list, a mailing list, or a shopping list, you create a simple flat database. Figure 11.7 shows a flat database created in Excel. Although it's common to use Excel to create simple databases, for more complex data and relationships, it's necessary to use a database management system such as Access.

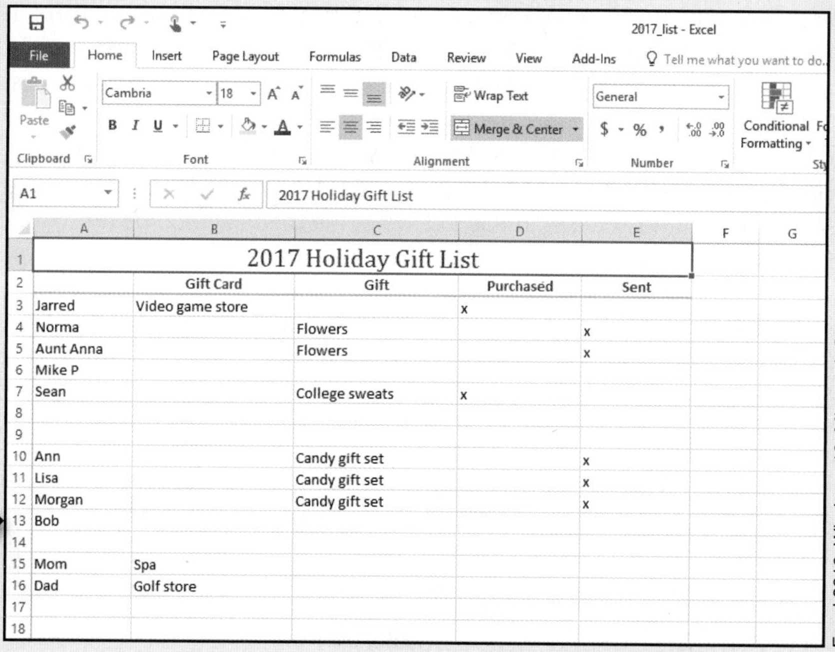

FIGURE 11.7 An Excel spreadsheet can be used to create a simple database.

Relational Databases

The majority of databases today are relational databases. A **relational database** consists of multiple tables that are related by common information. A large database might contain thousands of tables. This type of database reduces data redundancy. In Figure 11.8, the two tables are related by the fields describing the vehicle. The *Vehicles* table includes information such as color, purchase date, and price. The *Expenses* table includes vehicle service information such as service description, date, and mileage. Each vehicle record may link to multiple service records, but each service record is linked to only one vehicle record. When a single record in a table links to multiple records in another table, it's known as a **one-to-many relationship**—the most common type of relationship in a relational database.

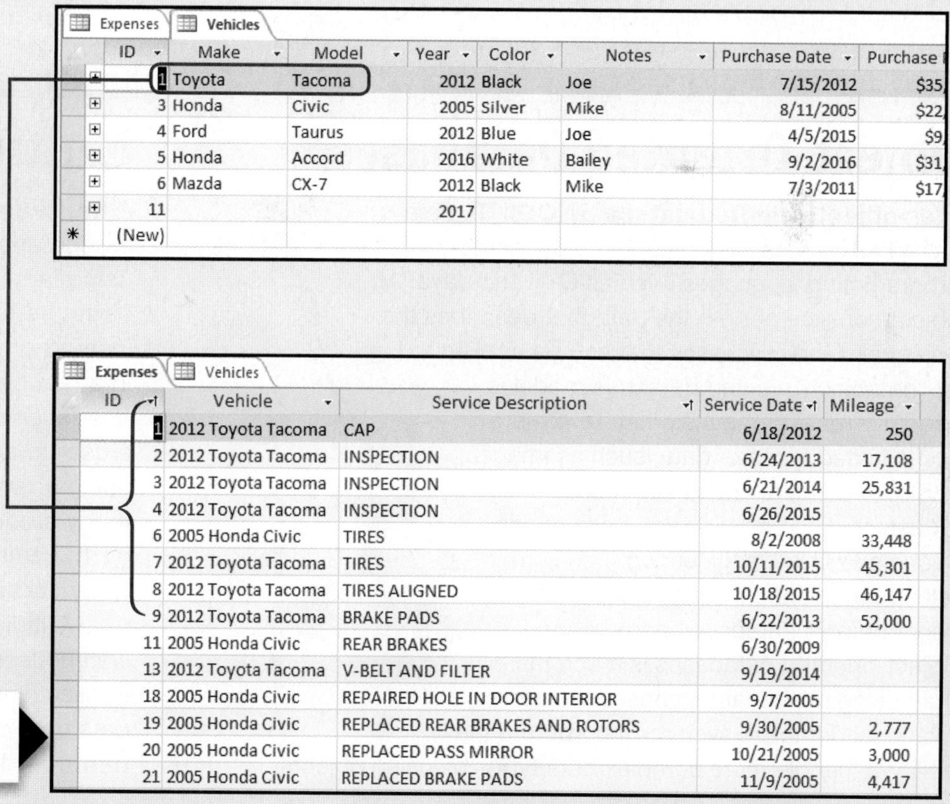

FIGURE 11.8 A one-to-many relationship exists between these two tables.

A less common type of relationship is a **one-to-one relationship**. In a one-to-one relationship, a record in one table is linked to a single record in another table. The two tables are linked by the same primary key. For example, a school might keep student medical records in one table and student academic records in another and then use the student ID number as the primary key in both (Figure 11.9). This is common when the data in a table requires restricted access. In this example, the medical records are confidential and restricted to the student health center.

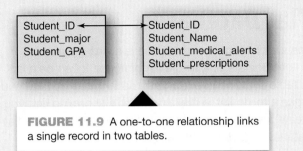

FIGURE 11.9 A one-to-one relationship links a single record in two tables.

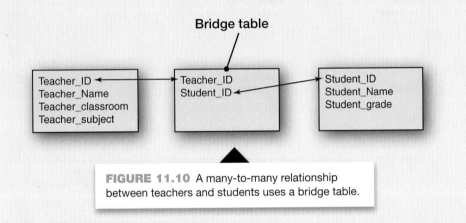

Bridge table

FIGURE 11.10 A many-to-many relationship between teachers and students uses a bridge table.

In a **many-to-many relationship**, multiple records from a table can link to multiple records in another table. In a library catalog, each author may have written multiple books, and each book can have multiple authors, creating a many-to-many relationship between an author table and a book table. In a school, each teacher has multiple students, and each student can have multiple teachers (Figure 11.10). The table between the teachers and students is called a **bridge table**, and it breaks up the many-to-many relationship into two one-to-many relationships.

Object-Oriented Databases

In an **object-oriented database (OODB)**, data is stored as objects, which are used by modern programming languages such as C++ and Java. An object consists of both the data that describes the object and the processes that can be applied to it. The object-oriented database model is used to create databases that have more complicated types of data, such as images, audio, and video, and is common in industries with complex database needs, such as science, engineering, telecommunications, and finance. For very complex database needs, using object-oriented databases is much faster than using relational databases. Some relational database systems incorporate the ability to handle more complex data types by using objects.

Africa Studio/Shutterstock

Multidimensional Databases

A **multidimensional database (MDB)** is optimized for storing and utilizing data. Such databases may be created using input from existing relational databases, but they structure the information into multidimensional data cubes instead of two-dimensional tables. The data can be accessed in a number of different ways, depending on the user's needs. One important feature of MDBs is the ability to allow a user to ask for information in question form rather than using a more complex query language. For example, "How many students visited the student health center on the north campus during the winter semester over the past four years?"

Multidimensional databases are ideal for use with data warehouses and **online analytical processing (OLAP)** applications, which enable a user to selectively extract and view data from different points of view. OLAP can be used for **data mining**—discovering relationships between data items.

A **data warehouse** is a central repository for all the data that an enterprise uses, including internal databases and external sources such as vendors and customers (Figure 11.11). The data is organized for use with queries, analysis, and reporting.

The best type of database to use depends on the type of data to be entered, the type of processing that's needed, and the expertise of the users and administrators. The relational database model is by far the most popular for most business applications. The object-oriented model has its niche in science and telecommunications, although it's also used in other industries, and the multidimensional model is used where query performance is critical. Many enterprises use a combination of these models to meet their needs.

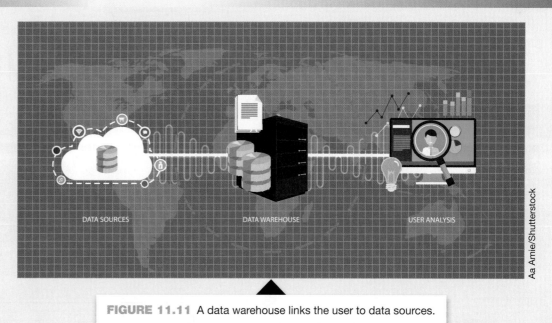

DATA SOURCES   DATA WAREHOUSE   USER ANALYSIS

Aa Amie/Shutterstock

FIGURE 11.11 A data warehouse links the user to data sources.

Running Project

Give an example of each of the four types of databases described in this article. Which of these have you used recently? Explain.

4 Things You Need to Know

- A flat database consists of a single list of items.
- A relational database consists of multiple tables related by common information.
- In an object-oriented database (OODB), data is stored as objects.
- A multidimensional database (MDB) structures the information into multidimensional data cubes.

Key Terms

bridge table

data mining

data warehouse

flat database

many-to-many relationship

multidimensional database (MDB)

object-oriented database (OODB)

one-to-many relationship

one-to-one relationship

online analytical processing (OLAP)

relational database

Create a Form Using Google Drive

Digital Literacy Skill

HOW TO VIDEO

Google Drive includes an easy way to create a form, distribute it, and then collect the results. In this activity, you'll create a form you can use to plan a study group with your classmates. You will need a Google account to complete this exercise.

1 Open your browser and go to **google.com**. If necessary, sign in to your Google account. From the Apps menu at the top of the screen, click *Drive*.

Google and the Google logo are registered trademarks of Google Inc., used with permission.

2 On your Google Drive page, click *New*; if necessary, click *More*, and then click *Google Forms*. At the top of the screen, on the toolbar, click the *Color Palette* icon, and then click the last icon to open the *Select Theme* dialog box. With Work and School selected, select the theme that includes a notepad and coffee cup. If this theme is not available, choose another appropriate theme.

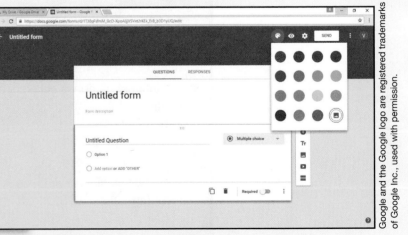

Google and the Google logo are registered trademarks of Google Inc., used with permission.

3 At the top of the screen, click *Untitled form* and rename the document **Study Group**. Click *Untitled form* in the form box to apply the title. Create the form using the following data:

Title	Study Group
Form Description	**Study group survey for CISC101**
Question Title	**Name and contact information**
Question Type	Paragraph

4 Click the *Required* slider and click the (+) to add a question.

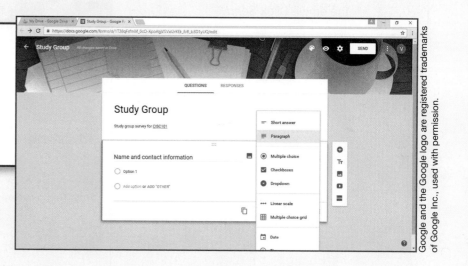

Google and the Google logo are registered trademarks of Google Inc., used with permission.

5 Enter the following question:

Question Title	Availability
Question Type	**Checkboxes**
Option 1	**Before class**
Option 2	**After class**

6 Select *Required* and at the top of the screen, click *Send*. Email the form to yourself and at least two classmates. Use the Subject **Study group survey** and type the message **Please complete by Friday.** Be sure to include the form in the email. Click *Send*.

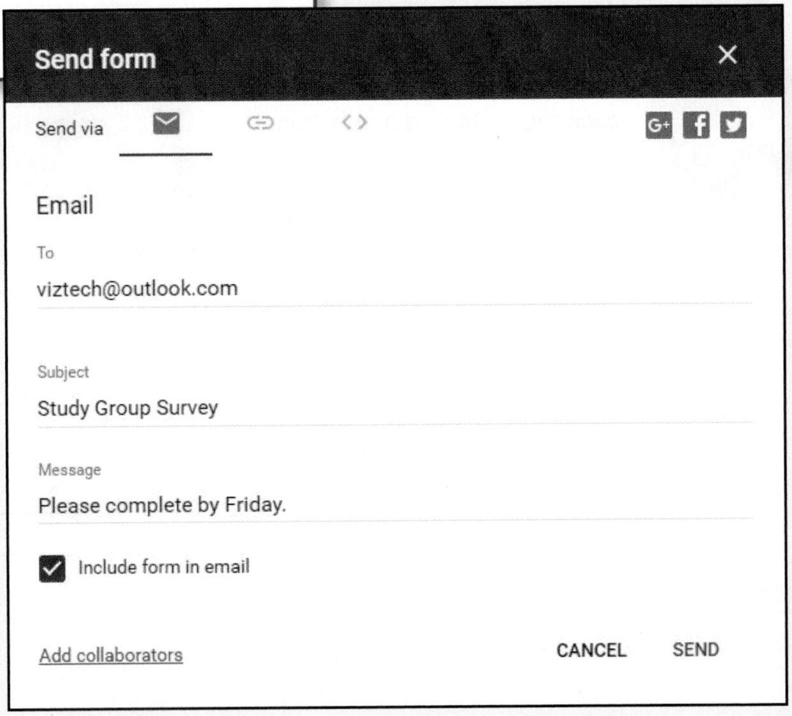

Send form ✕

Send via ✉ 🔗 < > G+ f 🐦

Email

To
viztech@outlook.com

Subject
Study Group Survey

Message
Please complete by Friday.

☑ Include form in email

Add collaborators   CANCEL   SEND

Google and the Google logo are registered trademarks of Google Inc., used with permission.

7 Open the email message you sent to yourself and click the link to *Fill Out in Google Forms*. Fill out and submit the form. Ask your classmates to do the same.

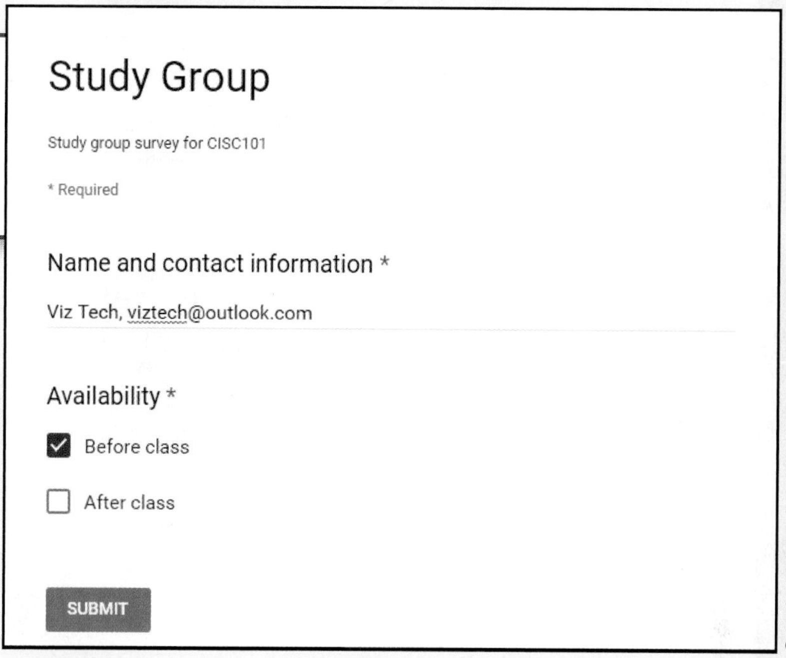

Study Group

Study group survey for CISC101

* Required

Name and contact information *

Viz Tech, viztech@outlook.com

Availability *

☑ Before class

☐ After class

SUBMIT

8 Return to the form, and then click the *Responses* tab. On the right, click the green *Create Spreadsheet* icon. Click *Study Group (Responses)* and replace the text with **lastname_firstname_ch11_howto1**. Click *CREATE*. Click *File*, point to *Download as*, and then click *Microsoft Excel (.xlsx)*. Locate the downloaded file and submit it as directed by your instructor.

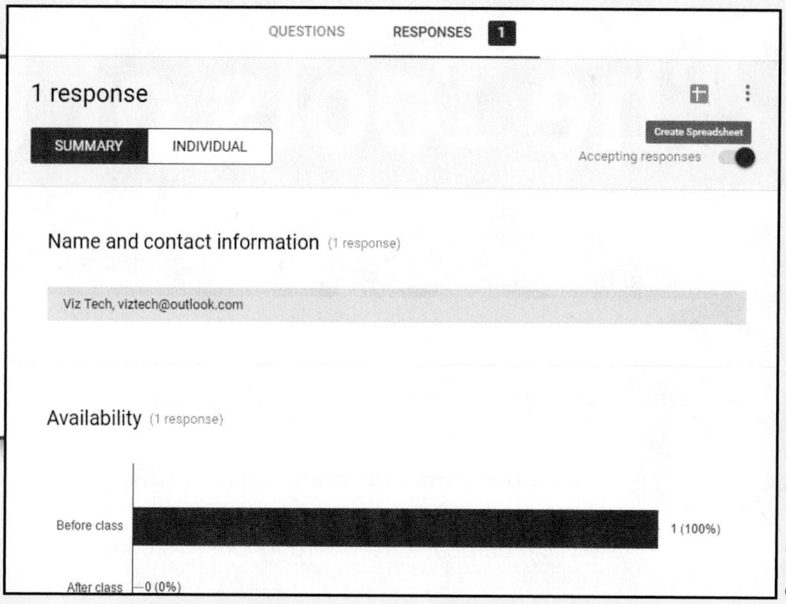

QUESTIONS   RESPONSES   **1**

1 response

SUMMARY   INDIVIDUAL

Create Spreadsheet

Accepting responses

Name and contact information (1 response)

Viz Tech, viztech@outlook.com

Availability (1 response)

Before class ████████████████████ 1 (100%)

After class — 0 (0%)

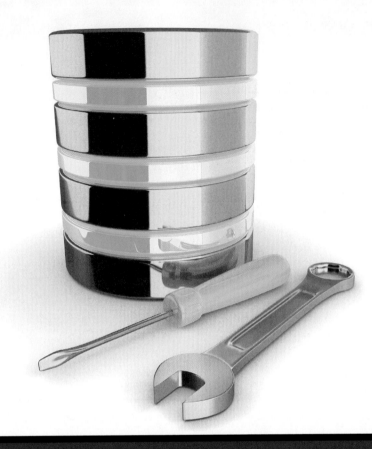

The Tools of the Trade

ctive

3 Explain Database Management Systems

A **database management system (DBMS)** is software used to create and manage data in a database. Microsoft Access, which is an example of a DBMS, was used to create the *Vehicle* database used throughout this chapter.

Creating a Database

A database management system such as Microsoft Access, Filemaker Pro, Oracle Database, or MySQL (Figure 11.12) is needed to create a database. The DBMS is used to create tables, reports, forms, and queries.

Planning is an essential first step to designing a database that can be used effectively. The design of a database starts with the data dictionary. The **data dictionary** defines all the fields and the type of data each field will contain. A field should be created for each independent piece of information. For example, first name and last name should be separate fields. This makes it easier to sort and filter the data. The **data type** defines the kind of data that you can enter in a field, including text, numbers, dates, images, and hyperlinks (Figure 11.13).

A major goal of good database design is to reduce data redundancy—that is, information duplicated in multiple places. This process is known as **data normalization**. Normalization reduces the size of a database, makes it easier to keep records up to date, and increases query speed.

FIGURE 11.12 MySQL is a popular open-source DBMS.

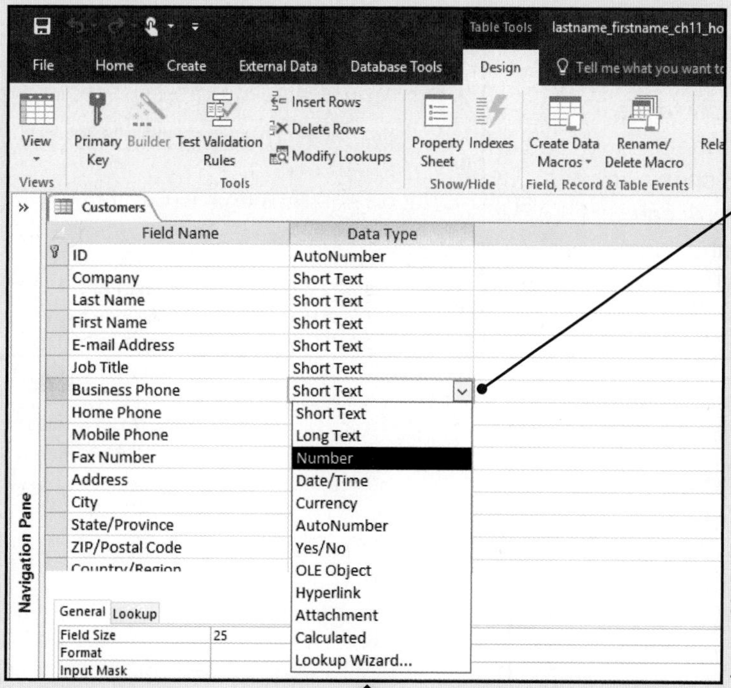

Set appropriate data type for each field

FIGURE 11.13 Set the data type for each field in a database.

Data Validation

Data validation reduces data-entry errors by using validation rules, such as data type, data length, acceptable values, and required fields. Specifying the data type, such as text, number, or currency, prevents a user from entering the wrong type of information into a field. You can create a lookup list that populates a drop-down list of items, such as state, year, or vehicle model, to choose from. In Figure 11.14, the data type for the *Service Date* field is Date/Time, and the data validation rule prevents the entry of dates before 1/1/1900. Figure 11.15 shows an error displayed when validation fails.

Once a table has been designed and the data dictionary created, data is entered into the tables. Data can be imported from other places, such as a Word table, an Excel spreadsheet, or another database. This is useful if the data is already in an electronic format. For example, I can import a file that contains the student roster I downloaded from my school website.

Manually entering data can be a tedious and error-prone activity. In addition to using data validation rules, an input form can be used to make it easier to enter data. The validation rules apply to the data entered into the form, further reducing the potential for data-entry errors. Figure 11.16 shows an input form for entering expense details. A form can contain drop-down lists and date pickers, and it can have some default information already filled in.

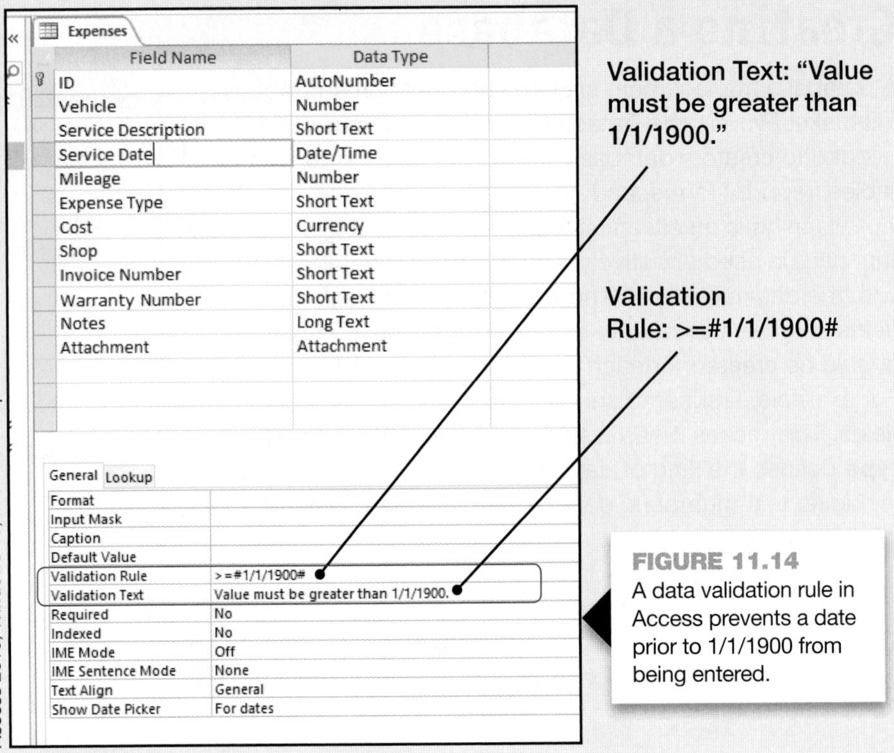

Validation Text: "Value must be greater than 1/1/1900."

Validation Rule: >=#1/1/1900#

FIGURE 11.14 A data validation rule in Access prevents a date prior to 1/1/1900 from being entered.

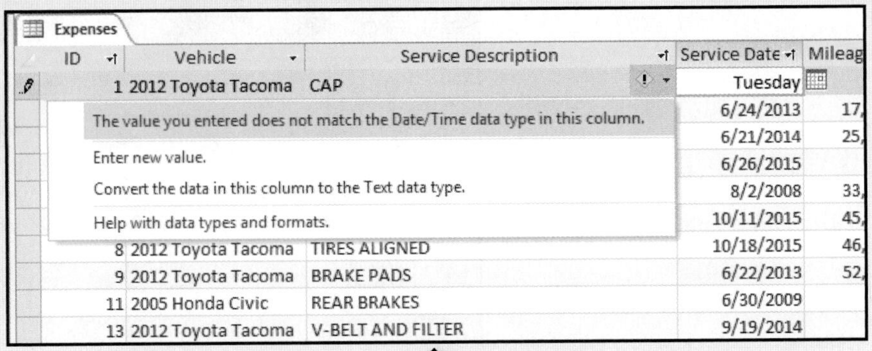

FIGURE 11.15 Data validation fails when the user enters invalid data.

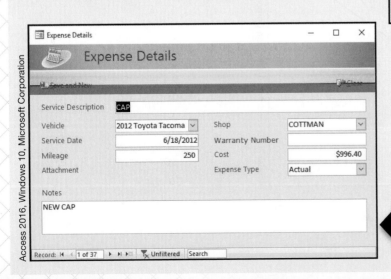

FIGURE 11.16 An input form simplifies data entry and reduces errors.

Access 2016, Windows 10, Microsoft Corporation

SQL

Once the data has been entered into a database, the DBMS helps to turn the data into useful information. To ask a question, a query is designed using a **query language**. Most DBMSs today—including MySQL, SQL Server, Access, and Oracle—use **Structured Query Language (SQL)**. In Access, you can use the Query Wizard or Design View to help form a query, and Access creates the SQL for you. In the example shown in Figure 11.17, the question asked is, "What are the expenses for vehicle 1?" In Design view, the tables, fields, and criteria for the query are chosen. Queries can draw from one or more tables within the database. In SQL view, you can see the SQL code created by Access. The results of a query are displayed in a new datasheet.

SQL statements use **relational keywords**, such as SELECT, FROM, WHERE, and AND, to manipulate, query, and update data in relational databases. It isn't necessary for ordinary users to be able to write complex SQL statements, but it's helpful to be able to understand them. In a large organization, a database programmer would be responsible for writing most SQL statements to create customized queries and reports.

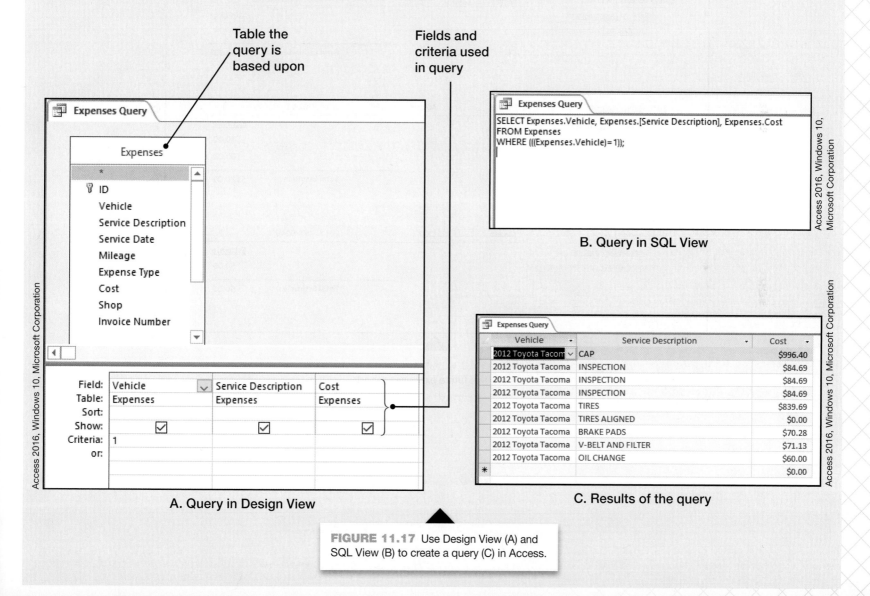

FIGURE 11.17 Use Design View (A) and SQL View (B) to create a query (C) in Access.

Output

A DBMS is also used to create reports that take information from tables or queries and organize it in a way that's easy to read and print. Reports can be designed to summarize information, and they can be distributed to others without those users having access to the database. Reports are often used to help in decision making. The report in Figure 11.18 includes information from both the *Vehicles* and *Expenses* tables.

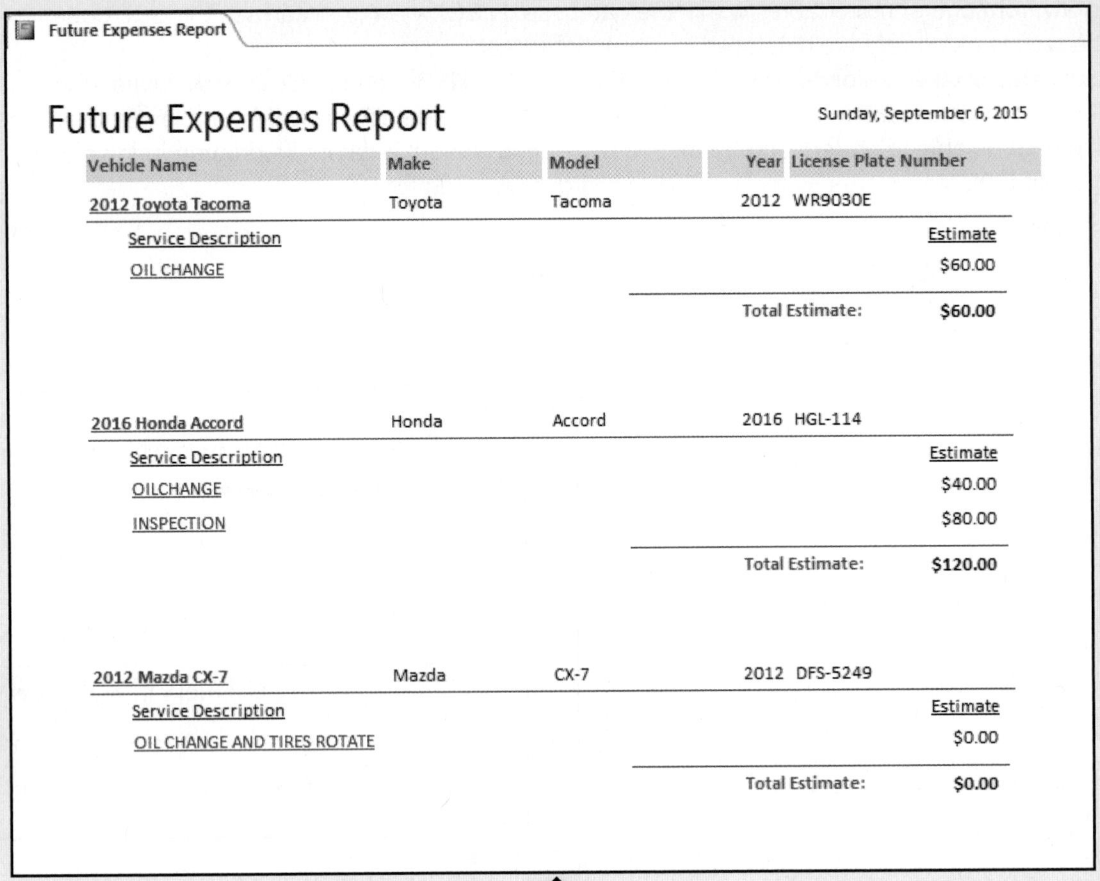

Future Expenses Report

Future Expenses Report

Sunday, September 6, 2015

Vehicle Name	Make	Model	Year	License Plate Number
2012 Toyota Tacoma	Toyota	Tacoma	2012	WR9030E

Service Description	Estimate
OIL CHANGE	$60.00
Total Estimate:	$60.00

Vehicle Name	Make	Model	Year	License Plate Number
2016 Honda Accord	Honda	Accord	2016	HGL-114

Service Description	Estimate
OILCHANGE	$40.00
INSPECTION	$80.00
Total Estimate:	$120.00

Vehicle Name	Make	Model	Year	License Plate Number
2012 Mazda CX-7	Mazda	CX-7	2012	DFS-5249

Service Description	Estimate
OIL CHANGE AND TIRES ROTATE	$0.00
Total Estimate:	$0.00

FIGURE 11.18 A DBMS is used to create reports like this future expenses report.

CAREER SPOTLIGHT

JOBS

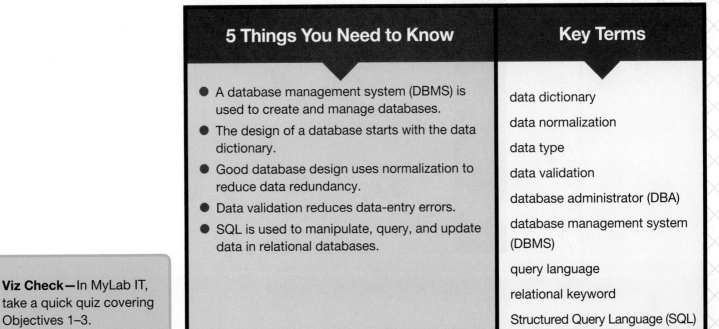

SQL

DATABASE ADMINISTRATOR   Databases are used in virtually every industry. As a result, there's a great need for people with expertise in designing, maintaining, and using them. According to the *Occupational Outlook Handbook*, jobs in this field are expected to grow much faster than the average for all occupations.

A **database administrator (DBA)** is a person who manages database systems. A DBA sets up databases, manages the installation and ongoing functions of the database system, upgrades database software, monitors performance, and performs maintenance, backup, and recovery of databases. A DBA may also create user accounts, manage database security, and provide login administration. A DBA generally requires at least a bachelor's degree. Industry certifications are also desirable.

Running Project

Many libraries use specialized database management systems. Visit your school or local library and find out what DBMS is used for the circulation desk. Do the librarians have special database training?

5 Things You Need to Know	Key Terms
• A database management system (DBMS) is used to create and manage databases. • The design of a database starts with the data dictionary. • Good database design uses normalization to reduce data redundancy. • Data validation reduces data-entry errors. • SQL is used to manipulate, query, and update data in relational databases.	data dictionary data normalization data type data validation database administrator (DBA) database management system (DBMS) query language relational keyword Structured Query Language (SQL)

✓ Viz Check—In MyLab IT, take a quick quiz covering Objectives 1–3.

How To?

Essential Job Skill

Create a Customer Database

HOW TO VIDEO

In this activity, you will use the desktop DBMS program Microsoft Access to create a customer database from a template. Note:

there is not a Mac version of Microsoft Access, this activity must be done on a Windows computer.

1 Open Access and type **customer database** in the *Search for online templates* box and press Enter.

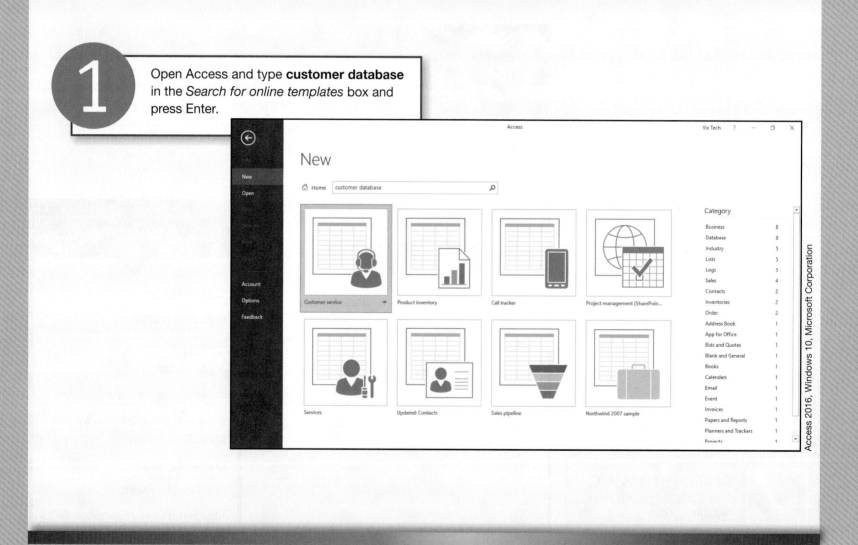

Access 2016, Windows 10, Microsoft Corporation

2

Click the *Customer service* template. In the *File Name* box, click the small yellow folder icon and browse to the location of your work for this chapter; name the file **lastname_firstname_ch11_howto2**, click *OK*, and then click *Create*. (If this template is unavailable, use the *vt_ch11_howto2* file provided in your student data files.) If necessary, click *Enable Content* on the yellow Security Warning bar. Expand the Navigation pane by clicking the *shutter bar*. Close the *Case List*.

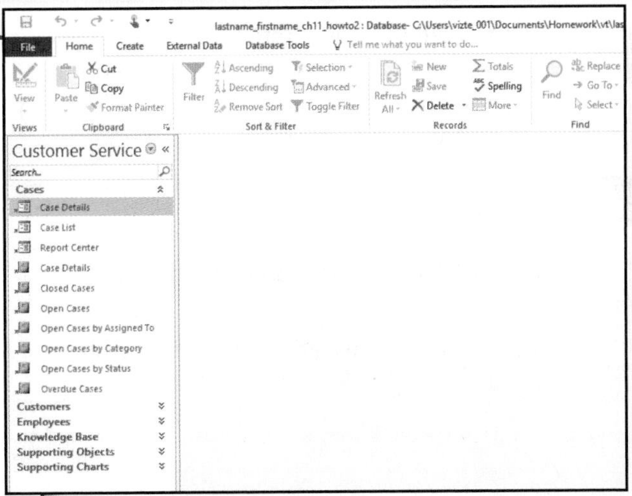

Access 2016, Windows 10, Microsoft Corporation

3

In the Navigation pane, expand the *Customers* section, and then double-click *Customer List*. Enter the following two customer records. If necessary, double-click the border between the Email Address and Business Phone fields to widen the Email Address column.

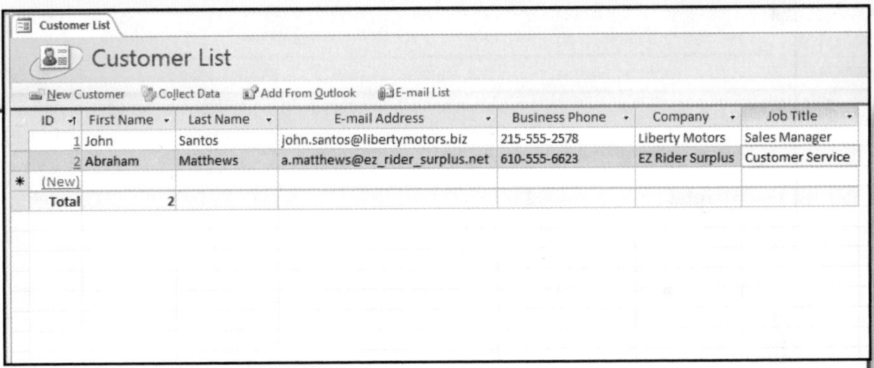

Access 2016, Windows 10, Microsoft Corporation

First Name	Last Name	Email Address	Business Phone	Company	Job Title
John	Santos	john.santos@libertymotors.biz	215-555-2578	Liberty Motors	Sales Manager
Abraham	Matthews	a.matthews@ez_rider_surplus.net	610-555-6623	EZ Rider Surplus	Customer Service

4 Close the Customer List. In the Navigation pane, expand Employees and open the Employee List table. Enter the following two employee records:

First Name	Last Name	Email Address	Business Phone	Company	Job Title
Cara	Johnson	cara.johnson@house_of_cars.biz	267-555-2321	House of Cars	Customer Care Manager
Angel	Ortiz	angel.ortiz@house_of_cars.biz	800-555-2275	House of Cars	Customer Care Associate

Sort & Filter	Records	Find	Text Formatting

Employee List

👥 Employee List

📧 New Employee   🔗 Collect Data   📇 Add From Outlook   📎 E-mail List

ID ▾	First Name ▾	Last Name ▾	E-mail Address ▾	Business Phone ▾	Company ▾	Job Title ▾
1	Cara	Johnson	cara.johnson@house_of_cars.b	267-555-2321	House of Cars	Customer Care Mar
2	Angel	Ortiz	angei.ortiz@house_of_cars.biz	800-555-2275	House of Cars	Customer Care Ass
* (New)						
Total	2					

Access 2016, Windows 10, Microsoft Corporation

5

Close the Employees List. In the Navigation pane, under *Cases*, double-click the first item, *Case Details*, to open the Case Details form. Enter the following information for fields in the top part of the form:

Title	**Barkley**
Assigned to	**Angel Ortiz**
Customer	**John Santos**
Opened By	**Cara Johnson**
Opened Date	Today's date
Due Date	Two months from opened date
Priority	**(3) Low**
Category	**(1) Category**
KB	Leave blank
Status	**Active**
Resolved Date	Leave blank

Access 2016, Windows 10, Microsoft Corporation

6 Click the *Category* arrow, and below the list, click the *Edit List Items* icon that displays. In the *Edit List Items* dialog box, select the text and then type the following items, pressing Enter after each:

Luxury Rental
Business Rental
Vacation Rental
Other

Case Details — □ ×

Case Details

🔲 Save and New   📧 E-mail   🖨 Print   📇 Close

| Title | Barkley | ID | 1 |

Assigned To   Angel Ortiz   (3) Low

Customer   John Santos   (1) Category

Opened By   Cara Johnson

Opened Date   Active

Due Date

Edit List Items   ?   ×

Type each item on a separate line:

Luxury Rental
Business Rental
Vacation Rental
Other

📎(0)

Case Information | Related Cases | Calls

New Comment

Default Value: Luxury Rental ▾

[OK]   [Cancel]

History

Record: ◄ ◄ 1 of 1 ► ►I ►❚ 🔾 No Filter   Search

Access 2016, Windows 10, Microsoft Corporation

7 Click *OK*. Change the category to *Luxury Rental*. In the bottom section of the form, in the Description box, type: **Needs a 6-8 passenger luxury vehicle and driver for charity event.**

8 Click the *Calls* tab. The Call Time field displays the current date and time. Click the *Caller* field and enter your name. In the Notes field, type **City Hospital Charity Ball** and then press Tab. Close the form. If necessary, save the change to the form design.

9 In the Navigation pane, double-click the fourth item, the *Case Details* report. Notice the case information you entered into the form is displayed in this report.

10 Click the *File* tab, click *Print*, and then click *Print Preview*. On the Print Preview tab, in the Data group, click *PDF or XPS*. If necessary, change the *Save as* type to PDF, name the file **lastname_firstname_ ch11_ report** and navigate to the location where you save your work for this class, and then click *Publish*. If necessary, close the PDF file. Close the Export – PDF window, and then on the Print Preview tab, in the Close Preview group, click *Close Print Preview*. Close Access. Unlike other applications, Access saves your database as you make changes, so you don't need to save the file before you close it. Submit the PDF file and the database file as directed by your instructor.

Access 2016, Windows 10, Microsoft Corporation

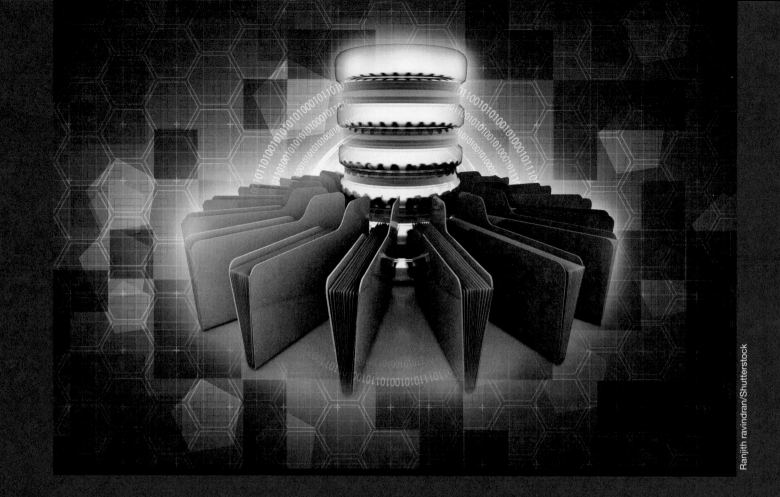

Data in ...
Information out

Objective

4 Discuss Important Types of Information Systems

An **information system** is the people, hardware, and software that support data-intensive applications, such as financial accounts, human resources, and other business transactions. Information systems include databases with special functions. In this article, we'll look at some of the most common information systems.

VIZ CLIP

Data Mining

Office Support Systems

Office support systems (OSS)—sometimes called office automation systems—include software and hardware that improve the productivity of employees by automating common tasks such as the exchange of information; management of documents, spreadsheets, and databases; collaboration; meeting; planning; and management of schedules. An OSS requires a network for electronic communication and storage. One example is an office suite, such as Microsoft Office. Systems that allow employees to work remotely are considered office support systems.

Transaction Processing

Businesses rely on **transaction-processing systems (TPSs)** to respond to user requests. Usually, a transaction involves the exchange of goods, services, or money. A single transaction may consist of multiple dependent operations. Transaction processing links multiple operations together and ensures that all operations in a transaction are completed without error.

Transaction-processing systems must pass tests for atomicity, consistency, isolation, and durability (the ACID test):

- **Atomicity:** A transaction is atomic—it will either happen or not. If one account is debited, then another account has to be credited. A TPS ensures that transactions are fully completed or aren't undertaken at all.
- **Consistency:** A TPS must always be consistent with its own operating rules (or integrity constraints). If errors occur in a transaction on either side, then the transaction will fail.
- **Isolation:** Each transaction must occur in isolation and must be independent.
- **Durability:** Transactions must be durable. Once transactions are completed, they can't be undone. This means, for example, that once an airline ticket is booked, it's permanently recorded.

An example of transaction processing is paying your tuition bill from your bank account. The process of paying a bill from your account consists of two operations: debiting your account and crediting your school's account. The TPS links these two separate operations in the transaction. The success of the transaction depends on both of the operations being successful. If the debit from your account is successful but the credit doesn't go through to the college's account, then the transaction fails. Your money would be lost somewhere in the transaction, so the TPS would roll back your debit, essentially undoing the operation (Figure 11.19).

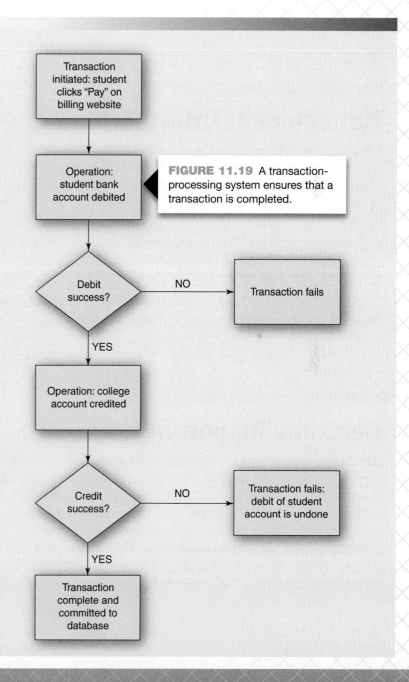

FIGURE 11.19 A transaction-processing system ensures that a transaction is completed.

Blockchain

Blockchain is a decentralized electronic database of digital currency transactions, first developed for bitcoin. The system is spread across a peer-to-peer network, making it extremely secure. The transactions are stored chronologically in blocks, which creates an accurate, indisputable transaction history. Future applications of blockchain are being developed in finance, healthcare, and other industries.

Elnur/Shutterstock

Management Information Systems

A **management information system (MIS)** includes software, hardware, data resources (such as databases), decision support systems, people, and project management applications. An MIS provides information on daily operations; takes data from the transaction-processing systems, other internal databases, and external sources; and puts the data into reports and simulations used by managers to organize, evaluate, and efficiently run their departments.

An MIS has two important functions:

- Generate reports—such as financial statements, inventory reports, and performance reports—needed for routine or non-routine purposes, putting unmanageable volumes of data into a form that can be used by decision makers.
- Create simulations of hypothetical scenarios that answer "what if" questions regarding alterations in business strategy.

MIS systems are typically used by midlevel managers. An MIS used by a marketing department might be used for product development, distribution, pricing, and sales forecasting. A human resources MIS might be used for hiring and recruiting decisions.

Decision Support Systems

Decision support systems (DSSs) are designed to help make decisions in situations where there is uncertainty about the possible outcomes of those decisions. For example, a local cookie bakery wants to begin selling its products nationally. Before making an investment in a website and online ordering system, the business manager needs to be sure that it's practical. The bakery business manager can use a DSS to gather information from internal sources (such as sales figures, account balances, and employees) to determine if the bakery has the ability to expand its business, as well as from external sources (such as industry data) to determine if there's a national market for cookies. The DSS organizes the data to help the manager analyze it and make the decision.

Business Intelligence and Big Data

Business intelligence (BI) tools are applications that are used to analyze data in information systems to help make decisions. BI applications include data mining, data warehousing, OLAP, and decision support systems. On a small scale, Excel spreadsheets and Access reports can be used for BI.

Big data is a term that means the collection of large amounts of data from multiple sources—both internal and external—that's used for ongoing analysis and decision making (Figure 11.20). It's big because there is so much data now available to collect and analyze, and it changes rapidly. Big data is too large to use desktop DMBSs effectively. Another characteristic of big data is that a lot of it is unstructured data such as social media posts, video, and images, which isn't already in a nice, neat database format. Posts on Twitter have been analyzed to predict election outcomes and flu outbreaks. **Clickstream data mining**, analyzing the links customers click as they visit a website, can help a company predict sales.

STATISTICS
DEMOGRAPHICS
CONSUMER HABITS TRENDS
STRATEGIC PLANNING
DEVELOPMENT
BIG DATA

Cyber Kristiyan/shutterstock

FIGURE 11.20 Big Data

Expert Systems and Artificial Intelligence

The branch of science concerned with making computers behave like humans is **artificial intelligence (AI)**. One important part of AI is the **expert system**—a computer programmed to make decisions in real-life situations (for example, diagnosing diseases based on symptoms).

An expert system simulates the judgment and behavior of a human expert and consists of two parts:

- **Knowledge base**—Contains expert knowledge and accumulated experience in a particular field.
- **Inference engine**—A set of rules for applying the knowledge base to each particular situation.

One of the most well-known examples of an expert system is IBM's chess program Deep Blue. In 1997, Deep Blue won a six-game match against Garry Kasparov, the reigning world champion (Figure 11.21). Deep Blue won because it was able to run through every calculation—derived from the rules of chess plus the expert's knowledge base—for every possible move.

In 2011, IBM's Watson computer (Figure 11.22) (**ibmwatson.com**) beat two reigning *Jeopardy!* champions. Watson is named for Thomas J. Watson, the founder of IBM. It is a **cognitive computing system** that was developed to play *Jeopardy!* A cognitive computing system gets better over time—it learns from its interactions. A cognitive system is designed to interact naturally with humans, using normal language. Unlike an expert system, a cognitive system does not have all the information in a knowledge base but rather can analyze outside data, both structured and unstructured. The system creates a hypothesis based on its analysis and functions as a decision support system. Today, Watson projects include healthcare, finance, research, and business applications.

In healthcare, the amount of information published every year is too vast for any physician to read it all. Watson can analyze information from numerous sources—journals, online publications, patient records, test results, and research and clinical trials from around the world—to help the physician make treatment decisions.

ADAM NADEL/AP Images

FIGURE 11.21 Deep Blue was an expert system designed to play chess.

Carolyn Cole/ Los Angeles Times/Getty Images

FIGURE 11.22 IBM Watson

Autonomous cars are a current and growing application of AI. To be fully autonomous the vehicle must not rely on human intervention at all. Self-driving vehicles have been developed by companies such as Google, Uber, and Tesla. Many car manufacturers have implemented a limited self-driving feature that allows cars to park themselves, but driving on crowded streets with other moving vehicles is much more of a challenge. Self-driving vehicles will cause major changes and disruption to industries that rely on the transportation of both people and goods.

Supparsorn/Shutterstock

Running Project

Research the current state of autonomous cars. What breakthroughs have occurred in the past five years? What manufacturers and models offer limited or full self-driving features?

5 Things You Need to Know

- Information systems consist of people, hardware, and software.
- Transaction processing links together multiple operations and ensures that all operations in a transaction are completed without error.
- An MIS generates reports and simulations used by managers.
- A decision support system is designed to help make decisions in situations where there's uncertainty about the possible outcomes.
- An expert system is programmed to make decisions in real-life situations.

Key Terms

artificial intelligence (AI)

autonomous car

big data

blockchain

business intelligence (BI) tool

clickstream data mining

cognitive computing system

decision support system (DSS)

expert system

inference engine

information system

knowledge base

management information system (MIS)

office support system (OSS)

transaction-processing system (TPS)

Nmedia/Fotolia

Real-World Databases

List Examples of Databases Used in Law Enforcement and Research

While a database to track your vehicle expenses or keep a home inventory is useful, many industries rely on databases for far more critical information. In this article, we discuss some of the exciting ways that databases are used in law enforcement and science.

Law Enforcement

You can hardly turn on the TV without hearing how DNA or fingerprints helped to solve a crime. It's on the news and in the plotline of every police drama. Law enforcement officers have technology on their side with two very powerful databases, CODIS and NGI, which are growing in size and helping in more cases every day.

INTEGRATED AUTOMATED FINGERPRINT IDENTIFICATION SYSTEM (IAFIS) AND NEXT GENERATION IDENTIFICATION (NGI)

The **IAFIS (Integrated Automated Fingerprint Identification System)** is a national fingerprint and criminal history system maintained by the FBI and used by local, state, and federal law enforcement. Launched in 1999, IAFIS is the largest biometric database in the world. It consists of a criminal database that includes the fingerprints of criminal subjects and a civil database of subjects who have served in the armed forces or work in the federal government, law enforcement, finance, and other sensitive industries. The records include not only fingerprints but also mug shots, criminal histories, and physical characteristics such as tattoos. As of September 2014, IAFIS has been replaced with the **Next Generation Identification (NGI)**, which improves upon, and adds new technologies to, the IAFIS system.

NGI is an automated system. It takes only minutes to search the massive database for potential matches. In the past, the process was done by hand and could take months to complete. Today, fingerprints can be taken from a suspect at a crime scene or from a suspected terrorist in a country across the globe using a handheld scanner (Figure 11.23) and sent to NGI remotely; results are returned in minutes.

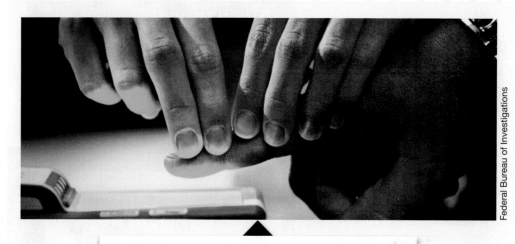

Federal Bureau of Investigations

FIGURE 11.23 A fingerprint technician takes a fingerprint using digital technology.

COMBINED DNA INDEX SYSTEM (CODIS)

The **CODIS (Combined DNA Index System)** searches across multiple local, state, and national DNA profile databases. It consists of three geographic levels: the National DNA Index System (NDIS) maintained by the FBI, the State DNA Index System (SDIS) maintained by individual states, and the Local DNA Index System (LDIS) (Figure 11.24) maintained by individual local authorities.

CODIS consists of five indices: Forensic, Arrestee, Detainee, Offender, and Missing Persons:

- The Forensic index contains DNA profiles obtained from crime scene evidence.
- The Arrestee, Detainee, and Offender indices contain DNA profiles of individuals arrested, detained, or convicted of various offenses, which vary by jurisdiction.
- The National Missing Person DNA Database (NMPDD) consists of several parts including Unidentified Human Remains, Missing Persons, and Biological Relatives of Missing Persons.

CODIS searches across these indices for potential matches. Matches found between the Offender and Forensic indices can identify a suspect. Matches found in the Forensic index can link crime scenes—and thus cases—to each other. According to the FBI, as of July 2016, CODIS contained more than 12 million offender profiles and more than 720,000 forensic profiles, and it had aided in nearly 325,000 investigations.

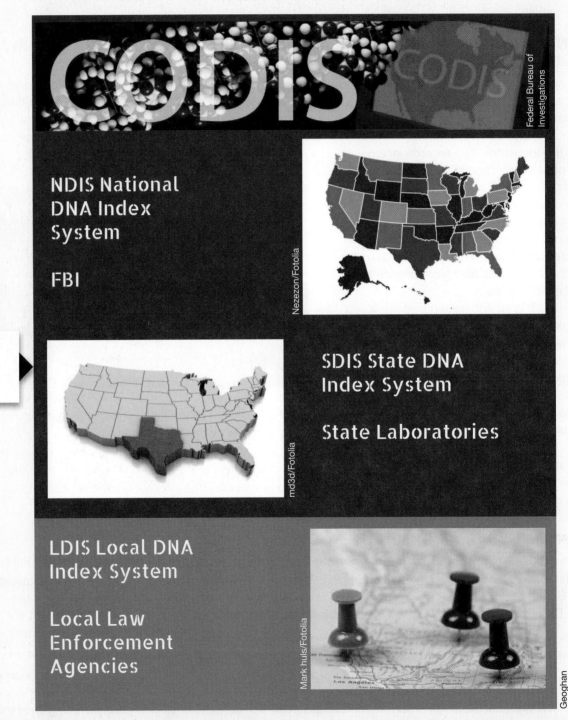

FIGURE 11.24 The CODIS is used by law enforcement to link cases and identify suspects.

Science

Modern advances in the sciences are closely linked to advances in technology. In some cases, the technology leads to scientific discoveries, and in others, the science drives technology development. Two areas where this is evident are bioinformatics and geography.

HUMAN GENOME PROJECT

Bioinformatics is the application of information technology to the field of biology. The **Human Genome Project (HGP)** (Figure 11.25) ran from 1990 to 2003 and was coordinated by the U.S. Department of Energy and the National Institutes of Health (NIH).

The goals of the Human Genome Project were to:
- Identify all the approximately 20,000–25,000 genes in human DNA.
- Determine the sequences of the 3 billion chemical base pairs that compose human DNA.
- Store this information in databases.
- Improve tools for data analysis.
- Transfer related technologies to the private sector.
- Address the ethical, legal, and social issues (ELSI) that may arise from the project.

When the project began, the technology to store and analyze the data collected didn't yet exist, and the field of bioinformatics was born. The project finished two years ahead of schedule, largely due to the advances in technology that the project produced. The data collected and analyzed from the project is being used in the development of new technologies and major advancements in biotechnology, agriculture, energy production, environmental science, and medical research.

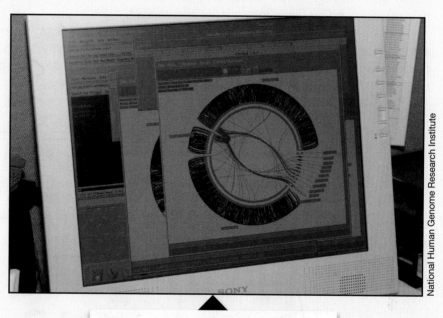

FIGURE 11.25 The HGP project combines biology and technology.

National Human Genome Research Institute

GEOGRAPHIC INFORMATION SYSTEMS (GIS)

A **GIS (geographic information system)** combines layers, or datasets, of geographically referenced information about Earth's surface. Each layer holds data about a particular kind of feature, such as rainfall, land use, land cover, census figures, or satellite imagery. The datasets may exist as graphic information, such as maps, or as database tables (Figure 11.26).

The U.S. Geological Survey has created the National Map (**nationalmap.gov**) that is available to the public on the web. You can use the free legacy online viewer, which is a simple GIS interface, to look at each of the GIS layers on the map. You can also download the map data into a desktop GIS program or mobile app. The National Map includes eight primary layers:

- Aerial photographs
- Elevation
- Geographic names
- Hydrography
- Boundaries
- Transportation
- Structures
- Land cover

A GIS applies database operations—such as queries—on different types of data to see patterns, trends, and spatial relationships. The analysis of GIS information is used in decision making. Municipalities use a GIS to design emergency routes, locate waste management facilities, and plan future development. Environmental management uses include natural resources management and environmental impact assessment.

The British Geologic Survey has created a Minecraft map of Great Britain (**bgs.ac.uk/minecraft**). Minecraft (**minecraft.net**) is a video game that allows players to build and explore virtual worlds using blocks of different materials. The Minecraft map of Great Britain and surrounding islands, based on real geographic data, consists of 22 million Minecraft blocks. Players can explore the geography of Great Britain above and below the surface.

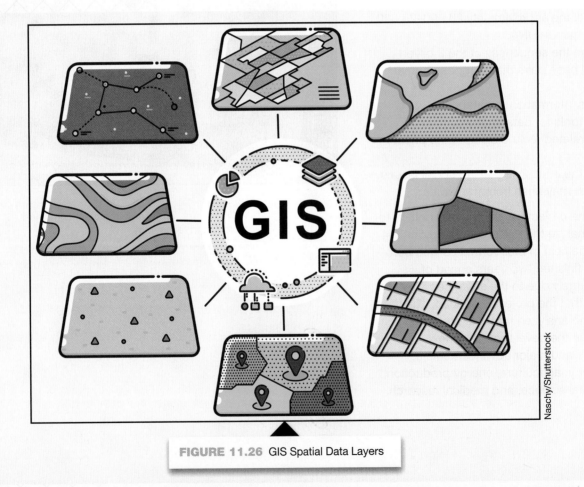

Naschy/Shutterstock

FIGURE 11.26 GIS Spatial Data Layers

ETHICS

Some states collect DNA profiles of convicted violent offenders, others collect samples from all convicted offenders, and still others collect DNA from anyone arrested. DNA samples may be collected from suspects who are never arrested—often simply to eliminate them as a suspect. What happens to the DNA of someone who is not convicted can be a cause for concern. Unlike fingerprints, which merely establish identity, DNA can be used to establish paternity, susceptibility to disease, and other genetic predispositions. The information in DNA profiles could potentially be used to deny someone a job or insurance. What do you think should be done with DNA samples from innocent persons?

Running Project

Visit the FBI website (**fbi.gov**) to find out how CODIS has been used to solve cold cases. Type **CODIS cold cases** in the search box and read through the results. Select one case and write a short summary of the investigation.

4 Things You Need to Know

- CODIS searches across multiple DNA indexes for a potential match.
- IAFIS, now Next Generation Identification (NGI), is a biometric database of fingerprints and other identifying information used by law enforcement.
- Bioinformatics is the application of information technology to the field of biology. The HGP mapped approximately 20,000–25,000 human genes.
- GIS combines layers or datasets of geographically referenced information about Earth's surface.

Key Terms

bioinformatics

CODIS (Combined DNA Index System)

GIS (geographic information system)

Human Genome Project (HGP)

IAFIS (Integrated Automated Fingerprint Identification System)

Next Generation Identification (NGI)

 Viz Check—In MyLab IT, take a quick quiz covering Objectives 4–5.

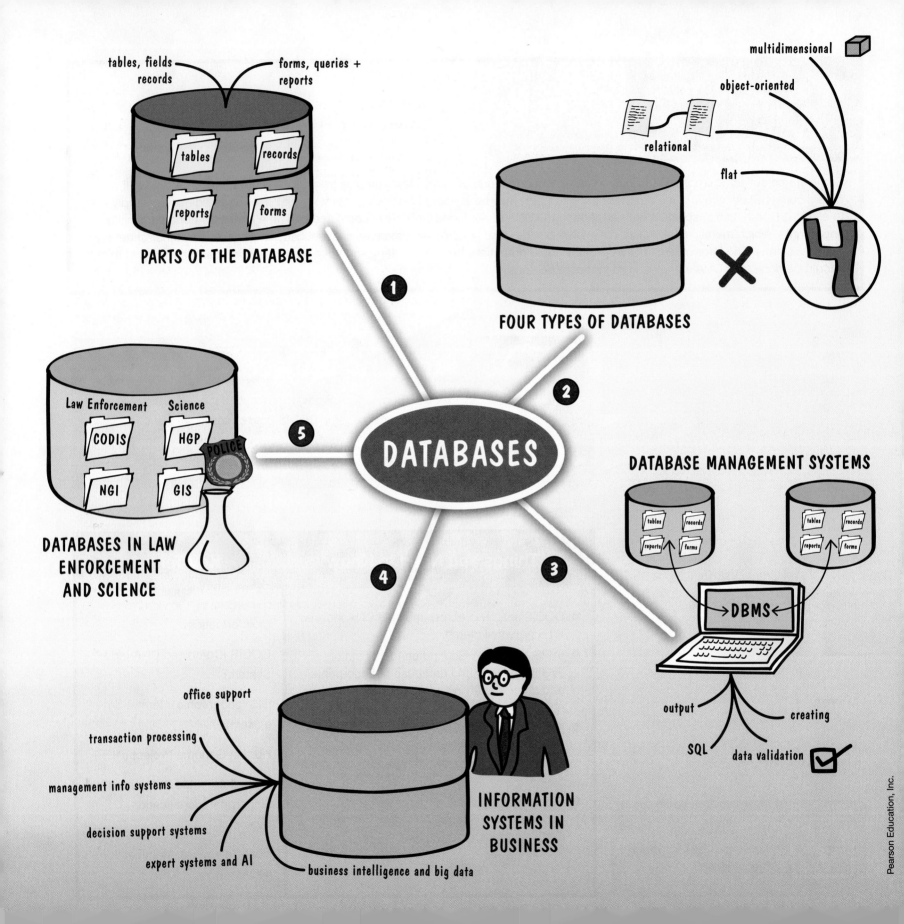

PARTS OF THE DATABASE

tables, fields records

forms, queries + reports

tables

records

reports

forms

FOUR TYPES OF DATABASES

multidimensional

object-oriented

relational

flat

4

DATABASE MANAGEMENT SYSTEMS

tables   records

reports   forms

tables   records

reports   forms

DBMS

output

creating

SQL

data validation

DATABASES

1
2
3
4
5

DATABASES IN LAW ENFORCEMENT AND SCIENCE

Law Enforcement   Science

CODIS   HGP

NGI   GIS

POLICE

INFORMATION SYSTEMS IN BUSINESS

office support

transaction processing

management info systems

decision support systems

expert systems and AI

business intelligence and big data

Pearson Education, Inc.

Objectives Recap

1. Identify the Parts of a Database
2. Compare the Four Types of Databases
3. Explain Database Management Systems
4. Discuss Important Types of Information Systems
5. List Examples of Databases Used in Law Enforcement and Research

Key Terms

artificial intelligence (AI) **579**
autonomous car **581**
big data **579**
bioinformatics **585**
blockchain **578**
bridge table **558**
business intelligence (BI) tool **579**
clickstream data mining **579**
CODIS (Combined DNA Index System) **583**
cognitive computing system **580**
data dictionary **565**
data mining **558**
data normalization **565**
data type **565**
data validation **566**
data warehouse **559**
database **551**
database administrator (DBA) **569**
database management system (DBMS) **564**
datacenter **555**
decision support system (DSS) **578**
expert system **579**
field **551**
flat database **557**
form **552**
GIS (geographic information system) **586**
Human Genome Project (HGP) **585**

IAFIS (Integrated Automated Fingerprint Identification System) **583**
inference engine **579**
information system **576**
knowledge base **579**
management information system (MIS) **578**
many-to-many relationship **558**
multidimensional database (MDB) **558**
Next Generation Identification (NGI) **583**
object-oriented database (OODB) **558**
office support system (OSS) **577**
one-to-many relationship **557**
one-to-one relationship **558**
online analytical processing (OLAP) **558**
primary key **552**
query **553**
query language **567**
record **551**
relational database **557**
relational keyword **567**
report **554**
Structured Query Language (SQL) **567**
table **551**
transaction-processing system (TPS) **577**

Summary

1. **Identify the Parts of a Database**

   A database consists of tables arranged in rows and columns. A row is a record that contains the information for a single entry. A column is a field, which is a single piece of information in a record. Forms, queries, and reports are database objects used to manage information in tables.

2. **Compare the Four Types of Databases**

   The simplest type of a database is a flat database consisting of a single list of items. The most common type of database is a relational database, which consists of multiple tables or relations related by common information. In an object-oriented database (OODB), data is stored as objects, which consist of both the data that describes the object and the processes that can be applied to it. A multidimensional database (MDB) is optimized for storing and utilizing data. It may be created using input from existing relational databases, but it structures the information into multidimensional data cubes.

3. **Explain Database Management Systems**

   A database management system (DBMS) is the software used to create and manage data in a database. The data dictionary defines all the fields and the type of data each field contains. Data normalization is used to reduce data redundancy, making it easier to keep records up to date and increases query speed. Data validation reduces data-entry errors using validation rules. A DBMS helps users design queries using a query language, such as SQL, and create reports.

4. **Discuss Important Types of Information Systems**

   Office support systems (OSS) include software and hardware that improve the productivity of employees by automating common business tasks. Businesses rely on transaction-processing systems (TPSs) to respond to user requests. Transaction processing links together multiple operations and ensures that all operations in a transaction are completed without error. A management information system (MIS) includes software, hardware, data resources (such as databases), decision support systems, people, and project management applications. Decision support systems (DSSs) are designed to help make decisions in situations where there's uncertainty about the possible outcomes of those decisions. Business intelligence (BI) applications, such as data mining, data warehousing, OLAP, and decision support systems, analyze data in information systems so it can be used to make decisions. An expert system is a computer programmed to make decisions in real-life situations—for example, diagnosing diseases based on symptoms. Cognitive computing systems learn from their interactions—they're designed to work with humans.

Summary continues on the next page

Summary *continued*

5. List Examples of Databases Used in Law Enforcement and Research

The CODIS (Combined DNA Index System) consists of multiple local, state, and national DNA profile databases and has five indices: Forensic, Arrestee, Detainee, Offender, and Missing Persons. The Integrated Automated Fingerprint Identification System (IAFIS), now the Next Generation Identification (NGI), is a national fingerprint and criminal history system maintained by the FBI and used by local, state, and federal law enforcement. It's the largest biometric database in the world. The Human Genome Project (HGP) determined the sequence of chemical base pairs that compose DNA and mapped the approximately 20,000–25,000 human genes. A GIS (geographic information system) combines layers or datasets of geographically referenced information about Earth's surface.

Multiple Choice

Answer the multiple-choice questions below for more practice with key terms and concepts from this chapter.

1. A _____ uniquely identifies a record in a database table.
   a. field
   b. primary key
   c. record
   d. table

2. A _____ retrieves specific data from one or more tables to answer a question.
   a. field
   b. form
   c. query
   d. report

3. Which is used to create databases that have more complicated types of data, such as images, audio, and video?
   a. Flat
   b. Multidimensional
   c. Object-oriented
   d. Relational

4. Which is the process of discovering relationships between data items?
   a. Data bridging
   b. Data mining
   c. Data normalization
   d. Online analytical processing (OLAP)

5. _____ is a decentralized electronic database of digital currency transactions.
   a. Blockchain
   b. Data normalization
   c. Online analytical processing (OLAP)
   d. Warehousing

6. A DBMS uses _____ to create a query.
   a. dictionaries
   b. forms
   c. schemas
   d. SQL

7. Collectively, applications that are used to analyze data in information systems so it can be used to make decisions are called _____.
   a. business intelligence (BI) tools
   b. decision support systems (DSSs)
   c. management information systems (MISs)
   d. office support systems (OSSs)

8. _____ is the branch of science concerned with making computers behave like humans.
   a. Artificial intelligence
   b. Bioinformatics
   c. Cognitive computing
   d. Expert systems

9. _____ is the part of an expert system that contains expert information and accumulated experience in a particular field.
   a. Artificial intelligence
   b. Bioinformatics
   c. Cognitive computing
   d. Knowledge base

10. A(n) _____ layers datasets that may include maps, imagery, and tables.
    a. CODIS
    b. GIS
    c. HGP
    d. IAFIS

True or False

Answer the following questions with *T* for true or *F* for false for more practice with key terms and concepts from this chapter.

_____ 1. Each database consists of a single table of information.

_____ 2. In a relational database, a bridge table breaks a many-to-many relationship up into two one-to-many relationships.

_____ 3. A query retrieves specific data from one or more tables to answer a question.

_____ 4. A report describes a particular entry in the database— for example, a customer or product.

_____ 5. An object-oriented database structures the information into multidimensional data cubes.

_____ 6. A data warehouse is a central repository for all the data that an enterprise uses, including internal databases and external sources such as vendors and customers.

_____ 7. Data normalization reduces data-entry errors.

_____ 8. SQL statements use relational keywords such as SELECT, FROM, and WHERE.

_____ 9. A GIS system combines layers—or datasets—of geographically referenced information about Earth's surface.

_____ 10. NGI and CODIS contain information only on convicted offenders.

Fill in the Blank

Fill in the blanks with key terms from this chapter.

1. A(n) _____ is a collection of information that's organized in a useful way.

2. A(n) _____ is a single piece of information in a record in a database.

3. A(n) _____ consists of multiple tables that are related by common information.

4. _____ analyzes the links customers click.

5. A(n) _____ database structures the information into multidimensional data cubes.

6. The _____ defines all the fields in a database and the type of data each field contains.

7. A(n) _____ learns from its interactions and interacts with humans using normal language.

8. _____ is the collection of large amounts of data from multiple sources—both internal and external—that's used for ongoing analysis and decision making.

9. _____ is the process of discovering relationships between data items.

10. A(n) _____ uses artificial intelligence rather than a human driver.

Running Project ...

... The Finish Line

Use your answers to the previous sections of the project. Why are databases important to you, and why is it important to be knowledgeable about them? Write a report describing how you use databases in your daily life and respond to the questions raised throughout the chapter. Save your file as **lastname_firstname_ch11_project** and submit it to your instructor as directed.

Do It Yourself 1

In addition to the physical collection in your library, many resources today are available in online databases. Visit your school library (in person or virtually) to find out what online databases are available to you as a student. From your student data files, open the file *vt_ch11_DIY1_answersheet* and save it as **lastname_firstname_ch11_DIY1_answersheet**.

> What databases are available to you? How many of these databases have you used in the past? Are any of the databases related to your chosen field? Select one that you haven't used before and create a query using the online form. Search for an article related to your career choice. If possible, use the system to create a citation. Write a summary of your results. How difficult did you find creating a query by using the online form? Paste your citation into your answer sheet. Save the file and submit it as directed by your instructor.

Do It Yourself 2

DBMSs have numerous templates that you can use to create your own database. In this exercise, you'll use an Access template to create a personal contact manager database. From your student data files, open the file *vt_ch11_DIY2_answersheet* and save the file as **lastname_firstname_ch11_DIY2_answersheet**.

1. Open Access. Type **personal contact manager** in the *Search for online templates* box and select the Personal contact manager template. Name the database **lastname_firstname_ch11_DIY2** then navigate to the folder where you save your work for this chapter, and click *Create*.

2. If necessary, close the Help window, click *Enable Content*, and expand the Navigation pane. Explore the database. List the objects that were created.

3. Close the *Contact List* table. Use the *Contact Details* form to add three new contacts (you can make up the data). Take a screenshot of one of them and paste it into your answer sheet. Open the *Contact Address Book* report and the *Contact Phone List* report, take screenshots of both reports, and paste into your answer sheet.

4. Type your answers in your answer sheet and include screenshots. Save the file and submit both your database and answer sheet as directed by your instructor.

File Management

Now that you have learned about databases, you can see that the file system on your computer is actually a database. From your student data files, open the file *vt_ch11_FM_answersheet* and save the file as **lastname_firstname_ch11_FM_answersheet**.

1. Open File Explorer and then open the Documents folder. If necessary, change the view to Details by using the View tab. If you are using a Mac, open Finder, click *Documents*, and change the view to list view. How does this view resemble a database table? What fields are in this table?

2. Right-click the *Name* column heading (on a Mac, Control-click). Click *More*. What are five additional fields that can be displayed in this window? List two that you think would be valuable to display.

3. Type your answers, save your answer sheet, and submit as directed by your instructor.

Critical Thinking

You have a large collection of DVD and Blu-ray movies that you often loan to friends and family members. You want to create a simple flat database to store information about your discs.

> Think about the information you'll need to organize. Design a simple flat database. It should have at least eight fields. Use a spreadsheet or DBMS of your choice to create your table. Define the data type to be used for each field and any data validation rules you think are needed. Save the file as **lastname_firstname_ch11_CT** and submit it as directed by your instructor.

Ethical Dilemma

It's standard business practice for a company to send you targeted advertisements based on information it has about you in a database. The information may be gleaned from your shopping habits, surveys you fill out, or information purchased from another company. From your student data files, open the file *vt_ch11_ethics_answersheet* and save the file as **lastname_firstname_ch11_ethics_answersheet**

Retailers competing for your loyalty offer club cards and other incentives for you to shop in their stores. Many people don't realize that when they use those perks, the company builds a profile that includes information about where and when they shop—and what they buy. This is so the stores can send targeted ads and offers. In 2012, a story broke about a large company that was data mining its customer databases to try to determine whether a woman was pregnant. This was a good time for the store to grab the customer with specials on baby items, maternity clothing, toys, and the like. If the information is public, is it okay for a business to use the information to send unsolicited emails or advertisements or to contact the people in other ways? How would you feel if you (or someone you are close to) received coupons for diapers before you told anyone that you (or she) were pregnant? Type your answers, save the answer sheet, and submit it as directed by your instructor.

On the Web

From your student data files, open the file *vt_ch11_web_answersheet* and save the file as **lastname_firstname_ch11_web_answersheet**.

1. Visit **w3schools.com/sql** and in the middle of the page, click *Start learning SQL now!* Read the Introduction to SQL and then click *Next*.

2. On the SQL Syntax page, read the information, click the *Try it Yourself* button, and then click the *Run SQL* button. What statement did you run, and what are the results? How many records are displayed? Click the tab to return to the SQL Syntax page and then click *Next*.

3. Repeat the procedure to learn about the SQL SELECT statement. What SQL statement did you test? What are the results? Repeat for the SQL SELECT DISTINCT statement. Compare the results of the three statements.

4. Type your answers, save the file, and submit it as directed by your instructor.

Collaboration

Instructors: Divide the class into four groups and assign each group one topic for this project. The topics are CODIS, IAFIS/NGI, HGP, and GIS.

The Project: Each team will prepare a poster for its database project. Use at least three references, only one of which may be this textbook. Use Google Drive or Microsoft Office to plan the presentation and provide documentation that all team members have contributed to the project.

Outcome: Prepare your poster using any tool that your instructor approves. In addition, turn in a final version of your file showing your collaboration, named **teamname_ch11_collab** and submit your presentation to your instructor as directed.

Application Project

Office 2016 Application Projects
Word 2016: Study Group Contact List

Project Description: In this project, you will create a flat file database using a Word table, apply a table style, sort a table, format text, and add a footnote. If necessary, download the student data files from **pearsonhighered** **.com/viztech**.

Study Group Contact List

Name	Cell Phone	Email
[1]Sandy Blackwood	267-555-2225	blackwoods@phhe.edu
Marty Fratelli	609-555-8663	fratellim@phhe.edu
Jake Giambi	215-555-9875	giambij@phhe.edu
Mary Koch	267-555-6345	kochm@ phhe.edu

[1] Group Leader

vt11_word_solution.docx

Step	Instructions
1	Start Word. From your student data files open the file *vt_ch11_word*. Save the file as **lastname_firstname_ch11_word**
2	Select the three contacts and convert the text to a 3 × 3 table.
3	Insert a row above the top row of the table. Enter the text **Name**, **Cell Phone**, **Email** in the three top cells.
4	Format table style Grid Table 4. Be sure Header Row and Banded Rows are both checked. Uncheck First Column.
5	Format the first line, *Study Group Contact List*, using the Title style. Apply the text effect Fill - Black, Text 1, Shadow and center-align the title.
6	Move the insertion point to the end of the last email address and press Tab to create a new row. Enter this record: **Sandy Blackwood** **267-555-2225** **blackwoods@phhe.edu**
7	Sort the table by Email ascending. If necessary, remove any hyperlinks from email addresses in the table.
8	Move the insertion point to the end of the document and press Enter two times. Search for an online image using the phrase **study time** and then insert an image of a student studying into the document, or use the image included in your student data files, *vt_ch11_image1*.
9	Resize the image height to 3 inches, lock aspect ratio. Position the image Middle Center, with Square Text Wrapping.
10	Adjust the color of the image to Grayscale and apply the Compound Frame, Black picture style.
11	Position the insertion point before Sandy and insert this footnote: **Group Leader**
12	Insert the file name in the footer of the document, using the File Name field.
13	Save the document and close Word. Submit the document as directed.

Application Project

Office 2016 Application Projects
Access 2016: Course Catalog

Project Description: In this project, you will add a second table to a database, add records through tables and a form, and change the field sizes in Design View of a table. You will also create a simple report. If necessary, download the student data files from **pearsonhighered.com/viztech**.

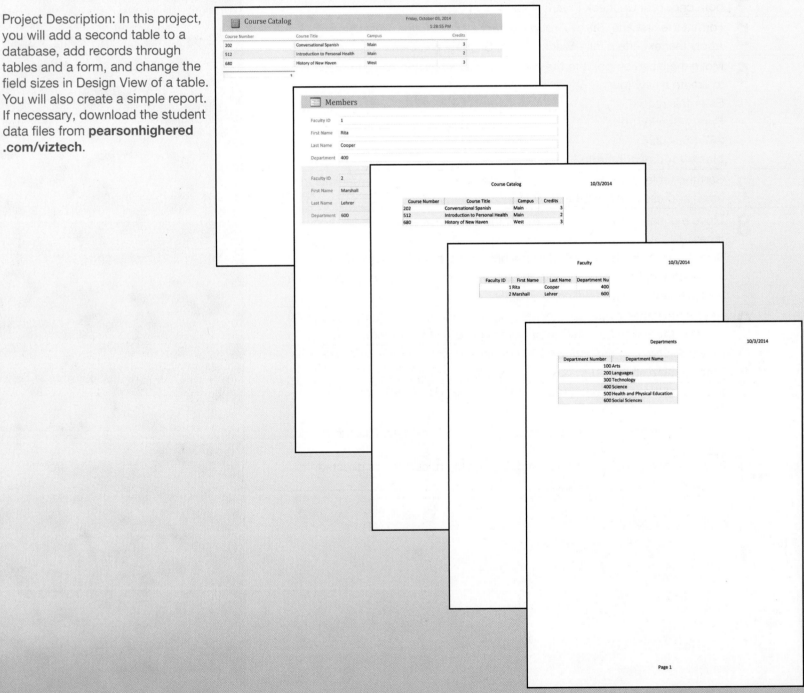

Step	Instructions
1	Start Access. From your student data files, open the file named *vt_ch11_access*. Save a copy of the database as lastname_firstname_ch11_access If necessary, click Enable Content.
2	Open the Faculty table. In Design View, change the First Name and Last Name field sizes to 20. Save and close the table.
3	Add the following two records to the Departments table: **500 Health and Physical Education** **600 Social Sciences**
4	Resize both columns to give the best fit automatically. Save and close the Departments table.
5	Open the Faculty Data Entry Form. Add a new record, entering **Rita** as the first name, **Cooper** as the last name, and **400** as the department number. Add a second record to the form, entering **Marshall** as the first name, **Lehrer** as the last name, and **600** as the department number. Close the form.
6	Create a new table in Datasheet View. Change the field name of the ID field to **Course Number** Using the Short Text data type, insert two new fields: **Course Title** and **Campus** (in that order). Add another field named **Credits** using the Number data type.
7	Switch to Design View and save the table as **Course Catalog** Change the Data Type of the Course Number field to Short Text, and ensure that the Course Number field is set as the Primary Key. Save the table and then switch back to Datasheet View.
8	Add the following three records to the *Course Catalog* table:

Course Number	Course Title	Campus	Credits
512	Personal Health	Main	2
680	History of New Haven	West	3
202	Conversational Spanish	Main	3

Step	Instructions
9	Resize all of the columns in the table to have the best fit. Save the table.
10	With the Course Catalog table open in Datasheet View, create a report that will open in Layout View. Sort the records from smallest to largest by the Course Number field.
11	Change to Design View and drag the right edge of the report to the 9.5-inch mark on the ruler. Save the report with the name **Course Catalog Report**
12	Close all database objects. Close the database and then exit Access. Submit the database as directed.

CHAPTER

12

Program Development

In This Chapter

VIZ INTRO

An information system is the people, hardware, and software that support data-intensive applications such as financial accounts, human resources, and other business transactions. When you have finished this chapter, you'll be familiar with the process of developing an information system and the tools used to create it.

Objectives

1 Describe the System Development Life Cycle

2 Describe the Program Development Cycle

3 Compare Various Programming Languages

4 Explain the Term *Artificial Intelligence*

Running Project

In this chapter, you'll learn about the processes and tools used to develop systems and programs. Look for project instructions as you complete each article. For most articles, there's a series of questions for you to research. At the conclusion of the chapter, you'll submit your responses to the questions raised.

BrunoWeltmann/Fotolia

Getting from Idea to Product

ctive

1

Describe the System Development Life Cycle

There are many different models for developing an information system. In this article, we look at the traditional model and also discuss some of the alternative models.

System Development Life Cycle (SDLC)

The traditional model for system development is known as the system development life cycle or the Waterfall model. As the name implies, it follows the system over time from inception to retirement or replacement. The **system development life cycle (SDLC)** consists of five phases (Figure 12.1) where each phase is completed in order before the next can begin. This method is rigid and doesn't allow for modification and revision to previous phases, but instead provides tight managerial control. The process begins when there's a request for a new system or a replacement for an old one in response to a business opportunity or problem.

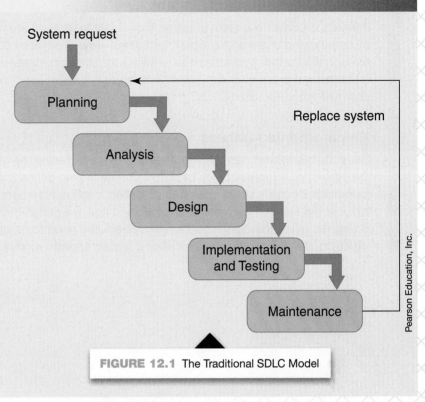

FIGURE 12.1 The Traditional SDLC Model

PLANNING PHASE

The SDLC begins in the planning phase. In this phase, the project team is assembled and feasibility studies are completed. Sometimes this phase is referred to as the *feasibility* stage.

Project Team

A **stakeholder** is someone who has an interest in and will be affected by the successful completion of a project, such as a manager, an owner, a user, a security professional, a telecommunications staff member, or a software developer. A **software developer** designs and writes computer programs. A project team consists of stakeholders from multiple areas. The leader of the project team is the **project manager (PM)**. Throughout the project, the PM coordinates the project team and keeps the project on track. A large project may include a business project manager and a technical project manager. The team tries to answer the questions: What are the purpose and goals of the project? How will we know if the project is successful? If the decision to proceed is made, then a project plan and budget estimates are produced.

Investigation and Feasibility Studies

The project team works to define the objectives and scope of the project. Feasibility studies are used to determine whether the project should proceed. A **feasibility study** involves several steps, including the creation of the terms of reference (or project charter), which state the objectives and scope of the project, the timeline for the project, risks, participants, deliverables, and budget. They typically focus on economic feasibility (Can we afford it?), technical feasibility (Do we have the technical resources to build it?), operational feasibility (Will it work within our business model?), and political feasibility (Can we get buy-in for the project?).

ANALYSIS PHASE

The goal of the analysis phase is to produce a list of requirements for the new system. This process involves evaluating the current system's weaknesses and strengths and defining the requirements of the new system.

Analyzing the Current System

If there's an existing system in place, the project team evaluates its strengths, weaknesses, and key features by interviewing users and support staff. **Data flow diagrams (DFDs)** are created to show the flow of data through the current system and to highlight the system's deficiencies. Figure 12.2 shows a DFD that illustrates the process of a student applying to a school. The "Approval process" circle could be broken down into more detailed DFDs.

Requirements Analysis

Once the old system has been analyzed, it's time to define the requirements for the new system. What will the system do? Tools such as data flow diagrams help define the flow of data in the system. Any deficiencies found in the current system will be addressed in the requirements of the new system. This process also looks at the existing business processes and how they might need to be changed. The system requirements generated guide the design of the new system and need to be as comprehensive as possible. The result is a logical model of the new system called a *system specification report*.

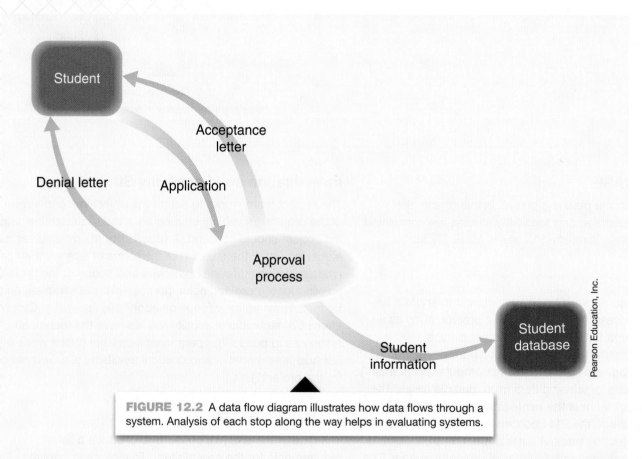

Student

Acceptance letter

Denial letter

Application

Approval process

Student information

Student database

Pearson Education, Inc.

FIGURE 12.2 A data flow diagram illustrates how data flows through a system. Analysis of each stop along the way helps in evaluating systems.

DESIGN PHASE

The analysis phase defines what the system will do, and the design phase defines how the system will do it. In the design phase, potential solutions are evaluated, and the best solution is selected for implementation.

Selecting a Solution

There may be many ways a system could be designed, including purchasing an off-the-shelf system and customizing it as well as building a system from the ground up. In this stage, potential solutions are proposed and evaluated against the system specifications. This

Ekaphon maneechot/Shutterstock

step involves research to look for systems that might meet the requirements. The option that best meets the requirements using the most cost-effective methods, hardware, software, and human resources is selected, and the designing of the system begins. Plans for any physical construction and hardware are laid out, as is a detailed design of the software.

Defining Application Specifications

If the project team determines that the system has to be built rather than purchased, then application specifications are written. Application specifications describe the software features and operations in detail—usability, reliability, interface, storage and processing, and output—using tools such as pseudocode and flowcharts. These tools are discussed in the article on programming.

IMPLEMENTATION AND TESTING PHASE

The implementation and testing phase is when the actual coding takes place and the system is installed and tested. During this phase, users are trained to use the system. Some versions of the SDLC break this into two phases.

Development and Testing

In the development and testing phase, the programmers use the designs and specifications to create the system. The documentation and help system are created, and the system is tested to ensure that it meets the project requirements. Programs are usually written in small pieces or modules that undergo individual unit testing. Integration or link testing ensures that the modules work together. Volume testing runs the system under normal usage conditions to ensure that it can handle the expected volume of data. Finally, acceptance testing ensures that the system does what it's supposed to do. If you've ever been a software beta tester, then you've participated in acceptance testing. During this phase, adjustments to the system are common.

Installation and Training

Next, the system is installed, and user training takes place. During training, the users learn how to interact with the system (Figure 12.3). This is a critical step to the success of the system. The implementation of the new system can occur in several different ways, depending on the needs of the business. Each method has pros and cons:

- The system may be phased in over time, bringing individual modules online one at a time or using a pilot group of users.
- The system may be run in parallel with the old system to ensure that the new system is working correctly before retiring the old one.
- The system may be brought online all at once, shutting off the old system at the same time.

Rawpixel/Shutterstock

FIGURE 12.3 User training is a critical part of the SDLC.

MAINTENANCE PHASE

The last phase of the SDLC is the maintenance phase. The system should undergo periodic reviews to ensure that it still meets the needs of the business. During this period, the system may be changed or updated, security holes and bugs may be fixed, and new features may be added. Users may need to be retrained and documentation updated as a result of these changes. Day-to-day operational maintenance includes monitoring performance, installing updates and patches, and creating and restoring backups. Helpdesk technicians support users in the use of the system and also collect feedback from them that can improve the system and identify bugs that were missed during testing. The maintenance phase is the longest phase of the SDLC and lasts until the system is retired or replaced.

Other Development Models

The SDLC is the oldest system development model, but because each phase proceeds in order, there's little opportunity to revise a project as it moves through the development process. Newer models include iterative steps—which means earlier phases can be revisited as needed.

JOINT APPLICATION DEVELOPMENT (JAD)

Joint Application Development (JAD) is a more collaborative process than the SDLC and involves the end user throughout the design and development of the project through a series of JAD sessions (Figure 12.4). Using JAD results in shorter development times because of the continued involvement of users throughout the development process. The user input throughout the process helps the developer better understand the users' needs and resolve any usability problems early in the process.

Nakophotography/Fotolia

FIGURE 12.4 JAD sessions are collaborative meetings throughout the design and development phases.

Nancy10/Fotolia

RAPID APPLICATION DEVELOPMENT (RAD)

Rapid Application Development (RAD) is an iterative process that uses prototyping and user testing of the designs. Multiple prototypes that look and behave like the final product are created using RAD tools and then tested. Once a prototype is approved, the real software is written. RAD uses object-oriented programming (OOP) with reusable software components to help speed up development. Unlike the traditional SDLC, RAD does not start with pre-defined requirements, making it more flexible and adaptable to users' needs.

GREEN COMPUTING
Programming Efficiency

Nakedcm/Fotolia

When we think of green computing, we usually think hardware—turn off your monitor, lower cooling costs, and recycle—but efficient programming is an important part of green computing too. Programmers can code efficiently so the program runs on the hardware with minimal impact—for example, using the processor efficiently and accessing data using the fewest interactions with the drives by using memory buffers. Think about how you perform a task as mundane as washing dishes. There are ways to do this inefficiently (washing each dish one at a time, leaving the water running continuously, drying each dish by hand) and methods you can use to make it more efficient (using a basin of water, washing a bunch of dishes, rinsing them all at once, and then allowing them to air-dry).

On a small scale, **green code**—which is written to be efficient so the program runs on the hardware with minimal impact—results in extending battery life for mobile devices, which have fewer resources to begin with. This is both a boon to the user and an energy saver in the long run. On a large scale, it's estimated that green code can lower energy requirements at data centers by 25–30%.

AGILE DEVELOPMENT

Agile Development, also called Extreme Programming, is an incremental and iterative process that uses short iterations or sprints, with the project team stopping and reevaluating the direction of a project every two weeks. At the end of each iteration, testing is done, and stakeholders review progress and reevaluate priorities. Projects are adjusted along the way as needs and business conditions change. Agile Development is a rapid and adaptive development model.

Other software development models include the V model (Verification and Validation), the Incremental model, the Iterative model, and the Spiral Method (SDM).

Different models are preferred for different types of applications. For example, Agile Development is the most frequently used model, particularly for time-critical problems. The traditional Waterfall SDLC is best used when the system requirements are very clear and structured, RAD is user-driven and so is ideal for developing software such as graphical user interfaces, and Spiral is best for high-risk projects.

Brian A Jackson/Shutterstock

Running Project

Another development model is Capability Maturity Model Integration (CMMI). Use the Internet to find out about this model. Explain how it works and detail its advantages. What advantages does CMMI have over the traditional Waterfall SDLC model?

5 Things You Need to Know

- The system development life cycle (SDLC) consists of five phases: planning, analysis, design, implementation and testing, and maintenance.
- A project team includes stakeholders from all the areas that have a stake in the successful completion of the project. The project manager is the team leader.
- Joint Application Development (JAD) involves the end user throughout the design and development.
- Rapid Application Development (RAD) is an iterative process that uses prototyping and user testing.
- The Agile Development model is iterative and incremental—using two-week-long increments.

Key Terms

Agile Development

data flow diagram (DFD)

feasibility study

green code

Joint Application Development (JAD)

project manager (PM)

Rapid Application Development (RAD)

software developer

stakeholder

system development life cycle (SDLC)

Coding the System

Objective

2

Describe the Program Development Cycle

A **computer program** is a sequence of instructions for a computer to follow. It's written in a language that the computer can understand and includes any data the computer needs to perform the instructions.

VIZ CLIP

Program Development

Program Development Cycle

The **program development cycle** is a set of five steps that a programmer follows to create a computer program (Figure 12.5). It's considered a cycle because the steps can be iterative—which means the programmer may go back and repeat them throughout the process.

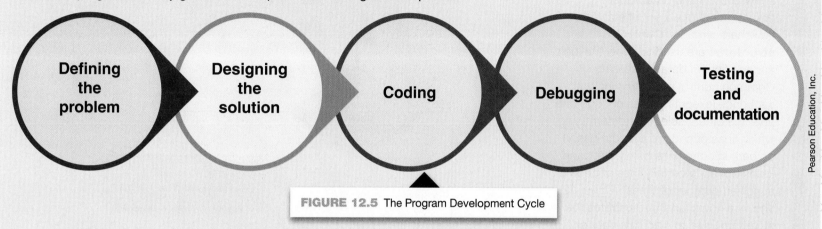

FIGURE 12.5 The Program Development Cycle

DEFINING THE PROBLEM

As with any other problem-solving exercise, the first step in the program development cycle is to define the problem. To a large extent, the success of the program depends on getting this step right. A programmer must determine what data will be provided (input) and what the program will do (processing and output).

DESIGNING THE SOLUTION

An **algorithm** is a set of steps to solve a problem. It should be a clear and simple statement that breaks down the solution into small modules, each of which performs a single task. A well-written algorithm lays out the logic and processes the program will include, the sequence of steps to be performed, and any choices or alternatives that might occur. An algorithm written in plain English for determining your grade in a class might look like Figure 12.6.

FIGURE 12.6 An algorithm to solve the grade problem shows the steps written in plain English.

1. Gather the grades for all assignments.

2. Add up the points earned.

3. Calculate average.

4. Look up grade based on the average.

5. End.

Once a good algorithm has been written, it can be mapped out using flowcharts and pseudocode. A **flowchart** is a graphic view of the algorithm. Flowcharts use arrows to show direction and other symbols to show actions and data. Most programmers use a set of standard flowchart symbols. **Control structures** are used to show the logic and the flow of data processing. Common control structures include sequence (executing lines of code one after the other), selection (determining which lines of code to execute based on certain conditions being met), and loop (repeating certain lines of code a specified number of times). Figure 12.7 shows a flowchart that illustrates the algorithm used to calculate your grade. The flowchart includes a selection control structure (*Have all grades?*) that leads to different steps depending on the answer.

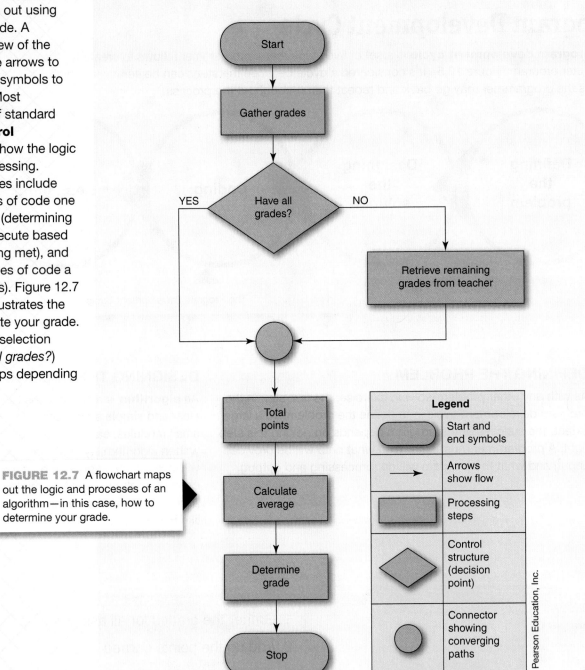

FIGURE 12.7 A flowchart maps out the logic and processes of an algorithm—in this case, how to determine your grade.

Legend	
Start and end symbols	
Arrows show flow	
Processing steps	
Control structure (decision point)	
Connector showing converging paths	

Pearson Education, Inc.

Pseudocode expresses the steps of an algorithm using English-like statements that focus on logic, not syntax. Although it is closer to what a program will look like, pseudocode is not specific to any one programming language and is not executable. Figure 12.8 illustrates the pseudocode for the grade problem. There's much more detail, with each step in the process defined and two control structures used to make processing decisions. The IF-THEN control structure asks the same questions as the *Have all grades?* selection control in the flowchart. The CASE control structure is used to complete the *Determine grade* process in the flowchart.

The design process helps create the organization for the coding to come. A poor design will lead to frustration and poor coding, so it's essential to take the time to do this right.

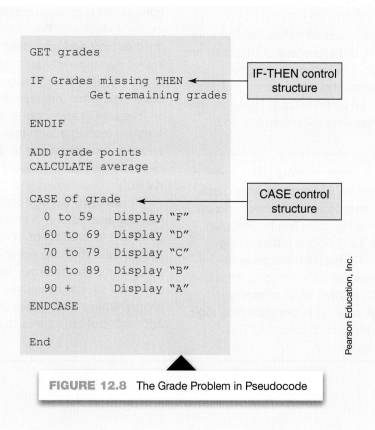

```
GET grades

IF Grades missing THEN          ◄──── IF-THEN control
        Get remaining grades              structure

ENDIF

ADD grade points
CALCULATE average

CASE of grade                   ◄──── CASE control
  0 to 59    Display "F"                structure
  60 to 69   Display "D"
  70 to 79   Display "C"
  80 to 89   Display "B"
  90 +       Display "A"
ENDCASE

End
```

Pearson Education, Inc.

FIGURE 12.8 The Grade Problem in Pseudocode

CODING

Computer programming (coding) is the process of converting an algorithm into instructions the computer can understand. First, the appropriate programming language must be selected, taking into account such factors as the type of task, the platform it needs to run on, and the expertise of the programmer. Different languages are optimized for different tasks, so choosing the right language will result in a better solution. Programming is accomplished using one of two models: **procedural programming**, which uses a step-by-step list of instructions, or **object-oriented programming (OOP)**, which defines objects and the actions or methods that can be performed on them. Objects can be reused in other programs, making OOP more efficient. Finally, the instructions are coded following the syntax of the chosen language. **Syntax rules** define the correct construction of commands in a programming language.

DEBUGGING

It's rare that a program runs error-free the first time through. **Debugging** is the process of detecting and fixing errors, or bugs, in a computer program. Debugging occurs throughout the coding process and can be considered alpha testing. There are three types of errors: syntax errors, logic errors, and runtime errors.

Syntax errors are errors in the way code is written. They may be typos, missing parameters, or incorrect use of symbols, such as brackets. Such errors are generally easy to spot. Syntax errors can be found by reviewing the code line by line; also, because they prevent a program from running further and each time generate a syntax error message that explains the error, spotting them can be easier than spotting other kinds of errors.

A **logic error** is an error in programming logic that results in an unexpected outcome. The commands may be syntactically correct but logically incorrect. For example, a mathematical formula may add up a column of numbers, but the wrong numbers are used. In this case, the formula is not a syntax error (because it's written correctly) but a logic error (because it uses an incorrect input, so it results in an incorrect result). A common logic error is creating a loop that has no end. Logic errors are more difficult to detect than syntax errors because they don't prevent a program from running.

A **runtime error** occurs when the program is running and data or a command that is entered causes it to crash. For example, a user may enter invalid data that causes the program to divide by zero. Computer memory issues are also a common cause of runtime errors. Good computer programming anticipates possible errors and adds control structures to trap or prevent them.

Raskjaer/Fotolia

TESTING AND DOCUMENTATION

Once a program has been debugged, it needs to be tested under actual working conditions. This is called **beta testing**, and during this process, undetected logic and runtime errors are often found. Documentation is created throughout the programming cycle and is written both for the user and for programmers (both those who work on the project and those who may maintain or update it in the future). Common documentation includes:

- For users of the system: user manuals (print or online)
- For programmers: comments within the code that explain what each section is designed to do as well as external documentation that outlines the project, problem, and design logic

Not every project follows all these programming steps exactly, and there's often much overlap and iteration in the process, but in general, programming requires good organization to result in a complete and stable program.

Viz Check—In MyLab IT, take a quick quiz covering Objectives 1–2.

Vector master/Fotolia

Running Project

Use the Internet to find out more about the differences between procedural programming and object-oriented programming. Review your college catalog and look at the computer programming classes offered. What languages are taught? Are they procedural or object-oriented? How do you know?

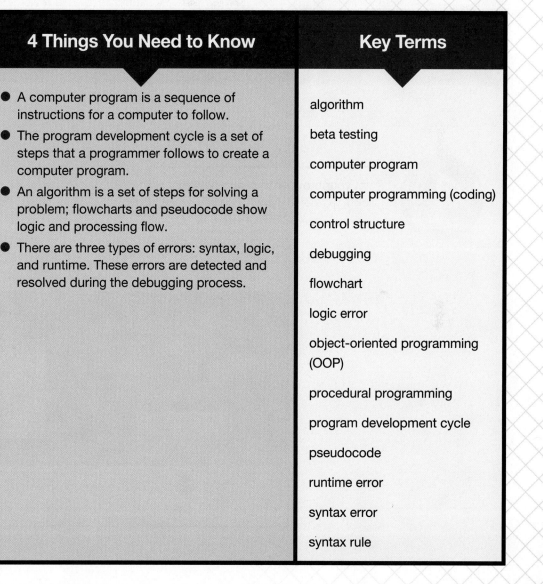

4 Things You Need to Know

- A computer program is a sequence of instructions for a computer to follow.
- The program development cycle is a set of steps that a programmer follows to create a computer program.
- An algorithm is a set of steps for solving a problem; flowcharts and pseudocode show logic and processing flow.
- There are three types of errors: syntax, logic, and runtime. These errors are detected and resolved during the debugging process.

Key Terms

algorithm

beta testing

computer program

computer programming (coding)

control structure

debugging

flowchart

logic error

object-oriented programming (OOP)

procedural programming

program development cycle

pseudocode

runtime error

syntax error

syntax rule

Create a Flowchart

Digital Literacy Skill

HOW TO VIDEO

Creating a flowchart using a word processor can be a tedious process. In this exercise, you will use Creately—a free online tool. If necessary, download the student data files from **pearsonhighered .com/viztech**. From your student data files, open the *vt_ch12_ howto1_answersheet* file and save the file as **lastname_firstname_ ch12_howto1_answersheet**.

1 Point your browser to **creately.com**. Click *Try Creately Now*.

Used with kind permission of Creately.com - online diagramming and collaboration.

2

On the Welcome screen, on the menu bar, click *New*.

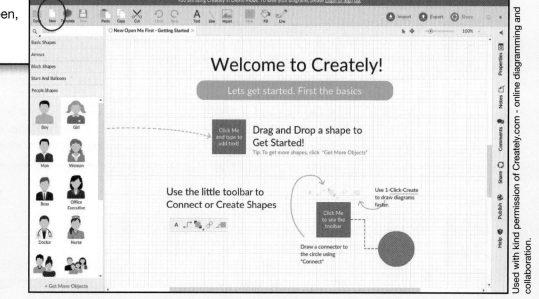

3

In the *What do you plan to draw*? box, type **flowchart**. If necessary click *Flowcharts*, and then click *Blank Diagram*. Name the flowchart **Chapter 12**, type your name in the description, and then click *Create Document*.

×

1. What do you plan to draw?

Flowcharts	×

2. What do you want to start with?

×

Blank Document

A blank document to start drawing from scratch.

3. What are you going to name it?

Chapter 12

Firstname Lastname

flow   flowchart   business   workflow

✔ Share with Community

Create Document

4 In the left pane, if necessary, click *Flow charts* to display the shapes used in a flowchart. Drag the Start/End shape onto the canvas. Using Figure 12.7 as a guide, create the flowchart that maps out the process of determining a grade. Add each shape either by clicking the *1-Click Create* option from the mini menu above a shape on the canvas or by dragging the correct shape from the left pane. As you add each shape, drag the corners to adjust the size and, if necessary, click on the *Connect* symbol above it to connect it to the next symbol. Type the correct statement in each shape. Don't worry if the shapes are not aligned exactly, but be sure they are placed and connected correctly.

5 On the toolbar above the canvas, click the *Text* button to add the YES and NO to the decision point. Click a blank area of the canvas to deselect.

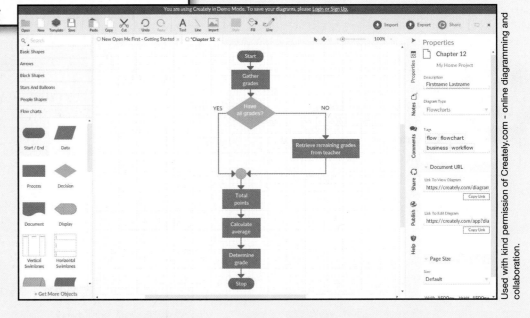

Used with kind permission of Creately.com - online diagramming and collaboration.

6 On the right-hand side, if necessary, click *Properties* to open the Properties pane. Take a screenshot of this window and paste it into your answer sheet. Save the file and submit it as directed by your instructor. Note: If you want to save your work, you will need to create an account on Creately.

CAREER SPOTLIGHT

JOBS

Iodrakon/Fotolia

SOFTWARE DEVELOPMENT According to the *Occupational Outlook Handbook*, computer software design and development is among the fields expected to grow the fastest over the next decade. The more experience and education you have, the better the job prospects and pay will be. Certifications also help to show your skills in specific platforms.

A computer software engineer is responsible for the design and development of computer software. Typically, the software engineer is responsible for the first parts of the SDLC—planning, analysis, and design. This field requires a minimum of a bachelor's degree, but a master's degree is preferred. A computer programmer writes the actual code based on the design work completed by the software engineer. A programmer should have at least an associate's degree, but a bachelor's degree is preferred. Often, the term *developer* is used instead of *programmer*. This implies that the person both designs and codes the system, and this is very often the case, especially on smaller projects or in smaller organizations.

Asha Sreenivas/Fotolia

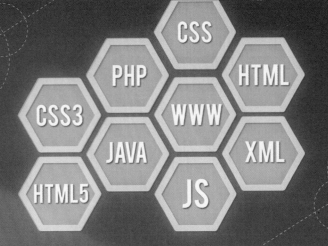

Tools of the Trade

Compare Various Programming Languages

The right tool gets any job done faster and better, whether you're building a deck or writing a computer program. There are many different programming languages to choose from, and selecting the right one results in a better product. In this article, we discuss several different ways a programmer might choose to code a program.

VIZ CLIP

Hello World!

Programming Languages

Programming languages can be divided into two levels: low level and high level. Within the levels, the languages can be further categorized into generations. Each generation is more sophisticated and moves from the 0s and 1s that a computer can easily understand (low level) to language that is more humanlike (high level). Table 12.1 lists some examples of each level.

TABLE 12.1 Programming Languages

Generation	Level	Examples
First	Low	Machine language
Second	Low	Assembly language
Third	High	Fortran C++ Java
Fourth	High	SQL Visual Basic
Fifth	High	Prolog LISP

LOW LEVEL

When the first computers were built, programs were wired directly into them. This was very inefficient and time-consuming. The first programming languages were written in the language a computer speaks—binary. A **first-generation language (1GL)** is a **machine language** written in binary that can execute very quickly but takes a lot of effort to write and debug.

A **second-generation language (2GL)** is an **assembly language**. It's written with statements closer to what humans speak and has to be converted into a machine language by an assembler before the computer can execute it. Assembly languages are difficult to use for large applications.

HIGH LEVEL

The majority of computer programming today is done using high-level languages for everything from small scripts and applets that make a webpage dynamic, to **macros** used to automate tasks in applications such as Word and Excel, to the creation of complex artificial intelligence systems. These languages are probably what you're most familiar with. The distinction between third-, fourth-, and fifth-generation languages isn't clearly defined, and some languages can fall into more than one generation.

Most modern programming languages are **third-generation languages (3GLs)**. These include both procedural and object-oriented languages, such as Fortran, C++, and Java. Programming in a 3GL requires a considerable amount of programming knowledge. Although simple programs can be written with just a few statements, complex applications can have thousands of lines of code. Large projects often involve multiple programmers working together. A **compiler** is needed to convert the code into a machine language the computer can read and execute.

A **fourth-generation language (4GL)** is designed to be closer to natural language than a 3GL; however, some programming knowledge is still needed to work effectively with 4GLs. Many 4GLs are used for accessing databases, such as SQL, PowerBuilder, and OLAP (online analytical processing) tools. Visual Basic is sometimes considered a 4GL. Visual Basic is an event-driven programming language, which means it responds to events such as a user pushing a button or selecting an item from a list.

Figure 12.9 shows a classic *Hello World!* program written in Java, and Figure 12.10 shows the same program in Visual Basic. The program simply displays "Hello World!" on the screen and is often used as a first program when learning a programming language. Although the syntax for these two programs is different, after compiling and running the programs, the results would be essentially the same.

A **fifth-generation language (5GL)** is a system a user can work with without writing code. The 5GL creates the code. 5GLs are primarily used in artificial intelligence applications and in combination with Platform-as-a-Service (PaaS) application development. Platform-as-a-Service (PaaS) is an online programming environment used to develop, test, and deploy custom applications.

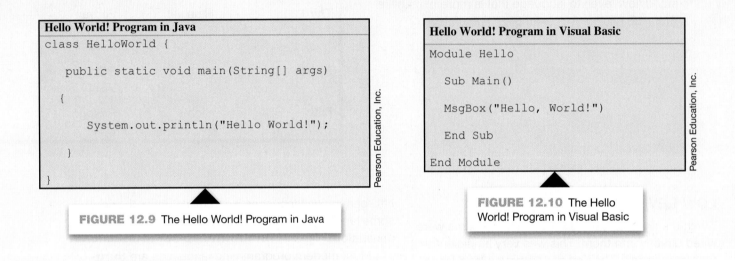

Hello World! Program in Java

```
class HelloWorld {

    public static void main(String[] args)

    {

        System.out.println("Hello World!");

    }

}
```

Pearson Education, Inc.

FIGURE 12.9 The Hello World! Program in Java

Hello World! Program in Visual Basic

```
Module Hello

    Sub Main()

    MsgBox("Hello, World!")

    End Sub

End Module
```

Pearson Education, Inc.

FIGURE 12.10 The Hello World! Program in Visual Basic

Programming Tools

Tools that help a programmer create programs include software development kits and integrated development environments.

A **software development kit (SDK)** is provided, often as a free download, to encourage programmers to develop software using a bundle of libraries and tools that are developed for a particular platform. For example, SDKs are available for creating iPhone and Android mobile apps and for developing Java and Facebook applications.

An **integrated development environment (IDE)** is a complete system for developing software, typically consisting of

- A code editor
- One or more compilers
- One or more SDKs
- A debugger

Popular IDEs include Eclipse and NetBeans—which are free and open source—and Microsoft Visual Studio. Each of these IDEs has support for multiple languages (Figure 12.11).

A few of the most popular PaaS systems are Salesforce.com, Windows Azure, Google App Engine, and Amazon Web Services. PaaS systems vary from those that require a lot of programming knowledge using 3GL and 4GL languages to those that have a point-and-click 5GL interface that requires little or no actual coding. The advantages to using a PaaS system are the same as for other cloud computing systems: the elimination of local administration, hardware, and software.

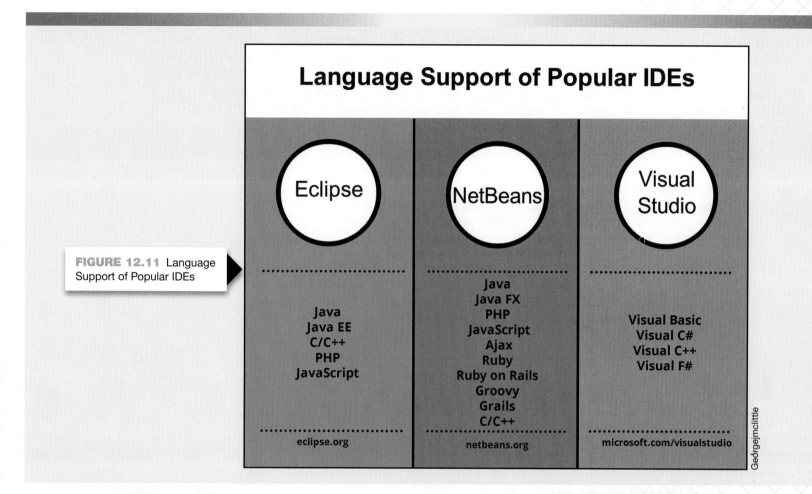

Language Support of Popular IDEs

Eclipse

Java
Java EE
C/C++
PHP
JavaScript

eclipse.org

NetBeans

Java
Java FX
PHP
JavaScript
Ajax
Ruby
Ruby on Rails
Groovy
Grails
C/C++

netbeans.org

Visual Studio

Visual Basic
Visual C#
Visual C++
Visual F#

microsoft.com/visualstudio

Gedrgejmclittle

FIGURE 12.11 Language Support of Popular IDEs

Web Programming

As with any other programming, developing web applications requires selecting the right language for the task. But there are different concerns when the application is designed for the web, such as the browser and device that will be used to interact with the programming.

The simplest form of a webpage is a static HTML page. The client browser requests the page, and the web server sends it. The browser then reads the HTML and displays the page. However, modern webpages are rarely static. Dynamic elements such as menus, rollovers, searches, videos, and animations make web programming more complex. HTML5 is the latest HTML standard. HTML5 includes support for audio and video.

SERVER-SIDE

A **server-side program** runs on a web server. An example of such a program is a web search. When a user types keywords in a search engine, the search is executed on the database on the server. The results are formatted into a new HTML page and sent to the client. The processing can't take place on the client side because the database isn't on the client computer. Because the processing takes place on the server side and the results are sent to the client in HTML, the client doesn't need to have special software—other than a browser—to see the results.

CLIENT-SIDE

A **client-side program** runs on the client computer. The coding is within a webpage, downloaded to the client computer, and compiled and executed by a browser or plug-in. Client-side programming (often called scripting) requires the user to have the proper browser and plug-ins installed. Because the processing takes place on the client system, it's not necessary to reload the webpage to see the changes. Many browsers are dropping support for, or restricting, client-side plugins such as Flash as they can pose security risks. Table 12.2 lists some common server-side and client-side technologies.

TABLE 12.2 Web Programming Technologies	
Server-side	**Client-side**
ASP	ActiveX controls
Java	Ajax
MySQL	Flash
Perl	Java applets
PHP	JavaScript
Python	

Mobile App Development

Apple and Google opened the first mobile app stores in 2008. Within five years, more than 50,000 developers were building apps for these stores. Making an app is the easy part. There are websites where you can use premade elements to create an app and publish it with ease. A professional developer uses more sophisticated tools and computer programming skills. Building a good app—one that works well, has market appeal, and generates income—is the hard part.

Revenue from mobile apps built for smartphones and tablets (Figure 12.12) is expected to reach $92 billion by 2018, so there is a lot of potential to earn income, but there are millions of apps in the Google Play store and in the Apple App Store, so the competition is steep.

There are four ways to monetize—that is, profit from—a mobile app:

- Pay-per-download: Charge an upfront fee for the app.
- Subscription: Charge a regularly recurring fee for use.

Georgejmclittle/Fotolia

FIGURE 12.12 Mobile devices are a huge market for development.

- In-app purchases: Charge for additional lives, levels, or other features from within the app. These are usually very small amounts, referred to as **micropayments**.
- In-app advertising: Charge a fee for displaying ads within the app. This is the most common way to monetize a free app.

Choosing the right programming language and tools is an important part of program development. A huge variety of options are available, and it's impossible to be an expert in every one of them. Although it's a good idea to be familiar with several programming languages, it's important to have in-depth knowledge of at least one, and good problem-solving skills are an absolute must. Even if you never intend to write a computer program, understanding how they're developed will help you make decisions regarding the purchase and development of software—perhaps as a member of an SDLC project team.

Running Project

Adobe Flash was an important web technology that is being phased out. Support for Flash was turned off by default in Chrome and Firefox in 2016 and it is not supported at all on iOS and Android devices. Why is support for Flash being removed? What are some of the newer technologies being used instead of Flash?

5 Things You Need to Know

- A 1GL is a machine language; a 2GL is an assembly language.
- Most modern programming languages are 3GL and require a considerable amount of programming knowledge.
- A 4GL is designed to be closer to natural language and is often used for accessing databases. 5GLs are primarily used in artificial intelligence and in PaaS development.
- Tools that help a programmer create programs include software development kits (SDKs), integrated development environments (IDEs), and Platform-as-a-Service (PaaS).
- In web programming, a server-side program runs on a web server, and a client-side program runs on a client computer.

Key Terms

assembly language

client-side program

compiler

fifth-generation language (5GL)

first-generation language (1GL)

fourth-generation language (4GL)

integrated development environment (IDE)

machine language

macro

micropayment

second-generation language (2GL)

server-side program

software development kit (SDK)

third-generation language (3GL)

Automate a Task by Using a Macro in Word

HOW TO VIDEO

Creating a macro is an easy way to automate tasks in applications such as Word and Excel, which include Visual Basic for Applications (VBA) to create and edit macros. In this activity, you'll record and edit a macro in Word.

1 Start Microsoft Word. Open a new blank document. On the File tab click *Options*, and then click *Customize Ribbon*. In the right pane, under Main Tabs, if necessary, select the Developer check box, and then click *OK* to display the Developer tab on the ribbon.

Word Options   ? ✕

General
Display
Proofing
Save
Language
Advanced
Customize Ribbon
Quick Access Toolbar
Add-Ins
Trust Center

Customize the Ribbon and keyboard shortcuts.

Choose commands from: ⓘ
Popular Commands ▾

Customize the Ribbon: ⓘ
Main Tabs ▾

Accept Revision	
Add Table ▸	
Align Left	
Bullets ▸	
Center	
Change List Level ▸	
Copy	
Cut	
Define New Number Format...	
Delete	
Draw Table	
Draw Vertical Text Box	
Email	
Find	
Fit to Window Width	
Font I▾	
A Font Color ▸	
A Font Settings	
Font Size I▾	
AB¹ Footnote	
Format Painter	
A˙ Grow Font	
Hyperlink...	
Insert Comment	
Insert Page Section Breaks ▸	
Insert Picture	
Insert Text Box	

Main Tabs
☐ ☑ Home
   ⊞ Clipboard
   ⊞ Font
   ⊞ Paragraph
   ⊞ Styles
   ⊞ Editing
⊞ ☑ Insert
⊞ ☑ Design
⊞ ☑ Layout
⊞ ☑ References
⊞ ☑ Mailings
⊞ ☑ Review
⊞ ☑ View
⊞ ☑ Developer
⊞ ☑ Add-Ins
⊞ ☑ Blog Post
⊞ ☑ Insert (Blog Post)
⊞ ☑ Outlining
⊞ ☑ Background Removal

Add >>
<< Remove

New Tab   New Group   Rename...

Customizations: Reset ▾   ⓘ

Import/Export ▾   ⓘ

Keyboard shortcuts: Customize...

OK   Cancel

2 On the *Developer tab* in the *Code group*, click *Record Macro*. Name the macro **ContactInfo** and then, under *Assign macro to*, click *Button*.

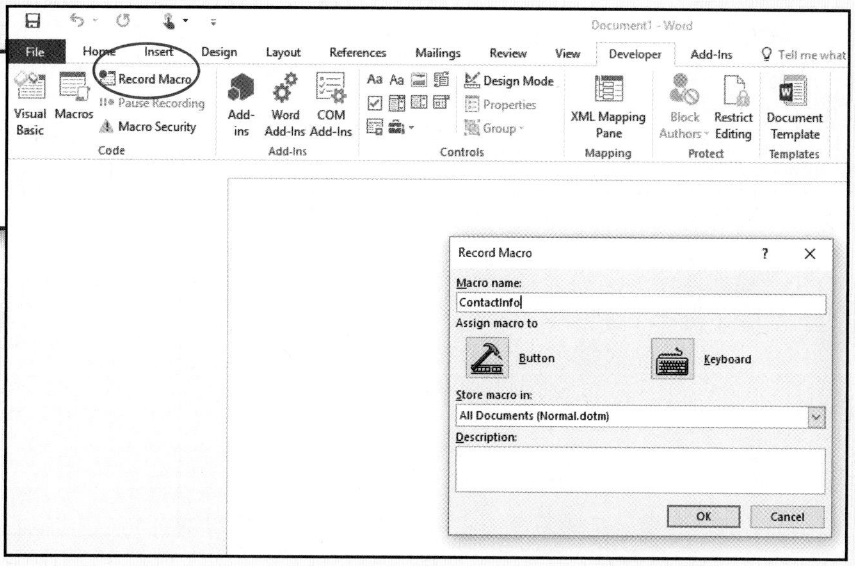

Microsoft Word 2016, Windows 10, Microsoft Corporation

3 Select your macro in the left column, click *Add* to place it in the right column, and then click *OK*. A new button will now appear on your Quick Access Toolbar, above the ribbon.

Select your macro

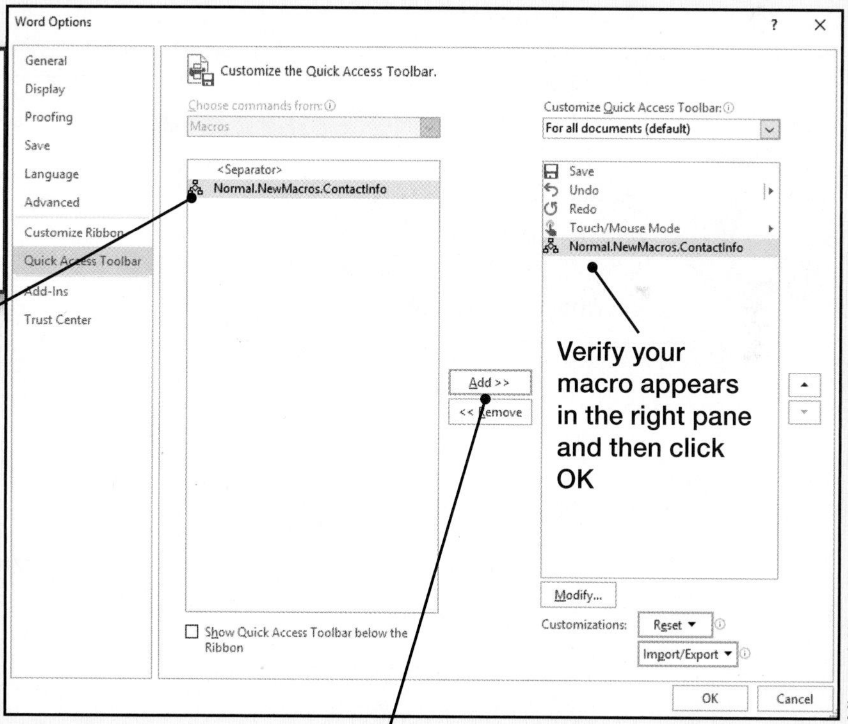

Verify your macro appears in the right pane and then click OK

Click Add

Microsoft Word 2016, Windows 10, Microsoft Corporation

4

On the *Insert* tab, click *Table*. Create a 1 × 1 table by clicking in the first box of the *Insert Table* menu.

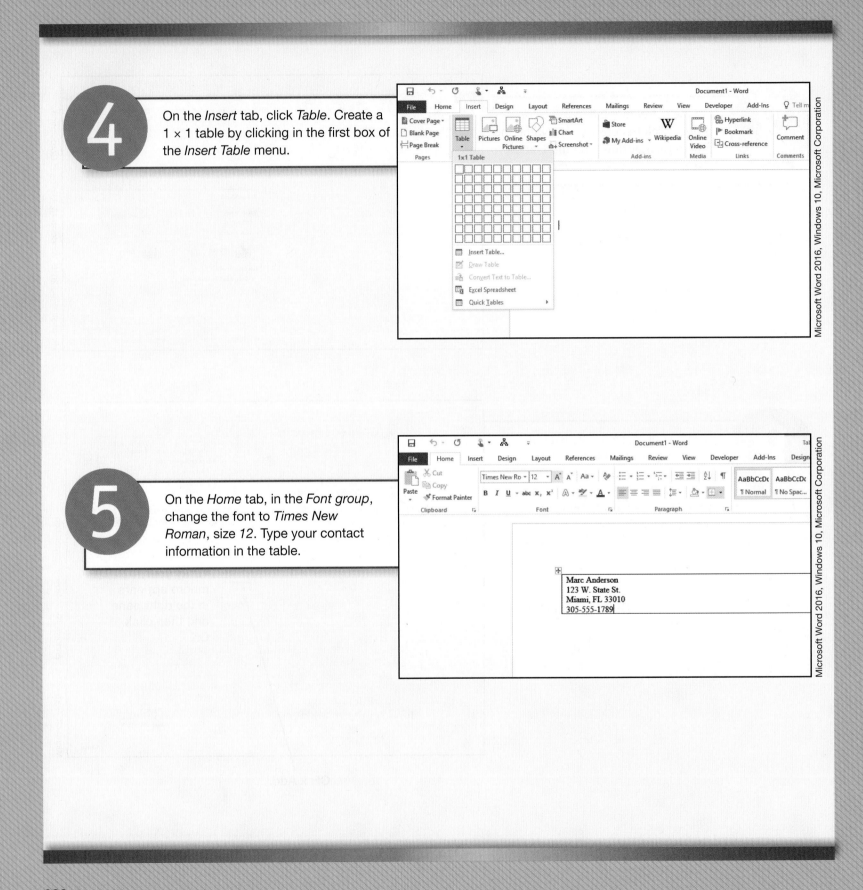

5

On the *Home* tab, in the *Font group*, change the font to *Times New Roman*, size *12*. Type your contact information in the table.

Marc Anderson
123 W. State St.
Miami, FL 33010
305-555-1789

6 On the *Table Tools Design* tab, in the *Table Styles group*, click *More* and then click the *Grid Table 4 - Accent 6* style.

Microsoft Word 2016, Windows 10, Microsoft Corporation

7 On the *Layout* tab, in the *Cell Size group*, click *AutoFit* and then click *AutoFit Contents*.

Marc Anderson
123 W. State St.
Miami, FL 33010
305-555-1789

Microsoft Word 2016, Windows 10, Microsoft Corporation

8

On the *Developer* tab, click *Stop Recording*. On the *File* tab, click *New* and then click *Blank document*. Save the file as **lastname_firstname_ch12_howto2**. Click the macro button you created on the *Quick Access Toolbar* to test your macro.

Your macro button

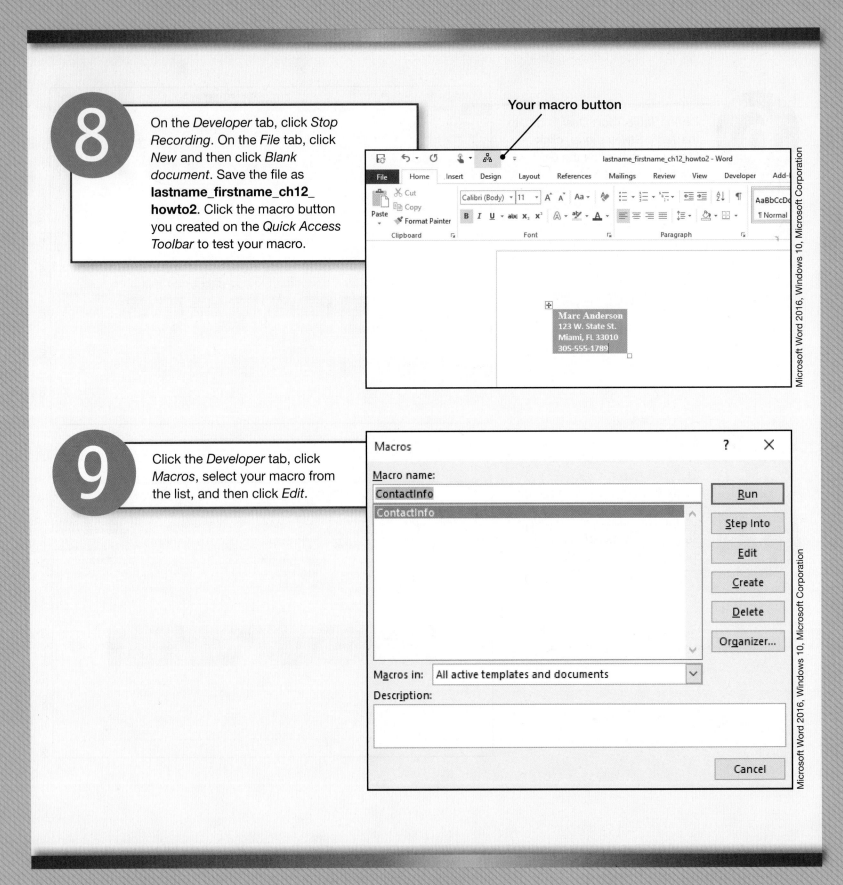

9

Click the *Developer* tab, click *Macros*, select your macro from the list, and then click *Edit*.

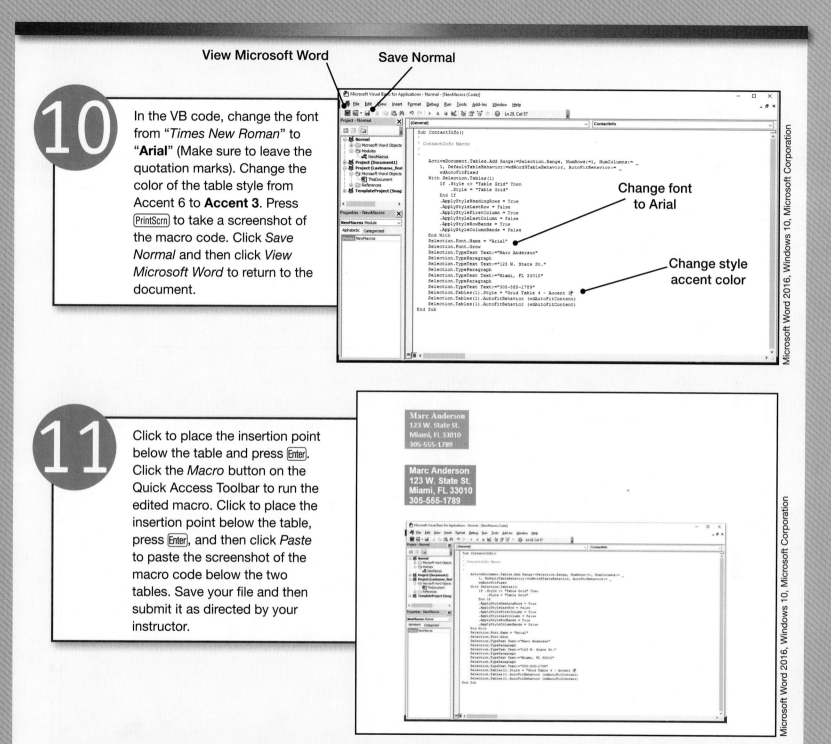

10 In the VB code, change the font from "*Times New Roman*" to "**Arial**" (Make sure to leave the quotation marks). Change the color of the table style from Accent 6 to **Accent 3**. Press PrintScrn to take a screenshot of the macro code. Click *Save Normal* and then click *View Microsoft Word* to return to the document.

Change font to Arial

Change style accent color

11 Click to place the insertion point below the table and press Enter. Click the *Macro* button on the Quick Access Toolbar to run the edited macro. Click to place the insertion point below the table, press Enter, and then click *Paste* to paste the screenshot of the macro code below the two tables. Save your file and then submit it as directed by your instructor.

To restore Word to its original configuration, on the Quick Access Toolbar, right-click the macro icon and then click *Remove from Quick Access Toolbar*. On the Developer tab, click *Macros* and then delete the macro. To remove the Developer tab, click the File tab, click *Options*, and then click *Customize Ribbon*. In the right pane, under Main Tabs, uncheck *Developer*. Click *OK*.

Microsoft Word 2016, Windows 10, Microsoft Corporation

If you are using a Mac:

1. Start Microsoft Word. Open a new, blank document. On the *Word* menu, click *Preferences*. Under *Authoring and Proofing Tools*, click *View*. Under *Ribbon*, if necessary, select the *Show developer tab* check box. Close the *View preferences* dialog box.

2. On the *Developer* tab, click *Record Macro*. Name the macro **ContactInfo** and then click *OK*.

Screenshot(s) reprinted with permission from Apple Inc.

3. On the *Insert* tab, click *Table*. Create a 1 × 1 table by clicking in the first box of the *Insert Table* menu. On the *Home* tab, in the *Font group*, change the font to *Times New Roman*, size *12*. Type your contact information in the table. On the *Table Tools Design* tab, in the *Table Styles group*, click *More* and then click the *Grid Table 4 - Accent 6* style. On the *Layout* tab, in the *Cell Size group*, click *AutoFit* and then click *AutoFit Contents*.

4. On the *Developer* tab, click *Stop Recording*. On the *File* tab, click *New* and then click *Blank document*. Save the file as **lastname_firstname_ch12_howto2**. On the *Developer tab* click *Macros*, select your macro from the list, and then click *Run*.

5. On the *Developer* tab, click *Macros*, select your macro from the list, and then click *Edit*. In the VB code, change the font from "*Times New Roman*" to "**Arial**" (Make sure to leave the quotation marks). Change the color of the table style from Accent 6 to **Accent 3**. Take a screenshot of the macro code. Click *Save Normal* and then click *View Microsoft Word* to return to the document.

6. Click to place the insertion point below the table and press Enter. On the *Developer tab*, click *Macros*, select your macro from the list, and then click *Run*. Click to place the insertion point below the table, press Enter, and then paste the screenshot of the macro code below the two tables. Save your file and then submit it as directed by your instructor.

To restore Word to its original configuration, click the *Developers* tab, click *Macros*, and delete your macro from the list. Close the dialog box. Click the *Word* menu and then click *Preferences*. Click *Ribbon* and uncheck *Developer*. Click *OK*.

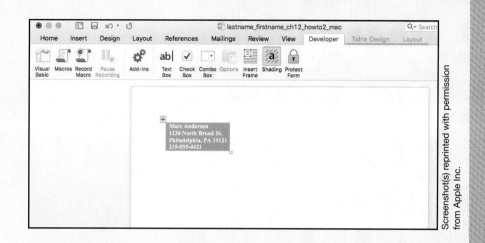

```
Sub ContactInfo()
'
' ContactInfo Macro
'
'
    ActiveDocument.Tables.Add Range:=Selection.Range, NumRows:=1, NumColumns:= _
        1, DefaultTableBehavior:=wdWord9TableBehavior, AutoFitBehavior:= _
        wdAutoFitFixed
    Selection.Font.Name = "Arial"
    Selection.TypeText Text:="Marc Anderson"
    Selection.TypeParagraph
    Selection.TypeText Text:="1230 North Broad St"
    Selection.TypeParagraph
    Selection.TypeText Text:="Philadelphia, PA 19121"
    Selection.TypeParagraph
    Selection.TypeText Text:="215-555-4421"
    Selection.Tables(1).Style = "Grid Table 4 - Accent 3"
    Selection.Tables(1).AutoFitBehavior (wdAutoFitContent)
End Sub
Sub Macro1()
'
' Macro1 Macro
'
'
    ActiveDocument.Tables.Add Range:=Selection.Range, NumRows:=1, NumColumns:= _
        1, DefaultTableBehavior:=wdWord9TableBehavior, AutoFitBehavior:= _
        wdAutoFitFixed
    Selection.TypeText Text:="Testing macors"
    Selection.TypeParagraph
    Selection.TypeText Text:="does it work?"
    Selection.Tables(1).Style = "Grid Table 4 - Accent 6"
End Sub
```

Kentoh/Fotolia

Artificial Intelligence

Objective 4

Explain the Term *Artificial Intelligence*

On the surface, it might seem that computers are smarter than people. After all, they can solve complex mathematical and scientific problems that humans couldn't solve without their help. The truth is, computers are really good at computation, but they can't think like humans—yet. Computers are just not that good at performing tasks that require human judgment, and that's what the science of **artificial intelligence (AI)** is all about: making computers behave like humans.

SIMULATION

Program Development

Applications

Humans can easily read something that another human scribbled on a piece of paper. You can figure out what the person meant, even if the words are spelled wrong, the handwriting is sloppy, and the paper is torn or wrinkled. This process is something you don't really have to think about, but a computer has a much harder time recognizing what's on the paper. When you're asked to fill out a CAPTCHA on a website to prove you are not a robot, the website security is based on the idea that a computer would not be able to decipher the CAPTCHA text, but a human could.

Facial recognition is even harder for a computer. When you see someone you know walking across the street, you can recognize that person even if he or she has a new haircut, has lost some weight, has gotten new glasses, and so on. Any of these changes are enough to confound a computer's facial recognition system. Contrary to what's portrayed in popular TV and movies, there's not a perfect facial recognition system currently available, although the technology is getting better all the time (Figure 12.13). Facebook's facial recognition algorithm suggests friends for you to tag in your images with over 80% accuracy.

Today, AI is being used in game playing, speech recognition, smart appliances such as air conditioners and refrigerators, medical and engineering research, weather forecasting, robots and automation, credit card fraud detection, and autonomous vehicles. Although we're a long way from a computer that has a mind of its own, AI systems are helping humans solve problems in areas that range from entertainment to saving lives. The most common programming languages used in AI development are Python, MATLAB, LISP, and Prolog.

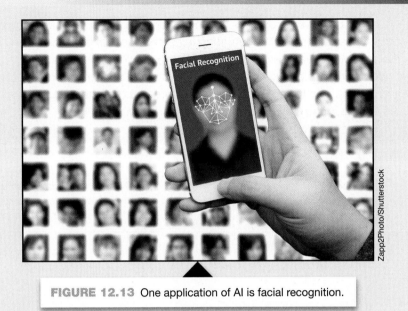

FIGURE 12.13 One application of AI is facial recognition.

Zapp2Photo/Shutterstock

Expert Systems

An **expert system** is a computer programmed to make decisions in real-life situations. It's developed by a knowledge engineer who studies the way humans make decisions in an area and translates that process into a set of rules that are programmed into the system. Expert systems are used to help diagnose illness, decide whether to approve a mortgage application, schedule delivery routes most efficiently, and even play chess (Figure 12.14). The more information the knowledge engineer has to program into the system, the more accurate the system will be. An expert system simulates human judgment to solve a problem using fuzzy logic.

Sergey Peterman/Fotolia

FIGURE 12.14 An expert system is used to program a computer to play chess.

Fuzzy logic recognizes that not everything can be broken down to a true or false answer. Some things fall somewhere in between. For example, answer the question "Is it sunny out?" The answer isn't necessarily a clear yes or no. Maybe it's partly sunny or partly cloudy—terms you often see on local weather forecasts (Figure 12.15). Fuzzy logic is similar to the way humans think.

FIGURE 12.15 Fuzzy logic helps determine whether the day is sunny, partly cloudy, partly sunny, or cloudy.

Machine Learning and Neural Networks

Machine learning (ML) is a form of AI that enables software applications to become more accurate at predictions by learning from data sets, rather than by being programmed. Computers can learn how to perform tasks themselves. **Deep learning** is a form of machine learning that relies on neural networks. A **neural network** is a system that simulates human thinking by emulating the biological connections—or neurons—of the human brain. A neural network consists of several layers. The input layer consists of the data that's put into the system, and the output layer is the results. The magic happens in the middle, hidden layer(s). A neural network is first trained by feeding it large amounts of data—both the input and expected output—that it then uses to create the processes (or weights) of the middle layer. Neural networks are used for pattern recognition, speech recognition, automation and control systems, and data-mining applications. Gmail Smart Reply is an ML application that offers users three possible replies to email messages (Figure 12.16). ML is also integral in Google's search algorithms.

FIGURE 12.16 Gmail Smart Reply

The field of artificial intelligence has been around since the 1950s. Norbert Wiener, a twentieth-century mathematician and researcher, cautioned in his book *The Human Use of Human Beings* "The world of the future will be an ever more demanding struggle against the limitations of our own intelligence, not a comfortable hammock in which we can lie down to be waited upon by our robot slaves." The idea of a computer that can think on its own and interact with us using natural language is still science fiction, but expert systems and neural networks are used in many applications, including voice and image recognition, robotics, data mining, and many scientific applications. Fuzzy logic systems are used in everything from camcorders to washing machines to smart weapons.

ETHICS

Whenever people start talking about making computers more human, there's controversy about just what that means. Ethical concerns about AI are common arguments against the research and have been the topic of many science fiction novels and movies. For many people, the images of HAL (*2001: A Space Odyssey*) or I, Robot are all too real and are frightening enough to prevent us from even continuing to pursue AI at all. There's fear that AI computers would soon become smarter than humans and eventually become sentient beings. What rights would they have? How would they be assimilated into our society? Do we have the ability to create such beings? Not yet certainly, but in the future it is likely. The ethical questions need to be addressed before that happens. What do you think?

Running Project

Visit the Association for the Advancement of Artificial Intelligence (AAAI) at **aaai.org**. Click *AITopics*. Under Topics, click *Games & Puzzles* and then click *Game & Puzzles Overview*. What are some of the ways AI is being used in games?

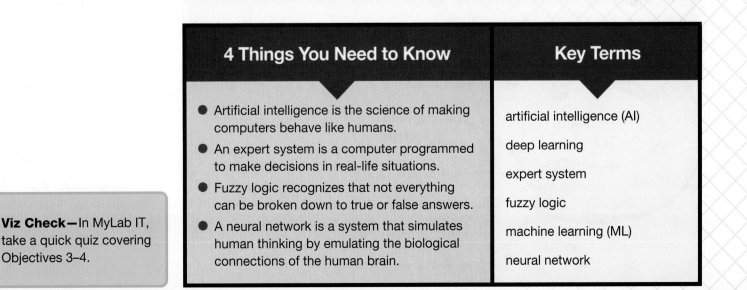

Viz Check—In MyLab IT, take a quick quiz covering Objectives 3–4.

4 Things You Need to Know

- Artificial intelligence is the science of making computers behave like humans.
- An expert system is a computer programmed to make decisions in real-life situations.
- Fuzzy logic recognizes that not everything can be broken down to true or false answers.
- A neural network is a system that simulates human thinking by emulating the biological connections of the human brain.

Key Terms

artificial intelligence (AI)

deep learning

expert system

fuzzy logic

machine learning (ML)

neural network

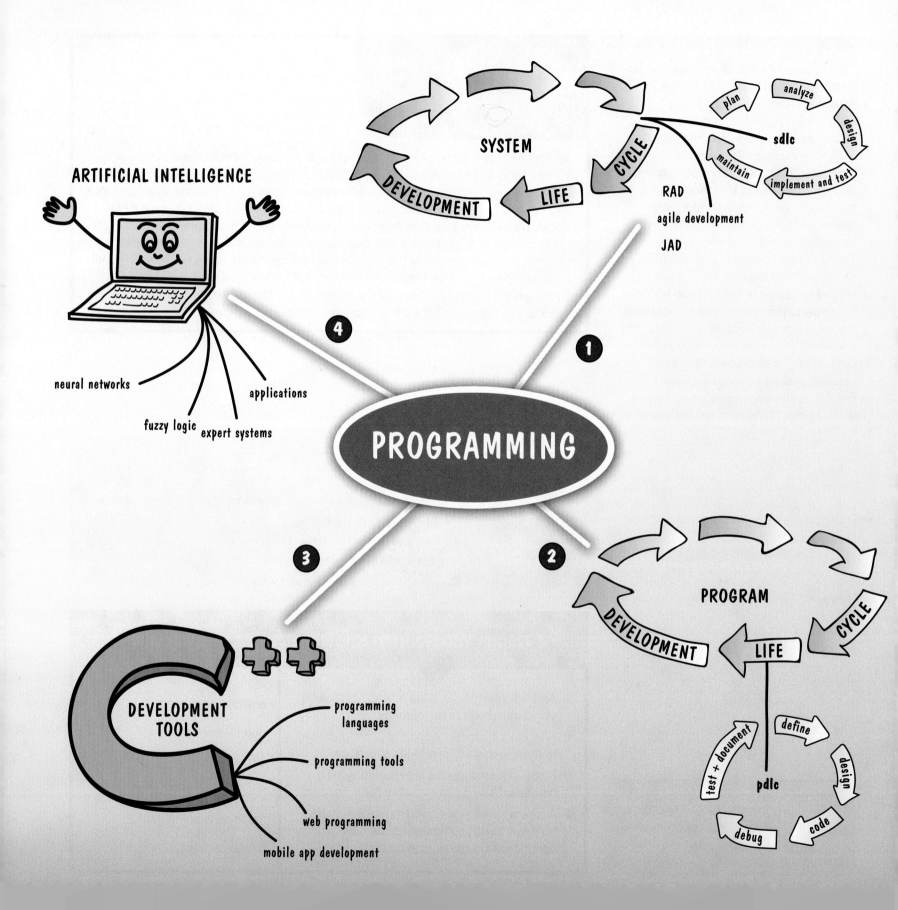

Objectives Recap

1. Describe the System Development Life Cycle
2. Describe the Program Development Cycle
3. Compare Various Programming Languages
4. Explain the Term *Artificial Intelligence*

Key Terms

Agile Development **607**
algorithm **609**
artificial intelligence (AI) **632**
assembly language **619**
beta testing **613**
client-side program **621**
compiler **619**
computer program **608**
computer programming (coding) **611**
control structure **610**
data flow diagram (DFD) **602**
debugging **612**
deep learning **634**
expert system **633**
feasibility study **601**
fifth-generation language (5GL) **620**
first-generation language (1GL) **619**
flowchart **610**
fourth-generation language (4GL) **619**
fuzzy logic **634**
green code **606**
integrated development environment (IDE) **620**
Joint Application Development (JAD) **605**

logic error **612**
machine language **619**
machine learning **634**
macro **619**
micropayment **622**
neural network **634**
object-oriented programming (OOP) **611**
procedural programming **611**
Program Development Cycle **609**
project manager (PM) **601**
pseudocode **611**
Rapid Application Development (RAD) **606**
runtime error **612**
second-generation language (2GL) **619**
server-side program **621**
software developer **601**
software development kit (SDK) **620**
stakeholder **601**
syntax error **612**
syntax rule **611**
system development life cycle (SDLC) **601**
third-generation language (3GL) **619**

Summary

1. **Describe the System Development Life Cycle**

   The traditional SDLC consists of five phases: planning, analysis, design, implementation and testing, and maintenance. The design phase includes the assembly of the project team and feasibility studies. During analysis, data flow diagrams help analyze the current system and highlight its deficiencies, and new system requirements are defined. The design phase defines what the new system will do and how it will do it. During the implementation and testing stage, coding takes place, and the system is installed and tested. The final and longest phase is maintenance, when the system is in place; during this phase, the system is periodically reviewed and updated and bugs are fixed until the system is no longer adequate and the cycle begins again. JAD, RAD, and Agile Development are other development systems in use.

2. **Describe the Program Development Cycle**

   The program development cycle consists of five steps: defining the problem; designing the solution using tools such as algorithms, flowcharts, and pseudocode; coding the program using the appropriate language and programming tools; debugging the code for syntax, logic, and runtime errors; and testing and documentation of the program.

3. **Compare Various Programming Languages**

   Computer programming languages can be classified into five generations. 1GL is a machine language, the binary code a computer can understand. 2GL is an assembly language that must be converted to machine language using an assembler. 3GL is a high-level language that can be procedural or object-oriented and requires a compiler to convert it to machine language. Most modern programming languages are 3GLs that require a lot of programming knowledge. A 4GL is closer to human language but still requires substantial programming knowledge and is often used to access databases. A 5GL uses tools that don't require programming on the user's part. 5GLs create the code and are used in AI applications.

4. **Explain the Term *Artificial Intelligence***

   Artificial intelligence is the branch of science concerned with making computers behave like humans. Modern applications include speech and pattern recognition, science and engineering applications, and financial predictions. AI uses fuzzy logic to help answer questions that don't have clear yes or no answers. Neural networks simulate the way humans think by emulating the biological connections in our brains. Machine learning allows computers to learn from data sets, rather than being programmed. Deep learning is ML that uses neural networks.

Multiple Choice

Answer the following multiple-choice questions for more practice with key terms and concepts from this chapter.

1. The traditional model for system development is the _____.
   a. DFD
   b. JAD
   c. RAD
   d. SDLC

2. The project team is assembled and feasibility studies are completed during the _____ phase of the SDLC.
   a. planning
   b. analysis
   c. design
   d. implementation and testing

3. A _____ is used to show the flow of data through a system and highlights the system's deficiencies.
   a. DFD
   b. flowchart
   c. RAD
   d. prototype

4. _____ is an incremental and iterative process that uses short iterations or sprints.
   a. Agile Development
   b. JAD
   c. RAD
   d. SDLC

5. _____ is a set of steps to solve a problem.
   a. An algorithm
   b. A data flow diagram
   c. A flowchart
   d. Pseudocode

6. _____ are used to show the logic and the flow of data processing.
   a. Control structures
   b. Flowcharts
   c. Data flow diagrams
   d. Beta tests

7. A _____ error results in an unexpected outcome.
   a. logic
   b. runtime
   c. syntax
   d. code

8. A _____ requires a compiler to convert the code into machine language that a computer can understand and execute.
   a. 2GL
   b. 3GL
   c. 4GL
   d. 5GL

9. Which of the following is an online programming environment used to develop, test, and deploy custom applications?
   a. Assembly language
   b. Software development kit (SDK)
   c. Integrated development environment (IDE)
   d. Platform-as-a-Service (PaaS)

10. _____ is a form of artificial intelligence that enables software applications to become more accurate at predictions by learning from data sets, rather than by being programmed.
    a. An expert system
    b. Machine learning
    c. A neural network
    d. Pattern recognition

True or False

Answer the following questions with *T* for true or *F* for false for more practice with key terms and concepts from this chapter.

_____ **1.** The SDLC consists of five phases: planning, analysis, design, implementation and testing, and maintenance.

_____ **2.** The program developer coordinates the team and keeps the project on track.

_____ **3.** Changes to the system cannot be made during the maintenance phase.

_____ **4.** The Rapid Application Development (RAD) system uses prototyping.

_____ **5.** Control structures are used in flowcharts and pseudocode to show logic and the flow of data processing.

_____ **6.** Procedural programming defines objects and the actions that can be performed on them.

_____ **7.** Many 2GLs are used to access databases.

_____ **8.** Micropayments are a common way to monetize a free app.

_____ **9.** An advantage to using a client-side program is that the client doesn't need to have special software to see the results.

_____ **10.** Fuzzy logic is a process used in artificial intelligence applications that recognizes that not everything can be broken down to true or false answers.

Fill in the Blank

Fill in the blanks with key terms from this chapter.

1. A(n) _____ is someone who has an interest in and will be affected by the successful completion of the project.

2. A(n) _____ shows the flow of data through an information system.

3. A(n) _____ is a graphic view of an algorithm.

4. _____ define the correct construction of commands in a programming language.

5. _____ is the process of detecting and fixing errors in a computer program.

6. _____ is the testing of a program under actual working conditions.

7. Most modern programming languages, both procedural and object-oriented programming (OOP), are considered _____.

8. A(n) _____ is a complete system for developing software, typically consisting of a code editor, one or more compilers, one or more SDKs, and a debugger.

9. Coding within a webpage that is compiled and executed by the browser or a plug-in is a(n) _____.

10. _____ is a form of machine learning that relies on neural networks.

Running Project ...

... The Finish Line

Use your answers to the previous sections of the project. Why is it important to understand the project development process? Save your file as **lastname_firstname_ch12_project** and submit it to your instructor as directed.

Do It Yourself 1

The w3schools.com website has free web development tutorials and a Try it Yourself editor that lets you try coding in your browser. In this exercise, you'll work with JavaScript. From your student data files, open the file *vt_ch12_DIY1_answersheet* and save the file as **lastname_firstname_ch12_DIY1_answersheet**.

1. Go to the **w3schools.com** website and, from the menu on the left, click *Learn JavaScript*. On the JavaScript Tutorial page, on the left, click *JS Output*, read the information under *JavaScript Display Possibilities*, and then, under *Using window.alert()* click the *Try it Yourself* button to open the editor in a new browser tab. If necessary, close the pop-up message. The JavaScript code on the left results in the output on the right. Replace *My First Web Page* in the left pane with **Hello! I wrote my first JavaScript!** (but do not delete the <h1> and </h1> tags—these are necessary to format the text). Press the *Run* button to see your results. Take a screenshot and paste it into your answer sheet.

2. Click the browser tab to return to the JavaScript tutorial page. On the left, click *JS Events*. Read the information under *HTML Events* and the click the *Try it Yourself* button. Edit the code in the left pane, using your own name, so the button displays *What time is it, your name?* Click the *Run* button, click the *What time is it, your name?* button, take a screenshot, and paste it into your answer sheet. Compare the lines of code in the two examples you tried. How are they different? Why is there more code in the JS events example?

3. Return to the JavaScript tutorial page. Click *JS Conditions* and try out the *if* statement and the *else if* statement examples and then compare them. Include screenshots of each. Which is a better control structure for the example tested, and why?

4. Type your answers in your answer sheet, including the four screenshots. Save your answer sheet and submit it as directed by your instructor.

Do It Yourself 2

Use an online mind mapper tool such as Creately.com, MindMeister.com, or Mindomo.com to create a mind map to compare the features of four models of system development. A mind map is a visual outline. More information about using mind maps can be found in Appendix B. From your student data files, open the file *vt_ch12_DIY2_answersheet* and save the file as **lastname_firstname_ch12_DIY2_answersheet**.

Your map should have four main branches: SDLC, JAD, RAD, and Agile Development. Each branch should have at least three leaves: process, advantages, and disadvantages.

> When you are finished with your map, take a screenshot of this window and paste it into your answer sheet, or, if available, export your mind map as a PNG or JPG file. Save your file and submit your work as directed by your instructor.

Critical Thinking

Your company needs software to track the inventory of its widgets. Your boss has asked you to help decide between using an off-the-shelf program and paying a programmer to create something new. From your student data files, open the file *vt_ch12_CT_answersheet* and save the file as **lastname_firstname_ch12_CT_answersheet**.

1. Write an algorithm to help make the decision to buy or create the software. What are the questions and decisions that need to be considered (cost, expertise, etc.)? List three, making sure each decision point is distinct.

2. Create a flowchart to show the steps in the algorithm. Use control structures to make decisions in your flowchart. You may sketch by hand and scan your chart or use another tool, such as Creately or Microsoft Visio, Word, or PowerPoint, to create it.

3. Write the pseudocode for the steps in your flowchart.

4. Save your file and submit it as directed by your instructor.

Ethical Dilemma

When creating a program, it is important to include detailed and accurate documentation within the code. This is crucial for a programmer who later might need to edit or debug the code. From your student data files, open the file *vt_ch12_ethics_answersheet* and save the file as **lastname_firstname_ch12_ethics_answersheet**.

Some programmers deliberately make code difficult to follow, using limited or cryptic documentation to protect their code. What are the implications of such practice? Is it legal? Is it ethical? Is it justified? Would this be beneficial or detrimental to business? Type your answers in your answer sheet, save the file, and submit it as directed by your instructor.

On the Web

Alice is a free scripting and prototyping environment program from Carnegie Mellon University for 3D object behavior. It was created as a tool for teaching programming. From your student data files, open the file *vt_ch12_web_answersheet* and save the file as **lastname_firstname_ch12_web_answersheet**.

Visit the **alice.org** website, and under The Alice Project? click *Read more*. … Watch the promotional video to learn about Alice. Do you think this is a good approach to engaging students in programming? Did it pique your interest? Type your answers in your answer sheet, save the file, and submit it as directed by your instructor.

Collaboration

With your team, create a presentation that explains the roles of the project team members: project manager, business manager, users, and programmers.

Instructors: Divide the class into groups of three to five students.

The Project: As a team, prepare a presentation that explains the roles of the team members. Use at least three references. Use Google Drive or Microsoft Office to prepare the presentation and provide documentation that all team members have contributed to the project.

Outcome: Prepare a presentation and present it to your class. The presentation may be no longer than three minutes. Turn in a final version of your presentation named **teamname_ch12_project_team** and submit your presentation to your instructor as directed.

Application Project

Office 2016 Application Projects
PowerPoint 2016: SDLC

Project Description: In this project, you will create a presentation about the SDLC. In creating this presentation, you will apply design and color themes. You will also insert and format a SmartArt graphic and apply animations to objects on your slides, and you will add transitions between slides. If necessary, download the student data files from **pearsonhighered.com/viztech**.

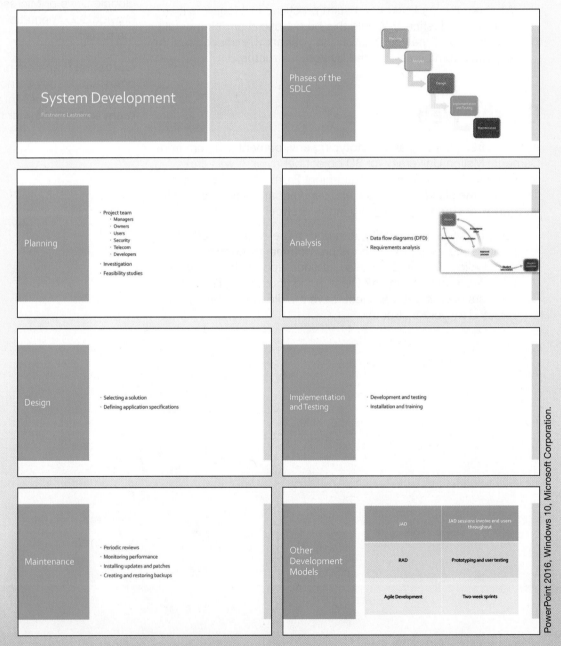

PowerPoint 2016, Windows 10, Microsoft Corporation.

Step	Instructions
1	Start PowerPoint. From your student data files, open the file named *vt_ch12_ppt*. Save the presentation as lastname_firstname_ch12_ppt
2	Apply the Frame theme to the presentation.
3	On Slide 1, in the subtitle placeholder, using your own name, type **Firstname Lastname**
4	On Slide 2, convert the bulleted list in the content placeholder to a Step Down Process SmartArt graphic. Change the SmartArt style to 3-D Inset and change the colors to Colorful – Accent Colors.
5	Open the Text pane and add two bullets to the list for a total of five shapes in the SmartArt graphic. Type the last two phases of the SDLC: • **Implementation and Testing** • **Maintenance** Close the Text pane.
6	On slide 3, under Project team, add the following six bullets: • **Managers** • **Owners** • **Users** • **Security** • **Telecom** • **Developers** Increase the List Level indent of the new bullet points.
7	On Slide 4, change the layout to Two Content. In the right content pane, from your student data files, insert the image file *vt_ch12_image1*.
8	Proportionally resize the image so that the height is 3 inches. Align the image to the middle and right of the slide. Apply the Center Shadow Rectangle Picture Style to the image.
9	On Slide 6, change the title font to 32 pt.
10	Insert a new Title and Content slide after Slide 7. On Slide 8, in the title placeholder, type **Other Development Models**
11	On Slide 8, in the content placeholder, insert a 2-column, 3-row table. Type the following text into the table: **JAD** — **JAD sessions involve end users throughout** **RAD** — **Prototyping and user testing** **Agile Development** — **Two-week sprints**
12	Resize the table so that the height is 5.5 inches. Distribute the rows in the table evenly. Center the text in the table both vertically and horizontally.
13	Apply the Push transition to all slides in the presentation.
14	On the notes and handouts pages for all slides in the presentation, insert the page number and the footer, **Firstname Lastname**, using your own name. View the presentation in Slide Show view from beginning to end and then return to Normal view.
15	Save the presentation and close PowerPoint. Submit the presentation as directed.

Application Project

Office 2016 Application Projects
Access 2016: Project Management Team

Project Description: In this project, you will manage a datasheet, build a form and query, and modify a query by defining query criteria. If necessary, download the student data files from **pearsonhighered.com/viztech**.

Vendors Form

Company Name	Contact	Title	Phone
Associated Developers	James Austin	Sales Manager	(609) 555-0667
Cressman Associates	Frank Miller	System Developer	(215) 555-2013
Extreme Solutions	Mark Worthington	Owner	(215) 555-5522
JAD Developers	Linda Aviles	Project Manager	(610) 555-2121
Jameson Systems	Patrick Jameson	Sales Associate	(609) 555-1936
LDP Data Security	George Tanaka	Sales Manager	(267) 555-1531
Northwest Security Specialists	Jessica Ruddy	Customer Service	(610) 555-4626
Systems Rescue Inc	Susan Mosely	Owner	(610) 555-4554

Created by Firstname Lastname

Projects Query   2/10/2014

Project Name	Project Manager	Start Date
Network Upgrades	Hudson, Kaplan	11/6/2014
Online Ordering System	VanSant, Cardenas	6/1/2015

Page 1

Step	Instructions
1	Start Access. From your student data files, open the Access database named *vt_ch12_access*. Save the file as **lastname_firstname_ch12_access** If necessary, click *Enable Content*.
2	With the Vendors table open in Datasheet View, sort the records in ascending order by Company Name. Use Filter by Selection to filter the records so that only those in *Software Development Services* are displayed.
3	Change the font size of the whole table to 12. Resize all of the columns in the Vendors table to get them the best fit. Save and close the table.
4	Use the Form Wizard to create a form based on the Vendors table. Add the Company Name, Contact, Title, and Phone fields to the Selected Fields list (in that order). Change to Tabular layout and name the form **Vendors Form**
5	View the Vendors Form in Design View. Change the theme to Organic. Change the font size of the title *Vendors Form* to 16 and apply bold formatting.
6	Increase the height of the Form Footer section to 0.5 inches. Add a label control to the Form Footer section so it is left aligned with the other controls in the form. Type **Created by Firstname Lastname** using your own name.
7	In the Detail section of the form, drag the right border of the Title control to the 6.5-inch mark on the ruler and then drag the left border of the Phone control to the 6.5-inch mark. Save the form.
8	View the Vendors Form in Form View. Add the following record to the form:

Company Name	Associated Developers
Contact	James Austin
Title	Sales Manager
Phone	(609) 555-0667

Save and close the form.

Step	Instructions
9	Use the Query Wizard to create a simple query based on the Projects table. Include the following fields (in this order): Project Name, Project Manager, and Start Date.
10	View the Projects Query in Design View. Modify the query criteria so that only records for Projects after **4/21/2014** are displayed. Run the query. Resize the columns to give the best fit. Save and close the query.
11	If directed by your instructor to export as PDF, open the Vendors Form and click the File tab, click Print, and then click Print Preview. On the Print Preview tab, in the Data group, click PDF or XPS. If necessary, change the Save as type to PDF, name the file **lastname_firstname_ch12_access_form** navigate to the location where you save your work for this class, and then click Publish. If necessary, close the PDF file. Close the Export – PDF window, and then close the Print Preview. Repeat the process for the query, saving the file as **lastname_firstname_ch12_access_query** Close all database objects. Close Access. Submit the database as directed.

Appendix A

Microsoft® Office 2016 Applications Chapter Guide
Visualizing Technology, Seventh Edition

CHAPTER	APP 1	PROJECT	APP 2	PROJECT
1. What Is a Computer?	Word Level 1	Intern Report	PPT Level 1	Business Technology Plan
2. Application Software	PPT Level 1	Introduction to PowerPoint design	Excel Level 1	Comparing Office Application Suite Costs
3. File Management	Excel Level 1	Municipal Waste	Word Level 1	Importance of File Management
4. Hardware	Word Level 2	Ergonomics	PPT Level 2	Comparing Printers
5. System Software	PPT Level 2	Should You Upgrade Your OS?	Excel Level 2	Worldwide Smartphone Sales
6. Digital Devices and Multimedia	Excel Level 2	Worldwide Digital Camera Sales	Word Level 2	Making the Most of Your Cellphone Camera
7. The Internet	Word Level 2	Cellular Internet Service	PPT Level 2	Internet Services
8. Communicating and Sharing: The Social Web	PPT Level 3	Browsers	Excel Level 3	Broadband Internet Growth
9. Networks and Communication	Excel Level 3	Mobile Cellular Subscriptions	Word Level 3	Secure Passwords
10. Security and Privacy	Word Level 3	Security Certifications	PPT Level 3	User Accounts
11. Databases	Word Level 3	Study Group Contact List	Access Level 1	Course Catalog
12. Program Development	PPT Level 3	SDLC	Access Level 2	Project Management Team

Note: Access projects are not available in MyLab IT

	WORD	POWERPOINT	EXCEL	ACCESS
Level 1	Enter and edit text Format text Insert and format graphics Check spelling and grammar Create headers and footers	Enter and edit text Format text Insert and format graphics Check spelling and grammar Create headers and footers Apply slide transitions Organize slides	Create and edit workbooks Format workbooks (themes) Format data (fonts, cell styles, number formats) Use basic formulas and functions Create headers and footers	Enter and edit table data Create forms and reports
Level 2	Level 1 skills plus: Format page and paragraphs (margins, line spacing, etc.) Find and replace text Use lists Create footnotes	Level 1 skills plus: Apply and modify themes Format text Use lists	Level 1 skills plus: Use absolute cell references Create column and pie charts	Level 1 skills plus: Generate queries
Level 3	Level 1 and 2 skills plus: Format graphics Create tables Use columns Incorporate borders and shading Create SmartArt	Level 1 and 2 skills plus: Insert and format graphics Use SmartArt Create tables Use charts Create animations	Level 1 and 2 skills plus: Use multiple sheets Apply more complex functions Use conditional formatting Create sparklines Sort and filter	N/A

Appendix B

Mind Maps

A mind map is a visual tool that's useful for taking notes and studying. It helps you organize information using images and keywords and see how the pieces are related to each other. To draw a mind map:

1. Write the main topic in the center of the page and then put a circle around it.
2. For each major subtopic, draw a line radiating out from the center.
3. Draw branches off the subtopics as you dig deeper into the material.
4. Draw dotted connecting lines between branches that are related.

Use single words and simple phrases, color, and images to help clarify the material.

Mind maps are used throughout this book to outline the basic structure of each chapter, but you can build on those beginning maps to delve deeper into the material. The figure below shows the mind map for Chapter 4. We can build on it by adding more detail to the branches.

The printer branch is a good place to expand. What topics and concepts would you list on the printer branch? Look at the chapter, and you'll see many choices that you might put here. The next figure shows a connection between the digital camera on the input branch and the solid-state storage (memory card) on the storage branch.

Pearson Education, Inc.

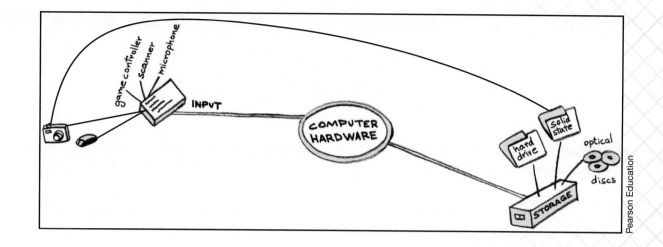

Because mind maps are used to help you remember and connect information, there's no right or wrong answer. Some people like to hand-draw mind maps; others use software to make maps cleaner. Mind maps help you review material and see connections between the topics. They're one tool you could use to take notes and study.

Glossary

AAC (advanced audio coding): An audio file type that is compressed in a manner similar to MP3 and is the default file type supported by iTunes.

acceptable use policy (AUP): A policy that computer and network users must abide by that forces users to practice safe computing.

adapter card: A card that plugs directly into an expansion slot on a motherboard and enables you to connect additional peripheral devices to a computer. Also called an expansion card.

adaptive technology: Software and hardware used by individuals with disabilities to interact with technology. Also called assistive technology.

ad hoc network: A network created when two wireless devices connect directly to each other.

add-on: An application that extends the functionality of a web browser.

adware: A type of malware that shows ads in the form of pop-ups and banners.

Agile Development: An incremental and iterative process that uses short iterations or sprints, with the project team stopping and reevaluating the direction of a project every two weeks.

algorithm: A set of steps used to solve a problem.

all-in-one computer A compact desktop computer with an integrated monitor and system unit.

alt text: Text description of an image that makes a website more accessible for visitors who use screen readers to read the content.

Analytical Engine: A mechanical computer designed, but not built, in the early 19th century by mathematician Charles Babbage that could be programmed using punch cards.

Android: A mobile Linux operating system that runs on many smartphones and tablets.

antispyware software: A form of security software that prevents adware and spyware infections.

antivirus program: A form of security software that protects against viruses, Trojan horses, worms, and spyware.

app: A self-contained program usually designed for a single purpose and that runs on smartphones and other mobile devices.

application programming interface (API): The feature of an operating system that enables an application to request services from the operating system, such as a request to print or save a file.

application software: A program that performs a useful task for the user, such as productivity, entertainment, and education software.

arithmetic logic unit (ALU): The part of a processor that performs arithmetic (addition and subtraction) and logic (AND, OR, and NOT) calculations.

ARPANET: The network developed by the U.S. Department of Defense in the 1960s that eventually became the Internet.

artificial intelligence (AI): The branch of science concerned with making computers behave like humans.

ASCII (American Standard Code for Information Interchange): An 8-bit binary code set with 256 characters.

assembly language: A programming language that is written with statements closer to language that humans speak, which must be converted into machine language by an assembler before the computer can execute it.

asynchronous online communication: A form of online communication that does not require the participants to be online at the same time—for example, email.

autofocus: A camera feature that automatically adjusts the focal length by using a small motor to move the lens in or out.

autonomous car: A self-driving vehicle that uses artificial intelligence rather than a human driver.

AutoPlay: feature of Windows that launches an application based on the type of files on the media.

avatar: A virtual body used to interact with others online in virtual worlds and games.

back up: The process of copying files to another location for protection.

bandwidth: The data transfer rate of a network, measured in kilobits per second (Kbps), megabits per second (Mbps), or gigabits per second (Gbps).

beta testing: The process of testing a program under actual working conditions.

beta version: A pre-release version of software.

big data: The collection of large amounts of data from multiple sources—both internal and external—used for ongoing analysis and decision making.

binary (base 2) number system: A number system that has only two digits, 0 and 1.

binary code: A system that represents digital data as a series of 0s and 1s that can be understood by a computer.

bioinformatics: The application of information technology to the field of biology.

biometric scanner: A scanner that measures human characteristics such as fingerprints and eye retinas.

BIOS (Basic Input/Output System): A program stored on a chip on a motherboard that is used to start up a computer.

bit: A binary digit; the smallest unit of digital information.

bitcoin: An anonymous, digital, encrypted currency.

blockchain: A decentralized electronic database of digital currency transactions such as bitcoin.

blog (weblog): An online journal.

blogosphere: All the blogs on the web and the connections among them.

Bluetooth: A technology that connects peripherals wirelessly at short ranges.

Blu-ray disc (BD): An optical disc that uses a violet laser to read and write data. The single-layer disc capacity is 25 GB, the double-layer disc capacity is 50 GB, and the triple-layer disc capacity is 100 GB.

Boolean operator: Term that defines the relationships between words or groups of words; used to create search filters: AND, OR, and NOT.

booting: The process of loading the operating system when starting up a computer.

bot: A computer that is infected with malware and is part of a botnet under the control of a master. Also called a zombie.

botnet: A network of computer zombies, or bots, controlled by a master, which can be used to send out spam and viruses or to launch a denial-of-service attack.

bridge table: In a relational database, a table that breaks a many-to-many relationship up into two one-to-many relationships.

broadband: Internet access that exceeds 25 Mbps as defined by the FCC.

browser hijacker: A form of malware that changes your home page and redirects you to other websites.

browser toolbar: A browser extension installed by an application that provides quick access to the application features from within the browser.

bug: A flaw in software programming.

burst mode: A feature on some digital cameras that enables you to take several pictures in quick succession by holding down the shutter button.

business intelligence (BI) tool: An application used to analyze data in information systems so it can be used to make decisions.

byte: Consists of 8 bits and used to represent a single character in modern computer systems.

cable Internet access: Internet access provided by cable companies.

cache memory: Fast memory that stores frequently accessed information close to the processor.

campus area network (CAN): A network that consists of multiple LANs located in the same location and connected to each other using routers.

captcha (Completely Automated Public Turing Test to Tell Computers and Humans Apart): A series of letters and numbers that are distorted in some way so that they are difficult for automated software to read but relatively easy for humans to read.

caption: The text of the audio in a video.

CD (compact disc): The oldest type of optical disc in use today, with a storage capacity of about 700 MB.

cell: The intersection of a row and a column in a spreadsheet.

cellular network: A network that uses cell towers to transmit voice and data over large distances.

central processing unit (CPU): A complex integrated circuit that contains processing circuitry that enables it to behave as the brain of the computer, control all functions performed by other components, and process all the commands it receives. Housed inside the system unit on the motherboard, it consists of two parts: the arithmetic logic unit and the control unit. Also referred to as the microprocessor.

chat: A real-time online conversation between multiple people at the same time in a chat room.

Chromebook: A subnotebook that runs the Chrome OS.

ciphertext: Text that has been encrypted.

clickbait: A link that teases you with just enough information to get you to click the link, driving traffic to a webpage.

clickjacking: A social network attack in which clicking on a link allows malware to post unwanted links on your page.

clickstream data mining: Analyzing the links customers click as they visit a website.

client: A computer that connects to or requests services from another computer called a server.

client–server network: A network that has at least one server at its center. Users log in to the network instead of their local computers and are granted access to resources based on that login.

client-side program: A program in which the coding is within a webpage, downloaded to the client computer, and compiled and executed by a browser or plug-in.

clock speed: The speed at which a processor executes the instruction cycle.

cloud: Another term for the Internet.

cloud computing: A type of computing that moves processing and storage off your desktop and business hardware and puts it in the cloud—on the Internet. Cloud computing consists of three parts: Infrastructure-as-a-Service (IaaS), Platform-as-a-Service (PaaS), and Software-as-a-Service (SaaS).

cloud service provider (CSP): A company that provides cloud (Internet-based) computing services: Infrastructure-as-a-Service (IaaS), Platform-as-a-Service (PaaS), and Software-as-a-Service (SaaS).

cluster: One or more sectors on a disk where data is stored.

CMOS (complementary metal oxide semiconductor): A volatile form of memory that uses a small battery to provide it with power to keep the data in memory even when the computer is turned off. It stores settings that are used by the BIOS.

CMYK: The standard ink colors used by printers: cyan, magenta, yellow, and key (black).

codec: Short for compression/decompression. An algorithm that reduces the size of digital media files.

CODIS (Combined DNA Index System): A system that searches across multiple local, state, and national DNA profile databases.

cognitive computing system: An information system that learns from its interactions and interacts with humans using normal language.

communication device: A device that serves as both an input and output device and enables you to connect to other devices on a network or to the Internet.

compact system camera (CSC): An advanced point-and-shoot camera with interchangeable lenses and other DSLR features. Also called a mirrorless camera.

compiler: A program that converts programming code into machine language that a computer can read and execute.

compression: The process of making files smaller to conserve disk space and make the files easier to transfer.

computer: A programmable machine that converts raw data into useful information.

computer fraud: A scheme perpetrated over the Internet or by email that tricks a victim into voluntarily and knowingly giving money or property.

computer network: Two or more computers that share resources such as software, hardware, and files.

computer program: A sequence of instructions for a computer to follow, written in a language that the computer can understand and including any data the computer needs to perform the instructions.

computer programming (coding): The process of converting an algorithm into instructions the computer can understand.

Control Panel: A Windows feature that allows you to change, configure, monitor, or troubleshoot most system settings, hardware, and software.

control panel applet: A program in the Control Panel that is used to configure, monitor, or troubleshoot settings, hardware, and software.

control structure: A structure (sequence, selection, and loop) used in flowcharts and pseudocode to show the logic and the processing flow of an algorithm.

control unit: The part of the processor that manages the movement of data through the CPU.

convergence: The integration of technology on multifunction devices such as smartphones.

convertible notebook: A type of notebook computer that has a screen that can swivel to fold into what resembles a notepad or tablet.

cookie: A small text file placed on a computer when you visit a website that helps the website identify you when you return.

Cortana: Windows built-in personal assistant.

Creative Commons (CC) licensing: A form of licensing that enables people to easily change their copyright terms from the default of "all rights reserved" to "some rights reserved."

crowdfunding: Project funding from multiple small investors rather than a few large investors.

crowdsourcing: Trusting the collective opinion of a crowd of people rather than the individual opinion of an expert.

CRT monitor: A legacy display technology that uses a cathode ray tube to excite phosphor particles coating a glass screen to light up the pixels.

cyberbullying: A form of computer harassment that happens between two minors.

cybercrime: Criminal activity on the Internet.

cyber-harassment: A form of computer harassment that happens between two adults.

cyber-stalking: A form of computer harassment that is serious in nature, with a pattern of harassment and a credible threat of harm.

cyber-terrorism: An unlawful attack against computers or networks that's done to intimidate a government or its people for a political or social agenda.

data: The unprocessed, or raw, form of information.

database: A collection of information that is organized in a useful way. Database records are organized into one or more tables.

database administrator (DBA): A person who manages database systems.

database management system (DBMS): Software used to create and manage data in a database.

data breach: A situation in which sensitive data is stolen or viewed by someone who is not authorized to do so.

data bus: A wire on a motherboard over which information flows between the components of a computer.

datacenter: A facility designed to house a company's servers and other equipment in a secure and controlled environment; sometimes called a server farm.

data dictionary: The part of a database that defines all the fields and the type of data each field contains.

data flow diagram (DFD): A diagram that shows the flow of data through an information system.

data mining: The process of discovering relationships between data items.

data normalization: The process of reducing data redundancy in a database.

data type: The kind of data you can enter in a field.

data validation: A rule designed to reduce data-entry errors by preventing invalid data from being entered.

data warehouse: A central repository for all the data that an enterprise uses, including internal databases and external sources such as vendors and customers.

debugging: The process of detecting and fixing errors—or bugs—in a computer program.

decision support system (DSS): An information system designed to help make decisions in situations where there's uncertainty about the possible outcomes of those decisions.

deep learning: A form of machine learning that relies on neural networks.

default browser: The browser that opens links you click from locations such as your desktop, email messages, and links in documents.

default program: The program associated with a particular file type and that automatically opens when a file of that type is double-clicked.

defragmenter: A disk utility that reorganizes fragmented files on a disk.

denial-of-service attack: An attack that sends out so much traffic that it could cripple a server or network.

desktop application: A computer program that is installed on your PC and requires a computer operating system such as Microsoft Windows; also known as a desktop app.

desktop computer: A personal computer that fits into a workspace such as a desk or counter.

device driver: A piece of software that acts as a translator, enhancing the capabilities of the operating system by enabling it to communicate with hardware.

Device Manager: A Windows tool that enables you to view and configure the settings of your system devices.

dial-up: Internet access over ordinary telephone lines.

digital device: A device that represents audio or video data as a series of 0s and 1s.

digital footprint: All the information that someone could find out about you by searching the web, including social networking sites.

digital rights management (DRM): A technology that is applied to digital media files, such as music, eBooks, and videos, to impose restrictions on the use of these files.

digital single-lens reflex (DSLR) camera: A digital camera that uses interchangeable lenses, can be manually focused, and can cost thousands of dollars. DSLR cameras give the user more control than point-and-shoot cameras.

DisplayPort: A digital video standard designed to replace DVI and VGA.

distributed computing: Processing of a task that is distributed across a group of computers.

DLP (digital light-processing) projector: A projector that uses hundreds of thousands of tiny swiveling mirrors to create an image.

DNS (Domain Name System): The service that allows you to use a friendly name, such as google.com, instead of an IP address, such as 74.125.224.72, to contact a website.

document management system (DMS): Software that enables a company to save, share, search, and audit electronic documents throughout their life cycle.

domain: A network composed of a group of clients and servers under the control of one central security database on a special server called the domain controller.

domain name: The part of a URL that precedes the TLD and is sometimes called the second-level domain. The domain name represents a company or product name and makes it easy to remember the address.

donationware: A form of freeware where the developers accept donations, either for themselves or for a nonprofit organization.

drive-by-download: A situation that occurs when you visit a website that installs a program in the background without your knowledge.

drive controller: A component located on the motherboard that provides a drive interface, which connects disk drives to the processor.

DSL (digital subscriber line): Internet access over telephone lines designed to carry digital signals.

DVD (digital video disc/digital versatile disc): An optical disc that can hold more information than a CD. A single-layer (SL) DVD can hold about 4.7 GB of information. A double-layer (DL) DVD has a second layer to store data and can hold about 8.5 GB.

DVI (digital visual interface): An older, digital video standard that was designed to replace VGA.

dye-sublimation printer: A printer that uses heat to turn solid dye into a gas that is then transferred to special paper.

e-commerce: Business on the web; often broken into three categories—B2B, B2C, and C2C, where *B* stands for *business* and *C* stands for *consumer*.

EIDE (Enhanced Integrated Drive Electronics): A legacy drive interface found on the motherboards of older personal computers.

email: A system of sending electronic messages using store-and-forward technology.

embedded computer: A specialized computer found in ordinary devices, such as gasoline pumps, supermarket checkouts, traffic lights, and home appliances.

embedded operating system: A specialized operating system that runs on GPS devices, ATMs, smartphones, and other devices.

emoji: A small image that represents facial expressions, common objects, and people and animals.

encryption: The process of converting unencrypted plain text into code, called ciphertext.

ENIAC (Electronic Numerical Integrator and Computer): The first working, digital, general-purpose computer.

enterprise server: A large computer that can perform millions of transactions in a day.

e-reader: A tablet designed primarily for reading.

ergonomics: The study of the relationship between workers and their workspaces.

Ethernet: The most commonly used standard that defines the way data is transmitted over a local area network.

EULA (end-user license agreement): A license agreement between a software user and the software publisher.

e-waste: Electronic waste, including old computers, cell phones, TVs, VCRs, and other electronic devices, some of which are considered hazardous.

expansion card: A card that plugs directly into an expansion slot on a motherboard and enables you to connect additional peripheral devices to a computer. Also called an adapter card.

expansion slot: An interface on a motherboard that expansion cards plug in to.

expert system: An information system programmed to make decisions in real-life situations—for example, diagnosing diseases based on symptoms.

feasibility study: A study created by a project team that includes the creation of the terms of reference (project charter) that state the objectives and scope of the project, the timeline for the project, risks, participants, deliverables, and budget. The four types of feasibility are economic, technical, operational, and political.

fiber-to-the-home (FTTH): Internet access over fiber-optic cables.

field: A single piece of information in a record in a database. For example, in a phone book record, the fields would be name, address, and phone number.

fifth-generation language (5GL): A system that a user can use without actually writing code. Primarily used in artificial intelligence applications and in combination with Platform-as-a-Service (PaaS) application development.

File Explorer: The window you use to navigate the file system and work with files, libraries, or folders on a Windows computer.

file extension: The second part of a file name. The extension is assigned by the program that is used to create the file and is used by the operating system to determine the type of file.

file fragmentation: Unorganized files that are broken into small pieces and stored in nonadjacent, or noncontiguous, clusters on the disk.

file management: The processes of opening, closing, saving, naming, deleting, and organizing digital files.

file name: The property of a file that's used to identify it using a name and file extension.

file property: Information about a file, such as authors, size, type, and date, which can be used to organize, sort, and find files more easily.

file system: The system that keeps track of files that are saved and where they're stored on the disk.

Finder: The tool you use to work with files and folders in macOS.

FiOS (Fiber Optic Service): The primary fiber broadband Internet service in the United States, provided by Verizon.

firewall: A device or software that blocks unauthorized access to a network or an individual computer.

FireWire: A hot-swappable port that can connect up to 63 devices per port. It also allows for peer-to-peer communication between devices, such as two video cameras, without the use of a computer. Also known as IEEE 1394.

first-generation language (1GL): A machine language written in binary that can be understood by a computer.

fixed-focus: A type of camera that has a preset focal length.

flash drive: A small, portable, solid-state drive with a USB interface.

flash memory: A nonvolatile form of memory that can be electrically erased and programmed.

flat database: The simplest type of database, which consists of a single list of items.

flowchart: A graphic view of an algorithm.

focal length: The distance at which subjects in front of the lens are in sharp focus.

folder: A container used to store and organize files on a computer.

form: A database object that makes it easier to enter data into a database table and displays information in an easy-to-read layout.

formatting: The process of preparing a disk to store files by dividing it into tracks and sectors and setting up the file system.

forum: An online, asynchronous conversation, also known as a discussion board.

fourth-generation language (4GL): A computer language that's designed to be closer to natural language than a 3GL. Many 4GLs are used for accessing databases.

freemium: Software offered for free that requires in-app purchases for additional content.

freeware: Software that can be used at no cost for an unlimited period of time.

fuzzy logic: A process used in artificial intelligence applications that recognizes that not everything can be broken down to true or false answers.

game controller: An input device that is used to interact with video games.

Gantt chart: In project management, a chart that shows the schedule and progress of a project.

geocaching: An electronic scavenger hunt played around the world. Geocachers hide geocaches and post GPS coordinates on the Internet.

geotagging: Adding location information to a digital photo.

gigahertz (GHz): A measure of the speed at which a processor executes the information cycle. 1 GHz is equal to 1 billion cycles per second.

GIS (geographic information system): An information system that combines layers—or datasets—of geographically referenced information about Earth's surface.

GPS (Global Positioning System): A system of 24 satellites that transmit signals that can be picked up by a receiver on the ground and used to determine the receiver's current location, time, and velocity through triangulation of the signals.

GPU (Graphics-Processing Unit): A processor found on a video card.

graphical user interface (GUI): The interface between a user and a computer. A GUI allows a user to point to and click on objects, such as icons and buttons, to initiate commands.

green code: Computer code written efficiently so the program runs on the hardware with minimal impact.

green computing: The efficient and eco-friendly use of computers and other electronics.

grid computing: Distributed computing using a group of computers in one location.

hacking: The act of gaining unauthorized access to a computer system or network.

hacktivism: Hacking to make a political statement.

hard drive: The primary mass-storage device in a computer that stores data magnetically on metal platters. Also called a hard disk or hard disk drive.

hardware: The physical components of a computer.

hashtag: A word or phrase preceded by a # symbol that is used to organize and make tweets searchable.

HDMI (High-Definition Multimedia Interface): A digital port that can transmit both audio and video signals. It is the standard connection for high-definition TVs, video game consoles, and other media devices.

headphones: Output devices that convert digital signals into sound. They come in several different sizes and styles, ranging from tiny earbuds that fit inside your ear to full-size headphones that completely cover your outer ear.

heat sink: A part of the cooling system of a computer, mounted above the CPU and composed of metal or ceramic to draw heat away from the processor.

hierarchy: The folder structure created by an operating system in which there are folders within folders, known as subfolders or children.

homegroup: A simple way to network a group of Windows computers that are all on the same home network.

home page: (1) The webpage that appears when you first open your browser. (2) The main or starting page of a website.

hotfix: A software update that addresses an individual problem when it is discovered. Also called a patch.

hotspot: A public wireless access point often available in a public location such as an airport, school, hotel, or restaurant.

hot-swappable: A device that can be plugged in and unplugged without turning off the computer.

HTML (Hypertext Markup Language): The authoring language that defines the structure of a webpage.

Human Genome Project (HGP): A research project that determined the sequence of chemical base pairs that compose DNA and mapped the approximately 20,000–25,000 human genes.

hyperlink: A connection between pieces of information in documents written using hypertext.

hypertext: Text that contains links to other text and allows you to navigate through pieces of information by using the links that connect them.

hyper-threading: A virtual form of parallel processing, used in processors built by Intel, which enables a single CPU to appear as two logical processors.

IAFIS (Integrated Automated Fingerprint Identification System): A national fingerprint and criminal history system maintained by the FBI and used by local, state, and federal law enforcement. The largest biometric database in the world. Now replaced by the NGI.

iCloud: A cloud storage and sync service from Apple.

identity theft: A form of cybercrime in which someone fraudulently uses your name, Social Security number, or bank or credit card number.

IEEE 1394: See FireWire.

IEEE 802.11: The standards that define the way data is transmitted over a Wi-Fi network.

image stabilization: A feature on some digital cameras that compensates for camera shake and therefore takes sharper images.

index: A list that Windows maintains that contains information about the files located on your computer to improve search speed.

inference engine: A set of rules for applying a knowledge base to each particular situation.

information: The processed, useful form of data.

information processing cycle (IPC): The process a computer uses to convert data into information. The four steps of the IPC are input, processing, storage, and output.

information system: The people, hardware, and software that support data-intensive applications such as financial accounts, human resources, and other business transactions.

infrastructure wireless network: A wireless network in which devices connect through a wireless access point.

Infrastructure-as-a-Service (IaaS): Part of cloud computing: the use of Internet-based servers.

inkjet printer: A printer that sprays droplets of ink onto paper.

input device: A device used to enter data into a computer system.

instant messaging (IM): A real-time online conversation.

instruction cycle: The steps a CPU uses to process data: fetch, decode, execute, store. Also known as the fetch-and-execute cycle or the machine cycle.

integrated circuit: A chip that contains a large number of tiny transistors that are fabricated into a semiconducting material called silicon.

integrated development environment (IDE): A complete system for developing software, typically consisting of a code editor, one or more compilers, one or more SDKs, and a debugger.

Internet: The global network of computer networks.

Internet backbone: The high-speed connection points between networks that make up the Internet.

Internet Crime Complaint Center (IC3): An organization that provides a website for victims to report cybercrimes.

Internet Exchange Points: The backbone of the modern Internet.

Internet of Things (IoT): The connection of the physical world to the Internet. Objects are tagged and can be located, monitored, and controlled using small embedded electronics.

Internet service provider (ISP): A company that offers Internet access.

Internet2: A second Internet designed for education, research, and collaboration.

iOS: A mobile operating system that runs on Apple mobile devices—iPods, iPhones, and iPads.

iOS device: An Apple device—iPad, iPhone, or iPod—that runs the iOS mobile operating system.

IP (Internet Protocol): The protocol responsible for addressing and routing packets to their destination.

IP (Internet Protocol) address: A unique numeric address assigned to each node on a network.

Joint Application Development (JAD): A collaborative system development process that involves the end user throughout the design and development of the project, through a series of JAD sessions.

joystick: An input device mounted on a base that consists of a stick, buttons, and sometimes a trigger.

keyboard: An input device that translates keystrokes into a signal a computer understands; the primary input device for entering text into a computer.

keylogger: A computer program or hardware device that captures information a user enters on a keyboard.

keypad: A small alternative keyboard that has a limited set of keys.

knowledge base: Part of an expert system that contains expert knowledge and accumulated experience in a particular field.

laptop: A portable personal computer. Also referred to as a notebook.

laser printer: A printer that uses a laser beam to draw an image on a drum. The image is electrostatically charged and attracts a dry ink called toner. The drum is then rolled over paper, and the toner is deposited on the paper. Finally, the paper is heated and pressure is applied, bonding the ink to the paper.

LCD (liquid crystal display): A flat-panel display type found on most desktop and notebook computers that consists of two layers of glass glued together with a layer of liquid crystals between them. When electricity is passed through the individual crystals, it causes them to pass or block light to create an image.

LCD projector: A projector that passes light through a prism, which divides the light into three beams—red, green, and blue—which are then passed through an LCD screen.

legacy technology: Old technology that's still used alongside its more modern replacement because it works and is cost-effective.

library: A tool used to gather files that are located in different locations on a Windows computer.

Linux: An open source operating system distribution that contains the Linux kernel and bundled utilities and applications.

local area network (LAN): A network in which all connected devices or nodes are located in the same physical location.

location services: A feature of computers and mobile devices that determines your location by using GPS or wireless networks.

logic bomb: An attack that occurs when certain conditions are met.

logic error: An error in programming logic that results in an unexpected outcome.

lossless compression: A compression algorithm that creates an encoded file by removing redundant information. When the file is decompressed, all the information from the original file is restored.

lossy compression: A compression algorithm used on files that contain more information than humans can typically detect (typically images, audio, and video files). That extra information is removed from the file. It's not possible to fully decompress such a file, as the information has been removed from the file.

LTE (Long-Term Evolution): A means of connecting to the Internet using cellular networks that provide 4G service.

Mac: A personal computer manufactured by Apple. Also referred to as a Macintosh.

machine language: A programming language written in binary that can be understood by a computer.

machine learning: A form of artificial intelligence that enables software applications to become more accurate at predictions by learning from data sets, rather than by being programmed, enabling computers to learn how to perform tasks themselves.

machinima: The art of creating videos using screens captured from video games.

macOS: The operating system installed on Apple Mac computers.

macro: A small program used to automate tasks in applications such as Word and Excel.

mainframe: A large multiuser computer that can perform millions of transactions in a day.

malware: A computer program that's designed to be harmful or malicious.

management information system (MIS): An information system that includes software, hardware, data resources (such as databases), decision support systems, people, and project management applications.

many-to-many relationship: A database relationship in which multiple records in one table link to multiple records in another table.

massively multiplayer online role-playing game (MMORPG): An online game in which players interact with people in real time in a virtual world using an avatar, or virtual body.

meme: A funny image or catchphrase, often of celebrity or pop culture reference, that is spread by Internet users across social media.

memory: Temporary storage that a computer uses to hold instructions and data.

memory card: A storage medium that uses flash memory to store data.

metasearch engine: A search engine that searches other search engines.

metropolitan area network (MAN): A network that covers a single geographic area.

microblogging: A form of blogging in which posts are limited to a small number of characters and users post updates frequently. Twitter is a microblog site.

micropayment: A small charge for additional lives, levels, or other features from within an app.

microphone: An input device that converts sound into digital signals and is used to chat in real time or as part of voice-recognition applications used in video games and for dictating text.

microprocessor: A complex integrated circuit that contains processing circuitry that enables it to behave as the brain of the computer, control all functions performed by other components, and process all the commands it receives. Also referred to as the central processing unit or CPU.

Microsoft Windows: The operating system found on most personal computers.

mobile application (mobile app): A program that extends the functionality of a mobile device.

mobile browser: A web browser optimized for small-screen devices, such as smartphones and tablets.

mobile device: A portable device such as a smartphone or tablet.

mobile operating system: An embedded operating system that runs on mobile devices such as smartphones and tablets and is more full-featured than other embedded OSs.

mobile payment system: Using a mobile device rather than cash or credit cards to pay for items.

modem: A communication device that modulates digital data into an analog signal that can be transmitted over a phone line and, on the receiving end, demodulates the analog signal back into digital data. Used to connect a computer to a telephone line, most often for dial-up Internet access. Modem is short for modulator-demodulator.

monitor: A video output device that works by lighting up pixels on a screen. Each pixel contains three colors—red, green, and blue (RGB)—and all colors can be created by varying the intensities of these three colors.

Moore's Law: An observation made by Gordon Moore in 1965 that the number of transistors that can be placed on an integrated circuit had doubled roughly every two years.

motherboard: The main circuit board of a computer, which houses the processor (CPU) and contains drive controllers and interfaces, expansion slots, data buses, ports and connectors, the BIOS, and memory. It provides a way for devices to attach to the computer.

mouse: An input device that may include one or more buttons and a scroll wheel that works by moving across a smooth surface to signal movement of the pointer.

MP3 (MPEG-1 Audio Layer 3): A common audio file type used for music files. MP3 is a lossy form of compression that works by removing some of the detail.

MP3 player: A handheld device that allows you to carry with you thousands of songs and podcasts, so you can listen to them wherever you are. Also called a portable media player if it supports photos and videos.

multi-core processor: A processor that consists of two or more processors integrated on a single chip.

multidimensional database (MDB): A type of database optimized for storing and utilizing data. It may be created using input from existing relational databases, but it structures the information into multidimensional data cubes.

multifunction device: A printer device with a built-in scanner and sometimes fax capabilities. Also known as an all-in-one printer.

multimedia: The integration of text, graphics, video, animation, and sound content.

multitasking: Doing more than one task at a time.

multiuser computer: A system that allows multiple, simultaneous users to connect to it, allowing for centralized resources and security.

municipal Wi-Fi: Wireless Internet access available in some cities and towns.

near field communication (NFC): A technology that enables devices to share data with each other by touching them together or bringing them within a few centimeters of each other.

netbook: A lightweight, inexpensive notebook computer designed primarily for Internet access; with built-in wireless capabilities, a small screen, and limited computing power and storage.

Network Access Point (NAP): One of the sites that make up the Internet backbone.

network adapter: A communication device used to establish a connection with a network. The adapter may be onboard, an expansion card, or a USB device and may be wired or wireless. Also called a network interface card (NIC).

network address translation (NAT): A security feature of a router that shields the devices on a private network from the public network (the Internet).

network administrator: The person responsible for managing the hardware and software on a network.

network interface card (NIC): See network adapter.

network operating system (NOS): A specialized operating system found on servers in a client–server network that provides services requested by the client computers, such as file services, printing services, centralized security, and communication services.

network resource: The software, hardware, or files shared on a network.

neural network: A system that simulates human thinking by emulating the biological connections—or neurons—of the human brain.

Next Generation Identification (NGI): A national fingerprint and criminal history system maintained by the FBI that has replaced IAFIS.

notebook: A portable personal computer. Also referred to as a laptop.

object-oriented database (OODB): A type of database in which data is stored as objects, which are used by modern programming languages, such as C++ and Java. Often used to create databases that have more complicated types of data, such as images, audio, and video.

object-oriented programming (OOP): A programming model that defines objects and the actions or methods that can be performed on them.

office application suite: A suite of productivity applications—such as a word processor, spreadsheet, presentation program, database, and personal information manager—integrated into a single package.

office support system (OSS): An information system that consists of software and hardware that improve productivity of employees by automating common tasks.

OLED (organic light-emitting diode): A monitor composed of extremely thin panels of organic molecules sandwiched between two electrodes.

OneDrive: Free online storage associated with a Microsoft account.

one-to-many relationship: The most common type of relationship in a relational database, in which a single record in one table is related to multiple records in another table.

one-to-one relationship: A database relationship in which a single record in one table is related to exactly one record in another table. The records are linked by a common primary key.

online analytical processing (OLAP): A system that enables a user to selectively extract and view data from different points of view and can be used for data mining or discovering relationships between data items.

open source: Software that has its source code published and made available to the public, enabling anyone to copy, modify, and redistribute it without paying fees.

operating system (OS): System software that provides the user with an interface to communicate with the hardware and software on a computer. The OS also manages system resources.

optical disc: A form of removable storage where data is stored by using a laser to either melt the disc material or change the color of embedded dye. A laser reads the variations as binary data.

optical network terminal (ONT): The device that connects a LAN to a fiber network.

OS X: The operating system installed on Apple Mac computers prior to the 2016 change to macOS.

output device: A device that returns processed information to the user.

overclock: To run a processor at speeds higher than it was designed to perform.

parallel processing: The process of using multiple processors, or multi-core processors, to divide up processing tasks.

patch: A software update that addresses an individual problem when it is discovered. Also called a hotfix.

path: The sequence of folders to a file or folder.

payload: An action or attack by a computer virus or other malware.

PCI (Peripheral Component Interconnect): A legacy type of expansion slot on a motherboard used to connect peripheral devices to a computer.

PCIe (PCI Express): A faster version of PCI used to connect peripheral devices to a computer.

peer-to-peer (P2P) network: A network in which all computers are considered equal. Each device can share its resources with every other device, and there's no centralized authority.

peripheral devices: Components that serve the input, output, and storage functions of a computer system.

personal area network (PAN): A small network that consists of devices connected by Bluetooth.

personal computer (PC): A small microprocessor-based computer used by one person at a time.

personal information manager (PIM): A program used to manage email, calendars, and tasks that is often part of an office suite.

pharming: A form of cybercrime that redirects you to a phony website even if you type the correct address into your browser.

phishing: A form of cybercrime in which email messages and IMs that appear to be from those you do business with—such as your bank, credit card company, social network, auction site, online payment processor, or IT administrator—are designed to trick you into revealing information.

photo printer: A printer designed to print high-quality photos on special photo paper. Photo printers can be inkjet printers or dye-sublimation printers.

piggybacking: Using an open wireless network to access the Internet without permission.

pipelining: A method used by a single processor to process multiple instructions simultaneously. As soon as the first instruction has moved from the fetch stage to the decode stage, the processor fetches the next instruction.

pixel: Short for picture element. A single point on a display screen. Each pixel contains three colors: red, green, and blue (RGB).

Platform-as-a-Service (PaaS): Part of cloud computing: an online programming environment used to develop, deploy, and manage custom web applications.

platform-neutral: An application that can run on all modern personal computing systems.

plotter: A printer that uses one or more pens to draw an image on a roll of paper.

Plug and Play (PnP): An operating system feature that allows you to easily add new hardware to a computer system. When you plug in a new piece of hardware, the OS detects it and helps you set it up.

plug-in: A third-party program that extends the functionality of a browser.

podcast: A prerecorded radio- and TV-like show that you can download and listen to or watch any time.

podcast client: A program used to locate, subscribe to, and play podcasts.

point-and-shoot camera: The simplest, least expensive digital camera type, which has the fewest features.

pop-up blocker: A browser feature that prevents webpages from opening a new window.

port: A connection point that is used to attach a peripheral device to a motherboard.

portable apps: Application software that can be run from a flash drive.

portable media player: A handheld device that allows you to carry with you audio files, photos, and videos, so you can enjoy them wherever you are. Also called an MP3 player.

primary key: A field that uniquely identifies a record in a database table.

procedural programming: A programming model that uses a step-by-step list of instructions.

processor: See central processing unit (CPU).

program development cycle: A set of steps that a programmer follows to create a computer program.

project management software: An application designed to help complete projects, stick to a budget, stay on schedule, and collaborate with others.

project manager (PM): The leader of a project team, who coordinates the team and keeps the project on track.

projector: A video output device typically used when making a presentation or sharing media with a group in such places as classrooms, businesses, and home theaters because they can produce larger output than a monitor.

protocol: The rules for communication between devices that determine how data is formatted, transmitted, received, and acknowledged.

pseudocode: The expression of the steps of an algorithm using English-like statements that focus on logic, not syntax.

punch card: A stiff piece of paper that conveys digital information by the presence or absence of holes.

QR (Quick Response) code: A two-dimensional bar code found in ads and on merchandise tags that can be scanned using an app on a mobile device to learn more about the item.

query: A database object that pulls out records that meet specific criteria. A query retrieves specific data from one or more tables to answer a question.

query language: A language used to design a database query.

RAM (random access memory): A volatile form of memory that holds the operating systems, programs, and data the computer is currently using.

ransomware: A form of malware that prevents you from using your computer until you pay a fine or fee.

Rapid Application Development (RAD): An iterative development process that uses prototyping and user testing of the designs. RAD tools use object-oriented programming (OOP) and reusable code modules to speed up the process.

record: A row of data in a database table that describes a particular entry in the database—for example, a customer or product.

relational database: The most common type of database, which consists of multiple tables related by common information.

relational keyword: A keyword used in SQL statements to manipulate, query, and update data in relational databases; examples of relational keywords are SELECT, FROM, WHERE, and AND.

report: A database object that displays data from a table or a query in a format that is easy to read and print.

resolution: The number of horizontal by vertical pixels—for example 1280×1024 or 1920×1080—on a display screen, expressed in megapixels.

retail software: The user pays a fee to use the software.

RFID tag: A tag that can be read by an RFID (radio-frequency identification) scanner. It contains a tiny antenna for receiving and sending a radio-frequency signal.

ROM (read-only memory): A nonvolatile form of memory that does not need power to retain data.

rootkit: A set of programs that allows someone to gain control over a computer system while hiding the fact that the computer has been compromised.

router: A device that connects two or more networks together. It uses address information to route the data packets it receives to the correct locations.

RSS (Really Simple Syndication): A format used for distributing web feeds that change frequently—for example, blogs, podcasts, and news—to subscribers.

runtime error: An error that occurs when a program is running and data or a command that is entered causes it to crash.

Safe Mode: A special diagnostic mode for troubleshooting the system that loads Windows without most device drivers.

SATA (Serial Advanced Technology Attachment): The standard internal drive interface.

satellite Internet access: A means of connecting to the Internet using communication satellites.

scanner: An input device that can increase the speed and accuracy of data entry and convert information into a digital format that can be saved, copied, and manipulated.

screen capture: A software tool used to create a video of what happens on a computer screen.

search engine: A website that provides search capabilities on the web.

search engine optimization (SEO): The methods used to make a website easier to find by both people and software that indexes the web and to increase the webpage ranking in search engine results.

second-generation language (2GL): An assembly language that must be converted into a machine language by an assembler before a computer can execute it.

second screen: Using a computer or mobile device while watching television to interact with other viewers or view enhanced content.

Secure Sockets Layer (SSL): A protocol that encrypts information before it is sent across the Internet.

security suite: A package of security software that includes a combination of features such as antivirus, firewall, and privacy protection.

server: A multiuser computer system that runs a network operating system (NOS) and provides services—such as Internet access, email, or file and print services—to client systems.

server-side program: A program that runs on a web server instead of the client computer. No special software is needed by the client.

service pack: A large, planned software update that addresses multiple problems or adds multiple features and includes previous patches and hotfixes.

service set identifier (SSID): A wireless network name.

Settings window: A Windows feature that enables you to change common settings.

sharebaiting: When users share posts, often without actually clicking them first, which can lead you to believe the links are safe.

SharePoint: A Microsoft technology that enables employees in an organization to access information across organizational and geographic boundaries.

shareware: Software offered in trial form or for a limited period that allows the user to try it out before purchasing a license.

shill bidding: Fake bidding by a seller or his or her accomplice to drive up the price of an auction item.

Short Message Service (SMS): A service used to send brief electronic text messages to mobile devices.

shutter lag: The time between pressing the shutter button and the camera snapping the picture.

signature line: A block of text that is automatically put at the end of an email message.

SIM card (Subscriber Identity Module): A small card found in cellular phones, which identifies the phone and includes account information and cellular carrier.

Siri: An intelligent personal assistant app that enables you to speak using natural language to interact with your Apple device.

smart appliance: A home appliance that monitors signals from the power company, and when the electric grid system is stressed, can react by cutting back on power consumption.

smart grid: A network for delivering electricity to consumers that includes communication technology to manage electricity distribution efficiently.

smart home: A house that uses automation to control lighting, heating and cooling, security, entertainment, and appliances.

smartphone: A small computer that combines a cellular phone with such features as Internet and email access, a digital camera, mapping tools, and the ability to edit documents.

social bookmarking site: A site that allows you to save and share your bookmarks or favorites online.

social media: Websites that use Web 2.0 technologies that enable you to create user-generated content, connect, network, and share.

social media marketing (SMM): The practice of using social media sites to sell products and services.

social network: An online community where people with common interests can communicate and share content with each other; a social network combines many of the features of other online tools.

social news site: An online news site that allows community members to submit content they discover on the web and puts it in one place for everyone to see and to discuss.

social review site: A website where users review hotels, movies, games, books, and other products and services.

software developer: A person who designs and writes computer programs.

software development kit (SDK): A bundle of libraries and tools that are developed for a particular platform.

Software-as-a-Service (SaaS): Part of cloud computing: the delivery of applications—or web apps—over the Internet.

solid-state drive (SSD): A small drive that uses flash memory to store data.

sound card: An expansion card that provides audio connections for both audio input devices and output devices.

spam: Unsolicited and unwanted email messages, also called junk mail.

spamming: The sending of mass, unsolicited emails.

speaker: An output device that converts digital signals from a computer or media player into sound.

speech recognition: A feature that enables users to use a device by speaking commands.

Spotlight: The search tool in macOS.

spreadsheet: An application that creates electronic worksheets composed of rows and columns. Spreadsheets are used for mathematical applications, such as budgeting, grade books, and inventory.

spyware: A form of malware that secretly gathers personal information about you.

SSID (service set identifier): The name of a wireless network.

stakeholder: A person who has an interest in and will be affected by the successful completion of a project.

standard: A specification that has been defined by an industry organization to ensure that equipment that is made by different companies will be able to work together.

storage area network (SAN): A network between the data storage devices and the servers on a network that makes the data accessible to all servers in the SAN; normal users are not part of the SAN but are able to access the information through the local area network servers.

streaming: Media, such as video or audio, that begins to play immediately as it is being received and does not require the whole file to be downloaded to your computer first.

Structured Query Language (SQL): The most common query language used to create database queries.

stylus: A special pen-like input tool that enables you to write directly on a touchscreen.

subject line: Part of an email message used to give the recipient some idea of the content of the email.

subnotebook: A notebook computer that is thin and light and that has high-end processing and video capabilities.

subscription: A software distribution model in which a customer pays a monthly or yearly fee for access to software for a limited time.

supercomputer: A very expensive and powerful computer system that is used to perform complex mathematical calculations, such as those used in weather forecasting and medical research.

switch: Hardware that connects multiple devices on a local area network and uses address information to send data packets only to the port to which the appropriate device is connected.

synchronous online communication: A form of online communication that requires the participants to be online at the same time—for example, chat and instant messaging.

syntax error: An error in the way code is written.

syntax rule: A rule that defines the correct construction of commands in a programming language.

system development life cycle (SDLC): The traditional model for system development, which consists of five phases—planning, analysis, design, implementation and testing, and maintenance—where each phase is completed in order before the next can begin.

System Preferences: A macOS feature that enables you to change system settings.

system requirements: The minimum hardware and software specifications required to run a software application.

system restore: A Windows tool that enables you to return the system to a previous state saved as a restore point.

system software: The software that makes a computer run.

system unit: The case that encloses and protects the power supply, motherboard, CPU, and memory of a computer.

table: A collection of related records in a database. It's arranged in rows and columns.

tablet: A handheld mobile device that falls somewhere between a notebook computer and a smartphone.

tagging: Labeling images or files with keywords to make it easier to organize and search for them.

Task Manager: A troubleshooting tool that enables you to view and stop processes that are running on a Windows computer.

TCP (Transmission Control Protocol): The protocol responsible for ensuring that data packets are transmitted reliably on a network.

TCP/IP protocol stack: A suite of protocols that define many types of data movement including the transfer files and webpages, sending and receiving email, and network configuration.

telephoto lens: A type of zoom lens that makes an object appear closer.

text messaging: Sending brief electronic messages between mobile devices using Short Message Service (SMS).

thermal printer: A printer that creates an image by heating specially coated heat-sensitive paper, which changes color where the heat is applied.

third-generation language (3GL): A computer language for which a compiler is needed to convert the code into machine language that a computer can understand and execute. Most modern programming languages, both procedural and object-oriented programming (OOP), fall in this category.

three-dimensional (3D) printer: A printer that can create objects such as prototypes and models.

Thunderbolt: A port that carries both PCIe and DisplayPort video signals on the same cable, so it can be used to connect many different types of peripherals to a computer.

time bomb: A form of logic bomb in which the attack is triggered by a specific time and date.

top-level domain (TLD): The suffix, such as .com or .edu, that follows the domain name in a URL and represents the type of website you're visiting.

topology: The physical layout of a computer network.

touchpad: An input device typically found on a notebook computer instead of a mouse. You move a finger across the touch-sensitive surface, and the computer detects and translates your motion.

touchscreen: An input device that can accept input from a finger or a stylus.

transaction-processing system (TPS): An information system that links together the multiple operations that make up a transaction and ensures that all operations in a transaction are completed without error.

transistor: A tiny electric switch used in second-generation computers.

Trojan horse: A program that appears to be a legitimate program but is actually something malicious.

Turing machine: A machine that can perform mathematical computations.

Turing test: A measure of a computer's ability to display intelligent behavior.

Tweet: A short message posted in Twitter, limited to 140 characters and spaces.

ubiquitous computing (ubicomp): Technology that recedes into the background and becomes part of the environment.

Unicode: An extended ASCII set that is the standard on the Internet and includes codes for most of the world's written languages, mathematical systems, and special characters. It has codes for about 100,000 characters.

universal design: Design principles that not only help create environments that accommodate people with disabilities, but also benefit those with no special needs.

Unix: A multiuser OS developed in the 1970s primarily used on servers and some specialized workstations.

unmanned aircraft system (UAS): An aircraft piloted by remote control or onboard computers. Also known as a drone.

URL (uniform resource locator): An address, such as http://google.com, that consists of three main parts: the protocol (http), domain name (google), and top-level domain (.com).

USB (Universal Serial Bus): A standard port type that is used to connect many kinds of devices, including printers, mice, keyboards, digital cameras, cell phones, and external drives. Up to 127 devices can share a single USB port.

user account: An account that grants a user certain rights and access to a computer system.

User Account Control (UAC): A Windows security feature that notifies you before allowing changes to be made on your computer.

user-generated content: Web content created by ordinary users.

user interface: The part of an operating system that you see and interact with.

utility software: A type of system software used to perform computer maintenance.

vacuum tube: A tube that resembles an incandescent light bulb and was used in first-generation computers.

VGA (video graphics array): A legacy, analog video standard.

video card: An expansion card that provides the data signal and connection for a monitor or projector. It may also include input ports to connect a TV tuner or another video device to the system.

video game system: A computer that is designed primarily for playing games.

viral video: A video that becomes extremely popular because of recommendations and social sharing.

virtual private network (VPN): A private network through the public network (Internet) that allows remote users to access a LAN securely.

virtual reality: An artificial world that consists of images and sounds created by a computer and that is affected by the actions of a person who is experiencing it.

virus: A program that replicates itself and infects computers. It needs a host file, such as a game, to travel on.

VoIP (Voice over IP): A service that allows phone calls to be transmitted over the Internet instead of over traditional phone lines.

volunteer computing: A form of distributed computing that relies on the processing power of hundreds or thousands of volunteers' personal computers.

wardriving: The practice of driving around and locating open wireless access points.

wearable: A computer worn on the body.

Web 2.0: Technologies used to communicate and collaborate on the web that enable you to be a creator, not just a consumer, of content.

web apps: Applications that run in a browser.

web browser: A program that interprets HTML to display webpages.

webcam: A specialized video camera that provides visual input for online communication, such as web conferencing or chatting.

webcasting: Broadcasting on the web.

webpage: Information on the Internet written in HTML, which can be viewed with a web browser.

website: One or more related webpages, all located in the same place.

wide-angle lens: A type of zoom lens that widens the view, making objects appear smaller and farther away.

wide area network (WAN): A network that spans multiple locations and connects multiple LANs over dedicated lines using routers.

Wi-Fi: A type of network found in homes and public hotspots, which uses radio waves to provide wireless, high-speed network connections.

Wi-Fi Protected Setup (WPS): A technique for setting up a secure wireless home network using a push button, personal identification number (PIN), or USB key to automatically configure devices to connect to your network.

wiki: A website that allows users to edit content, even if it was written by someone else.

WiMAX Mobile Internet: A means of connecting to the Internet using cellular networks that provide 4G service.

Windows Defender: Built-in antimalware software that protects against computer viruses and other malware on a Windows computer.

wireless access point (WAP): A device that allows wireless devices to join a network.

wireless encryption: A feature that adds security to a wireless network by encrypting transmitted data.

wireless LAN (WLAN): A network that uses Wi-Fi to transmit data.

word processor: An application that is used to create, edit, and format text documents. The documents can also contain images.

workgroup: A group of devices in a peer-to-peer network.

workstation: A high-end desktop computer or one that's attached to a network in a business setting.

World Wide Web: The hypertext system of information on the Internet that allows you to navigate through pieces of information by using hyperlinks that connect them.

worm: A form of self-replicating malware that doesn't need a host to travel. It travels over networks and spreads over network connections without any human intervention.

zero-day exploit: An attack that occurs on the day an exploit is discovered, before the publisher of the compromised software can fix it.

zombie: A computer that is infected with malware and is part of a botnet under the control of a master. Also called a bot.

zoom: Making objects appear closer or farther away.

Index

B

B2B (business-to-business), 423
B2C (business-to-consumer), 423
Babbage, Charles, 5
backup
  cloud, 134, 136t
  cloud storage, 135, 135f
  defined, 132
  external hard drive, 134, 134f, 136t
  macOS Time Machine and, 133, 133f, 267–268
  storage types comparison, 136t
  Windows File History and, 133, 133f, 264–266
bandwidth, 343
base 2 (binary) number system, 16
Basic Input/Output System (BIOS), 174
battery life, extending, 262
bcc (blind carbon copy), 394
BDs (blu-ray discs), 177, 177t
Berry, Clifford, 12t
beta testing, 613
beta version, 241
big data, 579
binary (base2) number system, 16
binary code, 16–18, 17t
binary storage capacity prefixes, 18t
bioinformatics, 19
biometric scanners, 190, 190f
BIOS (Basic Input/Output System), 174
bitcoin, 511
bits, 17
blind carbon copy (bcc), 394
blockchain, 578
Blogger, 414–417
bloggers, 432
blogosphere, 411
blogs, 411, 411f, 414–417
Bluetooth, 173, 455
blu-ray discs (BDs), 177, 177t
Boolean operators, 147, 147f, 362
booting, 174
botnets, 509f, 510, 511
bots, 510
Braille devices, 207, 208, 209f
bridge tables, 558
broadband connection, 344–345, 344f

Broadband Progress Report, 347
browser hijacker, 508
browser toolbar, 353
browsers. *See* web browsers
bugs, 99, 524
burst mode, 285
bus topology, 456, 456f
business intelligence (BI) tools, 579
business productivity software
  database, 59, 59f
  document management, 61
  financial, 61
  office suites, 55–60
  personal information manager (PIM), 60, 60f
  presentation, 58, 58f
  project management, 62
  spreadsheet, 57, 57f
  word processor, 55–56, 55f, 56f
business-to-business (B2B), 423
business-to-consumer (B2C), 423
bytes, 17, 18

C

C2C (consumer-to-consumer), 424
cable Internet access, 345
cache memory, 175
cameras
  digital, 188, 282–287
  video, 312–313, 312f
campus area networks (CANs), 458
captcha (Completely Automated Public Turing Test to Tell Computers and Humans Apart), 393, 633
captions, 310
carbon copy (cc), 394
Carbonite, 134, 134f
carbon nanotubes, 14f
careers
  bioinformatics, 19
  blogger, 432
  computer sales, 212
  database administrator (DBA), 569
  document management, 151
  healthcare, 314
  helpdesk specialist, 249
  IT security, 537

network administrator, 473
  software development, 617
  software trainer, 81
  web designer, 371
cc (carbon copy), 394
CDs (compact discs), 177, 177t
cells, spreadsheet, 57
cellular networks, 458
central processing unit (CPU)
  arithmetic logic unit (ALU), 164
  control unit, 164
  cooling system, 168, 168f
  defined, 13, 164
  GPU (graphics-processing unit), 166
  instruction cycle, 165, 165f
  multi-core processor, 166
  multiple processors, 166, 166f
  parallel processing, 167, 167f
  parts of, 164
  performance, 166
  pipelining, 167, 167f
  placement in computer, 165f
chat, 389–390, 389f, 390f
Check Disk utility (Windows), 256, 256f
Chromebooks, 23, 23f
ciphertext, 522
clickbait, 498
clickjacking, 498
clickstream data mining, 579
Client for Microsoft Networks, 467, 467f
clients
  in client-server network, 449
  defined, 33, 449
  email, 470f
  network operating systems (NOSs) and, 251
client-server network software, 469–470
client-server networks, 250, 449, 449f
client-side programs, 621
clock speed, 166
cloud
  backups, 134, 136t
  defined, 86
  file management, 118
  image transfer, 290–291
cloud computing
  defined, 86

Infrastructure-as-a-Service (IaaS), 87
  Platform-as-a-Service (PaaS), 87
  service types, 87, 87f
  Software-as-a-Service (SaaS), 88–89
cloud service providers (CSPs), 87
cloud storage, 135, 135f
clusters, 255
CMOS (complementary metal oxide semiconductor), 174
CMYK, 199, 199f
codecs, 305
coding, 611. *See also* programming
cognitive computing system, 580
Colossus computer, 11, 12t
Combined DNA Index System (CODIS), 583, 583f
communication devices, 210–211
compact discs (CDs), 177, 177t
compact system cameras (CSC), 286, 286f
compilers, 619
complementary metal oxide semiconductor (CMOS), 174
Completely Automated Public Turing Test to Tell Computers and Humans Apart (captcha), 393, 633
composing email messages, 394–395, 394f
compression, image file, 294
computer crimes. *See* cybercrime
computer fraud, 498–499, 498f
Computer Fraud and Abuse Act, 535
computer hardware. *See* hardware
computer networks, 446. *See also* networks
computer programming, 611. *See also* programming
computer programs, 608
computer software engineers, 617
computers. *See also* operating systems
  binary codes, 16–18
  defined, 4
  desktop, 21